MW01253031

The Praised and the Virgin

Philosophy of Religion

WORLD RELIGIONS

VOLUME 3

The titles published in this series are listed at *brill.com/prwr*

The Praised and the Virgin

By

Rusmir Mahmutćehajić

Translated by

Desmond Maurer and Saba Risaluddin

With an Introduction by

Gareth Jones

BRILL

LEIDEN | BOSTON

Cover illustration courtesy of the author.

Library of Congress Cataloging-in-Publication Data

Mahmutcehajic, Rusmir, 1948–
[Hval i djeva. English]
The praised and the virgin / by Rusmir Mahmutcehajic ; translated by Desmond Maurer and Saba Risaluddin.
pages cm. — (Philosophy of religion. World religions, ISSN 2210-481X ; volume 3)
Includes bibliographical references and index.
ISBN 978-90-04-25501-2 (hardback : alk. paper) — ISBN 978-90-04-27940-7 (e-book) 1. Islam—Relations—Christianity. 2. Christianity and other religions—Islam. 3. Mary, Blessed Virgin, Saint—In the Qur'an. 4. Mary, Blessed Virgin, Saint—Islamic interpretations. 5. Muhammad, Prophet, -632—In the Qur'an. 6. Islam—Bosnia and Hercegovina. 7. Christianity—Bosnia and Hercegovina. I. Title.

BP172.M28713 2014
297.2'83—dc23

2014030154

This publication has been typeset in the multilingual "Brill" typeface. With over 5,100 characters covering Latin, IPA, Greek, and Cyrillic, this typeface is especially suitable for use in the humanities. For more information, please see www.brill.com/brill-typeface.

ISSN 2210-481X
ISBN 978-90-04-25501-2 (hardback)
ISBN 978-90-04-27940-7 (e-book)

This book is printed on acid-free paper.

Printed by Printforce, the Netherlands

Contents

Preface

In *The Sorrowful Lament of the Noble Wife of Hassan Aga*, perhaps the best-known literary work of the Slavic South, Hassan Aga drives his faithful love from his halls and kin.[1] He does so because out of modesty she will not obey his command to deny God's apostle, the Praised. Having made clear why she rejects her husband's demand, she remains on the other side from him of the border between Ottoman-controlled Bosnia and Venetian-controlled Dalmatia, where Muslims were welcome only if prepared to deny the indissoluble confessional bond between God's unity and the Praised's apostolate. Hassan Aga addressed his children, saying:

Hod' te amo sirotice moje,	Come here, my little orphans,
Kad se neće smilovati na vas	There's no smile for you
Majka vaša srca ardžaskoga!	In your mother's Hagaric heart.

The otherwise unknown phrase, "Ardžasko srce," can with some certainty be read as "adžarsko srce" and as derived from the name "Hadžar" or Hagar.[2] This and related terms were used in areas bordering Christian states to refer to Muslims. An example from the works of the Montenegrin Prince-Bishop, Peter II Petrović Njegoš, will suffice. In his *Ogledalo Srbsko* [Serb Mirror], he wrote:

Da hristijanski narod izbavimo	To save the people of Christ
i Slavensko ime proslavimo,	and honour the name of Slav,
da slomimo jarma Agarjanska,	to shatter their Agarian yoke,
blagovjerja uzdignimo hrame.[3]	and raise up temples of pure faith

At another point in the poem, instructions are given for the slaughter of Agarians:

Poteći će krvave rijeke	Bloody rivers will run
Od nečiste krvi agarjanske,	of impure Agarian blood,

1 For this poem, see Fortis, *Viaggio in Dalmazia* and Mahmutćehajić, *Tajna Hasanaginice*.

2 For a fuller discussion of this, see Mahmutćehajić, *Tajna Hasanaginice*, esp. 152n9, 161n14, and 162n15.

3 Njegoš, *Ogledalo Srbsko*, 25.

Oprat Srbu ljagu sa obraza.[4]	to cleanse the scum from Serbian cheeks.

The other, who represents whatever stands against the good and beautiful, is constituted on the basis of self-witness in hope of better. There is no compromise with those who represent another aspect of existence. According to an anonymous monk, the Serbian Prince Lazar is said to have declared:

Ako i krv moja da se prolije,	Let first my blood be spilt,
ili ja da se pridružim,	before I join,
ili da se poklonim	or bend the knee,
nečastivom i gadnome,	to the impious and foul,
krvopiji Agaru.[5]	bloodsucking Agarian.

Muslims were berated for their *agarian* hearts or for being *Agars* or *Agarians*, condemned for their spiritual connection with Abraham through the Praised, his descendant out of Hagar. They were denied any right to bear witness to him as the truth of existence and judges did not allow accused Muslims to testify. They were guilty by being Muslim, by confessing no god but God and the Praised as His apostle, with neither defence nor appeal. And so it has gone.

What connects Abraham, Hagar, their son Ishmael and the Praised, on the one hand, with Abraham and Sarah and the Virgin Mary and Jesus, on the other? How is it that the Muslims of the Slavic South see in their Christian past, the Torah, Psalms, and Gospels their own sacred heritage and their main reason for confessing God's unity and the apostolate of the Praised?

The name "Muslims" is here used to refer to those individuals who, like existence as a whole and all things in it, are at peace, first through being creatures and then through their own individual acts of witness and striving to discover and confirm their authentic nature through the prophetic revelation, as their guide to return to the One. To discover this means leaving history for Spirit, but without rejecting the chronology of the waking state. We see it as leaving this lower level, but it involves passing beyond the boundaries of psychic envelopment into the world of the Spirit, where space and time have other meanings than quantity and measure.

The truth of seeing this other side is like the seer's faithfulness to self, to the oath to the Lord, given before all: who all gave one answer to one question. This response is actualized in the drama of our return. Faithfulness to the self is

4 Idem, *Lažni car Šćepan mali*, 155, verses 7–9.

5 Anonymous, cited in Radojičić, *Antologija stare srpske književnosti* (XI–XVIII *veka*), 119.

confidence in our higher potential as revealed and incarnate and exemplary, as first and last of all creation. It guides us on the upward path. Always the same, it is in each of us, albeit with difference. In the contemplation that unfolds from faithfulness to the self and our original nature and respect and loyalty to our guide, the self can free itself and bring about a rising up from our habituation to the dark.

The traveller passing through existence cannot know God, even if He is constantly revealing Himself. This self-revelation maintains us in existence, rather than nonexistence, in being, not nonbeing. Spirit, through which God reveals Himself, is a determination of His will, His revelation to duality. He told the Praised: "They will question thee concerning the Spirit. Say: 'The Spirit is of the bidding of my Lord. You have been given of knowledge nothing except a little.' "[6] The Concealed reveals Himself through the Spirit that descends from God to us through that little knowledge. All His names abide with Him, indistinguishable in His unity, but they have a constant desire to disclose themselves in what receives and manifests them.

Existence is the stage on which God's names are made manifest in space and time. They gather in us. We know ourselves and our Lord through them, for they are His. The Lord knows Himself through our knowledge: He is Creator only in creation. The scattered names are disclosed on the path of return and ascent from the many to the One. Our knowledge on this path is always little. The Praised said:

> Moses got up to deliver a speech before the children of Israel and he was asked: "Who is the most learned person among the people?" Moses replied: "I myself." God admonished him for he did not ascribe knowledge to God alone. So God revealed to him: "At the junction of the two seas there is a slave of ours who is more learned than you."[7]

Moses asked for instructions on how to find this servant[8] and travelled to and asked him:

> I came to you so that you may teach me of the truth which you were taught. Al Khadir said: "Is it not sufficient for you that the Torah is in your hands and Divine Inspiration comes to you, O Moses? Verily, I have a knowledge that you ought not learn, and you have a knowledge which

6 *Qur'an*, 17:85.

7 Bukhārī, 6:21.

8 On this see *Qur'an*, 18:60–82.

> I ought not learn." At that time a bird took with its beak from the sea. Al Khadir then said: "By God, my knowledge and your knowledge beside God's knowledge is like what this bird has taken with its beak from the sea."[9]

Moses as prophet knew the Torah, received as revelation. Al Khadir was more learned. As Al Khadir testified, their knowledge was mere drops from the sea of God's. The source might be the same, but they differed and were irreducible to each other, because God, Who has absolute knowledge, manifests differently from moment to moment and thing to thing. These forms of knowledge meant nothing, as negligible compared to their source, but were decisive for Moses and Al Khadir, as their link with Him Whose knowledge comprehends all things. Our little knowledge links any given condition of the self, any given thing in creation, with absolute knowledge.

The Sorrowful Lament of the Noble Wife of Hassan Aga relates the drama of a husband who has rejected the Praised's apostolate and driven his faithful love from his halls for continuing to view him as the only guarantee of redemption. He rushed to judgment on little knowledge:

Što se b'jeli u gori zelenoj?	What whitens that green height?
Al' su sn'jezi, al' su 'labutove?	Is it snow drifts or swans?
Da su sn'jezi već bi okopnuli,	Snow drifts would have thawed;
Labutovi već bi poletjeli.	Swans have taken flight.
Nit su sn'jezi, nit su labutovi,	They're not snow drifts nor swans,
Nego šator age Hasan-age.	But lord Hassan-Aga's tent.

The green height dominates. One rises to its peak out of the depth. The potential snows represent its purity, the white birds angels descending into the night of existence to lead us from our deep well to the peak, to that most beautiful upright form in which God sees Himself in us and we can see ourselves in Him. The scene stands for the world of the Spirit, the white robes of the Pilgrim in the act of sending and returning. Even the name Hassan Aga, the "beautiful gentleman," refers to our sublime potential – identification with the beauty God manifests in creation.

God, as Possessor of the most beautiful names, created us in beautiful uprightness. In our authentic condition, we announce His beauty and identify with it, as all we have is His. God reveals Himself in our beauty and sees Himself

9 Bukhārī, 6:217.

as Beautiful through us. When our will opposes His, the situation alters and we fall to the depth.

To return to authentic uprightness, we must turn to the mountaintop, the snows and the traces of angels. Our vision of the world is transformed into a vision of the self. Self-discovery, return, and realization are achieved on the path from depth to height. We go not east, west, north or south, but up, within the self, whose worldly signs remind us of the Self and Its valleys and peaks.

Our own little knowledge aspires to more and greater, as what little we do have connects us with the Creator. To know Him is to know the self. To cross the boundary of our knowledge is to travel into it, as the Praised said of our salvation: "O my Lord, increase me in knowledge!"[10] Increased knowledge is migration from depth to height and return to ourselves and our Lord.

There is nothing improper or shameful in calling the people of peace, linked to God as Peace by being-at-peace, Agarians or stressing their spiritual connection with the hand-maiden Hagar, who bore Abraham's son Ishmael, but detractors use the name to deploy distorted images. If Muslims are humiliated and offended, they should build up, in the ante-chambers of their own selves, a better understanding of being Agarian and assist their detractors to see how self-destructive their efforts at insult are, preventing their own self-realization after our common, authentic perfectibility.

Being of the people of peace is to migrate constantly in search of our perfectibility as human beings, which the Praised brought into focus and stood for as prophet. This migration is from lower to higher, darkness to light, evil to good, within the self reminded by the external world's horizons of the gradations from depth and darkness to most beautiful uprightness and light. Only signs can serve to recall our link with the One. At every stage on the path, we may expect assistance.

The peaceful way of life is determined by *hijra*, migration to follow the Praised as the maternal prophet, the light sent down, best example, and shining lamp. The path of self-realization is marked by movement, out of and with which the world reveals itself as the book of our redemption, not the concealment of our potential in worship of other gods than He Who said: "And We wronged them not, but they wronged themselves; their gods availed them not that they called upon, apart from God, anything, when the command of thy Lord came; and they increased them not, save in destruction."[11]

Our little knowledge stands against such destruction of the self through the worship of other gods, as the hidden God discloses Himself in the self of those

---

10 *Qur'an*, 20:114.

11 *Qur'an*, 11:101.

who love Him. Loving the Known and knowing the Beloved are faith, the path of migration, as the self opens to its higher potential. It encounters countless possibilities for orientation, but cannot pass on towards authentic perfection by any external path. So many paths offer themselves that are in reality mere shadows of what lies within.

Our quest for orientation towards an exit beyond the threshold of finitude and entry into the supersensible is the drama of the self. It takes place fully in the now as the only full reality. Issues related to signs in the world and their reference to images in the self, the meaning of the external orient compared to the orient of the self are decisive for this quest. God spoke of this openness through the Praised: "Do the people reckon that they will be left to say: 'We believe,' and will not be tried?"[12]

Temptations and experience are the path of freedom. We are not and cannot be free of God, as being creatures makes us servants-at-peace. God reveals Himself to his servants as Lord, Peace. We bear His confidence, a relationship possible only on free will. To realize our service manifesting His lordship and being-at-peace in manifestation of His being Peace, we must harmonize our will with His. Doing so, we cease to flee from the Real.

At peace in God, we bring our will into line with His and free ourselves of all things not God. Free for Him, we are free from all other things. We liberate ourselves from any association of other gods with God, realizing ourselves in and through our testimony of His unity, the apostolate of the Praised, and universal return. Freedom from the unreal entails freedom for the Real. Accordingly, our freedom is only possible if the self manifests the Self. This changes constantly. Our ascent from one manifestation to another, to draw nearer the Self in confession of no self but the Self, means our migration realizes freedom and self-possession. To be human is to be one's own, free. To be one's own and free is to be God's alone, for all things owe their reality, service and freedom to Him.

The stories of Hagar and Mary and their sons Ishmael and Jesus are normally put in geographical and historical context. More important than the knowledge such historicity gives, however, is the knowledge that answers this question: Who are they and why are they so significant for our quest for orientation within the expanse and history of the self?

---

12 *Qur'an*, 29:2.

List of Illustrations

Some Old Ways: Reuniting the Scattered Lines of Memory

Introducing The Praised and the Virgin

There are many old ways in Bosnia. If one heads out into the mountains east of Mostar, or north or south of that parallel, one can follow the shepherd tracks out into the wilderness, across the hills and valleys of Montenegro and eventually down onto the plains of Macedonia and Kosovo. These are the routes taken by the Ottomans in the fifteenth century and known far earlier by Greeks and Illyrians, travelled later by Sephardic Jews and Franciscans and then by many others. And some clichés remain true: for one may still hear wolves in the mountains up above Mostar, and one may still see bears and wild mountain goats in this wilderness.

More visceral realities also obtain, however. These same old ways are today often impassable not because of bears and wolves, but because of landmines. The ordnance left behind by the Serbian and Bosnian armies, and inadequately controlled by UN forces, now places physical, hidden barriers across these old ways. Official figures indicate that more than 220,000 unexploded devices remain buried in more than 13,000 locations in Bosnia. Landmine explosions in Bosnia have killed more than 500 people since 1996. Another 1200 individuals have been wounded.[1]

Such deaths and injuries are a constant physical reminder of the appalling crimes committed during the Croatian and Serbian attacks upon Bosnia. And yet the *physical* damage caused has been accompanied by a greater, *metaphysical* destruction. For these violent attacks upon the old ways have caused a deep blindness to pass over Bosnia, its peoples, and its neighbors. That deep blindness in turn has caused a deeper ignorance to prevail. This ignorance is not solely a geographical one, whereby people avoid the districts and regions that are "foreign" to them (though that instinct is common enough in Bosnia). Now people do not know the old metaphysical ways, their earlier practices and customs. They cannot see them. They are forgetting not only where these old ways go but also where they begin. Something of this situation can be seen in the isolationism that envelopes cities like Banja Luka, Tuzla, Mostar, and even Sarajevo, as well as the continuing, paralyzed hostility of Republika Srpska.

Bosnia sits not only on some old fault lines in European polity. It also occupies a unique position with respect to European religious traditions. For Christianity those traditions reside in the abiding presence of the Eastern and

1 Data from the Bosnia-Herzegovina Mine Action Centre.

Western Churches, as well as the historic role of the Franciscan order. For Islam the heritage is Ottoman. Sephardic Jewry arrived in the region after their expulsion from Spain in 1492, paradoxically hosted by the recently arrived Ottomans. Ashkenazy Jewry came with the Austro-Hungarian Empire in the 1870s and has left a physical imprint on Sarajevo. Each of these traditions has offered distinctive cultural and intellectual gifts to Bosnia, and each finds a presence in *The Praised and the Virgin*. These religious traditions form the spiritual and philosophical contexts both for Mahmutćehajić's work and the specific books that are being introduced here.[2]

The three volumes of *The Praised and The Virgin* – respectively, *Eternity in Prophetic Revelation; On Continuity and Discontinuity;* and *Reuniting the Scattered* – do not begin with Bosnia, however, though that country is always their landscape and memory. Rather, they constitute a series of extended reflections upon and around three themes that are crucial to the author's most passionate concern: first, how human beings come to know God through revelation; second, how this revelation is obscured by human confusions, most drastically in modernity's tropes; third, the recovery of authentic liminality (rather than its bogus forms) in the experiences of Bosnian social and religious pluralism.

These three themes also demonstrate the presence of European intellectual traditions in Mahmutćehajić's critical reflection. Though his thinking is far more eclectic than more straightforwardly academic positions, Mahmutćehajić's work occupies similar territory to other forms of the philosophy of religion, and the same questions – about ethical decision-making, the question of human identity, the character of both the Divine and the Good, and the determination of history – that one finds in other thought systems are also evidenced in *The Praised and the Virgin*. Some of those questions return to the broader areas of reflection that one finds in the European idealist and phenomenological traditions, for example in Hegel's *Phenomenology of Spirit* and its mediation in more recent literary and cultural media. Other questions return more deeply to Kant's three *Critiques* and strictly epistemological considerations. Each of these influences can be found in Mahmutćehajić's work,

2 Mahmutćehajić is by no means an exhaustive writer on the three monotheistic faiths in Bosnia, which in any case have received no systematic exposition that is available in English. Michael A. Sells' fine book *The Bridge Betrayed* does, however, have an excellent oversight of the important context here: *The Bridge Betrayed: Religion and Genocide in Bosnia*. London, University of California Press Ltd., 1998.

though one must note that his own overriding religious and intellectual compulsions always transform them into a unique narrative.[3]

This Introduction will draw out four main questions from the text in order to introduce both the religious and the philosophical themes with which Mahmutćehajić is concerned. They cannot be exhaustive but they should be critical, since being critical of self and community is a substantive part of what Mahmutćehajić regards as an ethical life. The four themes are: tradition; the "boundaries" of reading intelligently; revelation; and pluralism. They will be considered distinctly.

Authentic Memory

The Praised and The Virgin looks like a book "about" two key religious figures, and they are indeed the subjects of a great deal of material in these three volumes. Mahmutćehajić is not concerned, however, with solely debating the features of the historical discussion of Mary in Islam.[4] Rather, he offers a sustained, existential consideration of how humans encounter The Praised and The Virgin, how these figures speak and what they say to people, and more importantly what happens to individuals in these precise and detailed conversations.

It follows, therefore, that before Mahmutćehajić examines any of the questions he wants to write about, he has in mind what one might call an anthropology: a way of understanding the human condition, for want of a better expression.[5] His anthropology is not drawn from the material sciences and

3 It would certainly be wrong to attempt to categorize Mahmutćehajić's work according to the forms of the analytical philosophy of religion such as one finds, for example, in the English-speaking context. Nor, indeed, do I think his work is particularly grounded in similar areas. Thus, although there is a resemblance to John Hick's philosophy of harmonious and co-existing religious beliefs, in Mahmutćehajić they are always far more greatly traditioned than in Hick's work. Ultimately Mahmutćehajić is far more concerned with historical realities than logical possibilities: hence largely the absence of any explicit epistemology in his work and also its broader similarities with philosophers like Hegel and Heidegger.

4 On this question see especially Hosn Abboud, *Mary in the Qur'an: A Literary Reading*, London, Routledge 2013 and, older but still valuable, Aliah Schleifer, *Mary the Blessed Virgin of Islam*, Fons Vitae 1997. Another important study, albeit of a narrower question, is found in Mary F. Thurkill, *Chosen Among Women: Mary and Fatima in Medieval Christianity and Shi'ite Islam*, South Bend, University of Notre Dame Press 2008.

5 I intend this term "the human condition" in a general sense rather than any specific allusion to Malraux, Arendt, or others.

their analogues, however, but rather from what Mahmutćehajić knows instinctively on the basis of his years of study and reflection as a Bosnian, Muslim, and European intellectual.[6] We recognize such knowledge as tradition, and tradition is the starting point of Mahmutćehajić's understanding of the human condition.

"Tradition" is both a central part of Bosnian folklore in some distinctive ways, and a founding characteristic of religious experiences of the ethical monotheism of Judaism, Christianity, and Islam. It is, consequently, the basic material of *The Praised and The Virgin*, in that Mahmutćehajić's extended reflections are *actual* reflections upon what he has received as both a Bosnian and a Muslim and a European inheritor of ethical monotheism. One might say, therefore, that Mahmutćehajić is writing traditionally as much as he is reading tradition: indeed, that activity is as unavoidable to him as his material is specific.

"Tradition" is a slippery word, however, with Latin roots – *tradere, traducere* – in the nouns and verbs that accompany common understandings of trade, inheritance, translation, transportation, and betrayal. In a wider sense those same nouns and verbs gather around similar ideas of memory/remembering and ignorance/forgetting: for all notions of handing on/over or *not* doing so depend upon peoples' capacity or otherwise to take hold of what they have or to remember what they know. This understanding is not necessarily profound: indeed one might argue that it is literally *trivial* in the original Roman sense. It is, however, characteristic of how people engage with others, both those around them and those who have gone before and those who will come afterwards.

This understanding of tradition as *traditioning* is fundamental for Mahmutćehajić, so much so that one simply will not properly appreciate volume three without this insight. Mahmutćehajić's entire work, almost his entire intellectual life, is consumed by remembering, and his most passionate conviction in many ways is that the work of remembering, the work of *imagining* who they are through the act of remembering, is what makes people truly human and truly children of God. Tradition, therefore, is never solely the "stuff" one receives as a result of being in the right place at the right time. It is *always* the craft of identifying authentic existence and when we forget tradition, or when

6 Mahmutćehajić's most systematic treatment of the broad anthropological question can be found in his essay "On the Self," in: *Sarajevo Essays: Politics, Ideology and Tradition*, Albany, SUNY Press 200, pp. 133–48.

peoples' traditions are forced from them, then they forget rather than remember. Then they start to lose their identities.[7]

"Tradition," it follows, is a complex ecology, one in which many layers of meaning and allusion speak across, around, and alongside each other. The medieval palimpsest is a useful analogy here. Just as a palimpsest is used again and again, with each layer of writing erasing and yet adding text to the original base, so tradition is made up of many layers of diction and contradiction. "Realities" like Bosnia, Europe, and ethical monotheism are *traditional* in this sense of being extended complexes of layered meaning and allusion, diction and contradiction. Again this understanding is not necessarily profound in any intellectual sense: it is rather the way ordinary people live within *extraordinary* complexes of what Levinas called alterity and transcendence.[8]

Understanding these characteristics of how people live traditionally is crucial to Mahmutćehajić's entire work: for example in relation to volume three, his understanding not only of folklore and folk song, but more significantly their hold upon people, is dependent upon this sense of tradition. One may go further, however, and argue that Mahmutćehajić discovers a divine gift in these ways of living traditionally, and that that conception of divine gift is itself fundamental to his theodicy; i.e., his understanding of how one justifies the ways of God to humanity. Or, stated a little differently: folklore and folk songs tell us about ourselves because they are *presences* of the divine, which is why and how they are authentically traditional.[9]

How does that idea work? There are three stages to the argument. First, God hands over to human beings the gift of tradition as complex ecology: it is known by many different names – law, gospel, way – but the key point is that the gift's origin is divine. Second, the gift is contradictory because human relations with God are contradictory. Or better: different ways of *dictating* human traditions are inherently ambiguous over time and space; witness the located yet organic evolution of language and culture (witness, too, the metaphysics of Babel). Third, and crucially: only the good person acknowledges this complexity as divine gift because only the good person properly *values* this process of

7 On Heidegger and the philosophy of religion, see: Ben Vedder, *Heidegger's Philosophy of Religion: From God to the Gods*, Duquesne University Press 2006.

8 Emmanuel Levinas, *Alterity and Transcendence*, Columbia University Press (NYC), 1999.

9 There has been almost nothing available in English on Bosnian folklore until the recent publication of Richard marsh's very fine study: *The Tamburitza Tradition: From the Balkans to the American Midwest*, University of Wisconsin Press 2013. Whilst a monograph rather than a comprehensive study of the region, Marsh's book does provide now a very significant marker and origin for further work in this field.

navigating the old ways, through alterity towards transcendence. Or, to state it more provocatively: the good person is one who *remembers*, and *remembering* for good people means tracing their old ways back to God. Such ethical remembering is the defining human obligation and gift.[10]

Textuality and Liminality

For want of a better expression, therefore, tradition is about the human condition rather than particular "bits" of material that have "somehow" come down through time and space. Mahmutćehajić considers human lives *coram Deo* as people capable of living morally and spiritually complex and rich lives *provided* they are always seeking to understand themselves critically and relationally with others, and *provided* – paradoxically – that they understand the original Provision to be from God. As stated, this understanding is never a matter of factual knowledge but rather a remembering; a reception of gift.

This remembering and reception is the context for Mahmutćehajić's interpretation of Muhammad, The prophet, who is known in this book as The Praised (*Hval* in Bosnian). In a fine account in the first part of volume one, initially of Adam's fall but then of The Praised's own relationship with God, Mahmutćehajić articulates the individual's way from God, towards self and thereby annihilation, but then the return, through and beyond self, back to the eternal mystery of God's gift and love. That essentially is how Mahmutćehajić understands Islam: as the guidance sent down to lead us on this return to God.

If this part of volume one can be interpreted as a reasonably conventional Islamic theology, albeit a distinctive one, then the second part is more controversial. It brings together an extended consideration of the lives and devotions of Sarah, Hagar, and The Virgin Mary, creating an innovative typology that brings these three figures into a mutually indebted, faithful tension. That tension is, of course, strictly impossible historically, but is made intelligible here by Mahmutćehajić's understanding of tradition (see above) and his approach to textuality. Simply stated, he "folds" the stories of these women one into another, thereby eradicating the contingent differences and drawing out the essential identity that they all share. In this way Mahmutćehajić offers a genuinely differentiated understanding of the *origin* of the religious life: the embrace of liminality and thereby peoples' exposure to the unresolved debt they owe to the divine.

---

10 Mahmutćehajić's principal book of ethical reflection is *Bosnia the Good: Tolerance and Tradition*, Budapest, Central European University Press 2000.

This point influences the reading of *The Praised and The Virgin* in three ways. First, liminality in Mahmutćehajić's work is not solely an understanding of transition, threshold, and ambiguity, but rather a way of characterizing the entire idea of origin and the eternal. One may by faith have real clarity about human relationships with God, therefore: but one must always remain unclear about the specific source of that faith which is essentially mysterious. Second, Mahmutćehajić illustrates this point by drawing out the intimacy of Sarah, Hagar, and The Virgin. For rather than state baldly that Judaism, Islam, and Christianity are somehow descended from each of these women, he demonstrates how all three monotheistic faiths are inextricably woven together not historically but liminally. One might *think* that one's origin as a Christian is bound up with The Virgin, therefore: but Hagar is one's authentic Mother.[11]

Third, and more speculatively for Mahmutćehajić, this way of reading the textuality and liminality of the stories surrounding the Praised and the Virgin are models of how one must read all textuality. Or better: since all human life is traditioned textually and must be remembered and received as such, all peoples' stories become part of their indebted response to God. There is no escape, in other words, from peoples' lives *coram Deo*: for wherever one may go and whichever wilderness one's faith may take one to – Sinai, Arabian, or Judean – The Pillar of Fire always goes ahead.

For Jews and Christians much of Mahmutćehajić's reflection here is deeply reminiscent of the Psalms, and one can argue that his appreciation of poetry and folk song arises from more or less exactly the same human and religious instincts that one finds in those Biblical texts. It is an important point, for as one reads *The Praised and The Virgin* one needs to remember that everything Mahmutćehajić writes, everything he thinks, is part of his ongoing conversation with God. His text is always a profoundly scholarly and intellectual work that is also always profoundly devotional.

11 Again, this point illustrates the fundamental difference between Mahmutćehajić and a philosopher of religion like John Hick. Whereas for Hick the point here might be intelligible conceptually but certainly not in any literal sense, for Mahmutćehajić it is *literally* the case (as tradition) that Hagar is my mother as a Christian. To understand this point is to understand Mahmutćehajić's axiomatic reading of the original and originating materials of the monotheistic religions.

Truth

There is sufficient material here to make it worthwhile speaking of Mahmutćehajić's work broadly in terms of a "postmodern" interpretation, if by that idea is indicated not so much an anti-modernity or a specific era "after" modernity, but rather ways of thinking and reading and questioning traditions and textualities that engage with liminality, alterity, transcendence, etc. as ideas in flux.[12] And in that same context it makes a certain sense to speak of *The Praised and The Virgin* as a work of deconstruction, of deconstructing *imaginatively* the entire set of ideas one has when one speaks of God, faith, humanity and religion. The question of truth, therefore – "Are our stories about the Praised and the Virgin true?" – is for Mahmutćehajić meaningless if one does not first reflect deeply upon what one means by truth. *Of course they are true …* but who are human beings to ask that question?

Deconstruction is a way of asking this question philosophically, therefore. Limiting his work to deconstruction, however, does a profound disservice to Mahmutćehajić's ambition, which is so inherently *reconstructive* as to be identifiably pre-modern; i.e., to be engaging with the thought world and ideals of medieval romance. The evidence supporting this claim is palpable, since everything Mahmutćehajić says about the Praised and the Virgin renders their (textual, liminal) relationship a love story: *not* the doomed and sentimental capitulation of Romeo and Juliet, certainly, but rather the faith-full *recapitulation* of Abelard and Heloise. And just as the story of Abelard and Heloise embraces tragedy alongside a deeper consummation, so Mahmutćehajić is fully aware of the tragically unconsummated love between the Praised and the Virgin *and their believers*. It is the tragically unconsummated love of all Jews, Christians, and Muslims.[13]

This love story is not simply diverting or affecting, however, in the sense that any love story *might* cast light on how other human beings love. It is *original:* The Praised and the Virgin in themselves, their responses to God (and Jesus), and their own *sublime* relationship reveal the truth about God's will to love creation and to restore it and to be God in that gift. *The Praised and The Virgin* is in many ways Mahmutćehajić's retelling of that love story, not because he wants to demonstrate a scholarly discovery that had not been made by anyone

12 Cf. famously Jean-Francois Lyotard, *The Postmodern Condition: A Report on Knowledge*, Manchester University Press (Manchester), 1985, as a clear way into this distinction; see esp. pp. 71–85.

13 This aspect of Mahmutćehajić's work appears to be an entirely original contribution to the interpretation of the relationship between the prophet and the Virgin Mary.

else, but because his readers are also loved by the Praised and the Virgin *and they must learn to love Them too if they are to remember God and return to the old ways*. This love story is not an elective option, in other words. For want of a better word, it is of *ontological* significance because it is truth as revelation.

This insight is critical for any sophisticated reading of these volumes. For Mahmutćehajić the "truth" of his ideas, indeed the "truth" of his traditions and texts, can never be about accuracy. Speaking of the accuracy of his interpretation of these matters makes as much sense to Mahmutćehajić as limiting Christology to the death of the historical Jesus did to Hegel.[14] Truth as disclosure, as revelation, yes, as *aletheia* – wittingly or not Mahmutćehajić is following Heidegger on this point[15] – is the essential reconstructive turn that makes it possible for good men and women to imagine their memories and to turn their lives back to God. This truth has no content, if by "content" one means a Torah or a Cross or a Koran. It has rather an epiphany. Or better, *many* epiphanies: the mysterious disclosures of sincere and genuine human lives that lift them out of hypocrisy and help restore them to God.

European Tragedies

One recognizes in all of this critique, of course, that *Bosnia* remains the copingstone of Mahmutćehajić's work. He is by any account one of the greatest living European intellectuals: a priceless witness to our human condition and a giant champion of those central European heritages that bewitch the Balkan states. To read *The Praised and The Virgin* is to be introduced to an almost limitless treasure house of material that constitutes one of the greatest literary bequests of any culture. One of this text's most wonderful gifts to the reader is the sheer density of that material and how much of it is given for the reader to appreciate, enjoy, and understand.

Mahmutćehajić's passionate embrace of his Bosnian heritage has a price, however, in that it becomes necessary to recognize the enemies of that heritage as precisely that: enemies that are seeking to undermine peoples' spiritual

14 Cf. Eberhard Jungel, *God As The Mystery Of The World*, T & T Clark (Edinburgh), 1983, esp. p. 76, quoting Hegel: "In Swabia they say of something which had long since happened, it's so long ago that soon it won't be true anymore. Thus Christ died for our sins so long ago that soon it won't be true anymore." Thus famously Hegel's distinction between the historic and the speculative Good Fridays.

15 See Martin Heidegger, "Vom Wesen und Begriff der physis. Aristoteles, Physik B, 1," in: *Gesamtausgabe IX: Wegmarken*, Vittorio Klostermann (Frankfurt am Main), pp. 239–301.

disclosures and prevent their genuine return to God. These enemies are real and visceral threats, none more so than nationalism, which Mahmutćehajić recognizes as the greatest scourge of modern European political thought.[16] Modernity itself, however, is also such an enemy, as are all modern ways of thinking that seek to turn our minds towards accuracy and its objective, empirical calculation, and away from the deepest possible understanding of truth as *aletheia*. Again, there is much here that could be taken from Heidegger's criticisms of technology and its impact upon the human imagination.[17]

This sense of tragic conflict at the heart of European intellectual history returns to the old ways that can be traced across and through Bosnia; for in a very real sense the deepest tragedy that concerns Mahmutćehajić is what has befallen Bosnia and therein what is befalling Europe. Mahmutćehajić's genius is to preserve this metaphysics of Bosnia from political sentimentality by grounding it in the far greater religious traditions of ethical monotheism, which then in turn – through the Ottoman conquest and the disappearance of the Bosnian Church – also become part of the face of Bosnia. In this respect, and enormous though it be, *The Praised and The Virgin* is still only a fragment of a larger work. One can argue, for example, that one day Mahmutćehajić's metaphysics must embrace the fullest possible history of the Bosnian Church *as well as* the arrival and sanctuary of Sephardic Jewry after 1492 – controversial though that embrace and that critical narrative must inevitably be.[18]

Why this greater scope? Because the best way to understand the European tragedies that Mahmutćehajić argues against is as hypocrisy, as false witness to the self-disclosing God. Nationalism, for example, is hypocrisy because it falsely witnesses to peoples' identity in contingent political circumstances rather than remembered gift. Modernism in general is hypocrisy because it pulls people away from a deeply *sincere* understanding of their lives *coram Deo* towards a false witness to the sustainability of technological data. Indeed all "isms" are inevitably hypocritical if they become reified and homogenized as

16 Cf. Ivo Banac' deeply influential work on this question: *The National Question in Yugoslavia: Origins, History, Politics*, Cornell University Press (Ithaca), 1984.

17 Most obviously Heidegger's essay "Die Frage nach der Technik": *Gesamtausgabe VII: Vortrage und Aufsatze*, Vittorio Klostermann (Frankfurt am Main), pp. 5–36.

18 The question is controversial for several different reasons: the original reception then treatment of the Sephardic Jews; the heritage of *Ladino* in the Balkan countries and their folklore; the relative displacement of the Sephardic by Ashkenazi Jewry during the nineteenth century colonization by the Austro-Hungarian Empire; and Bosnia's compromised relationship – in the midst of many such relations – with national socialism in the period 1933–45, with its obvious consequences under Tito. See on this question Stephen Schwartz, *Sarajevo Rose: A Balkan Jewish Notebook*, London, Saqi Books, 2005.

things in themselves rather than as at best fleeting reflections of aspects of a deeper insight. Mahmutćehajić must reject these hypocrisies if he is to rediscover the old ways, just as people must reject and rediscover the same things if they are to exercise their ethical and spiritual affinities.

These points notwithstanding, *The Praised and The Virgin* has a genuine darkness to it, which is perhaps unavoidable: Bosnia may not be a land without hope but it is a land where hopefulness is hard to define. What redeems this part of his text, and indeed what may also redeem Bosnia, is Mahmutćehajić's insight that this ontic darkness is not essential but provisional. What people see around them in the contemporary world is not God's original face. It is what happens when the ghosts take over the machine. One likes to think those same ghosts disappeared in modern times but they did not; they simply went about their business. *Our* business is to struggle with them, not in order to seek their destruction but rather their liberty – and in their liberty, our own.

Conclusion

One of the greatest myths of modern Europe is that the old ways went away, therefore, like ghosts evaporating, never to return. It is a myth that has been rehearsed many times after evil has been seemingly exposed and consumed by the good, without conscious paradox. Europeans memorialize such events and celebrate their anniversaries, carefully avoiding moral equivalence so as not to offend; carefully ignoring the returning ghosts walking silently along the old ways.[19]

Dayton was solely the latest incarnation of this phenomenon, and that fact is profoundly depressing.[20] Yet the very provisionality of the Dayton Accords, and the certainty that Europe must someday once again confront their unfinished business, is itself a depressingly hopeful sign. For it means that once again Bosnia will provide Europe with opportunities to acknowledge its ghosts and restore them to their places in the world of living spirits.

---

19 Such specific literary and supernatural references continue to be a potent feature of popular belief and practice in this part of Europe, with an evident intelligibility in the folklore and customs of both the educated and uneducated. On this question in the Balkan countries see Tomislav Longinovic, *Vampire Nation: Violence As Cultural Imaginary*, Duke University Press (Durham, NC), 2011.

20 It remains to be seen, as of March 2014, how Russia and Ukraine resolve finally the crisis in the Crimea, and to what extent the USA and Europe are permitted any role in that resolution.

It is possible that Sarajevo in 2014, or Srebrenica in 2015, will initiate this latest process, in which case the patience of some might be rewarded.[21] As Mahmutćehajić's work teaches, however, true patience is not a human faculty that responds to deferred gratification. It is rather an authentic characteristic of love. And insofar as love can ever be authentic – as the Praised and the Virgin experienced it distinctly – it must originate with God. In this respect human patience is always an old way of being loved by God and loving Him in return.

Gareth Jones
Ming Hua College Hong Kong

21 Respectively the centenary of the assassination of Archduke Franz Ferdinand and his wife Sophie on 28th June 1914 and the twentieth anniversary of the genocide at the end of the Serbian war against Bosnia.

Foreword for the English Reader

The Praised and the Virgin is a three volume work, originally published in Bosnian as *Hval i Djeva* in 2011, by the publishing house of *Dobra Knjiga*, from Sarajevo, in Bosnia and Herzegovina. It is the result of several decades of reflection and study on key aspects of the Muslim intellectual tradition, against a background of oppression, war, ethnic conflict and interfaith dialogue. At its heart lies a committment to promoting greater understanding between the members of the three great religious communities that trace their origins back to the prophet Abraham and his covenant with God. It is an attempt to look at certain points of contact between the Muslim tradition, commonly referred to as Islam, and the Christian traditions, in their various current and past forms, particularly as present in Europe. Those points of contact include, but are not limited to the figure of Jesus, as God's Christ or Anointed, his mother, the Virgin Mary, and, of course, the prophet Muhammad or Paraclete, whom we call the Praised for reasons explained below. As such it has been used as the focal point for a series of interfaith seminars and discussions between representatives of all three traditions in Bosnia and the author gratefully acknowledges the additional insights gained from his Christian and Jewish interlocutors during them, some of which have been incorporated into this effectively revised edition.

The initial translation was largely the work of Ms. Saba Risaluddin, with some sections translated separately by Mr. Desmond Maurer for publication in academic journals. At the request of the publisher, the English edition is a moderately abridged version of the original, prepared by Desmond Maurer and the author. All three volumes are now published in one and their forewords combined. Otherwise the structure of the original has largely been preserved, but the translation has been thoroughly revised and condensed, with certain non-essential contents excised.

A particular aspect of the translation that has the potential to cause confusion is integral to the method being followed. This is the use of non-standard translations for common Qur'anic and Islamic terms. The author agrees with a strong current in modern academic religious studies which finds that all the religious traditions have been subject to major pressures of reification and ideologization, particularly under the conditions of modernity. These have seriously affected the way they view themselves, their adherents, their histories, their origins, how they are related to God, and even their view of God Himself. In extreme cases, they have become forms of idolatry, of the association of contingencies to the Essential. These deviations and deformities are deeply reflected in the language used to talk about the traditions, the major figures and the key concepts and to translate the texts. The author has therefore tried in Bosnian, and the same attempt is made in the English translations of his works, to use words and terminology that undermine this reification and ideologization in two ways.

The first is by returning to the semantic core in Arabic, or in some cases Aramaic and Greek, of the words used in the original texts and to find alternative translations that bring out the semantic associations they would have had for the authors and audiences of those texts, while also freeing the present-day reader from the accumulated baggage of centuries of petrification and distortion.

The second is by rejecting false dichotomies established between the Christian and the Muslim and the Jewish traditions. All too often, the different traditions use different words for concepts that are essentially identical in meaning. The author prefers to stress the common to the extent possible, as he believes only then can we come to see and appreciate what is truly different and value it for the richness it adds, rather than fear it for a merely apparent otherness.

Some of the most important examples follow.

The word *Allah* is not used in our English translation, because it is simply the Arabic for God.

The Praised is used to refer to *Muḥammad*, because that is what his name means in Arabic. It is also key to understanding the theology of the Muslim tradition, as the prophet is precisely what his name says and his name explains his role in God's creation. We refer to the Praised throughout as God's apostle, not God's Messenger. While this may seem to be substituting an archaism for a clearer term, in this case we feel that it points up the continuity between the traditions, which using the more modern term serves to conceal. Apostle is, after all, just Greek for messenger.

The Anointed is generally used to translate the *Christ* and *Messiah*, as it is what those titles mean. Translating it with an intelligible term that represents Jesus' place and function in God's plan, rather than one which puts meaning at a distance, is intended to create room for dialogue between the traditions.

Being-at-peace is the translation used for *islam*, as it and the various associated words, including *muslim* and *al-salam*, which just mean person of peace and peace respectively, are all semantically associated and derived from the same verbal root. In the author's view, the standard translation in terms of submission and surrender has been abused to create a completely false understanding of the Muslim tradition as a religion of fatalists and fanatics. It is possible to redeem the vocabulary of submission to God, but to do so would require parallel investigations of the theme of abnegation of the will to the Will in all three traditions – Christian, Jewish, and Muslim, as all three share a rich mystical heritage that has mined it extensively.

The most important other term is the use of debt or obligation to translate *al-din*, instead of the more usual religion. This is because religion has become a highly reified concept, refering to institutions, as well as doctrinal-ritual complexes, and even to communities of adherents grouped together in a quasi-ethnic fashion. What is in question is the proper way of relating to God, given that we are in debt or under an obligation to Him for our very existence and because of the sin committed in the Garden by Adam. This understanding forms the core of all three of the Abrahamic traditions. The Arabic word *din* means debt and is only secondarily used to refer to what we now call religion.

Central to the Debt is the Revelation, which the people of peace believe to have been sent down to the Praised in the Recitation. Recitation is the term we use to refer to the Qur'an, which simply means something recited, a lesson.

Covering and Coverers or Concealing and Concealers are used to refer to what is often called unbelief or infidelity. We do so because what is in question is a covering over of the innate knowledge we are all born with and which it is our task in life to uncover, to reveal our most beautiful authentic and original nature, as it was before Adam fell. The Arabic term *kufr* simply means covering or concealing.

When citing from the Recitation we have generally used Arberry's standard translation, adapted to conform with the above listed preferences. We have also adapted citations from the standard collections of traditions about the prophet and his life and from the Bible, which are normally quoted after the King James Version. Full details of editions used are given in the bibliography.

The author acknowledges the great contribution of the translators to the book in this form, as well as to many other friends and colleagues from all over the world, too numerous to mention, and amongst whom it would be invidious to single out individuals.

Prologue

Judaism and Islam can be difficult for Christian understandings of time, which connect past and future through the coming of Christ. Some find the continued Jewish presence inexplicable and the suggestion unacceptable that those who do not recognize the Christ as they do can still enjoy full relations with God. Much the same is held of Muslims, whose creed contradicts the Christian understanding of Christ. The Muslim confession of the Praised as key to pre-existence, history, and post-existence transformed Jewish and Christian witness of the Messiah. It does not deny him. It proposes a different narrative Muslims believe sent down by God as a revelation for all, its bearer foretold in all ages and places as representing our sublime potential and authentic nature. The Muslim story is consequently often formulated as one of intrusion, a distortion to be eliminated from the Christian trajectory.

Although Jewish, Christian and Muslim narratives all include accounts of a promised apostle and an anointed one (the literal meaning of Christ), interpretation of their canonical texts has produced apparently irreconcilable differences and controversies that are, for all that, integral to our world.

This book sets out a Muslim understanding of being as our relationship with God. Starting from wholeness, we enter plurality. We realize our humanity by recovering that unity. This involves two wills, human and Divine. Unity is the harmony of our will with God's. This unity is knowable. Jews, Christians and Muslims all agree that it both transcends existence and informs the duality of giving and receiving present throughout it. The One and duality bear mutual witness through the various sacred traditions, which are modes of overcoming difference to know the principle.

This essay investigates forms of tradition that do not treat the human instrumentally, seeing in the self a treasury of possibilities. It does so through the images of the Praised and the Virgin as the primordial revealed couple – "the seed and the fruit" of all revelation of the One. The Praised signifies God as Giving, the Virgin signifies Him as Receptive. The discussion draws on the perennial philosophy contained in Judaic, Christian and Muslim traditions and does so from a distinctly Bosnian perspective.

For Bosnian tradition, everything in space or time, passed down or to come, affirms divine unity and the role of the Praised. The prophets and their followers proclaim "the true apostolic faith" before humanity. Their acts of witness mean we can be that first human standing before God, mirroring Him, and so turn our backs on appearances that ape the Anointed and the Praised in an inverted chain of being. Just as the external world is one and many, our self is many and one. World and self are two faces of one principle they jointly disclose: the Lord. It is their meaning to reveal Him. That witness is integral to both, so that existence is totalized by manifesting Him, as epiphany. No matter where we turn, we are before the Face of the Lord, Which is beginning and end, outside and inside.

How can we know our Lord? Everything in the world and the self was created with truth. Recognizing that truth reveals the truth of our own creation, a truth we may then, and only then, realize. This potential is the uncreated core of our being. External knowledge – whether acquired by the senses or by contemplation or dreaming – serves to remind us of what is already present within us.

Contact with the world entails difference and flux, which we desire to transcend. Our origin and knowledge may be supposed to be this-worldly, received from outside, but this ignores that both we and the world are created in the same truth, a truth necessarily greater and more encompassing than its manifestations. We know this truth, the Lord of the worlds, only through speech, which comes from and leads to the unseen. All human speech is mythic, transcending the bounds of our finite knowledge.

> And when thy Lord took from the Children of Adam, from their loins, their seed, and made them testify touching themselves, "Am I not your Lord?" They said, "Yes, we testify" – lest you should say on the Day of Resurrection, "As for us, we were heedless of this," or lest you say, "Our fathers were associators aforetime, and we were seed after them. What, wilt Thou then destroy us for the deeds of the vain-doers?"[1]

Realizing our humanity does not depend on knowledge from outside, which can always mislead, as the knowledge at our core cannot. It is what it is, no matter how deeply buried, how absent from domains of being for which signs have lost their authentic meaning. The world, the prophets and the books exist only to remind us of what lies at the centre of our being. Meaning cannot be reformulated so as to alter that truth of creation. It is what links us as knowers to the knowable truth of creation, the double confession of no god but God and the Praised as His apostle.

The tenet that there is no god but God is irrefutable: it centres both world and self, independently of time and space, language and symbol. Bearing witness to it, we recognize ourselves as in the image of our Lord. This first tenet is inseparable from the second, the Praised as His apostle. The witness

1 *Qur'an*, 7:172–73.

that there is no god but God makes clear that all praise is in and from Him: the economy of praise passes from God through the world and the self back to the All-praised.

The self lies between degradation and rectitude. To realize the self as created is to discover that rectitude, a discovery through which God discloses Himself as All-praised. This disclosure bestows praise upon and draws praise from all in and to which He is manifest. Receiving His praise, we owe Him ours. Acknowledging this debt to God as Giver and repaying it in full, we too are praised, but even as praised, all we have is from Him. We are His servants. All existence receives His praise, and so glorifies Him with praise. All existence serves the All-praised, for all it has is from the Lord.

God's best servant, His apostle, is the perfect recipient and giver of praise, our best example, the mercy to the worlds. He represents the supreme potential of the self. There is no state of being to which he does not announce a higher potential, for us to turn to in knowledge and in love. This turn begins in free will, as testimony to Peace's presence in the self, through which we may be both at and of peace, linked with Peace through being-at-peace.

The Praised is first of the people of peace. The closer we are to Peace, the closer to him. As apostle, he is our guide on our path from the depths to the height. He is the supreme potential of every self. Return to God is through that potential alone. Being-at-peace, relationship to God as Peace, is the universal mode of existence and unity of outer and inner, first and last, is realized through it.

The Praised is the first principle of creation. He channels all manifestations of praise. He is in both manifest and unseen worlds, outer and inner, beginning and end. He encompasses every soul and all the worlds, in history and beyond it, within and beyond time, as when he said, pointing to his index and middle fingers: "I and the Hour were like these *two*."[2] This closeness with the Hour means that he is the first authentic manifestation of duality: the first male and the first female as the first joint manifestation of unity. His presence in history is a summons from duality to unity.

To reduce the Praised to his historical existence and ignore his presence in every instant is to reduce ourselves to transmitted knowledge, to information received from our forefathers, cutting ourselves off from God's unity and the Praised's apostolate. The import of these tenets is primarily for the self. The real is encompassed in the Hour, while the Praised is the real. He is of concern to every self. Nothing derived from past or future outweighs the potential for

2 Muslim, 4:1526.

sublimity at the core of the self: the Praised. Forgetting this, our knowledge of history and the history of that knowledge become motives for violence. We compete in externally derived knowledge, of no import for the realization of our core humanity. Such knowledge encourages us to forget and even deny the truth of creation.

The perennial wisdom we seek has thus been obscured over the centuries by forms of imported and alienated knowledge, forms invoked in defence against the most profound level of our consciousness. If our sublime potential is stunted, it is not by limits external to the self. Nothing past or to come can abrogate our reason for being in the world. Our "now" is the fullness of the real, heavy with past and future. Attaining our potential means eschewing what is not real and a return to the roots of the perennial philosophy offers a way to disperse the darkness and see the flux of existence in relation to the vertical axis that links the world with its principle.

Muslims – those at peace in God's will – do this through witness to God's unity and the Praised, as revealed in all things, great and small, inner and outer. So long as individuals or communities bear such witness, being and history are without rupture. If their testimony is informed by their sense of self, identity and of community and the marks they have left in and beyond history, the different resultant narratives of God's oneness map onto each other, opening up new vistas in the quest for self-realization and return to God through the best example.

We stand between the void, into which existence crumbles, and the absolute, which recollection offers and oblivion causes to withdraw. The rationalist claim to fill the void through revolutionary activity is a turn from the absolute. Its promise is vain and ruinous, a second separation from Intellect and our purpose of transcending finitude. We reach this purpose through the true core of the self, our authentic nature nothing can destroy. However obscured or displaced by substitute fantasies, our true human nature is always to be found both in and beyond language and tradition. They are signs that reveal our nature as a "link" to the supra-individual principle, above the laws of spatial and temporal extension. This is no flight from suffering and death, but a reorientation towards their absolute opposite. Revelation takes place in the act of distinguishing real from non-real, an act we are prepared for by our true nature, an act that is necessary but not sufficient.

Cleaving to the real is a journey along the axis of Being. No station on the journey can replace the goal: no apostle or law, book or institution, ritual or myth. They serve as reminders on our path, but once the dignity of Intellect has been acknowledged, no such limits confine us. Just as analytical reason is our guide to the point where higher possibilities are revealed, but not beyond, so text and ritual play a necessary role in discovering the absolute as answer to the void, but are not themselves the answer.

Bosnian culture contains a wealth of texts, redemptive beliefs, rituals and virtues. Their diverse threads are interwoven in the various interrelated religious traditions. As Bosnia has been caught up in global currents, new forms of knowledge, attitudes and behaviour have weakened the authority of oral tradition and the demand for traditional understandings. Reclaiming those despised experiences of orality and the findings of traditional intellectuality opens up exciting possibilities for rediscovering higher horizons of being, lost since the Renaissance. This is a move away from the dominant, narrow, materialist worldview, which denies, ignores, distorts, or simplifies traditional intellectuality. The collective rejection of ideology as a spent and empty promise has opened the possibility of a grand convergence of traditional knowledge. As obscure corners of the traditional world are illuminated and the scattered remains of its cultures rediscovered and brought together, we may hope for liberation from the violence of historicism, for which truth and deliverance had become mere bromides.

The world manifests the Creator's will perfectly. What is in heaven and earth and between them is in perfect harmony, but the world encompasses neither existence nor any particular in it, any more than we, the sum of all things, encompass the unity of the Principle in which duality and difference fade. The Creator's perfect relation to creation does not mean we can attain perfection in relation to ourselves, the world and God. Manifestation in descent is continuous, but this does not mean our attempts to ascend to our sublime potential are.

Creation is incessant flux, perpetually renewed. The reason is in His Self and to discover it we need more than the outside world. Our own self encompasses creation's reason and purpose. Absolute sincerity means acknowledging that disorder and the absence of ritual, orientation and rhythm lie in us. God alone puts order, ritual and rhythm on things. We need order and ritual to discover the unquantifiable world in the self as what links self to Self in confession of no self but the Self.

We have will and are aware of being in and facing the world. That there is will entails reconciliation or opposition to the Will. To be reconciled is to be part of the order of the self and outer horizons, to be in opposition to deny that order as given. The order of the world is thus inextricably linked with the will in the self.

Rites are how we participate in the universal order. Participation turns us towards spatial and temporal limits, which we acknowledge in order to pass beyond. No experience of staying, passage or return contains us. However sincere or immediate our experience of divorce from order, it does not interrupt the world's rhythm. Every experience is immediately manifest in memory and will, framed by self, society, universe and the next world.

Unity manifests in duality, flux and multiplicity. For those whose revelation is through the first duality, the Praised and the Virgin, present in the Word as Son and Book, there can be no ritual without hearing, speaking, writing and reading.

Gospel and Recitation are present throughout Bosnian history as crucially important elements of ritual. They inform where and how the hearing, speaking, writing and reading of the divine revelation appear in ritual, so that the universal order may be established in the self. The revelation of the Recitation confirms the Gospel, as what comes later cannot be accepted without what preceded it. These two modes of discourse manifest, in different ways, the same Principle and Revealer.

As created contingent beings, we forget there is no will but the Will, so that things disintegrate from moment to moment, losing orderliness, but they can be recovered in recollection. Ritual is the framework and means of return. It turns us to the Sacred, to renew our connection with It.

We constitute the order of existence in condensed form, in our witness that our every ritual action is dictated by connection with the Ultimate. The mihrab provides a frame for this ritual orientation through hearing and speaking. In it, the directed individual appears as writing and reading. All ritual involves the Book in some way, since the heard, remembered, spoken, written and read Book is how we become part of the order of things and as hearers, rememberers, speakers, writers and readers connect ourselves and our world with Unity as source and confluence of the entire order of things.

The world's order rests at the boundary where inanimate becomes living, living dead. Experience of death requires and sustains ritual, renewing our recollection of self and world as descending and ascending. When faced with the death of another, the living experience ritual as a way of resisting the descent of the self to a lower plane. The rituals of laying out the dead, accompanying the cortège, burying and mourning and maintaining the grave express our conviction that not even death is final mortification. This is evident in our attitudes towards the dead and their graves.

Rituals have two determinants – the doctrine that produces them and their meaning and the virtue expressed in humility and generosity that confirms it. Bosnia's long experience of doctrine, rituals and virtue encompassed by different revelations allows a number of interpretations: in some, differences are dispersed but related, in the other concentrated and united.

VOLUME 1

Eternity in Prophetic Revelations

∵

Introduction: "Whenever Zachariah Went in to Her"

Judaism, Christianity and Islam are sometimes represented as wholly discrete traditions, sometimes as variant responses to a single metaphysical question. Each has its sacred texts and rituals. Their origin is not of this world, but they are both in and with us.

When only "with" and not "in" us, analytical reason is mistaken as exhausting being, opening up a chasm between us and the world that we try to bridge with knowledge and power. In our desire to remake the world and stop the emptiness we have filled it with, we unveil the modern project of self-sacrifice for a future to be brought about by our actions alone.

This approach is evident in some modern and post-modern approaches to sacred texts and rituals, approaches based on rational reduction of supra-individual and supra-rational witness. Sacred tradition, ritual and text encompass each other. To objectify and subordinate them to reason alone is fatal to both. To divorce them from the living self is to condemn them to the dark of the grave.

1

Mary or Marija, Mara, Marica, Mejra, Merima, Mirjam, Merjema is the most common woman's name in Bosnia, particularly if one takes into account other names derived from the Virgin's attributes, like Abida, Sidika, Kanita, or Tahira. Commonly associated titles include Our Lady,[1] Virgin, Hazreti, Azra, Mother of God, Blessed, Saint, Most Holy, or Queen. Many churches are associated with her.

There has been no comprehensive study of her presence in Bosnian history or metahistory or of the forms it has taken.[2] At present, she is primarily

1 The girl's name Gospe (Lady) is still used in western Bosnia. There is clear evidence of diverse forms of veneration of the Virgin Mary in Bosnia, but more research is needed.

2 On Mary's meaning for believers, especially Christians, See Pelikan, *Mary through the centuries*; Markešić, "Crkva i Marija" and "Marija – Majka Kristova, Majka Crkve" in idem, *Crkva Božja*; Rahner, *Mary, Mother of the Lord*. For the veneration of Our Lady in Bosnia, see Šilić, "Stoljeće i po bosanskohercegovačkog vjerovanja u Marijino uznesenje"; anon., "Gospina svetišta u našoj domovini"; Markešić, "Štovanje Bl. Dj. Marije u bosanskohercegovačkoj tradiciji"; Duvnjak, "Razvoj teologije slike u otačkom razdoblju." On the Virgin, see Schuon,

 DOI 10.1163/9789004279407_002

associated with Christian sacred tradition. This is wrong, as the entire Muslim sacred tradition is imbued with respect for the Virgin and her son. She is present in almost every Bosnian mosque. The widespread ignorance of this presence is indicative of the ongoing erasure of such components of Muslim sacred tradition.

2

Nearly every Bosnian mihrab bears a calligraphic inscription of a partial Qur'anic verse, *Kullamā dakhala ʿalayhā Zakariyyā al-miḥrāba* (Whenever Zachariah went in to her in the sanctuary . . .).[3] It sums up the teaching sent down by God through His prophets. We and the world are two facets of His manifestation. We are created to know our Lord, independently of anything extrinsic. The world, the prophets and the books remind us of this inner knowledge.

Zachariah went in to the Virgin Mary at the Further Mosque, the Temple in Sion. He was a prophet of God, servant of the Temple, and father of another prophet, John. The Virgin was mother of the prophet Jesus. Between them, they bore witness to key events in the sacred history of the Judaic, Christian and Muslim traditions. They announced the full realization of humanity in the Praised.

To understand the Praised as a mercy to the worlds, we must first consider the meaning of the term *miḥrāb*, which means battlefield, and the ritual performed there (standing, bowing, prostration and sitting), and what befell the prophet Zachariah, his son John, the Virgin Mary and her son Jesus.

Every mosque centres on a mihrab.[4] Broadly understood, any place we turn to God is a mosque. The world is thus both mosque and mihrab. Every mihrab is for every individual and so for all – each of us as essentially human and

---

Dimensions of Islam; and idem, *Understanding Islam*. For an account of Marian studies, see Schleifer, *Mary the Blessed Virgin of Islam*; Chenique, *Le Buisson ardent, Essai sur la métaphysique de la Vierge*; Boss, *Empress and Handmaid*; Johnson, *Truly Our Sister*; Tatić-Đurić, *Studije o Bogorodici*.

3 *Qur'an* 3:37. Although this inscription plays an important role in Muslim sacred art, Hoyland does not discuss it in his standard work on *Qur'an*ic epigraphy. He considers verse 17:78 the most common Qur'anic inscription in mihrabs (Hoyland, "Epigraphy," 28), also noting the use of 2:144. Their use as inscriptions can only be understood in terms of how form, function, and content interact to create meaning. See Khoury, "The Mihrab: From Text to Form."

4 The word *miḥrāb* goes back a long way and has a range of meanings. It traditionally denotes a place of encounter between God and individuals (see Padwick, *Muslim Devotions*, 57–59). The Praised in the *miḥrāb* is supreme nearness to God. He is in the *hāʾ* of divine

as creation's quintessence. A mihrab can be simply or elaborately marked. Its counterpart in a church is the altar and they share certain features. Both direct us towards the sign of the Principle and our sublime potential,[5] from illusion to the Real, from the depths to the height.

The Praised is the first of the people of peace (*Muslims*). God is Peace (*salam*), and we relate to Him as Peace through being-at-peace (*islam*). War is the opposite of peace, the people of war the opposite of the people of peace. Everything in this world both reveals and conceals God. Perpetually at war, we are satisfied by Peace alone.

3

For the people of peace, witness to the Praised as principle and purpose of creation is inseparable from witness to Mary as most blessed among women and her son as the Word of God and the Spirit. Those who forget this let the boundaries of their world image contract, while those who deny the Praised as a mercy to the worlds deny the people of peace as a community, an unbroken course of life within a historical and metahistorical horizon and a constant but varying link to Essence.

The world is duality, both visible manifestation and invisible, higher horizon. So are we. This duality of visible and invisible determines what is possible for us in and beyond this world. The invisible is manifest through the

---

consubstantiality (*huwiyya*), lit by His light and dedicated to His sanctity, the first level of the reception of the Light of God, a Light-giving Lamp for all things in existence (Ibid., 59).

5 The geographer Ptolemy refers to Mecca as *Macoraba*, which some have interpreted as a form of the word *miḥrāb.* Moses is said to have experienced divine revelation on Mt. Horeb (Heb. *ḥōrēḇ*, "wilderness," "wasteland," "battlefield"), where God called him to be His apostle and gave His commandments and covenant to him (*Exodus* 3:1; *Deuteronomy* 4:10,15; 5:2). Elijah also received a revelation on Horeb (*1 Kings* 19:8, 11) and was later taken up to heaven from there. The name Horeb may be linked with the Hebrew word for altar, *mizbēaḥ*, which derives from the verbal root *z-b-ḥ* ("to slaughter, sacrifice"). The altar is the highest point of annihilation and abnegation. It symbolizes ascent from illusion to reality, which is self-realization by witness that there is no self but the Self, annihilation of the self in the Face of the Self. Such an ascent prevails over illusion, darkness and passion for Peace. We never attain final ascent, except through realization in Unity. Our every moment is a state of war against baseness for the sublime. The *miḥrāb* is the "place of *ḥōrēb* or *ḥarb* [war]," indicating that no human condition, even if turned towards Peace, actually attains It. None bring satisfaction, as only Peace justifies the journey. What is not Peace is wasteland, battlefield, baseness, death and suffering. We were created for the opposite – for Peace – and can always embark on our journey towards it, no matter our condition.

visible, but higher.[6] We and the world manifest Unity, most perfectly through the Praised. We realize our sublime potential by discovering him, as perfect humanity, within ourselves.

In finitude, suffering and death are inevitable, but we accept neither. We yearn for freedom from finitude, for felicity and life. Only God is plenitude, perfect felicity and full life and we must trust in Him: "Thee only we serve; to Thee alone we pray for succour. Guide us in the upright path, the path of those whom Thou hast blessed, not of those against whom Thou art wrathful, nor of those who are astray."[7]

The upright path links all existence. Its end is Peace. Whenever we turn to Peace, we are sent the prayed-for guidance. We cannot be Peace. Our longing to achieve It is an open, upward path. It is our goal and our focus on It reminds us we are on the battlefield, so long as we aspire to being-at-peace.

4

All things come from water and Spirit: "And the Spirit of God moved upon the face of the waters."[8] All living things are fashioned of water: "We unstitched [the heavens and the earth] and of water fashioned every living thing."[9]

---

6 God says in the Recitation, just after the Opening: "*Alif. Lam. Mim.* That is the Book, wherein is no doubt, a guidance to the conscious who believe in the Unseen, and perform the prayer, and expend of that We have provided them; who believe in what has been sent down to thee and what has been sent down before thee, and have faith in the Hereafter; those are upon guidance from their Lord, those are the ones who prosper." (*Qur'an*, 2:1–5). The modern inability to understand prophecy as a crucial source of knowledge leads us to exclude the Unseen as the principle of the visible. As Frithjof Schuon says, "The ideas of 'Great Spirit' and of the primacy of the Invisible are natural to man, which does not even need to be demonstrated; now what is natural to human consciousness, which is distinguished from animal consciousness by its objectivity and its totality – its capacity for the absolute and the infinite, we might say – what is natural to human consciousness proves *ipso facto* its essential truth, the reason for the existence of intelligence being adequation to the real." (Schuon, *From the Divine to the Human*, 6).

7 *Qur'an*, 1:5–7. After the profession of faith – there is no god but God and the Praised is His apostle – nothing so permeates Muslim character, individual and communal, as *ṣūra al-fātiḥa* (the Opening), the first seven verses of the Recitation, which every Muslim repeats at least forty times a day, during the five obligatory daily prayers. The Opening epitomizes the Recitation – and since the Recitation shaped the character of the Praised, our best example, in and beyond history, it also provides a concise summation of doctrine, ritual and virtue that springs from and flows into the profession of faith.

8 *Genesis*, 1:2.

9 *Qur'an*, 21:30.

The relationship between the Living God, represented by Spirit, and Essence, denoted by water, gives rise to life and all the diversity of existence. Spirit is the active principle, wholly subject to divine command. Water is at peace, receiving the Spirit. The resultant diversity is united in Spirit. The many comes from the One, its focus at all times. Reintegration in the One depends on the heart alone.

Mary signifies our integration of Spirit and Essence. She is water, receptive. The Spirit is upon her and she manifests her relationship with It as "full of grace, blessed [is she] amongst women and blessed is the fruit of [her] womb." The Spirit, received in her heart, manifests as her son, Jesus, the Word of God.

The Praised, perfect humanity through which God gathers the worlds and His foremost revelation as Peace, is that same receptive principle. He receives the Spirit, so that his nature is identical with the Recitation, the Word he speaks and to which his entire life attests: "The character of the apostle of God is the Recitation."[10] His apostolate is summed up in her example. She attests to and announces him, and he confirms and protects her.

5

What do the mosque and the Virgin mean for the tradition inherited from the Praised?

God's apostles all testify to the Praised as supreme principle and purpose of creation. He is with God both before and after. His coming is intimated in all human discourse. He is spoken of in the Torah, the Psalms and the Gospels, as well as in all metaphysical teachings. Insofar as the prophets reveal something of him, he is present throughout history, as a sign of higher levels of existence.

Our desire for life and happiness directs the soul to him as best model, defender, comforter and advocate, admonisher and guide. The tenet that there is no god but God is, moreover, the sublime core of the human self and depends on God alone. As manifest in us, it entails the apostolate of the Praised, insofar as it represents the sublime potential for witness within each of us.

These two fundamental tenets take many forms in language, ritual and virtue, but remain always the same, as that sublimity of human nature in which God's question and our response may be heard, affirming the perfection in which bliss is attained.

The world as a whole corresponds to our inner integrity. It is human being writ large, while human being is the world writ small. The principle externalised in the world is internalised in us. Both we and the world are forms of

10 Muslim, 1:359.

mosque, receiving being from God. Each of us focuses the world, the heart our focus. We and the world remain, however, just two facets of one revelation.

To build a mosque is to provide existence with a focus. The world is a mosque that owes its existence to God alone. The heavens, earth and everything between them have luxuriance of being with God. Without Him they are nothing. What we build is perfect only through its witness to God, Who created both us and our works.[11]

The world and the self are inextricable. All the world's meaning is in us since time began and will be for all eternity. We are creation's keystone, its reason, purpose and sum. Its meaning does not exist outside us. This relationship depends on our uncreated humanity, the heart from which and to which all multiplicity flows, as well as on the indivisibility of being, knowledge and happiness.

6

The mosque's centre is the mihrab – a place in which we are always alone, one to One, face to Face, with the testimony that there is no one but the One. But the world is a mosque: "Hast thou not seen how before God prostrate themselves all who are in the heavens, and all who are in the earth, the sun and the moon, the stars and the mountains, the trees and the beasts, and many of mankind?"[12]

Why were the prophet Zachariah, father of the prophet John, and the Virgin Mary, mother of the prophet Jesus, in the mihrab? Mary was in the mihrab and the prophet Zachariah came to her. She was a sign for him and us all, even more than the world. This book will suggest certain interpretations of this verse from the mihrabs of Bosnia, which is so similar to her presence in the churches of Bosnia and elsewhere.[13]

---

11 See *Qur'an*, 37:96.

12 *Qur'an*, 22:18.

13 The Virgin and her son are the most common and most important figures in Bosnian church murals. The original, sacred meaning of the icon is as representing them together. Their paired image was associated with the story of Jesus sending an imprint of his face to King Abgar of Edessa and the descent from heaven of a holy icon portraying Mary by Luke the Evangelist. Almost as significant are images of Zachariah and John. Zachariah is portrayed in the frescoes of several Bosnian churches: St. George's church in Lomnica monastery, 16th–17th centuries (see Kajmaković, *Zidno slikarstvo u Bosni i Hercegovini*, 336, 341); the presentation of the Virgin in Dobričevo monastery, 16th–18th centuries (Ibid., 348); the presentation of the Virgin in Zavala monastery, 16th–17th centuries (Ibid., 358, 360); the church of the Holy Archangel in Aranđelovo, 17th century (Ibid., 369);

The verse is to be found in mihrabs the world over, just as one finds images of Zachariah and the Virgin in many churches, but their presence always reveals certain distinctive features of the history and culture of the places it is found.[14]

The Virgin is a sign of integral existence, at least in Bosnian tradition. She is the Queen of Heaven. Nor should one overlook her peaceful response to her tribulations and the calumnies against her. Her seeming vulnerability and meekness are a source of sublimity and purity. No one can realize their own self without being humble and generous to her. The Virgin Mary belongs to everyone, but is never subordinate to any. Her inviolability preserves our original dignity.

7

The mihrab represents God's unity, the Praised's apostolate, and the return of all things to God. It is the stage on which being transforms into witness and vice versa. As a place of standing, bowing, prostration, and sitting, it comprehends all existence – seven heavens, seven earths and all between.

The world and we are one. The point of human life is to bring the self into harmony with the world and return to the source. Why are God's words "Whenever Zachariah went in to her in the sanctuary" inscribed at the centre of the mihrab? Our witness seems somehow linked with those words. The Praised is first in creation, God's first manifestation and seal to all things in existence. He is present in all things that come from and return to God. Everything on that path speaks of Him. Each one of us heralds and awaits him, and there are as many stories of him as people.

We can deny the sign and turn away from God as the goal of return, a temptation none is free from. The Praised says of Mary and her son: "No child is born but that Satan touches it when it is born, except Mary and her son."[15] Zachariah and his son John, "the voice of one crying in the wilderness," remind us of Mary's perfect reception of the Spirit and manifestation of the Word. Both

---

St. Clement's church in Mostaći, 17th century (Ibid., 372). The Lomnica painting shows Zachariah carrying Mary as a child (Ibid., 340–41). As God says in the Recitation, Mary was consecrated to the Temple in Sion and Zachariah, a servant of the Temple, took care of her.

14 No comprehensive study has been made of the appearance, construction and art of the *miḥrāb*. For Bosnian mihrabs, see Bećirbegović, *Džamije s drvenom munarom u Bosni i Hercegovini*, 148–55.

15 Muslim, 4:1261.

receiving and giving are signs of witness of the Praised. The Praised, to whom the prophets swore fealty in pre-existence, also said of Mary and her son:

> And when God took compact with the prophets: "That I have given you of Book and Wisdom; then there shall come to you an apostle confirming what is with you – you shall believe in him and you shall help him; do you agree?" He said, "And do you take My load on you on that condition?" They said, "We do agree." God said, "Bear witness so, and I shall be with you among the witnesses."[16]

The Virgin Mary and her son are thus the final prophetic foreshadowing of the Praised. When John accepted the charge of this compact, he knew of the Praised, whose presence in each individual was clear to him from Mary's words in the mihrab.

8

The Virgin and Jesus' prophecy of the Praised derived from their being without sin, wholly at peace in God. It includes both receiving and giving. We must ask ourselves where they gained their knowledge of him and in what it consisted.

The primacy of the Praised is manifest outwardly in history, through the prophets and humanity. It shines through the prophets from Abraham's son Isaac to the Virgin and her son. Their knowledge of him is a sacred legacy, rooted in their innate potential and their sublime expectation.

The apostle said that of all people he was closest to Jesus, and that there were no prophets between them,[17] while Mary's son Jesus said: "I am the door."[18] Return to God is through the Praised, who is closest to Him, as Jesus is closest to the Praised. To draw closer to God is to draw closer to both Jesus and the Praised. It epitomizes the paths of the prophets, who agree in their authentic witness to the apostle.

The Virgin Mary received the angel Gabriel and accepted her mission in complete acquiescence, saying: "Behold the handmaid of the Lord; be it unto me according to thy word."[19] She gave birth to Jesus, the Anointed, servant and prophet of God, His Word, who responded to severest trial thus: "Father, if

16 *Qur'an*, 3:81.

17 See Muslim, 4:1260–61.

18 *John*, 10:9.

19 *Luke*, 1:38.

thou be willing, remove this cup from me: nevertheless not my will, but thine, be done."[20]

9

Gabriel also visited the Praised, in his cave retreat, to instruct him regarding the Word sent down into his heart by God and pass it on, in reminder of the knowledge stored as treasure in our original nature.

God entrusted the descent of the Word into the heart of the Praised to Gabriel – the Spirit of Truth or Holy Spirit. This Word was passed on as the Recitation. ʿAbdullah ibn Masʾud, witness and companion of the Praised, called it: "...the banquet of God; take of it as much as you can, for I know nothing more unworthy than a house in which there is nothing of the Word of God. The heart which contains nothing of the Word of God goes to ruin like a house in which no one lives."[21]

When Zachariah, John, Mary and Jesus entered the world, they confirmed the expectations of some, denied the hopes of others. People either accepted or rejected them. Many views evolved, true and false. Those who heard them preach learned that the time of the sceptre in Judah's hands had passed[22] and that a prophet like Moses was to come, into whose mouth God would put His Words.[23]

The Praised bore witness to the Virgin and her son in accordance with what God had sent down about them. Placing his hands protectively over the icon of the Virgin and Child in the locked Kaʿba, he proclaimed no knowledge independent of the knowledge in our hearts, breathed into us in creation.[24]

The Praised made whole in the world what was rent when humans parted ways. He confirmed the words God sent down, breathing life into them with his breath and stamping them with his hands. He thus demonstrated, on the

---

20 Ibid., 22:42.

21 Dārimī, 2:521, tradition 3307.

22 Jacob, whom God named Israel, said: "The sceptre shall not depart from Judah, nor a lawgiver from between his feet, until Shiloh come; and unto him shall the gathering of the people be." (*Genesis*, 49:10). Jesus was of the line of Abraham, like Judah and David. With the coming of the Anointed, the sceptre of Judah thus departed from Israel. The Praised said: "I am al-Ḥāshir (Assembler) in that people shall be assembled after me. And I am al-ʿĀqib (the Last), after whom there will be no other prophet" (Mālik, 513).

23 See *Deuteronomy*, 18:18.

24 See Ibn Isḥāq, *Sīrāt Rasūl Allāh*, 552; Wüstenfeld, *Die Chroniken der Stadt Mekka*, 1:11, 4:104; Lings, *Muhammad*, 302.

example of his own soul informed by God's Word as brought by Gabriel, that learned knowledge is less than the knowledge innate to the self. He showed God's prophets assembled in his maternal self, which is the sublime potential of every self and the original nature that is our covenant with God. The Praised is the seal of this covenant, expressed in every language, whose essence is service of God and acceptance of His guidance.

In placing his blessed hands over their image inside the Kaʿba, the Praised bore witness to Unity, manifest as the Word through the perfection of recipient and giver throughout existence. Mary gave birth to Jesus, but it was God made him with His Word. The Recitation God revealed through the heart of the Praised is the same Word, manifest in speech. The Anointed and the Recitation are both manifestations of the same Word of God. The unity of the Praised's will with God's in His decree "Say!" is revealed by his words: "He is God, One, God, the Everlasting Refuge, who has not begotten, and has not been begotten, and equal to Him is not any one."[25]

10

The Praised said God married him to Mary in heaven.[26] To understand this claim one must consider his witness to God's unity, his own apostolate, and return to God. God chose the Praised as the principle of creation and sent him to the worlds and married him to perfect women in the Garden, revealing the place of Peace in its perfection.

25 *Qur'an*, 112:1–4.

26 The Praised said: "Many men reached the level of perfection, but no woman reached such a level except Mary, the daughter of ʿImrān, and Āsiya, the wife of Pharaoh." (Bukhārī, 4:428). The Praised is the first of the people of peace, so it is understandable that Paradise, as the world of Peace, includes his marriage to perfect women, as Ibn ʿAbbās related: "The prophet – peace be upon him – went in to Khadīja when she was on her deathbed. He said: 'Khadīja, when you meet others who are married to me, greet them in Peace for me.' She said: 'Apostle of God, were you married before you married me?' He said: 'No, but God married me to Maryam, daughter of ʿImrān, Āsiya, Pharaoh's wife, and Kaltham Mūsā's sister.'" (Ibn Kathīr, *Tafsīr*, 4:495). According to another similar tradition, Abū Umāma said: "The apostle of God – peace be upon him – said: 'Do you not know that God married me in the Garden to Maryam, daughter of ʿImrān, Kaltham Mūsā's sister, and Āsiya, Pharaoh's wife?' I said: 'May you be happy, O apostle of God.'" (Ibid.). The Praised said to ʿĀʾisha: "O ʿĀʾisha, God married me in Paradise to Mary, the daughter of ʿImrān, and Āsiya, Muzāḥim daughter." (Muttaqī, 12:273). "God married me in Paradise to Mary the daughter of ʿImrān and to the wife of the Pharaoh and the sister of Moses." (Ṭabarānī, 6:52, tradition 5485; Ibn Kathīr, 2:381). For further on this, see Schleifer, *Mary the Blessed Virgin of Islam*.

The Praised is first in creation. God is Light, the Praised the light shed, the light-giving lamp. God is All-praised, the light-giving lamp the revelation that He is All-praised. The Praised is thus first to receive God's praise and first to return it to source.

The Praised receives the Word from God through the Spirit of Truth. Recipient, he is the perfect servant, with nothing of his own. His poverty is absolute in the face of God's prosperity and generosity. His garments are white,[27] for he is a sign that reveals God as Light and Purity.

The Virgin is also a perfect servant, but her robe is blue as the sea and the vault of the heavens. She is the perfect recipient of the Spirit of Truth. She receives what the Praised receives, but her primary role is as recipient, his as giver. Mary gives her son as Word and News, incarnate. The Praised gives the Recitation, which he incarnates as a mighty morality and best example.

Mary is thus a perfect recipient, he a perfect giver. Heaven is the abode of Peace, of perfect equilibrium. Unity links Mary and the Praised through the Word given them by the Holy Spirit. Their union in heaven manifests God's mercy and friendship towards all things, as the Praised and the Recitation and Mary and Jesus are two manifestations of the Face, perfect images of each other.

11

The Word takes many forms. Once embodied, however, it separates from the source, which it serves to denote or to conceal. The authentic source of the Word, knowledge, is crucial for the discovery and realization of the self and return to God. Without such knowledge, the historical manifestations of the Word veil the self, laying a barrier between the light within and the signs without. The barrier is an actual historical, but reified and distorted form of the Word itself.

Both the people of peace and those not yet at peace commonly suppose that being-at-peace is a form of religion that begins with the historical manifestation of the Praised, as the Word of the Recitation was sent down into his heart. They forget the vow made by the prophets to God in pre-existence.[28] They also forget that all God's prophets bore witness of the Light God sends down to people as the Truth of the All-praised.[29] No valid reason can be found for this

27 The apostle said: "The best thing in which to visit God in your graves and in your mosques is white" (Tirmidhī, tradition 4382).

28 See *Qur'an*, 3:81–82.

29 Ibid., 7:157.

neglect or forgetting, for confining the Praised to history, whether through the Recitation or his historical legacy.

Being-at-peace in God takes many historical forms, but is not only in history. It is a universal relationship with God that began with existence. The word *islam* denotes it, as the universal condition of the creation before the Creator, as announced in the Recitation: "In Him has found peace whoso is in the heavens and the earth."[30] This is why bearing witness to God's unity is crucial for self-realization as part of every historical form of God's call to self-realization by relating to Peace through being-at-peace.

Each of us vows to God as Lord of creation, without intermediary,[31] out of free will, knowledge and love, with confidence.[32] Our vow places us on the upright path towards God, following the apostle. Travelling the path, we are friends of God, while our bond with the apostle is through our own prophets. This is a journey in the Kingdom of God, towards the Throne in the human heart. All things outside and within the self remind us of our Goal.

12

Confession of the Praised binds our witness to both First and Last in existence. Everything in existence relates to the All-praised through praise. Insofar as we epitomize existence, the Praised, who epitomizes our sublime potential, relates to the All-praised through praise. The differentiation of Unity in self-manifestation begins with the Praised, as does Its reassembly, for he is eternally closest to God.

Entering history, the Praised and the Recitation confirmed our witness of God's unity and his own apostolate as reality before God of all existence, seen and unseen. Prime Intellect is the Holy Spirit. Its human counterpart, the heart, is the sum of all manifestations of the Divine in the flux.

All that is in the heavens and on earth and our knowledge of it are there to serve self-realization through witness before God: "Yes, we testify."[33] This witness, the essence of our being before God, can hardly depend on learned knowledge or any external thing. No ignorance or appeal to tradition, to sources of knowledge extrinsic to God, excuses choosing to mask the perfect core of the self.

---

30 *Qur'an*, 3:83.

31 See *Qur'an*, 7:172.

32 Ibid., 33:72.

33 *Qur'an*, 7:172.

God says: "Muhammad is not the father of any one of your men, but the apostle of God, and the seal of the prophets; God has knowledge of everything."[34] The Praised and the Book are reminders, like the world, of the knowledge deep within us, whose purpose is return to God in realization of our perfection.

Zachariah and Mary are the last voices in the Further Mosque, informed by Gabriel of something inconceivable – that an old man and a virgin would both have sons. Both gifts are signs of God's mercy.

John and Jesus were connected with that mosque, but spoke outside it, warning people that their only covenant with God is in the heart and nothing can replace it – not buildings or heavens, kingdoms or armies, books or rites. They warned that our debt to God may be requited only in mercy and peace and that the walls of the mosque offer no succour against suffering or death.

God alone is Peace, peace from Him alone. In the Recitation, God says to the Praised, and so to us: "Recite what has been revealed to thee of the Book, and perform the prayer; prayer forbids indecency and dishonour. God's remembrance is greater; and God knows the things you work."[35] In that command, the integration of sacred text and ritual in the living person of speaker and worshipper is clear. This is how human being is preserved in fullness and not the void.

13

The Mosque of Sion has often seemed more important than the human heart to those who live around it. An inversion is imposed – the heart seeming to exist for the mosque, not the mosque for the heart. By supposing the mosque has value other than for the remembrance of His name, we veil our hearts with a darkness of ignorance, wronging ourselves and others.

In 70 AD, the Further Mosque was sacked and destroyed, its walls razed to the ground, its remains covered with the burnt ashes of the cedar beams. Alien troops marched over the holy place, trampling, plundering and laying waste everything people held sacred. Like its destruction five centuries earlier, this was a call never to cease remembering God, for remembrance is our greatest treasure.

The self that ceases to remember God becomes obscured. Acting out of obscurity, it does violence to itself and the world. It is unforgiveable sin, worse than the Antichrist. Standing in prayer can become association with God. It is

34 Ibid., 33:40.

35 Ibid., 29:45.

the horror, the Praised says, of "concealed idolatry," as one "rises in prayer and strives to make it good, because he is being watched."[36]

The Further Mosque remained in ruins until the Praised's night journey in 621 AD. The winds and rain cleansed it, as did the desire of the people of peace that it be revealed as a sign of ascent from the depths to the height. That year the Praised and the angel Gabriel came there, and all the prophets assembled around them and prayed with the Praised as their seal and champion.[37]

The meaning God gave the Praised when our stewardship on earth began was thus renewed in the Sion Mosque.[38] Some years later, his friend ʿUmar visited the mosque. He hallowed the place as a sign of the human heart and of the Ark of the Covenant. The sacred words of our covenant with God are inscribed on the inner and outer cornices of the Dome of the Rock.

The Golden Dome marks the Rock as symbolic counterpart of the Kaʿba. The Rock signifies Intellect and the beginning and consolidation of everything on the height; the Kaʿba marks the bottom of the valley and the descent of all things towards it. Consciousness of the depths signifies the dissolution of the individual, so that everything we do reflects our connection with the beginning or centre. From that dissolution there proceeds a gathering and a return to the One on the path from the depths to the height. Drawing attention to the indivisible link between his apostolate and the witness of Jesus and his mother, the Praised said:

> He who said: "There is no god but God, He is One, and there is no associate with Him, that the Praised is His servant and His apostle, that the Anointed is the servant and the son of His hand-maiden and he is His word which He communicated to Mary and is His spirit, that Paradise is a fact and Hell is a fact" – God would make him enter Paradise through any one of its eight doors which he would like.[39]

---

36 Ibn Māja, 2:146, tradition 4204.

37 For the night journey of the Praised referred to in Recitation (17:1), see Ibn Isḥāq, *Sīrāt Rasūl Allāh*, 181–87; Ibn Saʿd, *al-Ṭabaqāt al-kubrā*, 1:213–16; Asad, *The Message of the Qur'an*, 996–98; Hamidullah, *Muhammed A.S.*, 1:137–40; Lings, *Muhammad*, 113–16.

38 For more detail on the form and content of the Further Mosque through 13 centuries, see Grabar, *The Shape of the Holy*.

39 Muslim, 1:21–22.

14

Looking back to the suffering of Zachariah, Mary, John and Jesus, one cannot help wonder what felicity is. The Further Mosque, a holy place, was razed to the ground and turned into a midden. Zachariah, Mary, John and Jesus were humiliated and persecuted in the eyes of the world.[40] They were in the world for the sake of our happiness, but endured unimaginable suffering.

All things in existence are at peace in God. Our part lies in the felicity of return to Peace, with the Praised as guide and leader, who said: "I have been commanded to serve God, making my debt His sincerely; and I have been commanded to be the first of the people of peace."[41] God points to those who are at peace, "whose breast [He] has expanded for being-at-peace, so he walks in a light from his Lord,"[42] and says, through the Praised, "But woe to those whose hearts are hardened against the remembrance of God!"[43] Being-at-peace is connection with God as Peace. As first of the people of peace, the Praised said: "O God! Thou art Peace and Peace comes from Thee; blessed art Thee, O Possessor of Glory and Honour."[44]

We seek peace in God, and call out to Him: "Guide us in the straight path, the path of those whom Thou has blessed." The question of human felicity finds its answer in this relationship with God. It is only with God as Peace and His guidance towards Peace that we can realize ourselves in felicity and transcend death. God as Peace is the goal. We contain everything we need to attain this goal, including the guidance to remind us of it:

> People of the Book, now there has come to you Our apostle, making clear to you many things you have been concealing of the Book, and effacing many things. There has come to you from God a light, and a Book Manifest whereby God guides whosoever follows His good pleasure in the ways of peace, and brings them forth from the shadows into the light by His leave; and He guides them to an upright path.[45]

---

40 Regarding Mary as prophetess, two eminent Andalusian writers, Muḥy al-Dīn ibn al-ʿArabī and Abū ʿAbd al-Qurṭubī, were firmly of the view that Mary was a prophetess of God like other prophets. For more, see Schleifer, *Mary the Blessed Virgin of Islam*, 73–94.

41 *Qur'an*, 39:11–12.

42 Ibid., 39:22.

43 Ibid.

44 Muslim, 1:292.

45 *Qur'an*, 5:15–16.

15

Who are the people of the Book to whom God speaks through the apostle as His mercy to the worlds?

The key question is the question of the focus of the self. It is absolute and thus both internal and external – otherwise it would be limited. Our internal focus derives from the act of creation. Its presence depends on the Creator alone. God breathed His Spirit into us then and His Spirit cannot be limited by anything. This external focus, moreover, is simply a sign of the inner one. We discover this during the course of our life, through what is transmitted to us in language, signs and interpretations.

We wage constant battle to occupy a central position in the outside world and subjugate others. But the centre is impregnable. The claim that the centre is simply human power is a mere fabrication, one image amongst others. Those who identify themselves in thought with the centre may be peaceful or violent, loved or hated, good or evil. If peaceful, loved and good, they see themselves as such at heart. If violent, hated and evil, their selves will be constrained by their qualities.

God sends down His Word and it takes the form of a preacher or a Book. He sends no power with it. The Book is a reminder and a light, a warning and wisdom, a clear narrative of where we came from and why, a banquet we are invited to but free to decline. Though indebted, we are not compelled.

Only God knows the full and perfect interpretation of His Book, but we each find our own treasure in it, according to our station. None has full knowledge, but those with more owe a debt of witness in humility and generosity: the greater our knowledge, the greater our humility.

The people of the Book are those who bear witness that there is no god but God, that the Praised is His apostle, and that the Book is the warrant of our individual dignity – weak or powerful, hungry or sated, sick or healthy, frail and elderly. It comes with no power of any kind and no compulsion. Our will to cleave to it strips away the veils from the self and allows the light within to shine, to erase the darkness on our journey back to the authentic self, on the sublime height.

16

The Lord transported the Praised in a single night from the Inviolable to the Further Mosque. These places of worship symbolize the two extremes in the self, lower and higher.

When the Praised reached the Further Mosque, he took his place in the battlefield as leader (*imam*). The prophets prayed behind him, as their principle and seal, the light and mercy bestowed through them on the world. He and they all stood, bowed and prostrated themselves before God, with the Praised in first place, as the most humble of humankind. Everything in the world exists to remind us of God. It is all under constant threat of becoming wasteland and desert. When we forget it is there to manifest God, we fall on the battlefield. Remembering God raises us up to cross that field to Peace.

The Praised, like all else in existence, is mortal. Though a mercy to the worlds, God bade him say: "I am only a mortal the like of you; it is revealed to me that your God is One God."[46] That is why his acts of prostration and sacrifice, his life and death are before God. To attain life, he sacrifices all that is his as mortal. Renouncing all he owns, he returns to the Living as reason and purpose. His mortality denotes his creaturehood, but his inner self realizes sublime perfection and nearness to God, saying: "I have a time with God which I do not share with a cherubic angel or with any prophetic apostle."[47]

The mihrab of the Praised is existence as manifesting Unity. Mary and Muhammad are two facets of this manifestation of Unity – Mary as female, recipient and perfect servant, Muhammad as male, giver and perfect servant. Mary reveals a facet of the Praised, he a facet of Mary. They are two sides of the same perfection, a perfect pair announcing the One.

17

As first creature, the Praised is perfect recipient and maternal apostle. He manifests Mary's perfect nature. God is Light, first manifest as illumination through the lamp, Mary. But the Praised is light, too. As the light-giving lamp he bestows what he has received on the world. He is first to receive and first to return. There is no coming from or returning to God without the Praised – without the perfect man in whom differentiation into male and female, giver and recipient, is resolved.

The Praised is manifest as first recipient of Peace, apostle, as the niche that shows the path back, and the finest example of ascent along that path. A higher

46 Ibid., 18:110.

47 Mullā Ṣadrā, *The Wisdom of the Throne*, 149. For this well-known tradition, see Furūzānfar, *Ahādīs-i Masnavī*, 39. An associated tradition is: "The prophet was asked, 'When did you become a prophet?' He replied, 'When Adam was between spirit and body' " (Tirmidhī, *Sunan*, 5:585).

level descends toward a lower one, the lower ascends to the higher. As a mercy to the worlds and a light-giving lamp, the Praised descends and ascends. He is on both the most beautiful height and in the deepest depth.

The Praised comprehends this closeness of "two arcs," seeing everything in relation to the centre where beginning and end, inner and outer are one. The prophets are his witnesses. Only those who turn to him as our best and most perfect example can themselves lead. Their world is a battlefield on which the self realizes itself by confessing no self but the Self, as shown in the Recitation:

> Surely it is We who bring the dead to life and write down what they have forwarded and what they have left behind; everything We have numbered in a clear register.[48]
>
> We have honoured the Children of Adam and carried them on land and sea, and provided them with good things, and preferred them greatly over many of those We created. On the day when We shall call all men with their record, and whoso is given his book in his right hand – those shall read their book, and they shall not be wronged a single date-thread.[49]
>
> And when his Lord tested Abraham with certain words, and he fulfilled them, He said, "Behold, I make you a leader for the people." Said he, "And of my seed?" He said, "My covenant shall not reach the evildoers."[50]
>
> And We appointed from among them leaders guiding by Our command, when they endured patiently, and had sure faith in Our signs.[51]

Whenever we turn to face God, the Praised is our best example, first of the First and last of the Last. He is the clear register, the mighty morality shaped by the Word.

18

When not turned to God as First and Last, we are at odds with the Praised in existence. Given that the Praised is the very centre and essence of humanity, enmity towards him is resistance to God. The worst disfigurement of the self is ignorance of the Praised. Where there is ignorance, there is fear and

48 *Qur'an*, 36:12.
49 Ibid., 17:70–71.
50 Ibid., 2:124.
51 Ibid., 32:24.

violence. The source of all hatred is fear. Those who hate the Praised hate and fear themselves.

People of ignorance, fear and hate bind with the un-real. The real disappears from their world, dependent on them alone. They imagine themselves to be searching for a finitude to adopt as supreme. Their free will allows them to do so; but they did not receive their free will unconditionally. They will have to explain why they chose other gods than God and will respond: "They have gone astray from us: nay, but it was nothing at all that we called upon aforetime."[52]

The turn from the Praised can take various forms, but is in essence always the same – taking some nothing for the Real. Foremost are those who advocate multiplicity without Unity, the second level without the First. In the Recitation, God says: "And we appointed them leaders, calling to the Fire; and on the Day of Resurrection they shall not be helped."[53] He also says: "But if they break their oaths after their covenant and thrust at your debt, then fight the leaders of concealment; they have no sacred oaths; haply they will give over."[54]

To be in the world is to be in a theatre of war. We are at war for or against the self. Our goal is not of the world, but all it contains is a sign revealing or concealing the way to the Self. To annihilate the self as manifesting independently of the Self is war – a war won in Unity and return to the One. Multiplicity reveals Unity, but also distracts us from it. All things in plurality are with Truth; none replace It. Truth is why we wage war. We reach our goal only if we discover the perfect Giver and the perfect Receiver within ourselves, as two facets of one and the same perfection. This is to be in the theatre of war.

In the case of Mary, as perfect femininity and receptivity, God tells us of the donative principle she receives and manifests: "And when the angels said, 'Mary, God has chosen thee, and purified thee; He has chosen thee above all women. Mary, be obedient to thy Lord, prostrating and bowing before him.' "[55] And that: "...the angel came in unto her, and said, Hail, thou that art highly favoured, the Lord is with thee."[56] Mary is indeed full of grace and blessed among women of all the worlds; as the Praised was sent as a mercy to the worlds.[57]

---

52 Ibid., 40:74.

53 Ibid., 28:41.

54 Ibid., 9:12.

55 Ibid., 3:42–43.

56 *Luke*, 1:28.

57 See *Qur'an*, 21:107.

19

The world is our mihrab. Only in ourselves and our world can we realize the trust we bear[58] and bear authentic witness to God.[59] Only by war against violence, ignorance and false, extrinsic knowledge can we be sure of finding the real in the self and of returning to it. Every moment is thus a war, every place a battlefield. We remind ourselves of God's words: "In Him has found peace whoso is in the heavens and the earth."[60] Everything that has found peace bows down as God's other: "Before God prostrate themselves all who are in the heavens and the earth, willingly or unwillingly."[61]

We realize our supreme potential by confessing no will but the Will and that serving God is best, the only true freedom in which to realize our nature. We see ourselves in all existence, discovered and realized as a whole within the self: "None is there in the heavens and earth but he comes to the All-merciful as a servant."[62]

The mihrab symbolizes coming to the All-merciful in perfect freedom. We acknowledge we are mortal, but want life. For this reason, our love for and return to the Living is our only way to be delivered from death. Only perfect survival validates human suffering on the battlefield of the world. People recognize the battlefield and mark it out everywhere and at all times – in our homes and on the hills, on our carpets and in the fields, in our offices and schools, in our mosques and lodges (tekkes).

We do this in a variety of ways, with simple, barely discernible signs or through art, magnificent edifices, sumptuous decorations, and sometimes with the words: "Whenever Zachariah went in to her in the sanctuary." Even when these words are not inscribed, Zachariah and Mary, John and Jesus are present in the sanctuary, bearing eternal witness of no god but God and the Praised as His apostle. This witness is realized in the self, in the discovery of its perfect centre.

58 Ibid., 33:72.
59 Ibid., 7:172.
60 *Qur'an*, 3:83.
61 Ibid., 13:15.
62 Ibid., 19:93.

PART 1

Prophetic Sayings of the One

• •

Her Lord received the child
with gracious favour,
and by His goodness
she grew up comely;
Zachariah taking
charge of her. Whenever
Zachariah went in to her
in the sanctuary, he
found her provisioned.
"Mary," he said,
"how comes this to thee?"
"From God," she said.
Truly God provisions
whomsoever He will
without reckoning.

QUR'AN, 3:37

• • •

He is God;
there is no god but He.
He is the King, the All-holy, the All-peaceful,
the All-faithful, the All-preserver,
the All-mighty, the All-compeller,
the All-sublime.
Glory be to God, above that they associate!
He is God,
the Creator, the Maker, the Shaper.
To Him belong the Names Most Beautiful.
All that is in the heavens and the earth magnifies Him;
He is the All-mighty, the All-wise.

QUR'AN, 59:23–24

• • •

The seven heavens and the earth, and whosoever
in them is, extol Him; nothing is, that does not
proclaim His praise, but you do not understand
their extolling. Surely He is All-clement, All-forgiving.

QUR'AN, 17:44

• • •

An Anthropo-cosmological Prelude

Every self contains all of existence, all of space and time, in its now. There is no existence outside the self that knows it. This fact is so obvious it escapes us. Facing such clarity is like looking directly at the sun, until we avert our blinded and weary gaze to the shadows.

The present, properly understood, is not limited to a particular time, beginning or end. It exists in a moment without extension, for which past and future are just reflections, shadows for consciousness to show itself. These reflections may be reconstructed as images without number, but none comprehend or ground the self. Disregarding the self can make them seem independent, images of past and future ripped from their ground. The past appears to flow from one point towards another, governed by internal causes and effects, such that no individual self caught up in the current seems to play any role in the causal chain of world construction.

The self contains everything we can know. God reveals Himself to Himself through it. His will to be known caused the creation of the worlds that gather in us. Without the self, He would remain a hidden treasure. Self and world reveal Him, each through the other, no matter how distinct they seem.

This relationship is symbolized by the Kaʿba, a plain cube of a house, raised at the bottom of a wild valley, in the middle of a desert, and unlike anything in the natural world. It is quite clearly the work of human hands but who do those hands bear witness to? In spite of their work, the Kaʿba seems unnaturally uniform, logical. The human self is irreducible to mere number and logic. A black stone sits on one the house's walls. Placed but not fashioned by human hands, it came to earth from the heavens. To our eyes, it seems irregular, like the heavens. Its shape impresses our rational minds as belonging to a higher principle. We are drawn in by this relationship between house and stone, the one logical, constructed, the other of higher design, received into logic and construction. If the stone signifies the self, the Kaʿba is the work of the self that situates it in the world. The world gathers within the self through this very structure "sent down" through it into the world.

The stone, on the one hand, and the earth and heavens, on the other, are the Kaʿba's poles, witnesses that our activity takes place between two regular irregularities. The stone corresponds to the self, the Kaʿba to our action in the world. But the self is nowhere seen in authentic purity, except in human sanctity, the sacred arts and what they intimate.

What we build proceeds from the self. Cut off from their source in the self, our works can appear independent. We shrink in their shadow. Thoughts and

 | DOI 10.1163/9789004279407_003

imaginings and projects built upon them shrivel in the face of a regularity unconfirmed by either self or world.

The stone is black, the house draped in black cloth, to signify the bottom of the valley where we are at the lowest ebb of our powers, in the night of existence. Recognizing this is our first step in embarking on the upright path that transcends space and time for the Day.

Circuits of the house recall the "irregular regularity" of the heavens, earth, and everything in between, as against the regular irregularity of our own works. The circuit transforms the house into a globe or perfection, representing the search for the indestructible ray of light present in every dark. The circle is not squared, it is construed, as perfection, out of a square or fracture. A construction becomes the presence of perfection in a finite world and we renew ourselves in the openness of the self, able to see our works as signs on the path of witness to no self but the Self.

To pass beyond the limits of the constructed, we must first recognize the self's infinite potential, from being in the depths, where our works seem to exceed us, to being on the height, where light, illumination and enlightenment are one. We come to realize that the first steps of descent from the maternal prophet are also the final steps of ascent and return to him. Attaining him as our ever-present higher potential, we realize our own selves by confessing no I but His.

In our struggle to free ourselves from the self's darkness, signified by the black stone, we seek the abodes of light and knowledge. This goal is represented by the white stone of paradise, which needs no irregular regularity to guard it. Our innate need to distinguish light from dark, truth from falsehood, depth from height is satisfied only as the self attains its highest modality.

No particular condition of the self fully meets our need to distinguish truth from lie: the self strives constantly to transcend what the irreducibility of every now intimates. Nothing in the self or world meets this need, but the power of the Self does. We can become aware of our place in existence's perfect humility by facing and coming to manifest the Principle.

Baseness is always a possibility, close, remote, but never denied. We can rise closer or fall further from the transcendent Principle, Intellect, within Which our potential is gathered, signified by the luminous vault of heaven and the golden dome on the rock of our petrified and overshadowed heart. This is because our potential is in the self. What approaches the self from outside may bring darkness or light, but real Light is beyond the sensory veils of the self, to be drawn back for Its sake. In this way the self's true nature is revealed – its perfect formlessness, symbolized by the Rock on the Mount. We realize ourselves on two arcs, one upward, the other down, marking in the self centre and circuit, inside and all exteriorization.

Talking of His prophets, the wise, their followers and friends as part of history rather than in terms of the self renders them enigmatic, obscure fictions that tire and vex. Taking them as images of the self's potential, brought together in the fullness of the present, reveals them as a great dance in a cosmic symphony whereby the Self reveals itself without end.

The stories of Adam's fall, Noah's salvation from the flood, Abraham's faith, Moses' shaping of his people by the Book, David's work of praise, and Solomon's revelation through the Temple and its rituals are all well-known to our contemporaries, whether or not they follow a sacred tradition. These are, however, only a few of the stories of the 124,000 prophets.

All these stories, for all their difference, share a common core. Finding it is crucial for us as individuals and we can find it only within the self. External images remind us of its presence within, a crucial message in our present and absolute reality. These stories include at least three inextricable and irreducible mysteries regarding human nature and its realization.

The first is in the story of Abraham and his wife Hagar. When she conceived, it fulfilled God's promise to Abraham. The child still in her womb, she was driven from her husband's house, however, and God appeared to her through an angel in the desperation of her exile. She fled from God and His friend to find sanctuary in them and with them. After her child was born, she was driven away once more, to seek sanctuary in God, Who again appeared to her through an angel, at the place of the Kaʿba, which is the low point of existence. This relationship between Hagar and the angel took the form of a child called "God has heard" (*Ishmael*). A lineage of promise and covenant passes through Hagar and Ishmael to the Praised.

Abraham's wife Sarah also bore him a son, Isaac, whose name means "He laughed." A lineage of covenant and promise passes from him to Mary and her son. It can be traced in many details of the prophets and their revelations, like a river that flows unceasingly on the surface of the earth, never slipping below into the invisible underworld of the forgotten.

The second story is of the Nazarene virgin, Mary, whose childhood was in the Holy of Holies. An angel of God appeared to her in perfect human form and she sought sanctuary before Him in what was revealed to her. Out of Mary's relationship with God the Word was born into flesh, the Anointed, Jesus.

The third story is of the Praised, an orphan born near the Kaʿba and raised in close contact with the cruelties of the desert. He too sought refuge from

Him in Him. The Praised too received and passed on the Word in the form of the Recitation.

Both lines of descent point us towards the meeting of the arcs of the mysterious history of Unity manifest in existence. These arcs are brought together in the inseparable closeness of the Praised and Mary and in the one Word revealed through them in two ways, in the Book and in Person.

These three stories can be approached in two ways: as mythic-historical discourses fixed in time and place or as one discourse within the core of the self, knowledge of which allows us to discover the pure stone and the house built for it, in the hope of being revealed in the Word. These stories raise the question of self-realization in the One in His wish to be known.

The heavens and the earth reveal Him, through the scattered manifold, in space and time. This revelation is not complete. God has will, love, and knowledge. The heavens, the earth and everything between reveal Him because of His will that they do so. They were offered a relationship with the Faithful based on will and refused it. Their will was to have no will but His.

The manifold gathers in our embodied selves, the embodiment of Self. Individual things reveal Him partially; the world does so entirely. At the other extreme, in the depths and the narrows, everything gathers in us, as we willingly agreed our relationship with Him as the Faithful should be based on the confidence He offered us. We have free will, because we chose it. It entered the world, which is coextensive with the self, through the self.

The world and everything in it are signs by which the One self-reveals to Himself. We are both a sign and a sign of all the signs: the signs of the dispersed world gather in us, thanks to our knowledge of the divine names. We are servants who know their Lord, who have nothing not received first from Him, for what the Lord wishes to be known He has given His servant. There is nothing in the heavens or on the earth that does not relate to God as Peace through being-at-peace, nor anything which does not bow down to Him. We do so voluntarily and may equally refrain. This is why all of existence and everything in it concerns us.

To discover perfection as our reason, we must first discover the meaning of what exists. The turn towards perfection means taking part in praising the All-praised and discovering the Praised in each of us, the perfect individual as sublime exemplar. The revelation of Unity begins with his example, which leads us to God as Goal. Wherever we find ourselves between beginning and end, we are travelling towards our highest moment, the maternal principle. Return takes place by confessing Unity, perfectly revealed in the fullness and gathering of praise in the Praised.

We travel from a beginning to an end. We speak of them as comprising a whole, as two aspects of One. Origin and destination are one, manifest in existence. This manifestation is in quantifiable time and space, but its principle is beyond quantification. It is absolute quality.

Both quality and quantity exist in time and space – the first as principle, the second as manifestation. Nothing manifest entirely excludes quality and all knowledge involves a knowing self. All attempts to separate knowledge from quality isolate time and space from absolute "now" and absolute eternity. The apostle's wisdom is just that – the confession that the absolute "now" and absolute eternity orient our path on the way from and back to perfection.

CHAPTER 1

Nothing and Everything

When we say "I," we mean two things. The I is everything except the not-I. The boundary between the I as a person and the not-I as the world is unclear – they impinge upon each other. They have no eternal, independent existence, together or apart.

In our relationship with existence, including the self, we seek the ultimate reason and purpose all things possess. Our need is informed by witness to no god but God and the Praised as His servant and apostle. This witness is a feeling in our most profound core. It isn't knowledge from an external source, but the uncreated centre of our being, which can be shaped in countless ways without betraying its essence. It comprehends humanity and the world: what lies on the outer horizons speaks of it.

God is One and Only, Near and Remote, Like and Incomparable. All of existence, together and severally, owes Him existence. Existence is thus void, absolutely poor, in relation to God. Existence, in all its variety, manifests Him. Absolutely poor, it owes Him everything, as He is All-sufficient.[1] The forms of existence are not God, just as they are nothing without Him. If their existence seems independent, the signs in the world and self have in reality lost their transparency and their link to the Signified, Whom they then conceal.

Surrounded by the signs in which He is manifest, we vacillate between witness and forgetting. We experience the world as a desert, a battlefield, no worthy goal in it. The things in which God is manifest are traces to be kicked over as we journey towards our goal. The world is nothing, except in manifesting Him as Absolute.

God sent His chosen prophets to every nation[2] with tidings in their own languages.[3] Their messages had one essence, however many forms. The revelation conveyed is: "There is no god but I; so serve Me."[4] The messages have the form of learned knowledge about us, the world and God, rituals for building right relationships and the virtue that confirms being in such relationships.

1 See *Qur'an*, 47:38 and 35:15.

2 Ibid., 10:47.

3 Ibid., 14:4.

4 *Qur'an*, 21:25.

 | DOI 10.1163/9789004279407_004

Our right relationship with ourselves, our world and God is set out in the Recitation God sent the Praised through the Holy Spirit[5] as His Word, a blessing[6] and a warning:[7] "Hast thou not seen how before God prostrate themselves all who are in the heavens and all who are in the earth, the sun and the moon, the stars and the mountains, the trees and the beasts, and many of mankind?"[8] That all things prostrate themselves before God indicates their unreality without Him. Their existence is His will. This is and is not so for us, as we relate to God through trust: "We offered trust to the heavens and the earth and the mountains, but they refused to carry it and were afraid of it; and man carried it. Surely he is sinful, very foolish."[9]

Our relationship is based on both us and God being faithful – God in the plenitude of His mercy and knowledge, we in our finitude, which we transcend only by confessing His unity and the apostolate of the Praised as the finest example. When we suppose our power sufficient and exercise it out of little knowledge, we set our will against His. We fail to acknowledge our absolute poverty in relation to the All-sufficient. We are like those who refuse to prostrate themselves when receiving the debt of existence.

The self and the world are two aspects of one manifestation of God. The world, which is seven worlds, has no reality without the One it manifests. The descending order of existence – Non-Being confirmed by Being, the Unity of Being, the names, the imaginal and the sensate – represents the levels of the Manifest. We are at the bottom of the descending scale, but contain all we need to ascend. Ascent is within the self. The heavens, the earth, and all that lies between are merely a reminder that we contain everything for return to First and Last.

If we are aware of ourselves and the world as our base, the world becomes our mosque, into which God sends down His signs to make Himself known. By our own will we use it as a place of self-abnegation, annihilating in the self what

5 See *Qur'an*, 16:102.

6 Ibid., 2:122.

7 Ibid., 34:28.

8 *Qur'an*, 22:18. Another common translation of this verse is "Hast thou not seen how to God prostrate themselves…" To prostrate oneself means to express humility before God. The perfect response means acknowledging our total indigence in relation to God as All-sufficient, since only God as Peace represents sufficiency. One thus discovers the inseparability of *ḥarb* ("war") and *sajda* ("worship/annihilation"). The *miḥrāb* is the "theatre of war" and the *masjid* the "place of annihilation of false realities associated with God." Only those who have abandoned everything can gain everything. This is the essence of the testimony of no god but God.

9 *Qur'an*, 33:72.

is not the Self, discovering in it and the world the signs we use to turn ourselves into a manifestation of the Absolute. We build mosques to bear witness that God created both us and our deeds.[10] We stand in the perfection of creation by our own will, but without identifying created and Creator, Perfection and Its manifestation. There are no imperfections in the All-merciful's creation.[11] We are created in most beautiful uprightness.[12]

We take part in prostration, the abnegation of the will, but based on the knowledge and the way God sent us through His prophets. This participation, recognizing that all we have is from God, is confirmed by humility and generosity. Pride and arrogance exclude us from taking part.

World and self are the stage for our decision to participate or exclude ourselves. Participating in the universal prostration before God, we stand most beautifully upright. The world and all it contains manifest only God, confessing no god but God. In this position of abasement, we are on the sublime height, symbolized by Spirit or heaven or any high place. Excluding ourselves, we are in the depth, which the body, earth and valley symbolize.

Confessing no god but God and the Praised as His apostle, the self affirms itself in the manifold of existence from void to Peace. This affirmation is in the world and requires only what we already contain from our beginning. The world is there to remind us of our original condition. While earth and heaven manifest enduring order, they show infinite fragility before His glory and power. God offers any who seek to understand their place in the world and exit from it many images of transience and ending, of disintegration and disappearance that undermine the prevailing illusion of solid durability.

In accordance with the covenant stored in our inner self and our original nature, the Spirit He breathed into us, we are expected to bear trust and confidence as our relationship with God. It is our confidence in God and His perfect knowledge that allows us to transcend our finitude, our this-worldy abode. We can break free from our own violence against the self and world. Violence is action without knowledge. All action we take based solely on our own will is a form of violence.

We are without knowledge. What knowledge we do have is received from the All-knowing. Our knowledge links us with God. If the link is broken, we reorient ourselves on external sources of knowledge, adopting them as our supreme goal, instead of seeking the All-knowing through them. Accepting that only

10 See *Qur'an*, 37:95–96.

11 Ibid., 67:3–4.

12 Ibid., 95:4.

God's knowledge embraces all things, we turn towards and draw nearer the Goal, steadily discovering the higher potential within ourselves.

In the mihrab or battlefield of the world, we struggle to recall God as our reason and goal. Finite beings, we are at constant risk of forgetting the Real. Our memory can redeem, but forgetting, as the source of our suffering, undoes it. God said through the Praised: "So remember Me, and I will remember you"[13] and "they have forgotten God, and He has forgotten them."[14]

Recollection connects us with the Real, Which everything in existence was created to manifest. We must acknowledge the reality, truth and claim of God and his creation. It is our witness to Unity. Acknowledging the claims of all things, we find that what exists extols and praises[15] Him as the All-laudable.[16] We realize ourselves in praise. Being praised is our supreme potential, attainable in return to God: "And He is God; there is no god but He. His is the praise in the former as in the latter; His too is the Judgment, and unto Him you shall be returned."[17]

Praise is in all things. To receive praise is to recognize the God manifest in the signs in world and the self. Praising and extolling God, we discover our bond with Him. Allotting praise to individuals, He calls them exemplary. Praising and anointing are two ways God designates His chosen, the self oriented towards its best possibility regarding the Self.

When we forget God, He forgets us. Detached from awareness of the Real, we fall into illusion and unreality. Only thinking that conforms to the Spirit He breathed into us as the core of our consciousness is real. It helps us understand things as they are, but only when we know them as linked with the Creator, Who sustains them continuously. For real thought, things are inseparable from God. This is the meaning of confessing Unity, of recollection.

To be an example to the world is every self's purpose. What is outside us fulfils its purpose by being realized inside. We all expect absolution, individually and together, in the world and the self. Expecting this absolution in the world of the senses or in some political order clouds our self-realization. The kingdom of God is in the self. The worlds are its context, not its essence. When the children of Israel were under alien rule, hypocrisy and forgetting were everywhere and they looked forward to the redemptive coming of the Anointed, Elijah, or the promised prophet they knew of from the traditions of their

13 *Qur'an*, 2:152.

14 Ibid., 9:67.

15 See *Qur'an*, 17:44.

16 Ibid., 4:131.

17 *Qur'an*, 28:70.

forebears. They were puzzled by Zachariah's son John and Mary's son Jesus: which of the three they were expecting were these two – Elijah come down again, the Anointed, or the promised apostle?

Zachariah and the Virgin recalled God, in the Further Mosque, at a time and place far remote from the Valley. This time and place touched their inner selves, their connection with the one centre of humanity and the world. The Further Mosque at Sion symbolizes our goal of ascent from our basest condition. Its walls and roofs, cisterns and altars, rites and treasures do not exist for any other reason than the Name which is God's.

God answered Zachariah's prayers, giving him a son, John, when he and his wife were already advanced in years. He also decreed that the Virgin Mary be mother of the Anointed, His Word.

The lives of Zachariah, the Virgin and their sons are examples of almost incomprehensible suffering, but also of trust in God. These four lives are constantly before us in the matter of our confidence in God, the inevitability of suffering, confidence in the world and the things in it, and how to escape suffering. All four stand before us as witnesses and heralds of the Praised, through whom we discover our supreme potential, as we stand between abasement and Peace.

Our suffering and trials turn us towards the All-merciful and Ever-merciful, towards self-abnegation. Zachariah and Mary received sublime gifts from God, but their suffering and tribulations gave their being, knowledge and felicity new meaning, as self-realization and return, in comparison to others immersed in the things of this world and unmindful of Unity as source and confluence.

CHAPTER 2

Between Two Places of Annihilation of the Self

We begin in His will, the perfect Will, Which gives us our will. We and the world both manifest God, Whose Will is to be known. When we exercise this will, it turns us either towards or away from our original perfection. When it turns us towards Perfection, we ascend towards our highest potential. When we oppose our will to His, we turn away and approach baseness.

Our highest moment is self-realization that confesses only the perfect Will. Our will manifests in oppositional pairs – finding peace in Peace or opposing Him. Our will is received. Its real conforms to His will. Seemingly independent, it turns towards unreality.

The heavens seem subject to our knowledge but not our power. As an order that manifests His will, everything in them is perfect. The earth is a stage for our will, where we can oppose His. Our misfortunes result from this resistance. As Jesus said: "Our Father which art in heaven. Hallowed be thy name, thy kingdom come. Thy will be done on earth, as it is in heaven."[1]

One aspect of doing His will on earth and in heaven is return to our original condition. We were created perfect, our will and His originally one. In setting our will against His, we forfeited that position. What was lost can be found, however, as God said: "We indeed created Man in most beautiful uprightness, then We restored him to the depth – save those who believe, and do righteous deeds; they shall have a wage unfailing."[2]

We have known both most beautiful uprightness and the lowest depth: we enter the world on the sublime height, but have equal potential for the depth. Wherever we are, the sublime height remains in our memory as our original abode. We seek to discover and regain our beginnings, to realize our inner drive to life and happiness.

Everything around us, in heaven and on earth, has its level in existence, neither sinking lower nor rising higher. Our level can alter, however. Descent, ascent and wandering take place within the self. What the things in the world and self mean depends on the level the inner self has attained – as things are signs of God. The further we are from Him, the more the signs conceal Him; the closer to Him, the more transparent they are, revealing Him.

1 *Matthew*, 6:9–10.

2 *Qur'an*, 95:4–6.

 | DOI 10.1163/9789004279407_005

Our first experience was the covenant of the tree in the midst of the Garden. As long as its fruit was not eaten, God's will and ours satisfied each another, our perfection unconcealed.

Our next experience was of the depth, where we learned the consequence of our free opposition to God, turned to Him as Known and Beloved, and set off towards Him as our only Beloved, discovering ourselves within our Beloved's call: "O soul at peace, return unto thy Lord, well-pleased, well-pleasing! Enter thou among My servants! Enter thou My Paradise!"[3]

Our fall from most beautiful uprightness to the depth has its counterpart in ascent from the Inviolable to the Further Mosque, from the self in darkness to the Light, a possibility open to all.

The Praised is His perfect servant, the best example to those who believe and do good. He experienced both descent and ascent: "Glory be to Him, who travelled with His servant by night from the Inviolable Mosque to the Further Mosque, the precincts of which We have blessed, that We might show him some of Our signs."[4]

The two places of self-abnegation are body and soul, earth and heaven. Their great signs are the Inviolable Mosque, in the middle of the desert at the bottom of the barren valley of three branches known as Becca or Mecca, and the Further Mosque on Mount Sion in Jerusalem, in the land of milk and honey. The Praised is the perfect servant who ascends, in witness of no will but the perfect Will, from the depth of the Inviolable Mosque to the height of the Further Mosque. He is the finest example, through whom God says: "You have had the finest example in God's apostle for whosoever hopes for God and the Last Day and remembers God oft."[5]

The Praised is our highest potential, sent with guidance and the debt of Truth, to uplift that debt above all others.[6] All things, individually and together, are created with Truth: "It is He who created the heavens and the earth in truth; and the day He says 'Be,' and it is; His saying is true, and His is the Kingdom the day the Trumpet is blown; He is Knower of the Unseen and the visible; He is the All-wise, the All-aware."[7]

We encapsulate existence, from the depth to the height. For our self-realization in uprightness, we must acknowledge creation's Truth and claim. The Praised confirms that claim as the condition of our self-realization: "Verily

3 Ibid., 89:27–30.

4 Ibid., 17:1.

5 Ibid., 33:21.

6 See *Qur'an*, 9:33 and 61:9.

7 *Qur'an*, 6:73.

your soul has rights over you, your Lord has rights over you, your guest has rights over you, and your wife has rights over you; so give everyone who has rights his rights."[8]

We have an obligation or debt to acknowledge the rights, truth and dignity of all. Our first debt is to the self, for if we do not recognize its rights or truth, we cannot recognize those of the Lord or of anything in existence. This recognition is part of the key to consciousness, shaped by the profession of faith: "I confess that there is no god but God and that the Praised is His apostle." In the first part of this confession the self refuses to define itself as final and sufficient. It refuses any standpoint or state as final, remaining in unlimited openness and ascent towards the Self, the All-peaceful, All-faithful and Beautiful, without Whom there is no self. This ascent discovers the Praised as our way to the Self.

This first part centres on finding peace as the self's relationship to Truth and Peace in realizing itself and acknowledging its debt. The confession then has the following form: "I confess that there is no peace but Peace and that the first of the people of peace is the apostle of Peace."[9] This confession is the self's supreme reality, depending on nothing extrinsic. God as Peace is the ultimate goal of return and we find the greatest peace in God. Guidance on the path of return is given to the First of the people of peace,[10] the finest example,[11] a mercy to the worlds,[12] and our highest possibility. He is the maternal apostle, first in creation, its seal and keystone, our guide to God, Who told him: "Say, 'If you love God, follow me, and God will love you, and forgive you your sins; God is All-forgiving, Ever-merciful.' "[13]

To follow the first of the people of peace is to realize the self's original nature as the sum of all things through being-at-peace, as the manifestation of Peace. God said through the Praised: "What, do they desire another debt than God's, and in Him has found peace whoso is in the heavens and the earth, willingly or unwillingly, and to Him they shall be returned?"[14] We may follow the first of the people of peace, as our highest possibility, but we cannot surpass him.

---

8 Wensinck et al., *Concordance* 1:486.

9 In Arabic: *ashhadu an lā salāma illā al-salām wa ashhadu anna awwal al-muslimīn rasūl al-salām.*

10 See *Qur'an*, 6:163.

11 Ibid., 33:21.

12 Ibid., 21:107.

13 *Qur'an*, 3:31.

14 Ibid., 3:83.

The Praised is the apostle of God as First and Last, first in creation and first to return. The self cannot match him, as he is always at a higher level than we have attained; but he is also with every self, as its indestructible centre. What the self realizes in drawing nearer to God is the Praised. He is in it, its eternal guide in ascent, realization and return, as God said to the Praised: "How can you conceal, seeing you have God's signs recited to you, and His apostle among you? Whosoever holds fast to God, he is guided to an upright path."[15]

Mary's son said of those who relate to God as Peace through being-at-peace: "Blessed are the peacemakers: for they shall be called the children of God."[16] He said "be called," not "be," so they would know their being as bestowed and, knowing it, be on the path of the "blessed."

To love God is to know Him in all things, since all things are created with Truth. It is to ascend to Him for union with Him. The apostle represents our sublime potential for ascent and is nearer to us than our own selves, if we believe and see God in all things and love Him more than anything.[17] He is our centre, unexhausted by countless appearances. His self abides as the higher potential of the selves that follow him in their connection with the Self.

Everything in existence receives praise from and extols the All-praised in praise. In debt to Truth, existence is praised and returns to the All-praised what it received from Him. What God gives remains irrevocably His. Our highest potential is to be praised as part of return to and realization of what the self has received by extolling the All-praised. The apostle, the mercy to the worlds is the best example of this realization. So we confess, from our very core: "that there is none worthy of praise but the All-praised and that the Praised is the apostle of the All-praised."[18] This confession depends on nothing extrinsic, but everything in existence reminds us of it. The self can veil, but never destroy it. To realize our humanity is to discover it in the self and realize it in the entity we comprise with the world.

God's mercy embraces all things;[19] all mercy in the world is from Him. The Praised is His mercy to the worlds, "gentle to the believers, merciful."[20] The profession of faith could therefore be expressed as: "I bear witness that there is no mercy but the All-merciful and Ever-merciful and I bear witness

15 Ibid., 3:101.

16 *Matthew*, 5:9.

17 See *Qur'an*, 33:6.

18 In Arabic: *ashhadu an lā ḥamīda illā al-ḥamīd wa ashhadu anna muḥammadan rasūl al-ḥamīd.*

19 See *Qur'an*, 7:156

20 *Qur'an*, 9:128.

that the man of mercy is the apostle of the All-merciful and Ever-merciful."[21] We are in a relationship with God through trust and belief,[22] which can be expressed as: "I bear witness that there is no faithful but the Faithful and I bear witness that the Faithful is the apostle of the Faithful."[23]

The confession of no self but the Self is always present in peace and belief. Witness entails one of two abnegations of will – perfect harmony with God's will or total opposition to it. Confessing His will alone, we realize ourselves in return to God. We become a sign for Him to manifest Himself. Absolutely poor, as all things are His, we enter that state of prostration in which all things come from Him. All we have is received, perfect. Our state of prostration represents our supreme potential, our creation in most beautiful uprightness.

Supposing our will independent of His, we remove ourselves from our principle and descend towards the void, sinking ever deeper into a darkness we are unaware of, an illusion of self-sufficiency. But we cannot outrun our Creator's knowledge or mercy. What seems real is not, but the possibility of turning descent into ascent is. To recognize that this state of abasement does not lead to reality is our first step to redemption, to turning and recognizing the powerlessness of the will that represents itself as real, in opposition to His.

---

21 In Arabic: *ashhadu an lā raḥīma illa al-raḥīm wa ashhadu anna raḥīman rasūl al-raḥīm.*

22 See *Qur'an*, 33:72.

23 In Arabic: *ashhadu an lā mu'mina illā al-mu'min wa ashhadu anna mu'minan rasūl al-mu'min.*

CHAPTER 3

The Oath to the Praised

We are ever between two places of self-abnegation, one on the high rock of Sion, the other in the Kaʿba at the bottom of the valley of Becca. These two extremes reflect the heavens and the earth, the soul and the body. Only when fully aware of how they differ, as nearness and remoteness, can we return and realize ourselves throughout His manifestation.

Without His knowledge, our descent leads nowhere; we have nowhere to hide from Him. We never reach a condition where His wrath surpasses His mercy. We always remain in the embrace of His mercy, for there is nothing that it does not embrace. And so, the Praised, as our highest possibility, is always with us, regardless of the depth we have sunk to.

The Praised is our higher potential. Whatever our level, he calls us from above, as our guide on the ladder to most beautiful uprightness. He is manifest as creation's principle and purpose. He gives meaning to our being in this world, our passage through it and our return. He is God's first light, spoken of at the beginning of the Torah: "And God said, Let there be light: and there was light. And God saw the light, that it was good: and God divided the light from the darkness."[1]

We all carry witness in our core to the covenant in pre-existence, as sent down in the Recitation:

> And when thy Lord took from the Children of Adam, from their loins, their seed, and made them testify touching themselves, "Am I not your Lord?" They said, "Yes, we testify" – lest you should say on the Day of Resurrection, "As for us, we were heedless of this," or lest you say, "Our fathers were associators aforetime, and we were seed after them. What, wilt Thou then destroy us for the deeds of the vain-doers?"[2]

In this covenant, the self is the source of redemptive knowledge. All we need for self-realization is in us already; no received knowledge, even if passed on to us by our forefathers, is essential to our salvation. The very fact of being entails

---

1 *Genesis*, 1:3–4. Commentaries on the Light of the Praised (*al-nūr al-muḥammadi*) as the precursor of all creation are key elements of Muslim spiritual and intellectual heritage. See Böwering, *The Mystical Vision of Existence in Classical Islam*.

2 *Qur'an*, 7:172–173.

 | DOI 10.1163/9789004279407_006

knowledge and when we keep this knowledge at the centre of our being, the self can be realized in its original potential, answering our prayer: "Guide us on the upright path, the path of those whom Thou hath blessed."

All were offered trust and free will. All accepted. What they accepted was the possibility of tribulation, as knowledge is always limited. But God's mercy embraces all things[3] and exceeds His wrath,[4] so that all existence lies in His mercy, as in the womb. Our attempts in duality to realize ourselves in primal mercy entail perpetual war against seeming on behalf of truth. In that war, our ability to tell truth from lie and cleave to universal truth is constantly tested.

People are divided into nations. God sends His prophets to speak to each in their own language[5] and recall them to what lies at the self's core: the Spirit God breathed in, the knowledge of the names He taught, the primordial Light divided from the darkness, and the sublime potential sent as the ultimate sign of His perfection. This centre is the principle by which we attain what we are and discover the meaning of our creation.

We all share this core and redemption is open to all the children of Adam. Realization and ascent towards perfected humanity as the purpose of creation are enabled by what we know, what our original covenant with God gave us. It alone connects us with God. Everything else distracts from return and discovery of the self's core as the site of return. We find His light with us – the Light that ultimately receives the praise of the All-praised. Illumination and praise are manifest in the Praised's perfection.

The Praised is the prophets' best example and ours, apostle before them and all things. People are divided into nations and languages and God sends His prophets to remind them of the knowledge in their core that they may discover and realize their sublime potential, our maternal, receptive principle.

Everyone confesses God as Lord in pre-existence. Our return depends on no external source of knowledge, not our parents nor anything in the whole world.[6] We confess the apostle at the self's core, the perfection that is the measure for our every condition, the ever-present potential towards which we ascend in realizing life and discovering happiness.

Through His prophets, God reminds us of this original covenant, which the Praised, as perfect individual, exemplifies. All His prophets confessed the Praised in pre-existence. They addressed the people they were sent to through him, as is said in the Recitation:

---

3 See *Qur'an*, 7:156.

4 See Bukhārī, 9:482.

5 See *Qur'an*, 10:47 and 14:4.

6 Ibid., 7:172.

> And when God took compact with the prophets: "That I have given you of Book and Wisdom; then there shall come to you an apostle confirming what is with you – you shall believe in him and you shall help him; do you agree?" He said. "And do you take My load on you on that condition?" They said, "We do agree." God said, "Bear witness so, and I shall be with you among the witnesses." Then whosoever turns his back after that – they are the ungodly.[7]

That apostle is the Praised, whom all things manifest, receiving and returning praise to the All-praised. He is the perfect individual, receiving and refracting praise and extolling his Lord, the All-praised, in praise. All prophecy and all prophets gather in him at both beginning and end.

Humanity sets the seal on creation; everything dispersed in the world gathers in us. We are at the beginning and end of creation. Our perfect example as seal of creation is the Praised, of whom God said: "Muhammad is not the father of any one of your men, but the apostle of God, and the seal of the prophets; God has knowledge of everything."[8] God called him maternal prophet[9] because all existence and everything in it begin with him and confess him to be such. He is their reason and purpose.

The Praised as seal corresponds to existence's keystone, known from the beginning and present in all things. Without him there would be no true creatures. Without the headstone, known at the beginning and present at the end, all things are deficient, as the Psalmist says: "The stone which the builders refused is become the headstone of the corner. This is the Lord's doing; it is marvellous in our eyes."[10] Mary's son reminded his disciples of these words.[11]

The Praised described existence as a house and himself as the condition of plenitude:

> The similitude of mine and that of the apostles before me is that of a person who built a house quite imposing and beautiful and he made it complete but for one brick in one of its corners. People began to walk round it, and the building pleased them and they would say: "But for this brick your building would have been perfect." Muhammad (may peace be

---

7 *Qur'an*, 3:81–82.
8 Ibid., 33:40.
9 See *Qur'an*, 7:157.
10 *Psalm* 118:22–23.
11 See *Matthew*, 21:42.

> upon him) said: "And I am that final brick, and I am the last of the apostles."[12]

When the Praised lists his names, he is speaking of his position in existence: "I have five names. I am the Praised; I am the Most Deserving of Praise; I am the Eraser, by whom God erases concealment; I am the Gatherer, at whose feet the people shall be gathered; I am the Concluder."[13] Perfection is the why and wherefore of our existence. The Praised is that perfection. Approaching our better nature, we draw closer to the Praised, who is in and with us[14] and whose nature is of immense magnitude.[15] In our original nature, we all know God as Lord. The Praised is His first manifestation and our sublime potential. The prophets are his witnesses and the Praised is known to all peoples in all languages.

To bear witness to the Praised is to bear witness to the prophets. To bear witness to any prophet is to do so to all, including the Praised, as God says through him:

> What, do they desire another debt than God's, for in Him has found peace whoso is in the heavens and the earth, willingly or unwillingly, and to Him they shall be returned? Say: "We believe in God, and that which has been sent down on us, and sent down on Abraham and Ishmael, Isaac and Jacob, and the Tribes, and in that which was given to Moses and Jesus, and the prophets, of their Lord; we make no division between any of them, and in Him we find peace." Whoso desires another debt than being-at-peace, it shall not be accepted of him; in the next world he shall be among the losers.[16]

The Praised is the first of creation, our highest possibility, regardless of language, region or time. We all belong to some nation and each one contains a community of the guided and guiding by truth, and so is split into just and unjust, upright and crooked. The just speak and point to truth, discerning it in all things. They take the Praised for the possibility of perfection, the finest

---

12 Muslim, 4:1235.

13 Mālik, 513.

14 See *Qur'an*, 3:101.

15 Ibid., 68:4. This translates the Arabic *khuluq 'aẓīm*. Lings translates this into English as "Verily of an immense magnitude is thy nature" (Lings, *Splendours of Qur'an Calligraphy and Illumination*, 17).

16 *Qur'an*, 3:83–85.

example, sent to all, as the prophet of the Ummah, the Community, the communities of the just at all times and among all peoples:

> Say: "O mankind, I am the apostle of God to you all, of Him to whom belongs the kingdom of the heavens and of the earth. There is no god but He. He gives life, and makes to die. Believe then in God, and in His apostle, the maternal prophet of the common folk, who believes in God and His words, and follow him; haply so you will be guided."[17]

To follow the Praised is justice. He does not judge except with the knowledge God sent down to him. This knowledge is not of the world. It was revealed to him and through him everything is reshaped to speak of its reason and purpose. It is in each thing's centre, so that all the signs in the world and self recall him. This is why he is the Light divided from the darkness. Those who follow him follow the Light.

The Praised is present in every self, however veiled. He cannot be eliminated, since even in the uttermost depths, we are not beyond mercy and the Praised was sent as a mercy to the worlds. We never reach a condition in which the light of his lamp is forever extinguished.

The Praised is manifest in duality – receiving and giving. When God reveals Himself, He gives of His Light, the first of His gifts. As a form of existence, Light is at the highest level. First to be received, it is given to all other things. Receiving and giving, the female and the male principles are united in the Light-giving Lamp, the Praised.

---

17 Ibid., 7:158.

CHAPTER 4

Abraham, Ishmael and Isaac

God has sent 124,000 prophets.[1] Division into nations and languages, ages and regions neither enhances nor diminishes the fact that we are fitted for self-discovery by our original perfection, the inner knowledge God gave us in creation, of which the signs in world and self remind us, as do the prophets He sent to warn and serve us as examples. Every prophet serves a nation and a time, exemplifying realization in original knowledge, our covenant with God. They all confessed the Praised as the best example and a mercy to the worlds.

As first man and first prophet, Adam is the Praised as model for us and all the prophets. In original purity in the Garden, the tree still inviolate, Adam realized the Praised perfectly as best example. Once he had eaten the fruit God forbade, Adam went down from the sublime height, the acme of existence denoted by the summit of a hill, to the depth, denoted by the bottom of a valley. The Praised's initial image was submerged in Adam's depths, as he sank from the height. The clarity of the Praised's presence in self and world was lost – but his presence was not.

The heavens and earth are, like the hilltop and the valley floor, outward signs of what is within. Our "I" encompasses existence's spectrum, from the body of clay to the Spirit breathed into it. At existence's lowest degree, in the valley of the uttermost depths, after our fall, we turned to God, Who decreed these signs to orient our path back. With them, we turn ego into humility before God and lamentation for our sin of setting our will against His. We rediscover ourselves through the Praised as the principle of our perfection. The signs He discloses to us become the time and space in which we renew our original covenant with Him. Abu Dharr recalled a conversation with the Praised about the signs of return and ascent:

> I said: "Apostle of God, which was the first place of annihilation and self-abnegation to be built on earth?"
> "The Inviolable Place of Annihilation (*al-masjid al-ḥaram*)," he said.
> "And then which," I asked?
> "The Further Place of Annihilation (*al-masjid al-aqṣā*)," he said.
> I further asked, "What was the time span between the two?"
> "Forty years," he replied.

1 See Bayhaqī, 9:4, tradition 17489.

 | DOI 10.1163/9789004279407_007

> And he added, "Wherever you may be at the time of prayer, pray there, for that is best."[2]

These two places of self-annihilation are signs of our ascent and return to God. We can return at anytime from anywhere, as we are always somewhere between depth and height. To pray is to confess this duality and turn to the self's uncreated centre, Intellect or Spirit, which shows the upright path from Inviolable to Further Mosque, from the signs to the Signified.

The upright path is the sending down of Unity, Its manifestation in plurality, and the universal return to Unity. The path ends in uncreated Peace. All things in existence turn towards Peace as source and confluence, but nothing attains It by its own will. Both descent and ascent are embraced by His mercy. As Peace and Mercy He links all things to Himself through mercy and being-at-peace. The Praised too is merciful,[3] a universal mercy,[4] the first of the people of peace,[5] utterly dedicated to the All-merciful and Ever-merciful and uncreated Peace.

When the Praised entered history, he confessed all the prophets, who had confessed him in pre-existence as their sublime potential and who revealed him as such in their earthly mission. God connected their existence and their prophecy through the Praised: "We sent apostles before thee; of some We have related to thee, and some We have not related to thee. It was not for any apostle to bring a sign, save by God's leave."[6]

Time passed and prophets came, one after another, who knew of the Praised and the places of self-abnegation in Becca and on Sion. They made their vow to God through the Praised as their seal. The houses built on the sites of those two signs were derelict and destroyed, repaired and rebuilt. At times only piles of stone were to be seen; at others the original worship was wholly distorted or destroyed. The seven heavens mark out the degrees of our ascent to Peace, ascent that is within us, from our depths to our height, from margins to centre.

In the valley, God taught us the rite of the seven circuits of the house of the Kaʿba. With six sides corresponding to six directions in space, the house manifests the apostle as the centre of both humankind and the world. He is the point of origin and convergence of all six directions, the seventh through which Peace manifests its connection to all things and all things return to It.

---

2 Bukhārī, 4:383.

3 See *Qur'an*, 9:128.

4 Ibid., 21:107.

5 Ibid., 6:163.

6 *Qur'an*, 40:78.

The seven circuits denote our ascent to the lost height, as we confess: "There is no self but the Self and the Praised is the apostle of the Self." This confession is the essence of the discourse of all of God's prophets.

One of these prophets was Abraham, the friend of God.[7] Two things were clear in his soul – the impotence of the will isolated from His will and His perfect guidance of the self that remains pure and true to Him. Committed to God's guidance, Abraham travelled the road revealed, and earth and heaven and Sion and Becca were signs free of distortion. He knew God as the Faultless Guide, found refuge in Him as Peace and was true to Him as True, discovering the Praised as best example within himself.

His wife Hagar bore him a son, Ishmael,[8] and thirteen years later his wife Sarah bore another, Isaac.[9] God's promise to him came true in his descendants: "And I will make of thee a great nation, and I will bless thee, and make thy name great; and thou shalt be a blessing."[10]

Hagar and Ishmael left Abraham's home, as Sarah wished and God willed. Guided by Him, mother and child made their abode in the ruins of the house at Becca, while Sarah and Isaac remained with Abraham, close to the ruins of the house on Sion. Abraham was close to both sons to the end of his life, visiting Ishmael in the valley and returning northwards to Isaac and Sion. The Recitation records Abraham and Ishmael's witness of the Praised:

> And when Abraham, and Ishmael with him, raised up the foundations of the house: "Our Lord, receive this from us; Thou art the All-hearing, the All-knowing; and, our Lord, bring us to peace in Thee and make of our seed a community at peace in Thee, and show us our holy rites, and turn towards us; surely Thou turnest, and art Ever-merciful; and, our Lord, do Thou send among them an apostle, one of them, who shall recite to them Thy signs, and teach them the Book and the Wisdom, and purify them; Thou art the All-mighty, the All-wise."[11]

The house in Becca was the first. God's call to go there and walk around it includes all we need to recover what we have lost. The prophets told their peoples of the rites of pilgrimage and circumambulation and, when we respond today, it is with Abraham and Ishmael in mind: "The first house established for the people was that at Becca, a place holy, and a guidance to all beings. Therein

---

7 See *Qur'an* 4:125, cf. *Isaiah* 41:8; *2 Chronicles*, 20:7.

8 See *Genesis*, 16:15.

9 Ibid., 16:16 and 21:5.

10 *Genesis*, 12:2.

11 *Qur'an*, 2:127–29.

are clear signs – the station of Abraham, and whosoever enters it is in security. It is the duty of all men towards God to come to the house a pilgrim, if he is able to make his way there."[12] Abraham and Ishmael restored the house in the valley to its purpose, as God recalled: "And We made covenant with Abraham and Ishmael: 'Purify My house for those that shall go about it and those that cleave to it, to those who bow and prostrate themselves.' "[13]

The nation God promised Abraham as his seed had two branches through his two sons, both prophets. Ishmael's twelve sons gave rise to twelve tribes[14] who dwelt in the land, while Ishmael "died in the presence of all his brethren."[15] These brethren were the descendants of Isaac, who founded twelve tribes from the twelve sons of his son Jacob, whom God called Israel.

Again and again the prophets of these two branches of the nation God promised Abraham spoke of the two places of annihilation of the self. The Ishmaelites were associated with the first, the Israelites with the second, brethren separated to confess and find Unity manifest in multiplicity, from earth to heaven, body to Spirit, the Inviolable to the Further Mosque, on our path of ascent to God.

Abraham and Ishmael cleared and rebuilt the Inviolable Mosque as a legacy to all people. This undertaking is inseparable from Abraham as the friend of God and traveller between two extremes, from Mount to Valley and back, from wandering to ascent, from the younger Isaac to the older Ishmael, and back again. This shows that the lowest level we sink to is the beginning of our return, as nothing is ever wholly lost. His mercy encompasses all things.

The rebuilding of the house and the rite of pilgrimage direct us towards the sublime height we lost. At the lowest level of existence, human perfection is like a pure, fresh spring welling up from the dark depths of the earth into which it once sank.

Abraham and Isaac directed their descendants, the children of Israel, to the Further Mosque. They lived close to the house on Mount Sion, but ascent to the House was deferred for future generations, who would discover in themselves the indivisibility of depths and height, earth and heaven, body and Spirit. These two streams of consciousness in Abraham's descendents share a single source and confluence, as these words make clear: "Surely we belong to God, and to Him we return."[16]

12 Ibid., 3:96–97.
13 Ibid., 2:125.
14 See *Genesis*, 25:16–17.
15 *Genesis*, 25:18.
16 *Qur'an*, 2:156.

In this, Abraham is the finest example, uniting within himself the depths and height:

> You have had the most beautiful example in Abraham, and those with him, when they said to their people, "We are quit of you and that you serve, apart from God. We deny you, and between us and you enmity has shown itself, and hatred for ever, until you believe in God alone."[17]

The two branches of Abraham's posterity, the Ishmaelites and the Israelites, may seem divided, but this is mere illusion in their earthly divagations. The Ishmaelites and the Israelites were travellers on the same path in discovery of their orientation towards the One. On that path, none of us can avoid the rite of setting off from the depths or of turning to face the height as our Goal. As the two branches are inseparable, so the two mosques are facets of our ascent to Peace.

Postscript

Abraham, Ishmael and Isaac and all their children were circumcised, as God commanded:

> This is my covenant, which he shall keep between me and you and thy seed after thee; every man child among you shall be circumcised. And ye shall circumcise the flesh of your foreskin; and it shall be a token of the covenant betwixt me and you. And he that is eight days old shall be circumcised among you, every man child in your generations, he that is born in the house, or bought with money of any stranger, which is not of thy seed.[18]
>
> And as for Ishmael, I have heard thee: behold, I have blessed him, and will make him fruitful, and will multiply him exceedingly; twelve princes shall he beget, and I will make him a great nation.[19]
>
> And Abraham was ninety years old and nine, when he was circumcised in the flesh of his foreskin. And Ishmael his son was thirteen years old, when he was circumcised in the flesh of his foreskin. On the selfsame day was Abraham circumcised, and Ishmael his son. And all the men of

17 Ibid., 60:4.

18 *Genesis*, 17:10–12.

19 Ibid., 17:20.

> his house, born in the house, and bought with money of the stranger, were circumcised with him.[20]

Circumcision is the sign of our covenant with God. Ishmael was thirteen years old when circumcised. God granted him twelve sons, so that he and they together were thirteen. This number is the sign of the Praised as the principle of the covenant of all the prophets with God.

---

20 Ibid., 17:24–27.

CHAPTER 5

Israel and Moses

We return to our beginning, find ourselves in our first principle. Our original form is Adam, the first incarnation of human perfection and pure image of the Creator.[1] But Adam's model is the truth of the Praised. Our path thus goes from the Praised, seal of the prophets, through the prophets, admonishers of the nations, through and beyond history to the Praised and, in ascent, to God as First and Last.

The path is described in the stories of the prophets and nations, as is said in the Recitation: "These are they whom God has blessed among the prophets of the seed of Adam, and of those We bore with Noah, and of the seed of Abraham and Israel, and of those We guided and chose. When the signs of the All-merciful were recited to them, they fell down prostrate, weeping."[2]

Abraham's son Isaac had a son, Jacob. All three were prophets. After a mysterious happening one night, God renamed Jacob Israel,[3] and all Abraham's descendants through Isaac and Jacob are named for him: the entire nation of the children of Israel.

---

1 The terms "divine image" or "God's image" are used through the book. This translates the Arabic *ṣūra*, which means "picture," "shape," or "form." Some of the writer's friends have confessed their uneasiness regarding this term in the Muslim tradition. This feeling is understandable because of the difference between the Muslim understanding of the image of God, Who is like nothing and strictly incomparable, and the Christian doctrine of the Word which "became flesh." Contemplation of God's image forms an important part of the Muslim intellectual heritage, however, about which Ibn al-ʿArabī writes: "The thing the Shapegiver gave shape to is the same thing as Him and nothing but Him, because it is not without Him. There is no doubt that God gave to the cosmos its shape in accordance with showing His substance. Man, who is Adam, is made up of individuals in whom the cosmos is gathered (*majmūʿ*), because he is a small man, an abstract of a 'great man' (macrocosmos). Man cannot observe the whole cosmos because of its size and vast span. Opposite of that, man is of small span and observation covers him due to his shape, his body build and spiritual capability he empowers. God ordered in him all that is outside of him but Him. The reality of God's name (*Allah*), that caused Him to show and out of which He became shown, is linked to every one of His acts, which is the reason why every God's name is in relation with Him; and why none of them circumvents Him. That is why Adam was made according to the shape of the name Allah, because that name includes all of God's names." (*al-Fūtūḥāt al-makkiyya*, 2:123.35; in Chittick, *The Sufi Path of Knowledge*, 276).

2 *Qur'an*, 19:58.

3 See *Genesis*, 32:29.

 | DOI 10.1163/9789004279407_008

Abraham bequeathed his legacy to his sons Ishmael and Isaac, and later Jacob did the same to his sons: "My sons, God has chosen for you a debt; see that you die not save in peace."[4] In accepting this charge, the children of Israel became a chosen people, with the memory of our original perfection and of the depths to which we fell after violating our first covenant with God. They are aware of both extremes – the remote depths and the height close by. The regions around holy Mount Sion were given them, as part of their covenant with God.

No covenant is unconditional. The call to the Israelites to ascend towards the height, symbolized by the Further Mosque, requires acceptance of first and second covenants – the initial covenant and the one from the depths, when God took pity on fallen humankind. It is only from that state of abasement revealed to Ishmael that the journey can begin to the summit of the Mount, towards the younger brother, Isaac, their separation revealed in their paternity, sons of one father and sign of God's unity.

It was necessity, as well as His guidance deep within, that compelled the Israelites to settle in Egypt and endure Pharaoh's rule. Both the covenant and God's promise were with them, as He said: "Now, therefore, if ye will obey my voice indeed, and keep my covenant, then ye shall be a peculiar treasure unto me above all people."[5]

Pharaoh ruled in coercion, based on ignorance of First and Last. His supremacy was fictitious and people were forced to limit their selves within his notions of authority. They were subjugated to things of this world, not their Lord. The Israelites recalled their debt to God under their covenant and this preserved them from accepting Pharaoh's rule as valid. God sent them one of their own as prophet, to restore their memory to full consciousness and lead them from the darkness towards the Light. God told the Praised: "And We delivered the Children of Israel from the humbling chastisement, from Pharaoh; surely he was a high one, of the prodigals; and We chose them, out of a knowledge above all beings, and gave them signs wherein there was a manifest trial."[6]

It was while delivering the children of Israel, a people at peace with their covenant with God, that Moses was sent with a book to guide their ascent by the upright path from the depths to the height. Its signs, inseparable from each other, are the Inviolable Mosque in the sacred valley of Becca and the Further Mosque on holy Mount Sion.

---

4 *Qur'an*, 2:132.

5 *Exodus*, 19:5.

6 *Qur'an*, 44:30–33.

Since we fell from the sublime height to the depth, our ascent must be from the depths we fell to. Not just this or that individual, but every one of us fell to existence's depths in Adam's fall, which is imprinted on our very nature. In these depths, our covenant with God is renewed, as we rediscover how to relate to All-faithful God as faithful through faith. There is no ascent if we are not aware of both extremes – the height and the depths. At any given point, there are brethren below, in the depths, and above, on the height. We cannot make our journey if we disregard this difference. The Ishmaelites and the Israelites are one example of differentiation between brethren, in which participants both lose and find their father, as sign of one origin and of the Praised, our original nature and sublime potential.

To remind them of the oath sworn by all the prophets, God spoke to the children of Israel through Moses about the Praised. It is a clear revelation in two utterances. In the first, Moses speaks to them about the Praised, while God tells them the same through Moses' mouth:

> The Lord thy God will raise up unto thee a prophet from the midst of thee, of thy brethren, like unto me; unto him ye shall hearken; according to all that thou desirest of the Lord thy God in Horeb in the day of the assembly, saying, Let me not hear again the voice of the Lord my God, neither let me see this great fire any more, that I die not. And the Lord said unto me, They have well spoken that which they have spoken. I will raise them up a prophet from among their brethren, like unto thee, and will put my words in his mouth; and he shall speak unto them all that I shall command him. And it shall come to pass, that whosoever will not hearken unto my words which he shall speak in my name, I will require it of him. But the prophet, which shall presume to speak a word in my name, which I have not commanded him to speak, or that shall speak in the name of other gods, even that prophet shall die.[7]

---

7 *Deuteronomy*, 18:15–20. In the Muslim view, God's announcement to Moses of the Praised's entry into history is echoed in several places in other books of the Bible (See, e.g., Bukhārī, 6:345–46). God says in the *Qur'an*: "Surely We have sent thee as a witness, good tidings to bear, and warning." (48:8). This revelation and the commentary on it in Bukhārī are associated with several biblical passages. One of them is expressed by the prophet Isaiah: "Behold my servant, whom I uphold; mine elect, in whom my soul delighteth; I have put my spirit upon him: he shall bring forth judgment to the Gentiles. He shall not cry, nor lift up, nor cause his voice to be heard in the street. A bruised reed shall he not break, and the smoking flax shall he not quench; he shall bring forth judgment unto truth. He shall not fail nor be discouraged, till he have set judgment in the earth; and the isles shall wait for his law." (*Isaiah*, 42:1–4). This passage is also associated with the coming of Jesus, the Messiah (cf. *Matthew*,

Nor did God raise up any prophet like Moses again among the children of Israel:

> And there arose not a prophet since in Israel like unto Moses, whom the Lord knew face to face, in all the signs and the wonders, which the Lord sent him to do in the land of Egypt to Pharaoh, and to all his servants, and to all his land, and in all that mighty land, and in all the great terror which Moses shewed in the sight of Israel.[8]

The same Book sent down through Moses says that the brethren of the children of Israel are the children of Ishmael.[9] The prophet of whom God spoke to Moses is thus of the children of Ishmael. Abraham and Ishmael renewed and bequeathed the teachings, ritual and virtue whose sign is the first house in the Valley and its connection with the second house on the Mount. The first house corresponds to the low darkness from which we hope to escape and return to the authentic beauty in which we were created. This return and revelation in the self corresponds to the house on the Mount. These two houses are indivisible signs of our return to God.

Leading the children of Israel from slavery to the Further Mosque and renewing their covenant, Moses pointed to God in their centre and left them with that as their only warrant of redemption. Frightened and alone, unable to see Him in their centre, they collected gold and made a molten calf: in giving up their gold to merge into a common centre, they were trying to express their commitment to the place they thought of as Moses' and thus God's.

When Moses returned and found them dancing around the golden calf, his "anger waxed hot" and he commanded those loyal to him to slay their brothers, companions and neighbours. Some three thousand were killed. God spoke of this through the Praised in the Recitation:

> And when Moses' anger abated in him, he took the Tablets, and in the inscription of them was guidance, and mercy unto all those who hold their Lord in awe. And Moses chose of his people seventy men for Our appointed time; and when the earthquake seized them, he said, "My

---

12:18–21). Nor should one forget that the Anointed and the Praised are intimate and inseparable witnesses to one another, as this book indicates. Both of them, in similar but different ways, are the sum of the historical experience of Israel and bestow it as God's revelation on all of us. For more on how Isaiah's prophecies relate to the coming of the Praised see Graham, *Divine Word and Prophetic Word in Early Islam*, 203–204.

8 *Deuteronomy*, 34:10–12.

9 See *Genesis*, 16:12 and 25:18.

> Lord, hadst Thou willed Thou wouldst have destroyed them before, and me. Wilt Thou destroy us for what the foolish ones of us have done? It is only Thy trial, whereby Thou leadest astray whom Thou wilt, and guidest whom Thou wilt. Thou art our Protector; so forgive us, and have mercy on us, for Thou art the best of forgivers. And prescribe for us in this world good, and in the world to come; we have repented unto Thee." Said He, "My chastisement – I smite with it whom I will; and My mercy embraces all things, and I shall prescribe it for those who are mindful and pay the alms, and those who indeed believe in Our signs, those who follow the apostle, the prophet of the common folk, whom they find written down with them in the Torah and the Gospel, bidding them to honour, and forbidding them dishonour, making lawful for them the good things and making unlawful for them the corrupt things, and relieving them of their loads, and the fetters that were upon them. Those who believe in him and succour him and help him, and follow the light that has been sent down with him – they are the prosperers."[10]

To lead is to go ahead on the path of ascent from darkness to Light, ignorance to the All-knowing, the depths to the All-high. He who precedes is closer to God. The Light was originally sent down with our perfect potential. Every prophet leads with and towards it, as his original vow to God.

God said of Moses: "And We sent Moses with Our signs – 'Bring forth thy people from the shadows to the light and remind thou them of the Days of God.' Surely in that are signs for every man enduring, thankful!"[11] The Book and salvation[12] were given to Moses to lead them forth, and he himself was shown to the people as God's perfect art, of which God says: "I shaped you as a work of art for Myself. I have chosen thee for My service."[13]

Moses was thus a witness to the Praised as the apostle, testifying as one of the prophets who swore an oath to him in pre-existence. His people are the children of Israel, to whom he brought the Book and the Salvation, and to whom he testified as the first of the believers.[14] Those of his people who

---

10 *Qur'an*, 7:154–57.

11 Ibid., 14:5.

12 See *Qur'an*, 2:53.

13 *Qur'an*, 20:41. This translation follows Martin Lings, *Splendours of Qur'an Calligraphy and Illumination*, 17.

14 See *Qur'an*, 7:143.

followed him were a maternal nation: "Of the people of Moses there is a maternal nation who guide by the truth, and by it act with justice."[15]

Moses led the children of Israel out of Egypt towards the Further Mosque. His bodily presence came to an end on the way, but he remained their best example. That journey requires his example and following Moses entails following the Praised. The warrant is the nation that guides by the truth.

Moses spoke to his people, bringing the Torah as light and guidance,[16] and told them a prophet would come from among their brethren. God dictated their undifferentiated covenant by maintaining the connection with their brethren. All that takes place among the Israelites remains eternally linked with the destiny of the Ishmaelites; in no war or peace is the link wholly broken. Does not His instruction to the Praised to direct all his followers towards the Israelites also show this?

> So, if thou art in doubt regarding what We have sent down to thee, ask those who recite the Book before thee.[17]
>
> It belongs not to any mortal that God should give him the Book, the Judgment, the prophethood, then he should say to men, "Be you servants to me apart from God." Rather, "Be you masters in that you know the Book, and in that you study."[18]

The prophet Moses confessed a prophet like him, through Whom God spoke to people. When He spoke to him, the voice and the fire of Horeb were manifest as the Recitation sent down through the Spirit of Truth, the Holy Spirit. By warning people with Himself and the Recitation, and sending down the Praised as the prophet like Moses, God announces him as a mercy to the worlds: "Say: 'Have you given thought if this be truly from God and yet you deny its truth? – even though a witness from among the children of Israel has already borne

---

15 *Qur'an,* 7:159. The original contains two terms – *al-qawm* and *al-umma.* The first is translated as "people," the second as "maternal community." This could also be "matrix" or "mother." The Praised is the best example of community in every nation and at all times. See *Qur'an,* 7:158. The queen bee is a symbol of his confirmation on coming out after his instruction, the corresponding Arabic name for which is *al-Mahdi.* In the upper chamber of the lodge of the Mevlevi order of dervishes in Sarajevo there was a mural of a queen bee, which signified the hidden presence of that principle of truthfulness and righteousness.

16 See *Qur'an,* 5:44.

17 *Qur'an,* 10:94. See also 16:43 and 21:7.

18 Ibid., 3:79.

witness to one like himself, and has believed in him, the while you glory in your arrogance? Verily, God does not grace evildoing folk with His guidance.' "[19]

What is more, the prophet Moses blessed the children of Israel and told them that descent and ascent are connected. Though we fall to the depth, we are not fallen into utter ruin, for even there the Praised remains with us in our inner self, as our perfect nature to discover which restores us to our original condition. Moses told the children of Israel their future was inseparably linked with their brethren, the children of Ishmael, and spoke to them of the Praised as a pledge between them, saying: "The Lord came from Sinai, and rose up from Seir unto them; he shined forth from Mount Paran, and he came with ten thousands of saints: from his right hand went a fiery law for them."[20] In saying that the Lord "shined forth from Mount Paran," Moses confirms the old annunciations and enduring human expectation of the Praised, who manifests sublimity in humility and humility in sublimity.

"The Lord's coming" from three places, three high places, points to three different revelations of His Word. The prophet Moses speaks of the future, but directs his listeners towards the prophet Abraham and the two streams that flowed from him. *Genesis* relates how Hagar wept over her son Ishmael, fearing that he would die of thirst in the wilderness.

> And God heard the voice of the lad; and the angel of God called Hagar out of heaven, and said unto her, What aileth thee, Hagar? Fear not; for God hath heard the voice of the lad where he is. Arise, lift up the lad, and hold him in thine hand; for I will make him a great nation. And God opened her eyes, and she saw a well of water; and she went, and filled the bottle with water, and gave the lad drink. And God was with the lad; and he grew, and dwelt in the wilderness, and became an archer. And he dwelt in the wilderness of Paran.[21]

The Praised is a Light-giving Lamp. His rising is in Paran, in the land of Ishmael, among his descendants; and Ishmael's descendants are the brethren of the Israelites.

---

19 Ibid., 46:10. The translation of this verse quite closely follows that given in Asad, *The Message of the Qur'an*, 771.

20 *Deuteronomy*, 33:2. For the history of the Muslim understanding of this verse as heralding the Praised, see Peters, *A Reader on Classical Islam*, 48.

21 *Genesis*, 21:17–21.

CHAPTER 6

The Ark of the Covenant

We are the sum of His creation. All the levels of existence, earth, heaven and what lies between or beyond were created in six days. When everything had already been dispersed in existence, God reassembled it all in human plenitude as His goal. He revealed Himself on the seventh day, the Sabbath, as Peace, the source and confluence of all things.

We are the only beings to relate to God through trust. This requires both us and God to be faithful and true and to enjoy free will. God offered His confidence in absolute knowledge and mercy. We accepted it out of little knowledge, but in the love that binds us to the Absolute.

That trust, offered and accepted, is our covenant with God, which has many expressions. In our finitude, we forget and remember and our covenant lies between remembering and forgetting. To remember is our sublime potential, whereby we transcend finitude. It is remembering that makes us bearers of the trust He offered and we accepted. Forgetting, we are nothing. But forgetting does not destroy the Spirit received at creation.

In pre-existence, we confessed God as Lord and the elect from all the people agreed to confess the Praised as their seal, impressed upon them by God as King and Judge.

Adam, as first man, was allowed to dwell in the Garden so long as he obeyed the command not to eat the fruit of one tree. The forbidden fruit was the central sign of this covenant, but Adam and Eve broke it and fell from the height to the depths. There Adam turned again to God and the covenant was renewed. The houses in the Valley and on the Mount are the central signs of the renewed covenant.

The house faces us, exterior to interior. It has six surfaces, twelve edges; two surfaces on the vertical axis, up and down, four on the horizontal axes, forward and back, left and right. These three dimensions and six directions converge on and arise from a single point. This point is the ineffable seventh, uncreated Stillness as the principle of motion. Exteriority manifests interiority as its principle, as multiplicity manifests Unity. All speech is of one Word.

Our original condition meant perfect harmony between inner and outer. The things in the world reflected the things in the self, and vice versa. When we violated what was not to be eaten, that unity split into duality. The inner became obscured, while the signs in the world remained clear, but no longer

 | DOI 10.1163/9789004279407_009

legible. The perfect order of the Garden was split into earthly opposites – poisonous and healing, cold and hot, ugly and beautiful, dark and light.

God offered us and we accepted a covenant of confidence, but forgetful creatures, we forgot it. The houses were reduced to piles of stone, their facets, the inner and unseen and the outer and visible, divorced by our forgetting, so that the outer aspect seemed all of existence, and we the master, not the servant. The signs in world and self came to seem independent of their reason for existing. Our bond as knowers with God as Known was broken and Unity lost in multiplicity, which seemed increasingly sufficient, the only reality.

When we succumbed to forgetting, the houses, signs of the renewed covenant, fell derelict. Their fracture was due to our obliviousness of them and of our reason and purpose in the world. We stopped seeing the signs of our original perfection, our vow to God, in the house's six visible surfaces.

God chose Abraham and his sons to rebuild the houses as signs of His eternal covenant with us, and of Unity's significance as source and confluence of multiplicity. Abraham and Ishmael rebuilt the house in the Valley and left it to their descendants in witness of the Praised, who was to arise in the Valley, beside the house, as the maternal seal of the prophets, first and last among them. That renewal began at the depths, since the first station on the path of ascent lies on the desert valley floor.

Only when we understand where we stand in the Valley can we begin to know our goal. The Praised is the sublime core within each one of us, to which the house bears witness. Only with the perfect Praised and his mighty morality at the heart of existence can we comprehend the worlds' praise of God and remind ourselves of the Praised in and with each of us.

Abraham directed his other lineage to discover and restore the house on the Mount. Both facets of our orientation towards the houses, in the Valley *and* on the Mount, manifest the same humanity, united by our covenant with God. Our centre is the inner selfhood whose potential spans the worlds, from the depth to the height, darkness to the Light, body to Spirit.

The Houses symbolize our fall from height to depth and ascent back to Him, our sublime potential in following the Praised as warrant for our love of Him and His of us. They are mere stones unless we see in them our heart as His house and the Praised as our best example.

People – a given community in a given nation – accept and bear witness to their prophet as their link with God. But no prophet is God, Who left an empty space at the heart of the nation to be filled with remembrance of Him and of our covenant with Him. Moses' people put the golden calf in that space, because they could not stand the void or their fear of it. Those same people's descendents asked their prophet to appoint a king for their centre and he warned them with the Word or Moses' pledge:

> And their prophet said to them, "The sign of his kingship is that the Ark will come to you, in it a Shekhinah from your Lord, and a remnant of what the folk of Moses and Aaron's folk left behind, the angels bearing it. Surely in that shall be a sign for you, if you are believers."[1]

God told the Israelites, while still in the wilderness, to build a sanctuary for Him to dwell among them.[2] The sanctuary was in their midst, the Ark of the Covenant, containing the Stone Tablets of God's Word. A rite was prescribed for the sanctuary to serve our eternal covenant with God, for which our heart was created. Nothing about sanctuary or rite means anything without our heart as abode of the Word. Everything placed with the Israelites – the Tabernacle and the Ark in all their magnificence and the Tablets of Stone and all the rites around them – had no purpose but to recall the Word.

The Israelites were thus reminded of God's presence among them on their journey to the Further Mosque as God guided them from the depth to the sublime height.

And God gave His prophet David the honour of placing the Ark in the Further Mosque, where Adam had built a House in sign of ascent, as the Psalm says:

> Sing unto God, ye kingdoms of the earth; O sing praises unto the Lord; Sellah: To him that rideth upon the heavens of heavens, which were of old; lo, he doth send out his voice, and that a mighty voice. Ascribe ye strength unto God: his excellence is over Israel, and his strength is in the clouds. O God, Thou art terrible out of Thy holy places: the God of Israel is He that giveth strength and power unto His people. Blessed be God.[3]

As long as they have a prophet in whose speech God is manifest as Speaker, the people feel secure. The prophet listens and acquiesces to and then relates His Word as a person of peace. But His Word is greater than the prophet. People know It in their heart and It reminds them of what God gave them in creation, of Spirit, and of being taught all the names. All we need on our journey is this primordial gift. Our outward self is just a manifestation of the inner.

1 *Qur'an*, 2:248.

2 See *Exodus*, 25:31.

3 *Psalm* 68:33–36.

The house in the Valley and the Ark in the house on Sion recall our inner self as His house and the world as the manifestation of Unity's constant presence in multiplicity. Only this knowledge of the extrinsic as manifestation of the intrinsic, of the secondary as manifestation of the primary, and of multiplicity as revelation of Unity allows us to discover and realize our original nature, knowledge of all His names and His Spirit within us.

Our life is of the Living, yet we experience death which cannot touch Him. Our link with what manifests Him must be transferred to the Living, as we sacrifice all we own to Him, to Whom our real belongs: "My prayer, my ritual sacrifice, my living, my dying – all belongs to God, the Lord of all Being. No associate has He."[4]

Not the Tabernacle nor the Ark nor the Tablets of Stone are equal to the Word they receive and whose abode they are. Nor are any of the places that receive the Word, except only our uncreated core, the Spirit God breathed into us. Our core thus houses both Word and speaker:

> In the beginning was the Word, and the Word was with God, and the Word was God. The same was in the beginning with God. All things were made by him; and without him was not anything made that was made.[5]

4 *Qur'an*, 6:162–63.

5 *John*, 1:1–3.

CHAPTER 7

David and the Tabernacle

Chains link the 124,000 prophets, branches that reach through all peoples and times. The history of some is known and all such knowledge has the same meaning. It confirms we come from perfection, to pass through this world and return to God. No time is repeated. Let those who claim otherwise provide proof some past day has been.

The accounts of the prophets let us recognize the eternal issues that concern the living. We are expected to look after our own concerns and direct our will to life and being happy. Our self-ignorance is burden enough, our forgetting our original perfection our greatest concern. Redemption lies in memory. Everything – world, humankind, and revealed books – is for memory, to recall our original nature, the Spirit breathed into us and the names taught us. This nature cannot be wholly lost, only concealed by veils of forgetting. We can always remove the veils and rediscover the treasure God entrusted to us at our beginning.

The accounts of the prophets descended from Abraham through his two sons serve this same need and concern us all, in our quest for the road to perfection. God's pledges to the children of Israel are our heritage, their narratives an example and remembrance for every age. Each prophet demonstrates his discovery of God's pledge in us all.

In principle, we are the same from our beginning and shall so remain. The world is one from its beginning. But neither we nor the world are set fast in that sameness. We are in constant flux, one essence manifesting differently each moment. This enduring sameness is there in each of us at any moment, concealed or unrealized, distorted or denied, but never absent.

Our original nature is indestructible. All things perish but His face and we are in His image, so let everything perish but the Real, Whose image is in us. This is our path back, of which all things in world and self remind us.

Everything that comes to us from outside is known through the self, which is in constant flux. The signs in the world also manifest to us in ever-changing ways and no manifestation is final. Their purpose is to remind us of the riches in the heart of our being, the Spirit breathed into us and our knowledge of the names. Only with them, as our uncreated Light, do we accomplish return or realization. Our inner knowledge is key to our destiny; everything else – the worlds, the prophets, and the Book – serves that original, pledged knowledge.

 | DOI 10.1163/9789004279407_010

David was a prophet of the children of Israel. He like the rest can only be understood as part of the community of prophets. They and the world, individually and together, are signs of God, Who, although One, is manifest in many ways.

> We have revealed to thee as We revealed to Noah, and the prophets after him, and We revealed to Abraham, Ishmael, Isaac, Jacob, and the Tribes, Jesus and Job, Jonah and Aaron and Solomon, and We gave to David Psalms, and apostles We have already told thee of before, and apostles We have not told thee of; and unto Moses God spoke directly – apostles bearing good tidings, and warning, so that mankind might have no argument against God, after the apostles; God is All-mighty, All-wise. But God bears witness to that He has sent down to thee; He has sent it down with His knowledge; and the angels also bear witness; and God suffices for a witness.[1]

The Psalms were the praise of God revealed to David. God is All-praised in and by Himself. He received His laudability from no one, owes it to no one. But manifesting Himself in His creation, all of creation, together and severally, manifests Him as All-praised. All things receive their praiseworthiness from Him and owe it to Him. There is nothing that does not glorify Him with praise. All things thus manifest and return what they received in creation. The world as a whole is Praised and is related to God the All-praised through praising.

When we gather all the praise of the world and acknowledge it as God's, returning it to Him as our debt by proclaiming His praise, we are praised and praiser. Absolute glorification of God in praise is our supreme potential. The perfect Praised is our finest example, the principle of humanity, the first manifestation of God to Himself. Those who praise Him discover and confess the Praised as their supreme potential within themselves. Proclaiming praise is ascent and return to the All-praised. Our guide is the Praised as the perfect recipient of praise from God and glorifier of Him in praise. David follows the Praised in his glorification of God in praise:

---

1 *Qur'an*, 4:163–66. The word *Psalms* from the Greek *Psalmoi* ("songs") corresponds to the Arabic *Zabūr* and the Hebrew *tᵉḥillîm* ("praise" or "songs of praise").

> And with David We subjected the mountains to give glory, and the birds, and We were doers. And We taught him the fashioning of garments for you, to fortify you against your violence; then are you thankful?[2]
>
> The seven heavens and the earth, and whosoever in them is, extol Him; nothing is, that does not proclaim His praise.[3]

Taking our glorification of Him for garments, we protect ourselves from the source of our fears and tribulations. What proclaims His praise received it as goodness and beauty; our awareness of this is our finest garment.[4] God said to David:

> David, behold, We have appointed thee a viceroy in the earth; therefore judge between men justly, and follow not caprice, lest it lead thee astray from the way of God. Surely those who go astray from the way of God – there awaits them a terrible chastisement, for that they have forgotten the Day of Reckoning.[5]

As a prophet recalling us to relations with God through praise and through the Praised, David spoke of how the place of self-abnegation in the valley was related to the height:

> Blessed are they that dwell in thy house: they will be still praising thee. Selah. Blessed is the man whose strength is in thee; in whose heart are the ways of them. Who passing through the valley of Baca make it a well; the rain also filleth the pools. They go from strength to strength, every one of them in Sion appeareth before God. O Lord God of hosts, hear my prayer, O God of Jacob. Selah. Behold, o God our shield, and look upon the face of thine anointed. For a day in thy courts is better than a thousand. I had rather be a door-keeper in the house of my God, than to dwell in the tents of wickedness. For the Lord God is a sun and shield: the Lord will give grace and glory: no good thing will he withhold from them that walk uprightly. O Lord of hosts, blessed is the man that trusteth in thee.[6]

---

2 *Qur'an*, 21:79–80.

3 Ibid., 17:44.

4 See *Qur'an*, 7:26.

5 *Qur'an*, 38:26.

6 *Psalm* 84:4–12. The Hebrew word *bāḵā'* is usually translated as "dry valley" and may be connected to *bakā* which means "weeping." In the Recitation (3:96), *Becca* is referred to as the site of the first house built for people. Abraham prayed (*Qur'an*, 14:37): "Our Lord, I have made some of my seed to dwell in a valley where is no sown land by Thy holy house; Our

David is in the sanctuary, the mihrab where victory must be won over all that seems other than a sign of God. He is irrevocably oriented towards Peace. The heavens and the earth and all that lies between are expected to offer a doorway to God, as we are expected to stand face to Face with our Lord, to annul what seems to come from other than God, to accept no baptism but His, for none baptize fairer than God.[7] In his attitude to God, in his constant battle for Peace, David is His anointed, an example of true baptism. Two disputants entered the sanctuary to seek judgment from him and he thought to try them by his own will. Realizing his mistake, "he sought forgiveness of his Lord, and he fell down, bowing, and he repented."[8]

As God willed, David received the Ark and carried it with him on his journey to the Further Mosque, where he set it up in a tabernacle. For him, as for every prophet, the Ark is a sign of our original nature, which houses Spirit and the names and from which God sent His Word into existence that we might return to our original, sublime height. The site of the Further Mosque received the Ark with the Shekhinah from the Lord, and David placed it under a tabernacle, but not in that Mosque. The Ark on the site of the Further Mosque showed that both signs on the path of return to God, the houses in Becca and in Sion, are an indivisible reminder from God of our fall from and ascent to the height through His Word. God told His prophet David:

> Behold, a son shall be born to thee, who shall be a man of rest; and I will give him rest from all his enemies round about: for his name shall be Solomon, and I will give peace and quietness unto Israel in his days. He shall build a house for my name; and he shall be my son, and I will be his father; and I will establish the throne of his kingdom over Israel for ever.[9]

Lord, let them perform the prayer, and make hearts of men yearn towards them, and provide them with fruits; haply they will be thankful."

7 See *Qur'an*, 2:138.

8 *Qur'an*, 38:24.

9 *I Chronicles*, 22:9–10. The Hebrew name *šᵉlōmōh* means "peace." In the quotation the decisive "Father – son" metaphor is used to picture the "God – man" relationship. This metaphor receives its fullest use with regard to the relationship of God and his prophet Jesus. Their closeness is emphasized by the use of the metaphor to show Jesus' messiah-hood as a central point in all existence. In the Muslim intellectual tradition, this metaphor is avoided, but not refuted. This is in order to emphasize the metaphor's nature and to avoid any strict equation of the metaphor and its content. The Praised says that God's apostles are all brothers, albeit by different mothers. (Muslim, 4:1260–61) That passage contains indirect reference to the closeness of God and His apostles in the metaphor of God as their common Father. On the metaphorical "sonship" of the Israelites, see Idel, *Ben: Sonship and Jewish Mysticism.*

CHAPTER 8

Solomon and the Temple

The name Solomon contains the root *s-l-m*, or *sh-l-m* present in the Arabic nouns *al-muslim, al-islām* and *al-salām*. To understand God's messages, as sent down to His prophets, we need these words, but their meaning often eludes us, slipping into obscurity and oblivion, into ignorance. Where ignorance is, so is violence. Action not based on full knowledge is violence.

The words *muslim, islām* and *salām* mean one at peace (in God's will), being-at-peace, and Peace. Solomon means "person of Peace." His name is emphatic, in the diminutive, just as an individual's beauty may be stressed by calling him Most Beautiful or Little Beauty.

Solomon shaped his inner self after his name in relation to Peace. His self confessed no peace but Peace and Solomon knew that peace and stillness link all things with God. His name means one who is at peace, but the Praised is the first of the people of peace,[1] the maternal beginning of the prophets, the seal God set upon them and on us all.

Obeying God's revelation and his father's will, Solomon built a great temple on the site God had shown Adam as the Further Mosque, as sign of our original rectitude. Solomon did this a thousand years after his ancestor Abraham and his son Ishmael had hallowed and rebuilt the Inviolable Mosque at Becca.[2] Both lines of Abraham's posterity, Ishmaelites and Israelites, were thus recalled to signs of our origin and fall, the violation of the inviolable, and our return to God.

As prophet and king, Solomon built the temple where God told him to, rendering manifest the wisdom and knowledge God had revealed to him, as God says in the Recitation:

> And to Solomon [We subjugated] the wind; its morning course was a month's journey, and its evening course was a month's journey. And We made the Fount of Molten Brass to flow for him. And of the jinn, some worked before him by the leave of his Lord; and such of them as swerved away from Our commandment, We would let them taste the chastisement of the Blaze; fashioning for him whatsoever he would – places of worship, statues, porringers like water-troughs, and anchored cooking-

1 See *Qur'an*, 6:162.

2 See Lings, *Mekka*, 8.

 | DOI 10.1163/9789004279407_011

> pots. "Labour, O House of David, in thankfulness; for few indeed are those that are thankful among My servants."[3]

Solomon used the wisdom, knowledge and skills received from God to erect an edifice centred on the rock that welcomed the Ark of the Covenant, as a sign of God's Word. The Ark and the Temple with its rituals are there simply to strengthen our calling – realization of our original nature, our original affirmation of God[4] and our acceptance of His confidence.[5]

Our heart is the world's centre. Split internally, it is marked by two places of self-abnegation, the Inviolable and the Further Mosque, signs on the earth-heaven, body-Spirit, us-God axes, sent down for our sake. Acknowledging them, we are on the upright path through heaven's gates.

We fell from most beautiful uprightness to the depth.[6] And we can rise again, to find what we lost. Confessing His unity and the Praised as apostle in all the signs of world and self lets us ascend from the depths towards the height and realization of our original nature. We are led through heaven's gates to union with the Beloved, the Known. To deny these signs is to remove from Unity: "And those who cry lies to Our signs We will draw them on little by little whence they know not,"[7] and again: "Those that cry lies to Our signs and wax proud against them – the gates of heaven shall not be opened to them."[8]

God twice showed the people around the Further Mosque the consequences of denying His signs and waxing proud against them. The edifices Solomon built on the site of the Further Mosque were destroyed, a new temple built, and that too was destroyed. God said:

> And We gave Moses the Book, and made it a guidance to the Children of Israel: "Take not unto yourselves any guardian apart from Me." The seed of those We bore with Noah; he was a thankful servant. And We decreed for the Children of Israel in the Book: "You shall do corruption in the earth twice, and you shall ascend exceeding high." So, when the promise of the first of these came to pass, We sent against you servants of Ours, men of great might, and they went through the habitations, and it was a promise performed. Then We gave back to you the turn to prevail over

---

3 *Qur'an*, 34:12–13.

4 See *Qur'an*, 7:172.

5 Ibid., 33:72.

6 Ibid., 95:4–5.

7 *Qur'an*, 7:182.

8 Ibid., 7:40.

> them, and We succoured you with wealth and children, and We made you a greater host. "If you do good, it is your own souls you do good to, and if you do evil it is to them likewise." Then, when the promise of the second came to pass, We sent against you Our servants to discountenance you, and to enter the Temple, as they entered it the first time, and to destroy utterly that which they ascended to. Perchance your Lord will have mercy upon you; but if you return, We shall return; and We have made Gehenna a prison for the concealers.[9]

The children of Israel spent centuries in exile in Egypt, oppressed, with Pharaoh for overlord, not God. God recalled them, through Moses, to their original covenant, which, like every other covenant that binds us, demands immediate recognition of God as Lord. Moses led them from slavery to service, telling them God's message of God as Peace and peace from God.

Moses passed on the Word as revealed to him, as a full and clear inscription on Tablets of Stone. The Tablets received the Word, demonstrating in their cold passivity that human hearts are also recipients and bearers of the Word. No tablets nor all the worlds can replace the heart as house of the Word. The Stone Tables, the Ark, and the Mosque, like all else in existence, are merely reminders of what the human heart holds from and for always: His Word.

The Tablets were given to the Nation for each and every heart, sealed in the Ark to mark the Unity in the heart. The Word was a guide for the children of Israel towards their highest potential – most beautiful uprightness on the original height, where God is our only friend.

Solomon, the Man of Peace, confirms our relationship to God as Peace through being-at-peace. Perfectly acquiescent, the heart at peace becomes house and city of Peace. Solomon built his temple on that rock of the Ark on Sion to guide us on the upright path into the self. What world and self contain are signs on that path of self-discovery and realization in Peace.

The Stone Tablets, mounted in gold in the Ark, the most sacred part of the Mosque, inner sanctuary of the tabernacle, Holy of Holies, surrounded by walls and vaults of stone and cedarwood. Beneath are Mount Sion's foundations, above the seven heavens as Footstool of the Throne.

In and beyond is the Spirit of the One Who is, Whose house is the heart. All the signs in the world and self recall Him in that house. He sent prophets to remind us of His Spirit at our core, as He revealed through the Praised: "And We send not the envoys, but good tidings to bear, and warning. Yet do the

9 Ibid., 17:2–8.

concealers dispute with falsehood, that they may rebut thereby the truth. They have taken My signs, and what they are warned of, in mockery."[10]

When the prophets and their tidings and the signs are considered extrinsic to their Sender, they are distorted, corrupted in the self of those who take them so. The prophets, tidings and signs lose none of their nature as good tidings and warning. It is the self of the mocker that is veiled, obscured and distorted. When such a self expresses life, will, power, knowledge, speech, hearing and sight in relation to the external world and not God, it is violent and unjust towards self and others and the world. Of such people God says:

> And who does greater evil than he who, being reminded of the signs of his Lord, turns away from them and forgets what his hands have forwarded? Surely We have laid veils on their hearts lest they understand it, and in their ears heaviness; and though thou callest them to the guidance, yet they will not be guided ever.[11]

No sign in existence – neither Valley nor Mount – guides us. Nor do life, will, power, knowledge, speech, hearing or sight. Only God does. All things are void without His guidance.

---

10 Ibid., 18:56.

11 Ibid., 18:57.

CHAPTER 9

Zachariah

The line of prophets descended from Abraham through Isaac and Jacob ended with Zachariah and his son John and Mary and her son Jesus. This was not seen as a completion, but as announcing a new beginning. Most people sought in it the fulfilment of their hopes for the long-promised coming of three – the Anointed, Elijah and the prophet.

We all have our own lives and no one can bear another's burden, but their lives cannot be understood apart from the connection between them. They are the end of a sequence of prophecy, but also mark a new beginning, the realization of their predecessors' prophecies and a turning to the Further Mosque.

The Virgin Mary and the elderly Zachariah are two selves in the mihrab of the Further Mosque. The Virgin's self is entirely pure and open to intellectual knowledge, the image of the supreme potential in Zachariah's self. Both are in the Further Mosque, the house of His Word, built that the Name of God might abide there. But the abode of the Name is the heart, the Mosque merely an image of the Portico of God, where His Name is constantly mentioned. All is void without the mention of His Name – this is our most profound nature. In line with the supreme reality of that nature, the unseen world is the principle of all visible things. When this is denied or forgotten, error enters the world and the self.

Jesus son of Mary, as Messiah, and John, son of Zachariah, as prophet, are two manifestations of His Word. The Virgin received the Word God bestowed on her as pure and chosen, while Zachariah received the Word as God's response to his prayer:

> O my Lord, behold the bones within me are feeble and my head is all aflame with hoariness. And in calling on Thee, my Lord, I have never been hitherto unprosperous. And now I fear my kinsfolk after I am gone; and my wife is barren. So give me, from Thee, a kinsman who shall be my inheritor and the inheritor of the House of Jacob; and make him, my Lord, well-pleasing.[1]

1 *Qur'an*, 19:4–6.

 | DOI 10.1163/9789004279407_012

Before Imran's wife bore Mary, she had vowed her child to serve in the Temple, the Further Mosque, expecting it to be a boy. Girls were not regarded as suitable for temple service. God told the Praised this:

> When the wife of Imran said, "Lord, I have vowed to Thee, in dedication, what is within my womb. Receive Thou this from me; Thou hearest and knowest." And when she gave birth to her she said, "Lord, I have given birth to her, a female." (And God knew very well what she had given birth to; the male is not as the female.) "And I have named her Mary, and commend her to Thee with her seed, to protect them from the accursed Satan."
>
> Her Lord received the child with gracious favour, and by His goodness she grew up comely, Zachariah taking charge of her. Whenever Zachariah went in to her in the Sanctuary, he found her provisioned. "Mary," he said, "how comes this to thee?" "From God," she said. Truly God provisions whomsoever He will without reckoning.
>
> Then Zachariah prayed to his Lord saying, "Lord, give me of Thy goodness a goodly offspring. Yea, Thou hearest prayer." And the angels called to him, standing in the Sanctuary at worship, "Lo, God gives thee good tidings of John, who shall confirm a Word of God, a chief, and chaste, a prophet, righteous."
>
> "Lord," said Zachariah, "how shall I have a son, seeing I am an old man and my wife is barren?" "Even so," God said, "God does what He will." "Lord," said Zachariah, "appoint to me a sign." "Thy sign," God said, "is that thou shalt not speak, save by tokens, to men for three days. And mention thy Lord oft, and give glory at evening and dawn."[2]

This is the account of Zachariah, an elderly priest in the Further Mosque, and the Virgin Mary, whose mother vowed her to the temple. Mary thus became the centre of the Further Mosque and recipient of God's mercy, through whom He also spoke to His prophet Zachariah.

The Further Mosque on Mount Sion denoted humankind as the centre of creation, the purpose of what God created in six days. But the centre was not in the magnificence of stone, timber and metal, which was merely a reminder of the heart as world centre and house of the Lord and of the Unseen as higher than the visible. Even Zachariah was a reminder of this: God gave all things as reminders of our original covenant, the Spirit we receive direct from Him and our heart-knowledge of Him as Lord.

2 Ibid., 3:35–41.

Both Zachariah and Mary are in the mihrab. Ultimately this denotes not their physical surroundings, but their commitment to pass through every veil and every barrier impeding service in our original knowledge of God as One and Lord. They are in a constant battle with forgetting or mistaking any sign for the Signified. They expect peace from Peace alone. None of the beauties of the world has any meaning for them except to manifest Beauty. However the world seems, whatever reaches their senses or thoughts from outside, they confess only what they once knew, in pre-existence, directly as their response to the Lord: "Yes, we testify." This is their response to God's question: "Am I not your Lord?"

Zachariah and Mary knew clearly, not from the will but from their profoundest core, that every sign in the world or self was there to confess and intimate the Signified. When the Signified is forgotten in the sign, the sign becomes opaque. It ceases to shine with received Light, concealing Him for Whose revelation we were created. Our self is thus obscured and evil enters the world.

That the sign can always lose its transparency is what kept both Zachariah and the Virgin on the battlefield, fearing to leave it, since, so long as they were in this world, that would mean turning from God, from Real to unreal. All they did – in silence and speech, stillness and movement – was out of knowledge they regarded as received, to safeguard themselves from action out of ignorance and the violence God loves not.

This safeguarding is constantly, relentlessly facing trials and temptations. The signs are under constant threat of obscurity, of concealing Him. The good demonstrate their recollection by suffering what seems, to ordinary folk, as bad as anything that can be experienced. The visible world for them is just passage to the Unseen as our higher, nearer Reality.

Zachariah was an old man without heir, entrusted with the care of a child, Mary. She was in the Temple, close to the Holy of Holies, vowed to service while still in her mother's womb. While in that sumptuous edifice built to remind people of their original perfection, she was exposed to the contempt of those who found no source of Light or remembrance of God as our most profound reality in their knowledge of sacred history and the material presence of the house in Sion. They saw nothing in this maid in the Temple of what God manifested to the world through her.

Zachariah was in the Further Mosque, waiting for his son John, given him by God. He called upon the people to turn to their Lord. The visible glory of the Mosque had one purpose, to recall the Unseen as the principle of all things. John called for renewal of the order that had become obscured in the self. He did so from the Judean desert, on the banks of the Jordan, to show that the walls of the Further Mosque were become veils over the eyes of the heart and that people no longer heard what was given shape in the Word God had bestowed from His Spirit.

Zachariah was murdered so brutally that even his murderers might conclude his life without mercy, his election a mere illusion on the part of those who do not see the world as it really is. His murderers killed him by cutting to pieces the log pile where he had hidden.[3] Mary testified before him: "Truly God provisions whomsoever He will without reckoning."

But God gave Zachariah, already aged, a son, John, "who shall confirm a Word of God, a chief, and chaste."[4] If his life ended horribly, God reveals to us that Zachariah was one whom He remembered, who was with Peace. Does not the whole enigma of humanity lie in the illusion of the duality of opposites, suffering and Mercy, persecution and Peace?

---

3 See Thaʿlabī, *ʿArāʾis al-majālis fī qiṣaṣ al-anbiyāʾ*, 637–38.

4 *Qurʾan*, 3:39.

CHAPTER 10

Mary

Zachariah and Mary were in the Further Mosque on Mount Sion, an old man protecting a young girl. They both considered the Mosque the holiest place in the world, the house of the Name of God. The sanctuary never concealed the Holy or Named from her, just as the purity, beauty and humility of the unforgetting heart remain unconcealed. The house can only be inhabited with a heart open to Him and creation is like a house whose only purpose is for the Creator to be known. We are similar, as epitomes of that manifestation. The Creator's entire purpose is imprinted on what we do. Realizing ourselves in knowledge of and return to God, we become that house, that fullness of creation.

Mary urged Zachariah to pray to God for a child, to believe in God's mercy and knowledge as embracing all things, even his old age and his wife's barrenness. Only the heart of the faithful servant is so broad as the house of the All-merciful and All-knowing.

God answered Zachariah's prayers. His wife received the Spirit and, through it, life in her womb. The Spirit also descended on Mary, as God said in the Recitation:

> And when the angels said, "Mary, God has chosen thee, and purified thee; He has chosen thee above all women. Mary, be obedient to thy Lord, prostrating and bowing before Him."[1]
>
> When the angels said, "Mary, God gives thee good tidings of a Word from him whose name is Anointed, Jesus, son of Mary; high honoured shall he be in this world and the next, near stationed to God. He shall speak to men in the cradle, and of age, and righteous he shall be." "Lord," said Mary, "how shall I have a son seeing no mortal has touched me?" "Even so," God said, "God creates what He will. When He decrees a thing He does but say to it 'Be', and it is. And He will teach him the Book, the Wisdom, the Torah, the Gospel, to be an apostle to the Children of Israel saying, 'I have come to you with a sign from your Lord. I will create for you out of clay as the likeness of a bird; then I will breathe into it, and it will be a bird, by the leave of God. I will also heal the blind and the leper, and bring to life the dead, by the leave of God. I will inform you too of what things you eat, and what you treasure up in your houses. Surely that is a

1 *Qur'an*, 3:42–43.

 | DOI 10.1163/9789004279407_013

> sign for you, if you are believers. Likewise confirming the truth of the Torah that is before me, and to make lawful to you certain things that before were forbidden unto you. I have come to you with a sign from your Lord; so be mindful of your God, and obey you me. Surely God is my Lord and your Lord, so serve Him. This is an upright path.' "[2]
>
> So she conceived him, and withdrew with him to a distant place. And the birthpangs surprised her by the trunk of the palm-tree. She said, "Would I had died 'ere this, and become a thing forgotten!"
>
> But the one that was below her called to her, "Nay, do not sorrow; see, thy Lord has set below thee a rivulet. Shake also to thee the palm-trunk, and there shall come tumbling upon thee dates fresh and ripe. Eat therefore, and drink, and be comforted; and if thou should'st see any mortal, say, 'I have vowed to the All-merciful a fast, and today I will not speak to any man.' "
>
> Then she brought the child to her folk carrying him; and they said, "Mary, thou hast surely committed a monstrous thing! Sister of Aaron, thy father was not a wicked man, nor was thy mother a woman unchaste."
>
> Mary pointed to the child then; but they said, "How shall we speak to one who is still in the cradle, a little child?"
>
> He said, "Lo, I am God's servant; God has given me the Book, and made me a prophet. Blessed He has made me, wherever I may be; and He has enjoined me to pray, and to give the alms, so long as I live, and likewise to cherish my mother; He has not made me arrogant, unprosperous. Peace be upon me, the day I was born, and the day I die, and the day I am raised up alive!"
>
> That is Jesus, son of Mary, in word of truth, concerning which they are doubting. It is not for God to take a son unto Him. Glory be to Him! When He decrees a thing, He but says to it "Be," and it is. Surely God is my Lord, and your Lord; so serve you Him. This is an upright path.[3]

Mary received the Word. The miracle of its reception and birth in the person of Jesus, the Anointed, confronts us all. To understand we must see the virginity of the self it took place in, like the pure water over which the Spirit moves. That self received the Word in virginal purity, not impurity and sin. No one is immaculate, without sin, but the Virgin and her Son, signs of the sublime potential towards which the Praised leads us out of the depths. His guidance begins in the perfection of our authentic nature, to which alone it is directed.

---

2 Ibid., 3:45–51.

3 Ibid., 19:22–36.

The Praised and his guidance encompass our origins and purpose, coming and return, fall and ascent.

In Mary's receptive nature, Essence is revealed as purity, beauty and humility: pure, since the inner self, her perfect humanity, is open to reception at any moment; beautiful, as connected to Spirit, which transcends every boundary between visible and unseen, in constant witness to the All-high; humble, as knowing all things come from God and our only debt is to Him.

When the angels washed the Praised's heart in the desert, he was yet a boy. They revealed the purity, beauty and humility of his virginal nature to him.[4] The black drop they took from his heart showed his immense nature encompassing all of existence, from the depth to the height, the Inviolable to the Further Mosque. The black drop stands for the depths, the "valley where is no sown land."[5] The other extreme of our potential is represented by his absolute purity, the Further Mosque and Mary.

The contrary to the "valley where is no sown land" is the "land that floweth with milk and honey."[6] The two houses, in the Valley and on the Mount, represent the extremes between which the self's fall and ascent take place, the perfect unity of His names of harshness and tenderness, majesty and beauty, wrath and mercy. On his night journey, the Praised chose to drink milk, to show he led to the All-merciful and Ever-merciful, Resolver of all oppositions.

Both Mary and the Praised exemplify the expression "In the name of God, the All-merciful, the Ever-merciful." Mary was merciful as recipient,[7] most merciful in giving her son to the world as Word. She was chosen, purified, at peace, and confident in the Word of her Lord.[8] As recipient, the prophet

4 On the washing of the heart of the Praised with snow, see Ibn Isḥāq, *Sīrat Rasūl Allāh*, 72.

5 *Qur'an*, 14:37.

6 *Deuteronomy*, 26:9.

7 "Merciful" is the usual translation of the Arabic noun al-*raḥīm*, al-*riḥm* (pl. *arḥām*). The literal meaning of that word is "womb," "uterus," "belly," the "female generative organ." In the broader sense it represents the importance of relations and blood ties. The verbal root *r-ḥ-m* generates the noun *raḥma*, meaning "grace" or "compassion" and the divine names *al-raḥmān* and *al-raḥīm*, which we translate as "the All-merciful" and "the Ever-merciful." These divine names are indicative of the feminine character of God's mercy. Through the Praised, He says: "I am the All-merciful, and I created the tie of (blood) kinship. I have derived its name from My name. Whoever strengthens it, him I strengthen; whoever severs it, him I sever and cut off" (in Graham, *Divine Word and Prophetic Word in Early Islam*, 134). It should also be mentioned that in old Bosnian the word for heart was sometimes used for the uterus.

8 Frithjof Schuon writes of the link between Mary and the Praised in these terms: "Just as the Virgin Mary, fecundated by the Holy Ghost, is 'Co-Redemptress' and 'Queen of Heaven,' created before the rest of the Creation, so the prophet, inspired by the same Paracletic Spirit, is

is praised (*Muḥammad*), a mercy to the worlds. As giver, he is most praised (*Aḥmad*), most merciful.

While Mary's name appeared in different forms in different languages over the centuries, the original form was sent down from heaven and allows a deeper understanding of her nature – of the pure, absolute potential that God's creative Word descended upon. "Her name is thus associated with the waters over which moved the Spirit of God."[9] As is the name Muhammad.

When Mary was born, she confirmed the potency and impotence of her mother's expectations. Her purpose was to restore the centre of the Further Mosque as house of the Spirit of God, in which His Word would be shaped, and to correct our errancy in preferring the visible and denying the Unseen. Her experience was unendurably painful for all those who witnessed her and her times – their standards were confined within a closed world that existed only

---

'apostle of Mercy' (*Rasūl ar-Raḥmān*) and 'Lord of the Two Existences – this world and the next' (*Sayyid al-Kawnayn*), and was likewise created before all other beings. This priority of creation signifies that the Virgin and the prophet incarnate a principial or metacosmic Reality; they are identified – in their receptive function, though not in their Divine Knowledge, nor, in the case of Mohammed, in his prophetic function – with the passive aspect of universal Existence (*Prakriti*; in Arabic *al-lawḥ al-maḥfūẓ*, 'the Guarded Tablet'), and it is for this reason that the Virgin is 'immaculate' and, from the merely physical standpoint, 'virgin,' while the prophet, like the apostles, is 'illiterate' (*ummī*), that is to say, pure from the taint of human knowledge or knowledge humanly acquired." (Schuon, *The Transcendent Unity of Religions*, 120–21)

9 "In Hebrew this name is not Mary but *Mariam*, which was retained intact in the Greek of St. Luke (1:28 and 30), and it is a pity that this manner of writing her name was thereafter neglected, for its already mentioned secret sense only becomes apparent in the Hebrew form. Mariam, in Hebrew, is written MRIM, since vowels are omitted (I or Y is a semi-consonant). The word itself is divided up in this way: MIM on the one hand and R on the other. By articulating the vowel A in the first component, we obtain Maim, which means 'the waters.' The M (*mem*) is the hierogram for universal passivity, pure receptivity, symbolized by water and the waters in Jewish cosmogony, as elsewhere in nearly all traditions; the I or Y (*yod*) is the hierogram for divine activity, the principle of manifested activity, and the R (*resh*) the deployment of energy, energy in motion. The Hebrew character corresponding to R was, originally, the hieroglyph of a serpent with its head raised to strike forward. Thus the name MaRIaM is nothing less than a translation of the creative act: RI is the *ad extra* emission of the divine creative energy which is unleashed on cosmic Substance, that is to say on the totality of potentialities and their receptive surroundings, represented by the primordial Waters as brought out in the first verses of *Genesis*: 'The Spirit of God was moving over the face of the waters.' And so the Name of Mary is, in its way, a divine Name, one connected with the *ad extra* divine activity, which means that Mary is a manifestation of what this divine Name represents." (Hani, "The Rosary as Spiritual Way," 58–59).

so far as their senses reached. Suffering meant something different to them than how she experienced it.

When she said "Would I had died 'ere this, and become a thing forgotten!" her words indicated the miraculous separation of recipient and received. Compared to the received, the recipient seemed superfluous, but was not so. Unity is manifest in duality. Speech has meaning in listening. Many vilified Mary and spread calumny, but how else could she have borne the Word in her womb, how shown that God lives only in the heart, not in buildings or the world? Within the heart He encompasses all things.

When people condemned her, she remained silent, pointing to her son as the Word and the Anointed himself told them to listen, since his mother had received and given birth to the Word. She believed in the Word and it is up to us whether we listen to or deny him.

Mary was always in struggle, fighting for each sign in the world or self to retain its transparency and light – transparency to the All-high and light received from Him.

When all supposed her son dead on the cross, in her purity, Mary knew that the Living does not let His servants who confess Him with their entire being die: "Yet they did not slay him, neither crucified him, only a likeness of that was shown to them. Those who are at variance concerning him surely are in doubt regarding him; they have no knowledge of him, except the following of a surmise; and they slew him not of a certainty – no indeed; God raised him up to Him; God is All-mighty, All-wise."[10]

God sent the Holy Spirit to Mary, and she received It gladly. It was enfolded within her as she received It. She gave birth beneath a palm tree to His Word. Beauty was made visible through Mary and her son, the world made manifest as the revelation of the Principle, the reshaping of valley into height.

Our speech is breath made manifest in sound. Neither sounds nor words transcend that breath, which is just the manifestation of Spirit breathed into us by God. When the son was born as Word incarnate, the Spirit revealed the Essence in his body that it might ascend through speech, breath and Spirit to the Speaker. The ascent is not by our will. God sends down and raises up, gives and takes. He breathes in the Spirit and all that receives it is His, and no condition transcends, no form confines it.

The sensory world is a consequence or revelation of the higher and is nothing without it. Those who thought the visible independent of the Unseen were under the illusion they could slay Word and Spirit. Illusion is a revolution that takes sign for Signified. The sensory world ceases to be a mihrab, a gateway to

---

10 *Qur'an*, 4:157–58.

the Unseen, but a realm of illusion, degeneration and decadence, a theatre of war, a wilderness on our path back. From the furthest star to Mary's mantle there is only Essence, which abides deep in her heart. This is the confession of no self but the Self, realized in receiving provision from God in the world-mihrab: "God is the best of providers."[11] The blue of the sky and of Mary's mantle are evidence of our only centre in the house that is there to receive and host the All-high.

---

11 Ibid., 62:11.

CHAPTER 11

John

Zachariah served God as prophet in the Further Mosque, extolling the Lord in praise in the magnificent edifice on the Mount. Many extolled the magnificence itself, glorifying themselves. They did not see their inner self as a veil over the face of the Self. They saw nothing behind that veil. It seemed to them that they defined their own existence. The signs in the Further Mosque direct us through the veil and prompt us to open ourselves to confess no self but the Self.

Zachariah reached old age as a servant in the Mosque, where the Virgin spent her childhood with him. Knowledge of the Torah and the prophetic narratives seemed to have been part of her inner self always. The prophecies – the coming of the Anointed, of Elijah, and the apostle – came true. The Temple, its walls, roofs, doorways and cisterns, altars, censers, lamps and rituals merely reminded her of the mystery of the heart, where God manifests Himself.

Mary's dedication to God and her having received everything from Him prompted the elderly Zachariah to pray for a child to follow him in the Temple. God heard and granted his prayer, telling him as he stood in the Holy of Holies: "O Zachariah, We give thee good tidings of a boy, whose name is John. No namesake have We given him aforetime."[1]

John's birth was announced by an angel to Zachariah, burning incense in the Temple. In Luke's account, the angel told him:

> Fear not, Zachariah: for thy prayer is heard; and thy wife Elisabeth shall bear thee a son, and thou shalt call his name John. For he shall be great in the sight of the Lord, and shall drink neither wine nor strong drink; and he shall be filled with the Holy Ghost, even from his mother's womb. And many of the children of Israel shall he turn to the Lord their God. And he shall go before him in the spirit and power of Elijah, to turn the hearts of the fathers to the children, and the disobedient to the wisdom of the just; to make ready a people prepared for the Lord.[2]

1 *Qur'an*, 19:7.

2 *Luke*, 1:13–17.

 | DOI 10.1163/9789004279407_014

Six months passed between the prophet John's conception in his mother Elisabeth's womb and that of the prophet Jesus in his mother Mary's.[3] The close relationship between Zachariah and Mary, their service in the Temple, marks the closeness between John and Jesus. Luke tells the story of Mary's visit to Elisabeth, while both were with child:

> And Mary arose in those days, and went into the hill country with haste, into a city of Judah; And entered into the house of Zachariah, and saluted Elisabeth. And it came to pass, that, when Elisabeth heard the salutation of Mary, the babe leaped in her womb; and Elisabeth was filled with the Holy Ghost. And she spake out with a loud voice, and said, Blessed art thou among women, and blessed is the fruit of thy womb. And whence is this to me, that the mother of my Lord should come to me? For, lo, as soon as the voice of thy salutation sounded in mine ears, the babe leaped in my womb for joy. And blessed is she that believed: for there shall be a performance of those things which were told her from the Lord.[4]

Elisabeth praised Mary, but Mary is the perfect recipient of all reality from God, and she replied: "My soul doth magnify the Lord, And my spirit hath rejoiced in God my Saviour."[5]

After Zachariah and Mary, John and Jesus, who recognized each other in the womb, are the last of the prophets descended from Abraham through Isaac. Their task was to clarify what people did not understand and dissented over and to fulfil the long-awaited prophecies. Mary's was to keep silent and point to her son as the one to answer all questions. Zachariah was dumb when told his son would speak to the people.

Mary's *magnificat* reveals her soul or self's relationship with the All-praised as magnification of Him. It was the self of one who received praise from the All-praised and gave what it had received back to the All-praised, true possessor of all praise. Before Elisabeth and two still unborn prophets, Mary confessed the Praised as Light-giving Lamp, finest example, maternal seal and original oath of every prophet, heart into which the Holy Spirit descended as Spirit of Truth, our sublime potential. With him, the Kingdom of God is near.

The Praised is disclosed in Mary's self as that potential. She follows it in her love of God, as Zachariah does in his joy at his son's birth: "Blessed be the Lord

---

3 See *Luke*, 1:36.

4 *Luke*, 1:39–45.

5 Ibid., 1:46–47.

God of Israel; for He hath visited and redeemed His people. And has raised up an horn of salvation for us in the house of His servant David."[6]

Praise and anointment express the relationship of creature and Creator. God is the All-praised and the Anointer, Who praises and anoints in Himself and the Spirit all that manifests Him. All things that exist receive both praise and anointment from Him. Their reception is summed up in our perfection, manifest in the Praised and the Anointed as perfect recipients. The prophets all remind us of these two facets of our common perfection.

God remembered Zachariah. He also said through the Praised: "So remember Me, and I will remember you."[7] The name John means "The Live One." Zachariah remembered God, and his son cried out to Him throughout his life: "O Living!"

Zachariah provided for the Virgin in the temple, who carried the fruit of her womb, the Word John knew. He cried out to the Word from the wilderness, not the Temple, calling on us to turn towards that of which the Temple and all things that exist and the prophets and God's friends remind us. He called us to see and confess our Lord through the signs in the world and self: "Repent ye: for the kingdom of heaven is at hand."[8]

Zachariah, Mary, John and Jesus all lived at the same time, entering a history in which three comings were awaited – the second coming of the prophet Elijah, the coming of the Anointed, and the apostle God told Moses would be raised up from among the brethren of the children of Israel.[9] The crucial question for them all was realization of God's kingdom.

All three were initially outside history, their coming announced in signs that preceded them, signs interpreted variously. For some, these signs were entirely outside, in the world, in an uncertain future. But we are concerned with our time, our here and now, as the kingdom of God.

When the Anointed entered history, some saw their expectations confirmed in him, others did not. People still looked for the coming of Anointed, Elijah and apostle, in their need for a guide from the depths to the height. The prophecies of their coming were part of sacred heritage. Those who recognized the Anointed joined him, others distanced themselves. All wondered about John and the Anointed: who they might be, as three were prophesied to come?

---

6 *Luke*, 1:68–69.

7 *Qur'an*, 2:152.

8 *Matthew*, 3:2.

9 See *Deuteronomy*, 18:18.

> And this is the record of John, when the Jews sent priests and Levites from Jerusalem to ask him, Who art thou? And he confessed, and denied not; but confessed, I am not the Anointed. And they asked him, What then? Art thou Elijah? And he said, I am not. Art thou that prophet? And he answered, No.[10]

The prophet John is the witness closest to the prophet Jesus. They knew each other when still in their mothers' wombs. Existence in the womb denotes our pre-existence in God's mercy. That they were chosen and sent was not concealed from them. As John's words reveal, he was not the Anointed nor Elijah nor that apostle.

He affirms as a prophet that he is not "that prophet," the apostle. Nor is he the Anointed, whom he recognizes in Jesus. But Elijah had already been in Israel. The great mystery of his prophecies, framed by the cries from the wilderness, the theatre of war, is his fore-knowledge of the Anointed and the Praised. To eliminate any doubt that the promised apostle would soon come, John – as a prophet contemporary to the Anointed – states he is neither. Zachariah and Mary and John and Jesus prepare the wide world and the self to receive an apostle like Moses. God will put His Word in his mouth and he will reveal the imminence of the Hour and that realization of the Kingdom of God is within us.

John was a witness, a voice crying in the wilderness: "Prepare ye the way of the Lord, make his paths straight."[11] He bore witness before the Virgin and the Anointed for all people: "There cometh one mightier than I after me, the latchet of whose shoes I am not worthy to stoop down and unloose. I indeed have baptized you with water: but he shall baptize you with the Holy Ghost."[12]

Jesus, the Anointed, was not after him, but with him. While the Anointed spoke to the people, John was in prison. Not long before Jesus' mission ended, John was beheaded.[13] Both Zachariah and John gave their lives confessing what they were, before the Virgin and her son.

---

10 *John*, 1:19–21. According to the Biblical narrative, the prophet Elijah ascended to heaven alive. The Anointed speaks of the prophet John as Elijah (See *Matthew*, 11:14; 17:12). Since John himself says he is not Elijah, these two verses should be understood in the light of the annunciation by the angel to the prophet Zachariah that he would have a son: "And he shall go before him in the spirit and power of Elijah, to turn the hearts of the fathers to the children, and the disobedient to the wisdom of the just; to make ready a people prepared for the Lord." (*Luke*, 1:17).

11 *Mark*, 1:3.

12 Ibid., 1:7–8.

13 See *Mark*, 6:17–29.

Both Zachariah and John were killed by leading figures of a ruling order that hid behind the walls, wealth and rituals of the Further Mosque, who elevated signs above the Signified, and concealed Him from themselves and others. Both called upon the people to look behind surface and wall, written and spoken word, for the Spirit that gives life and is not subject to anything, of Whom it was said: "The wind bloweth where it listeth."[14]

The Spirit's unconquerable nature, obedient to God alone, is what allows our freedom through service to Him. The Spirit is our only guide on this unbounded path to the Lord. Blaspheming against It is the same as associating an idol with God or thinking our knowledge sufficient and our will independent of anything higher. God does not forgive blasphemy against the Holy Ghost,[15] nor association of idols with Him.[16]

The Praised said he and the Anointed were closest of all, with no prophets between them. Just as John confessed the Anointed, whom he saw and knew, he foresaw the apostle to come after Jesus.

John was tortured in prison for following the Spirit in his speech and refusing to recognize any authority not given us in God's service. The powerholders, who existed to blaspheme against the Spirit and associate idols with God, ordered his beheading and his head was brought on a salver to those he had warned of their unforgivable violation of the law.

The powerful appealed to their learning and what they considered its sources, using them to justify the killing of two prophets, Zachariah and John. They rejected knowledge irrefutable by external authority, knowledge innate to us through our original covenant with God. Their suffering confirms the righteousness of God's witnesses. Zachariah, Mary, John and Jesus are clear examples, who suffered almost unimaginable injustices. The perpetrators saw the world and themselves as finite and what lay beyond temporal and spatial boundaries as meaningless. Their suffering thus had meaning in transcending those boundaries. God said through the Praised, of those who suffered injustice: "By My glory, I shall aid you, even if at a later time."[17] This help transcends space and time, where the righteous call on us to turn towards the sublime height. It transcends even the boundaries of existence.

---

14 *John*, 3:8.

15 See *Matthew*, 12:31.

16 See *Qur'an*, 4:48.

17 In Graham, *Divine Word and Prophetic Word in Early Islam*, 145.

CHAPTER 12

The Anointed

God said in the Recitation: "And We made Mary's son, and his mother, to be a sign, and gave them refuge upon a height, where was a hollow and a spring: 'O apostles, eat of the good things and do righteousness; surely I know the things you do. Surely this community of yours is one community, and I am your Lord; so mind Me.' "[1]

People have understood the sign of Jesus and his mother on the height in various ways, taking different paths as a result. God speaks to them through the Praised:

> People of the Book, go not beyond the bounds in your debt, and say not as to God but the truth. The Anointed, Jesus son of Mary, was only the apostle of God, and His Word that He committed to Mary, and a Spirit from Him. So believe in God and His apostles, and say not, "Three." Refrain; better is it for you. God is only One God. Glory be to Him – that He should have a son! To Him belongs all that is in the heavens and in the earth; God suffices for a guardian.[2]

1 *Qur'an*, 23:50–52. When Jesus son of Mary admits to his disciples that he is the Anointed, he tells them not to tell anyone (See *Matthew*, 16:20; *Mark*, 8:30). What Jesus revealed to his disciples as a secret, God revealed to the entire world through the Praised, thus confirming Jesus' words (*Luke*, 4:18, referring to *Isaiah*, 61:1): "The Spirit of the Lord is upon me, because he hath anointed me to preach the gospel to the poor; he hath sent me to heal the broken hearted, to preach deliverance to the captives, and recovering of sight to the blind, to set at liberty them that are bruised."

2 *Qur'an*, 4:171. When God instructs us not to say "Three" in reference to Him, the Holy Spirit and His Word, He is emphasizing that the Revealer and His Revelation are indistinguishable in essence from whoever received the Revelation to pass on to others. All this is demonstrated with the utmost subtlety in the case of the Virgin Mary, the Holy Spirit, and her son Jesus. Mary receives the Word through the Holy Spirit and gives birth to Jesus as the Word. Prophesying the Praised, Jesus speaks of the Paraclete or Holy Spirit, the Comforter and Spirit of Truth. Muslims believe that the Paraclete is one of the many forms of the name of the Praised (see Cutsinger, "The Virgin," 146–47).

 | DOI 10.1163/9789004279407_015

To God belongs what is in the heavens and on earth, including Mary's son, as determined by witness to God "Who has not begotten, and has not been begotten, and equal to Him is not anyone."[3]

There was debate over who the Anointed would be before his appearance in history and over who he was during and since. The prophets spoken of by Moses were known: Elijah, a historical figure, who left this earth to come again, and the Anointed – for all the prophets had spoken about them.

Zachariah, Mary, Jesus and John all entered history at the same time. People saw and heard and accepted them as already known because they prophesied and were prophesied. Their appearance in history met their expectations for some, but not for others.

> Jesus asked his disciples, Whom say the people that I am? They answering said, John the Baptist; but some say, Elijah; and others say, that one of the old prophets is risen again.
>
> He said unto them, But whom say ye that I am? Peter answering said, the Anointed of God.[4]

People asked John whether he was the Anointed, Elijah, or "that prophet."[5] And John sent his followers to ask Jesus, son of Mary: "Art thou he that should come, or do we look for another?"[6]

If, as Jesus said, John was Elijah come again,[7] and if the speaker was the Anointed, then the identity of the third remained, the prophet the people sought and he and John prophesied.

Of the Anointed and the expected prophet there are various interpretations, various opinions and many reasons for and against them all. Councils have been held on Jesus' nature as a person in and outside of history. Those attending had to choose and decide his nature by majority vote to justify some opinion as truth. God spoke to the Praised of these interpretations:

> And when God said, "O Jesus son of Mary, didst thou say unto men, 'Take me and my mother as gods, apart from God?' " He said, "To Thee be glory! It is not mine to say what I have no right to. If I indeed said it, Thou knowest it, knowing what is within my soul, and I know not what is within Thy

3 Ibid., 112:3–4.

4 *Luke*, 9:18–20.

5 See *John*, 1:19–21.

6 *Matthew*, 11:2.

7 On the prophet Elijah see note 233 in chapter 11.

> soul; Thou knowest the things unseen. I only said to them what Thou didst command me: 'Serve God, my Lord and your Lord.' And I was a witness over them, while I remained among them; but when Thou didst take me to Thyself, Thou wast Thyself the watcher over them; Thou Thyself art witness of everything. If Thou chastisest them, they are Thy servants; if Thou forgivest them, Thou art the All-mighty, the All-wise."[8]

Some of these views have crossed permissible limits of dissent and one might have expected them, with their horrific consequences for the world, to be resolved with the coming of the Praised, as prophesied by the Anointed. Some of these views are contrary to God's unchanging truth:

> And they say, "The All-merciful has taken unto Himself a son." You have indeed advanced something hideous! The heavens are well nigh rent of it and the earth split asunder, and the mountains well nigh fall down crashing for that they have attributed to the All-merciful a son; and it behoves not the All-merciful to take a son.[9]

Mary's son, the Anointed is a servant of God,[10] a prophet,[11] an apostle,[12] renowned in this world and the next, one of the closest to God.[13] God anointed him with the Holy Spirit.[14] He is His Word.[15]

The Father,[16] the Son (of Mary) and the Holy Spirit are Three. Understanding their relationship is key to answering the question of humankind, the world and God. God told the Praised:

---

8 *Qur'an*, 5:116–118.

9 Ibid., 19:88–92.

10 See *Qur'an*, 4:172.

11 Ibid., 19:30.

12 Ibid., 3:49.

13 Ibid., 3:45.

14 Ibid., 2:87.

15 Ibid., 4:171.

16 The Arabic noun *rabb* covers a wide range of meanings, not easy to translate into another language with a single term. It includes the notion of having the right of ownership over something, and consequently the right to rule it, as well as that of providing for, supporting and provisioning someone or something from its conception or inception to its completion. The head of a household is known as the *rabb al-dār*, because he has authority over it and is responsible for its maintenance. But God is the only provider, supporter and provisioner of all things. The Slav word *otac*, father, as the childish *ota* reveals, derives from the Indo-European *atta*, designating the child's dependence on the older and more

> They are concealers who say: "God is the Anointed, Mary's son." For the Anointed said, "Children of Israel, serve God, my Lord and your Lord. Verily whoso associates with God anything, God shall prohibit him entrance to Paradise, and his refuge shall be the Fire; and wrongdoers shall have no helpers."
>
> They are concealers who say, "God is the Third of Three." No god is there but One God. If they refrain not from what they say, there shall afflict those of them that deny a painful chastisement. Will they not turn to God and pray His forgiveness? God is All-forgiving, Ever-merciful.
>
> The Anointed, son of Mary, was only an apostle; apostles before him passed away; his mother was a just woman; they both ate food. Behold, how We make clear the signs to them; then behold, how they perverted are![17]

God is not the Third of Three. He is First and Last, Outer and Inner.[18] Whatever thing or throng one may consider, God is its First and Last, its Inner and Outer. So it is and so it has been for all time and everywhere. If confessing Three calls into question our confession of Unity, it is flawed and inadmissible. So long as God is confessed as One and Only, manifest in multiplicity, the trinity of Father, Son and Spirit can be a way of bearing witness to Unity. If we affirm God as Third of two, Other to all, this is entirely in accordance with His revelation to the Praised:

> Has thou not seen that God knows whatsoever is in the heavens, and whatsoever is in the earth? Three men conspire not secretly together, but He is the fourth of them, neither five men, but he is the sixth of them, neither fewer than that, neither more, but He is with them, wherever they may be; then He shall tell them what they have done, on the Day of Resurrection. Surely God has knowledge of everything.[19]

The history of Jesus' presence in the world is a history of unresolved debates on his nature, differences resolved only in return to God. Remembrance of God

---

powerful, not their blood relationship. The father-son relationship may thus have two different meanings, one of blood relationship, the other not. The latter is much broader and is thus the initial image of the term.

17 *Qur'an*, 5:72–75.

18 See *Qur'an*, 57:3.

19 *Qur'an*, 58:7.

is greater than anything we do. No circumstance in which we act, no time or place, is essential to the undeniable remembrance of God as the essence of our core. Neither heavens nor earth, neither Inviolable nor Further Mosque, replaces its primacy. Our value on the height is greater than anything else. Remembering God as the discovery of our original nature has priority over all else. Nothing external answers the question of the Anointed. We find our truth about him in the self: "There is not one of the People of the Book but will assuredly believe in him before his death, and on the Resurrection Day he will be a witness against them."[20]

Any attempt to resolve these divisions over the Anointed without acknowledging the primacy of remembrance of God resorts to arguments justified by something other than God, by some external knowledge. Such knowledge is not sufficient in itself. It differs from our core and requires power to advance and sustain it. This shows that such knowledge is incomplete. Our core, our original nature has all knowledge. All things serve to recall this votive, absolute knowledge in the Intellect or Heart.

Were knowledge of the Anointed found only in history, contingent on transmission, it would refute that the kingdom of God is within us.[21] Power and a system would be needed to sustain such knowledge. Knowledge whose source is in the heart has a different form. People of power, who belong to the system set up to protect their knowledge, cannot abide difference. They subjugate, persecute and kill any who prefer inner knowledge to outward authority. We self-realize by knowing and loving God. Love and knowledge united in the self's centre are belief. Believing in God, we accept no authority but His. When knowledge is contingent on human power, those who believe will be persecuted:

> By heaven of the constellations, by the promised day, by the witness and the witnessed, slain were the Men of the Pit, the fire abounding in fuel, when they were seated over it and were themselves witnesses of what they did with the believers. They took revenge on them only because they believed in God the All-mighty, the All-praised, to Whom belongs the

---

20 Ibid., 4:159. In the Muslim tradition this verse is usually understood to be God relating the second coming of Jesus in the last days. The Praised is explicit about Jesus' second coming. (See, e.g.: Muslim, 4:1501)

21 Jesus said: "The kingdom of God cometh not with observation: Neither shall they say, Lo here! Or, lo there! For, behold, the kingdom of God is within you." (*Luke*, 17:20–21)

> Kingdom of the heavens and the earth, and God is Witness over everything.[22]

The ways and places God is remembered are inviolable so long as they serve their purpose. None has precedence over any other except in being open to those who remember. The differences between people are reflected in the differences in how and where they remember God, as God reminded the Praised: "Had God not driven back the people, some by the means of others, there had been destroyed cloisters and churches, oratories and mosques, wherein God's name is much mentioned."[23]

When the question of the Anointed, Elijah or the prophet mentioned by John and Jesus is considered in the light of the Revelation to the Praised, the following mystery remains:

> And after six days Jesus taketh with him Peter, and James, and John, and leadeth them up into a high mountain apart by themselves: and he was transfigured before them. And his raiment became shining, exceeding white as snow; so as no fuller on earth can white them. And there appeared unto them Elijah with Moses: and they were talking with Jesus.[24]

If Jesus is the Anointed and John Elijah's second coming, who is the prophet they wonder about? Here he is called Moses, elsewhere Jeremiah.[25] According to John and Jesus, he had not yet come and the people did not know him like Elijah, Moses and Jeremiah, who had been, or John and Jesus, who were then among them. Describing the three on Mount Tabor, the writer saw the Anointed, Elijah, and Moses.

Through Moses, God announced the coming of a prophet like him: "I will raise them up a prophet from among their brethren, like unto thee, and will put My words into his mouth; and he shall speak unto them all that I shall com-

---

22 *Qur'an*, 85:1–9.

23 Ibid., 22:40.

24 *Mark*, 9:2–4.

25 See *Matthew*, 16:14. Associating the expected apostle with Moses and Jeremiah is a convincing illustration of the mission of the Praised. If the lives and missions of these two prophets are considered in the light of those of the Praised, it is hard to imagine a more convincing way of prophesying the One made manifest in history by the coming of the promised apostle whose Arabic name is *Muḥammad*.

mand him."[26] Moses and Elijah, Zachariah and Mary, John and Jesus are all of the children of Israel. But the prophet God spoke to Moses of was not of them, but of their brethren[27] and so of the line of Ishmael, for, Moses says, God never raised a prophet like him in Israel.[28]

Postscript

Glorifying God as she acknowledged being chosen, the Virgin said:

> He hath shewed strength with his arm; he hath scattered the proud in the imagination of their hearts. He hath put down the mighty from their seats, and exalted them of low degree. He hath filled the hungry with good things; and the rich he hath sent empty away. He hath holpen his servant Israel, in remembrance of his mercy; As he spake to our fathers, to Abraham, and to his seed for ever.[29]

Magnifying God, the fruit of Whose mercy was in her womb, the Virgin affirmed her knowledge of Abraham and his line. Circumcision is a sign of our covenant with God renewed through Abraham. The Praised is its seal: "And when eight days were accomplished for the circumcising of the child, his name was called Jesus, which was so named of the angel before he was conceived in the womb."[30]

The Anointed assembled twelve disciples at a last supper to reveal Thirteen to them and that we must acknowledge our plenitude, the reason for our creation, to discover it:

> And in the evening he cometh with the twelve. And as they sat and did eat, Jesus said, Verily I say unto you, One of you which eateth with me shall betray me. And they began to be sorrowful, and to say unto him one by one, Is it I? And another said, Is it I? And he answered and said unto them, It is one of the twelve, that dippeth with me in the dish. The Son of man indeed goeth, as it is written of him: but woe to that man by whom

26 *Deuteronomy*, 18:18.

27 See *Deuteronomy*, 18:18.

28 Ibid., 34:10.

29 *Luke*, 1:51–55.

30 Ibid., 2:21.

> the Son of man is betrayed! Good were it for that man if he had never been born.[31]

The Son of man is betrayed when we fail to confess the Praised as maternal seal, the Thirteenth by whom the One is revealed to the prophets and all people. Thirteen is the path back to our original perfection, the Praised as pure manifestation of God.

Matthew,[32] Mark[33] and Luke[34] all describe that supper, Jesus' revelation of Thirteen. John does not, but speaks of Jesus' prophesying the Paraclete, which the other evangelists do not. The Last Supper is an image of the Paraclete, of the Thirteen we realize as our supreme potential.

In the Hebrew and Arabic alphabets, the letters have numerical values. *Mim* is the thirteenth letter, its value forty. In the Arabic alphabet, the sacred divine name *al-aḥad*, which means "One," corresponds to the numerical value thirteen. The sum of thirteen and forty is fifty three. That is the numeric value of the name *Aḥmad*, which means "the Most Praised." In a saying frequently quoted by Muslim mystics, God says: "I am *Aḥmad*, without *mim*." The sacred name of Ahmad thus contains both thirteen and forty – the One and the Praised, inseparable, but distinct.

---

31 *Mark*, 14:17–21.

32 See *Matthew*, 26:20–29.

33 See *Mark*, 14:17–25.

34 See *Luke*, 22:14–30.

CHAPTER 13

Paraclete

All God's prophets bore witness of the Praised, as maternal and the truth of their original nature. Their tidings included that witness in their own languages, in which they called him by different names, each corresponding to our original perfection and potential to know the Lord through direct experience. His name can be translated into every language and he has as many names as there are languages. He alone, however, is our one true sublime potential with direct knowledge of God.

That his name is so recognizable, as our sublime potential and first and last of God's creation, becomes particularly evident in translation from Arabic into other languages, or the converse. *Muḥammad* means the Praised, *Aḥmad*, the Most Praised. That he is the Praised derives from his relationship with God as All-praised.

The Praised, God's first manifestation in creation, receives praise from God. The Praised returns in full to God what he has received, including the world as praised. The Praised is the servant who joins the universal praise of his Lord as All-praised. Praise is how the world relates to God as All-praised, and how we relate as the sum of all things to the Lord Who taught us the names.

In Aramaic, Jesus' language, the Praised's name would be *Mauhamana*, in Greek, the term used of him is *Parakletos*. These correspond to the Arabic *Aḥmad* or *Muḥammad*. God told the Praised:

> And when Jesus son of Mary said, "Children of Israel, I am indeed the apostle of God to you, confirming the Torah that is before me, and giving good tidings of an apostle who shall come after me, whose name shall be *Aḥmad*."[1]

Soon before leaving this world, perhaps at the Last Supper, Jesus told his twelve disciples:

> If ye love me, keep my commandments. And I will pray the Father, and he shall give you another Comforter, that he may abide with you forever. Even the Spirit of truth; whom the world cannot receive, because it seeth him not, neither knoweth him: but ye know him; for he dwelleth with you, and shall be in you. I will not leave you comfortless: I will come to

1 *Qur'an*, 61:6.

 | DOI 10.1163/9789004279407_016

you. Yet a little while, and the world seeth men no more; but ye see me: because I live, ye shall live also. At that day ye shall know that I am in my Father, and ye in me, and I in you. He that hath my commandments, and keepeth them, he it is that loveth me; and he that loveth me shall be loved of my Father, and I will love him, and will manifest myself to him.[2]

If a man love me, he will keep my words: and my Father will love him, and we will come unto him, and make our abode with him. He that loveth me not keepeth not my sayings: and the word which ye hear is not mine, but the Father's which sent me. These things have I spoken unto you, being yet present with you. But the Comforter, which is the Holy Ghost, whom the Father will send in my name, he shall teach you all things, and bring all things to your remembrance, whatsoever I have said unto you. Peace I leave with you, my peace I give unto you: not as the world giveth, give I unto you. Let not your heart be troubled, neither let it be afraid. Ye have heard how I said unto you, I go away, and come again unto you. If ye loved me, ye would rejoice, because I said, I go unto the Father: for my Father is greater than I. And now I have told you before it come to pass, that, when it is come to pass, ye might believe. Hereafter I will not talk much with you; for the prince of this world cometh, and hath nothing in me. But that the world may now that I love the Father; and as the Father gave me commandment, even so do I.[3]

But when the Comforter is come, whom I will send unto you from the Father, even the Spirit of truth, which proceedeth from the Father, he shall testify of me; And ye also shall bear witness, because ye have been with me from the beginning.[4]

But now I go my way to him that sent me; and none of you asketh me, Whither goest thou? But because I have said these things unto you, sorrow hath filled your heart. Nevertheless I tell you the truth; It is expedient for you that I go away: for if I go not away, the Comforter will not come unto you; but if I depart, I will send him unto you. And when he is come, he will reprove the world of sin, and of righteousness, and of judgment: Of sin, because they believe not on me; of righteousness, because I go to my Father, and ye see me no more; of judgment, because the prince of this world is judged. I have yet many things to say unto you, but ye cannot bear them now. Howbeit when he, the Spirit of truth, is come, he will guide you into all truth: for he shall not speak of himself; but whatsoever

2 *John*, 14:15–21.

3 Ibid., 14:25–31.

4 Ibid., 15:26–27.

> he shall hear, that shall he speak: and he will shew you things to come. He shall glorify me: for he shall receive of mine, and shall shew it to you. All things that the Father hath are mine; therefore said I, that he shall take of mine, and shall shew it unto you.[5]

The Anointed spoke to his disciples about the Praised: "Ye know him; for he dwelleth with you, and shall be in you," telling them that he came from and would return to God and that this was linked to the coming of the Praised and his own return: "Yet a little while, and the world seeth men no more; but ye see me: because I live, ye shall live also." He said his departure was a condition for the coming of the Praised, who "shall not speak of himself; but whatsoever he shall hear, that shall he speak."

The Praised also reported what he had heard from God about the Anointed: "There is not one of the People of the Book but will assuredly believe in him before his death, and on the Resurrection Day he will be a witness against them."[6]

As these sayings reveal, Jesus as the Anointed and the Praised as apostle are joined in the core of every self. Jesus confesses and prophesies the Praised as our sublime potential. Jesus' role, like every other prophet, is to call us to that potential and remind us of the knowledge, ritual and virtue that guide our ascent to the All-praised. Loving Jesus and keeping his commandments are preconditions for realizing the self in knowledge and loving the Praised as best example, which, as both said, is within us.

In the tradition historically derived from the Praised, the Greek term *Parakletos* is understood to refer to him.[7] Every one of God's prophets bore

---

5 Ibid., 16:5–15.

6 *Qur'an*, 4:159.

7 Knowledge of Jesus' prophecy is to be found in the best-known biography of the prophet Muhammad, written by Ibn Isḥāq. (See Ibn Isḥāq, *Sīrāt Rasūl Allāh*, 103–104) In the Bosnian Church, the name Paraclete was rarely translated. For the connection between Paraclete and the Praised in a later Bosnian manuscript of the *Apocrypha*, Codex no. 3488 in the University Library of Bologna, see Bojanić-Lukač, "Un chant a la gloire de Mahomet en Serbe," 57–63. See also Rycaut, *The present state of the Ottoman Empire, containing the Maxims of the Turkish Politie, the most material points of the Mahometan religion, their sects and heresies, their convents and religions votaries, their military discipline with and exact computation of their forces both by land and sea, illustrated with diverse pieces of sculpture, representing the variety of Habits among the Turks*, 2:131, and Solovjev, "Engleski izvještaj XVII vijeka o bosanskim poturima," 101–109; idem, "Nestanak bogumilstva i islamizacija Bosne," 66–69. Rycaut wrote of the Bosnians: "they believe that Muhammad was the Holy Spirit whom Christ promised and that the descent of the Holy Spirit on the day of Pentecost was the image and likeness of

witness to the Praised and this witness is the seal of his original nature. Jesus' prophecy of the Paraclete emphasizes his connection with the Spirit of Truth and the Holy Spirit. According to the Recitation, Jesus is the Anointed, the Word and the Spirit, the Truth, with whom the Holy Spirit is. The Praised speaks the Word brought to him by the Spirit of Truth and the Holy Spirit:

Muhammad, believing that in each verse the word παράκλητος designates their prophet, into whose ear the White Dove revealed the infallible guidelines of felicity." (In Solovjev, "Engleski izvještaj XVII vijeka o bosanskim poturima," 104–105.)

This interpretation of the gospel Paraclete is common, but not the only one. The story of Radin Butković, a Bosnian Church leader who died in Dubrovnik in 1467, allows different interpretations and readings. Unfortunately, the sources do not support definitive conclusions on his understanding of the Paraclete, the true nature of "the faith he believes in," his views of "other faiths," or his attempts to preserve his astonishingly large mobile assets under highly complex political circumstances. In his will, written in Dubrovnik, and a letter to the Venetian authorities, he pleads with them to give him and his company refuge. It is, however, mere conjecture when Marko Šunjić writes of his beliefs: "Radin's krstjans or at least those sixty or so that attempted to pass under Venetian protection had no intention of comparing their religion to Islam or looking for similarities between these two faiths or seeking in Muhammad that mysterious Paraclete promised by Jesus and sent by God." (Šunjić, "Jedan novi podatak o gostu Radinu i njegovoj sekti," 268). This conjecture is directed against Solovjev's view ("Nestanak bogumilstva i islamizacija Bosne," 68–69) and represents just another example of the prevalent "colonization of the history" of the Bosnian *krstjani* and the Bosnian Muslims, a colonial perspective that does not accept the evident close connection between these two phenomena, the Bosnian *krstjans* and the Bosnian Muslims, one close enough for Cardinal Torquemada to write two treatises implicitly linking them – *Abjuratio trium bosnensium* and *Tractatus contra principales errores perfidi Machometti sive Saracenorum* (MS Vat. Lat. 976); see Kamber, "Kardinal Torquemada i tri bosanska bogumila (1461)," 30. This is because the historian decides what sources to use and how to interpret them. He chooses examples and organizes ideas, trying to impose his meaning on the past. To understand the "colonization of the history" of Bosnian *krstjani* and Muslims we must have some insight into the historian's self. (On the "colonization of history" see Hill, *Rethinking History and Myth*). The Paraclete has often been a key symbol for Muslims to view their indisputable linkage with their Christian heritage. The discovery of ancient records in 1588 in Granada called the *Libros plúmbeos* was an example of this linkage. They were written in Latin and Arabic. The Cardinal of Granada declared that "they are sacred relics which supplement the true prophecies of St. John with the commentary of St. Cecil the Arab, who wrote in Arabic" (Perry, *The Handless Maiden*, 142). In 1682, however, Pope Innocent XI declared the texts forgeries, "condemning the Arabic passages as attempts to stain the Catholic faith" (Ibid.). See López-Baralt, *Islam in Spanish Literature*, 199ff; Harris, "Forging History: The Plomos of Sacromonte of Granada in Francisco Bermúdez de Pedraza's *Historia Aclestiàstica*," 945–66.

> Truly it is the revelation of the Lord of all Being, brought down by the Spirit of Truth upon thy heart, that thou mayest be one of the warners, in a clear, Arabic tongue.[8]
>
> Say: "The Holy Spirit sent it down from thy Lord in truth, and to confirm those who believe, and to be guidance and good tidings to the people of peace.[9]
>
> He has sent down upon thee the Book with the truth, confirming what was before it, and He sent down the Torah and the Gospel aforetime, as guidance to the people, and He sent down the Salvation.[10]

The Anointed foretold the Paraclete. He said that what he had revealed would only be fulfilled with his coming. When the Paraclete, that is the Praised, did come, he brought the fullness of his manifestation in this-worldly time. His presence cannot be revoked: "It is He who has sent His apostle with the guidance and the debt of truth, that he may uplift it above every debt, though the concealers be averse."[11]

Jesus' supreme legacy is his confession of the Praised, as foremost in creation, the avowal of all the prophets of God. Jesus spoke of the Praised to his disciples, saying that any questions about himself, God and the prince of this world would be resolved through him on his entry to this world and that his presence in people would be more important that his presence in history. He told his disciples that they knew the Praised as with them and in them. He may be known through history and on the basis of inner knowledge, as Jesus said: "But when the Comforter is come, whom I will send unto you from the Father, even the Spirit of Truth, which proceedeth from the Father, he shall testify of me."

Jesus' followers, who loved him and kept his commandments, included some who knew of and looked for the historical coming of the Praised. They knew when and where he would come, his origins and signs, what he would say and

---

8 *Qur'an*, 26:192–95. The Arabic *al-rūḥ al-amīn* ("Spirit of Truth") may also be translated as "True Spirit" or "Trustworthy Spirit." The Hebrew noun *ᵓᵉmeṯ*, usually translated as "true," is connected with the verb *ᵓᵉmûnâ* ("to support," "to maintain," "to establish") and with the noun *ᵓemûnâ* ("steadfastness," "fidelity"). If the Arabic phrase *al-rūḥ al-amīn* is considered in the widest possible sense, there is no doubt it can rightly be translated as "Spirit of Truth." Among the 201 names of the apostle are Spirit of Truth (*rūḥ al-ḥaqq*) and Holy Spirit (*rūḥ al-qudus*). (See Jazūlī, *Dalāʾil al-khayrāt*; Qāḍī, *Kitāb al-shifāʾ bi-taʿrīf ḥuqūq al-muṣṭafā* and Dé Clais, "Names of the Prophet," 504).

9 *Qur'an*, 16:102.

10 Ibid., 3:3–4.

11 Ibid., 61:9.

do. There is evidence for every aspect of his history in the heritage of Jews and Christians and all other nations. The books of his life offer many examples of foreknowledge and prediction of his coming, of which two will suffice.

A monk named Buhayra or Bahira, who lived as a hermit in Busra, recognized the prophet while still a boy. He questioned and examined him, discovering the seal of prophecy between his shoulder-blades, and realized he was the prophet spoken of in the books of the Christian heritage. He told the boy's uncle, Abi Talib, "a great future lies before this nephew of yours, so take him home quickly."[12]

Another Christian monk from Syria recognized Muhammad as the expected prophet. Seeing him in the shade of a tree near his cell, he told one of his companions: "None but a prophet ever sat beneath this tree."[13] Maysara witnessed the event and told Khadija, the owner of the caravan Muhammad was leading, who told in turn her cousin Waraqa, a learned Christian priest of the line of Ishmael, who said: "If this be true, Khadija, verily Muhammad is the prophet of his people. I knew that a prophet of this people was to be expected. His time has come."[14]

When the apostle received his first revelations, Khadija told Waraqa. Meeting the Praised close to the Kaʿba, Waraqa questioned him and, on hearing his reply, said: "Surely by Him in whose hands is Waraqa's soul thou are the prophet of this people! There hath come unto Thee the greatest Namus, who came unto Moses. Thou wilt be called a liar, and they will use thee despitefully and cast thee out and fight against thee. Verily if I live to see that day, I will help God in such wise as he knoweth."[15]

This coming of the third announced before the coming of the Anointed or John is part of Christian heritage. Salman the Persian, a Magian convert to Christianity, said his teacher had told him: "that he knew of no one who followed his way of life, but that a prophet was about to arise who would be sent with the debt of Abraham; he would come forth in Arabia and would migrate to a country between two lava belts, between which were palms. He has unmistakable marks. He will eat what is given to him but not things given as alms. Between his shoulders is the seal of prophecy."[16]

The Praised instructed his first disciples to seek refuge with the Christian king of Abyssinia from persecution in Mecca. His mission thus reached the

---

12 Ibn Isḥāq, *Sīrat Rasūl Allāh*, 81.

13 Ibid., 82.

14 Ibid., 83.

15 Ibid., 107.

16 Ibid., 96.

Christians there and the king later rebuked one of the Praised's Meccan opponents as follows: "By God, he is right and will triumph over his adversaries as Moses triumphed over Pharaoh and his armies."[17] When Daghatir, bishop of Syria, heard of the Praised, he told the envoy: "Your master is a prophet who has been sent; we know him by his description and we find him mentioned by name in our scriptures."[18] News of the Praised as the expected prophet spread far and wide and many bore witness to him as such.

The Praised was first confessed as prophet in pre-existence and in this world by God's other prophets and then His friends. He is the perfect example, the pure centre of realization in confession of no god but God and the Praised as His servant and apostle, manifest throughout creation, seen and unseen, differently at different times and places, but always of the same essence, human perfection, our original and ultimate purpose.

During his own lifetime, knowledge of him changed, without being exhausted. His historical manifestation reminds us of the eternal knowledge of him in every inner self, of the Praised who abides with those who know him. Our most sublime expectation before and after the Anointed's first coming, such will he remain until his second coming.

Speaking of this presence in time after his historical incarnation, the Praised said: "If only one day were to remain in the life of this world, God would prolong that day until He sent into the world a man from my community and my family. His name would be the same as mine. He would fill the land with equality and justice where it had been full of oppression and violence."[19]

The Paraclete or Praised has two faces. The first is in prophecy: all the prophets confessed him in pre-existence, as maternal seal, and in history told their peoples of him as our sublime potential.[20] The second is in friendship: after his immediate appearance in history, he passed on his presence to the friends of God for whom the Paraclete is the guide or hidden leader.

Knowing these manifestations of the Paraclete's face – that to which the prophets swore their oath in pre-existence and then foretold as our supreme potential while in history, that which appears as the historical figure of Muhammad, son of ʿAbdullah, and that to come at the end of history to realize

---

17 Ibid., 484.

18 Ibid., 656.

19 This saying of the Praised is reported by ʿAbdallāh ibn Masʿūd and quoted by Ibn Ṣabbāgh in *al-Fuṣul al-muhimma*, 271; quoted from Ṭabaṭabāʾī, *Shīʿa*, 211. For more on the transmission of the sayings of the Praised on the end of time, see Corbin, *Face de Dieu, Face de l'homme*, chapter "L'idée du Paraclet en Philosophie Iranienne," 309–358.

20 See *Qurʾan*, 3:81–82.

his promises and demonstrate the impotence of the prince of this world – is symbolized by an old Bosnian seal made of yew wood, a holy wood, preserved through the centuries as a treasure of the sacred legacy of the Bosnian Muslims.[21]

Postscript

God told Abraham to circumcise himself and his male children as a sign of their renewed covenant. The Anointed was circumcised in accordance with this, while consciousness of the Praised as first principle of creation, maternal prophet, mercy to the worlds, light-giving lamp, mighty morality, fairest example and prophetic seal was restored by this circumcision as sign of that covenant. The Praised was born circumcised, entering history as the perfect man that he be known to be the seal of the prophets. His uncle, al-Abbas, Abdul Muttalib's son, said: "The apostle – may Peace be upon him – was born circumcised and joyous. This delighted Abdul Muttalib, who came to love him,

---

21 The inscribed surface of the yew-wood seal is diamond-shaped. The top is in the form of a *fleur-de-lis*, ramifying upwards and downwards. The words inscribed on it are: *huwallāh* ("He is God") and *Muḥammad al-muṣṭafā* ("The Praised is chosen"), those inscribed in a circle in the centre are: *al-mulku lillāh* ("God's is the kingdom"), *Muḥammad rasūlullāh* ("The Praised is the apostle of God"), and *ʿAlī waliyyullāh* ("The High is the friend of God"). Twelve circles form a ring around the central circle, in which, reading clockwise, are the words: *wa ṣalli ʿalā ʿAlī al-Murtaḍā* ("And blessings on the High, the Satisfied"), *wa ṣalli ʿalā al-Ḥasan al-Mujtabā* ("And blessings on the Handsome, the Distinguished"), *wa ṣalli ʿalā Ḥusayn sayyid al-shuhadāʾ* ("And blessings on the Most Handsome, foremost of the witnesses"), *wa ṣalli ʿalā ʿAli Zayn al-ʿabidīn* ("And blessings on the High adornment of the servants"), *wa ṣalli ʿalā Muḥammad al-Bāqir* ("And blessings on the Praised, the Opener"), *wa ṣalli ʿalā Jaʿfar al-Ṣādiq* ("And blessings on the Lavish, the Sincere"), *wa ṣalli ʿalā Mūsā al-Kāẓim* ("And blessings on the Navigating, the Maintained"), *wa ṣalli ʿalā ʿAli al-Riḍa* ("And blessings on the High, the Contented), *wa ṣalli ʿalā Muḥammad al-Taqī* ("And blessings on the Praised, the Conscious"), *wa ṣalli ʿalā ʿAli al-Naqī* ("And blessings on the High, the Pure"), *wa ṣalli ʿalā Ḥasan al-ʿAskarī* ("And blessings on the Handsome, the Soldierly"), *wa ṣalli ʿalā Muḥammad al-Mahdī* ("And blessings on the Praised, the Guided"). The bottom of the seal bears the year 932. Imprints of the seal on paper are used as precious amulets. The seal was housed in western Bosnia until World War II, when it was taken to Sarajevo, where it has been kept ever since as a sacred Bosnian treasure. The author of the main published treatise on the seal did not understand its meaning, although he did see it as an old and precious part of Bosnia's heritage (see Kosta Hörmann, "Stari drveni muhur").

and said, 'this son of mine will surely be someone!' and he was someone."[22] As the perfect example, the Praised is always the same potential in every self on its return to original perfection and the realization of what it received from God. He emphasizes circumcision as reawakening our awareness of our original nature and return to it.[23]

22 Ibn Sa'd, *al-Ṭabaqāt al-kubrā*, 1:103.

23 See Muslim, 1:159.

CHAPTER 14

World Axis and Axis of Humanity

God shaped our original nature by teaching Adam the names. The core of the self is those names together: this centre is the Heart, Spirit or Intellect. We realize our humanity by discovering that centre, with its inexhaustible potential for knowing the names and the things that manifest them. This knowledge places us constantly in Unity, our only perfect haven.

Discovering knowledge relates the discoverers and what they learn. What is there to discover? The answer lies in directing the question back at the questioner – this is seemingly the greatest enigma of existence. He who discovers knowledge is what he discovers. Knowledge is how we relate to ourselves.

Our greatest task is to know the self of one who has discovered such knowledge. We know the world, insofar as we know ourselves; but both we and the world are given. They are not just what we see, but also what lies beyond, the unseen from which we derive. Everything visible is a sign or speech of the Unseen. Discovery of the Unseen liberates us from confinement. The Unseen speaks to us as the higher level of the self. Such speech prompts the self to split into giving and receiving, male and female, darkness and light, base and sublime.

The Self as One reveals Itself in multiplicity and speech:

> Mankind, mind your Lord, who created you of a single soul, and from it created its mate, and from the pair of them scattered abroad many men and women; and be mindful of God by whom you demand of one another, and the wombs; surely God ever watches over you.[1]

Our original nature, most beautiful uprightness, became known through descent and differentiation into multiplicity, which has no end in the depth. We and the world differentiate along the vertical axis of descent, which is also the axis of ascent – descent from Unity to its fullest manifestation in multiplicity and ascent from the depths to most beautiful uprightness. In our descent and return, we realize God's intention to create a vice-gerent on earth.

Our path of descent and ascent is from and towards Unity. The Praised is our finest example on the path of return. Descent and ascent include our bond

1 *Qur'an*, 4:1. For the connection between the words "womb" and "mercy" see note 7 of chapter 10.

 | DOI 10.1163/9789004279407_017

with him as the self's perfect potential. Affirming God's unity and the Praised's apostolate is the entire teaching on humankind, but not just the teaching, as it is also our inner self, of which the signs of both visible and unseen worlds remind us. The purpose of our confession is to realize the self in it.

Trust is how we relate as faithful believers to God the All-faithful. The Praised must be dearer to the faithful believer that all else, including the self. As he said: "None of you will have faith till he loves me more than his father, his children and all mankind."[2] And God said through the Praised: "The prophet is nearer to the believers than their selves."[3]

The Praised is at the beginning of creation, for creation manifests God as All-praised. Creation is Praised, having only what it has received from the All-praised. It relates to God through praise. What is in heaven and on earth returns what it has received, praising God as the Lord of all the worlds. Praise is how all things as praised, for they have received praise from God as All-praised, relate to the All-praised, Who owes His laudability to none.

The world is praised thanks to God the All-praised, to Whom it owes that debt. To praise God is to acknowledge and repay our debt to the Giver. The principle of reception and so first thing in creation is the maternal prophet from whom the differentiated world starts, to whom it returns. There is no path to the One except through him. All the world serves God, Who speaks of it through the Praised: "None is there in the heavens and earth but he comes to the All-merciful as a servant."[4]

We can realize existence as praised. This is our sublime potential, manifest in the Praised as best example. This potential can only be realized in Unity. It sets the seal on every prophet and every prophet pledged his oath to it in pre-existence.[5] Not one of them or of us is satisfied by anything but God, Who is satisfied by return to Him and satisfies those who return to Him. Only thus is return to God, our confession of no self but the Self and of the Praised's night journey from depth to height, realized.

The Praised is the original form of our perfection. The one hundred and twenty four thousand prophets are likenesses of it, the only essence of God's revelation, as God told the Praised: "And We never sent an apostle before thee except that We revealed to him, saying, 'There is no god but I; so serve Me.' "[6]

2 Muslim, 1:31.

3 *Qur'an*, 33:6.

4 Ibid., 19:93.

5 See *Qur'an*, 3:81.

6 *Qur'an*, 21:25.

For: "It is He who has sent His apostle with the guidance and the debt of truth, that he may uplift it above every debt, though the concealers be averse."[7]

The confession of God's unity and the apostle's mission contains the knowledge of all things, expressed in different ways by every sign on the horizons or in the self. One is God's command to the Praised to tell the people: "Say: 'If you love God, follow me, and God will love you, and forgive you your sins.' "[8] This reminder to follow the Praised in loving God, so that God may love us, cannot concern any outward thing. They are mere signs. Our sublime potential is within. To follow our perfect potential is to follow the Praised as our finest example. To love ourselves in that potential, in that authentic confession of God as Lord, is to love the Praised who leads to God, One and Only.

God says all things serve Him,[9] bound to Him through being-at-peace, as the apostle is His servant,[10] first of the people of peace.[11] That he is an apostle includes all of existence as his image, and since all things extol their Lord with praise,[12] he is praised and praiser in the image of the All-praised.

God created all things and then guided them.[13] The apostle is guided and guidance is his relationship with God as Guide.[14] That he was sent by God places him in a relationship with God as Sender. As the first of the people of peace, our realization in confessing God as Peace and Peace as from God[15] includes him as our link with God. This connection is through the self and the world, the two faces of one manifestation of Peace. The Anointed told his disciples: "Peace I leave with you, my peace I give unto you: not as the word giveth, give I unto you."[16]

Jesus the Anointed left his disciples Peace, but God is Peace and Peace from God. When he says "my peace," he is telling them what they know in themselves: that the Praised, who is to come, is the first of the people of peace and frees us from fear and resolves what is obscure.

The expression that "there is no god but I" is the first part of the Confession. The command "so serve Me" points to its second part: the Praised as His servant

---

7 Ibid., 61:9.

8 Ibid., 3:31.

9 See *Qur'an*, 19:93.

10 Ibid., 72:19.

11 Ibid., 6:163.

12 Ibid., 17:44.

13 Ibid., 20:50.

14 Ibid., 22:54.

15 See Muslim, 1:292. In full, this saying of the apostle's reads: "O God, Thou art Peace, and peace comes from Thee; Blessed art Thou, O Possessor of Glory and Honour."

16 *John*, 14:27.

and apostle. Our existence and the world's manifest God. We are indebted to His desire to be known and our acknowledgement of that indebtedness repays our debt. Return of the debt is manifest in our being peaceful and at peace, receiving and returning confidence, praised and praising. The world gathers in us. When the self, split between depth and height, is realized as praised and praising, it becomes the world axis and the axis of humanity, the self called from its original nature:

> Praise the Lord. Praise the Lord, O my soul. While I live will I praise the Lord; I will sing praises unto my god while I have any being. Put not your trust in princes, nor in the son of man, in whom there is no help. His breath goeth forth, he returneth to his earth; in that very day his thoughts perish.[17]

This call to the self to praise God makes Him manifest as All-praised. He is the Creator of the self and its deeds. His being All-praised is contingent on no other. He is All-praised in and by Himself. The self's capacity to praise Him is its recognition that it too is praised, owing its existence to the All-praised. When the self is revealed in this potential, it is praised and realizing the confession of no self but the Self. The Praised, as the perfect human self, is thus the finest example to every self. It is the most important aspect of our relationship with the Self. The call to praise God is a call to follow our best example, in the footsteps of the Praised.

Referring to his manifestation in the world and to our selves, the Praised said: "I am the Praised; I am the Most Deserving of Praise; I am the Eraser, by whom God erases concealment; I am the Gatherer, at whose feet the people shall be gathered; I am the Concluder after whom there is no prophet."[18]

There is no prophet before or after him, as he is the first manifestation of God in creation, the profound nature of every prophet, their maternity, seal and purpose. Every prophet corresponds to some level in descent from and ascent to Unity. All bear witness to the Praised as one manifestation with different names in different languages. The Praised said: "I was a prophet when Adam was between water and clay."[19] He also said: "I am the nearest of all the people to the son of Mary. The prophets are paternal brothers, their mothers

---

17 *Psalm*, 146:1–4.

18 Muslim, 4:1254–55. The relationship between the name the Praised (*Muḥammad*) and the Most Praised (*Aḥmad*) may be seen as follows: *Muḥammad* denotes being filled with praise, being highly praised, while *Aḥmad* denotes the superabundance of being praised.

19 Ibn Ḥanbal, 4:66.

are different, but their debt is one. And there has been no prophet between me and him."[20]

All creation is split between the invisible and visible, with God at its beginning and end, One and Only. We are split between body and Spirit and our ascent on the axis of the self is our confession of no self but the Self, as all existence reminds us. Our angelic nature is in our centre, and, on our return to God, we pass through the unseen or illuminated side of the self, affirming no light but the Light.

No human condition, no achievement on our journey stands as goal, if we confess no self but the Self. This is why we are perpetually at war, on the battlefield. No human condition satisfies us. Let it seem otherwise – let us forget our witness to no self but the Self – and we must abase ourselves and perform prostration in the mihrab. Only thus can we realign the axis of our inner self to the world axis. Any other witness deforms us and renders impossible return to God.

Return is from the depths. Becoming aware of the depths and turning to God, we begin our ascent and the black drop is cleansed from the heart. Our new awareness helps us understand our origin in mercy and renew our openness to the presence of names and praise of God: "In the name of God, the All-merciful, the Ever-merciful: Praise belongs to God, the Lord of the worlds, the All-merciful, the Ever-merciful, the King of the Day of Debt."[21]

Our original nature is the most beautiful status and corresponds to the peak of existence, the Rock and Garden, where the fruit of the forbidden tree is within reach. At once available and forbidden, it signifies free will as the condition of our relation of confidence with God as beings of faith. We transgressed of our own free will and what had been within reach withdrew. We fell to the depths, whose boundary registered God's mercy and our renewed covenant and, turning from that depth, we cried out: "From the depths of despair, O Lord, I call for your help. Hear my cry, O Lord."[22] The Kaʿba marks that low place and our cries. Ascent leads back to the summit and most beautiful uprightness, signified by the Rock. The Praised is our guide on that upright path, which he crossed with God in the night of being.

---

20 Muslim, 4:1260.

21 *Qur'an*, 1:1–4.

22 *Psalm* 130:1–2.

CHAPTER 15

Two Mosques

Two mosques, in the Valley and on the Mount, mark our descent and ascent. They are signs, as are the heavens and earth. On the axis of ascent, they denote the Throne, as revealed to David: "The Lord is in His holy temple, the Lord's throne is in heaven: his eyes behold, his eyelids try, the children of men."[1] God told the Praised: "His Throne comprises the heavens and earth; the preserving of them oppresses Him not; He is the All-high, the All-glorious."[2]

That differentiation of existence – between depths and height, earth and heavens, fallen and risen, body and Spirit, darkness and Light, rationality and Intellect, sign and Signified, concealment and revelation, visible and invisible, hell and heaven[3] – is resolved first and last by Intellect as the first of creation. Intellect is concomitant to our core or heart as Unity, manifest in feeling, thought, speech and motion. It is always at a higher level than its manifestations, with the One, as Its first expression, the womb or treasury of what exists in the flux of being. All things are sent down from, illuminated by, united within, and dispersed outside Intellect.

So long as those things are seen as linked with the signs in the self and manifesting the unseen as the other face of the visible, we and the world are two facets of one existence, whose truth is Unity as their source and confluence. We cannot know multiplicity without knowing Unity, in Which we realize ourselves, being what the self knows, knowing what it is.

---

1 *Psalm* 11:4.

2 *Qur'an*, 2:255.

3 The association between the Inviolable Mosque and the lowest depth, corresponding to darkness and hell, may seem questionable to some. The lowest depths, the depths of hell, are potential in each of us; but even in those depths, God's mercy is primal, for it embraces all things. Whatever our human condition, we are always in need of God's mercy and the guidance of the Praised. The Praised is therefore with us through every experience from the lowest depth to the sublime height; he is our guide out of whatever state we find ourselves in, but is himself always perfect, sinless, a mercy to the worlds and the finest example. It should also be remembered that both the Anointed and the Praised descended to hell in their experience of ascension, the former from the tomb, the latter from the Inviolable Mosque. The enigmatic fall to the lowest depth cannot be understood without taking into account their intimate connection and their role of redeemer or mercy to all people, even those who are in the uttermost depths.

 | DOI 10.1163/9789004279407_018

With multiplicity divorced from Unity, something – anything – can occupy the centre, so that the world is closed off. Its closure isolates us too, in a state of corruption, all Reality hidden.

Abraham was a man of peace related to God as Peace through being-at-peace. He defined his will in witness of no will but the Will, acquiescent in God's guidance, infallibly guided through the wastes of the world, revealing through himself the perfect paths of return.

Abraham's posterity turned in different ways to the Inviolable and Further Mosques. Ishmael and his children settled by the house in the Valley and they included the Praised as transmitter of God's Word. The children of Isaac settled by the house on the Mount. God sent down His Word for them to Moses, who placed it in the Ark to be carried on their journey to that Mosque. David housed the Ark where it belonged in Sion, on the Rock, as a sign of return, gathering, and unification. Solomon built the buildings of that Mosque around the Ark. Both signs were thus connected with His Word, which is us. When we are perfect, in and through us God's "Be"[4] is manifest at every moment.

The two houses, in the Valley and on the Mount, have the Word as their foci. The former was empty; the latter housed Stone Tablets inscribed with His Word as revealed to Moses. Both houses fell to ruin, but their emptiness did not. It is the heart's full and inviolable presence.

"The earth and everything in it is damned," said the Praised, "except for the remembrance of God, and what attends it, and its teacher and its student."[5] Nothing in world or self is without the original Divine "Be." Everything recalls God; nothing is damned. The alchemy of remembrance transforms damned into blessed. The heart is the site of remembrance, in which God is truly present, for which we are blessed, but only knowledge can bring the heart to life and enable most beautiful uprightness. This is why Ibn 'Arabī wrote:

> The greatest sin is what kills hearts. They do not die except through the absence of the knowledge of God. This is what is named ignorance. For the heart is the house that God has chosen for Himself in this human configuration. But such a person has usurped the house, coming between it and the owner. He is the one who most wrongs himself because he has deprived himself of the good that would have come to him from the owner of the house had he left the house to Him. This is the deprivation of ignorance.[6]

---

4 *Qur'an*, 36:81.

5 Tirmidhī, 4:561, tradition 2322.

6 Ibn al-'Arabī, *Fūtūḥāt al-makkiyya*, 3:179.6, in: Chittick, *Ibn 'Arabī: Heir to the Prophets*, 67.

The houses at the bottom of the Valley and atop the Mount denote the poles of the self. They manifest the heart and are united only within it. After seven circuits of the house, the Praised went in to pray, destroying first all three hundred and sixty idols around it, saying: "The truth has come, and falsehood has vanished away; surely falsehood is ever certain to vanish."[7]

Before the witnesses there with him, the Praised cleansed the Inviolable Mosque, for gods had held court there and it was an image of the heart in which gods hold court instead of God. We are constantly at risk of gods ruling in our hearts and they cannot be cleansed unless we follow the Praised as he journeys from Inviolable to Further Mosque, which he does at all times. When we cease to follow the Praised, our heart is revealed as in the state of those two places of worship, the one at the bottom of the Valley and the other on top of the Mount. The cleansing of the Inviolable Mosque is described by the inscriptions on the octagonal, gold-clad Dome of the Rock on the Mount of the Further Mosque:

> Outer face
>
> In the name of God, the All-merciful, the Ever-merciful; there is no god but God, One, without partner. Say: He is God, One, God, the Everlasting Refuge, who has not begotten, and has not been begotten, and equal to Him is not any one.[8] The Praised is the apostle of God, Peace be upon him. In the name of God, the All-merciful, the Ever-merciful; there is no god but God, One, without partner. God and His angels bless the prophet. O believers, do you also bless him, and pray him peace.[9] In the name of God, the All-merciful, the Ever-merciful; there is no god but God, One, without partner. Praise belongs to God, who has not taken to Him a son, and who has not any associate in the Kingdom, nor any protector out of humbleness. And magnify Him with repeated magnificats.[10] The Praised is the apostle of God, may God bless him and His angels and His prophets, and Peace and the Mercy of God be with them. In the name of God, the All-merciful, the Ever-merciful; there is no god but God, One, without partner. His is the Kingdom, and His is the Praise;[11] He gives life, and He makes to die, and He is powerful over everything.[12] The Praised is the apostle of God, may God bless him, and accept his intercession on the

7 *Qur'an*, 17:81.
8 Ibid., 112.
9 Ibid., 33:56.
10 Ibid., 17:111.
11 Ibid., 64:1.
12 Ibid., 57:2.

Day of Resurrection for his maternal community. In the name of God, the All-merciful, the Ever-merciful; there is no god but God, One, without partner. The Praised is the apostle of God, may God bless him. There built this dome the servant of God ʿAb[d al-Malik, commander] of believers, in the year seventy-two, may God accept [it] from him and be pleased with him. Amen. Lord of the worlds. Praise be to God.

Inner face

In the name of God, the All-merciful, the Ever-merciful; there is no god but God, One, without partner. His is the Kingdom, and His is the Praise;[13] He gives life, and He makes to die, and He is powerful over everything.[14] The Praised is the servant of God and His apostle. God and His angels bless the prophet. O believers, do you also bless him, and pray him peace.[15] People of the Book, go not beyond the bounds in your debt, and say not as to God but the truth. The Anointed, Jesus, son of Mary, was only the apostle of God, and His Word that He committed to Mary, and a Spirit from Him. So believe in God and His apostles, and say not, "Three." Refrain; better is it for you. God is only One god. Glory be to Him – that he should have a son! To Him belongs all that is in the heavens and in the earth; God suffices for a guardian. The Anointed will not disdain to be a servant of god, neither the angels who are near stationed to Him. Whosoever disdains to serve Him, and waxes proud, He will assuredly muster them to Him, all of them.[16] Blessed be Your prophet and Your servant Jesus, son of Mary, and peace be with him on the day he was born and the day he died and the day he was raised up alive. That is Jesus, son of Mary, in word of truth concerning which they are doubting. It is not for God to take a son unto Him. Glory be to Him! When He decrees a thing, He but says to it "Be," and it is. Surely God is my Lord, and your Lord; so serve Him. This is an upright path.[17] God bears witness that there is no god but He – and the angels, and men possessed of knowledge – upholding justice; there is no god but He, the All-mighty, the All-wise. The true debt to God is being-at-peace. Those who were given the Book

13 Ibid., 64:1.
14 Ibid., 57:2.
15 Ibid., 33:56.
16 Ibid., 4:171–72.
17 Ibid., 19:33–36.

were not at variance except after the knowledge came to them, being insolent one to another. And whoso disbelieves in God's signs, God is swift at the reckoning.[18]

East entrance

In the name of God, the All-merciful, the Ever-merciful: Praise be to God, than Whom there is no god but He, the Living, the Everlasting, Creator of the heavens and the earth and Light of the heavens and the earth,[19] Guardian of the heavens and the earth, the One, the Only; who has not begotten, and has not been begotten, and equal to Him is not any one,[20] One, Master of the Kingdom, Thou givest the Kingdom to whom Thou wilt, and seizest the Kingdom from whom Thou wilt.[21] All power is Thine and comes from Thee, our Lord, and returns to Thee, Master of the Kingdom, the All-merciful, the Ever-merciful. He has prescribed for Himself mercy. His mercy embraces all things.[22] May He be glorified and exalted. As for what the polytheists associate [with Thee], we ask Thee, O God by Thy mercy and by Thy beautiful names and by Thy holy Face and by Thy great majesty and by Thy perfect word, on which are based the heavens and the earth and through which we are preserved by Thy mercy from Satan and are saved from Thy punishment on the Day of Resurrection and by Thy abundant favour and by Thy great grace and forbearance and omnipotence and forgiveness and liberality, that Thou blessest the Praised, Thy servant, Thy prophet, and that Thou acceptest his intercession for his people, the blessing of God be upon him and peace be upon him and the mercy of God. This is what was decreed by the servant of God, imam al-Ma'mun, commander of the faithful, may God prolong his life, in the reign of his brother the commander of the faithful Abū Isḥāq, son of the commander of the faithful al-Rashid, may God prolong him. By the hand of Ṣāliḥ ibn Yaḥyā, protégé of the Commander of the faithful, in Rabi' al-Akhira 216.

18 Ibid., 3:18–19.

19 Ibid., 2:255, in part, or 3:2, 6:101 and 24:35, in part.

20 Ibid., 112.

21 Ibid., 3:26.

22 Ibid., 6:12 and 7:156.

North entrance

In the name of God, the All-merciful, the Ever-merciful: Praise be to God, than Whom there is no god but He, the Living, the Everlasting.[23] There is no other god than He,[24] the One, the Only, who has not begotten, and has not been begotten, and equal to Him is not any one.[25] The Praised is the servant of God and His apostle, whom He sent with the guidance and the debt of truth, that he may uplift it above every debt, though the concealers be averse.[26] We believe in God, and that which has been sent down on us, and sent down on the prophets of their Lord; we make no division between any of them, and in Him we find peace.[27] God bless the Praised, His servant and His prophet, and Peace be with him and mercy from God, His pleasure, His forgiveness and His satisfaction.[28]

23 Ibid., 2:255, in part, or 3:2.

24 See *Qur'an*, 6:163.

25 *Qur'an*, 112.

26 Ibid., 9:33 or 61:9.

27 Ibid., 2:136 or 3:84.

28 The translation of the inscription is from: Grabar, *The Shape of the Holy*, 59–61.

CHAPTER 16

The Mihrab

Always and everywhere, we are in multiplicity, but multiplicity manifests Unity as First and Last, Inward and Outward. In multiplicity, any condition not fully confessional of Unity and the Praised's apostolate is a mihrab or battlefield.[1] The war in multiplicity for unification with Unity and the Praised's perfection has no solution that does not pull back that in the world which veils Unity. To pull back the veils is to reveal them as signs through which to see or know the Signified. Confessing Unity and the Praised's apostolate we are in mihrab and mosque, the battlefield and the place of annihilation of the self.

The theatre of war is to face the world as veiling. We have Spirit or Light in our centre and reject concealment of Unity, striving to draw away the veils and reveal the world as manifesting Truth. In so doing, we find our original nature outside ourselves, in the knowledge of the names our Lord taught us.

Existence is nothing compared to God but everything when God is manifest in it. It ranges from nullity to plenitude, from earth, or the depths, to the heavens, or the height. The range outside is mirrored by the range in us from body to Spirit. We fell from Spirit to the body. Spirit and the height remain the goal of our return, so we pray to God: "Guide us on the upright path, the path of those

1 The Arabic noun *miḥrāb* means "theatre of war" or "battlefield"; and the noun *masjid* means "place of prostration" or "place of *sajda*," a place of self-abnegation. The Arabic *miḥrāb* (pl. *maḥārib*) designates the niche or recess in the wall of a mosque, opposite the entrance door, oriented towards the Kaʿba. In fact, there are two doors – one for us to pass through in the body, the other for our spiritual passage. The mosque is entirely formed, both literally and meaningfully, around the *miḥrāb*. The word *miḥrāb* derives from the root *ḥ r b* of the verb *ḥariba*, the primary meaning of which is to be furious or enraged. In another form, it means to fight, combat or wage war. Commentators associate this root meaning with the great war against the self, the war against evil and malign influences. Linguists state that the word *miḥrāb* can also mean a building, a recess or a room. In the fact that, in the prophet's Mosque in Medina, where, as God's apostle, he dictated all the forms and contents, there had once been a *miḥrāb* where a door was later opened and doors where the *miḥrāb* would later be "closed," one should recognize the relationship between bodily and spiritual passage to the Ultimate, or emerging from war into Peace, from illusion into Reality. The original decree to face in prayer the Further Mosque on Mount Sion in Jerusalem, the second mosque built, was later altered to one to face the Inviolable Mosque in Becca, the first mosque built. This meant that all things face the First, which is also the Last, for all time.

 | DOI 10.1163/9789004279407_019

whom Thou hast blessed, not of those against whom Thou art wrathful, nor of those who are astray."[2]

Our goal is the end of that path, the direction of realization in the testimony to His Unity and the Praised's apostolate. On earth, we are bound to its surface. The heavens above and the earth we live on are two signs of one path of return to God. Nothing in them fails to signal that path. The signs may be more or less clear, but together, they reveal nullity in the face of God. That we may the more willingly participate in that nullity in the place of worship of creation, God decrees the path of our ascent from the depth to most beautiful uprightness.

The bottom of the valley in the midst of the desert corresponds to the depth. Each of us is called upon to acknowledge and become aware of our baseness and turn from it to God, as God said through the Praised: "The first house established for the people was at Becca, a place holy and a guidance to all beings."[3] God calls on us all to turn towards that house and become aware of our baseness as where ascent begins: "Turn thy face towards the Inviolable Mosque; and wherever you may be, turn your faces towards it."[4] Those who accept that call and turn towards the Inviolable Mosque form a circle around it. Those who visit it walk around it seven times, then walk seven times from one of the two nearby hills to the other, and stand on the plain of Knowledge.

To face the house and journey towards it is the turn to the centre of the self that knows its Lord in its original nature. The seven circuits signify ascent to the Lord throughout existence, through all seven heavens, while walking seven times from one hill to another designates our liberation from duality and realization in Unity. Standing on the plain of Knowledge affirms our faith in God and the Day of Judgment.

The bottom of the Valley corresponds to the depth or existence after violating the inviolable. Turning towards it and relating to it at all reminds us of our violation of the inviolable, which must be restored as the inviolability of the vulnerable. As a sign of the nadir, the Kaʿba is a visible work of God's hands, a reminder that He created us and our works. Our highest option is to journey to Him.

The opposite to baseness is most beautiful uprightness, remote, beyond all seven heavens and the entire visible world. It is signified by the house

---

2 *Qur'an*, 1:6–7.

3 Ibid., 3:96.

4 Ibid., 2:144.

inhabited[5] and the Lote-Tree of the Boundary.[6] On earth, its sign is the Further Mosque in Sion.

The Praised is the perfect realization of ascent from the depth, or Inviolable Mosque, to most beautiful uprightness, or Further Mosque. This is why he is a maternal prophet, a mercy to the worlds, a light-giving lamp, an immense nature, and the best example. Loving God, we follow the Praised, and God loves those who follow him.

Turning our face from the depth to most beautiful uprightness begins our journey, whose goal is realization in witness of no self but the Self. Each point we reach is a place of worship or annihilation of the self. Travelling on, we leave behind the wastelands of the attained for a higher place, in a constant process of liberation from duality. Existence is the place of worship, the mosque, where we turn towards Reality. Doing so, we attempt to abandon the sign for the Signified, self for the Self, and transcend duality for Unity. This is being in the world as mosque, facing Reality, in the theatre of war to break free from un-Reality.

Our presence in the world always involves two questions. The first is our relationship with things: "What is that?" The second is our relationship with them as an incalculable multitude of the at once similar and different: "What is it really?"

There are as many answers to the first question as things, for it arises in regard to everything. Everything has its own shape, place and time and is in perpetual flux, with features that dictate the response as to its thingness. The second question has only one answer, the sum of our witness of no god but God. All things owe their existence to God; their specific features manifest as place, time and form are their debt to Unity, which is in and with all things. Everything is an unmediated manifestation of Unity. We are the sum of that manifestation, so that every individual thing is also us. Only the first question makes an object of manifestation. The second makes it indivisible from seer and knower.[7]

The first question is inseparable from rationality; the second, from Intellect. Rationality or analytical reason is wholly focused on multiplicity, with its concomitants, cognition and the brain. Intellect is eternally with Unity, and its

---

5 See *Qur'an*, 52:4.

6 Ibid., 53:14.

7 This kind of knowledge of things is open to all of us, but only a few realize it, as God says: "And those firmly rooted in knowledge say, 'We believe in it; all is from our Lord;' yet none remembers, but men possessed of minds." (*Qur'an*, 3:7, see also: 3:18, 58:11, 47:16.)

concomitant is the heart.[8] Our whole involves both – the brain as seat of rationality and the heart as seat of Intellect.

We always know something and all we know, regardless of how much our gaze takes in, manifests Unity. Unity is full knowledge, being a full person being what we know – Unity.

Our opening up to Unity is the purpose of all knowledge, every path and every virtue: this is realization in the heart. And the mihrab is the sign of our turning from multiplicity towards Unity,[9] of our overcoming mere rationality, which scatters what is summed up within us. It is the sign of the gathering in Unity, or of being what we are, or of union with what we love.

The mihrab signifies our transition from the first question to the second and our self-realization in the response to it. All that we are manifests as division and dispersion, but also as duration and completion. Neither is possible without Intellect and Eternal Life, both of which we desire. The world is our mihrab, we its. The meaning of both questions and their answer depends on how this duality is resolved.

We expect the world of things to open up to Unity, manifest in both the world and the things in it. We expect to open ourselves to discovery of Unity in what our ego embraces.

As a sign, the mihrab reveals part of the circumference on which we always are, in the world outside. We stand on the earth's surface, but our verticality connects us to the heavens. A mihrab arch is normally composed of segments of seven circles or rings with pendants, denoting the seven heavens. The entire mihrab, with us in it, speaks of heaven's gates.[10]

We and the world are only apparently split into two separate entities. Neither has reality except in the confession of no god but God. Our relationship with the world, as two facets of Reality's manifestation, is resolved in the mihrab as where we wage war against delusion. This is the war that enables us to pass from earth to heaven, from reality to Reality, from mind to Intellect.

---

8 For more on the relationship between the Intellect and the rational mind, see Nasr, *Islamic Philosophy from its Origin to the Present*, 93–103. For more on the heart as the seat of knowledge and intellectuality, see idem, "The Heart of the Faithful is the Throne of the All-Merciful." See also Chittick, *Science of the Cosmos, Science of the Soul*, 29–30.

9 In the Sufi tradition, it is held that the roots of the nouns *miḥrāb* and *raḥma* (*ḥrb* and *rḥm*) can be connected through the key provided by two forms of the name of the Holy Valley, Becca and Mecca. The two roots thus become *ḥrm* and *rḥm*. This is none other than the first spilling over of the Mercy that embraces all things. (See Izutsu, *Sufism and Taoism*, 116).

10 See *Qur'an*, 7:40.

Wherever we are rooted in knowledge, there is a mihrab.[11] The earth, as our place of abode, and the seven heavens above it are a mihrab. We show our turn to Unity in how we remember we are both outward and inward. We build mihrabs to strengthen that recollection.

As a battlefield, the mihrab directs us towards God's all-encompassing mercy. Our war in the world and the self is one of liberation, to free ourselves from illusion and transience and to comprehend all of being as Mercy. We do this by striving for self-realization. The more we know, the readier we are to realize ourselves beyond the veils of thingness. Nothing on that journey deserves to serve as goal, but everything reveals the Goal. We are forever between multiplicity and Unity, rationality and Intellect.

Duality can be resolved through witness of Unity in multiplicity and return to It. Waging war and journeying keep rationality subject to Intellect as its principle. Intellect is wholly subject to God's will. Thus, rationality, Intellect and intuition[12] correspond to levels of being, which are distinguished in descending or ascending order. As Frithjof Schuon wrote:

> Intellectual intuition communicates *a priori* the reality of the Absolute. Reasoning thought infers the Absolute by starting from the relative; thus it does not proceed by intellectual intuition, though it does not inevitably exclude it. For philosophy, arguments have an absolute value; for intellectual intuition their value is symbolical and provisional.[13]

The mihrab denotes this duality as question and answer. When in it, we are simultaneously peripheral and central, on the surface and on the axis. To realize the self on the surface is to set it upright on the vertical axis through the levels of existence. Annihilation is the union of centre and periphery, of the depths and the height. We are ever in multiplicity or duality, always related to an Other, Unity, Which appears to us as multiplicity. We acquiesce in the Other as Peace. Our knowledge of the Other is how we relate to It as All-knowing and loving It is our aspiration to unite with It as Beloved and All-loving. But Peace is unknowable in multiplicity and war, as are knowledge and loving. Peace is salvation from war, knowledge redemption from ignorance, and loving salvation from fear and hatred.

---

11 In 1664, there were fifty mihrabs in Nevesinje, then a major Bosnian town (see Čelebi, *Putopis*, 416).

12 The term "intuition" denotes the direct experience or knowledge of phenomena, their "taste" (Ar. *dhawq*, Lat. *sapientia*).

13 Schuon, *Spiritual Perspectives and Human Facts*, 112.

The heart is the centre of the world, veiled by the visible. When revealed, it is what the signs in the world and self recall. Mary's reception of Spirit, as blessed amongst women, appeared as a centre enfolded in seven heavens and placed in the house and the Ark and on the Tablets of Stone, but never closed off. The centre illuminates existence, but nothing can illumine it, as it is the confession of no light but the Light.

CHAPTER 17

Becca and Sion

The floor of Becca valley marks our fall to the depth, the summit of Mount Sion our most beautiful uprightness. Every valley and hill indicates this split. It is by confessing God's unity and the Praised's apostolate that we ascend the path of rectitude from that depth to the height.

If the valley and the mount are mere signs of descent and ascent, they in turn are mere indications of the self, all-embracing in its original creation as witness and bearer of His trust. As creatures of infinite potential, given us by the Spirit breathed into us and our knowledge of the names, obscured by our will to defy His will and pluck what was forbidden, we lie between two extremes – original and perfect and obscure and finite.

The Praised encompasses the span. When Adam fell to the depth, the Praised was his finest example even there, to help him understand the meaning of the house God had sent down as a reminder of the house in paradise. The angel Gabriel taught him of it and led him to Becca to outline with his foot on the earth the shadow cast by a white cloud, the size of a heavenly mosque, whose purpose, like that of the rituals associated with it, would be to reveal the mysteries of our original nature and of return to the Garden.

The Praised is in that house. Realization in the heart attains our sublime potential through following him – but this takes place invariably between two loves – the self's love for the Self and the Self's love for the self. Love is simply yearning for union. Nothing satisfies it but Unity as attested in confessing no self but the Self.

Only the Self knows the self fully, offering countless obstacles and challenges on its path of return or union, but never depriving it of His love or mercy. The Self knows all things in the self, which cannot, however, know all things in It. Jesus the Anointed, son of Mary, said to God: "Thou knowest it, knowing what is within my soul, and I know not what is within Thy soul."[1]

The Praised travelled one night with God from the Inviolable to the Further Mosque.[2] This night ascent was the path of our self-realization in the One. The floor of Becca valley and the summit of Mount Sion are its signs within us,

1 *Qur'an*, 5:116.

2 See *Qur'an*, 17:1.

 | DOI 10.1163/9789004279407_020

from analytical reason to Intellect, from the manifest self to its centre, from the world and us to God.

Neither of the two signs or places that God's finger showed Adam after the fall means anything if not to the heart. They are signs of the door to the Garden and the key to the door. The Garden is not lost, as though still out there on an undiscovered island, under the same sky. It was and remains within us. The door is closed to our awareness, since we reached for the forbidden fruit. Both Garden and door lie within and the path to the door and the key to open it were given us through Gabriel; in travelling the path, we must know that guidance is God's alone.

The house at the bottom of the valley of Becca, in which the Praised dwells, whose heart received the Spirit of Truth from the Word of God, and the house on Sion, whose heart was the Ark of the Covenant, are but ruins, the habitations of idols, when we turn from God. Was not the house at the bottom of Becca valley a mere heap of stones when Abraham came there with his son Ishmael? Was it not an abode of dead gods when the Praised came there on his camel? Was not the house on Sion a "den of thieves"[3] when Jesus came there? Did not John leave the house to be a voice calling from the wilderness to the children of Israel to turn to God? And did not Jesus say to them, pointing to himself: "But I say unto you, That in this place is one greater than the temple."[4] And did he not add: "Destroy this temple, and in three days I will raise it up."[5]

The ruination of the house stems from the condition of our hearts. When the stones and decorations, rituals, chanting, robes and multitudes cover His true house, the heart, ruination follows, as the Bible relates: "And as some spake of the temple, how it was adorned with goodly stones and gifts, [Jesus] said, As for these things which ye behold, the days will come, in the which there shall not be left one stone upon another, that shall not be thrown down."[6]

Despite the magnificence of the house and the precious things in it, God gave Zachariah, "whom God remembers," a son to be His prophet, to show how the house and the covered self are sullied by the rejection of God. John called on us to consider what is our hearts:

> O generation of vipers, who hath warned you to flee from the wrath to come? Bring forth therefore fruits meet for repentance: And think not to

3 *Luke*, 19:46.

4 *Matthew*, 12:6.

5 *John*, 2:19.

6 *Luke*, 21:6.

> say within yourselves, We have Abraham to our father: for I say unto you, that God is able of these stones to raise up children unto Abraham. And now also the axe is laid unto the root of the trees: therefore every tree which bringeth not forth good fruit is hewn down, and cast into the fire.[7]

John showed the people the purity of Mary's heart into which the Holy Spirit had descended to manifest His Word. Both house and Ark point unmistakably to the inner self, the house of our sublime potential and the source of our self-realization – the Praised, who descends from the sublime height to the depths, for God does not allow us to fall into utter ruin. Moses ascended the Mount to descend again with God's reminder to His people.

The Ark is the sign of the heart, as is the Kaʿba. It epitomizes the teaching on the cosmos and on us, as the two facets of His revelation.[8]

The world stretches from earth to heaven, just as the path runs from the bottom of the valley to the summit of the mount. We too run from body to Spirit, from surface to heart, from darkness to light. We came with the Spirit, and so we return. Thus God inspired Moses' mother to put her child into an ark and send him down river. The ark contained the focal point through which He would manifest Himself in human language, a manifestation whose shattered remains would be laid in the Ark, like a dead body to rest, that we might know that the heart of the living is the house of the Living God. God reminded us through the Praised:

> Already another time We favoured thee, when We revealed what was revealed unto thy mother: "Cast him into the ark, and cast him into the river, and let the river throw him up on the shore. An enemy of Mine and his shall take him." And I loaded on thee love from Me, and to be formed

7 *Matthew*, 3:10.

8 The Kaʿba, the Ark and the house are key symbols of the entire content of the perennial philosophy. There is an extensive discussion of the meaning of the Kaʿba as God's speech on Himself, the world and man in *Kitāb asrār al-ḥajj*, by Qāḍī Saʿīd Qummī (1639–1691), discussed in turn by Henry Corbin. God as the All-praised and Lord manifests Himself through the unseen and the visible world as the All-praised Who encompasses the whole of existence, all summed up in the Praised as the first of the people of peace, represented by the Kaʿba with its twelve visible edges. For more see Corbin, *Temple and Contemplation*, in particular the chapter entitled "The Configuration of the Temple of the Kaʿba as the Secret of the Spiritual Life," 183–262.

> in My sight, when thy sister went out, saying, "Shall I point you to one to have charge of him?"[9]

God told Moses: "I have chosen thee for My service."[10] The self and the Self are related so that the witness of no self but the Self is never bypassed. God chose Moses for that witness to His Unity and the Praised's apostolate: "The Lord came from Sinai, and rose up from Seir unto them; He shined forth from Mount Paran, and He came with ten thousands of saints: from His right hand went a fiery law for them. For their sake He came from the Kadesh multitudes, from His south all the way to the Hills."[11]

The shining forth from Paran is the light of the Praised, who is the pledge of all the prophets. Whenever a prophet appeared on valley or mount, hill or shore, he brought the light of the apostle as the only light in at the centre of the self, to remind us that the mosque of the world was given us for the sake of the mosque within, the mosque filled with Light.

The four corners of the Kaʿba correspond to four prophets, and each prophet to a height: the Syrian corner – Abraham and Safī, the Western corner – Moses and Sinai, the Yemeni corner – Jesus and Seir, and the Iraqi corner – Muhammad and Paran.[12]

One cannot understand the two mosques or places of self-abnegation, the first in Becca, the other on Sion, without Unity, revealed and confirmed by duality. The earth and heavens were one mass.[13] We are all of a single soul.[14] The differentiation of unity entailed descent: two are lower than one. No given feature of multiplicity is reducible to any other. Comparison leaves a remainder known only to God. The purpose of separation is to manifest Him. It is only in separation that we can return to Unity. Where separation is, there is love, a yearning for union.

Both places remind us of this separation. To explain their meaning, the sage Salih said:

> Imagine a bowl full of soup, with a lid topped by a rosebud. Take the rosebud between finger and thumb and remove the lid. Put it down beside the bowl. Now you can see and smell the soup. Once you have drunk it all,

9 *Qur'an*, 20:37–40.
10 Ibid., 20:41.
11 *Deuteronomy*, 33:2.
12 See Corbin, *Temple and Contemplation*, 222–24.
13 See *Qur'an*, 21:30.
14 Ibid., 4:1.

you are at the bottom of the bowl. You may think there is no way out from the bottom of the bowl. You reverse the process. You take hold of the rosebud on the lid and put it back onto the bowl. What was in the bowl is now inside you. It all began with the rosebud. The whole thing began with and came back to it. Can you rise to the whole? Do not forget that the rose is the symbol of the Virgin Mary and the prophet Muhammad.[15]

15 The author first heard this saying in one of those encounters which seem more than the sum of their parts. That is why only some indication of the tradition's origin has been given. It belongs equally to all who know it.

CHAPTER 18

Covered by the Hands of the Praised

Abraham was led to the Inviolable Mosque and so the mosque in the self. Its signs of heavenly reality were veiled over when Adam took the fruit. Abraham guided both posterities to that inner mosque, recalled by Valley and Mount together, hoping they would meet there, where only Light, Spirit and Intellect are. He guided them as he had been guided. Our earthly condition is manifest in countless dualities, but return affirms Unity in duality.

The Inviolable and Further Mosques are signs with one centre, one heart that corresponds to all hearts: "The hearts of all the sons of Adam are between the two fingers out of the fingers of the Ever-merciful Lord as one heart. He turns that to any (direction) He likes."[1]

God revealed the mystery of the mosques to Adam through Gabriel, as a story of return to the lost garden, Peace's heavenly city. We are guided to Peace by being-at-peace, confessing His Unity and the Praised's apostolate, standing in prayer, giving alms, fasting, and visiting the house (generally supposed to refer to the house at Becca, but its deeper, more sublime meaning is the heart as containing Light). Achieving peace is necessary for belief in God, His angels, His Books, His prophets, the Day of Resurrection, and His determination of good and evil.

The prophets used the two mosques to indicate the mystery of return to the inner mosque, the all-encompassing centre. This encompassing realizes our witness of His unity, but mistaking the signs for the Signified delivers the self over to outward forms in stone and it cannot enter the inner mosque to join the angels around His Throne.

Turning away from our core, the mosque of the Spirit, towards mere forms without the Living, had consequences: statues erected around the Kaʿba and destruction of the Further Mosque on the Mount. Both resulted from obscuring the heart and taking signs for the Signified.

Through the Virgin, God made manifest the Truth of His creation: our heart as His house. Everything in the universe, rituals and books serves to remind us of this. Our purpose is perfect realization, our best example the Praised, ever in us, whom Jesus called Paraclete or Comforter.

The choice of the Virgin to birth the Word in the world and recall the heart, as immeasurably greater than all the world's expanses, shook every authority

1 Muslim, 4:1397.

 | DOI 10.1163/9789004279407_021

and order. We return alone to God, each bearing our own burden, called singly, on our battlefield, expected to annul whatever meaning in world or self does not recall us to our Lord or serve our return to Him.

The Praised realizes the meaning of both mosques, Becca and Sion. He says nothing for himself. His Word is God's Word as much as Jesus is. Just as God revealed Jesus as His Word through Mary's heart, He revealed His Word through the Praised's heart as the Recitation.

Jesus is closest to what God said through the Praised, the Virgin to the Praised as a mercy. Both offer a path across the battlefield to the Word, Whom they reveal as first and last.

The Praised led his companions north from Becca, towards the Mount, indicating the duality resolved in confessing His unity and the Praised as apostle. Both signs must be cleansed of what obscures their discourse on the self's Light, so as to reveal the original covenant, whose core is the Praised. His witness of Unity unites both signs. This is why he led his companions to Becca and entered the house to reveal himself as the core and finest example of every self. He taught what the angel Gabriel taught Adam after he fell to earth: return to the Garden.

When he entered the Kaʿba, the centre of the Inviolable Mosque, the Praised found its walls covered with images of angels and gods, including one of Mary and her son. He covered them with his hands, while ordering the other images to be effaced.[2] This is why that image in the Kaʿba is under the palms of the Praised. His breath was filled with the Spirit of Truth in which God reveals His Word. Our only heart, of which both Inviolable and Further Mosque speak, is revealed in four revelations – the Virgin, Jesus, the Praised and the Recitation – in the house at Becca and in the Praised, who made himself known as the core of our ascent from the depths to most beautiful uprightness.

The Praised prayed in the Kaʿba with three companions, with the door closed, and then spoke from its door to those assembled: "There is no god but God alone. He has kept His promise, and aided His servant. He alone has put the confederates to flight. Every prerogative now lies with me save two – the

2 See Ibn Isḥāq, *Sīrāt Rasūl Allāh*, 552; Wüstenfeld, *Die Chroniken der Stadt Mekka*, 1:111, 4:104; Lings, *Muhammad*, 302. In references to Constantinople, Haghia Sophia is usually seen as its principal symbol and the name is clearly associated with the Virgin Mary. The Praised spoke to his followers of the city: "Surely, Constantinople will be conquered (by my community); how blessed the commander who will conquer it, and how blessed his army." (Ibn Ḥanbal, 18:189). When Sultan Mehmed the Conqueror entered the church, he felt it his duty to establish a *miḥrāb* there with reference to the prophet Zachariah and the Virgin Mary. Both the *miḥrāb* and the inscription are still there.

guardianship of the Kaʿba, and the office of providing water for pilgrims."[3] He spoke of life and death, honour and dishonour, and God's warning: "O mankind, We have created you male and female, and appointed you races and tribes, that you may know one another. Surely the noblest among you in the sight of God is the most mindful of you. God is All-knowing, All-aware."[4]

The Virgin is the most mindful of women, the Praised the best example and the mightiest morality. They reveal the world's duality in which God is manifest, out of love to be known. Together, they manifest Unity perfectly.

Our existence, like all that preceded us in creation, is acceptance of debt: God is the Giver, we the recipients, related to Him by our debt. The recipient is to return the received on the Giver's terms. We repay our debt by recognizing our original confession that God is Lord. This entails finding and actualizing the Word.

Our being in this world and acceptance of God's confidence make existence a battlefield. The image of the world as theatre of war is inherent to mihrab and altar, indicating our arrival as creatures and our return as individuals. We were equipped at creation to enter this theatre of war, in order to ensure our return to God. Redemptive knowledge is within; teachings, rituals and virtue mere reminders. The worlds and prophets and revelation serve the realization of what is in our hearts from time immemorial – confession of His unity and the Praised's apostolate.

Returning to God of our own free will is no easy task. The path is hard, uphill, with countless obstacles and traps. Everything returns to God, willingly or no. We can do so freely and escape the violence to be levied on us as just judgment for violence we have done ourselves. The proof our return is by our own free will is our persistent struggle against ascent. Those who return of their own will remain on the battlefield, on that steep ascent towards the height.

In repaying our debt to God, nothing has meaning except as a sign manifesting Him. Forgetting this, we fall to the depth. Mindful of it, we begin our ascent. The Virgin heralds the persistence of memory, as witness that not world, prophets, nor most sacred mosque have any purpose but to recall us to our original covenant with God, the treasure in every heart. She is a sign of existence as a whole, the heavens and the earth. She is the Word's recipient, the infinite azure vault of the heavens which embraces existence and from which the Word emerges as Light-giving Lamp. Her heart encompasses more than

3 See Ibn Isḥāq, *Sīrat Rasūl Allāh*, 552–53.

4 *Qur'an*, 49:13.

both the heavens and the earth, than that wherein the Lord is.[5] God manifests His Word through Mary, through her heart, as Jesus, His Anointed.[6]

The Virgin thus announces the Praised as recipient of the same Word she revealed as her son, Jesus, God's anointed. The same Word is revealed in two ways – in Jesus, the perfect man, and in the Recitation, revealed through the heart of the Praised.[7] It is inseparable from Mary as sign of perfect receptivity or maternity and from the Praised as the second aspect in the One's revelation through duality. As perfect, the Virgin and the Praised both receive and give the Word. In giving and receiving, they manifest the fullness of our nature.

Placing his blessed hands over the image of the Virgin and her Son, the Praised revealed the world as manifestation of Unity: the Anointed is part of the Recitation.

Mary and the Praised, dual principles of receiving and giving, female and male, left and right, manifest their indivisibility from Unity, Which they bear witness to and serve.[8] In their indivisibility, they are what they are – absolute humanity, through whom God reveals His Word, perfect and for perfection, sent down for our ascent. The mihrab turns us towards the Kaʿba, which signifies the heart. It contains their perfect humanity in and of the Word.

---

5 God said through the Praised: "My earth and My heaven embrace Me not, but the heart of My believing servant does embrace Me." (Related by Abū Ḥāmid al-Ghazālī, *Iḥyāʾ ulūm al-dīn*, 3:12.) This well-known tradition is cited by almost every Sufi author, but the chain of transmission from the Praised is not well attested (see Chittick, *The Sufi Path of Knowledge*, 107).

6 See *Qur'an*, 4:171.

7 Ibid., 26:192–94.

8 Mary is often portrayed with her Son on the altar of the churches of Eastern Christianity. She wears a blue mantle, while the Son is sometimes in white, sometimes in gold. The Virgin thus represents the whole of creation at the centre of which is the Word made manifest.

CHAPTER 19

The Debt

Nothing is more evident than that all things owe their existence to the Creator. Nothing can be its own cause or there would be no world order to satisfy our need to understand.

If all things owe their existence to God, they are in His debt. This debt is the Word. With the Word as Unity and multiplicity, things receive form, time and place. The path from each thing leads towards the Word as source and principle. The Word is originally with God.

All existence and everything in it owe a debt to God, the Only Creditor, Who creates and guides the worlds as His manifestation. Their entire debt is summed up in us:

> Belongs not the sincere debt to God?[1]
>
> He has laid down for you as a debt that He charged Noah with, and that We have revealed to thee, and that We charged Abraham with, Moses and Jesus: "Do the debt, and scatter not regarding it." Very hateful is that for the associators, that thou callest them to. God chooses unto Himself whomsoever He will, and He guides to Himself whosoever turns, penitent.[2]
>
> They desire to extinguish with their mouths the light of God; but God will perfect His light, though the concealers be averse. It is He who has sent His apostle with the guidance and the debt of truth, that he may uplift it above every debt, though the concealers be averse.[3]
>
> That which you serve, apart from Him, is nothing but names yourselves have named, you and your fathers; God has sent down on authority touching them. Judgment belongs only to God; He has commanded that you shall not serve any but Him. That is the right debt; but most men know not.[4]
>
> Today have I perfected your debt for you, and I have completed My blessing upon you, and I have approved being-at-peace for your debt.[5]

1 *Qur'an*, 39:3.

2 Ibid., 42:13.

3 Ibid., 61:8–9.

4 Ibid., 12:40.

5 Ibid., 5:3.

 DOI 10.1163/9789004279407_022

> And Abraham charged his sons with this and Jacob likewise: "My sons, God has chosen for you the debt; see that you die not save in peace."[6]

We are just if we confess Truth, for God is Truth.[7] Justice is how the just relate to God as Just. It is manifest as human action, from perception and thought to opposition and construction in the world. Action out of ignorance is unjust, but full knowledge is beyond us. Imperfect knowledge is not in itself unjust, but it is unjust to suppose incomplete knowledge to be perfect and act on that basis. The more ignorant we are, the more violent and disorderly.

Knowing that our knowledge's limits are part of our humanity and that only the Creator knows all stimulates us to humility and generosity and a need to know the One, draw closer to Him and grow in knowledge. Humility, being-at-peace and generosity are impulses to knowledge of an undeniable reason to love the Good and Beautiful, the infinite source of goodness and beauty in the self.

Truth is in all things. Its affirmation depends on the state of the self, whose potential to recognize Truth in all things is its original nature.

We learn to confess no god but God and the Praised as His apostle from teachers and authorities, but this witness originally exists in the self's uncreated centre, Intellect, our common nature, the Spirit God breathed into Adam. This knowledge is our common but several nature. Learning it from an external source is to be reminded, a stimulus towards what we all possess in our uncreated core, our original knowledge of the names received in Spirit.

To realize our humanity is to affirm from the self's centre that the signs in world and self are an account of Truth. If we are what we confess, no attained state can exhaust what the centre receives. The apostle is our best example, guided and guiding, the sum of all our aspirations to life and happiness, our highest potential in relating to God through trust and faith. When we are faithful, God is All-faithful.

God said: "The prophet is nearer to the believers than their selves."[8] He meant that the prophet and apostle is the self's highest possibility, our goal in loving God. Loving God means drawing ever closer to Him. As the apostle is always a higher potential, drawing nearer to the Beloved means following the apostle. This is no this-worldly journey. It is discovery of the apostle as our highest potential in ascent along the upright path.

---

6 Ibid., 2:132.

7 See *Qur'an*, 22:62.

8 *Qur'an*, 33:6.

The Praised is within us, our immaculate centre. His discourses, disposition and sublime morality were informed by the Spirit of Truth God sent down into his heart, as He told us: "How can you conceal, seeing you have God's signs recited to you, and His apostle among you?",[9] and: "But God would never chastise them, with thee among them; God would never chastise them as they begged forgiveness."[10] The Praised wrote that the self is one:

> God has not assigned to any man two hearts within his breast; nor has He made your wives, when you divorce, saying, "Be as my mother's back," truly your mothers, neither has He made your adopted sons your sons in fact. That is your own saying, the words of your mouths; but God speaks the truth, and guides on the way.[11]

This centre is manifest by countless unique expressions of life, will, power, knowledge, speech, hearing and sight, differently each moment. All our individuality does not exhaust Unity. Existence is Unity's varying image, an image in constant flux whose understanding in the self also constantly changes. The world's image is never twice the same in the same person, nor at any moment the same in two different people.

Whenever speech is linked to the centre, heart or Intellect, it is with Truth and manifest as such. The lie lacks connection to the centre, mistaking the unreal for the source. The self's second heart is a lie. Just as there is no god but God, there is no heart but the Heart. When we take a heart for something other than the Heart, we take for a god what is not God.

Intellectual truth is one, from and for always. Its various expressions require no external authority, which serves only to recall what is in the self. As William C. Chittick has written:

> [...] according to the masters of the intellectual tradition, you cannot gain intellectual understanding by listening to others or reading books. You have to find it in yourself. Nonetheless, it is useful to listen to what the great teachers have to say in order to grasp the nature of their quest. When we do listen to them, we find that they agree on a large number of points, though they tend to use a diversity of expressions.[12]

---

9 Ibid., 3:101.

10 Ibid., 8:33.

11 Ibid., 33:4.

12 Chittick, *Science of the Cosmos, Science of the Soul*, 31.

What is manifests Unity as Principle. All things come from Him, return to Him, depend wholly on Him; He on nothing. This dependency is absolute. God gives creation and guidance to what exists.[13] He breathed Spirit into us[14] and taught us the names.[15] Everything in the world has its image in us. Images are constantly being differentiated and sent out from the uncreated centre, the heart, and constantly returning to one centre, without which no sign is real. The heart is source and confluence; Unity is manifest perfectly in it, and, however concealed or obscured, return is always possible. Our aspiration to life and happiness is recollection of this lost but recoverable potential in the self.

Our unique position in creation, which derives from the trust God offered and we accepted, means there must be two free wills, our and His. Otherwise, there could be no trust. Our free will is manifest as our sublime potential when the self confesses no will but the Will, no self but the Self. Realizing this is our willing return to God.[16] Finding peace in Him, we return to God beyond existence, in love and felicity, realizing ourselves in the affirmation of His unity and the apostolate of the Praised.

God said that the noblest of us is who is most conscious of Him.[17] We are all conscious in different ways, uniquely reflecting the Absolute in creation. We contain something no other element of creation has, something unique and of inestimable value.

That the self's condition is unique means each self is equivalent to all. The Absolute guarantees their individual value. We have nothing of our own, as it is all from our Creator. We are at every instant indebted for existence and awareness, which is a never-ceasing flux. The self captures something of that flux, always the same, always unrepeatable. Consciousness is never the same for two moments or two people. At any given moment our consciousness manifests all of existence, but in entirely new and different ways in each of us.

Divine creation is not in the remote past, but our being in every moment. Nothing repeats. Everything is ever renewed, including our grasp of Unity, which is not transposed from world or self, but in each of us at every instant, in different, unrepeatable ways, confirmed by multiplicity's flux.

After breaching the limits imposed by God, Adam began to stitch leaves to cover himself.[18] He and wife Eve now saw their nakedness and tried to conceal themselves. Visibility of the self is the converse of awareness of the

---

13 See *Qur'an*, 20:50.

14 Ibid., 15:29.

15 Ibid., 2:31.

16 Ibid., 3:83.

17 Ibid., 49:13.

18 Ibid., 7:22.

debt. Aware, we are turned towards our Creditor, seeing ourselves in Him, Him in us. When we lose sight of this, we seek our principle in ourselves and obscure our knowledge. Adam could not hide from God, Who knows all. Adam's awareness was concealed after breaching the limits laid down. In his turn to his self, he affirmed a self other than the Self.

To discover the self is to turn from self to Self. Wherever we are, we can always turn to ourselves in debt, restoring our bond with Him in Whose debt we are. As creatures, we can never satisfy that debt. We can only be conscious of it, always, everywhere, in every thought and deed. Self-discovery in debt is our response to God's question: "Where art thou?" God does not ask to find out, but because it is crucial for our knowledge of God. Being aware Who asks and what He is asking and replying to Him allows any place to be a valley to ascend from, since ascent begins at the time and place when and where we respond to that question.

The Praised reports God saying to Moses: "Moses, I am thy Lord; put off thy shoes; though art in the holy valley, Towa. I Myself have chosen thee; therefore give thou ear to this revelation. Verily I am God; there is no god but I; therefore serve Me, and perform the prayer of My remembrance."[19] Knowing our place as unmediated contact with the earth and being aware of it at every instant are that response to the question "Where art thou?" It is the turn to the self, descent and ascent, the discovery that all things are created with Truth and that we discover Truth by determining what belongs to it independently of the created, the recognition that everything is "in the name of God, the All-merciful, the Ever-merciful."

Confessing God's unity and the Praised's apostolate, we turn to our higher potential. We are not turning from ourselves, but striving to realize ourselves in ourselves on our only possible stage, the Real. The debt to God is to ourselves, any debt to ourselves a debt to God. Honouring the debt is to stand our ground and find our reason for existence.

We may imitate what is in and beyond existence, but not Truth. This is why our being is the epitome of creation at all times and in every place, as there is nothing that is not created with Truth. Even when the inner self is deformed to the limit, we cannot destroy our own creation with Truth. Our creation gives us unique and indestructible value. It enables us to repay our debt to God, despite the poverty of our original nature.

Awareness of our poverty lets us see His gift in all things and their claims. All things in existence have claims on us. Recognizing them, we recognize our own debt to God and may realize our only right: to return to the Absolute and realize ourselves in perfection.

---

19 *Qur'an*, 20:11–14.

Postlude: Finding the Sacred Centre

God sent prophets to all nations[1] with His tidings in their languages.[2] Despite all the forms it can take, prophecy's principle is one – the maternal prophet they swore their oath to in pre-existence. A prophet's heart contains only the knowledge God gave us all as our original covenant of Lordship and service. Their knowledge is realized and clarified to remind us of that covenant.

Prophecy belongs to all peoples and languages. It fits our original nature. In pre-existence we bore witness to His lordship[3] and the prophets remind us of this. Their every admonishment confesses the Praised, received from the Lord as maternal seal[4] in pre-existence.[5]

To confess the Praised is to confess God. He is our link between existence and the Creator.[6] All things can know this, existence manifests it, and God reveals in the Recitation: "We shall show them Our signs in the horizons and in themselves, till it is clear to them that it is the truth."[7] This clear knowledge is realized in acknowledging that all things reveal His unity and the Praised's apostolate. God and His apostle are the Reality of the self. Learned knowledge reminds us, but is not sufficient for self-realization. The Praised sums up the world and the prophets. Created with Truth, he confirms every sign in history. The Recitation records:

> He has laid down for you as debt that He charged Noah with, and that We have revealed to thee, and that We charged Abraham with, Moses and Jesus: "Honour the debt, and scatter not regarding it." Very hateful is that for the concealers that thou callest them to. God chooses unto Himself whomsoever He will, and He guides to Himself whosoever turns, penitent."[8]

1 See *Qur'an*, 10:47.

2 Ibid., 14:4.

3 Ibid., 7:172.

4 Ibid., 33:40.

5 Ibid., 3:81.

6 Ibid., 33:56.

7 *Qur'an*, 41:53.

8 Ibid., 42:13.

 | DOI 10.1163/9789004279407_023

> He has sent down upon thee the Book with the Truth, sent down the Torah and the Gospel aforetime, as guidance to the people, and He sent down the Salvation.[9]

Every people and individual has always and will always realize knowledge through two confessions that manifest one Truth: God's unity and the Praised's apostolate, the only path to God:

> My chastisement – I smite with it whom I will; and My mercy embraces all things, and I shall prescribe it for those who are mindful and pay the alms, and those who indeed believe in Our signs, those who follow the apostle, the maternal prophet, whom they find written down with them in the Torah and the Gospel, bidding them to honour, and forbidding them dishonour, making lawful for them the good things and making unlawful for them the corrupt things, and relieving them of their loads, and the fetters that were upon them. Those who believe in him and succour him and help him, and follow the light that has been sent down with him – they are the prosperers.[10]

Following the Praised determines prosperity in two ways. First is our conduct in the world as the theatre of success, where "following the apostle," obeying his "bidding to honour and forbidding dishonour," "making lawful the good things and making unlawful the corrupt things," and "relieving us of our loads" are applied to nature, society, the political order and the cosmos. Second is following him as inner, return through the self to the world of angelic presence, the lost abode which the signs, prophets and revelations recall. This prosperity depends on realization in the angelic light of the self, the lost abode. Each of us returns to God alone.

The angels are created of light and circle the Throne of God, the Light of the heavens and the earth. Those who follow the light of the Praised follow the angels. His Throne is in the heart, and the Kaʿba and the circuit remind us of our covenant with Him, Who revealed His lordship to us directly and entered a covenant with us by revelation. As He said, He sent the Kaʿba into the world as a sign of return to that perfect state, lost with the original covenant: "God has appointed the Kaʿba, the holy house, as an establishment for men."[11]

---

9 Ibid., 3:3–4.

10 Ibid., 7:156–57. The difference in translation of the two verses given here from the translation given above serves to indicate possible differences of interpretation.

11 *Qur'an*, 5:97.

In the garden on the heights, an angel recalled Adam to the covenant. God trusted that angel with swallowing the record of our covenant and obtaining renewal each year. Thus, we confirmed our share in the glorification of God as King.

When Adam forgot the covenant, ate the fruit, and fell from the garden, he forgot his oath as the light of his self's very core. God turned to him[12] and sent down that forgotten angel as a white pearl. All Adam saw was a stone, so God let the pearl speak:

> "O Adam, do you recognize me?"
>
> "No."
>
> "Surely Satan has triumphed within you, since he makes you forget the memory of your Lord."
>
> At this point the pearl regains its original form of the angel who was Adam's companion in the Garden, asking, "Where are your promises and your undertaking?"
>
> Adam awakes, recognition of God's covenant is coming back to him and he weeps. He kisses the white pearl, angel, and renews his agreement to the covenant.[13]

Adam was told to visit the house, that the knowledge and rituals of his return might be revealed. He took the pearl, which God now made seem a Black Stone, and Gabriel guided him and helped him carry it. This is how Adam came to Becca. He was shown how to renew his covenant and return to God, to show us how we can renew our original covenants with God.

The Black Stone built into the Iraqi corner of the Kaʿba reminds us of our covenant with God, our better angel, the light in the self, what makes the Praised our best example, the original Garden, and the sublime height for which the ritual of return holds the key.

Our senses cannot see the angel of the white pearl, the constant reminder of our original covenant. They see a Black Stone. Break the bounds of the mihrab to rise above it and the white pearl reveals itself as our centre. Through it, we know our Lord. Discovering the pearl, we remember our witness to that covenant. When the covenant became a burden and we grew weary and fell into forgetfulness, God sent His angel Gabriel to relieve us of our burden.

---

12 See *Qur'an*, 2:37.

13 A saying of the Sixth Imam, Ja'far al-Ṣādiq, cited in Majlisī, *Biḥār al-anwār*, 7:339; in Corbin, *Temple and Contemplation*, 237.

Every one of Adam's descendants must make that journey to the Kaʿba and perform the ritual of circumambulation, to lead him to the forgotten self and enter his original nature. Each of us must rebuild the house in spirit to reach that centre, discover the secret of the Black Stone and the mystery of the angel. The Black Stone, which pilgrims kiss as they pass, represents for the material Kaʿba what the angel does for us. This is the meaning of the journey to and entry into the house, through the mihrab of passage from the material world to the spiritual house.

PART 2

The Time of the World and the Time of the Self

Hagar and Mary as Images of Maternity

• •

•••

Jesus said: If those who lead you say to you:
"See, the Kingdom is in heaven," then the birds
of the heaven will precede you. If they say to you:
"It is the sea," then the fish will precede you.
But the Kingdom is within you and it is without you.
If you know yourselves, then you will be known
and you will know that you are the sons of
the Living Father. But if you do not know yourselves,
then you are in poverty and you are poverty.

THE GOSPEL ACCORDING TO THOMAS, 3

∴

Prelude on Human Perfection

Traditional teachings tell us redemption and self-discovery are conditional on confessing God's unity, the Praised's apostolate, and universal return to God. The first two are conditions of the third, as the Praised is just a name for the perfect sign of perfected humanity, inseparable from confession of Unity.

The Praised's name is part of the world as a signifying whole. It has a corresponding translation in every language, as the One's first manifestation, but people have recently become accustomed to two Arabic forms, *Muḥammad* and *Aḥmad*, and come to neglect his eternal presence at all times and all regions and even in their own languages.

The discovery and realization of most beautiful humanity is the primary intention or core of God's self-revelation. All existence derives from or proceeds towards it, much as the tree from the fruit. The first and last in creation is related to the possibility that a consequence may be a cause, a cause a consequence, as a decisive aspect of liberation from confinement within mono-perspective.

Being in the world is witness of difference – between us and what is outside us, a difference that is conditional and conditioned, because the world is in us, just as we are in it. No boundary gives this difference the aspect of clear-cut duality. Both world and we manifest the same essence in ways both similar and different. The self comprises everything in the worlds, while being parallel to them. Understanding our reason and purpose requires that we see past this apparent contradiction.

Viewed from our perspective, the external world must, due to extension, have limits. We relate to it within them through sensory cognition. The things and horizons of the world may be seen, heard, grasped, loved, and experienced and we can develop assumptions and images of them and our relationships to and with them. What is within these spaces has measure and proportion and may be attributed quantity. We relate to it through comparison, measurement and analytical rationality.

However dispersed and durable the things of the world, we cannot think of them or it without assigning limits. Our rational capacity, comparison and quantification, extends to those limits, but the world does not recognize them. It stops at them in one form, begins in another. Analytical reason cannot comprehend the world beyond those quantifiable limits, but Intellect, the integrative principle of creation as intended by the Creator, comprehends all.

Intellect does not depend on any particularity. All are contained within it. It is like the unifying point from which all rays of light originate, to which they

 | DOI 10.1163/9789004279407_024

return, and in which they meet again. Analytical reason relates to this dispersion and re-gathering, as external to the integrative principle. However minute that point may appear compared to the universe, it is immeasurably more comprehensive than the external.

The visible world renders the invisible manifest, two aspects in which the One regards and reveals Himself. All the visible signs are linked to the reality of that other world. Through them, we can conceive of its reality. These worldly signs, like their archetypes in the invisible world, have a certain pre-existence within perfected humanity, which is coeval with Intellect, and both aspects function to manifest what is already present within us.

The external world holds nothing whose name we do not know. Truth, as the principle of creation, is our and their master. All things abide with Truth, making It manifest, belonging to It. Integral humanity contains all these things in the integrated self, both as essences and names known from the beginning and as the forms given them in space and time.

Each thing within the world and in difference recalls its presence in the self, where it is brought together and gathered with the rest. This is our debt to them, their claim on us. Their claim comes from accepting spatial and temporal form and so recalling what lies within us from the beginning. All existence is reflected in us in one way, while we are reflected in existence in another. This pair is indestructible, because through it the One reveals Itself.

Our knowledge of the names determines our having been created as existence's epitome. All existence lies within us, because, as the Creator intended, the names precede manifestation. We can know them and are treasure houses of their faculty of appearance, of coming into and leaving existence. Each thing thus reveals a name or attribute of the Creator.

God's names are most beautiful and all things participate in their own way in the perfect order of His self-revelation. Names lord over things. Existing in the world, they are subject to a different time than that of the self. Gathered within the intellectual centre of the self is like being in the eternal now.

The things within the world are dispersed from nearest to furthest. Places and times correspond, as measures of relationship, to these proximities or distances. Neither space nor time exists in the absence of things which take up space. One may trace a path from thing to thing in more or less time and speak of very short or very long time periods and distances. Differences in speed, different time periods and different paths correspond to different phenomena. Neither space nor time exists apart from beings. All things, including nearness and remoteness, take on different meanings and magnitudes within the self. Everything dispersed in worldly time and space comes together within the self.

As we discover all the names within the self, we realize our nature as in God's image, as the servant in whom He is manifest as Lord. While the worlds reveal Him in extension, even in concert they are not masters of all the names. They have no free will and are not related by trust to the Creator they reveal. They renounced their will and subordinated their existence to His. They possess neither oblivion nor love, but are absolutely subject to being-at-peace. God is revealed within them as Lord and Peace. Ultimately they gather within our form of being, but we have more than that.

As creatures, we do not possess full knowledge. The knowledge in us is always and necessarily small compared with His, but nonetheless sufficient for us to love Him Who irresistibly attracts us and to stimulate our return. No return is possible, however, without original perfection as a pure image in which God regards Himself. Our growth in knowledge is potentially boundless, insofar as it leads to ascent to the higher self. The disclosure of our potential and our original knowledge of all the names is growth in knowledge and return to God.

Coming to know God through His creation, we come to know His beautiful names in their various manifestations. He reveals Himself through beauty and attracts all who know Him, so that He and the knower love each other, because love is the mutual attraction of lovers. Knowledge with love of the known is faith, which is the path of return, the realization of the self in the Self.

Faith is crucial for return, as the connection that links the faithful with the God of Faith. God's faithfulness abides with absolute knowledge and absolute love, ours relies on little knowledge and on the love that transcends and comprehends all knowledge. This love connects us with the Beautiful Who sees Himself in it. It manifests as irresistible attraction, as the image seeks to identify with Him Whom it reveals. This is the desire of the self to draw near to God and so its own self, to see with ever-increasing clarity Him we love and to love with ever great force Him we see. When He told the angels He would create us His viceroys on earth, God called the worlds and their meanings a stage our creation would complete. Humanity, created from clay, with its knowledge of the names, brings together all the worlds. We carry within all the forms of knowledge as part of our authentic perfection, as Rumi said:

> The father of mankind, who is the lord of "He taught the Names,"
> hath hundreds of thousands of sciences in every vein.
> To his soul accrued (knowledge of) the name of every thing,
> even as that thing exists (in its real nature) unto the end (of the world).[1]

---

1 Rūmī, *The Mathnawī*, 1:1234–1235.

Adam, our common father, was originally perfect, but his archetype was the Praised, the reason and purpose of creation. Asked when he was created, the Praised said: "When Adam was between spirit and body."[2] This is why he is Adam's maternal principle as well as ours, his appearance in time just a confirmation that he is perfect redeeming light even at our nadir.

Able to rise up in knowledge, we reveal the Creator's perfect intention, higher and more sublime than we, who are finite thanks to our endowment with space and time in the world of things. His intention is prior to manifestation, the reason and purpose of all that manifests it. Every manifestation is a sign sent down from higher to lower. Perfect humanity is on a higher level, as Intellect, Spirit, or Light. Everything that descends into existence is brought together in this perfect humanity, our principle and the goal of our return.

Adam is the Praised's first perfect manifestation. The world and Adam are perfect, everything in his self visible in the things outside, and vice versa. Before he violated the one restriction in paradise, Adam's self knew no distinctions. Everything arose from it and with regard to it. This is the import of confessing the light and spirit of the perfect individual as first and foremost of God's self-manifestation.

Perfect humanity is the principle and essence of each individual. We all contain a treasure house of the hidden and disclosed Creator. Through witness to His Unity, we discover ourselves in our perfect potential. This potential is our maternal and most sublime principle. Incarnate in existence, it becomes a sign of spirit. All the prophets bore witness to it and the light of the Praised is its eternal essence.

In this vision, time and space take on different meaning. Fully comprehended within the perfect self, they correspond to the all-encompassing day. The path towards this gathering is in the self alone. The name for finding it and returning is the Praised, who links the self at its highest with the worlds.

As soon as God reveals Himself, the worlds praise Him as All-praised. Focused in its own absolutely pure image, the act of praise appears as perfect humanity. Descent and dispersal of the signs within the world's horizons denote the self-revelation of the One within duality. He has no other and duality has no reality aside from Him. Existence is a night in witness of the Light dark cannot destroy.

The descent or self-differentiation of the One into countless things through which to reveal Itself continues to the furthest boundary, but never passes beyond His knowledge or His mercy, for there is nothing real but the Real. Our

2 Ibn Ḥanbal, 4:66, 5:59, 379.

essential knowledge of the names lets us comprehend the entire world of difference, but we are split between absolute light and absolute dark. Not even there, in the depths of the dark, do we lose our original humanity, because the truth of our creation cannot be undone.

Sending down His revelation into the dark, God initiated our capacities, which are from always and forever. The Word descended that all who achieve self-realization might leave the dark for authentic fullness. Earth is a sign of our baseness, heaven of the height. Two signs on earth correspond to this – the inviolable place of self-abnegation in the Valley and the further one on the Mount. The path of ascent is passage from matter to spirit, from the inviolable to the further place of self-abnegation. Each stage on that path represents a possible condition of the self. Journey's end lies in none of them, for the goal is the One.

When God said He sent down the Recitation at night into the heart of the Praised, it was to rise up and pass through all the levels of existence in accordance with the confession of no self but the Self and the Praised as His apostle. This experience of receiving what is sent down in order to rise up and return produces recognition of our capacity to discover perfection as what is closest to us and so find our Lord. Following perfection, we embark on a path of redemption, of discovering the Praised within as the most beautiful model of our primordial nature and the seal of creation. Rumi wrote:

> So it is realized that the Praised was the foundation. "But for thee I would not have created the heavens." Everything that exists, honour and humility, authority and high degree, all are of his dispensation and his shadow, for all have become manifest from him.[3]

We are unrelated to world or God except through the self. In discovering our own pure essence, we discover the signs in world and self as Truth's discourse. Nothing serves our redemption but the self's essence, nor will God accept us without it, as the worlds were created for it. God told the Praised:

> They swear to you by God, to please you; but God and His apostle – more right is it they should please Him, if they are believers. Do they not know that whosoever opposes God and His apostle – for him awaits the fire of Gehenna, therein to dwell forever? That is the mighty degradation.[4]

---

3 Arberry, *Discourses of Rūmī*, 117.

4 *Qur'an*, 9:62–63.

The nocturnal descent of the Book through the Holy Spirit and the self's ascent confirm the perfection of the reason we were created. The Garden, the condition of the self that has achieved peace and is pleasing to the Creator, corresponds to rising under guidance. The duality of dark and light or of bliss and suffering are done away with. The alternative is the fires of hell and a condition of the self in which the passions and suffering predominate.

We can always choose to approach either paradise or hell. To draw closer to paradise is to follow the Praised and to accept that the essence of the self, its authentic perfectibility, is always at a higher level than we are. The goal of return lies outside of place and time, as it is a passage through all the darkness to the day that comprehends all things. Thus, humanity is simply being on the axis, on the upright path, the very possibility that we may rise out of a given condition to a higher one.

Two further possibilities are open to us – to descend to the lowest level of the self or to wander within one level of existence. When perfectibility is denied within a self, it is forced to descend further and further from the One to Whom all things return. All suffering proceeds from the opposition between these forms of action, one from our very core, the other from its denial.

The beasts are of the Creator's this-worldly signs and we are beasts. We differ from them and all existence only in our ability to descend or rise. Hell and the garden are the extremes of these processes. While the other animals realize themselves on one level, we can realize ourselves only through a ceaseless striving to rise between levels until we reach the One.

The two forms of time, of the self and of the world, are inextricably linked, just like the self and the world. All the worlds are brought together and gather in the perfect self, as do all forms of time. Our self-realization is in the now, through the union of the external forms of time in our essence. All conflict with ourselves, the world, and God arises out of the supposition that these two forms of time can be separated.

CHAPTER 1

On Self and World

The tenets on divine unity and the apostolate of the perfect individual as reason and end of existence make a whole that encompasses witness and witnessed. If the whole is in constant flux, yet remains one as revelation of the One, we reflect it, being and abiding with it in constant flux. Our understanding is confirmed by the presence of the object of our witness. We belong to existence and encompass it. To reveal the whole requires both us and existence.

Existence gathers in the perfection of the apostle. Sent by the whole, his beginning and end are the One. We experience perfection as a potential at a certain remove, to which we can nonetheless return as to the reason and end of our being in the world. The Praised guarantees this possibility, as maternal, sealing principle – a name for our original condition, our having been sent into the world, and our capacity to return from alienation to the principle.

The One is absolute. His abundance is replete with life, will, power, knowledge, discourse, hearing, and vision, goodness, beauty, glory, praise, mercy, wisdom, and justice. In Unity, this abundance is His names in absolute indistinction. He is absolutely Self. Nothing can receive His abundance of praise or return the received, unless He manifests Himself to Himself. Creation is the revelation of His being Praised.

Creation is thus praised, as He praises and knows Himself as Praised through His revelation. What reveals God as All-praised must somehow be with Him, absolutely close, but also different and absolutely remote. This fullness of revelation is our highest potential – the Praised as God's intention in whom all of existence gathers.

Our exile in the strange land of existence and our return to our perfect place of origin both require God. He is concealed in and by His fullness. His love for Himself is His desire to be manifest. Realizing it requires differentiation and distinction in which the One nonetheless remains One, showing Itself in and through duality, as Creator in His creation. His creation reveals Him as Lord and serves Him perfectly. Perfect Lordship produces perfect service as it is only through service that Lordship appears.

Return from alienation comprehends existence in its perfection, from the One as first confirmation of the Ineffable to the lowest degree of distinction and back to the One. At each level, whether in ascent or descent, perfect humanity provides the measure and best example. We were given knowledge

 | DOI 10.1163/9789004279407_025

of the names.[1] The perfect individual recognizes their dispersion in the world and provides a focus for them in his own self, informed by the witness to no self but the Self.

With God concealed, His names are indistinct and undifferentiated. They desire to be manifest, things to name and be named by. The Beloved needs a lover, the lover a Beloved. Their love connects them. God is absolute Self. Any self that loves Him is a means of revelation of the Self. God knows each self absolutely, in all its original potential. He loves it, as His creature, leading it from Himself to Himself.

A thing's name is its master in the flux. Through their names, things gather in the One, Who is without other.[2] This gathering affects all things through which He reveals Himself to Himself: the One in the many and the many in the One. Coming from the One to the many and returning entails discovering all the names within the self, so that God sees Himself in us, we ourselves in Him.

No self is barred access to the full range of possibilities, from the perfect principle to maximum remoteness. They are laid out on the path from the principle toward the depth. They have corresponding possibilities in the cosmos. This experience of downward motion frames our actions of focusing, finding ourselves, and returning to authentic unity. This is why we are all involved in each other's experiences, in their stories. The self faces options on this path that are neither new nor old. They have always been and will always be. Their stage, time and place lend them alternate form.

Everyone knows the story of Abraham, who abandoned home and kin for God, to discover his authentic nature and reconcile his will to the Lord's. However remote in history the events or different the variants and interpretations, the story retains its impact from age to age. It speaks to the inner self and only the self searching for its authentic nature can remedy the obscurities due to transmission.

Abraham went from Ur, where he was born, to Haran, a city far to the northwest. Obedient to God's call,[3] he set off again towards the south and, wandering, arrived in Egypt. From there he later returned and settled in Hebron, whence he sent out both posterities, one south, the other north.

Hebron is south of Jerusalem, but north of Mecca. Medina also lies approximately on this north-south line. Abraham sent his posterity by Hagar and Ishmael from Hebron to Mecca and his posterity by Sarah and Isaac towards

1 See *Qur'an*, 2:31.

2 Ibid., 6:163.

3 See *Genesis*, 15:7.

Jerusalem. The two key symbols within these towns are the Inviolable and the Further places of self-abnegation, one at the bottom of a valley, the other atop a hill. There is constant coming and going between them, ascending and descending, and circuits made around them, confirming their link to the One through the axis of existence and the path of universal return.

The inviolability of the Becca Mosque marks the limits of our fall, the extremity from which our covenant is renewed, opening up our path back along the arc of ascent towards our authentic creaturehood, the pure nature represented by the maternal prophet and his fulfilment of humanity.

The remoteness of the mosque on the Mount marks our openness to return in ascent to finest rectitude or uprightness, realizing absolutely the maternal nature through which the Lord is revealed in His servant, the servant in his Lord. The mosque is on a hill crowned by a rock. Many ways lead from the depths to the peak. All meet at a single point, their Orient. The rock symbolizes our original uprightness, the beginning from which we descended to the depths, the peak as goal of ascent and return to the One.

This pair of buildings symbolizes the split in the self between dark and light. To realize the self by confessing the Self is to ascend. We must first recognize the depths and find the Ray of light that is our guarantee that God abides with us, wherever we are, before may ascend the upright path through the levels of existence, from multiplicity to the One, from the sensory world to what transcends it.

In his travels Abraham was accompanied by Sarah and their followers. He sought confirmation in events of God's promise to be his Guide and return them to Himself, to fulfil the purpose of their creation. He expected this in his descendants. Abraham stood between principle and consequences, the one revealing the other, so that everything that passed within him or in the world was out of love for the principle and its consequences. Even in old age, he trusted in God's guarantee – in His oath as All-faithful to the faithful amongst us. His dedication was realized, as the impossible became possible.

Abraham's love for God was reflected in his desire to see himself through God and for God to see Himself through Abraham. Abraham was born, his Beloved was not. In his attraction to Sarah, he saw a revelation of God, to Whom all beauty belongs. His love of God was tested by the lack of a child, a third, through whom God might be revealed as First and Last. God delayed this confirmation, testing His beloved to cleave to his vision of the as yet invisible.

The Egyptian bondwoman Hagar is also part of his story. She was given to Sarah in their Egyptian exile. Unable to bear that her connection with her beloved husband was yet unconfirmed, Sarah gave Hagar to her husband Abraham to be his second wife and to bear a child as their heir and confirm them as a revelation of the One within duality.[4] But they were three, not two, and no confirmation was possible. Only pairs reveal the One, as mother and father are a pair in relation to their child, who is a sign of the One revealed in duality. Sarah desired Hagar's child, but also to exclude its mother.

Hagar did not will her flight or wanderings. Others did. She was bound in destiny to Abraham, who freely left his kin and home to dedicate himself to God's guidance, accepting that His friendship should govern his fate and witnessing his Lord by accepting His yoke and erecting his halls in an alien land.

When Hagar conceived, her mistress drove her from those halls, in envy and in anger. In the desert, beside a well, she turned to heaven in despair and an angel appeared and announced the birth of a son to be named "God has listened." Submitting to the One, she returned to her husband's halls, only to be driven off again with her newborn son.

Abraham, whose only desire was to trust in God's will, accepted their expulsion. For him, the unknown paths he put his wife Hagar and son Ishmael on did not lead to the dark, but towards the Face of God Who knows all in His infinite mercy, the Light of the heavens and the earth.[5]

In the desert of Paran, Hagar and Ishmael reached the dry infertile valley of Becca and the ruins of the first house raised on earth. They ran out of water and the mother left her dying son so as not to look upon his suffering. An angel again appeared to tell her that God had heard their sighs. He pointed to a spring at the boy's feet and repeated God's promise of a posterity to come from this suffering.

Their despair and sufferings in fact uncapped the spring at the house. The axis was revealed to them that links the lowest depth with heaven, the upright path from the worlds of exile to the garden of our original home. Unthinkable suffering transformed exile, wandering, and abandonment into entry, settling, and finding the fruit for and from which the tree of existence was planted. Servitude, exile, and suffering were turned to liberation, sanctuary, and blessedness.

Their story relates to our condition of coming and going, entering and exiting, bringing in and expelling, loss and recovery. Full awareness of our humanity means accepting this continuous process of sojourning in strange lands, between two poles of existence, one fixed in damnation, the other in redemption. The same story is told by the unbroken procession from Sarah and Isaac to the Virgin Mary and her son. Whatever the apparent differences, these two

---

4 See *Qur'an*, 6:163

5 Ibid., 24:35.

currents are inextricable: each guarantees the other, being revealed in and through it.

In the inner kernel of the story of Abraham, his progeny through Hagar and Sarah, humanity's loss in the darkness of the self and recovery in the light that transcends every particular, we see the same pattern as in the stories of Hannah, the prophet Samuel's mother, of Elizabeth's infertility and God's promise of a son in old age, and of the Virgin Mary and her Son.

When Gabriel told Mary the Holy Spirit would descend and the power of the Almighty cover her with its shadow and she would bear a son,[6] she praised God: "He hath holpen His servant Israel, in remembrance of His mercy; – As he spake to our fathers, to Abraham, and to his seed for ever."[7]

Her encounter with Gabriel as a perfect man and her realization through the revelation of the Word in her son Jesus and the Praised's encounter with the same Archangel and his realization through the Recitation as the Word should be seen as imaginally simultaneous, as part of a history of the self that brings together all space and time. In saying that God caused Jesus to ascend or took the Praised to Himself during the night, we recall the perfection of the self that comprehends all existence and all times. The Virgin Mary praised God as All-praised, revealing the Praised as the maternal principle through which she discovered her openness to mercy. The Praised told the Archangel he did not know how or what to recite, signifying his desire to receive and pass on the Word.

Supposing Gabriel took the form of the Praised in appearing to the Virgin, one recalls the ancient Bosnian tradition that he appeared to the Praised as the Virgin:

> When the angel came down to the Praised,
> he approached him gently in the likeness of the virgin.
> Recite, O chosen one, O Praised,
> the faithful angel told him.
> The fair virgin embraced the Praised,
> and gave him her words into his heart.
> The Word that all the world be praised.[8]

---

6 See *Luke*, 1:34.

7 *Luke*, 1:54–55.

8 These seven verses are cited from a Bosnian text written in Arebica, a local adaptation of the Arabic script, in the manuscript book *Injil ayetleridir*. All the texts in this manuscript are in old Turkish, except the 56th page which contains Bosnian verses written consistently in Ekavian. The Praised and the Virgin are mentioned in these verses. Seven units end with the

The Virgin saw Gabriel as perfect man, the Praised saw him as perfect maid. They abide in perfect union in paradise, where God celebrated their wedding feast. Praising God, Mary mentioned Abraham and his posterity. Seeing the Virgin and the Praised progress from perfection towards the levels of manifestation, their relationship offers a key to the mystery of Sarah and Hagar revealing Abraham through their sons Ishmael and Isaac, who in turn affirm Abraham-Hagar and Abraham-Sarah.

---

verses "The Praised and the Virgin are our refuge." It was in part on the basis of the contents of this ancient Bosnian text that the author decided to use the name "Hval" as the Bosnian form of the Arabic name *Muḥammad/Aḥmad*, here translated as the Praised. Hval is a name form used in the Bosnian middle ages. The author had previously used a Bosnian adjectival form Hvaljeni, which is literally the Praised. The manuscript belonged to hajji Mujaga Merhemić (1877–1959).

CHAPTER 2

Departure and Return

The prophet Abraham is a key symbol of Jewish, Christian, and Muslim discourses of how we relate to God, as summed up in God's command and promise to Abraham:

> Leave your country, your people, and your father's household and go to the land I will show you. I will make you into a great nation and I will bless you. I will make your name great, and you will be a blessing. I will bless those who bless you, and whosoever curses you I will curse. And all peoples on earth will be blessed through you.[1]

At the heart of this discourse, which treats the drama of the self, is a highly dynamic symbol of importance for every metaphysically grounded tradition,[2] that has been developed into a myth embracing both the divine Revelation and the self understanding of the time-bound individual.

A kernel common to the many stories of Abraham is God's self-revelation to him, which transformed his understanding of kin and social affiliations. Saying: "I love not the things that go down,"[3] or appearances, he posed the question of the self that conceals nothing, neither going down nor disappearing. Exploring the self's connection with God, Abraham leaves one order of values, to enter another. The sacralised social order he was born into is revealed as a distortion of the truth of existence in its metaphysical, cosmological, anthropological, and psychological aspects.

---

1 *Genesis*, 12:1–3.

2 Many versions and interpretations have been developed of the Torah story of Abraham in both Jewish and Christian traditions. These stories receive fresh confirmation and new form in the *Qur'an*, as well as a fresh stream of reworkings and interpretations. For more on the treatment of Abraham and his son in the Muslim tradition, see, Ṭabarī, *Tā'rīkh al-rusul wa'l-mulūk*, 2:48–131; Kisā'ī, *Qiṣaṣ al-anbiyā'*, 136–59; Tha'labī, *'Arā'is al-majālis fī qiṣaṣ al-anbiyā'*, 124–73; Firestone, "Abraham's journey to Mecca in Islamic Exegesis: A form-critical study of a tradition," 5–24.

3 *Qur'an*, 6:76. This stage in Abraham's dramatic quest for the Lord within the horizons of the world is described thus: "Then, when the night overshadowed him with its darkness, he beheld a star; he exclaimed, 'This is my Lord!' – but when it went down, he said, 'I love not the things that go down.' "

 | DOI 10.1163/9789004279407_026

His native land has become an unacceptable order of evil. Those who desire salvation must leave their native land, turning flight into migration and returning to their authentic nature. That our revealed maternal and authentic nature is in irreconcilable conflict with the politics of kinship is true not just of Abraham's self, but of all creatures. Nowhere in the world or self do we find anything real that is not the Real, because there is nothing real but the Real. Our migration to the Real means leaving everything we know for what those things reveal as Real.

We inhabit a spatial cross, forward, backwards, left, right, up, down, which we cannot move outside. It is anchored in the self, entirely dependent upon the body, but with an external framework – east, west, north, south, zenith and nadir. We orient ourselves by harmonizing the cross in the self with the worldly one, normally by the rising sun.

The sun rises and lights up the horizons at the preordained time. The sun sets and dark falls. The roads on the earth's surface are open. The path of ascent and descent is different, a vertical axis to heaven. So we pray to God: "Guide us upon the upright path, the path of those whom You have favoured, and not of those against whom You are wroth or of those who are in errancy!"

To embark upon the upright path is to discover order within the self, of which the external horizons are signs. Our original, perfect nature and our confession of God's lordship over human service, in which the One is manifest, are like the Northern Star. East, west, north and south, zenith and nadir no longer refer to space, any more than dawn, day, twilight, night, and the Northstar refer to time as the external world knows it.

The self in gloom knows its position by the Northstar and can find its way back to its best potential. It finds succour in its authentic reason, its haven in heaven. To set off it must first orient itself, as God told the Praised: "It is not piety, that you turn your faces to the East and to the West."[4] The light in the darkness of the self is like "a niche wherein is a lamp (the lamp is a glass, the glass as it were a glittering star) kindled from a Blessed Tree, an olive that is neither of the East nor of the West."[5]

To realize the self means connecting with that tree not of east or west, since we require a lamp of perfect nature, a Northern Star in the night of the self. God told us: "From whatsoever place thou issuest, turn thy face towards the Holy Mosque. And wherever you may be, turn your faces towards it."[6]

---

4 *Qur'an*, 2:177.

5 Ibid., 24:35.

6 Ibid., 2:150.

In God's divine call we see all people turn towards the earthly sign in the desert valley. Countless paths lead to it, so that some journey east, others west or north or south. The sun rises and sets above it and it is placed in the centre to show we will find our star, not to east nor west, not rising or setting, but in that night of the self when the dark is thickest. By its light, the self find the perfect potential beyond all limits, the full union of the lights of the Praised and the Virgin.

The Inviolable Mosque marks the move from society to individual, from the passing to what stays, from the plane of existence to the axis of ascent. This meta-cosmic heaven, with its Northern Star, is within the self, of which the external world is a sign or image.

Just as the valley of the Kaʿba in the south and the hill of the Rock to the north mark the axis of ascent, so the west, where the sun goes down, and the east, whence it rises, signify the nature of ascent. The Real Orient is our goal, on the axis, where perfect humanity abides, atop the hill of the Self, covered by an eternal snow, from which the angels descend and to which they ascend.

Earthly east and sunrise, like earthly west and sundown, belong to the self's sensory exterior. The interior is in night. Its Orient is the Northstar, high above the world of darkness, in which the midnight sun rises, as God told the Praised:

> Behold, We sent it down on the Night of Power. And what shall teach thee what is the Night of Power? The Night of Power is better than a thousand months. In it the angels and the Spirit descend, by the leave of their Lord, upon every command. Peace it is, till the rising of dawn.[7]

God also says:

> *Ha. Mim.* By the therein Book, We have sent it down in a blessed night (We are ever warning) therein every wise bidding determined as a bidding from Us, (We are ever sending) as a mercy from thy Lord (surely He is the All-hearing, the All-knowing), Lord of the heavens and earth, and all that between them is, if you have faith.[8]

The Holy Spirit, the Spirit of Truth, descends from the suprasensible to the sensible world, from the heart of the Praised to his spirit or breath, becoming speech. The Word sent down linked the depths to the height that its recipient might arise and ascend: "Glory be to Him, who carried His servant by night

---

7 Ibid., 97:1–5.

8 Ibid., 44:1–7.

from the Holy Mosque to the Further Mosque the precincts of which We have blessed, that We might show him some of Our signs. He is the All-hearing, All-seeing."[9]

We are always between two extremes – the original and authentic light of the height and the deep dark of the depths. There are always two possibilities – to descend further or to turn back to the light. For the Praised, the prophet Abraham's myth is a perfect circle of descent and ascent, annunciation and realization, loss and finding. Being-at-peace brings Abraham to the perfect humanity of the person-of-peace at peace in God who is Peace.

At peace in this truth, Abraham accepted its guidance and judgment, transcending the kinship-based social order he inherited through no will of his own to enter another which is the will of the Creator and Governor of all things. Abraham left one world to return to another better fitted to our true nature. He destroyed the lie that the truth was immediately visible and left to be alone and await his deserts as a friend of the Most High.

Abraham's story reveals the discovery of the self as set between extremes – the primordial unity of the Creator's plan and the absolute dispersion of creation, the arc of descent and the arc of ascent, which together close the circle of existence so that everything in either heavens or self is seen to reveal the One.

Both ascent and descent are often sorted by receptive and donative, female and male aspects. This duality is how the One is revealed as the principle. The arcs frame creation in both its forms, cosmic and human. This whole is like a circle on which the prophets may be found, each connected to the centre and to all the other prophets. And there is only one centre.

Abraham as a key dynamic symbol and the entire mythic narrative of departure and return turn our attention to humanity as spread over time and divided into communities of kin and language, social and political orders with varying degrees of recollection of their perfect origin, an origin each and every self is capable of regaining.

Our one authentic homeland we yearn for all our lives. Not being what God is, we discover our duality and that of humankind. From duality's union a child is born, a sign of the One Who is neither begotten nor begetting. These memories have not faded entirely from any time, place or people. Within them and with them abides the truth of creation.

God sent apostles to all peoples to recall us to our authentic human nature in our own tongues and exhort us to abandon oblivion for recollection and seek the higher potential within. Despite the ages and languages and lands in

---

9 Ibid., 17:1.

which they taught and the responses of those they warned, the prophets did not waver from their maternal principle, our perfectibility as reason and end of creation.

Perfect nature is in us all and cannot be introduced from outside. The prophet's role is to remind us of it and return us from the depths to our original nature on the sublime height. The prophet knows that what is truly his is what he has received from the One, Who gives Himself out of His desire to be known. No prophet has ever spoken against the principle expressed by God to each and every prophet: "There is no god but I; so serve Me."[10]

God's unity is revealed through His names. All things in existence reveal and testify to one or more of them. The world is the stage of their dispersed revelation, but human beings focus them as images of our Creator. To discover our own selves is to discover our Lord, and vice versa. Leaving the world of appearance is to return to the self and the Lord, as commanded: "I will flee to my Lord."[11]

Our migration to the Lord is a return to our original condition. Completing it is our highest moment, thanks only to Him Who is revealed through the truth of creation as Truth. Perfect service to Him entails confessing His unity. All existence points to this confession in two parts, of God's unity and of the apostolate of perfect uprightness as maternal principle and the goal of creation. It contains the irrefragable truth of creation and of guidance by perfect reason to the perfect goal, the God Who gave us both creation and guidance.[12]

The gift of creation and guidance is revealed in the self that confesses no god but God and the Praised as His servant and apostle. The Praised manifests God the All-praised perfectly in both creation and guidance, standing for both the reason and purpose of creation. All the prophets, known and unknown, confess him, directing us, in a move from apparent to real, towards the Lord to Whom we are bound by the Praised in most beautiful uprightness.

Abraham's prophetic testament is a clear realization of service leading to the discovery of our created nature and the Creator's perfect guidance. Abraham left his kin and halls for strange roads and the guidance of the All-knowing. His journeys led him through fertile, pleasant plains, but also barren and wild desert lands with little water or sustenance, lands full of dangers and of enemies.

Some joined him, some left him. Stories of him endured with friend and enemy alike. A sign of our connection to God through perfection, he is known in his maternal aspect, his witness of the Praised as the maternal prophet and

---

10 Ibid., 21:25.

11 Ibid., 29:26.

12 See *Qur'an*, 20:50.

principle of human perfection: "Surely, Abraham was a maternal community obedient unto God, a man of pure faith and no associator, showing thankfulness for His blessings. He chose him, and He guided him to the upright path."[13] He was a maternal community as the fount of the peoples of God, who share God's gift as the basis of all community – their authentic nature.

Abraham left all his attachments, including his own self, for that other he was seeking. Leaving himself, he discovered himself and his Lord's image in each abandonment. No image satisfied, as he turned from those he had received, one by one. God revealed Himself through His names, as He is inscribed in the self, alongside His names. We must discover them, ourselves and our Lord.

Coming to know God through His names as innate to the self has no end. At no hour does He cease to reveal Himself in some way or form. The flux within creation offers new refuges and new exiles. Giving and receiving, ascending and descending, fleeing and taking refuge, moving and staying are under the presence of the One, Near and Far, Whose revelation never ceases. Each time we discover or realize one of His names within us, it links us to the others.

The Lord rules over His servants and the Creator reveals Himself in His creation, as it finds reality in Him. The One is manifest in two that love each other irresistibly, attracted and satisfied only by the constant return to the Self, which is always through another. Faithful, their faith connects them. Faith is the love of the known and the knowledge of the beloved. The Lord sees Himself in us, loves us for revealing Him. We love God, Who reveals Himself to us in all things, so that we recognise our love of God in what attract us.

The love shown through Sarah, Hagar, and Mary has two inseparable levels – one physical and visible, the other spiritual and invisible. The second is reached through the first. "For just as a divine Name can be known," Henry Corbin has written, "only in the concrete form of which it is the theophany, so a divine archetypal Figure can be contemplated only in a concrete Figure – sensible or imagined – which renders it outwardly or mentally visible."[14]

---

13 *Qur'an*, 16:120–21. *Maternal community* is used instead of the more common *nation*, as it is a closer translation of the Arabic noun *umma*.

14 Corbin, *Creative Imagination in the Sūfism of Ibn 'Arabī*, 139.

CHAPTER 3

In the Torah

Hagar's story is marked out in ways that make it a sort of mythic pattern for other narratives in the biblical books. God addresses her twice through His angel, at moments of tension which inform her ineradicable presence in prophetic wisdom. At the heart of this tension is a child – a third term to confirm the husband and wife pair and so the transcendence of duality.

Hagar was an Egyptian woman given to Abraham's wife Sarah as bondwoman. She figures strongly in Abraham's role as prophet. Her name signifies migration, separation, and the transition of the self from one earthly order to another. As a servant in Abraham's house, Hagar becomes his consort and the mother of his first son, producing tensions, separations, and departures. He took her for wife, however, at the suggestion of his barren first wife Sarah, who wanted a child from her.

Abraham saw and loved himself in Hagar, who mirrored the elements of his own orientation: service of the Beautiful, finding peace in Him on the path of return, and realizing inner lordship through His most beautiful names. Only in this way can one realize oneself in authentic service to God. As He says: "There is no one in the heavens and in the earth that does not come to the All-merciful as a servant"[1] and "in Him finds peace everything in the heavens and in the earth."[2]

As Sarah's servant, Hagar was inviolate. Two wills protected her – hers and Sarah's. By asking her husband to take Hagar, Sarah subordinated her servant's will to her own, but God guaranteed the girl's inviolability: "And constrain not your slave girls to prostitution, if they desire to live in chastity, that you may seek the chance goods of the present life. Whosoever constrains them, surely God, after their being constrained, is All-forgiving, Ever-merciful."[3]

The servant girl's very lack of power was her claim to inviolable dignity. Those with power owe protection to the dignity of the powerless. The stranger, the orphan, the dead and the sick, the sleeper and the slave are all inviolate, not to be touched, as is woman during her period, when she is a whole in the process of manifesting selfhood to itself.[4] Hagar is inviolate, as foreigner and

1 *Qur'an*, 19:93.

2 Ibid., 3:83.

3 Ibid., 24:33.

4 See *Qur'an*, 2:222.

 | DOI 10.1163/9789004279407_027

slave. She manifests Sarah's will to find herself in a son for Abraham and his will to beget his own self in the perfection of the divine image. Thus, the prophet and the servant girl reveal the self in quest of a higher possibility and co-presence with the Lord through service.

When Hagar conceived, Sarah told her husband: "My wrong be upon thee: I have given my maid into thy bosom; and when she saw that she had conceived, I was despised in her eyes: the Lord judge between me and thee."[5] Sarah then persecuted Hagar, who fled into the desert. At a well, an angel of the Lord said to her: "Hagar, Sarai's maid, whence camest thou? And whither wilt thou go?"[6] She replied: "I flee from the face of my mistress Sarai."[7] The angel of the Lord then told her: "Return to thy mistress, and submit thyself under her hands,"[8] adding: "I will multiply thy seed exceedingly, that it shall not be numbered for multitude,"[9] and further: "Behold, thou art with child and shalt bear a son, and shalt call his name Ishmael; because the Lord hath heard thy affliction. And he will be a natural man; his hand will be against every man, and every man's hand against him; and he shall dwell in the presence of all his brethren."[10]

As a couple, Abraham and Sarah reveal His unity. The child of their love would affirm their witness. They have grown old in dedication to the One, but are without child. This child is Sarah's desire, his beloved but barren consort in wandering. When she sees her desire quicken in Hagar's womb, she understands that it affirms their pairing, her only role being to have imagined the impossible. So, overcome by envy and wrath, she hopes to restore her pair, which does not yet affirm unity of witness. But in the self, only the full hour, the absolute now is real.

5 *Genesis*, 16:5.

6 Ibid., 16:8.

7 Ibid.

8 Ibid., 16:9.

9 Ibid., 16:10.

10 Ibid., 16:11–12. We have used "natural man" where other translations used "wild man," or "wild ass of a man," etc. This locus allows of a variety of interpretations. Wild asses were untameable. If taken metaphorically, the term may refer to our original nature as the treasury of all knowledge of our origin and purpose, of the world and everything in it, and as a reminder of what we carry within our innermost being, which does not depend on anything external. On certain possibilities for interpreting this crux, see Douglas, *Jacob's tears*, 55. One can read the raising of all hands against him and his against all as raising hands in sign of peace, as our link with the God of Peace.

It is not just that Sarah wants to return from a reality she has imagined. She now understands the revealed One transcends any claims of servitude and mastery and is affirmed by countless pairs. Sarah renounces her plan for a vicarious child through Hagar to wait for her own pair to have its own child in sign of union in and return to God. She sees that her problem cannot be resolved fictitiously through Hagar and her return to waiting patiently reveals an entirely other aspect of existence to her. Her husband has access to two different pairs and so two different affirmations of the One.

In her relationship with Abraham and display of mastery over Hagar, Sarah brings together and represents a world whose essence is both revealed and hidden. When not related to essence, the world is not other, it is nothing. Essence's desire to be revealed continuously produces images. It gives itself to them and they constantly produce new images in duality. Abraham is both essence and its image, as are Sarah and Hagar.

When Abraham and Sarah overcame duality in marital communion, their images would fade in union and they would taste essence. Return to the world of images causes mourning and is comforted by conception, as the child is an image that can manifest essence. But there was no conception. Sarah turned to rational scheming, fantasizing of lordship over her serving girl so as to accentuate her own being and the serving girl's nullity.

Sarah withdrew, removing her participation from the two images facing her – Abraham's, with whom she is in love, and Hagar's, whom she considers a possession. With Sarah withdrawn, Abraham saw in Hagar his true love, an image he wanted to receive and give himself to. For him as prophet and friend of God, she was no mere slave. Their marital union could only be out of love or violence. But Abraham did only what was just, loving what he knew, knowing what he loved.

Their experience of essence through marital union annuls the images. The light of return to Essence makes them reappear in their own images. The conception of a child is a sign of that experience. In it, Abraham and Hagar felt and saw the Essence Whose images they were. Return to duality renews feelings of exile and alienation. The world has received us, but also pushes us from itself, as we have received it and push it from ourselves. With all this receiving and leaving, the Essence's inviolable presence nonetheless abides in its images. It is the breath of the All-merciful, in which all images come into and leave being.

Hagar fled, hoping to leave one condition for another, and reached the well – the depth, in contrast to the heavenly heights. Self-realization is on the axis or upright path by which we return to the One. But she was on the earth's surface, with all its places and times and directions, only one of which is straight upward and leads towards the One. It is to be found within the self or not at all. That is where the Lord appeared to her through his Angel, asking: "Hagar, Sarah's serving girl, whence have you come and whither will you go?"

This was the first time God or an angel addressed a woman in the Torah. Her goal was revealed, sent down from her most sublime potential, her heart and uncreated kernel of humanity. God reveals Himself as present and merciful in every hour. His friends are not consumed by worries of "whence?" or "whither?" or the sorrows they bring. He told her to return and submit to the seeming source of her woes, because what happens here is also before the Face of the All-merciful.

Hagar told the angel of the Lord: "Behold, I am fleeing from my mistress Sarah." She fled from what is everywhere. Taking an image created in His breath for the All-merciful, leaves the fugitive without refuge, but to recognise the claims of all things on the self is to discover refuge in exile and a world pregnant with Essence.

Sarah realized that the desired-for child was not hers, while Hagar saw her love realized through others. Shame, the desire to be alone and annihilate the self before Him, made her flee into the desert. In that waste, an angel, a herald of God, appeared and spoke to Hagar. She had fled in the desire to reduce the transcendence we accept only by supposing the revealed Lord to be an angel of the God we cannot know directly. Faith in the angel He reveals Himself through is surrender to His guidance towards the goal which is the why and wherefore of existence.

Hagar returned to her husband's house to submit to Sarah's will that she be Abraham's concubine and bear his child. Hagar's awareness of the One transcended her suffering, giving her inviolable meaning through the child. For every child is a sign of the One.

In seeking her own child, Sarah could no longer tolerate either Hagar or her son. She asked Abraham to take them away, as the will of the mistress of those halls gave them no place there. There was no place, since Hagar could no longer be a mere serving woman nor Sarah her mistress, as before. The prophet Abraham, loyal to the guidance of his God, was unsure regarding her will, responding with regret and concern. Then God came to him:

> Let it not be grievous in thy sight because of the lad and because of thy bondwoman; in all that Sarah hath said unto thee, hearken unto her voice; for in Isaac shall thy seed be called. And also of the son of the bondwoman will I make a nation, because he is thy seed. And Abraham rose up early in the morning, and took bread, and a bottle of water, and gave it unto Hagar, putting it on her shoulder, and the child, and sent her away: and she departed, and wandered in the wilderness of Beersheba. And the

> water was spent in the bottle, and she cast the child under one of the shrubs. And she went, and sat her down over against him a good way off, as it were a bow shot: For she said, let me not see the death of the child. And she sat over against him, and lifted up her voice, and wept. And God heard the voice of the lad; and the angel of God called to Hagar out of heaven, and said unto her, What aileth thee, Hagar? Fear not; for God hath heard the voice of the lad where he is. Arise, lift up the lad, and hold him in thine hand; for I will make him a great nation. And God opened her eyes, and she saw a well of water; and she went, and filled the bottle with water, and gave the lad to drink. And God was with the lad; and he grew, and dwelt in the wilderness, and became an archer. And he dwelt in the wilderness of Paran.[11]

Hagar fled heavy with child, as an undifferentiated pair, seeking a way out of her difficulties and God appeared to her through an angel and told her He was with her and her unborn son. Driven out and abandoned to despair in the desert, she again saw God through an angel and was told He was with her. He reminded her that what we see as rejection may in fact be return to Him – our rejection of things in existence cannot remove them from God's mercy; nothing is so hidden that He cannot see; the human self's condition is always a stranger to its potential, a wayfarer on the path towards it.

What Hagar experienced as unbearable suffering, withdrawing and weeping, was revealed to be a holy message to the generations: free yourselves of fear of rejection, abandonment, and contempt and focus on Him Who gives purpose to existence. Hagar returned to her son and the water God sent in answer to her cries, which two are a well in the desert of our oblivion.

When Ishmael was thirteen, Isaac was born to manifest the pairing of Abraham and Sarah. The pairings of Abraham and Hagar and Abraham and Sarah were confirmed in Ishmael and Isaac, two separate unities. As Unity has no other, these two unities cannot be reconciled in their duality. Abraham could not know his image in his posterity, but he did know that it would never outrun absolute knowledge of the Lord, the Unity all things come from and return to.

Surrendering his sons to sacrifice or to the cruelty of the desert, at His command, Abraham knew God would not break His promise and that He knows what His servants cannot, as there is nothing in His creation without fullness of purpose. Abraham had full faith in His mercy which comprehends all. His friendship with God may seem inexorable cruelty, but only if Hagar's

---

11 *Genesis*, 21:12–21.

story is isolated from its majestic issue in human perfection as a mercy to all the worlds.

The biblical narratives of Hagar and Sarah and their sons make clear that Abraham's seed produced two lineages, whose chiefs were two brothers, Ishmael the elder and Isaac the younger. The quotation above refers to the former. In it, God reveals Himself to Hagar through His angel twice, both times with a message regarding her son.

From Isaac's posterity through Jacob came the nation known as the sons of Israel. God raised up his prophets amongst them, including Joseph, Moses, and Aaron, David and Solomon, and Malachi, the last. Then, the Jews believe, the Holy Spirit, the Spirit of Truth, ceased to descend amongst them, but Christians and Muslims believe that It came down once more upon the Messiah, Jesus, and Muslims believe also upon the Praised.

Looking back at the forks in the lineages of Abraham's posterity, they all meet in his love for God, through Sarah and Hagar. Both forking and gathering take place at the same time. What begins with one prophet passes into many tongues, as the stories spread amongst people of different times and places. They nonetheless remain focused on Unity which, as the One Word, brings them together in the time of the self.

As gatherers of creation, we relate to God the Gatherer. He reveals Himself in unity and multiplicity, gathering all things to Himself. We, in His image, are that same unity revealed by multiplicity and its gathering. The perfect self, realized after the Praised, reveals the simultaneity of unity and multiplicity and our own original simplicity and purity. Fully at home in our own hearts, we appear unconcealed, reason undivorced from intellect, sensory from spiritual knowledge.

The integrity of inner and outer in the self requires an openness no ambient changes can close. Our heart is made to mirror external change, but a mirror that doesn't reflect can't find its principle in the One. All things in multiplicity gather in Him, as He manifests in it in new ways.

The heart is sensitive to all change. The Praised said: "The heart is like a feather in a desert of the earth. The wind blows it to one side and the other."[12] And also: "The hearts of all the children of Adam are like a single heart between two of the fingers of the All-merciful. He turns it wherever He desires. O God, o Turner of Hearts, turn our hearts toward obeying Thee!"[13] And God said

12 Ibn Ḥanbal, 4:419.

13 Muslim, 4:1397.

through him: "My earth and My heaven embrace Me not, but the heart of My believing servant does embrace Me."[14]

God's authority comprehends creation as His self-revelation. Not a gust of wind escapes. Our heart knows that authority as the Living, Willing, Powerful, Knowing, Speaking, Seeing, and Hearing. With absolute knowledge, life, will, power, knowledge, speech, sight, and hearing reveal the One. The multitude in the self is revealed as a simple and harmonious discourse of Him.

To the many gathering in the One and the One revealed in the many corresponds language's simple but comprehensive nature. Each language is originally whole, a unit and a flux of countless signs. Sever a sign from the whole and it ceases to be a sign. A child's use of language, in the internal harmony of its elements, does not disintegrate the whole into its elements. Only through the serious study of grammar does one learn how and why the elements relate to the whole, never betraying the principles of unity in multiplicity or multiplicity in unity.

Each breath contains the potential for new unique ways of expressing the speaker's heart. All words come originally from silence, mystery, and the absence of distinction and ultimately return there again, beyond material limitation. Each word is authentic, original, at the absolute centre of the self, perfectly and absolutely corresponding to the Creator's command. Any whole expression necessarily reflects the heart as the centre of the self and so with the Word as one.

Language's simple and holistic nature is not unlike sacred art: each encounter yields something not experienced before, though the form remains the same. Its mystery is not exhausted in one or any number of encounters. A work of sacred art, properly understood, manifests both simplicity and multiplicity, integrates and differentiates, and leads towards and away from Unity.

Everything the self has – including our innate knowledge of His names and of what the One reveals Himself through and so of Him – is in the One and His revelation in language. The manifest is like a finger pointing to Him, a sign of countless distinctions. Language reflects this potential for distinction as multiplicity revealing Unity. He is constantly revealed through multiplicity in language, with the heart representing the principle of harmony and meaning within multiplicity.

In the Recitation, God says of languages and colours: "And of His signs is the creation of the heavens and the earth and the variety of your tongues and hues.

---

14 Tradition cited in: Ghazālī, *Iḥyā' 'ulūm al-dīn*, 3:1.5. See also: Chittick, *The Sufi Path of Knowledge*, 107, 396n20.

Surely, in that are signs for all living beings."[15] God's revelations to the Praised speak to this role of each language and disposition of each individual amongst the nations: "Every maternal community has its apostle"[16] and "We have sent no apostle save with the tongue of his people, that he might make all clear to them."[17]

---

15 *Qur'an*, 30:22.

16 Ibid., 10:47.

17 Ibid., 14:4.

CHAPTER 4

In Galatians

The angel of the Lord appeared one more time to a woman of Abraham's descendants by his wife Sarah – to the Virgin Mary to whom he announced the birth of a son. Some of the sons of Israel accepted this as truthful, others rejected it. Both did so freely and neither possibility excludes God's mercy, which always exceeds His wrath. Such a principle of freedom is difficult to understand within a linear concept of time not centred on the all-comprehending heart. Without such comprehension, there would be neither world nor Creator. With it, the revelation of God through creation becomes possible. Only through creation can the Creator affirm Himself as Manifest.

The many forms of witness and ritual confirm faith in God. Their plurality speaks to the One. Whether one calls them Jewish, Christian, Sabaean, or some other name, these acts of focusing facilitate self-realization by highlighting our perfect potential as reason and end of existence. This entails responsibility for every atom of good and every atom of evil done, for which account will be rendered and just judgment done. The differences between the forms are irreducible, their underlying harmony due to their common connection to the transcendental centre revealed by all levels of existence, times and places.

Just judgment speaks and shows the truth that binds everything in existence. He Who knows all is the only just judge and He judges us for our actions and our failures to act. That this is so is guaranteed by God, Who told the Praised:

> Surely they that believe, and those of Jewry, and the Christians, and those Sabaeans, whoso believes in God and the Last Day, and works righteousness – their wage awaits them with their Lord, and no fear shall be on them, neither shall they sorrow.[1]

God's promise to Abraham for his posterity by Sarah came about in the faith of those who accepted the Virgin's confession that her son was the Word. Those who denied it were refused a part in the covenant with Abraham for his posterity out of Sarah. According to the apostle Paul, they forfeited their genetic and spiritual connection with Sarah for descent from Hagar. Paul wrote of this approach to the miracle of the Virgin, as a reversal of expectations:

1 *Qur'an*, 2:62.

 | DOI 10.1163/9789004279407_028

> For it is written, that Abraham had two sons, the one by a bondmaid, the other by a freewoman. But he who was of the bondwoman was born after the flesh; but he of the freewoman was by promise. Which things are an allegory: for these are the two covenants; the one from the mount Sinai, which gendereth to bondage, which is Agar. For this Agar is mount Sinai in Arabia, and answereth to Jerusalem which now is, and is in bondage with her children. But Jerusalem which is above is free, which is the mother of us all. For it is written, Rejoice, thou barren that bearest not; break forth and cry, thou that travailest not: for the desolate hath many more children than she which hath an husband. Now we, brethren, as Isaac was, are the children of promise. But as then he that was born after the flesh persecuted him that was born after the Spirit, even so it is now. Nevertheless what saith the scripture? Cast out the bondwoman and her son: for the son of the bondwoman shall not be heir with the son of the freewoman. So then, brethren, we are not children of the bondwoman, but of the free.[2]

By this reversal, Sarah's descendants, including Jacob's twelve sons, Moses and Aaron, Samuel, Saul and David and Solomon and all the others who did not accept the Virgin Mary and her son as the Anointed, became Agarians. For Paul, these Israelites were no longer Sarah's children, but of Hagar. This was because Sarah was a freewoman through whom God's promise came to fruition, while Hagar was a bondwoman.

Paul clearly considers Hagar, to whom God spoke through His angel, a symbol that exceeds univocal interpretation. He does not address the symbolic meaning of the free and the bondwoman, however. When God reveals Himself as Lord, it is perfectly received in maternal service, absolute patience, and purity. Only such patience can receive the Word and pass it on as received.

Does this not recall Hagar's wandering on roads whose end only God knew, while Sarah remained in the halls where all things served her habitual confusion of wilfulness and freedom? Service is the perfect approach to the Lord, in Whom alone our authentic nature is seen as His self-revelation. Only the absolute servant is absolutely free, as he alone reflects absolutely the Free.

Once He had taught us all the names, God showed us their dissemination from Unity to the depth, to gather them on our ascent to most beautiful uprightness of being. We cannot extirpate our openness towards perfection. Its principle is uncreated, the Spirit God breathed into us. His perfect lordship is what confirms the perfection of our service out of the freedom given us. Only

2 *Galatians*, 4:22–31.

through absolute service to God do we fully realize our own freedom, as His perfect mastery confirms our service out of the freedom allowed us as our only perfection.

Paul says nothing about Abraham's children by Hagar nor of her herself whom God led through the desert to be the treasury of his greatest warrant, the keeper of the keystone of the world. The descendents promised by God to Abraham and Hagar bear witness to Jesus as Anointed, Word, and Spirit and the Virgin Mary as chosen above all other women. Paul also says that the revelation on Sinai, which denotes Jerusalem, corresponds to Hagar's service and that her descendants' covenant is based on the covenant of Mount Horeb. Developing an allegory of the promise to Abraham, he recognises Hagar and Sarah as complementary in the order of salvation.

With her son Ishmael, Hagar was driven into the desert, on roads which, in human terms, must lead to death. They were however led by the perfect guide to the holy Valley of Becca, of which the Psalmist says:

> Blessed is the man whose strength is in thee; in whose heart are the ways of them. Who passing through the valley of Becca made it a well; the rain also filleth the pools. They go from strength to strength, every one of them in Sion appeareth before God. O Lord God of hosts, hear my prayer: give ear, O God of Jacob. Selah. Behold, O God our shield, and look upon the face of thine anointed. For a day in thy courts is better than a thousand. I had rather be a doorkeeper in the house of my God, than to dwell in the tents of wickedness. For the Lord God is a sun and shield: the Lord will give grace and glory: no good thing will he withhold from them that walk uprightly. O Lord of hosts, blessed is the man that trusteth in thee.[3]

The valley Hagar and her son Ishmael reached marks the lowest depth. Not even there, in the deepest dark of the self, is God's mercy absent, for it comprehends all.[4] This is why the Psalmist points from the Valley towards Sion, the top of the mount at which all upward paths meet. This ascent marks the quest for our perfect potential, sent down by God, for which Abraham, with his son Ishmael, prays:

> Our Lord, receive this from us; Thou art the All-hearing, the All-knowing; and, our Lord, let us be-at-peace in Thee, and let our seed be a maternal community at peace in Thee; and show us our holy rites, and turn towards

3 *Psalm* 84:5–12.

4 See *Qur'an*, 7:156.

> us, surely Thou turnest, and art Ever-merciful; and, our Lord, do Thou send among them an apostle, one of them, who shall recite to them Thy signs, and teach them the Book and the Wisdom, and purify them; Thou art the All-mighty, the All-wise.[5]

Abraham and Ishmael's prophetic prayers at the house, raised in sign of renewed covenant, point forward to the apostle as goal and fruit of existence. Intimation is given of the turn from appearance to Real, from the world to the comprehending nature of the heart, and from the luxury of the temples to the Virgin's heart. Only the humble are so raised up, as God says: "We desired to be gracious to those that were abased in the land, and to make them leaders, and to make them inheritors, and to establish them in the land."[6]

Both Anointed and Praised direct us towards the hour as the reality of His kingdom. If Hagar means slavery and poverty, it is because her self-realization lies in them, as mastery and abundance are from the Abundant. This is one meaning of the Praised's answer to Gabriel regarding the hour: "The slave girl will give birth to her mistress."[7] Sarah is the mistress, her love for Abraham as yet unconfirmed in a posterity. Considering herself absolute mistress and Hagar absolute slave, Sarah projects her desire for the One onto Abraham and Hagar. She expects confirmation in what is, but her muddied desire gives her a taste of the service in which the One's lordship is manifest. Hagar is silent, content in her service, which is why God spoke to her through His angel. Sarah speaks out, lording over Hagar and blind to her own authentic nature as servant, but God is silent towards her. She fantasizes of an heir from her servant girl's womb, seeking it of her husband Abraham, God's prophet and friend.

Paul says that those descendants who reject the Anointed are no longer Sarah's children, but Hagar's. He calls this an allegory.[8] Sarah's freedom, as what determines who inherits the Anointed, and Hagar's servitude, in which God spoke to her as the bearer of His promise, are both allegorical or symbolic relations, which have played a decisive role in our quest for meaning, the meaning of our creation, resulting in the grand split between the sphere of angels and our own earthly destiny.

---

5 *Qur'an*, 2:127–29.

6 Ibid., 28:5–6.

7 Muslim, 1:3.

8 Allegory is discourse in which concepts and thoughts are expressed in a way that does not rely on the basic meaning of the words used. It is figurative speech or the figurative explanation of concepts and thoughts.

The primacy of Intellect, in which all things since come to the visible world first gathered, and our humanity, as the supplementary gathering in intention, manifestation and revelation, joining first and last in creation, allow us to see the options open to humanity in Hagar's silence and receptiveness to the angel's words, on the one hand, and Sarah's discourse of command, on the other – or in modern terms, the privilege of gnosis and universal intellectuality as the essence and heart of existence, on the one hand, and belief in the sufficiency of analytical reason, on the other.

Hagar symbolizes the feminine as receptive and focusing aspect of humanity, Sarah the active instrumental reason with its illusory offer of a self-sufficient and finite world that underwrote her scorn for the angel's promise of a son to be born to her. With faith in instrumental reason predominant, the consciousness that transcends the quantifiable world's boundaries is rejected, along with the openness of the self to realization in the One.

As a rational operation, allegory allows no transition to new levels of being or of consciousness. It presents what can be known in any case. In contrast, the symbol reveals a different level of consciousness from rational evidence. It expresses a mystery, the only way to say what cannot be understood otherwise. A symbol is never "explained" once and for all; it is explicated over and over.

A work of sacred art emerges through acts of listening, watching, and performing, with full participation by audience, viewers, and performers, its mystery never fully revealed, always being revealed. Existing outside of simple temporal limitations, it is pregnant with prophetic wisdom, so that everything in the world of the senses intimates higher levels of existence and of consciousness. Each prophet relates to the One through the angels of the higher levels, as in Him all the things of the world and the self are connected, descending from and ascending to Him.

Ascent and descent involve two inextricable worlds – the sensory and suprasensory. Knowledge of these relationships is wisdom, in which what was sent down is linked with its source, to which it may return. Both sending down and returning involve the angels and imaginal perspectives on creation. Within these perspectives, the angels descend and ascend, as does the Spirit, linking God and His prophets. In both God's and His prophets' imagination, symbols appear and are of decisive importance in discourses of witness and mystery, external and internal.

That things are symbols allows gnosis, unmediated relationships with signs in world and self as "indices" of the higher and mysterious reality of existence. When an index, or existence in its visible aspect, is taken for existence in all its aspects, Intellect is reduced to analytical reason at this level of existence and the revealed laws and rituals, rules and institutions to their social context.

Then essential humanity will revolt, as the prescriptive forms of the revelation only satisfy when properly grounded within the self as means for recalling us to and realizing our authentic nature.

Nothing in existence – not the cosmos or what transcends it, not the books or what transcends the attainable levels, not social institutions and what goes with them – is possible without the self. Existence acts as a reminder of the self's comprehensive nature. With humanity as his servant, God is Lord. The self's claim on God is indistinguishable from His claims on the self. Our debt to the Lord comprises all the self's relations to itself and the world. These debts constitute God's claim as Creator and Guide of all things. But He has bound Himself to receive us in the fullness of His mercy for our recognition of those debts as His rights.

The revolt is denial of mediation by institutionalized interpretation of God's unity, the apostolate of the Praised, and the return of all things to Him. Through revolt, the self can return to itself and its Lord, Who is unlike anything, with us always, closer than the jugular vein, without Whom nothing exists. Knowledge of God cannot be separated from love of Him, the attraction through which each thing strives to discover and find itself in and with Him.

God calls His lovers to follow the Praised so that He may love and forgive them their sins. From this it is clear that God loves the Praised who loves Him. The loving servitude of the Praised is perfect confirmation of God's lordship. The Praised has nothing not received from Him. For what he has received, he is the perfect image of God, Who manifests Himself through the Praised in His love to be known. The Praised is thus the perfect possibility in each individual of realizing the self after the Praised as our most beautiful example, of which he said:

> I saw my Lord in the most beautiful image. He said to me: "What does the most sublime company discuss?" I said: "Lord, that You know best." Then He lowered His hand between my shoulder blades and I felt its cold on my breast, and I knew what is in the heavens and on the earth. And I recited: "So We were showing Abraham the kingdom of the heavens and the earth, that he might be of those having sure faith."[9]

Certain faith is sure knowledge of the Beloved and sure love of the Known. What the Praised and Abraham knew so surely was a vision of the Lord in the most beautiful image, which made Him manifest in spatial and temporal fini-

---

9 Dārimī, 2:170. The final quotation is *Qur'an*, 6:75.

tude. Everything in heaven and earth presents this vision. We see, hear, smell, and touch it. Each such experience reveals God, Who is unlike anything.

Without experiencing this love of God and finding Him in every sign in world and self, there is no love between servant and Lord. The Praised, the perfect servant, says that of worldly things he loves women, scents, and worship.[10] The Praised's relationship with them is a relationship with the Lord, manifest always and only in the most beautiful image. The image reveals and conceals Him – reveals because everything in existence is His face, conceals because He transcends all images.

God is both lover and beloved.[11] This duality affirms His unity in His being Creator and through revelation in creation. Loving to be Known, He is manifest in the act of creation, without being two. He loves Himself in creation, His love serving as its inner essence, reason, and purpose. Creation turns towards original Unity, the concealed treasury from which a ceaseless procession takes place into and back from existence.

Two forms of nostalgia, for the self as known and for the concealed reason of all revelation, bear constant witness to no self but the Self. Both simultaneously contain disassembly and assembly. These two aspects of the One are like looking eye to eye. He Who looks is seen by him who looks, He who is seen looks at Him Who sees him. The One looks out of concealment at Himself through Himself as revealed. Union enters duality constantly, but the lookers-on see themselves in the One: all His revelations turn towards Him, for He alone is Real.

Before finding the Beloved in the self, the lover seeks Him everywhere outside. What he finds beautiful in the world he takes for a sign: finding and losing, discovering and hiding, seeking refuge and being persecuted may all be felt in satisfaction from the beautiful which nonetheless fails to transcend the sensory surface of the self. In the attempt to transform inevitable loss, lack, and exile into finding, discovering, and residing, sensory beauty serves us as a ladder leading to what lies inside, the Lover and the Beloved Who is closer than the jugular vein.

---

10 Versions of this tradition are given in Nasāʾī, 1; Ibn Ḥanbal, 3:128, 199, 285; and Ghazālī, *Iḥyāʾ ʿulūm al-dīn*, 2:2.1. See also: Murata, *The Tao of Islam*, 345n43.

11 See *Qurʾan*, 5:54

CHAPTER 5

Hagar's Posterity

God promised Sarah's posterity the land of milk and honey in the west. Their brothers from Hagar's posterity settled in the desert to east and south. Two lineages of one man and two wives – two affirming One. The gifts of prophecy, the books and the land might seem to belong to one, oblivion, the desert and want to the other. They are represented by two houses, in the Valley and on the Mount. Without obvious historical connection, they nonetheless symbolize the unity of earth and heaven, matter and spirit, a precious guarantee for all in uncovering the history of the self.

Both these spiritual and genetic lineages assume the guise of mastery over poverty, memory over oblivion. But oblivion is ours alone. Nothing outruns the knowledge of God. We remain poor, the Lord abundant.[1] When the lineages seem to diverge, His wealth comprehends and unites them, as He comprehends and composes all contradictions. Reconciling all things through which He makes Himself manifest, God allocates each its perfection, both inner and outer.

Both posterities of Abraham bore a promise from God. The promise to the line through Isaac seems clear, that to the line through Ishmael less so. These promises appear irreconcilable to many and the decisive question for salvation becomes: how is the promise made to Hagar to be fulfilled?

The answer lies in the intertwined progress of both lines and their prophetic progeny, as they relate to the centre where they meet again, their source and confluence. This answer lies in the time of the self and that of the world. The best starting place is the revelation of God as inner and outer. That the lineages meet again becomes the key to the gates of existence for the self before them.

The meaning of Hagar's name is clear. It safeguards the essence of prophetic destiny. Anyone seeking self-discovery must shuck off their habits and attachments and depart normality, as the hour, which the self's condition reflects like the shadow its source, is not repeated. If we try to grasp it in a form of being, it creates a rift between centre and periphery, traveller and goal, as "God never discloses Himself in a single form to two individuals, nor in a single form twice."[2]

1 See *Qur'an*, 35:15.

2 This tenet was often repeated by Ibn al-ʿArabī. It was coined by Abū Ṭālib al-Makkī, a famous Sufi teacher. See Chittick, *The Sufi Path of Knowledge*, 103.

 | DOI 10.1163/9789004279407_029

We can always disconnect from our own condition, connect with another. We become separated, because all appearance must fade. It changes from moment to moment, as we come and go ceaselessly, exiting and entering, fleeing and arriving, finding and losing, falling and standing. We are refugee and settler, vagabond and follower and find connection only with the Real, for only the Real serves as support and fulcrum. Any other connection is with the non-real, a form of descent and a drawing away from authentic humanity.

Our capacity from creation to connect with the Real is guaranteed by our authentic nature, which has the nature of a debt, the debt of nature. In our deepest core, we are directly aware that we owe our existence to the Creator alone. This is why knowledge is our nature.[3] It is always accessible, but unconfined to spatial or temporal boundaries.

The self is split between two extremes, one tending towards nothing, the other towards the absolute. The absolute is the self's essence, fully realized only once the tension between these extremes has been transcended, the dark abandoned for the self's own higher regions and return to the absolute. To return is to follow the Praised as perfect exemplar, present in every self, who represents ascent on the upright path. God said of the drama of the self:

> And know that the apostle of God is within you. If he obeyed you in much of the affair, you would suffer; but God has endeared to you belief, decking it fair in your hearts, and He has made detestable to you concealment and ungodliness and disobedience. Those – they are the right-minded, by God's favour and blessing; God is All-knowing, All-wise.[4]

The faithful relate to God the Faithful through faith. Of course, to believe one must know, but not all forms of knowledge serve for faith. Only love of what we know makes us faithful, as each increase in knowledge leads to confirmation of our love. When we love the revelation of the Real, knowledge of it, however little, connects us to the Real and that alone, while love attracts to Him, as the self's essence is the Absolute Which reveals Itself.

God reveals Himself through His creation, without ceasing to be Hidden or Concealed. We know God only through what He manifests Himself in and love Him as such. A little knowledge is enough for absolute love, the lover's irresistible desire to unite with the Beloved. He Who both knows and loves absolutely

---

3 "The debt of nature" or "natural debt" (ar. *dīn al-fiṭra*) is a standing capacity we are endowed with that allows us to distinguish the Real from the unreal. This capacity is part of our individual nature, so that each self is equal indignity. See *Qur'an*, 30:30.

4 *Qur'an*, 49:7–8.

makes Himself manifest through the knowledge of those who love Him. For, whatever our condition, we are never beyond the Creator's knowledge or love.

God's love for us and our love for God is clear in the apostle's presence in every self and our rejection of the siren call of the depths of the self. His role is to lead us from the depths towards the height and the light. As a mercy to the worlds, to which he announces All-merciful and Ever-merciful God, the apostle rejects the subordination of the self oriented towards nothing and the deepest dark. He calls us to migrate from the depths towards the authentic and most beautiful height. Faith entails consciousness of the beauty of the signs in the world and the self that bear witness to the Lord as bearer of the most beautiful names. Everything but the goal of this path is nothing, in which all things are absent, even beauty, and especially the relationship of the faithful to the Faithful.

Saying that He is One and Flux, neither begotten nor begetting, to Whom nothing is equal,[5] and that every self shall experience death,[6] God exempts His Own Self from death, even though He is manifest through selves that are born and beget. God's desire to reveal Himself is neither born nor begets, but manifest in a self realizing It as a stimulus to birth. Conscious of revealing God, the self knows that it is the Revealed's own consciousness of Its self-revelation. What the self wants in this knowledge is clarity of revelation of the One it reveals: it wants to leave duality for the Self within itself.

Every self is pregnant with desire for the Self, Which it itself reveals. But a self begets a self, as the Self neither begets nor was born. The complete or perfect self contains the Self, while the Self sees Itself in and beyond that self. The perfect self is a polar star, a maternal principle for every other self, a light of the light sent down to the lowest heaven within each self that it may exit the gloom for the Light that transcends all light.

The self's desire to give birth to the Self produces only a self that manifests the Self as like nothing,[7] but also near[8] and always present within the self.[9] After experiencing birth resulting from its desire for the Self, the self finds a father in its own child, as the only unborn self was the first from which all others derive.[10] And even the first self, in desire for the Self, gave birth to its own mother, since the Creator neither begets nor was born. In its own child it

5 See *Qur'an*, 112:1–4.

6 Ibid., 3:185, 21:35, 29:57.

7 Ibid., 42:11.

8 Ibid., 2:186.

9 Ibid., 57:4.

10 Ibid., 4:1, 6:98, 7:189, 39:6.

saw the incarnation of its desire, an image of its own perfect image from which an image of an image was born out of the desire of the self.

The heart is desire's native domain, where desire lies concealed, albeit constantly trying to reveal itself. No form it takes exhausts concealment and no desire fails to confirm recollection of the One. The desire for revelation is a desire for the self. Revelation does not sweep away the unity of the heart; it enables it to see into itself and for itself, as the sacred tradition says: "My heavens and My earth embrace Me not, but the heart of My believing servant does embrace Me."[11]

The heart of the believing servant is, for Muslim esotericism, the Anointed, the child fed on the milk of its own maternal principle, which is recollection of God filling out the entirety of a self made equal to the Word. The Holy Spirit brought down that word to the heart of the Praised, as the maternal principle of all perfected prophecy, the authentic image for each one of us. This is why many Muslim mystics consider the Virgin a sign of primordial maternity and the self that finds the Lord manifests its own spiritual child.

Hagar was separated from her home three times – first her parents' home in Egypt, then twice in Canaan the home of her mistress and husband. She had no one to rely on but the Guide in Whose will she trusted, making of separation connection, of exile refuge. Those who give themselves over to absolute service know the absolute free will of the Guide. Taken from those halls, she was with Abraham's family as entirely passive. Her will to submit or resist was not considered.

She is thus linked to Abraham's finding peace in Peace. Respite from her travails in the desert came with the voice from heaven that she could accept or reject. That same voice stopped Ishmael's death. Even as it seemed silent before his death, the heavenly voice pointed out the saving spring at his feet.

Fleeing Sarah, at a desert well Hagar met the angel who comforted her with news of a son. When she abandoned that promised son, unable to bear his dying, the angel again appeared to say that God was with her and the boy. What form did he take before Hagar? He was the desire of her own essence, which comprehends all things – perfect humanity, the nature of the Praised, the mercy to the worlds. Thus, the Praised said to his companions: "If you want to see Abraham, then look at your companion."[12]

Hagar's suffering includes three things. First, she suffers constant separations and connections. Second, she is constantly being freed from one form of

11 For this tradition and its source, see p. 127, note 5.

12 Bukhārī, 4:367.

servitude for another. Third, she submits to the machinations of an infertile female eager for confirmation by the One by excluding her as mother.

In Sarah's mind, contempt for Hagar the bondwoman justified abuse. It was how she could expect a child born to Hagar to confirm her own pairing with Abraham. Returning contempt for contempt, Hagar fled to unknown parts to save herself from what she knew too well, accepting exile out of loyalty to a son who confirmed her and her husband as a sign of the One.

Her fear of how her exile might end was, however, based on little knowledge. God's view of things and their relations differs from ours. Our understanding is a mere sign of His. Misfortune through unjust exile confirms – as does any undeserved and patiently borne suffering – spiritual gain for the person afflicted, as the Praised said: "No fatigue, nor disease, nor sorrow, nor sadness, nor hurt, nor distress befalls a person-of-peace, even if it were the prick he receives from a thorn, but that God expiates some of his sins for that."[13]

Abraham's seed by Hagar travelled far from the land of milk and honey and its distress, continuing until long after the watershed of the Virgin and the Christ, to a time in a savage desert valley when Amina bore a son she called Praised, bringing about God's promise through Moses:

> I will raise them up a prophet from among their brethren, like unto thee, and will put my words in his mouth; and he shall speak unto them all that I shall command him. And it shall come to pass, that whosoever will not hearken unto my words which he shall speak in my name, I will require it of him. But the prophet, which shall presume to speak a word in my name, which I have not commanded him to speak, or that shall speak in the name of other gods, even that prophet shall die.[14]

When this long-awaited prophet bore witness before his folk that he was the one, he invoked his ancestral mother Hagar.[15] He encouraged his followers to follow her path. They were to leave their place of refuge, as Abraham's seed, for thousands of years, as there is no return without leaving, no finding without loss. He showed them, in their focus on the last things beyond the dust of the

---

13 Ibid., 7:371–72.

14 *Deuteronomy*, 18:18–20.

15 The Praised told his followers: "Show piety in dealing with the protected peoples, those of the settled lands, the black, the crinkly haired, for they have a noble ancestor and marriage ties" (Ibn Isḥāq, *Sīrat Rasūl Allāh*, 691). According to the account of those who passed down these traditions, the reference to "a noble ancestor" is to Hagar, while the "marriage ties" referred to are through Mary, the prophet's wife (Ibid.).

grave, two directions – one back, one forward – where all things lie between seed and fruit: each seed contains its fruit, each fruit its seed.

Those who answered God's call to follow the Praised were called migrants,[16] marking their link to Abraham, who said though Lot: "I will flee to my Lord!"[17] Their migration signifies that the conditions of the self are stations on the way from lower to higher stages on the upright path and none is the principle or source of memory.

In what our love for God discovers we see the Praised raised above his brothers, the sons of Israel. In the Recitation, he is said to be maternal and the seal, a mercy to the worlds, the most beautiful example, the light sent down and the shining lamp. God said through him: "If you love God, follow me, and God will love you, and forgive you your sins."[18] While the prophet said of himself: "I have five names. I am the Praised. I am the Most Praised. I am the Effacer, by whom God effaces the covering. I am the Gatherer, before whom people are gathered. I am the Last."[19]

The Praised's "I" is our highest potential, dearer to us than our own attainments, as God said: "The prophet is nearer to the believers than their selves."[20] His "I" cannot be outstripped. It manifests the Real, even at the lowest depth. Calling himself Praised and Most Praised, he marks two different levels of participation of the self. The first reflects existence as a whole glorifying the Lord with praise. The second is his link by praising and being praised with God the All-praised.

Through this standing privilege of the self over all other aspects of our personality we discover things as signs of the One. In any other configuration, they remain concealed. In concealment, they no longer connect us with higher levels of existence. All that remains are their mutual connections, their confinement in a single level of existence. Myth, ritual, and symbol become history, allegory, and things. They are unconcealed only by the self of the Praised, the Most Praised, the light sent down forever and eraser of all concealment. Calling himself gatherer, the Praised simply meant that all our hearts are as one held between God's fingers.[21] To realize our humanity is to discover the self in that common heart.

---

16 The followers of the Praised referred to themselves as migrants, as did their contemporaries. See Hoyland, *Seeing Islam as others saw it*, 548n.16.

17 *Qur'an*, 29:26.

18 Ibid., 3:31.

19 Mālik, 513.

20 *Qur'an*, 33:6.

21 See Muslim, 4:1397.

The Praised also calls himself the last, the last fruit of the seed of creation, the presence of the Real in the depth that connects all things to the First. Properly understood, "last" is "first." Priority serves all things in existence as maternal principle, as connection with the Principle. Although first, the Praised is dual, recipient and donor, male and female, as his sacred relationship with Mary tells us.

The orders and the prophetic heritage in all its forms are naturally oriented towards the maternal, primal, and original nature of the Praised. Redemption and emergent truth are only possible through the discovery of human perfection. At the end of his life, the prophet Jacob told his 12 sons the treasures of salvation and accepted their oath: "We will serve thy God and the God of thy fathers Abraham, Ishmael and Isaac, One God. In Him we find peace."[22]

Similarly, every order established within that heritage serves our perfection, its reason, measure, and purpose, as, according to the Torah, Jacob said: "The sceptre shall not depart from Judah, nor a lawgiver from between his feet, until Shiloh come; and unto him shall the gathering of the people be."[23]

---

22 *Qur'an*, 2:133.

23 *Genesis*, 49:10. On the link between this annunciation and the Praised, see Vidyarthi, *Muhammad in World Scriptures*, 155–75.

CHAPTER 6

In the Recitation (1)

The Praised bore witness of a particular connection with Abraham that was both spiritual and by blood. He is a maternal prophet, as well as a principle for humanity. The prophecies and all associated matters are realized through the maternal prophet, as a link with original perfection. The Praised was thus Abraham's most sublime desire, the son he desired.

The Praised is the son who represents for Abraham, his father, the principle. Like all the prophets, Abraham was a man of peace,[1] but the Praised was the first of them.[2] Being-at-peace connects whatever reveals God as Peace with any human being thus made manifest. We may deny or affirm our nature, depending on whether we accept or reject the confidence God offered as our relationship. The Praised accepted His will as his own and never betrayed it.

Abraham's desire for the Praised is expressed in his prayer: "Our Lord, do Thou send among them an apostle, one of them, who shall recite to them Thy signs, and teach them a Book and the Wisdom, and purify them; Thou art the All-mighty, the All-wise."[3] Facing posterity, Abraham hitched his desire to the God Who sends down signs and the Books and wisdom and purification, towards what is highest, without which nothing exists or has reason or purpose. The Praised is a higher level of his own self, pre-announced in history.

The first house was established to mark our covenant with God at the centre of our earthly present, the rediscovery of our high potential.[4] Adam lost his original fullness, in which his being-at-peace and Peace were undifferentiated and being praised, praising, and the All-praised were a whole reflected in all things. He travelled to the lowest depth, repented, and was offered the house as a sign of the covenant's renewal and of return by the upright path.

The renewed covenant was offered to recall us to our primordial oath as servant to God as Lord. The house in Becca is just a sign of this. Oblivion has brought us far from this memory and the house's meaning. The self has darkened, as the circuit of the house, worship, and prostration have lost meaning. Oblivion is cast over the world's essence, as we are increasingly reduced to the surface, cut off from the heart's authentic comprehension of all things.

---

1 See *Qur'an*, 2:128; and 3:67.

2 Ibid., 39:12.

3 *Qur'an*, 2:129.

4 See *Qur'an*, 3:96.

 | DOI 10.1163/9789004279407_030

Oblivion of God is oblivion of the self, and vice versa – recollecting God means recollecting the self. The self's authentic nature is service in which God is revealed as Lord. He uses us for revelation, so that our authentic condition is the highest of sublimities. Divine lordship is manifest in it. Oblivion was near universal when God Whom all things serve at peace called Abraham to wander the paths of the world and submit to His guidance. God called Abraham to free himself from the things that cover his Creator's will: "And We made covenant with Abraham and Ishmael: 'Purify My house for those that shall go about it and those that cleave to it, to those who bow and prostrate themselves.' "[5]

The covenant is how the faithful relate to Faithful God. Our faith derives from love for Him we always know insufficiently. God's knowledge is absolute. He loves us who love Him entirely, in both His revealing and concealing Himself from us. The covenant is for those who love Him, who have not forsaken their faith with Him.[6] Aligned by the ritual of the first house, the self enters the order of the world, split like itself between the depths and the most beautiful height, which includes all of Creation as His revelation.

Abraham's desire for the Praised is our eternal higher potential issued in two posterities. This is why the Praised is first and last. His connection with Abraham, expressed through their like selves, marks the Praised's maternity as inner principle of humanity. The Praised referred to this thus: "May God bestow His mercy on the mother of Ishmael! Had she not hastened, Zam-zam would have been a stream flowing on the surface of the earth."[7]

Still there by the house, the spring of Zam-zam marks the axis of the upright path towards the frequented house in the seventh or ultimate heaven. Abraham links these two houses, earthly and heavenly: with Ishmael he restored the house on earth and now resides beside the house in the seventh heaven. The Praised said of passing through all the heavens: "And there was a man sitting on the throne of the gate of the immortal mansion"[8] and elsewhere that "Gabriel said: 'This is your father; pay your greetings to him.' So I greeted him and he returned the greetings to me and said: 'You are welcomed, O pious son and pious prophet.' Then I was made to ascend to the Lote-Tree of the utmost boundary."[9]

The Praised ascended from the lowest depths to the highest height, through all the heavens, to meet the patriarch Abraham. But he passed beyond even

5 *Qur'an*, 2:125.

6 See *Qur'an*, 2:124; 4:54–55; 37: 113; 57:26.

7 Bukhārī, 4:372.

8 Ibn Isḥāq, *Sīrat Rasūl Allāh*, 186.

9 Bukhārī, 5:147.

that patriarchal level. He showed himself beyond the patriarch's desire, first and last for it too. He is the maternal principle of the prophets.

These houses at the extremes represent Adam's presence in and expulsion from paradise and Abraham's restoration of the earthly house as a sign of its heavenly model. The Praised comprehends and surpasses them both. When he met Abraham, he said to him: "O Praised, convey my peace to your community and tell them that paradise is a vast plain of pure soil and sweet water and that its trees proclaim: 'Glory be to God, and praise be to God, and there is no God but God, and God is great.' "[10]

Indicating his link as maternal prophet with all the other prophets, the Praised calls on his witnesses to connect with Abraham and his posterity:

> Oh God! Pray for the Praised and the family of the Praised, as You prayed for Abraham and the family of Abraham, for You are the All-praised, the All-magnificent. O God! Bless the Praised and the family of the Praised, as You blessed Abraham and the family of Abraham, for You are the All-praised, the All-magnificent.[11]

Linking the Praised's followers with Abraham and his family brings together Hagar's and Sarah's posterities. Their places in history appear clear enough. They link people back to Abraham. But how can they appear as a whole in one self on the day that embraces all time? What is Hagar's place in this whole and why is it so consistently denied?

Although a key symbol of the discourse of His unity and the apostolate of the Praised, Hagar's name is not in the Recitation. This is problematic, as God says: "We have neglected nothing in the Book!"[12] In fact, the silence is only apparent. There is indirect reference to Hagar, for those who look.

One might resolve this contradiction and failure to mention Hagar by supposing her to be mentioned through her husband and her son, the prophets Abraham and Ishmael, and their line down to the Praised, the seal of the prophets, particularly given how much the destinies of those through whom she is indirectly mentioned – Abraham, Ishmael, and the Praised – resemble her own: they all left or were driven from their homes, separated from their folk, leaving the close for the remote.

It is also fruitful to compare her destiny with Mary's, as the key myth of the entire Recitation, and see how Hagar's destiny is reflected in it. Their destinies,

---

10 Tirmidhī (b), 7:248–49.

11 Bukhārī 4:385.

12 *Qur'an*, 6:38.

like every other quest for the inviolate dignity inherent in all created things, are brought together and revealed in the very name of Hagar. In her lonely exile God spoke to her through angels, giving her unborn child the name "God has listened." We should therefore look for Hagar in the Recitation in and through semantic fields associated with the verbal roots *h-j-r* and *kh-r-j*, from which her name is derived.

The term *hijra* derives from *h-j-r*, which means "cutting of friendly or social relations," "ceasing to talk to the other," "leaving," "denial," "abandonment," and "avoiding." It also signifies "leaving the desert for a settlement" or the reverse. Its most common meaning is "leaving home to live abroad" or "emigrating." Forms derived from *kh-r-j* are similar in meaning.[13]

Every language reflects existence as a whole. Relations between things in world and self are all faithfully imaged in language. Everything dispersed within the horizons of the world gathers in the self, whence it is disseminated again. The space and time of the external world are faithful images of their archetype in highest innerness. They are united in the essence of the self. Sent down to existence, they receive extension. All distance and every period matures in the now of the self. Our darkening knowledge of these two inseparable times, in the self and outside it, cuts us off from our principle, God as the One and the Flux.

The One confirms Essence, duality the One. When the One manifests in duality, flux moves, placing the receptive and donative aspects of duality in constantly changing relations. Existence is departing and arriving, fleeing and taking refuge, ascending and descending. In any revelation of the One, the balance of coming and going, giving and receiving, male and female may be lost or found.

As God's revelation the Recitation – sent down to the heart of the Praised and expressed in the language of his people, so that it might be transferred into any other language – reflects this ceaseless flowing in and out, begetting and dying, arriving and leaving, through which the One and Flux manifest. This continuous act of revelation reveals Hagar's place and meaning. She accepted Abraham and made manifest the meaning of the One in her son Ishmael, as part of a journey of coming and leaving, receiving and giving.

Each self bears, in principle, all of language and existence. This includes Hagar as a symbol of abandonment and acquiescence, losing and finding, and seeing in the world the meaning sought in abandonment. Abraham came

13 In the Recitation, seven forms are derived from *h-j-r* and they occur in thirty one places (see Badawi, *Arabic-English Dictionary of Qur'anic Usage*, 979); there are fourteen forms derived from *kh-r-j*, found in one hundred and twenty two places (Ibid., 257). The second root is simply a form of the first (see Faruque, "Emigration," 18).

with her and their son Ishmael to the middle of the desert, where he left them, his human fear mastered by fear of God. If He is not Merciful, where shall we seek refuge? The Praised said of Abraham's abandoning Hagar and Ishmael: "She called to him from behind: 'O Abraham! To whom are you leaving us?' He replied: 'To God.' She said: 'I am satisfied to be with God.' "[14]

The discourses on going in and coming out, flight and refuge, leaving and returning in the Recitation offer many expressions which use these words with different meanings: they are like jewels refracting light differently from each facet, while each facet remains part of the whole.

In exploring Hagar's symbolic implications, one should distinguish from the semantic fields and chains formed around the verbal root *h-j-r* in the Recitation those expressions that shed light on the integrity of language. The following examples are presented for the insight they provide into wider semantic fields throughout the book, beyond the said into the unsaid, beyond the seen into the unseen.

> O thou shrouded in thy mantle, arise, and warn! Thy Lord magnify thy robes. Purify and defilement *flee*![15]
>
> And bear thou patiently what they say, and *forsake them graciously*.[16]
>
> Whoso *emigrates* in the way of God will find in the earth many refuges and plenty; whoso *goes forth* from his house an *emigrant* to God and His apostle, and then death overtakes him, his wage shall have fallen on God; surely God is All-forgiving, Ever-merciful.[17]
>
> And those that *emigrated* in God's cause after they were wronged – We shall surely lodge them in this world in a goodly lodging, and the wage of the world to come is greater, did they but know.[18]
>
> Those who believe, and *have emigrated*, and have struggled in the way of God with their possessions and their selves are mightier in rank with God; and those – they are the triumphant.[19]
>
> And those who *emigrated* in God's way and were slain, or died, God shall provide them with a fair provision; and surely God is the best of providers.[20]

14 Bukhārī, 4:379–80.

15 *Qur'an*, 74:1–5, *fahjur*.

16 Ibid., 73:10, *wahjurhum hajran jamīlan*.

17 Ibid., 4:100, *yuhājir* (...) *yakhruj min baytihi muhājiran*.

18 Ibid., 16:41, *hājarū*.

19 Ibid., 9:20, *hājarū*. See also: 8:72 and 8:74.

20 Ibid., 22:58, *hājarū*.

It is for the poor *emigrants*, who *were expelled* from their habitations and their possessions, seeking bounty from God and good pleasure, and helping God and His apostle; those – they are the truthful ones.[21]

And those who made their dwelling in the abode, and in belief, before them, love whosoever *has emigrated* to them, not finding in their breasts any need for what they have been given, and preferring others above themselves, even though poverty be their portion. And whoso is guarded against the avarice of his own soul, those – they are the prosperers.[22]

But the believers, and those who *emigrate* and struggle in God's way – those have hope of God's compassion; and God is All-forgiving, the Ever-merciful.[23]

And their Lord answers them: "I waste not the labour of any that labours among you, be male or female – the one of you is as the other. And those who *emigrated* and *were expelled* from their habitations, those who suffered hurt in My way, and fought, and were slain – them I shall surely acquit of their evil deeds, and I shall admit them to gardens underneath which rivers flow."[24]

The prophet is nearer to the believers than their selves; his wives are their mothers. Those who are bound by blood are nearer to one another in the Book of God than the believers and the *emigrants*; nevertheless you should act towards your friends honourably; that stands inscribed in the Book.[25]

And those who have believed afterwards and *emigrated*, and struggled with you – they belong to you; but those related by blood are nearer to one another in the Book of God; surely God has knowledge of everything.[26]

Let not those of you who possess bounty and plenty swear off giving kinsmen and the poor and *those who emigrate* in the way of God; but let them pardon and forgive. Do you not wish that God should forgive you? God is All-forgiving, Ever-merciful.[27]

God has returned towards the prophet and the *emigrants* and the Helpers who followed him in the hour of difficulty, after the hearts of a

21 Ibid., 59:8, *al-muhājirīna alladhīna ukhrijū min diyārihim.*

22 Ibid., 59:9, *hājara.*

23 Ibid., 2:218, *hājarū.*

24 Ibid., 3:195, *hājarū wa ukhrijū*. See also: 16:110.

25 Ibid., 33:6, *al-muhājirīna.*

26 Ibid., 8:75, *hājarū.*

27 Ibid., 24:22, *al-muhājirīna.*

> part of them well nigh swerved aside; then He turned towards them; surely He is Gentle to them, and Ever-merciful.[28]
>
> And those the angels take, while still they are wronging themselves – the angels will say, "In what circumstances were you?" They will say, "We were abased in the earth." The angels will say, "But was not God's earth wide, so that you might *have emigrated* in it?" Such men, their refuge shall be Gehenna – an evil homecoming![29]
>
> They wish that you should conceal the truth as they conceal it, and then you would be equal; therefore take not to yourselves friends of them, until they *emigrate* in the way of God; then, if they turn their backs, take them, and slay them wherever you find them; take not to yourselves any one of them as friend or helper.[30]
>
> The apostle says, "O my Lord, behold, my people have taken this Recitation as a *thing to be shunned.*"[31]
>
> But Lot believed him; and he said, "*I will flee* to my Lord; He is All-mighty, the All-wise."[32]
>
> O believers, when believing women come to you as *emigrants*, test them. God knows very well their belief. Then, if you know them to be believers, return them not to those who conceal the truth. They are not permitted to the concealers, nor are the concealers permitted to them.[33]
>
> And the Outstrippers, the first of the *emigrants* and the helpers, and those who followed them in good-doing – God will be well-pleased with them and they are well-pleased with Him; and He has prepared for them gardens underneath which rivers flow, therein to dwell forever and ever; that is the mighty triumph.[34]

Everything in existence relates to God as Peace through being-at-peace, as peace comes from Him.[35] Being-at-peace is the original and authentic nature of all created beings, including us. Our free will, as the precondition of relating to God the Faithful through faith, allows us to oppose our nature or discover and realize ourselves freely in it.

---

28 Ibid., 9:117, *al-muhājirīna.*

29 Ibid., 4:97, *fatuhājirū.*

30 Ibid., 4:89, *juhājirū.*

31 Ibid., 25:30, *mahjūran.*

32 Ibid., 29:26, *muhājirun.*

33 Ibid., 60:10, *muhājirātin.*

34 Ibid., 9:100, *al-muhājirīna.*

35 See Muslim, 1:292.

Nothing in existence is not at peace: even if manifest in motion, peace is never deposed as our principle nature. It can only be suppressed by a will against God's. We realize our nature by accepting peace as ever-present in the essential core of our being and all forms in which we present through movement as affirming peace, as well as denying it. We are constantly spurred toward our goal of realizing our authentic nature by the possibilities of moving within the world and of the world moving within us. That goal is our path back through the surface of the world, along the vertical axis, towards the centre or peace within the self.

Passing through countless possible conditions, we nonetheless remain on a path. We journey from the depths to the height, darkness to light, surface inwards. Our nature spurs us, as do the things of the outside world, whether we take them as signs of Peace or opaque, as the emphasis given above to certain semantic fields in the Recitation makes clear: defilement *flee*!; *forsake them graciously*; Whoso *emigrates*; whoso *goes forth* from his house an *emigrant* to God and His apostle; those that *emigrated* in God's cause; Those who believe, and *have emigrated*; those who *emigrated* in God's way; the poor *emigrants*, who *were expelled* from their habitations and their possessions; those who *made their dwelling* in the abode, in belief, and love whosoever *has emigrated* to them; those who *emigrate* and struggle in God's way; those who *emigrated* and *were expelled* from their habitations; nearer to one another in the Book of God than the believers and the *emigrants*; And those who have believed afterwards and *emigrated*, and struggled with you; and *those who emigrate* in the way of God; God has returned towards the prophet and the *emigrants* and the Helpers; "But was not God's earth wide, so that you might *have emigrated* in it?"; until they *emigrate* in the way of God; my people have taken this Recitation as a *thing to be shunned; I will flee* to my Lord; when believing women come to you as *emigrants*; And the Outstrippers, the first of the *emigrants* and the helpers.

Postscript

"God and His angels pray for the prophet."

A translation of the text known as the *tasliyah* was given above. The speaker prays for God to take a similar attitude to the Praised and his progeny as He did to Abraham and his. The text is connected to something God says through the Praised in the Recitation: "God and His angels pray for the prophet. O believers, do you also pray for him, and greet him with peace!"[36] The statement that

36 *Qur'an*, 33:56.

God and his angels "pray for the prophet" corresponds to the part of the translation given in the text, "O God, pray for the Praised and the family of the Praised (…)"

The translation is literal and accurate, but has been a source of confusion, denial, "correction" and interpretation for centuries.[37] Reading it literally raises certain issues. How can God or his angels be said to pray for the prophet? How can we ask God to do so? Why are we asked to do so, when God Himself says that He is doing it already?

All of existence – heaven and earth and everything between them, sun and moon, stars and mountains, trees and animals – prostrates itself before God.[38] Only we and the djinn can refuse, as our relationship to God is through faith. We can participate in existence, through which God knows Himself, or oppose it and Him.

Voluntarily participating in the prostration of all things makes us the central seal of creation, with two possibilities to chose from – to be the most sublime thing in existence or the lowest. Time and space take on absolutely different aspects depending on our choice. Either they gather in fullness, as the things of the external world gather in the self, or time and space are spread thin, appearing to the self as its destruction and reduction.

In their prejudice against the sacred traditions, many interpreters interpret the verbal form *ṣallā ʿalā* in this verse and prayer in ways quite inconsistent with normal usage in the sacred text. Failing to understand its literal meaning or see it as a challenge to entrenched perspectives, they claim it is unintelligible because of a mistake in the text, rather than in the self. As knowledge can always be improved, when facing the apparently unintelligible, it is best to try our ignorance first.

The cognate noun *salāt* means "worship" and is a key concept for the Muslim sacred tradition. A look at how this "challenging crux" is treated in other discursive frameworks may offer some prospect of understanding in a way faithful to the literal text, which is always the same under countless interpretations. Knowledge is not increased by radically distinguishing the knowing subject from *salāt* as an external object of knowledge. We transcend duality by participating in worship, not reifying it.

Toshihiko Izutsu has written: "As to the basic meaning of *salāt* we know that the verb *sallā* meant 'to invoke blessings upon someone' in both pre-Koranic and the post-Koranic literature."[39] This meaning derives from the form that

---

37 See Patton, *Religion of the Gods*, 282–306.

38 See, for example, *Qurʾan*, 22:18.

39 Izutsu, *God and Man in the Koran*, 149.

signifies worship, incorporating both spoken and non-spoken attitudes. As our way of relating to God, worship is fully formed ritual with nothing arbitrary about the time or place, the positions taken, or what is said.

This ritual contains nothing from the world, even while entirely located in it. God determined that our worship should be our voluntary doing of His will, the self voluntarily excluding its own will in order to manifest the will of the Self. It is denying denial and making affirmation manifest within it. Therefore, God calls on us to establish an act of worship that resides within our nature. To realize ourselves through worship is to identify external and internal in us. Entering worship, we leave the arbitrary and participate fully in a form of existence that is God's will. We consciously bear witness to no self but the Self and His apostle the Praised.

The discomfort over the literal translation is probably due to thinking duality in terms of the God-world and God-humanity pairings as two different realities. The modern age is highly sensitive to this distinction and action based on it. It leads to the claim that, if God is, He has abandoned His creation to flux and independent causality.

The world image entailed by causality presupposes two principles. God is one of them, but outside the world, remote. The second is that the laws of the world govern existence independently of the Creator. One may, thus, know the world's truth without knowing its Creator.

Accepting the unity of the Principle and the principle of Unity means that we and the world are not an admissible counterweight to God. We would then determine Him, Who is One. Existence reveals Him. Nothing can add to or take away from Him. Humanity epitomizes this revelation, both as concealment and revelation. When God told him this, the Praised replied: "My prayer, my ritual sacrifice, my living, my dying – all belong to God, the Lord of all Being. No associate has He."[40]

The One God reveals Himself in His creation, duality, and confirms Essence as ineffable and indeterminate. Essence does not oppose, it reveals Him. Duality is first the reception of the One and then giving. Both receiving and giving are ways the One reveals Himself. They are in perfect harmony, but not reducible to each other. They are just signs of the One. Neither involves anything not from Him.

What reception and giving contain bears witness to the One's absolute closeness and remoteness. The One is present in all things so that the relations of giving and receiving are constantly changing, constantly producing new

---

40 *Qur'an*, 6:162–63.

manifestations of the One: what was received becomes what is given, what was given what is received in an infinite chain of signs indicating the Creator as both Near and Present. None of this is against or outside the One, Who is absolutely close to all things as well as absolutely remote, absolutely similar and absolutely different.

Central to all that reveals the Creator, we focus creation. We are first receivers, as we have only that in which God reveals Himself by the world to it. We are only real in the Real, however, as images of Him Who shows Himself to Himself through us. All of creation gathers in us, out of our desire to relate to the Faithful through confidence. God reveals Himself to Himself in any individual that has attained perfect potential: the perfect individual is the perfect image of the Lord. God has no other. To whom shall He reveal Himself, whom love, if not His own self?

In worship, properly understood, we manifest our love of God with all our being. Our act of worship is not ours; it is a revelation of God worshipping His own manifestation in and through us. Existence is like a mirror in which God regards Himself. When existence worships in and through the perfect individual, it is actually God worshipping in and through us and existence. Worshipping, we rise within the self from depth to height.[41] This is our reason and purpose in our most beautiful example, which connects us to God as the holder of the most beautiful names.

The Praised received the form of worship during his absolute return to God in Whom the world's limits are transcended. Raised up in perfection from the night of the world into full light, he brought together the arcs of existence. Descending again to reach the depth, he brought the form of worship with him as a received way for us to rise towards our own potential. God is absolutely near to the world in its absolute prostration, as we return to Him in our own acts of prostration.

After God had raised him to the height to receive the act of worship, the Praised, the perfect epitome of creation, confirmed the real intention of divine self-revelation. God gave the form of worship by which He reveals Himself to Himself in us as His perfect images. Saying that He and the angels worship the

41 The most sublime experience of the Praised was his being drawn up from the lowest depth to the One, as symbolized by the journey from the Inviolable to the Further Mosque. This is when he received the act of worship from the One. He then returned into the world with it so that he might give it to us as our means of ascent. His words have been handed down: *al- Ṣalāt miʿrāj al-muʾmin*, which mean "Worship is the rapture of the faithful." Cited in Rāzī, *al-Tafsīr al-kubrā wa mafātīḥ al-ghayb*, 1:213.

Praised, God reminds us that what He, the only Real, worships in His perfect image is Himself. God's calls for us to do the same and the Praised's explanation of how both reveal our sublime potential: "O God, pray for the Praised and the family of the Praised as you prayed for Abraham and the family of Abraham, for you are the All-praised, the All-highest!"

One joins integral worship, but not as if entering another world. Two inextricable aspects of the same manifestation of God, we and the world are in space and time. Worship transforms our relationship with the world. There is nothing arbitrary about any aspect of worship. The worshipper is oriented freely with regard to existence as a whole, in the space and time of the external. The time of the external world and that of the worshipping self align in mutual regard. Nothing in how the worshipper acts or moves can be treated separately from the words pronounced, thought, listened to.

Prostration is one element of worship. The worshipper moves towards prostration from the first moment of the act. From standing and reciting, the worshipper then stretches out, straightens up and finally falls in prostration. The worshipper's focus rises up to seven foundations (head, hands, knees, and feet) that symbolically characterize the world as a whole, with its seven earths and the seven heavens. Lowering oneself in prostration is to rise up, sublimity within humility. In this position, the face is on the surface of the earth, as are the palms of the hands, the knees, and the tips of the toes. The worshipper brings together earth and heaven and everything they contain in the act of prostration.

God told us of the universal prostration through the Praised: "For do you not see that everything that is in the heavens and on the earth, the sun and the moon, the stars and the mountains, the trees and the animals, and many amongst people too, do prostrate themselves before their God?"[42] All of existence and every individual thing in existence prostrate themselves. All of existence is a place of worship. We humans comprehend existence in its totality. In prostration, we are images of existence: all the worlds brought together within us, we made manifest in them. In the duality of our existence – gathering and dispersion – the perfect individual manifests God. As the Praised said: "The nearest a servant comes to his Lord is when he is prostrating himself, so make supplication."[43]

When God and the angels worship the prophet and He calls on the faithful to do the same and be at peace with him in Peace, this is the One's self-revelation through perfect humanity, unifying existence so that God and no

---

42 *Qur'an*, 22:18.

43 Muslim, 1:254.

other is manifest in it. We see in the Praised our own redemptive and supreme potential, manifest perfectly for all time, at each and every moment.

Our relationship as faithful worshippers to the Praised, whom we are told to keep faith with,[44] is our perfected relationship with God as Faith. Our act of worship resembles the divine revelation of His act of worship: our service reveals His mastery. God said through the Praised: "Worship is divided into two parts between Me and My servant – half is for Me, and half for My servant."[45]

Worship is an integral act, revealing the One in and through two – in the worshipping Self and the worshipping self as Its perfect image. Taking in all of existence, the self of the Praised makes manifest the confession of no self but the Self and no praised but the All-praised, as suggested by his prayer: "O God, our Lord, unto Thee be praise that would fill the heavens and the earth and fill that which will please Thee beyond them!"[46]

All existence and every self share in the Praised's nature as sublime created principle and purpose of creation: he is the mercy to the worlds, the maternal prophet. Calling on God to worship the Praised, we affirm our witness of no self but the Self and the Praised as His apostle. One may therefore say that the divine act of worship is made manifest in the human act of worship. This is because all of being – life, will, power, knowledge, speech, sight, and hearing – is but His manifestation as Living, Willing, Powerful, Knowing, Speaking, Seeing, and Hearing. When He loves His servant, any individual self-realizing through worship, God is that individual's act of looking, hearing, grasping, and walking.[47]

The clear statement that God and the angels worship the prophet is not difficult for an initiate who accepts His proximity is inextricable from His remoteness, His similarity from His difference, and who knows the Real as Him always with us,[48] as He creates doer and done.[49] Not God, but we can be absent, and can return, as God said through the Praised: "When somebody remembers Me in himself, I remember him in Myself."[50] Perfect worship, symbolized by the

---

44 See *Qur'an*, 10:104.

45 Muslim, 1:216.

46 Ibid., 1:252.

47 See Bukhārī, 8:336–37.

48 See *Qur'an*, 57:4.

49 Ibid., 37:96.

50 This sacred tradition is included in most of the collections of the traditions about the prophet of the first rank. See Graham, *Divine Word and Prophetic Word in Early Islam*, 127 ff.

Praised, manifests Him, as Ibn al-ʿArabi said.[51] In Henry Corbin's words: "If a mental theophany is attached to the practice of Prayer, it is because Prayer is first of all 'Prayer of God' (it is God who prays and shows Himself to Himself)."[52]

God does not cease to be One by His self-revelation to Himself in creation. Perfection is manifest in all things, in their freedom. No matter how great or small, nothing escapes perfection. That He worships Himself in His self-manifestation through worship of the Praised, giving creation the meaning of His self-regard also appears as existence's universal worship of His truth of being:

> God most High informed His worshippers of the rank which His prophet holds with Him in the heavenly host, by praising Him in the presence of the angels of access, and by the *salat* of those angels for Him. Then He commanded *salat* and a greeting of peace from the people of the world below, so that the people of both worlds, above and below, might unite in His praise.[53]

Worship is precisely what links manifestation with the Praised as maternal and sealing prophet. Only he, in fullness of purity, is worthy that God regard Himself in him. All others who address God pray to the Praised as the merciful principle whose maternal mercy is their refuge. Creation is with and through him, the link with God, His most sublime manifestation, confessed by the signs in world and self, who said of those with him: "We are the last, but the foremost on the Day of Resurrection."[54]

Praying for God to worship the Praised and his family, we affirm our individual desire to participate in universal worship and bear witness in the prophet as maternal principle to our own relationship with God. The Praised and Abraham are joined in the self that participates in this universal act of worship. Reference to the All-praised in prayer recalls the acts of praise, of manifesting Him and of receiving manifestation, and so the light of the Praised. Through it, each of us is connected with All-praised God, as the Praised receives and gives only His self-manifestation.

---

51 See Ibn al-ʿArabī, *al-Futūḥāt al-makkiyya*, 1:431, cited in Robson, "Blessings on the Prophet," 366.

52 Corbin, *Creative Imagination in the Sufism of Ibn ʿArabī*, 264.

53 al-Suyūṭī, *al-Ḥirz al-manīʿ min al-qawl al-badīʿ fī al-ṣalāt ʿalā al-ḥabīb al-shafīʿ*, 12, cited in Padwick, *Muslim Devotions*, 156.

54 Bukhārī, 2:9–10.

The Praised's link to Abraham, so frequently reflected in the external world, demands re-examination of how their historical existence in time and self is interrelated. Both arcs of Abraham's posterity meet in the historical Praised, whose historical presence was in the depths and heavenly presence on the height. The Praised, as created principle of existence, comprehends and transcends everything in that span from the depths to the seventh heaven. From his transcendence of existence, he descended with the act of worship to reveal and manifest God.

> Someone asked Rūmī: "What is the meaning of 'greetings' and 'blessings' upon the prophet?" The master replied: "It means that these acts of adoration and service and worship and attention do not come from us and we are not free to perform them. The truth is that 'blessings' and 'prayers' and 'greetings' belong to God; they are not ours, they are wholly His and belong to Him."[55]

---

55 Arberry, *Discourses of Rūmī*, 79.

CHAPTER 7

In the Recitation (II)

The Praised said we sleep in this world to wake up on dying.[1] This sleep lasts from the fourth month of pregnancy, when the Spirit is breathed into the child, until death.[2] Our dreams during our earthly sleep lie on the boundary between worlds, where both worlds are present, as they are in the soul. Dying, we enter that boundary area to await universal resurrection and the introduction of the dead before the Judge. The day of reckoning for our debt to our Lord, which we have either returned to or failed to, is another boundary area, between the garden and the fire.

Our condition always involves such a boundary area, from which to rise up towards Spirit, approach the One, and distance ourselves from all that is other than Him. These areas are like steps on the upright path. What leaves a boundary area must enter it, what enters must have left somewhere else. This is the case with death – what dies was born. But God was neither born nor begets and every born thing is real in Him, returning as living to Him, Who is untouched by death.

This world and the other are connected by the boundary area. This is so for all the worlds: there are boundary areas between all of them, but their Lord is one. The worlds are in orders of descent and ascent. To see them all together shows the closeness of the arcs.[3] Existence forms an integral unit made up of the arcs of descent and ascent. The One is the beginning of descent and end of ascent. Descent's final point is in this world. Everything we see in it has descended from the unseen. Ascent is transition into the boundary area to climb the stations of the arc of return.

The boundary area is a higher level of reality than the world below it, the world above higher again. To enter the boundary area is to leave this world. The dead are in it or on a higher level of reality. The resurrected are at a higher level than the sleeping dead. If we awaken in death from our dream in this world, then it is the dream of death we wake from in resurrection.

---

1 Ibn al-ʿArabī and other Muslim writers cite this expression as the Praised's, even though it is not included in the main collections of his traditional teachings. See Chittick, *The Sufi Part of Knowledge*, 119.

2 See Musallam, *Sex and Society in Islam.*

3 See *Qur'an*, 53:8–9.

 | DOI 10.1163/9789004279407_031

Resurrection to gather before the Lord for judgment is like the removal of veils that stop us finding and confessing our claims against ourselves, or the Lord's, or the claims of all things in creation. Of the judgment, Ibn al-ʿArabi said: "God will come in order to decide and to judge; so He will only come under [the guise of] His Name, 'Light.' The Earth will be made radiant with the lights of its Lord, and through that light every 'soul will know its works, the former and the latter,'[4] for it will find them present, unveiled by that light."[5]

Where we stand will be seen in the full light cast into the recesses of the self and it will reflect our behaviour from when we came into this world until we leave it for the ante-chamber. To have served in this world, which is to know that we only have what we have been given, is revealed as the real prize in this new order, since God is never absent, but with us wherever we are.

We think of existence as His absence, to which we have become accustomed, our movements no longer migrating from apparent to Real. When we discover His face before us always, shame occupies the self, whose essence makes known to us that single reality cannot involve two presences. Aware of being images of God, we are ashamed of our possessions, since there can be no god but God.

Shame, the desire to wane and fade from existence, is admission of the Real, as our sense of "I am" loses meaning in the face of His "I am." This is because our feelings are just images through which the divine "I am" is manifest. The fully enlightened self encounters the opposite of what it wished in the shadows: the self-desiring self is far from its Lord, the self that wants Him returns to itself. The self saved for something other than the Lord has no desire. The answers it receives to its desires are but signs through which the desired Lord reveals Himself. The self that, in shame before the Lord, would be nothing and desires death, accepts His presence and enters life. He gives Himself as the Living.

The self realizes itself by confessing: "God, there is no god but He, the Living, the Standing. Slumber seizes Him not, neither sleep!"[6] Three evident proofs remind us of this – first, breath, which, on arrival in this world out of mystery, we know by being and not out of conscious witness of the beginning; second, the ceaseless alternation of sleeping and so-called waking, which we know as repeating, passing into sleep from waking and returning from it; and third, death, whose certainty we know through the death of others.

---

4 *Qur'an*, 82:5.

5 Ibn al-ʿArabī, *al-Futūḥāt al-makkiyya*, 2:485.32; cited in Chittick, "Death and the World of Imagination: Ibn al-ʿArabī's Eschatology," 66.

6 *Qur'an*, 2:255.

These three evident proofs range from waking to death and slumber to reawakening. That waking is lower than sleeping and death is clear from the degrees of individual will involved. We feel that the waking will can imagine and inform desire, deciding on its outcome. Sleeping offers transition into a world the will of the sleeper no longer rules over. Returning to the waking world, the sleeper can freely compare waking and sleeping events. There is no return from death, but our experience of sleep intimates a world where the will as the waking state knows it ceases to be. These three degrees – waking, sleep, and death – are thus relations with God Whom slumber and sleep comprehend not. His will comprehends our every condition, so that sleep and death are higher levels of manifestation than wakefulness in a waking world.

The self enters this world with its full endowment. The Lord has not withheld, nor given more. He reveals Himself in every self at every moment, with ever-present difference. As the self leaves this world for the antechamber to attend and be sorted before the Lord, it carries its image of the Lord. Its self-realization by confessing no self but the Self then leads it from the self as the Self's image, which we upend in our desire to see the Self beyond it and confirm that He has no other, as witnessed: "The truth has come, and falsehood has vanished away; surely falsehood is ever certain to vanish."[7]

Riding a camel, the Praised passed seven times around the Kaʿba, and then turning to the 360 idols arrayed around it, he smashed these incarnate images of gods with his prophet's staff.[8] He overturned them, since no image is worthy of Him, no matter that He reveals Himself through images or signs. If established as independent of Him, the image becomes an obstacle on the self's path upward from humility to the sublime, slumber to reawakening, matter to Spirit.

Ascent and entry are also descent and exit. It is possible for the condition we reach through ascent to be transformed into a petrified image. It will not be, however, so long as the self continues to transcend, passing from form to form, intent on the goal beyond. Possibilities surround us in the external world. To reserve our heart for God alone, we must direct our staff against the images of the external world, transform them into transparent signs of truth.

Whenever truth is manifest before the Lord Who shows Himself to Himself through us, we feel the most profound shame. Feeling that God needs us, we are more modest than a covered virgin, as He depends on nothing, He is abundant, we poor. Only with absolute poverty can we be what we are – His

---

7 Ibid., 17:81.

8 For the Praised's circuit around the Kaʿba and his destruction of the statues, see Ibn Isḥāq, *Sīrat Rasūl Allāh*, 552.

revelation to Himself in His unity and flux. We give ourselves to God in absolute poverty, as only thus may we receive His revelation.

Our need to escape the images of our Lord, Who reveals Himself without cease to us, showing Himself to His own, leads us to the Hour in which He shows Himself to all people so that they will remember.[9] He is manifest in our awakening from death to finding our place in the order that follows the two previous forms of slumber, the first during life here, the second during death or being in the antechamber of that other world.

Thought and memory are forms of our presence in existence. They require the spatial and temporal expanses of this world and mediate the One, Who has no other. What thought and memory attain fades. What they establish in firm images is seeming, fictions that veil the truth of creation, without past or future. They are one, always in the absolute hour, even though their forms are numberless.

Of course, none alone nor all together can displace the one, self-identical Hour. The forms do not mediate the Hour. Otherwise, there would be something more than truth. But God is Truth and He has no other. Travelling from the forms of appearance is the path of realization in truth. This is why thought and memory are only signs on that path. They are never what the Goal is, even though they have no reality without it. The traveller leaves them behind for the sake of the Goal whose signposts they are.

God is manifest in creation at every moment, so that existence constantly experiences coming into and going out of being, death and animation. Through the Praised, God said He is constantly concerned with something.[10] He is always Creator. He reveals Himself in the Hour through new creation, so that each individual is always a new image of Him. In His constantly being One, as one image disappears, another appears.[11]

The self connects with what is coming into being and what is leaving it so that the non-existent appears existent, the unreal real. Desiring what it does not have, it introduces lack of peace into existence as the revelation of Peace, turning towards the images as the solid places of his inner existence. Such a self is closed, incapable of passing over its limits. Entering and exiting, it does not recognise the One, Who flows in and out, entering and exiting, outside and inside. By realizing the self and being face to Face, we receive the Creator as our own condition. In a tradition of the Praised, God says to the blessed: "I say

---

9 See Muslim 1:124.

10 See *Qur'an*, 55:29.

11 For the Muslim traditional viewpoint on the continuity of new creation, see Izutsu, *Sufism and Taoism*, 205–215.

to a thing, "Be!," and it is;[12] now I have given to you that you should say "be!" And it will be."[13]

The discourse of the Recitation faithfully reflects this entry and exit, leaving and taking, which comprise all existence. A look at forms derived from the verbal root *kh-r-j* in the Recitation may help show that the concepts of "wandering," "abandonment," "exile," "leaving" and so forth change meaning depending upon the discursive context. These concepts are spread throughout existence, from earth to the seventh heaven, and as they ascend they receive new content from the concealed treasury.

> It is He who sends down upon His servant signs, clear signs, that He *may bring you forth* from the shadows into the light. Surely God is to you All-gentle, Ever-merciful.[14]
>
> And of His signs is that the heaven and earth stand firm by His command; then, when He calls you once and suddenly, out of the earth, lo *you shall come forth.*[15]
>
> And when We took compact with you: "You shall not shed your own blood, neither *expel* your own from your habitations"; then you confirmed it and yourselves bore witness. Then there you are killing one another, and *expelling* a party of you from their habitations conspiring against them in sin and enmity; and if they come to you as captives, you ransom them; yet *their expulsion* was forbidden you.[16]
>
> And God caused you to grow out of the earth, then He shall return you into it and *bring you forth.*[17]
>
> *Alif. Lam. Ra.* A Book We have sent down to thee that thou *mayest bring forth* mankind from the shadows to the light by the leave of their Lord, to the path of the All-mighty, the All-praised.[18]
>
> And if they had patience, until thou *comest out* to them, that would be better for them; and God is All-forgiving, Ever-merciful.[19]

---

12 *Qur'an,* 16:40 and 36:82

13 This tradition is cited by Ibn al-ʿArabī, *al-Futūḥāt al-makkiyya,* 3:295.16. See Chittick, "Death and the World of Imagination: Ibn al-ʿArabī's Eschatology," 71.

14 Ibid., 57:9, *liyukhrijakum.*

15 Ibid., 30:25, *takhrujūna.*

16 Ibid., 2:84–85, *tukhrijūna* (...) *tukhrijūna* (...) *ikhrājuhum.*

17 Ibid., 71:17–18, *yukhrijukum ikhrājan.*

18 Ibid., 14:1, *litukhrija.*

19 Ibid., 49:5, *takhruja.*

If you do not help him, yet God has helped him already, when the concealers *drove him forth* the second of two, when the two were in the Cave, when he said to his companion, "Sorrow not; surely God is with us." Then God sent down on him His Shekhinah and confirmed him with legions you did not see; and he made the word of the concealers the lowest; and God's word is the uppermost; God is All-mighty, All-wise.[20]

Indeed they were to startling thee from the land, *to expel thee* from it, and then they would have tarried after thee only a little – the wont of those We sent before thee of Our apostle; thou wilt find no change to Our wont.[21]

And say: "My Lord, lead me in with a just ingoing, and *lead me out with a just outgoing*; grant me authority from Thee, to help me."[22]

Will you not fight a people who broke their oaths and purposed *to expel* the apostle, beginning the first time against you? Are you afraid of them? You would do better to be afraid of God if you are believers?[23]

O believers, take not My enemy and your enemy for friends, offering them love, though they have disbelieved in the truth that has come to you, *expelling* the apostle and you because you believe in God your Lord. If you *go forth* to struggle in My way and seek My good pleasure, secretly loving them, yet I know very well what you conceal and what you publish; and whosoever of you does that, has gone astray from the right way.[24]

As thy Lord *brought thee forth* from thy house with the truth, and a part of the believers were averse to it, disputing with thee concerning the truth after it had become clear, as though they were being driven into death with their eyes wide open.[25]

Thou makest the night to enter into the day and Thou makest the day to enter into the night, Thou *bringest forth* the living from the dead and Thou *bringest forth* the dead from the living, and Thou providest whomsoever Thou wilt without reckoning.[26]

Out of the earth We created you, and We shall restore you into it, and *bring you forth* from it a second time.[27]

---

20 Ibid., 9:40, *akhrajahū.*

21 Ibid., 17:76–77, *liyukhrijūka.*

22 Ibid., 17:80, *akhrijnī mukhraja ṣidqin.*

23 Ibid., 9:13, *bi ikhrāj.*

24 Ibid., 60:1, *yukhrijūna* (…) *kharajtum.*

25 Ibid., 8:5–6, *akhrajaka.*

26 Ibid., 3:27, *tukhriju* (…)*tukhriju.*

27 Ibid., 20:55, *nukhrijukum.*

He knows what penetrates into the earth, and what *comes forth* from it, what comes down from heaven, and what goes up to it; He is Ever-merciful, the All-forgiving.[28]

From them *come forth* the pearl and the coral.[29]

He who appointed the earth to be a cradle for you, and appointed ways for you therein, that haply you may be guided; and who sent down out of heaven water in measure; and we revived thereby a land that was dead; even so you *shall be brought forth*.[30]

Surely in that is a sign for a people who remember. It is He who subjected to you the sea, that you may eat of it fresh flesh, and *bring forth* out of it ornaments for you to wear.[31]

And every man – We have fastened to him his bird of omen upon his neck; and *We shall bring forth* for him, on the Day of Resurrection, a Book he shall find spread wide open.[32]

Then We said, "Adam, surely this is an enemy to thee and thy wife. So *let him not expel you both* from the Garden, so that thou art unprosperous."[33]

Then Satan caused them to slip therefrom and *brought them* out of that they were in; and We said, "Get you all down, each of you an enemy of each; and in the earth a sojourn shall be yours, and enjoyment for a time."[34]

Said He, "*Go thou forth* from it, despised and banished. Those of them that follow thee – I shall assuredly fill Gehenna with all of you."[35]

"Our Lord, *bring us forth* out of it! Then, if we revert, we shall be evildoers indeed."[36]

The movement of the self from one state to another is double, in the world as our temporary abode and in the self split between the depth and the sublime. If this movement is upwards, towards God, it activates our perfect potential,

---

28 Ibid., 34:2, *yakhruju.*

29 Ibid., 55:22, *yakhruju.*

30 Ibid., 43:10–11, *tukhrijūna.*

31 Ibid., 16:13–14, *tastakhrijū.*

32 Ibid., 17:13, *nukhriju.*

33 Ibid., 20:117, *lā yukhrijannakumā.*

34 Ibid., 2:36, *akhrajakumā.*

35 Ibid., 7:18, *ukhruj.*

36 Ibid., 23:107, *akhrijnā.*

realization of our authentic nature. In any case, we are moved to change the condition of the self by what is in and what is around us.

With countless potential movements, back and forth, right and left, up and down, only one leads towards the most beautiful height. That is movement with God in our perfected humanity. It never appears twice in the same way. The forms God appears to us in are forms of self-realization. Persecution by others and suffering to free ourselves from servitude other than service to God can become redemptive migration and return in which both self and Self find satisfaction, realizing the confession of no self but the Self. Then, we have revealed the authentic self and discovered our Lord.

Redemption through persecution and suffering reveal the world and the signs in it as belonging to the God from and to Whom we flee, as there is no refuge from God but in God. Examples exist in the Recitation of migration that is not exile, suffering that redeems, persecution that ends in refuge, and separation which makes connection possible. There are things in the world that correspond to every sentence of the Recitation, in terms of their connection to the whole.

Persecution involves at least two aspects. Our authentic nature harries us to move from seeming to Real. This is migration from depth to height, dark to light. In it, the Praised stands above, leading us on up the path of ascent. Separation from the Real is either following or abandoning the Praised: He *may bring you forth* from the shadows into the light; out of the earth, lo *you shall come forth*; neither *expel* your own from your habitations; and *expelling* a party of you from their habitations; Yet their *expulsion* was forbidden you; and *bring you forth*; that thou *mayest bring forth* mankind; until thou *comest out* to them; when the concealers *drove him forth; to expel thee* from it; *lead me out with a just outgoing*; and purposed *to expel* the apostle; *expelling* the apostle ... If you *go forth* to struggle in My way; As thy Lord *brought thee forth* from thy house with the truth; Thou *bringest forth* the living from the dead and Thou *bringest forth* the dead from the living; and *bring you forth* from it a second time; and what *comes forth* from it; From them *come forth* the pearl and the coral; even so you *shall be brought forth*; and *bring forth* out of it ornaments; and *We shall bring forth* for him a book; So *let him not expel you both* from the Garden; and *brought them* out; *Go thou forth* from it; Our Lord, *bring us forth* out of it!

CHAPTER 8

In the Recitation (III)

In our world of waking and sleeping, we experience suffering and bliss, ignorance and knowledge, death and life, none of which exceeds its contrary. Each pair is mixed, but it is our orientation towards bliss, knowledge, and life that marks out our higher value in the hierarchy of existence and our greater closeness to God, whose mercy exceeds His wrath.[1]

This deployment of the levels of existence begins with Essence as Ineffable, revealed by the One, like or equal to nothing, whose names reveal Him. In the imaginal, these names connect the individual trapped in the material with God. Our being has five levels – Essence, God, the names, the imaginal, and sensory existence – through which God reveals Himself as real. Ibn al-ʿArabi said:

> God created the cosmos in its essence only for felicity; wretchedness occurs to whom it occurs as an accident, since Sheer Good untouched by evil is the Being of God, who bestowed existence upon the cosmos; and nothing emanates from Him except that which corresponds to Him, which is good alone.[2]

Sheer good is in all things, revealed in contrast to evil, which is not a principle. In the moment as indivisible reality, good appears in contrast to its contrary. God has no other, no contrary. Talk of a contrary refers to the nature or form of His revelation. We, like everything else in existence, are constantly coming and going – coming from and returning to good. Good is a principle, evil is not. Distinguishing one from the other and cleaving to good, we realize ourselves according to our principle, which is constantly being revealed to and concealed from us. We are strangers to what is not by the principle, and, called by our higher potential and spurred on by its bafflement, we constantly struggle with forces keeping us from the principle, which thereby reveal what they are not and can never be.

God gives examples in the Recitation of how appearance and reality, loss and finding relate: word pictures of our capacities from our original and most beautiful sublimity to our lowest depth, and back in the return of all things to

1 See Bukhārī, 9:482.

2 Ibn al-ʿArabī, *al-Futūḥāt al-makkiyya*, 3:389.21.

 | DOI 10.1163/9789004279407_032

the principle. The splitting of the self between the extremes of the empty dark and full light corresponds to how un-real relates to Real. The world is manifestation of the Real and our only possible essence. We stand before It from moment to moment and fade, with the world, as un-real, since only the Real is real. We bear this knowledge within. Everything in the world and the self reminds us of our original nature.

Acting to maintain both world and self with all their distinctions, language can comprehend the self's conditions, reflecting all the changes in God's revelation. A single root yields unlimited forms, each meaning something different in different sentences. Meaning derives from the context of sentence and speaking and listening subjects. When a form is repeated, the subjects are different. Existence is flux, never ceasing, ever new. Nothing limits God, not even the condition of the manifesting self.

God spoke to the people of the Praised through him in their own language, a claim that can be accepted or not. Either entails obligations. To discover the meaning of Hagar's name or such concepts as "Hagaric heart," "muhajir" and "hijra," particularly in terms of traditional teaching about our entry into, passage through and exit from this world, we must consider their appearances in the Recitation.

> God is the Protector of the believers; He *brings them forth* from the shadows into light. And the concealers – their protectors are idols, that *bring them forth* from the light into the shadows; those are the inhabitants of the Fire, therein dwelling forever.[3]
>
> From whatsoever place thou issuest, *turn thy* face towards the Inviolable Mosque; and wherever you may be, turn your faces towards it, that the people may not have any argument against you, excepting the evildoers of them; and fear you them not, but fear you Me; and that I may perfect My blessing upon you, and that haply so you may be guided.[4]
>
> Satan has decked out fair their deeds to them and he has barred them from the way, and therefore they are not guided, so that they prostrate not themselves to God, who *brings forth* what is hidden in the heavens and earth; and He knows what you conceal and what you publish.[5]
>
> Hast thou not regarded those who *went forth* from their habitations in their thousands fearful of death? God said to them, "Die!" Then He gave

3 *Qur'an*, 2:257, *yukhrijukum* (…) *yukhrijūnahum*.

4 Ibid., 2:150, *kharajta*.

5 Ibid., 27:24–5, *yukhriju*.

them life. Truly God is bounteous to the people, but most of the people are not thankful.[6]

When they come to you, they say, "We believe"; but they have entered in concealment of the truth, and so they *have departed* in it; God knows very well what they were hiding.[7]

But had We prescribed for them, saying, "Slay yourselves" or "*Leave* your habitations," they would not have done it, save a few of them.[8]

How is it with you, that you do not fight in the way of God, and for the men, women, and children who, being abased, say, "Our Lord, *bring us forth* from this city whose people are evildoers, and appoint to us a protector from Thee, and appoint to us from Thee a helper"?[9]

(...) and *expel* them from where they *expelled* you.[10]

They said: "If thou givest not over, Lot, thou shalt assuredly be one of the expelled."[11]

"Hast thou come, Moses," he said, "*to expel us* out of our land by thy sorcery?"[12]

They say, "If we return to the City, the mightier ones of it *will expel* the more abased"; yet glory belongs unto God, and unto His apostle and the believers, but the hypocrites do not know it.[13]

God forbids you not, as regards those who have not fought you in the cause of the debt, *nor expelled* you from your habitations, that you should be kindly to them, and act justly towards them; surely God loves the just.[14]

And We sent Moses with Our signs – "*Bring forth* thy people from shadows to the light and remind thou them of the Days of God." Surely in that are signs for every man enduring, thankful![15]

You are the best nation ever *brought forth* to men, bidding to honour and forbidding dishonour, and believing in God.[16]

---

6 Ibid., 2:243, *kharajū*.

7 Ibid., 5:61, *kharajū*.

8 Ibid., 4:66, *ukhrujū*.

9 Ibid., 4:75, *akhrijnā*.

10 Ibid., 2:191, *akhrijūhum min ḥaythu akhrajūkum*.

11 Ibid., 26:167, *mukhrajīn*.

12 Ibid., 20:57, *litukhrijanā*.

13 Ibid., 63:8, *la yukhrijanna*.

14 Ibid., 60:8, *lam yukhrijūkum*.

15 Ibid., 14:5, *akhrij*.

16 Ibid., 3:110, *ukhrijta*.

Hast thou not regarded the Council of the Children of Israel, after Moses, when they said to a prophet of theirs: "Raise up for us a king, and we will fight in God's way." He said: "Might it be that, if fighting is prescribed for you, you will not fight?" They said: "Why should we not fight in God's way, who *have been expelled* from our habitations and our children?" Yet when fighting was prescribed for them, they turned their backs except a few of them; and God has knowledge of the evildoers.[17]

Leave is given to those who fight because they were wronged – surely God is able to help them – who *were expelled* from their habitations without right, except that they say: "Our Lord is God." Had God not *driven back* the people, some by the means of others, there had been destroyed cloisters and churches, oratories and mosques, wherein God's name is much mentioned. Assuredly God will help him who helps Him – surely God is All-strong, All-mighty.[18]

As for the wall, it belonged to two orphan lads in the city, and under it was a treasure belonging to them. Their father was a righteous man; and thy Lord desired that they should come of age and than *bring forth* their treasure as a mercy from thy Lord.[19]

God only forbids you as to those who have fought you in the cause of the debt, and *expelled you* from your habitations, and have supported in *your expulsion*, that you should take them, for friends. And whosoever takes them for friends, those – they are evildoers.[20]

The hypocrites are afraid, lest a sura should be sent down against them, telling thee what is in their hearts. Say: "Mock on; *God will bring forth* what you fear."[21]

They will question thee concerning the holy month, and fighting in it. Say: "Fighting in it is a heinous thing, but to bar from God's way, and conceal the truth of Him, and the Inviolable Mosque, and *to expel* its people from it – that is more heinous in God's sight; and persecution is more heinous than slaying." They will not cease to fight with you, till they turn you from your debt, if they are able; and whosoever of you turns from his debt, and dies a concealer – their works have failed in this world and the next; those are inhabitants of the Fire; therein they shall dwell forever.[22]

17 Ibid., 2:246, *ukhrijnā*.

18 Ibid., 22:39–40, *ukhrijū*.

19 Ibid., 18:82, *yastakhrijā*.

20 Ibid., 60:9, *akhrajūkum* (...) *ikhrājikum*.

21 Ibid., 9:64, *mukhrijun*.

22 Ibid., 2:217, *ikhrāju*.

> Man says: "What, when I am dead *shall I then be brought forth* alive?"[23]
> On the day they hear the Cry in truth, that is the *day of coming forth.*[24]
> No fatigue is there shall smite them, neither shall they ever be driven forth from there.[25]

Being-at-peace, faith, and doing what is good and beautiful connect us with God as Peace, Faith, and Beauty. It is our way, on which we realize our nature as peaceful, faithful, and beautiful. Otherwise, our authentic nature is covered over and deformed. We have what is needed for salvation through being-at-peace, faith, and beauty. God reveals Himself through His names and all things reveal that beauty. The self that discovers the signs in itself, expresses virtue, humility and generosity.

God is hidden, but loves to be known, *Deus absconditus ac revelatus* – and He is incomparable, infinitely far, His face set against all things in existence, revealed in them all. The decision to establish us as His viceroys on earth and give us knowledge of all the names comprises both aspects of the One Self, revelation and concealment. Looking at both aspects, as the Self hides and reveals Itself in them, splits our self between its lowest depth and most beautiful height. No depth eradicates our authentic nature, as determined by our answer to the Creator's question: "Am I not your Lord?"

Deus absconditus is *Deus revelatus* in the attribute of Beauty. *Deus absconditus* reveals Himself through Beauty as *Deus revelatus.* Revelation is constant and continuous, but constantly changing. It cannot be established in beauty. This is how He is both One and Flux. Commenting on Razi's teachings on the phenomenology of light, Henry Corbin has written:

> Majesty (i.e. rigor, inaccessible, sublimity) and Beauty (fascination, attraction, graciousness): these are the two great categories of attributes which refer respectively to the divine being as *Deus absconditus* and as *Deus revelatus,* beauty being the supreme theophany, divine self-revelation. In fact they are inseparable and there is a constant interplay between the inaccessible Majesty of Beauty and the fascinating Beauty of inaccessible Majesty. The interplay is even such that Najm Kobrā, when comparing their relation to that of the masculine and feminine principles, perceives a transference corresponding to a mutual exchange of the masculine and feminine attributes. And to suggest that their twofoldness

23 Ibid., 19:66, *lasawfa ukhraju.*

24 Ibid., 50:42, *yawm al-khurūj.*

25 Ibid., 15:48, *mukhrajīn.*

> is necessary for the spiritual individuality to be born, he quotes this saying of the Sufi Abu-Bakr Wasiti: "The attribute of Majesty and the attribute of Beauty intermingle; from their union the Spirit is born. The son is an allusion to partial reality; the father and mother an allusion to total reality." According to Najm Razi, photisms, pure lights and colored lights, refer to attributes of Beauty; the "black light" refers to the attributes of Majesty. He outlines the "physiology of the man of light" concurrently with the theory of the "unveilings of the suprasensory world."[26]

Asked about his vision of his Lord, the Praised said: "He is a Light. How could I see Him?"[27] Absolute light is *Deus absconditus*. Invisible, it is shining darkness. In contrast to the dark, it is *Deus revelatus*. Essence is unhindered, because God has no other. Absolute light is the Face of the Real, revealed by contrast to the dark side of the self. Henry Corbin has written:

> Their black face, the one the mystic perceives, is their poverty: they have nothing with which to be, they cannot be sufficient unto themselves in order to be what they have to be, it is the *inessence* of their essence. The totality of their being is their daylight face and their night face; their daylight face is making of essence out of their inessence by the absolute Subject. This is the mystical meaning of the verse in the Qorān: "Everything perishes except His Face",[28] that is except the face of light of that thing.[29]

What disappears existed. God is not such. He never existed and will never disappear. His revelation is His constant presence. When He says that He was, it means He is; when He says that He will be, it means He is. In His self-revelation to Himself, the fullness of gathering becomes the presentation of His face in the manifold and concealment in it. Concealment and discovery take place at once, as He is First and Last, Outer and Inner.[30] Otherwise, how could He teach Adam the names?

The mystery of our instruction in the names involves constant revelation and concealment. Their synchronicity recalls the constant presence of two names – in the self and in the world. Time in the self comprehends all within an hour, this world and the other, hell and paradise. Time in the world derives

26 Corbin, *The Man of Light in Iranian Sufism*, 103–104.

27 Muslim, 1:113.

28 *Qur'an*, 28:88.

29 Corbin, *The Man of Light in Iranian Sufism*, 113.

30 See *Qur'an*, 57:3.

from time in the self. What appears in it is just a sign of what is in the self. Seen from the self, Adam, Noah, Abraham, Moses, David, Jesus, and Muhammad represent possible conditions of the self.

In the external world, they all had their own formalized traditions, with their histories and signs, spread across different regions, languages, and times in causal sequence. It is hard to conceive their interconnection through the axes of world and self in terms of a history of events separate from the history of the self, which comprehends all things. Each self returns individually to the Self, under its own burden of debt. Through tradition, the prophets act as signs to remind us of return and the reckoning.

All the prophets abide in their maternal principle, in that prophet they swore their oath to in pre-existence, the perfect self and first light given by Light, first reception, first giving, in affirmation of the One. To realize him in the self is to find in him all humanity epitomized, a heart that comprehends all.

The path of redemption means rising up from the depth through the seven levels of being to the corresponding seven heavens. This ascent takes place within the self and is recalled by the seven circuits around the Kaʿba. The first house on the sacred desert valley floor was raised as a sign and signifies the heart as the centre of all seven levels of being.

The centre is also an all-embracing whole, integrity without limit. The seven circuits mark the seven levels of ascent towards the heart, recalled by the seven letters, ways, and levels of the Recitation.[31] The Recitation that entered the heart of the Praised is the Spirit of Truth.[32] Any who seek realization within the Word must first pass through all seven levels to the one which contains Its immediate reception, fullness, the absolute. This ascent is without stop, as anything less than the One falls short. We were made for perfection. Our hearts are Hagaric, exiles for the sake of the One.

According to the mystic Semnānī, rising through the levels of the self may be represented by seven prophets – Adam, Noah, Abraham, Moses, David, Jesus, and Muhammad. Each is a level of the self that manifests the centre. They form a descending and a rising arc. Henry Corbin explicates this hermeneutic physiology in his *The Man of Light in Iranian Sufism*.[33] A simplified account follows:

There are seven levels or heavens in each individual heart or at the centre of each self. The immediate impact of the self in the world is the first level. It requires a new self, even though on a higher level than physicality. This level is

31 See Muslim, 2:391; Bukhārī, 3:355; and Tirmidhī, 2:215.

32 See *Qur'an*, 26:192–94.

33 See Corbin, *The Man of Light in Iranian Sufism*, 124–25.

the purely spiritual conception of the new self, the spiritual frame of its physicality. In mystical physiology, it is called Adam's being.

The passionate self, which encompasses the unharmonized stimuli of life and close relations of dark and light, life and death, corresponds to the second level – the self that leads to evil. At this second level, one can travel in three potential directions – deeper into darkness, on the surface, or towards a higher level. The level the traveller orients himself towards, passing from lapsarian state to redemption, enemy to God, having broken all ties except those that bind us to God, given over all habits, and journeyed towards the unfathomable regions of return in accordance with His guidance, corresponds to Noah. Standing up to the lower self corresponds to Noah's conflict with his people.

At the third level, the heart, a mystical posterity is conceived, a pearl in the shell. The pearl is the true self. This level of the heart is Abraham. The fourth level is mystery or supra-consciousness, involving a close and confidential conversation and corresponding to Moses. The Spirit is the fifth level of the heart, as God's viceroy at that level of the world of descent and ascent. This is David.

A fitting Latin name for the sixth level is *arcanum*. Here, we receive the help and stimulus of the Holy Spirit. This corresponds to approach to the Praised and is the Jesus of the traveller's heart, just as in the Recitation it is Jesus, as the penultimate prophet of this cycle, who announced the last prophet.[34]

The seventh and last level relates to the divine centre, the eternal seal. This is the Praised, the precious pearl, the true self, the one conceived in Abraham. In a discussion of the linkages between the Praised and Abraham, Henry Corbin has written:

> Every passage in the Qorān which defines the relationship of Muhammad with Abraham then offers us an admirable example of the inward movement actualized by Semnānī's hermeneutics, the transition from "horizontal time" to the "time of the soul." It ends by actualizing, in the person of the human microcosm, the truth of the meaning according to which the religion of Mohammad originates in the religion of Abraham, for "Abraham was neither Jew nor Christian, but a pure believer (*hanīf*), a *Moslem*"[35] which is to say that the "Abraham of your being" is led through the subtle centres of higher consciousness and of the *arcanum* (the Moses and the Jesus of your being) until he reaches your true Ego, his spiritual progeny.[36]

34 See *Qur'an*, 61:6.

35 *Qur'an*, 3:67.

36 Corbin, *The Man of Light in Iranian Sufism*, 125.

CHAPTER 9

Witness

Taking the upright path through the levels of the self from Adam to Muhammad is return to the perfection in which everything began. As passage on the arcs of descent and ascent, it is perfect integration of outer and inner, first and last. In paradise, Adam is the most sublime image of the Praised, as the first or principle of creation, while in Becca he is the image of one whose praiseworthy core is a redemptive light on the path back to the One.

Rising through the levels and realizing the internal prophets that correspond to them, the mystic associates with each a different coloured light. These lights disclose the degrees or stations he has passed. Corbin explicates this hermeneutics of light as follows:

> The stage of the subtle body at the level of its birth, still very close to the physical organism (the "Adam of your being"), is simply darkness, a *blackness* sometimes turning to smoke-gray; the stage of the vital soul (Noah) is *blue* in colour; that of the heart (Abraham) is *red*; that of the superconscious (Moses) is *white*; that of the Spirit (David) is *yellow*; that of the *arcanum* (Jesus) is *luminous black* (*aswad nūrānī*); this is the "black light," the luminous Night about which we were informed by Najm Rāzī as well as by the *Rose Garden of Mystery* and its commentator; lastly the stage of the divine centre (Mohammad) is brilliant *green* (the splendour of the Emerald Rock) for "the colour green is the most appropriate to the secret of the mystery of Mysteries (or the suprasensory uniting all the suprasensories)."[1]

God told the Praised that He is Light.[2] God asks us to turn from confusion and follow the Light sent down through the Praised, the maternal prophet.[3] The Light was sent down from the core of the Praised, the peak of the emerald rock, through the heavens, each with its prophet who swore allegiance to the peak as to his own maternal nature or womb.[4] Redemption from the depths involves two motions – lowering and rising. Neither is separate from the other.

---

1 Corbin, *The Man of Light in Iranian Sufism*, 126.

2 See *Qur'an*, 24:35.

3 Ibid., 7:156–57.

4 Ibid., 21:107.

 | DOI 10.1163/9789004279407_033

Our darkness is never without light. God's knowledge and mercy are all encompassing. To follow the light sent down with the Praised is to discover signs of our essence and rise back through them to the self's fullest potential. God leads us out of the dark into the light,[5] so that the light remains even in the self in the thickest gloom. Descent does not mean God's incarnation or our ascent will bring about deification. We descend into existence because of God's wish to know Himself. In that descent, we are servants, with or against our will. Only voluntary service satisfies voluntary mastery. Our authentic nature took on service in realization of mastery, so that it entails knowledge of all His names. Wherever we find ourselves between the height and depths, we retain our nature, in and through which God makes Himself manifest.

God is One. His manifestation in duality, which affirms His love, satisfies Him as Lord and us as servant. Love, the manifestation of the One in the many, overcomes all obstacles: suffering and persecution, weakness and death. Nothing satisfies Lord or servant but full realization in the One, as He said: "O soul at peace, return unto thy Lord, well-pleased, well-pleasing! Enter thou among My servants! Enter thou My paradise!"[6]

We master His names in what has received and bears them. Existence as a whole has received all of His names, in order to suppress its own will and have only His. This is the meaning of the revelation that all things are servants and at peace, continuously prostrate before Him. We focus the names, as servants of the Lord of lords. We also differ from the rest of existence in our relationship of confidence with God. The heavens and the earth refused such a will that could differ from His, as a constant occasion of suffering and ruin. We accepted due to our little knowledge and so are subject to His mercy and knowledge.

God reveals Himself to Himself out of self-love. What else could He reveal Himself to? What else could love Him but Himself? He regards Himself through His act of creation in His creature as His manifest form. He knows His concealed through His revealed self. Nothing is real without Him, even in the Creator-creation pair, so He remains One. His lordship is manifest in creation's service, but neither creation nor service is real without Creator and Lord, nor Creator or Lord without creation and service.

In ever-mysterious fullness, God reveals Himself to Himself through the names, both in that fullness and manifest in creation. Each thing reveals some name of God. That He is Creator is not limited by space or time. He is Creator now, always and forever whose creation is always and forever.

5 Ibid., 2:257.

6 *Qur'an*, 89:27–30.

God is Lord now, always and forever. His mastery requires service, now, always and forever. His act of creation is now, unconditioned by anything past or future. God's revelation is His act of creation. The many, which He calls His own face, does not affect His unity, but manifests It in the boundlessness of His self-presentation.

His unity comprehends the visible and invisible. Only in unity do the names reveal Him. As we discover all the names, we externalize knowledge in ritual, ritual in knowledge, and move from partial to full, hidden to revealed, outer to inner. We love God and follow the Praised. We approach Him gradually, seeing ourselves increasingly through Him, knowing that He sees Himself through us. When we love Him, God is the eye we look through, the ear we hear through, the hand we catch with, the leg we walk on.[7]

This vision of mastery in service, service in mastery, does not reduce the distinction of Creator from creature. We and the world exist in the perfect relationship of Creator and creature, the confession of no god but God and the Praised as His apostle. Any self may discover this, its essence as His image revealed. God says in the Revelation: "And when thou throwest, it was not thyself that threw, but God threw."[8]

Realization in Unity lies in the self as epitome of creation. The self remains bound to society, even as it hopes to exit it, rising out of the world towards its highest possibility. The Recitation contains images of this exodus. One is the servitude and liberation of the sons of Israel from Egypt and their wandering in the desert. The Israelites were subject to the social order of Egypt, with Pharoah at the centre. God spoke through Moses, who led them out of their condition. He showed them God as real centre, humiliating the Pharaonic one. The Israelites left Egypt for the cruel waste between the land they were leaving and that they were promised.

Between these two lands, Moses left his people to receive a book from God on Mount Horeb. The emptiness of the centre then began to seem an unfathomable ignorance and fear filled the people. The fearful followers of the absent prophet gathered their gold and heaped it up into a common possession, placing it over the unbearable void. They prepared for themselves a social order by placing the fused parts of their individual possessions in the common centre.

Returning from Horeb with his book, Moses found his people and their order made without him or his book. He threw down and smashed the tablets of this book. He was expressing the irreconcilability of the order the people had made for themselves and the order God was offering them.

7 See Bukhārī, 8:336–37.

8 *Qur'an*, 8:17.

No prophet remains bodily with the people he is sent to. God revealed through Moses the constant need for a maternal prophet and a book if a social order is to allow access to the upward path. The maternal prophet is in every self, always and forever, as its highest capacity. Mentioned in all the revealed books, he appeared in history, but it was to remind of his eternal presence in us and that he is closer to us than the condition of our own selves.

The Praised, whose father was called "Servant of God" and mother "Faith," was a husband and father of many daughters and sons. He withdrew from his family to the solitude of a cave. The world, with its luxuries and wants, pleasures and suffering, comings and goings, seemed a stain in a desert in which Truth reveals Itself to Itself.

The archangel Gabriel appeared to him in that cave. What revealed Itself was thus Essence. Appearing as Gabriel, the Holy Spirit, the Spirit of Truth, Its image is our most sublime experience of Essence. In it, the Praised saw himself, while Essence saw Itself in him. The Praised was afraid:

> While he was in the cave of Hira, the angel came to him and asked him to recite. The prophet replied: "I do not know how to recite." The prophet added: "The angel caught me and pressed me so hard that I could not bear it any more. He then released me and again asked me to recite and I replied: 'I do not know how to recite.' Thereupon he caught me again and pressed me a second time till I could not bear it any more. He then released me and again asked me to recite, but again I replied: 'I do not know how to recite.' Thereupon he caught me for a third time and pressed me, and then released me and said: 'Recite: In the name of thy Lord who created, created man of a blood-clot. Recite: And thy Lord is the Most Generous, who taught by the Pen, taught man that he knows not.'[9] Then the apostle of God returned with the Inspiration and with his heart beating severely." Then he went to Khadija bint Khuwaylid and said: "Cover me! Cover me!"[10]

Returning from this experience of Essence to the world of images, in which Essence ceaselessly announces Itself, the Praised was ashamed. He hid under his robe. All in this world seemed mere seeming compared to his experience in the cave. All seemed full of sorrow after he had attained his highest capacity. The Holy Spirit loved, knew, talked, listened, looked in, and transformed him, commanding: "Recite: In the name of thy Lord who created!"

---

9 Ibid., 96:1–5.

10 Bukhārī, 1:3.

He Who addressed him revealed Himself in his heart and the Praised came to know his core as the Spirit of Truth, the Holy Spirit, who spoke in him. He recited God's discourse, brought by the Spirit of Truth to his heart: "Truly it is the revelation of the Lord of all Being, brought down by the Spirit of the Truth upon thy heart."[11] The Praised became the expression of God's discourse, His command through the Spirit of Truth, while the book he recited was an image of the heart in which God speaks.

God said of the Praised's experience of Spirit: "His heart lies not of what he saw"[12] and that: "He stood poised, being on the higher horizon, then drew near and suspended hung, two bows-length away, or nearer."[13] The Praised's maternal prophecy comprehends all things. He says nothing out of whim. All he says reveals Essence, as Its images come into and go out of being.[14]

In Gabriel the Praised saw the self he loved as a revelation of God, the fullness of his own readiness. This is why he saw Gabriel as the Recitation. The Recitation reveals the perfect couple of the Praised and the Spirit of Truth, the connection binding each of us to the Praised and the Spirit of Truth, the pairing in which the One reveals Itself. This is why our love of God is contingent upon following the Praised. Only in our shared nature with the Praised can we receive the Spirit of Truth and through it appear as one who loves God and whom He loves.

Gabriel, the Spirit of Truth, appeared to the Praised and, after their embrace, impressed the Word on his heart. He was the image which represented the manifestation of God to the heart of the Praised. God refers us to the same image in His narrative of the Virgin Mary, to whom the Spirit of Truth also appeared as Gabriel, as a perfect human being. The Arabic word *al-ruh*, which means *spirit*, is of feminine gender. Its incarnation may be either male or female. That it appeared as a perfect human reminds us of the relationship between image and Essence: the image manifests Essence, Which is disclosed and hidden, remains and disappears in it.

The tenet "I bear witness that there is no god but God and I bear witness that the Praised is His servant and His apostle" is the final word for the project of the people of peace to realize the self after the prayer: "Guide us onto the upright path, the path of those whom Thou hast blessed, not of those against whom Thou art wrathful, nor of those who are astray!"[15]

11 *Qur'an*, 26:192–94.
12 Ibid., 53:11.
13 Ibid., 53:6–9.
14 See *Qur'an*, 53:1–5.
15 *Qur'an*, 1:6–7.

These two confessional principles are the "word of witness." Although they are two and comprise some 15 words in Arabic, they are referred to as if one. This may seem strange, but one should recall that all existence was originally just a Word, which all the dispersed things reveal. The discourse of existence is that Word sent down and differentiated.

For Bosnia's oral poets, a *word* is a whole expression, an entire meaningful utterance, regardless of how many elements it comprises.[16] An utterance derives from the transcendent Word, the source of meaning it refers to, bears witness of, and directs us to. Each element included in the whole falls short of the absolute word. Participating in multiplicity and contributing to an utterance, the element eases affirmation of the original dispersed word.

The upright path mentioned in the above prayer leads the self from a given condition towards a higher one, at its core, in the divine presence, entirely near and absolutely remote. No condition of the self may be finally attained or entirely lost. The self cannot outrun His mercy. Descent cannot remove it from the real, as only the Real is real. At no point in descent, no stage in humiliation, does the self stop being able to rise and grasp the cord of salvation, for, as God says: "My mercy precedes My wrath."[17]

In every situation, the self hopes to progress. If it is moving from appearance to the real, following our ever-present perfect potential, the wanderer's will comes into harmony with the principle. But if in the opposite direction – from the Real to the non-real, light to darkness, authentic enlightenment towards the darkening self, then that will stands against the principle.

Our perfect potential cannot abandon us. Concealed, it cannot be destroyed. Concealment of the Word forces us into action in the dark and ever more certainly action out of ignorance, violence against our own selves. The light in our minds cannot be extinguished. It accompanies us on our path down to the worst extremities. Recalling our descent into the dark, we are sure to make every attempt to leave the dark for a higher level. We find ourselves at war with any form of the self as distorted as our lower levels, the self that tempts to evil.

The self's potential is enveloped in seeming and habit, the comfort and ease of home, protection by kin, property, and power. Called to rise up, it sees each aspect of existence as both peripheral and a potential sign of the centre. Rising up and moving forward never end, as the goal of return has no limit in time or space. They press upon us, enclose us, but are, nonetheless, our allies in becoming conscious of our move forward from finitude to what transcends it.

---

16 See Foley, *Traditional Oral Epic*, 44.

17 Bukhārī, 9:482.

Since our perfection is uprightness, being on the most beautiful height, we need it to return to the One and the first tenet is inseparable from the second. To return we must know we have departed. Otherwise there is no ascent or descent and the traveller neither leaves authentic potential behind, nor draws closer to it. Both ascent and descent take place in the self, as part of the war the higher levels conduct against the lower. The war is for return to where God appears as Peace. As Peaceful, all being in duality involves relationship to Him. Both sides of the self, that turned towards Peace and that set against It, receive something from the One they affirm as Peace, thanks to which they can give.

No pair in existence can be cancelled. That would require comparison without remainder or difference. Duality is in ceaseless flux – each side yields to the other and their positions shift. The receptive becomes donor, donor recipient. This flux, with its coming and going, attaining and relinquishing, leaving and settling, is with regard to the house of Peace, our first authentic home.

This flux embraces the heavens and the earth and what lies between, spirit and body and what lies between, drawing them into ceaseless discovery and veiling of the One Who is and before Whom all things wane.[18] We left the house of Peace, but carry it with us and within us. We can withdraw from it or approach it, but we cannot escape its presence within the self: it mourns its departure from the self and hopes for return to it.

The self offers two possibilities at every moment, ascent and descent. But there is only one moment, manifest in these possibilities. Viewed from the stable and full presence of the self, both possibilities offer a way to ascent from the depth to uprightness. No condition is without this possibility. The Self's simultaneous absolute closeness and absolute remoteness mean we are always partly in paradise, partly in hell: in paradise, because we can always fall lower; in hell, because we can always climb higher. Descent intimates hell, ascent paradise. To understand this possibility, our act of ascent must bring self-realization through the confession of no self but the Self. The alternative is death, which cannot comprehend the Self. Leaving offers one more confirmation that the only real guidance is already within the self.

18 On the potential for providing an *intrepretatio neo-confuciana, buddistica,* or *taoistica* of the main ontological, cosmological, anthropological, and psychological aspects of this current, as incorporated in the divine discourse of the Recitation, see Murata, *Tao of Islam*; idem, *The Sage Learning of Liu Zhi.*

CHAPTER 10

Patterns

Ascent and descent, migration and persecution, dying and reviving are ways the One self-reveals in creation. All things were created in pairs.[1] That each thing has aspects that move and change indicates they were created with Truth. Truth is One and reveals Itself only through the ceaseless alteration of the duality that confirms It.

Comparing change in itself with things in the world, the self engages in giving and receiving, persecution and flight, growth and shrinkage. None of these changes reduces its core, which is absolutely Real. Knowledge relates the knowing subject to the All-knowing, realizing its own love and desire to see itself in the Other and confess that the One is one.

The self's condition, manifest in and through motion, determines its place on the upright path, as the path of the blessed, or on the path of those God is wroth against. The upright path passes through the manifest planes, the levels of existence. All the directions of a given ontological plane meet at that vertical, as the focus of links to higher and lower levels of Being. Rising up is to realize this vertical in the self, from the lowest depth that tempts to evil to the most beautiful height of the self at peace. No station on it evades comparison of lower and higher, as the higher self, closer to the Self, constantly rebukes the lower.

To ascend is to follow the Praised, loving God and being loved by Him. This relationship informs our integrity, as God said: "God and His angels bless the prophet. O believers, do you also bless him, and pray him peace."[2] Blessing the Praised is to bond with him and turn towards our highest potential, transcending death.

Sincere thought offers clarity to anyone confused about worshipping God: God is with us, wherever we are; in our perfection, He is our eye, ear, hand, and foot; He calls us to worship and has given us the Praised as our best example. For should He not be with His perfect servant? Confessing God's unity and the Praised's apostolate assumes resurrection after death. The Praised is closest to God and furthest from death: "The prophet of God is alive and given provision."[3]

1 See *Qur'an*, 36:36.

2 *Qur'an*, 33:56.

3 Ibn Māja, 1:524.

 | DOI 10.1163/9789004279407_034

God says of Himself: "Verily I am God; there is no god but I; therefore serve Me and perform the prayer of My remembrance."[4] His witness of Himself is through our I, which confesses no I but His. There is no knowledge outside the knowing self, so our witness makes God manifest. Everything in world and self is a sign of the Creator. That we hear, see, and smell them is God seeing Himself within His inexhaustible revelation through Himself in His creation.

We know ourselves through His knowledge of us. He knows Himself through our knowledge of Him. Henry Corbin, writing about Ibn al-ʿArabi, discusses this mystery:

> To say that one of our thoughts, sentiments, or desires is concretized in a form specific to the intermediate plane of Idea-Images of subtile matter (*ʿalam al-mithal*), is the same as to meditate before a flower, a mountain or a constellation in order to discover not what obscure and unconscious force they manifest, but what divine thought, flowering in the world of Spirits, is epiphanized, is "at work" in them. Shall we then, succumbing to the doubt which the "imaginary" arouses in us, ask, for all our wonder at the beauty of these forms in which the best of ourselves is epiphanized, "Do they exist?" If, giving in to our habits, we demand a guarantee, a rational proof that these forms existed before us and will continue to exist without us, this will amount to closing our eyes to the epiphanic function of our every own being, to the very thing that constitutes the validity of our Creative Imagination. Of course these forms pre-exist, since nothing begins to be that was not before.[5]

God is One, hidden and invisible, revealed and visible. These pairs are forms of His being. They do not trouble His unity, as He is not other to anything.[6] His disclosure, visibility, finality, and externality are not equal to His concealment, invisibility, priority, and interiority.

His I is revealed in these ways. Our I, whose service, worship, and recollection reveal His lordship, also takes part in disclosure, seeing, and being last and external: forms revealing the One. As Ibn al-ʿArabi said: "We have given Him to manifest Himself through us, whereas He has given us (to exist through Him). Thus the role is shared between Him and us."[7]

---

4 *Qur'an*, 20:14.

5 Corbin, *Creative Imagination in the Sūfism of Ibn ʿArabī*, 236.

6 See *Qur'an*, 6:162–63.

7 In Corbin, *Creative Imagination in the Sūfism of Ibn ʿArabī*, 247.

Joseph said to his father Jacob: "Father, I saw eleven stars, and the sun and the moon. I saw them prostrate themselves before me."[8] With his father, mother, and brothers before him in Egypt, Joseph said: "See, father, this is the interpretation of my vision of long ago. My Lord has made it true."[9] The first vision was a dream, the second waking. The Praised said that we sleep in this world to wake when we die. What we see asleep is higher than what we see awake.

What Joseph said about the proper interpretation of his sleep vision must be understood as relating higher and lower levels of existence in both directions: everything on the higher level is manifest on the lower, while sensory experience is meaningful in how it indicates and leads towards the higher level. The levels are connected in Intellect. When one level is in bondage to the quantifiable, to analytical and instrumental reason, it excludes the other. Analytical reason that denies Intellect as unifying the ontological levels offers no knowledge of life beyond death.

Both visions indicate the Praised's maternal nature. Jacob's sons prostrate themselves, with Joseph as their leader. Their father makes 13. This suggests the letter *mim* (م), the 13th in the Arabic alphabet, whose value is 40: 13 and 40 make 53,[10] the number of books in the Hebrew and Christian Bibles. The Praised is a shining lamp, whose number is 13.

We may think of Joseph in this way, starting from his vision on the lower, sensual level, passing through his dream, and reaching the hidden treasury, God's now that comprehends all things. This treasury is meant by the confession of no god but God and the Praised as His servant and apostle. The visible world manifests the invisible. The dream leads into the invisible. Being in the dream is a way of gaining knowledge to interpret the things of the lower world.

The semantic clusters around the roots h-j-r and kh-r-j come together particularly clearly in Hagar's story as Sarah's bondwoman, Abraham's consort, Ishmael's mother. In the Recitation, forms derived from them tend to designate the metaphysical, cosmological, anthropological, and psychological aspects of prophetic wisdom that give her story context.

The associated semantic fields generally relate to suffering, persecution, loss, and abandonment in the world of waking, which the Praised said is really sleeping. Looked at as signs of the world, of dreaming and death or awakening to the real, these semantic fields are present in the world of our refuge to help

---

8 *Qur'an*, 12:4.

9 Ibid., 12:100.

10 For further detail on such numerological interpretations of the sacred name of *Aḥmad*, including its relationship to the Greek name of the Paraclete, see Mahmutćehajić, *Tajna Hasanaginice*, 115.

us realize our right to life and happiness. They are like Joseph's vision of the stars, sun, and moon, properly understood.

In the exile she embraces, Hagar turns towards the house in Becca. It symbolizes the heart as centre of existence – the Unity all things spring from and flow back to. She and her husband are affirmed by and manifest in their son, in a turn to a principle deeper than any depth, closer than any closeness. Ishmael is a sign that God listens, an indication that there is no god but God.

Abraham and Hagar turn towards Him, Near and Far. Confident in her tomorrow, Hagar knows its confidence in her, as tomorrow and yesterday are just forms manifesting the One. God listened to her, pregnant, beside a desert well, as he did to a dying boy by another well, near a house in a valley. That He listens to every call does not contradict His remoteness or closeness.

The One affirms Mystery, duality the One. The One is constant towards Mystery and duality. Although manifest in duality, the One has no other, just as no duality is real except in heralding the One. The One is unlike anything, comparable to none.[11] Its appearance in infinite pairs going back to the First incorporates duality as pairs of related but separate aspects – receptive and donative, passive and active, female and male. Severally and together, they have no principle but the One. They may be compared, but not measured. These differences in aspect cannot be surmounted, as a pair's members are not subtracted or divided without remainder.

Each is confirmed in descending fashion by the appropriate pair. An element in each pair becomes a mediate principle for the next. Each thing finds an aspect of its duality in a higher level or preceding pair, as well as something inseparable from what is sought, since everything in existence is part of some pair. Thus, each element in a pair is part of a higher pair in ascent and a lower pair in descent. The downward path leads towards differentiation and dispersion, the upward towards coming together. The One is never Third of three, but of two.

The first pair includes receptivity as its maternal side. The received may be given: this is the paternal side. Each pair is both maternal and paternal. Its nature as revelation of the One derives from this, so that what enters exits, what flows in, flows out, what moves in, moves out, what is born, dies.

Paradise was the first duality. It had two aspects – us and the not human. Distinct, but inseparable, we and the rest fit each other like object and reflection, affirming Unity. We had nothing of our own, only what we had received. That was all we had to give. All things in the garden belonged to us, except the inviolate tree. This was the duality we were created into. We and the rest were

---

11 See *Qur'an*, 42:11; 112:4.

united, without prior distinction, in clear revelation of the One and there was no difference between what we knew and what was, no judgment that preceded difference.

When our freedom, as the precondition for confidence, caused us to reach for some other duality, then judgments arose regarding duality, and measurement, and guessing, and judgment itself. The self stood at the centre, turning what wasn't into its object. Duality multiplied, with increased distancing from the first, absolute affirmation of the One. This was the consequence of our will to do away with the difference that underwrote the duality we were created into. Pairs became differentiation of space and time; paradise withdrew.

Withdrawing, paradise gave ground to hell, as hell mustered against it. The dark seemed to win against the light. This was no external accident. It took place in the self, far from the principle. But our recollection of origin, of absolute closeness to the One, never quite fades.

In this closeness the names of the things of the dissolute world gather, while descent causes them to be revealed in things in the manifold of duality. Nothing in duality fails to announce a name. The name has priority over annunciation, as the latter's owner or lord. The names, which possess the things of the world, lie in the self, as the horizons themselves do. The self is thus the stage of the Self's full revelation and we are Its image, Its vicar in the manifest.

When God says through the Praised that praising is His – as Lord of worlds, All-merciful, Ever-merciful, Emperor of the day of debt[12] – He comprehends existence. Everything reveals His names, as Lord of worlds. Things take part in His praise, constantly manifesting the light of the Praised as first of creation, the universal womb.

That God is All-merciful and Ever-merciful is revealed through the Praised, the mercy to the world, as the coming from and return to Him of all things. Our arrival in, passage through, and exit from the world again are measured against our consciousness of the Praised as a mercy and our link to the Lord. In this His lordship and our service are revealed ceaselessly.

Lordship requires service, as reflects God's will, so that mercy and knowledge embrace all lordship. In this embrace, the Lord reveals Himself in countless masteries that correspond to His most beautiful names. Without them, His love to be known would be unrealized. Only in manifestation does He have One to love and love Him back, to know and know Him back. He is All-praised and the world receives and returns His praise.

As praise gathers in integral perfection and knowledge of the names reflects His lordship, the gathering self loves Him and He sees Himself in it. As the

12 Ibid., 1:2–4.

gathering of His will for self-manifestation, we share pre-existence, where He has neither beginning nor end. We too have a will to be known and knowing, loved and loving, and to manifest Him, as Lord, in ourselves, as servants. Only service affirms Lordship, as His names have one to receive and bear them.

In Eden, the inviolate tree signified the irreducible differences of aspects of this duality. Our insult to the tree introduced previously inexistent oppositions, making impurity visible against purity, darkness against light, ignorance against knowledge, evil against good, ugliness against beauty.

Impurity, darkness, ignorance, evil, and ugliness are states of the self, remoteness from the principle. They have no place in proper witness. When such oppositions become apparent, we find ourselves outside our original condition. Resolving them, we return to our original condition, turning from impurity, darkness, ignorance, evil, and ugliness. The act of descending from Eden to earth gave us valuable experience of the path we must rise on. As God said: "We indeed created Man in most beautiful uprightness, and then We restored him the lowest of the low – save those who believe and do righteous deeds; they shall have a wage unfailing."[13]

No longer upright, our authentic nature is in eclipse and internal and external beauty no longer coincide. In descent, we stand between possibilities – the depth or return to the height.

To be conscious of ascent, we must accept that the depth and concealment of selfhood in the dark involve separation from our original condition on the height. What proceeds from our loss intimates ascent, like the house in the centre of the valley. We turn towards it to cleanse ourselves and return, at least symbolically, to our original station. There are such houses and sacred precincts at every level on the upright path.[14]

Turning from dark to light, we purify ourselves of the depth, accepting the ritual that points to the upright path. On it, we are turned towards our principle, the abandoned home to which we are returning. This path is no straight line, beginning and ending in infinity, but a circle, whose centre is both infinitely near and far.

---

13 *Qur'an*, 95:4–6.

14 The apostle of God said: "This house is one of fifteen, seven in the heavens up to the throne and seven up to the limits of the lowest earth. The highest situated one, which is near the throne, is the 'frequented house'. Every one of these houses has a sacred territory, like that of the Kaʿba. If anyone of them fell down, the rest would fall down, one upon the other, to the limits of the lowest earth. And every house has its heavenly or earthly worshippers, like the Kaʿba" (Wüstenfeld, *Die Croniken der Stadt Mekka*, 6, 1, cited in Wensinck, "The Ideas of the Western Semites Concerning the Navel of the Earth," 51–52).

Bosnian Muslim oral tradition speaks of a flower whose petals are four letters the faithful read clearly and unambiguously on their path home. The petals are represented by the Cyrillic letters ББББ (BBBB) or the Arabic ones م م م م (MMMM). They express different sounds, the first opening the lips in gentle exhalation, the second in inhalation. They stand for Muhammed-Mary-Messiah-Mushaf. Mushaf is book, particularly the Book of the Revelation. Its original recipient, Muhammad exhaled gently, while Mary inhaled the Spirit and gave it to the Messiah. They make up the Mushaf or fullness of discourse.[15]

---

15 In citing the evidence for this tradition, some refer to the appearance of four letters ББББ on a *stećak* at Radimilja, on a number of carvings of flowers on Bosnian Muslim furniture, and the appearance of the flower in certain manuscripts. The flower is sometimes made up of repeated Cyrillic letter Бs forming a counter-clockwise circle, while between the four positions of the letters so derived the Arabic letter م is inscribed, producing a flower with eight petals. When the letter Б is rotated, it may be read as the Arabic م. This tradition found expression in the poetry of Bosnia's national poet, Mak Dizdar. See Dizdar, *Stone Sleeper*, 80–94.

CHAPTER 11

Stranger and Host

Hagar's tale involves multiple interruptions of our links to the world. The more emphatic the interruption, the more terrible it seems. Becoming accustomed to it, in oblivion and descent into ever darker precincts of the self, we depart on a journey towards a goal beyond finitude. In the dark, we can only feel this unknown goal, but the mercy and knowledge of the universal Creator and Guide comprehend it, secretly illuminating the darkness. If we are not our own principle, neither is our redemptive goal contingent on anything outside us.

Our connection to our goal lies in order and ritual, which we enter upon as migrants out of impurity. We must first seek purification. The break between the perfect cosmic order of Eden and the world's actual condition is in the consciousness of the traveller bound to and healed by recollection: at the heart of the self is the Ark of the Covenant, the fullness of knowledge, the original promise, the table at which all guests are pure and God the Host. The ritual of ascent requires admission of our impurity, compared to our original purity,[1] as well as ablutions and preparations for the feast to come.

The call to prayer is a call to consciousness of the balance between separation and return. We think in terms of pairs, by comparison or analogy, and the call to worship begins by reminding us of a quantity without pair, to which nothing can be compared.

The unity of contraries is important here – quantity in the minute, duration in the moment, sublimity in humility, wealth in poverty, life in death, and mastery in service. The things of the world and self, of the physical world of duality, are preformed towards the confession of no god but God.

We are thus reminded of His unity, though our entire existence takes place in duality. We are established so that we look on duality as the revelation of the One, achieved insofar as we accept the perfection sent down in a pure image of the One and expressed by confessing the Praised as His apostle, our link with Him and our salvation from this disjointed state. Calls for ritual incorporation and redemption in the fullness of majesty and unity suggest this. Nothing on our path is worth stopping for and lingering, as there is no god but God.

Worship and revelation were both sent down to us. The Praised received them at the summit of his ascension, while the Holy Spirit sent down the Recitation to him. Recognizing the true nature of the lowest depth, signified

1 See Douglas, *Purity and Danger*, 209.

 | DOI 10.1163/9789004279407_035

by ritual purification, is a precondition for embarking on ritual and recitation. Turning towards the house in the Valley, the inviolable place of self-abnegation, is to affirm the link between Eden, as our original home, and the earthly realm of migration. This vertical connection is between earth and heaven, body and spirit. The human drama of separation takes place on the path between these extremes.

That we were created on the most beautiful height and sent down to the depths entails that belief and doing good deeds are a way to maintain our link with our original condition and to recover it. Nothing else in creation is ever said to have been sent down or to have a condition set to its redemption. In most beautiful uprightness, we have no impurity. Absolutely pure, we bring together all the most beautiful names of the One and are revealed in our authentic condition. Beauty reveals eternity and infinity within finite time and space. It is quality's victory over quantity. When we recognise beauty in the horizons of the world, amongst the signs of heaven and earth and what lies between them, we discover our self in it, as in our original and yearned-for absolute closeness to the Creator. This reflects our acceptance of confidence, offered to us as to every other thing. Everything else in existence rejected the offer of confidence, recusing themselves of free will and remaining only what the Creator's will made them: their will is His, and they are at absolute peace in and with Him.[2]

We accepted the offer and can therefore relate to the Faithful through faith. As a result, we have free will, but based upon a knowledge that is always limited, as it has been received out of eternity and infinity in a world of temporal and spatial limitations. Given that we make our decisions on the basis of this free will, it is always possible for us to commit evil and to oppose the will of God. It is of this aspect that God said in the Recitation: "Surely he is sinful, very foolish."[3] One may be redeemed from such a condition only by voluntary obedience to the Creator's will, the Hagaric heart in which are to be found the unknown ways of the Lord comprehended only in His knowledge and mercy.

Although always little,[4] our knowledge links us to God, Whose knowledge comprehends all.[5] Every sign bears a revelation of this knowledge, since creation served the Creator's love to be known.[6] The sign is both separate from

---

2 See *Qur'an*, 33:72.

3 *Qur'an*, 33:72.

4 See *Qur'an*, 17:85.

5 Ibid., 4:176.

6 In a well-known sacred tradition, frequently cited in the texts of the Muslim intellectual tradition, God says: "I was a hidden treasure so I loved to be known. Hence I created the

and connected to what it signifies. Serving as link with the Signified, the sign must always transmit something of the Creator's beauty. Once this beauty is known, knowledge of it changes its role and place. Beauty is not subject to limitation. Reason is powerless before it. Beauty is entirely immediate. Whatever causes us to feel it, wherever it appears, beauty is an experience of the most profound level of the self. Its presence at the surface of sensory knowledge is just an intimation of a limit which never encompasses it.

Worldly times and places at which beauty appears are attractive. Our little knowledge recognizes this beauty, which gives its objects irresistible attractiveness. Little knowledge combines with beauty to become love. Faith requires knowledge and love. As knowing subjects we love what we know, while as loving subjects we know what we love, and the faithful relate to the Faithful through belief or faith. This relationship has no surety. Both sides are free to deny the link. Only in freedom do those who love remain on paths of mutual attraction, open towards the One.

In this insecurity, the lover tries to get nearer the beloved: the greater the insecurity, the more powerful the attraction. The lover is travelling a path to the beloved. He burns with desire to be a guest in the beloved's house or to host the beloved in his own and discovers himself in the countless aspects through which beauty attends from eternity and infinity and enters the conditional world.

Nothing satisfies the lover but union and assimilation with the Beloved, so that these beauties are felt deep within the self's recesses and revealed upon the face of the Beloved. Offering witness of his own mighty character as the best example, the Praised stated how close he and the Anointed are to each other: "I am most akin to the son of Mary among the whole of mankind. And the prophets are of different mothers, but of one debt, and no prophet was raised between me and him."[7] He also said:

> He who said: "There is no god but God, He is One and there is no associate with Him, that the Praised is His servant and His apostle, that the Anointed is His servant and the son of His hand-maiden and he is His Word which He communicated to Mary and is His Spirit, that Paradise is true and Hell is true," God would make him enter Paradise through any one of its eight doors which he would like.[8]

---

creatures that I might be known." See Chittick, *Sufi Path of Knowledge*, 250–52. The past tense may be seen as referring to present and future, as all human time is one in the One.

7 Muslim, 4:1260.

8 Ibid., 1:21–22.

The discovery of the self in the garden depends, according to the Praised, on the spoken word, which comprehends him and the Anointed. The self's most sublime moment is the heart of the Praised, which is Hagaric in stubbornly cleaving to the perfection of our creation. The world's horizons are linked to our bodies and self and heart through the Praised. God sent down the Holy Spirit, His Word, upon the heart of the Praised. That heart houses a discourse, mysterious, ineffable, yet revealed by the Recitation. Each self can move from the depth, sin and ignorance, through the Word, to the Praised's Hagaric heart, who: "is a migrant who abandons evil, a warrior who does battle against his passions."[9]

The migration and wars the Praised refers to came about because of him. He is the maternal prophet to whom the other prophets pledged allegiance in pre-existence, more immediate to us all than the condition of our own selves, the mercy unto the worlds. Consequently, all of existence lies within his maternal grace, the womb of all things. Saying the Anointed was closer to him than anyone else from this or a future world, the Praised was drawing attention to his own mighty character, found in countless images in finitude.

The finite is mortal. The Praised, as image of the Living, makes manifest the limits of images. He limits the Anointed, with whom he manifests God. As Moses said: "The Lord came from Sinai, and rose up from Seir unto them; he shined forth from Mount Paran."[10] If God did appear three times, through Moses, Jesus, and Muhammad, it was through finite images. Their finitude confesses Him as Infinite. Descent and ascent, which correspond to the images of Moses and Jesus, meet in the Praised, as the two arcs of descent and ascent.

Earthly acts of descent, down hills into valleys, or ascent, towards the mountain peaks, are just images of possibilities in the self. Through creation, God made Himself manifest as Creator, seeing Himself through His faithful servant's heart. An individual in love with God knows in his heart each of His manifestations: His now is eternal. That is why all the worlds exist within the perspective of the faithful servant through whom the Lord sees Himself.

Anxious to explain to his disciples how all things exist together in and through him, Mary's son, Jesus, led them to the Mount: "and he was transfigured before them. And his raiment became shining, exceeding white as snow; so as no fuller on earth can white them. And there appeared unto them Elijah with Moses: and they were talking with Jesus."[11] His disciples could only know the individuals they saw were really Moses and Elijah if Jesus told them so.

---

9 In Ghazālī, *Iḥyā' ʿulūm al-dīn*, 4:70.

10 This tradition passed down from the Praised relates to *Deuteronomy* 33:2–3.

11 *Mark*, 9:2–4.

The Anointed knew this in his perfect heart. He said to God: "Thou knowest it, knowing what is within my self, and I know not what is within Thy Self."[12] What Jesus Knew in His heart was, for him, God's self-revelation, in which space and time are different than they appear in the external world. For such knowledge, the prophets are synchronous and scattered in time. A prophet may call on them and talk with them, whenever he or she wants.

During his night journey, the Praised rose up from the place of self-abnegation at Becca towards the place on sacred Mount Sion. The second mosque signifies the extremity of the divine apparition. The Praised met the prophets there, looked at them and talked with them. Before him, they were the same revelation of God as was gathered in his own heart. The Praised is the supreme possibility each of us carries within. Any who realize his nature within their own selves shares time with God and experiences the universal apparition in its most focused mode. Sadruddin Qunawi said of his master, Ibn al-ʿArabi:

> Our *shaikh* Ibn ʿArabī had the power to meet the spirit of any prophet or Saint departed from this world, either by making him descend to the level of this world, or by making him in an apparitional body (*ṣūrat mithālīya*) similar to the sensible form of his person, or by making him appear in his dreams, or by unbinding himself from his material body to rise to meet the spirit.[13]

The Recitation is the Word sent down by God through the Holy Spirit to the Praised as His servant and apostle. It is originally and authentically in God and with Him. In God and with Him, it is uncreated, but becomes manifest in creation. It was sent down with a view to our potential range, from most beautiful uprightness to lowest baseness. Its first form is as the Preserved Tablet which is the Holy Spirit or Spirit of Truth. As the perfect recipient of the Word, the Praised is that Tablet. Otherwise, we could not resolve the question of God's Word, which came into the world on his breath and lips.

No self can receive the Word without being linked with the breath, lips, and discourse of the Praised. Whatever imprint being listened to or spoken or written or read makes on it, its source in creation is his lips. Between the lips that form speech and its source are many levels of being. The levels in the world, from earth to heavens and beyond, are their images.

12 *Qur'an*, 5:116.

13 In Affifi, *The Mystical Philosophy of Muḥyid-Din Ibn al-ʿArabī*, 133, cited in Corbin, *Creative Imagination in the Ṣūfism of Ibn ʿArabī*, 224.

As an individual, the Praised is not the source of the Word. The Word is God's. But, as a human being, he bore God's breath inside, so that fullness was already present in finite creation and appearance. The Word is within and with this fullness. It is, in principle, beyond the particular, but its descent entails reception. It can only be given through the lips and only if already received. The Recitation as God's authentic Word was received by the self of the Praised, in an act unshared with any other thing. This is why he is maternal.

This maternal nature is present in all of us, as creatures. It is manifest as the highest level of existence. God's revelation as All-praised begins with it, while descent and ascent are marked by its presence, which is like the essence of mercy. All the signs of creation are decked out upon it. It was in the face of the revealed fragility of the world, its lack of reality without the Real, as Moses prayed and God replied:

> And when the earthquake seized them, he said, "My Lord, hadst Thou willed Thou wouldst have destroyed them before, and me. Wilt Thou destroy us for what the foolish ones of us have done? It is only Thy trial, whereby Thou leadest astray whom Thou wilt, and guidest whom Thou wilt. Thou art our Protector; so forgive us, and have mercy on us, for Thou art the best of forgivers. And prescribe for us in this world good, and in the world to come; we have repented unto Thee." Said He, "My chastisement – I smite with it whom I will; and My mercy embraces all things, and I shall prescribe it for those who are mindful and pay the alms, and those who indeed believe in Our songs, those who follow the apostle, the maternal prophet, whom they find written down with them in the Torah and the Gospel, bidding them to honour, and forbidding them dishonour, making lawful for them the good things and making unlawful for them the corrupt things, and relieving them of their loads, and the fetters that were upon them. Those who believe in him and succour him and help him, and follow the light that has been sent down with him – they are the saved."[14]

Moses was praying to God in front of 70 chieftains of Israel. God's response reminded him of the oath he and the other prophets had sworn. Part of that oath is the Praised, as the seal of creation and the mighty character against which each and every self is measured, the most beautiful example, supreme potential and essence of every self. God said of this oath:

---

14 *Qur'an*, 7:155–57.

> And when God took compact with the prophets: "That I have given you of Book and Wisdom; then there shall come to you the apostle confirming what is with you – you shall believe in him and you shall help him; do you agree?" He said, "And do you take My load on you on that condition?" They said: "We do agree." God said, "Bear witness so, and I shall be with you among the witnesses." Then whosoever turns his back after that – they are the ungodly.[15]

This is God's speech, as is the entire Recitation, revealed through the Praised. We receive it as both his and God's. It contains all selves, all times, all worlds, all creation in which the Creator is manifest. The history of the self comprehends that of the world. When Moses prayed to Him, God revealed Himself as Speaker in that very act. He chose Moses to manifest Himself and He descended to the lowest depth, as absolutely near, the only reality of that through which He manifests Himself.

In His mercy, God threatens us with destruction. This is to turn us towards Him, as it is the greatness in beauty, tenderness in severity, forgiveness in punishment, guidance in temptation, love in anger, and compassion in power. When God says He punishes whom He will, He also says His mercy comprehends all, including all He punishes. All of existence lies within this womb of mercy. Just as a mother preserves the growing seed in her womb until ready to enter the world, the Lord preserves each self through the prophet, the mercy to the worlds.

As maternity is mercy, sent down to recall us to the path, the world becomes a discourse on the reason and purpose of being in this world and redemption from it into fullness of life and happiness.

---

15 Ibid., 3:81–82.

CHAPTER 12

Hannah and Mary

The first book of Samuel contains the story of Elkanah of the hill country of Ephraim and his two wives. Hannah was beautiful and beloved, but had borne him no child. Penninah had born a child and despised and abused Hannah for her infertility. In desperation and hope, Hannah went to the temple on the height at Shilloh to pray for a son to deliver her from persecution in her own house into the freedom a successful birth might confirm.

In her humble prayer, Hannah vowed to dedicate any son from God to serve in His temple at Shilloh. He granted her prayer and she brought the son she bore, called Samuel, to the temple and gave him to the priest Eli, to praise God and confirm his mother's gratitude. Affirming her duality with her husband, Hannah renewed her connection with her heart.

This mosque kept the Ark of the Covenant, so that Hannah's prayer and God's response took place under the sign of the Holy Spirit's descent and our own return. God appeared to Samuel there, who lay in the temple, and called him prophet, telling him of the mysteries of Eli the priest and his sons and revealing the truth of the Praised hidden in the self.

At a time when the Philistines ruled over them, the Council of the sons of Israel called on Samuel to nominate a king. The Recitation tells us that he told them to take Saul for king and of the signs for this choice:

> The sign of his kingship is that the Ark will come to you, in it a Shekhinah from your Lord, and a remnant of what the folk of Moses and Aaron's folk left behind, the angels bearing it. Surely in that shall be a sign for you, if you are believers.[1]

Anointing Saul and raising him up to be king over Israel, he said:

> Is it not because the Lord hath anointed thee to be captain over his inheritance? When thou art departed from me today, (...) Then shalt thou go on forward from thence, and thou shalt come to the plain of Tabor, and there shall meet thee three men going up to God to Beth-el, one carrying three kids, and another carrying three loaves of bread, and another carrying a bottle of wine. And they will salute thee, and give thee two loaves of

1 *Qur'an*, 2:248.

 | DOI 10.1163/9789004279407_036

> bread; which thou shalt receive of their hands. After that thou shall come to the hill of God, where is the garrison of the Philistines: and it shall come to pass, when thou art come thither to the city, that thou shalt meet a company of prophets coming down from the high place with a psaltery, and a tarbet, and a pipe, and a harp, before them; and they shall prophesy: And the spirit of the Lord will come upon thee, and thou shalt prophesy with them, and shalt be turned into another man.[2]

So, Saul became king under a condition laid down by God through His prophet. When Saul broke it, Samuel revoked his anointment, transferring it to the boy David, prophet of Israel, Solomon's father and the Virgin's ancestor, confirming what was said of anointment: "The baptism of God!? And who is there that baptizes more beautifully than God?"[3]

Before his elevation, David had served Saul and borne his faults patiently. He knew of Saul's anointment and its revocation and the debt of his own anointment by God. He had crossed the river in the king's army, of whom the Recitation says: "How often a little company has overcome a numerous company, by God's leave! And God is with the patient!"[4]

This small group of faithful fought a great army of concealers. God said: "And David slew Goliath. And God gave him the kingship, and wisdom, and He taught him such as He willed."[5] God promised David his kingdom would last through his posterity forever.[6] The Anointed was from this posterity.[7] David, like his descendant Jesus and ancestor Abraham, is on the wheel of Time, on which every tomorrow is yesterday and exile, migration and suffering are signs of potential mercy. Each prophet participates in praising the All-praised and the truth of the Praised as the truth of creation.

Hannah and Penninah's destinies and Samuel's affirmation of Hannah and Elkanah's pairing bear comparison with Ishmael's story affirming the pairing of Hagar and Abraham. Hannah faces the void, searching for a sign to affirm the pair she is a term of. God gives her one in Samuel, showing that He hears

---

2 1 *Samuel*, 10:1–2, 3–6.

3 *Qur'an*, 2:138.

4 Ibid., 2:249.

5 Ibid., 2:251. The Sabre of the prophet David later came into the possession of the prophet of the Praised. See Dhahabī, *Siyar a'lām al-nubalā'*, 2:429–30; cited in Wheeler, *Mecca and Eden*, 38.

6 See 2 *Samuel*, 7:1–17.

7 See *Matthew*, 1:6.

everything. This suggests a pattern where unilinear time is a distorted image of the circle of time in which beginning and end are One.[8]

Hannah prayed God to show Himself through a son to fulfil her womb. She vowed that son to His service. This is the mystery of Samuel's link with God through the Holy Spirit. The gift Hannah received was the Holy Spirit's descent upon her son, as the Holy Spirit is connection with the One. Any desire informed by His desire is realized through that Spirit. Those who share in it have time with God, the day that comprehends all things.[9]

The Virgin Mary's story also reflects Hagar's path. Her parents vowed her to the mosque in Sion at birth, as was the custom with the first child, in recognition of our authentic and most beautiful sublimity and the truth carried by the Praised. According to the Recitation, her mother said: "Lord I have vowed to Thee, in dedication, what is within my womb. Receive Thou this from me; Thou hearest and knowest."[10] Once she had given birth, she said: "Lord, I have given birth to her, a female. (...) And I have named her Mary, and commend her to Thee with her seed, to protect them from the accursed Satan."[11]

Mary served in the temple, where the prophet Zachariah looked after her. The mosque – for all its holy scrolls and incense burners, banqueting table and choirs, size and solidity – is just a dwelling or house recalling God's dwelling in creation. Amongst all its luxury, however, the truth of the Praised, as our authentic, culminating nature, to which the signs in world and self testify, was in danger of being forgotten.

Given how the celebration and glorification of his name in the mosque was disfigured, God decided to reveal His majesty in the heart of the Virgin and through her to make manifest the Word. Through His angel He announced to her: "Mary, God gives thee good tidings of a Word from Him whose name is Messiah, Jesus, son of Mary; high honoured shall he be in this world and the next, near stationed to God. He shall speak to men in the cradle, and of age, and righteous he shall be."[12] The Holy Spirit came to her, the Spirit of Truth, to announce a miracle to her – the birth of the child who is the Word.

Mary is perfect in purity, absolute femininity, absolutely prepared to receive herself in fullness, to be realized in the desire for donative masculinity and to

8 For an inter-textual reading of the stories of Hagar and Hani, see Nikaido, "Hagar and Ishmael as Literary Figures: An Intertextual study."

9 See *Qur'an*, 11:84.

10 *Qur'an*, 3:35.

11 Ibid., 3:36.

12 Ibid., 3:45–46.

be seen in the Word which is perfect humanity, the entity anointed by the Holy Spirit. God said through the Praised:

> And mention in the Book Mary when she withdrew from her people to an eastern place, and she took a veil apart from them; then We sent unto her Our Spirit that presented himself to her a man without fault. She said: "I take refuge in the All-merciful from thee. If thou art heedful of God." He said: "I am but an apostle come from thy Lord, to give thee a boy most pure."[13]

The image to be seen in Mary's pure receptive nature is perfect masculinity, the apostle, the most beautiful example.[14] She withdraws from people and seeks solitude in a place to the east. She gives herself over to the light of the Praised through which God reveals Himself and through perfect externalization she sees her own interior, which becomes unbearably attractive to her. Loving this beauty, she sees herself in it and it in herself. Mary, together with the Spirit, brings into the world the purest of boys as God's Word. The Praised, receiving the Holy Spirit, is manifest in the Recitation, in His Word.

In his humanity and so in the Virgin's desire, the Anointed is closest to the Praised. The Holy Spirit appeared to the Virgin as a faultless man, a most beautiful example. The Virgin and the Praised form a pair through which the One is manifest in two forms of the Word – as the complete human being and as the Recitation. Both recall our perfect nature, which begins in and returns to mercy.

The drama of the Messiah's birth took place in a desert, under a palm tree, in desperate loneliness, as Mary cried out: "Would I had died 'ere this, and become a thing forgotten!"[15] Her exclamation is due to perfect shame. God's appearance in the Word is realized in and through her. Both Mary's I and God's I are conscious of this. The latter in the former, which, as recipient, would rather not exist as I, as the personal I is unsustainable in the face of His I. Mary wishes not to exist, because truly she cannot. Her exclamation is perfect witness that there is no I but God's. His I is revealed to her and she becomes entirely His. Her exclamation confesses the One and the Praised as His perfect servant and apostle.

And in her desperation before the majesty of His I, another angel appeared to her. He directed her towards the fruits of the palm tree and the new-flowing spring at her feet:

---

13 Ibid., 19:16–19.

14 See *Qur'an*, 33:21.

15 *Qur'an*, 19:23.

> Nay, do not sorrow; see, thy Lord has set below thee a rivulet. Shake also to thee the palm-trunk, and there shall come tumbling upon thee dates fresh and ripe. Eat therefore, and drink, and be comforted; and if thou shouldst see any mortal, say: "I have vowed to the All-merciful a fast, and today I will not speak to any man."[16]

The Virgin and Jesus are a sign of the worlds, as we are told in the Recitation: "And she who guarded her virginity, so We breathed into her of Our spirit and appointed her and her son to be a sign unto all beings."[17]

The angels and the Spirit, as God's revelation to us, appeared to Hagar and Hannah and Mary. They appear to each prophet, in ways attuned to his or her self. The prophets were of their place and time, reflecting their interpersonal relations. Reduced to quantities, these relations belong to history. But linked to God through angels and Spirit, their relations transcend separation and dissolution in history and the prophets exist together in the supra-individual world of names and images. There, they meet and talk, as in the story of the Transfiguration on Mount Tabor:

> And after six days Jesus taketh Peter, James and John his brother, and bringeth them up into an high mountain apart, and was transfigured before them: and his face did shine as the sun, and his raiment was white as the light. And, behold, there appeared unto them Moses and Elijah talking with him.[18]

This scene of Jesus, Elijah, and Moses together on the seventh day, a trio separated by many centuries in history, refers us to a world of names and synchronicity, in which place and time are absolute. The night gathering of the prophets at Sion to be led in prayer by the Praised is the same. They had sworn their oath to him, their maternal prophet, in pre-existence, the world of absolute attributes. The Praised was carried from the holy Valley of Becca to the sacred mount at Sion by a light incarnate on a winged steed led by the Angel Gabriel. At Sion "he found Abraham, the friend of God, Moses, and Jesus assembled with a company of the prophets, and he prayed with them".[19]

---

16 Ibid., 19:24–26. On various interpretations of the role of the Virgin Mary in the Muslim intellectual tradition, see Smith, "The Virgin Mary in Islamic tradition and commentary."

17 Ibid., 21:91.

18 *Matthew*, 17:1–3.

19 Ibn Isḥāq, *Sīrat Rasūl Allāh*, 182.

Their synchronous appearance intimates our own first and last gathering before God. We were all gathered, with the prophets, in the beginning, as God said in the Recitation:

> And when thy Lord took from the Children of Adam, from their loins, their seed, and made them testify, touching themselves, "Am I not your Lord?" They said, "Yes, we testify" – lest you should say on the Day of Resurrection, "As for us, we were heedless of this," or lest you say, "Our fathers were associators aforetime, and we were seed after them. What, wilt Thou then destroy us for the deeds of the vain-doers?"[20]

The prophets were selected from this gathering to take an additional oath to the Lord to bear witness, accept, and assist His apostle[21] as the maternal seal, the first of the people of peace, shining lamp, mercy to the worlds and closer to the faithful than their own selves. On the day of resurrection, when we all face God, the apostle will be first. In front of the Incomparable, Who is absolutely close and absolutely remote, the expanses of space and time will become manifest in the moment, one all-comprehending day.

Her son dying of thirst, Hagar said: "Let me not see the child's death." Seized by labour, Mary wished: "Would I had died 'ere this, and become a thing forgotten!" On meeting Gabriel in the cave, the Praised went home and told Khadijah: "Cover me, cover me!"[22] The Praised called himself more bashful than a covered maid.[23] The inability to face Essence's images is shame.

Essence reveals Itself in images. They come into and go out of being as determinations in which the indeterminate shows Itself, stimulating a desire for self-annihilation in the witness, to submerge the I in the revelation of the Creator's I. This always carries a sense of the image mediating relationship with the One. This is why Hagar and Mary and the Praised would deny their own to receive what is as the apparition of the One. Whatever the condition of our consciousness, we remain with but outside the One. Being outside Him seems separation or sufficiency. Being with Him makes us ashamed of our separation. We know we are an image wanting to be what it reveals; we know our finitude and want out of it.

---

20 *Qur'an*, 7:172–73.

21 See *Qur'an*, 3:81.

22 Rūzbehān Baqlī cites a tradition in which the Praised says "If only the Lord of Muhammad had not created Muhammad." See Ballanfat, *Quatre traités inédifs de Rūzbehān Baqlī Shīrāzī*, 101.

23 See Bukhārī, 8:89.

According to Rūzbehān Baqlī, the desire for annihilation perfects shame against the pre-eternal and the post-existent.[24] Shame is essentially prophetic. Whenever Essence is revealed in an image, we see it as constantly revealing and hiding. The prophet is ashamed of feeling Essence and Its revelation in the determinate image, in being only to die. Evidence reveals and conceals itself through its image. Prophetic experience discovers the self as revelation of Essence, manifest in shame and the need to cover all images to find It in one only,[25] as in Moses' conversation with God:

> And when Moses came to Our appointed time and his Lord spoke with him, he said, "Oh my Lord, show me, that I may behold Thee!" Said He, "Thou shalt not see Me; but behold the mountain – if stays fast in its place, than thou shalt see Me." And when his Lord revealed Him to the mountain He made it crumble to dust; and Moses fell down swooning. So when he awoke, he said, "Glory be to Thee! I repent to Thee; I am the first of the believers."[26]

Conversation is a relationship between a self and another. While the self is speaking, the listener is thou. Conversely, when the listener is speaking, the self is thou. Addressing God, Moses presents his self to the Thou Whom he yearns will manifest in his self. Given that Moses' self contains his vision of the world, sun and moon, stars and mountains, and trees and animals, his vision of God calls for their disappearance, as existence is made up of signs of Him, as is Moses' own self, in absolute shame before the Self.

Confessing no god but God, the I affirms itself as in God's image. Understanding God as manifest only in images, the witness embraces silence and waiting. Whatever the self desires, no image remains: Essence extracts and destroys each one. Appearing as Spirit, the image is and is not the same as God. The I then wants to self-annihilate, as there is no god but God, no I but

---

24 In Ballanfat, "Mary as a melting of spiritual significations: the case of Rūzbehān Baqlī (d. 1209)," *Forum Bosnae 51*, 233–34.

25 Petar Skok considers the noun *stid* "modesty" to come from *stūd*, which means "cold," "winter," "frost" (Skok, *Etimologijski rječnik hrvatskoga ili srpskoga jezika*, 3:352). In the face of God's revelation, the self withdraws, shrinks, and annihilates itself. Things shrink in the cold, while living creatures die. The connection between the words "stid" and *stūd* is therefore an understandable one. While shame (sram) and modesty (stid) are close in meaning, the difference between them in Bosnian is obvious: stid or modesty is an inner response to the revelation of the sacred, while shame or sram is the opposite – the suppression of stid or modesty and the violation of the sacred.

26 *Qur'an*, 7:143.

His. That is prophetic shame. All the Praised's followers share in it to transcend the imaginal order, as his Light is the first determination no order or institution can comprehend, though it comprehends them all. With it, all existence is prostrate before God.

All things annihilate themselves to receive existence as His revelation. This is why the Praised, as the perfect epitome of existence, the maternal prophet, mercy to the worlds, is more bashful than a covered virgin. God is revealed to him and he confesses no god but God. This is why he is His apostle. Confessing that he is the Praised, linked to the All-praised by praise, he is God's apostle, whose nature and mighty character are shame and prostration. The Praised relates to God, Who came to him through an angel, both through the image and beyond it, both mediately and immediately. The Recitation confirms him, as simultaneously the self's undifferentiated interiority and within differentiated externality.

Faced with Spirit as his own nature, his own sublime capacity, the Praised is filled with shame. He desires self-annihilation so as to be only the Word and its Recitation, images revealing Essence, from which the ashamed self is indistinguishable. His shame is a desire to fade away before what it sees, desiring to be it and nothing else. God said of this: "Indeed, he saw him another time by the Lote-Tree of the Boundary nigh which is the Garden of the Refuge, when there covered the Lote-Tree that which covered; his eye swerved not, nor swept astray. Indeed, he saw one of the greatest signs of his Lord."[27]

The Praised's vision of a major sign of the Lord by the Lote-Tree is Spirit, the Light of the Praised, which he regards without averting his eye, realizing himself in what he sees and annihilating himself in all else. Anyone who follows the Recitation may have a similar experience, participating in his vision. Essence's image is determinate: the Beautiful revealed in signs that link to Him.

Firm in their desire to establish images in the social order, laws and interpretations, people posit their own finite selves as mediating revelation and the self ashamed at its immediate experience of Spirit. Confessing no self but the Self, as every image comes and goes, recalling what has died and intimating what is being born, we encounter the obstacle of the church as incarnate order or prophet as objectified construct of historians and interpretations that depict revelation as insufficient and contingent.

To strip us of our refuge in the knowledge brought by the Praised, who has "seen Him enough" and was ashamed, the Church, as incarnate order and law, and the prophets of the historians' constructs, as mediators of our relationship

27 Ibid., 53:13–18.

with God, declare us in violation of that order, apostate of their firm establishment of Essence's image, Who abides in no image.

The Praised's vision of the two arcs in their remoteness and proximity makes manifest the heart that comprehends God. When following the Praised informs our love of Him, we see how the Praised's vision was independent of anything but the Book and his own immense nature. The Praised leads us on the upright path, the path of the blessed, and his time differs from that of the historians. In their image, all things are laid out on a single plane of existence, objects insofar as they are dead traces of the dead.

During the time of immediate experience, inhabiting the imaginal world of the living and relating to the living God, every now is linked to the heavenly council through God's constant interest. This time corresponds to our journey on the upright path. We know it thanks to perspective gained by ascending and looking down from above. Only from that position do we see the links between the things of existence.

When God says that the heavens are seven, it means each of them offers a different view of our earthly home. These views are from different conditions of the self. Each image withdraws as lower and expiring compared to the higher that is being born. The self raises itself up with the help of these images through the seven heavens, not to occupy the highest and comprehend the things of existence, but to break free of perspective, since He Who comprehends them is not comprehended by them. No perspective is His nor is there any without Him.

CHAPTER 13

The Union of the Praised

In the infinity of space and time, it can be difficult to fathom the reason or end of the world, our existence in it, or where its expanses begin and end. The order in them suggests a reason, while our confusion and this-worldly pettiness cry out for an end. One may suppose them perfect and discoverable, but what profit order in the world, without order in the self?

How the self and the world's expanses are related can be posited many ways: as opposition, mutual encapsulation of world in self and self in world, or, for modern science's fetish of quantification, exclusion of the self. The physicist, Max Planck, said: "We must forget about man, in order to study nature, and discover and formulate her laws."[1]

Forgetting ourselves, we forget God. Modern science wants a world with neither human nor divine. Hannah Arendt wrote of how our relationship with the world and God interacts with our understanding of metaphysics:

> (…) in increasingly strident voices, the few defenders of metaphysics have warned us of the danger of nihilism inherent in this development; and although they themselves seldom invoke it, they have an important argument in their favour: it is indeed true that once the supersensual realm is discarded, its opposite, the world of appearances as understood for so many centuries, is also annihilated. The sensual, as still understood by the positivists, cannot survive the death of the supersensual. No one knew this better than Nietzsche who, with his poetic and metaphoric description of the assassination of God in Zarathustra, has caused so much confusion in these matters. In a significant passage in *The Twilight of the Idols*, he clarifies what the word God meant in Zarathustra. It was merely a symbol of the supersensual realm as understood by metaphysics; he now uses instead of God the word true world and says: "We have abolished the true world. What has remained? The apparent one perhaps? Oh, no! With the true world we have also abolished the apparent one."[2]

1 Cited in Cassirer, *Substance and Function*, 306.

2 Arendt, "Thinking and Moral Consideration," 420–21.

 | DOI 10.1163/9789004279407_037

This relationship between sensual and supersensual is central to the question of metaphysics underlying both traditional science and modern physics. Traditional science considers Planck's conclusion profoundly mistaken.

Traditional science teaches that the heavens and the earth and everything between are there for us, the universal keystone. They cannot be thought in whole or part without us. They serve as a constant reminder that we are existence's reason and purpose. The time of the self is more decisive than those on the horizons. Wanting a world that exists beyond our open selfhood as its keystone, we reduce ourselves to the sensual and superficial, the shallows of existence, where we seek death.

God said through the Praised: "Thee only we serve; to Thee alone we pray for succour. Guide us on the upright path, the path of those whom Thou hast blessed!" The path ends in realization and bliss as the self finds peace in Intellect, the light of the Praised. Looking at the signs on the horizons, we see their forms, but not their meaning. Our failure to understand is due to the condition of the observing self and the obstacles within.

We owe our reality to God. Our debt is His sabre for us to overcome those obstacles. The lower self is enlightened by the higher, so that all we require for return and to settle our debt is already within our essence, our authentic nature, as Rumi said:

> The "sword of debt" is he who enters combat for the debt's sake and whose efforts are totally for God. He discerns correct from incorrect and truth from falsehood. But, he first struggles with himself and rectifies his own character traits. As the prophet said, "Begin with your own self!"[3]

God is Light, above and beyond, as well as within illumination. He is remote and near and like and unlike all things. Sent down, His light dwells in our perfection. The dark cannot destroy It. It may be less visible, but remains. God, as Light, gave the arcs of the perfect circle of His revelation. Calling the apostle the maternal prophet, He used the word *ummiyy*, translated as "virginal," "pure," and "without sin," but literally "maternal."

The Arabic noun *rahma* means "womb" and is derived from the same root as two of God's most common names in the Revelation – *al-rahman* and *al-rahim*, "All-merciful" and "Ever-merciful." The maternal prophet is a mercy to the worlds. God is pointing out that we relate to Him through the merciful womb, signifying the Praised's closeness to the All-merciful and Ever-merciful. God also says: "I am God, for I am the All-merciful. I created the merciful womb

3 Arberry, *Discourses of Rūmī*, 179.

and gave a name derived from My name. For, any who separate from the merciful womb, will I separate him too; but he who seeks connection with it, I will provide him connection with Me."[4]

The prophets all swore an oath to the Praised as their principle, the centre they gather around before scattering across existence and returning. God's unity is not made dual or created in revelation. He is One, Flux. He manifests being All-praised to Himself through the Praised as the womb of all things. God is above language, while the Praised's prophetic maternity bears within itself all language, as the oath of the prophets, together and severally.

In the Recitation, God says He made creation subject to us together and severally.[5] Each of us gathers all of existence, as do we all together. He also said that to create, raise up or animate one is to do so for all.[6] He calls on us to obey Him and His prophet,[7] a call of which the Praised said: "There is no obedience except to what is good."[8] He also told us: "Do not obey a creature against his Creator."[9] These commands are for all and for each. Nothing in existence absolves the self of the responsibility to obey Him and His apostle or the responsibility to disobey the merely created, if it stands against the Creator. God said: "Every soul earns only to its own account; no soul laden bears the load of another."[10]

Torn between the depth and darkness and the most beautiful height and illumination which satisfies and completes it, the self realizes itself through obedience to the Praised and God. The Praised is our highest possibility, the essence in which our original oath to God as Lord of all the worlds lies. The self gathers all God's self-revelations to Himself, so that we realize ourselves only through witness to His Unity and the apostolate of the Praised. Through this witness, we return to our essence, of whose perfection the Praised is the finest example.

The Praised is the goal, path, and means of our redemption. The only possible source for the book he received was the One Who said:

---

4 Ibn Ḥanbal, 1:191, 194.

5 See *Qur'an*, 31:20; and 45:13.

6 Ibid., 31:28.

7 Ibid., 4:59; 5:92 and 24:56.

8 Bukhārī, 5:441.

9 Ibn Ḥanbal, 1:131.

10 *Qur'an*, 6:164.

> Not before this didst thou recite any Book, or inscribe it with thy right hand, for then those who follow falsehood would have doubted. Nay; rather it is signs, clear signs in the breasts of those who have been given knowledge; and none denies Our signs but the evildoers.[11]

Faced with the written and recited book, we can either follow a lie or receive knowledge. If it seems incompatible with our assumptions, the claim of God as source may cause doubt, prompting us to seek reasons and corroborate our beliefs as knowledge, corroboration that needs our knowledge to be based on a lie we believe like the truth.

For others, the Book, whose entry into the world through the Praised is a matter of history, is confirmed within the self by its knowledge of the world and human beings, of reason and purpose. It does not contradict what was received. This call from without seems to have been ever-present within the self. The Praised, who first received it, is a sign, a stranger come amongst them to recall that the Book is already in them and that there are "signs, clear signs in the breasts" on the path to the centre of the self, our real homeland, from which the Praised entered world and self, descending into darkness to ascend again, with his followers.

The Book is only possible within the self, where it was sent, like light, knowledge, recollection, and warning. Entering the self from outside, its boundaries are where it is experienced as wisdom. Realizing the Book as the revelation of the Wise and understanding the reason and purpose of all things, based on the claims and debts of all things, the self acquires wisdom, discovering its authentic nature. Wisdom is how the wise relate with God as Wise. Our knowledge came down to us from God through the Praised, the first recipient of intellectual integrity. God says of this: "God has sent down on thee the Book and the Wisdom, and He has taught thee that thou knewest not; God's bounty to thee is ever great."[12]

Self discovery begins by recalling the self from oblivion, the empire of death and darkness. This is a precondition for even seeing the upright path and the way back. The Praised is the Light's first shining revelation, before even Adam, guaranteeing his sublime capacities. Temptation means moving from or covering over the light. The full moon and its waning to a dry palm frond signify this light and its eclipse.

---

11 Ibid., 29:48–49.

12 Ibid., 4:113.

Having lost everything, we are ever more remote from any clear principle of the self. To rediscover its potential after the principle we must first confess the Praised as culmination of our return. Following him from the depth to most beautiful uprightness, we move from the dry palm frond to the full moon. Awareness of the self's condition is like the fullness of the moon, allowing constant adjustment to witness that our reality is the Self.

God's unity is evident, but witness to it entails another tenet – the Praised as His prophet. The unity of the principle and the principle of Unity are fully evident in our nature and the forms it leads to, including consciousness. What seems self-evident generally requires no proof, but many do not consider the second tenet so.

The dominant forms of contemporary knowledge consider the Praised essentially an historical fact, a trace on the film of time that stretches from indeterminate beginning to indeterminate end. Knowledge of him depends on transmission, so how can he be both servant and apostle, determining our salvation and self-realization?

The bond between second and first tenets suggests a fault in the prevalent image. If confessing the Praised's apostolate entails God's unity, his appearance in history is surely a major ontological, cosmological, and anthropological sign. The first tenet is part of our nature, as he is our truth. The prophet's truth is first and final in revealing God's priority and finality.

His revelation cannot be confined to beginning and end in measurable time. Its start is inseparable from its end, as He is One. The primal and absolute purity of His revelation, the primacy of creation, is seed and fruit. The confession of the Praised's apostolate includes this primacy and finality of the revelation of things as so many signs.

The sensory world is liminal, where lower and higher levels of the self meet. The full self cannot be reduced to it without murdering God and our own selves in a darkening condition, bereft of reason for hope. The Praised's truth is with all things, excluded from none. Otherwise, the All-praised, revealed by existence's praise, would not be in all things, nor they His everlasting self-revelation before His face.

Obeying God's command, the Praised said: "I have been commended to be the first of the people of Peace."[13] And: "In Him has found peace whoso is in the heavens and the earth, willingly or unwillingly, and to Him they shall be returned."[14] This revelation says Abraham and Ishmael are people of peace,[15]

13 Ibid., 39:12.

14 Ibid., 3:83.

15 See *Qur'an*, 2:127 and 3:67.

like Mary and Jesus and his disciples,[16] as clearly follows from the claim that everything in existence is at peace in God.

The claim that the Praised is one of the people of peace thus seems clear, as he entered the world after Abraham and Ishmael, Mary and Jesus. But how can he be first, preceding even existence? He is a servant, created and guided, like existence, as God said: "There is no one in the heavens and the earth that does not come to the All-merciful as a servant."[17]

He is the Praised, as his mother was told to name him.[18] He is at-peace, a bringer of peace, faithful.[19] These three names reflect his relationship with God of the most beautiful names. God's names include Peaceful, All-praised, and Faithful. Realizing them within us through being-at-peace and faith, we are at-peace, bringers of peace and faithful. In the act of praise we establish a relationship with the All-praised through the person of the Praised.

Confessing no god but God and the Praised as His servant, we declare our participation in the act of praise of every created thing, as revealed by the Creator: "The seven heavens and the earth, and whosoever in them is, extol Him; nothing is, that does not proclaim His praise, but you do not understand their extolling. Surely He is All-clement, All-forgiving."[20]

Our original creation in most beautiful uprightness corresponds to the Praised and signifies absolute purity and being-at-peace, as a bringer of peace and faithful. The truth of the Praised is our core and belongs to us all as the why and wherefore of our creation. The signs in the world remind us of this. It is how what is relates to God the All-praised. The Praised's majestic nature[21] is our goal, calling us to the road back to the One.

Except in most beautiful uprightness, we are removed from purity, which spurs us to discover ourselves in the reason and purpose of our creation, the truth of the Praised. Removed, not absolutely remote, our beautiful uprightness and his truth are a hidden treasure, to which the upright road leads and from which our descent into duality begins.

---

16 Ibid., 3:52–53.

17 *Qur'an*, 19:93.

18 Amina, the mother of the Praised, said that while she was pregnant she heard a voice which told her, "You are pregnant with the lord of this people and when he is born say, 'I put him in the care of the One from the evil of every envier; then call him the Praised.'" (Ibn Isḥāq, *Sīrāt Rasūl Allāh*, 69)

19 It is usual to cite 201 names for the Praised. In a well-known Sufi work, the *Dalā'il al-khayrāt*, compiled by Muḥammad Sulaymān al-Jazūlī, these names are brought together for use in ritual.

20 *Qur'an*, 17:44.

21 See *Qur'an*, 68:4.

Return and self-realization lead toward this treasure house. Without it we are nothing. It links us to the Peaceful and All-praised and is more precious to us than our own selves. The self's conditions are just signs of its presence, as are the signs on the horizons. As absolute treasure house of our perfectibility, the Praised is reason and goal of creation. This is a meaning of God's exclamation: "But for thee I should not have created the heavens!"[22]

Saying that no prophet comes between him and the Anointed, the Praised is pointing out their union in confessing God's unity and our perfectibility. The things in world and self point to this in different ways, linked with God as Peace and Lord through being-at-peace and service. The Praised focuses this connection and is nearer the faithful than their own selves.[23]

The Messiah is both Word and child, a principle even for her who bore him. She received the Word, rendering it incarnate. The case of the Praised is similar. The Word was delivered to humanity through him, but as prior to him. He received it thanks to his maternal prophethood: moulding himself to it, he brought it into this world as divine discourse. All the worlds are in his nature, it in them. His nature is majestic in its original fitness to receive the Word. Nothing in the created world is or can be more beautiful than it, because he is the first of creation, the beginning of all things that descend from God and the end of return to Him.

The Praised's nature is like the Word revealed in the Recitation.[24] In a pattern of causes and consequences joined in his primordial nature, the path from Abraham through Hagar leads through the Praised to the Virgin Mary, and back again, whether through Hagar or Sarah.

This view of temporal progress can be reversed, with the Praised and the Anointed together at the beginning, closer to each other than any others, while Abraham and his sons are at the end. This cycle of seed and fruit, fruit and seed, as described in the revealed texts and their interpreters, represents the two arcs, one upward, the other downward, on which time and space are qualities, their quantitative expressions mere shadows. The Messiah and the Recitation are the Word, uncreated, spoken by God. Its manifestations were

---

22 'Ajlūnī, *Kashf al-khafā' wa muzīl al-ilbās 'ammā ishtahara min al-aḥādīth 'alā alsinat al-nās*, 2:214. This tradition is a common one in the Muslim intellectual tradition. The source cited notes it is not in the main collections of the Praised's traditions, but its meaning is clear. Rūmī does not question its authenticity and cites it frequently. See Rūmī, *The Mathnawi*, 2:974 i 5:2737.

23 *See Qur'an*, 33:6.

24 'Ā'isha, the prophet's wife, said: "The prophet's nature is the Recitation" (Muslim, 1:359).

created. This One Word is confirmed in the receptive and donative pair of the Praised and the Virgin.

Rashid al-Din Maybudi wrote a commentary on the verse of the Recitation that relates the well-known and distressing accusation of adultery against the Praised's wife 'Ā'isha:[25]

> "Those who came with the slander are a band of you; do not reckon it as evil for you; rather it is good for you."[26] It has come in the stories that paradise has an outskirt, and tomorrow the Lord of Exaltation will gather the faithful in the outskirt and, before they go into paradise, He will host them in a perfect invitation, a fitting bestowal of eminence, and a complete caressing. Then He will place a favour on Mustafâ: "O Muhammad, this invitation is the banquet for your contract of marriage with Mary, daughter of 'Imrân, and Âsiya, daughter of Muzâhim. O Muhammad, I kept Mary away from companionship with men and brought forth from her a child without a man for the sake of your honour and jealousy. I kept Âsiya next to Pharaoh, but I took away Pharaoh's manliness and never let Pharaoh be with her. I conveyed her to you pure, without defect, no one's hand having touched her." Now listen to a subtle point: He honoured Mary and Âsiya, who tomorrow, in the next world, will be the spouses of Mustafâ, and He praised them for purity and guarded them from the people. 'Â'isha, the truthful, who was his spouse in this world, who pleased him, who was his companion, whose love was in his heart, and who will be betrothed to him tomorrow in paradise – what wonder if He honoured her, sent Koranic verses and revelation exonerating her, and if He himself gave witness to her purity and approved of her.[27]

The Praised told his wife Khadija that God had married him in the garden to the Virgin Mary and to Āsiya. In one tradition, the event has already happened, in another it is yet to come. It could not be otherwise, as it presents final achievement which is perfect beginning.

---

25 On this case, see further Lings, *Muhammad*, 243–46, and Ibn Isḥāq, *Sīrāt Rasūl Allāh*, 493–99.

26 *Qur'an*, 24:11.

27 Maybūdī, *Kashf al-asrār wa 'uddat al-abrār*, 6:514–15. The author owes this English translation of the Persian original to William C. Chittick (personal communication).

Postlude: The Time of the World in the Time of the Self

When an intention is realized, its final act or key lies in its beginning. The fruit is the beginning and end of the tree, which does not at first exist in material form, but suprasensibly, as archetype.

The Praised is the keystone left to one side and his is the central position in existence.[1] There is nothing not oriented towards or determined by him. The Praised is first in the Creator's Self. He seals creation. He was before Adam, but sent down into the world as his descendant. In him both time and space are seen in both aspects – descending and ascending.

God established Adam in paradise, bringing together in him all of creation. By reaching for the fruit of the inviolate tree, Adam forfeited his purity of self, in which both outer and inner signs pointed to the One. This is why he was sent down, but not beyond his Lord's mercy or knowledge.

In remorse, Adam turned again to God to confess his mistake. His God took mercy on him and renewed our original covenant, in sign of which, the first house was raised in the sacred valley of Becca,[2] and, forty years later, the second house on sacred Mount Sion. The seven circuits of the Kaʿba in the valley signify the linkage of depth and height, earth and seven heavens, and return to God by the upright path through the garden. This is the discovery of the Praised's nature in every self as the principle Adam clearly reflected in his original purity and turned to again after the restored covenant.

That restored covenant allowed ascent from the depth but was again forgotten in Adam's posterity. Forgetting is neglect of the heart, symbolized by the ruined house and the lost or corrupt ritual. From generation to generation, God sent prophets to remind us of that covenant as the condition of pure nature. Age followed age, as some ascended to the height and others descended into ever thicker dark. Then God sent Abraham and his son to clear the house's foundations and call to the ritual of circumambulation.

God again indicated the potential in the self, signified by the house in Becca, and the authentic perfection of the Praised, signified by the house on Sion. Abraham's restoration of house and of ritual is marked where he stood

1 See *Psalm* 118:22–23 and *Matthew*, 21:42. The Praised says of himself that he is the keystone of the perfect building. See Muslim, 4:1235.

2 See Bukhārī, 4:383.

 DOI 10.1163/9789004279407_038

by a stone that bears the imprint of his feet.[3] From there, he recalled us to the Praised's purity of nature and begged God to renew our consciousness of creation's purpose by sending the maternal prophet to be a mercy to the worlds and our most beautiful example.

When the Praised passed, during his night journey, from the Inviolable Mosque of the depth to the Further Mosque of the height, he was led up along the upright path through the heavens, from earthly exile to the garden of the blest. He gathered within himself all the worlds. In the seventh heaven, he met Abraham, but continued on, past the Lote-Tree, the garden of blessedness and the frequented house, demonstrating that he is the maternal principle of existence to whom the prophets swore their oath. As our most beautiful example, he is the sign of two times – that of the things of the world and that whereby they are comprehended within the now of the perfect self.

The space and time of the external world are derived from the sacred time of the perfect self of the Praised. The confession of no god but God and the Praised as His apostle entails the affirmation of the primordial substance of what is created. The Spirit is of this essence. It is the first reception of God's breath, received and passed on as creation, the discovery of the Hidden. The Praised carries out both these actions, reception and passing on, as a mercy to the worlds. Acknowledging this, we confess him as the maternal prophet. The first essence is his essence: Intellect, the Pen, the coming of Light.

God is the Holy.[4] His exhaled breath is the Holy Spirit, the Praised's first or receptive aspect. Passing on the received is the form his prophecy takes. The essence of existence has two aspects, receptive and donative, female and male, a duality that confirms and reveals Unity. In a perfect union, they journey down through the levels of existence, in constant witness of the One, bringing joyful news of Him.

Sacrality is the inner, prophecy the external aspect of his apostolate. The Anointed referred to them when he told his disciples that the Praised was the Paraclete, the Holy Spirit,[5] and again that the Paraclete was the Spirit of Truth.[6] Sacrality and prophecy relate to each other so that sacrality is the inner aspect of prophecy, itself in turn the external aspect of sacrality. They are aspects of the Praised: at the level of reception he is the Holy Spirit, of donation the Spirit of Truth.[7] God says of him: "We have not sent thee save as a mercy to all

3 See *Qur'an*, 3:97.

4 Ibid., 59:23.

5 See *John*, 14:26.

6 Ibid., 16:13.

7 See Nasafi, *The Furthest Goal*, 82–83.

worlds";[8] "thou, surely thou, guide onto the upright path – the path of God";[9] and "O prophet, We have sent thee as a witness and good tidings to bear a warning, calling unto God by His leave and as a light giving lamp."[10]

Faith is the relationship of the believing individual with God, Who believes and keeps faith. That this is so follows from God's will to reveal Himself as Faithful to Himself. He therefore offered us confidence or faith as the form of the relationship of the One with Itself, but in His twofold unity: faith, the correlative of our partial knowledge, and the love for the Real to which it leads. The more we know it, the more we love it; the more we love it, the more we know it.

All the signs in world and self point to the Real. They are sufficient for love of what they signify and so for faith. God told the Praised: "And in the earth are signs for those whose faith is sure and in yourselves. Can ye then not see?"[11] and: "We shall show them Our signs on the horizons and in their own souls until it becomes clear to them that He is the Truth."[12]

The earth and the horizons and everything in them are perfect creatures revealing their perfect Creator, Who said: "Thou seest not in the creation of the All-merciful any imperfection."[13] Humanity is part of this perfect totality and He said of us: "Surely We created man in the most beautiful uprightness."[14] That creation is predicated upon duality – female and male, receiving and giving. So it must be, as everything is created in duality, as symbolized by the Praised and the Virgin as one perfect revelation of the One.

The Christian and Muslim views of the Virgin and her son agree over their final and ultimate meaning. For Christians, this view is not to be questioned or relativized. For them, the Virgin and the Messiah are the reason and end of existence. As Anointed, Jesus is the light of lights. The Muslim perspective does not question these claims, but considers them subordinate to the primacy of the Praised and his truth, firstly in the divine intention, but also as the goal of the entire revelation.

In saying that of everyone in this or any future world the Anointed was closest to him, the Praised was stressing the inseparability of the *Muhammad-Mary-Messiah-Mushaf* complex. From this perspective, the Praised and Mary form a pair constituted by receiving and giving, while the Anointed and the

---

8 *Qur'an*, 21:107.

9 Ibid., 42:52–53.

10 Ibid., 33:45–46.

11 Ibid., 51:20–21.

12 Ibid., 41:53.

13 Ibid., 67:3.

14 Ibid., 95:4.

Recitation are the Word God revealed through them as one in two different instances. This helps explain certain difficult questions of the Muslim intellectual tradition, questions that confuse even Muslims, never mind outside observers, and can have very serious consequences.

These reflections on the Praised's claim that there were no prophets between him and the Anointed and that their closeness was unmediated raise the question of the dominant image of time for most of the past millennium. According to this image, time flows from indeterminate beginning towards indeterminate end, between which it takes on the form of a causal chain that can somehow be reduced to quantity.

Such a progression from cause to consequence, where every cause is also a consequence, every consequence a cause, can afford to ignore the principle, since it allows that the lower may be cause of the higher, the lesser of the greater. This false expression may be found in the absolutization of the quantifiable world and the construction of history against the open self, which this vision holds forcibly closed. One consequence is that the truth of the Praised is necessarily reduced and confined to history.

His truth must first be enclosed to then be reduced to the quantifiable. Time increasingly loses the attribute of quality, appearing to be quantity, which it is not. One consequence is the absolutization of the ascending presence of all existence on a single time line, extending from lower to higher. It is forgotten that any line is just part of a circle and that countless circles may share the same centre. This centre is, properly, always and everywhere One, regardless of how may images He reveals Himself in.

These thoughts on closing the circle with Abraham and his two sons on one side and the Virgin Mary, the Praised, the Anointed and the Recitation on the other lead us to an image of circular time in which nothing on the edge or circle of existence can be severed from the Centre, his truth.

From this follows that the two times – that in the external world and that within the self, cannot be separated. Only in the self do worldly space and time have the hour for principle. But, the hour comprehends all existence, as the stage of sacred history within the mighty nature of the self of the Praised. The hour is within the self. There, one does not wait for it, for time is a mere attribute to it. But in the external world we must wait for it. Considering existence's turn from its reason towards its purpose, which are that same nature of his self, and returning to it again and again in his tour of human perfection, Rumi says:

> That is why the Praised said: "Adam and the prophets
> are behind me under my banner."
> That is why the prophet, possessor of myriad virtues,

spoke the mystery, "We are the last and the foremost."
"Although in form I am born of Adam,
in meaning I am the ancestor of my ancestor.
For the angels prostrated themselves to him for my sake,
and he followed me to the seventh heaven.
So in meaning, the first father was born from me;
in meaning the fruit gave birth to tree."
The first thought comes last into actuality:
especially the thought that is the Attribute of Eternity-without-beginning.[15]

---

15 Rūmī, *The Mathnawi*, 4:525–30.

VOLUME 2

On Continuity and Discontinuity

PART 1

The History of Religion

• •

CHAPTER 1

The One

As the first, indelible manifestation of the Not-One, the One is irreducible. All things reduce to It. Multiplicity manifests, comes from and returns to the One. Every self is in its sublime potential One person, epitomizing all manifestation of the One. We are images of the One and self-realization lies in discovering that image within ourselves.

Self-realization in that One person depends on witness to Unity, which sets us on the upright path. Those not on it seek their horizon in society or nature. But there is no one but the One, no person but the Person. The in and out of everything is One and everything we achieve manifests the Person, in and out.

If we manifest the One, it is necessarily as duality. That is how the One manifests. We are always dual, images manifesting Unity. Human duality is masculinity and femininity, receiving and giving, descent and ascent, departure and return. There is Unity in every form duality takes. No dual state to which the infinity of things reduces reveals anything real but Unity: duality is from and returns to Unity. This is what was meant by saying all things are created in pairs.[1]

Every self experiences itself as both one and two, a single core split between lower and higher, conscious and shadowed, joyful and dismal. It can move in either direction, down, away from Unity, or up, towards the principle and goal.

If this divided self is an image of Being, then Being is also divided into multiple states. Multiplicity reveals Being as one.

No level of being is independent of the others; singly or together, they manifest and confirm Unity. Multiplicity always contains Unity. Every manifestation remains linked to It, owes its principle to It. Every level of Being is always repaying its debt to Unity. Otherwise, they would be their own principle.

We all owe a debt to that inner person who epitomizes all manifestation of the One. The world and we are two aspects of one manifestation of the One. There can be no world without us, nor we without the world. We contain nothing it doesn't, the world nothing we don't, for God is One and Flux, incomparable and similar, remote and close. To speak of Him is to acknowledge mystery; to say nothing of Him is to acknowledge His speech:

1 See *Qur'an*, 43:12.

 | DOI 10.1163/9789004279407_039

> Foremost in the debt is knowledge of Him, and the perfection of this knowledge is believing in Him, and the perfection of this belief is affirming His Oneness, and the perfection of this affirmation is to purify one's devotion to Him, and the perfection of this purification is to divest Him of all attributes – because of the testimony of every attribute that it is other than the object of attribution, and because of the testimony of every such object that it is other than the attribute. So whoever ascribes an attribute to God – glorified be He – has conjoined Him [with something else], and whoever so conjoins Him has made Him twofold, and whoever makes Him twofold has fragmented Him, and whoever does fragment Him is ignorant of Him. And whoever points to Him confines Him, and whoever confines Him counts Him; and whoever asks "in what?" encloses Him, and whoever asks "upon what?" isolates Him.[2]

Debt relates recipient to giver. We receive existence, but not in order to be other than God; then, God would not be one, but two, God and man. Confessing Unity rejects this possibility. But we continue to see ourselves in duality, no matter how illusory.

We are entirely in God's debt. Everything in us is received; what is received from God is real – God's self-disclosure. From our perspective, it presents as an object. The seer and the seen are two, bound by seeing. Witness to Unity turns us towards the overcoming of duality, as reality is just Unity seen in that way.

If knowledge derived from duality exists for Unity, then overcoming the separation of knower from Known is seeing duality as the manifestation of Unity, humanity in perfect masculinity and perfect femininity, whose mutual attraction and yearning to transcend separation is love. To know separation and wish realization in Unity is to love the known and know what is loved. This is faith, how we relate to the Faithful.

This relationship of faithful to Faithful, knower and Known, lover and Beloved, aims at the One. Only the One can resolve the self's inner divisions. But the self is always divided. It is constantly struggling not to confuse the One with the means of Its self-disclosure. None of the self's stations resembles the Goal, each one being erased in turn for the next one up. Only the One resolves division.

2 From the first discourse of imam ʿAli ibn Abī Ṭālib, in *Nahj al-balāgha*, cited after Shah-Kazemi, *Justice and Remembrance*, 208.

This process of transcending the attributes through which the One discloses Himself is the way out of closure and fragmentation, a journey of ascent without end, as there is no end to anger and mercy, suffering and joy. Nothing on that upward path even potentially marks attainment of our goal. At every stage, the goal remains present and absent. So long as we can speak of ourselves, we remain within the duality that abides with speech and silence and owes the confession that there is no real but the Real.

CHAPTER 2

Witness

We define ourselves by the object of our acts of witness, positioning ourselves in our present, aware of coming from the past and facing the future. Different acts define our position differently. Witness is valid so long as the witnesses possess irrefutable reasons or inner knowledge so sure that no external evidence can shake it.

Confessing God's unity, the Praised's apostolate and return to God, we willingly and consciously define ourselves in relation to our neighbours. They differ, in principle, from us and their witness to God, the Praised, and return is never the same as ours, for two key reasons. The first is that the witnessing self is in constant flux, so that nothing in the world seems the same from moment to moment, including our neighbours. This inconstancy of theirs is the second reason. They too change from moment to moment. They may appear constant to themselves and others, but this is just appearance and is the reason for the concealment of the One manifested by diversity.

Confession of God, the Praised, and return takes many forms in history. It happens through God's apostles, who are many – twice as many as the Israelites who left Egypt and crossed the Red Sea.[1] They are 124,000, according to a saying of the Praised.[2]

Many are forgotten, a few only remembered for how they focused and preserved God's message. Among them are Abraham, Moses, David, Jesus, and Muhammad. Prophets have been raised up in every people to speak the same truth in different languages, among them Confucius, Lao Tze, Buddha and Socrates. They received their revelations in different times and places, but from the same God. As God revealed His speech to them, they expressed it in their languages to their peoples. Speech presupposes a listener to assimilate and pass on.

This potential to assimilate incorporates each of us in the stream of tradition. Bearing witness denotes that inclusion. Since all God's apostles reveal the same message in different forms, bearing witness to one embraces them all, knowingly or not. However historically remote, Abraham, Moses, David, Jesus or Muhammad remain immediate to us, for the speech they received in

1 *The Babylonian Talmud*, Megillah, 14a.

2 Bayhaqī, 9:4.

 | DOI 10.1163/9789004279407_040

human tongue is actually the speech of the one God before Whose face all things stand.

The followers of a divine apostle confess out of their free will. This links them to the one God, in and beyond history, and to an apostle, with a clear historical status. This double witness, to God's oneness and the apostle's exemplary nature, may be treated synchronically, in relation to others in our own time, and diachronically, through the generations, back to the first ancestor.

We may bear our witness through being-at-peace, knowledge, love, and beauty, and our purpose is always to pass from duality into Unity. However impossible it may seem, our salvation depends on this.

Each person of peace is oriented towards Peace by their very being-at-peace. Only Peace can satisfy the person of and at peace; but not so long as differentiation remains, as the Creator continues to disclose Himself in creation. If we seek to know, only perfect knowledge of all things can satisfy us. Knowledge is decisive only when the knower becomes one with reality of the known. The apostle's call to acknowledge the truth, reality, right and dignity of whatever their knowledge can attain evokes that union attained in return to God as Truth. Love is what binds lover to Beloved. Mere knowledge of the Beloved is not sufficient; for the lover, only union will suffice. Only then will the differences indicated by separation be known and removed.

As speaking beings, we and our speech both have meaning. We discover our meaning in speech, making speech the meaning of meaning. This leads to key questions regarding how the person of and at peace relates to Peace, the known/knower to the Known, and the beloved/lover to the Beloved. Can being-at-peace and Peace, knowing and the Known, loving and the Beloved have being, distinct from the person of and at peace, the known/knower or the beloved/lover?

The short answer is no. Every duality, the entire manifest world, has Unity as principle and confluence with the Flux. Giving and receiving, male and female, the Praised and the Virgin are one in Peace, the Known, the Beloved, the Beautiful, two inextricable manifestations of the One, His first symbol in creation.

All this is said in language appropriated from our parents. Without some such process of transmission, where would we get language from? The knowledge set out in this book might seem derived wholly from external sources, appropriated and assimilated, then expressed and written down. But this "might seem" is vital in directing us to the purpose of this presentation.

Our witness of no god but God and the Praised as His servant and apostle is expressed in language and so shares in the logic of giving and receiving; it is a social expression of witness. It comes from and returns to the supreme potential of the self. It is realized, independent of any proof outside the witness' own self, as tautegorical: we know it in and of ourselves, independent of form or even language. As knowledge it is both logical and mytho-logical.

As the self is constantly changing, our witness to God's unity, the Praised's apostolate, and return to God can take any number of forms without betraying its essence, which transcends each individual expression and all of them combined.

CHAPTER 3

Religions

In reviewing these synchronic and diachronic aspects of individual experience in Muslim, Christian and Jewish relations, one must keep both in view, but distinct. In principle, no Muslim does or could live without Christian and Jewish neighbours. Living with them is what determines selfhood dialectically. Ignorance of them is ignorance of self; fear of them, fear of self; hatred of them, hatred of self. If "Muslim, Christian and Jew" are names for people oriented towards the One, they all share one authentic essence. Any who bears them is that other to deny whom is to deny oneself.

This coexistence is not just a historical or geographical fact. However Judaism, Christianity and Islam differ as religions, they share one metaphysical essence. One cannot discuss their languages, meanings or symbols, their teachings, rites and art, and ignore that unity of metaphysical origin.

The metaphysical core is one, eternal. It takes different forms in different religions. When a religion becomes unmoored from this core, the ritual and virtue become increasingly meaningless. They, nonetheless, continue to point the self towards the source of teaching at its core, the perennial source of its religious knowledge. Persisting with ritual and virtue necessarily leads to the source in the self.[1] Even if from without, they serve to reveal and reinvigorate our core.

In terms of temporal continuity, Muslim witness to God's unity and the Praised's apostolate dates from the time of the historical Praised. This is, however, eternity descending into time, infinity into space. As revelation, there is no rupture in time or space; in it everything, past and present, gathers, is ordered, explained and presented in new form.

Those facing this new revelation of old truth can either embrace and confess it or repudiate it as false and alien. Its reality is unaffected by either. Both are weighed within the self and no one else, near or far, can bear our burden of witness or denial for us. The source of the sacred teachings is not in history, it is eternal and unchanging, whatever temporal and spatial forms it may take. It is up to us to discover it in the Hour of the self.

---

1 The Bosnian word for ritual, *obred*, which means "order," is cognate with Latin *ordo* and Sanskrit *ṛta*. Ritual is fulfilled by order. The entire trajectory of the revelation of Mystery is an ascent from chaos to order. Ritual is therefore inseparable from life, as what opposes entropy. Our every effort aims to enter ritual and order to approach the First Principle.

 | DOI 10.1163/9789004279407_041

For this reason, confessing the Praised's apostolate in the historical person of Muhammad, son of ʿAbdullah, comprehends past and future fully. As witness, it can be shouldered or refused, but only through free will. This is also true of witness of Jesus, son of Mary. Each of us chooses to confess or deny his historical person as truth of Divine revelation. Both possibilities are reflected in the selves of witness and denier. Those who do confess see no rupture between Jesus' historical existence and what preceded it. Witness to him affirms the Law and the prophets, if it is based on free will.

If Jews refuse to confess Jesus, that too is out of free will. Their refusal to confess Jesus as Anointed and Word of God causes no break in their continuity. Both past and future meet in their confession. By recognizing Jesus, they would cease to be what that confession makes them.

Christians add the earlier books of the Jewish tradition to their own as part of their fundamental heritage, finding in them countless reasons for their own witness. They read them in a way that reveals references and witness to Mary and Jesus on almost every page. Jews read these same books, but what they see is different from what Christians have for the past two thousand years. This relationship between Christian and Jew, Jew and Christian, applies equally to Muslim and Christian, Muslim and Jew, Christian and Muslim, Jew and Muslim.

In God's revelation to the Praised, Muslims see a summation and a new expression of what God had already revealed. They read the Christian and Jewish books as addressing their inheritance. Like Christians with the books of the Jewish tradition, Muslims find confirmation in the books of the Christian and Jewish traditions. They find mention of the Praised as our supreme potential and best example of relationship with God on every page of the Gospels, Psalms and Torah.

Their readings are based on free will and the confession of God's unity, the Praised's apostolate and return to God. For Muslims this is *the* way, encompassing all and excluding any other. They allow others the same courtesy, however, of an entirely different way to God. God says explicitly to the Praised: "To every one of you We have appointed a right way and an open road."[2]

Viewed in terms of temporal process, the spiritual thread connecting Jews, Christians and Muslims may be considered to share, however obscurely, a history from Adam to Abraham. With Abraham, it forks – one line passing through Ishmael, the other through Isaac and from Isaac through the prophets to the Anointed, Jesus, or perhaps to the last prophet before him to be accepted by Jews and Christians alike, where another fork appears – the Jews are still

2 *Qur'an*, 5:48.

waiting for the Messiah that Christians see in Jesus, through whom they interpret past and present.

Muslim witness holds that both branches of spiritual sequence from Abraham meet again in the Praised and in Mary, but only to split again, as one branch runs from Malachi towards the Messiah still-to-come, the other from Jesus and Mary, for which the Praised and the Recitation are the new revelation.

These three spiritual sequences continue in history as the Jewish, Christian and Muslim traditions. Muslims perceive these sequences differently from Christians and Jews. These differences cannot be glossed over. They may be troubling and painful, but life involves their challenge. At any given time, we are both guest and host of these differences: guest, because others bring what we lack; host, by receiving those who bring us news of God. We are all simultaneously both guests and hosts of God, and that is a difference that cannot be reconciled without return to God, when we shall all be His guests. Jews, Christians and Muslims all affirm this return.

All shall stand before one God, Who will judge justly. The more conscious we are of return, the nearer it is. Difference exists to guarantee our dignity as individuals, but not as something attained through our rational formation. Each one of us, a creature of God, is worth all the rest together, as God told the Praised: "We prescribed for the Children of Israel that whoso slays a soul, not to retaliate for a soul slain, nor for corruption done in the land, shall be as if he had slain mankind altogether; and whoso gives life to a soul, shall be as if he had given life to mankind altogether."[3]

3 Ibid., 5:32.

CHAPTER 4

Ascending

Modern interpretations of Bosnian historical continuity are dominated by notions of rupture. Historical representations of Christian history that serve ideological purposes treat the Muslim presence as intrusion by force followed by a break. Such essentially ideological images underpin anti-Bosnian and anti-Muslim projects. They break down, however, under a history of religion that entails an image of world and self together with ever-present God.

God's ever-presence as creator and ruler cannot be regarded as a source of history; it is essential to each instant, each thing. Exclude it and you may associate temporal duration with any of the countless things which one may term a "first cause" or "source." The modern absolutization of reason views the world in time in this way. It entails silence about the other aspect of existence over which reason has no power. Histories without God therefore proceed under their own steam, determined by causes that can be described once and for all. Historical phenomena are thus bodies for which the other is a disease from which to be freed.

Rule God out of the world, however, and history of religion, properly understood, becomes impossible. Then the variety of religious forms takes on quite a different meaning, on the assumption of the potential reification of phenomena in history, as postulated by modern science. For such views, the religions are forms of the perennial religion, which admits countless religions over time, while always remaining the same. Central to this view is that the perennial symbols of religion perdure, from tradition to tradition.

To better understand the continuity of Bosnian history, let us look at how two key symbols of the Muslim faith, the links between the valley of Becca and Mount Sion and the Virgin Mary and her son Jesus have been approached. Our treatment is based on the heritage of old Bosnian Christianity and its assimilation into Muslim religious forms. Our purpose is to show that the constant process of losing one and discovering other sets of meanings for symbols and myths is inextricable from presence in religion.

What was forgotten can be remembered, what was lost found. God created us in His image and our authentic nature encompasses all knowledge. In it we know everything, but our time as a created being constantly reminds us that we are not God. Our potential for perfection is perfect service of God; only then do we receive everything from God as our Lord. Remembering the forgotten and finding the lost presuppose admitting that we forget and knowing that

 | DOI 10.1163/9789004279407_042

we seek, and bearing witness to God's ever-presence in all things, including us. The teachings and rituals are there to help us recall the forgotten and to cleave to our eternal essence, from ever, forever.

As One, God reveals Himself through His most beautiful names.[1] He created us and taught us those names,[2] preparing us to be His steward, as He said Himself.

> It is God who made the earth a fixed place for you, and heaven a building; and He formed you, He made your forms beautiful, and He provided you with the pleasant things.[3]
>
> He created the heavens and the earth with the Truth, He formed you, and He made your forms beautiful; and to Him is the homecoming.[4]

We have received His most beautiful names, as has existence as a whole, which manifests them. Our return to God means realizing the received, revealing our service as the reception and return of what is beautiful from and to our Lord. God asks only being-at-peace in payment of our debt, but this requires self-realization through His names. This is how we return to, find or discover ourselves in authentic nature. Our final goal in return is to be God's steward, as one of the good.

Our debt is service and being-at-peace. From it derives our right to develop in perfection and to expect forgiveness for betraying what we received. This correlation between debt and right is God's revelation to humankind. From it derives the tradition that encompasses all times and places. The debt is personal. It affects each of us individually. It is being in the instant, without past or future, or anywhere but where one is. The revelation is inextricable from Unity, infinity and perfection. Tradition encompasses all time and place. Our debt to God, as He reveals it, is the source of tradition, so tradition can never replace the debt itself.

There are many revelations, but one source. Only that source is real. We may see it in anything and discern it against the unreal. Each revelation appears all-comprehensive, but each differs from the rest. And whatever touches revelation appears as perfect in its beauty.

We are in the depths, in the manifold. Realization lies in ascent, return to the initial height, where we received existence and knowledge of it. Height

1 See *Qur'an*, 59:24.

2 Ibid., 2:31.

3 *Qur'an*, 40:64.

4 Ibid., 64:3.

and depths, One and many, near and far are at once. Discover one and cover the other. Return and gathering mean accepting God's commandment: "And look that thou make them after their pattern, which was shewed thee in the mount."[5] The mount is our original station on the "sublime height." The tastes of the valley call us back to the tastes of that height.

What we receive in existence may appear at various levels, the highest and lowest being the summit of the mount and the valley bottom. Wherever our search for their meaning takes us, we can always distinguish real from unreal and confess His revelation: "Naught is there, but its treasuries are with Us, and We send it not down but in a known measure."[6] To receive what was sent down we must first join the self-abnegation of all things before God in demonstration of His glory, for all things glorify Him with praise.[7]

We receive and discover our potential link to God the All-praised through praise by making His apostle the Praised a reality within our selves. The Praised's nature is our supreme potential. Approximating it, we rise up from the depths in the valley to the height on the mount. This is our path back to God and the essence of His revelation in all its forms. It touches the self. Everything else is a mere reminder of our authentic perfection and our desire to discover and realize it.

Every form of His revelation and its transmission from generation to generation connects us with Unity as our principle and ultimate purpose. We have only what we have received from and must return to that source, as our final confluence. Receiving and returning presuppose that willing self-abnegation of which God says: "Hast thou not seen how before God prostrate themselves all who are in the heavens and all who are in the earth, the sun and the moon, the stars and the mountains, the trees and the beasts, and many of mankind?"[8]

Recalling Unity as our reason and purpose and revealing our supreme potential in that relation to Unity mean always being in a place of self-abnegation. Then we can see the signs in all things and through them God as Signified. Confessing openly that "there is no god," we can rise from the depths of forgetting to the height of remembrance and the affirmation "but God." That is always being in a place of self-abnegation and on a battlefield. Negating illusion, we discover the Real. Ascending from the depths towards our potential, we confess the Praised as our best example, His perfect servant and apostle. To be always in a place of self-abnegation, on a battlefield, is to steadily free

5 *Exodus*, 25:40.

6 *Qur'an*, 15:21.

7 See *Qur'an*, 17:44.

8 *Qur'an*, 22:18.

ourselves from illusion and move towards Peace. No point we reach ends this attempt at liberation and return to the Abode of Peace.

Ascending, after the Praised, transforms the signs in the world and the self so that they bring the traveller nearer the Signified. Joy and suffering take on a new aspect at each stage of the ascent – the attraction of enjoyment and the repulsiveness of suffering become stronger. We repent for all we have been, acknowledge our frailty, and trust in God's mercy.

CHAPTER 5

Historiosophy

In modern times, the idea that past and even future events form series of quantifiable causes and effects visible in the facts they leave behind has the sheen of scientific truth. Historians are supposedly observers outside the course of history, the object of their science. They encourage this assumption of detachment, presenting themselves as immaterial eyes recording the indisputable reality of historical events.

The modern assumption of a single, finite, quantifiable world also excludes openness of self. The closure of the world within limits, anything beyond which is disregarded, implies a closed self too. This self can attain a level of command over both the world and its sciences, but the real world resists it, given the indefiniteness of its limits. In consequence, action is preferred to knowledge.

The preference for action suggests that anything undesirable may be eradicated by action, like a disease from the body of history. But only knowledge frees. Unlike action, based on little knowledge and tending to multiply the effects of ignorance, knowledge is a possession forever.

Historians do not generally discuss this detachment, but the perspective informs how they present or interpret history. They are outside the course of events being observed, neither participating nor disturbing. The laws governing history are taken as axiomatic, discernable by the "right" historian. They are read from quantifiable, self-evident facts, whose self-evidence renders "evident" the course in question.

Causal chains of action supposedly determine the course of events and historians try to discern history's onto-topology though their imprint on things. These traces betray no personality, not even that of the historians. They are accepted as unproblematic evidence for reconstructing history's course and the deception lies therein: that the freer they are of the historian's presence, the more accurate the representation of history.

Kicking the historian out of history is to deny the irreducible mystery in all that exists, including us. Denying that mystery means closing the "I" and so a contradiction: the historian's "I" is at once impartial observer of the past and an entirely negligible factor in the process of observation. Let the historian's "I" become involved and everything acquires an irreducible mysteriousness. Observers are alive and their "I," open to mystery, is a factor in the life of the

 | DOI 10.1163/9789004279407_043

moment. It shocks the historical object out of its lifelessness. Henry Corbin has written of the consequences of ignoring the living, involved observer:

> By contrast, that which certain Western philosophers, like Baader and Schelling, have called *Historiosophy* would not be able to do without a metaphysics, for if one ignores or excludes the hidden, esoteric sense of things, the living phenomena of this world are reduced to those of a cadaver.[1]

Elsewhere he says:

> Take note! When a man lets himself be thrown into history he can go through all the philosophies of history he likes, he can legislate in the name of a historical causality which ignores all metaphysics, he can behave like a complete agnostic. This is no longer possible when history is interiorised, integrated into man's consciousness. The events are the events of the soul; they have a transcendental dimension. One can no longer play at whatever agnostic philosophy of history you like. Only that which theosophists like Franz von Baader or Schelling have so rightly named "historiosophy" can now be pursued.[2]

This "interiorization" of history – or any other world-view – introduces a new "no" for non-mystery, restoring the representation of time to the reality of the moment. Only the absolute "now" is real and the self's reality is reality's self, beyond the confines of manifestation. Nothing subordinates the moment, but everything in time is subordinate to it.

Even scientists who accept God set Him apart from the world. They allow Him the beginning and the law, not absolute proximity or ever-presence. The laws by which things subsist and change in time and space are sufficient for the scientific world-view. There is no mystery in such being. God is remote from it, absent.

When he says that the Hour is nearer than the sunset of the already setting sun or the gap between two fingers,[3] the Praised is telling us that any representation of time must be aware of the Hour at the heart of existence. The turn to the self is a turn from appearance toward reality. Return to God is realization in

1 Corbin, "For the Concept of Irano-Islamic Philosophy," 121.

2 Corbin, *The Concept of Comparative Philosophy*, 25.

3 See Muslim, 4:1526.

the Hour: the nearer the Hour, the greater our realization and liberation from appearance. The apostle is a sublime sign of this supreme potential in each of us. It is within, the things of the world mere reminders of it.

God told the Praised: "The people will question thee concerning the Hour. Say: 'The knowledge of it is only with God; what shall make thee know? Haply the Hour is nigh.'"[4] The Hour cannot be thought without Flux. Time flows into and out of the absolute moment, or so it appears, for the self has no experience except in the moment. Images of what is past derive from the reality of the moment. Our consciousness lies in that constant slipping into an apparent past and future. To be free of appearance we must be in the moment. This supposition or illusion the self never manages to escape.

Influx and outflow are an ever-present duality. The moment, where influx becomes outflow, is what duality confirms and shows. The moment is one, but is also Flux. Outflow appears to be begotten by influx, but is not: Flux is one, neither begetting nor begotten. And so it is clear that Flux is the same as the absolute density symbolized by solid rock.

The moment is like absolute light. When his companions asked if he had seen God, the apostle replied: "He is a light. How should I see Him?"[5] But only light can be seen. This apparent contradiction of seeing God in all things and not seeing Him in any is the beginning of theosophical wisdom. What cannot be seen has no reality. To be aware of something's invisibility is to confess no real but the Real.

---

4 *Qur'an*, 33:63.

5 Muslim, 1:113.

CHAPTER 6

The Hour

Like any other, the revelation to the Praised is a reminder of God's unity and Resurrection Day. God's unity is a principle, confirmed, manifest in existence. It is in the Hour. Time, split between past and future, is the descent of the Hour, in which only the real and eternal are revealed. The Hour is certainty, no eternity outside it. The Day of Resurrection relates us to the Hour, which contains the self's zenith and nadir, our placement on the height, descent to the depths, and return to origin.

All the ways the self relates to the Self are tried in that descent-ascent towards the Day. Only confessing no self but the Self proves more than appearance or the turn from the Hour towards illusions of past and future.

The Hour makes clear the difference between knowledge and action. Knowledge abides in the hour of the self, but action eludes it, pretending to extend from past into future. It abandons the actor, who, to keep possession of it, assigns a clear and certain cause and a predictable effect. The self, forgetful of the Hour's reality on the heavenly vertical, becomes increasingly bound to the horizontal plane of time. Within this plane of the quantifiable, the self loses its belief in the other higher world or in the Spirit that descends. The hidden is unimportant, irrelevant. Perennial wisdom inverts this view: "The present life is naught but a sport and a diversion; surely the Last Abode is better for those that are mindful. What, do you not understand?"[1]

For this view of two worlds separated by the Day of Resurrection, each thing's time is limited, but the truth of all things' creation is not, and the Hour is judgment on all things. Existence derives order from the Hour and remains contingent on it. There is no order on the earth, heavens or between them independent of the Hour's imminent judgment. All things disintegrate and warp in its absolute proximity and ever-presence. The world's days are each but a part of existence, but the Hour of the Day of Resurrection is all, and in it Unity is revealed as the principle of all.

Each revelation is a mysterious meeting of eternal and temporal, eternity assuming temporal form and appearing as word and sign. Viewed from time, word and sign link with Speaker and Signified. Through that link, those who listen to His discourse and interpret the signs can exit time. Entering and leaving time are crucially important aspects of every revelation. Each self's "now"

1 *Qur'an*, 6:32.

 | DOI 10.1163/9789004279407_044

appears as a stream of consciousness – a disordered stream. To awaken to this is to realize oneself in the Hour and transform the disorder of consciousness into a manifestation of Unity. René Guénon has said: "He who is unable to leave the viewpoint of temporal succession and see everything in simultaneity is incapable of the least conception of the metaphysical order."[2]

Where history ends, sociology begins. This is the precondition of both. History is sociology's warrant, sociology history's, and the sequence of time where flow denies instant cannot be escaped. The revelation and presence of the sacred contradict the closure of history and sociology. According to Mircea Eliade: "The structure of the sacred in the human consciousness is built on the structure of synchronicity, as opposed to the diachronic structure of radical historicism."[3]

This contradiction must be understood to distinguish inner from outer in the religions. As Eliade put it: "The total present, the eternal present of the mystics, is stasis or non-duration. Expressed in spiritual symbols, the non-durational eternal present is immobility."[4] Attaining this state takes the form of escape from individuality. This good instant encompasses the entire finite world and Intellect, the Heart, then, like a flash, lights up the levels of existence.

Causality, as what links phenomena, comes to be seen as law, applicable regardless of time and place. God appears as law, but law is created and may be treated so as to exclude or include His presence. A variety of answers exist in historical and historiosophical discourse. For Henry Corbin, the causal link that figures in the predominant understanding of physical phenomena does not exist.

> The fundamental idea is this: visible, apparent, outward states, in short, phenomena, can never be the causes of other phenomena. The agent is the invisible, the immaterial. Compassion acts and determines, it causes things to be and to become like itself, because it is a spiritual state, and its mode of action has nothing to do with what we call physical causality; rather, as its very name indicates, its mode of action is *sympatheia*.[5]

---

2 Guénon, "Oriental Metaphysics," 50.

3 Eliade, "The Sacred in the Secular World," 105; also in Rennie, ed., *Mircea Eliade: A Critical Reader*, 61.

4 Eliade, *Images and Symbols*, 81.

5 Corbin, *Alone with the Alone*, 119.

The Hour is beyond time. In it the principle descends into the flux of space and time, without losing connection with eternity. That vertical of descent and ascent to the Hour is what makes religion: without it, religion becomes meaningless. Without the Face of God constantly before us, so that all things vanish but Him, we too are without purpose.

Thanks to the loss of Paradise and our fall to the depths, we can redeem and rediscover our authentic selves. This is the Hour, deliverance from history, of which Corbin said:

> The time of prophets and of prophetic visions was not *within* the time of History. The Copernican reversal of the question is made necessary by the existential phenomenology of the *Imago Templi* that we are attempting to elucidate. Faced with a Church which had become a historical power and a society in the time of this world, the longing for the Temple is a longing for the "place" where, during the liturgical mystery and at "the meeting-place of the two seas," eschatology was realized in the present – a present which is not the limit of past and future in historical time, but the *nunc* of an eternal Presence. This "realized eschatology" was the restoration of Paradise, the restoration of the human condition to its celestial status.[6]

The revelation to the Praised and his experience of it signify the Hour's transcendence of time split into past and future. God said of the experience of the Hour: "he stood poised, being on the higher horizon, then drew near and suspended hung, two bows'-length away, or nearer, then revealed to his servant that he revealed. His heart lies not of what he saw; what, will you dispute with him what he sees?"[7]

"The two arcs" designate the circuit of ascent and descent, departure and return, so that the viewer sees it all as One. When the arcs are experienced as a closed circle, the hour seems to take in all things, so that the Praised, in the Hour, left night for day and descended to the depths to be a mercy there, a lamp, an example for all. The Buraq on which he travelled is the flash of the Hour in which all things appear in the One, the One in all things.

---

6 Corbin, *Temple and Contemplation*, 338.

7 *Qur'an*, 53:6–12.

CHAPTER 7

Symbol

The idea of a causal-temporal chain of events presupposes God's absence from this world. Insofar as thing causes thing, Corbin says God's presence and proximity have been surrendered:

> If the chronological succession does not suffice to give us knowledge of a causal historical filiation between these recurrences, at least we see arising between them the continuity of a "hierophanic time," which corresponds not to the external history of the sects and schools connected with the Gnosis, but to the cyclical presence of their "archetype," to their common participation in the same cosmic dramaturgy.[1]

Only the Hour is real, demarcating past and future and depending on nothing beyond that boundary. What is past or present simply points to it. History is its sign, but not it, as Gershom Scholem concludes: "The history of the world unfolds according to an inner law that is the hidden law of the divine nature itself. Every gnosis transforms history into a symbol of cosmic processes."[2]

A symbol thus indicates the Hour. It is independent of anything external, past or future. It affects us with its reality, which is like ours, whether we know it or not. Consciousness includes symbols of the outer horizons and of the self and life involves their meanings. They convey their message and perform their role even when the meaning is not conscious.

Past and future are signs of the Hour. Reality is in the Hour, contact with it through the Hour. As Corbin put it:

> Past and future thus become *signs*, because a sign is perceived precisely *in the present*. The past must be "put in the present" to be perceived as "showing a sign." (If the wound, for example, is a sign, it is so because it indicates not that such and such a one *has been* wounded, in an abstract time, but that *is* having been wounded.) The genuine transcending the past can only be "putting it in the present" as *sign*.[3]

---

1 Corbin, *Avicenna and the Visionary Recital*, 17.

2 Scholem, *Origins of the Kabbalah*, 474.

3 Corbin, "The Time of Eranos," xvii.

 | DOI 10.1163/9789004279407_045

Both world and self are here and now. The signs in them are as they were and will be. If we seek an image of the past, we must read the signs in the world and self. The past is essentially an element of our present reflections. Ernst Cassirer reminds us that knowledge that does not start with and culminate in symbols is impossible:

> The historian, like the physicist, lives in a material world. Yet what he finds at the very beginning of his research is not a world of physical objects but a symbolic universe – a world of symbols. He must, first of all, learn to read these symbols. Any historical fact, however simple it may appear, can only be determined and understood by such a previous analysis of symbols. Not things or events but documents or monuments are the first and immediate objects of our historical knowledge. Only through the mediation and intervention of these symbolic data can we grasp the real historical data – the events and the men of the past.[4]

No sign in world or self is at once first and last of the Signified. Knowledge lies with the beholder, but is received from the Signified. Every sign has two aspects, one facing the knower, the other the known. Let this relationship of knower, sign and Signified be seen as our supreme potential and all the signs in world and self are imbued with one principle.

> All that exists, in whatever mode this may be, necessarily participates in universal principles, and nothing exists except by participation in these principles, which are the eternal and immutable essences, contained in the permanent actuality of the Divine Intellect. Consequently, it can be said that all things, however contingent they may be in themselves, express or represent these principles in their own way and according to their order of existence, for otherwise they would be purely and simply nothingness. Thus, from one order to another, all things are linked together and correspond, to come together in total and universal harmony, for harmony is nothing other than the reflection of principial unity in the manifested world; and it is this correspondence which is the veritable basis of symbolism.[5]

---

4 Cassirer, *An Essay on Man*, 175.

5 Guénon, *Autorité spirituelle et pouvoir temporel*, 22.

In principle, consciousness is in chaotic flux, with no saying where it begins or ends. Through memory and expectation, there is a constant dissipation, but it never ends predictably. This constancy of chaos attests to the existence of its hidden centre; if there were no centre, chaos would cease to be. The discovery of the centre and awakening into Unity give order to chaos. Consciousness then appears as perfect order confirming its principle. This curbing of chaos takes place in the Hour, when everything in word and self is linked to the centre and becomes a symbol to which the Centre gives meaning.

Everything in world and self is created with Truth and confirms the principle of creation. To confess this to world and self is to see everything as interconnected, manifesting Unity in perfectly harmonious multiplicity. The prophetic reminder that our most profound nature is a treasury containing all knowledge of the world means we can, always and everywhere, see the diversity of this revelation of order as confirming a single metaphysical knowledge – knowledge without origin in history or us. It is in our uncreated essence, of which Jesus said: "It is the spirit that quickeneth; the flesh profiteth nothing: the words that I speak unto you, they are spirit, and they are life."[6]

All the signs in the outer world manifest the One, Intellect. When the Spirit descends into the self, the signs in world and self take on linguistic form, so that the unique order of all things takes many forms amongst us. Symbols, natural or man-made, become a language connecting us to the principle. If languages, meanings and symbols differ, they can be translated through the centre or principle of the order they are manifest within, from any given language to any other.

There do seem to be many traditions, each starting from the One and Its revelation in the Word. Each prophet's role is to remind us of our original fitness for purpose, return to the One. The traditions share one essence, even as names and forms change from generation to generation. The same symbols are found in many traditions, regardless of how they differ temporally and spatially, linguistically and ritually. This cannot be due solely to borrowing; the symbols derive from a single source, the immutable essential connection between the universe and ourselves, created and Creator.

6 *John*, 6:63.

CHAPTER 8

The Anointed and the Guided

Religious communities become ideological ones quite simply. As they do so, one part of society splits off, to lay down and enforce the laws required by its focus on a goal within history. The move beyond this-worldly boundaries is either denied or displaced. For a minority, esotericism remains a haven fostering knowledge and hope. As Corbin said:

> If a certain science of our time views Nature in this way, it may be said in return that it is this transgression which all esoterisms have subsequently tried to redeem, and that is their significance for a spiritual history invisible to historians of external events. However, because the triumph cannot occur except with the manifestation of the Imam-Paraclete, no esoterism, until the coming of the Imam, can be anything more than a *witness*, recognized by a small number, ridiculed by all the others, and not progressing except in the night of symbols.[1]

The coming of Imam Muhammad al-Mahdi, that is the Rightly Guided One, is associated with the second coming of Jesus the Anointed. The apostle says of the Mahdi that he will be of his descendants and name,[2] while of the Anointed he said: "I am most akin to the son of Mary among the whole of mankind."[3] The coming of both Jesus and Muhammad is thus a manifestation of the apostle. From an historical perspective, this coming is continuous: it is with the Hour and so potential to every now.

The meeting of the Anointed and the Rightly Guided is deliverance from history, salvation in the Hour. This meeting heals and bridges the rift across which our redemption, the realization of our Covenant with God, must take place. Our most profound nature is informed by knowledge received from the Lord. This knowledge is unmediated and fully represents our free will. As God said in the Recitation:

---

1 Corbin, *Swedenborg and Esoteric Islam*, 110.

2 See Ṭabaṭabāʾī, *Shiʿa*, 211.

3 See Muslim, 4:1260. The relation between Jesus and Muhammad has been given various historical interpretations. Their role from an eschatological perspective has largely been overlooked. On how their similarities have been transformed into irreconcilable difference and variously interpreted, see Winter, "Jesus and Muhammad: New convergences," 21–38.

 | DOI 10.1163/9789004279407_046

> And when thy Lord took from the Children of Adam, from their loins, their seed, and made them testify touching themselves: "Am I not your Lord?" They said: "Yes, we testify!" – lest you should say on the Day of Resurrection: "As for us, we were heedless of this." Or lest you say: "Our fathers were associators aforetime, and we were seed after them. What, wilt Thou then destroy us for the deeds of the vain-doers?"[4]

We are this seed, in all our generations and languages, everywhere. We all share, in our hearts, this knowledge of His authentic lordship and our service. Our parents give us care, language and meaning, but not as theirs originally. They mediate their worldly presence and connection with their ultimate, non-human source. Metaphysically, this witness is simultaneous for everyone, but it is experienced differently in time. Its historical images are necessarily distortions.

Whatever the society of our birth, all the Children of Adam share the same original nature and witness to God's lordship. In the Recitation, God says that He sent an apostle to every nation.[5]

This variety of languages is itself a sign of God.[6] Prophets address people in their own languages.[7] That news of God takes so many forms is evidence that its essence is independent of time and place. Our original covenant with God is thus always reflected in symbol, one in many forms. The prophets, in their witness to our potential relation to God, announce their essential witness of the apostle. Their covenant with God preinforms our primordial oath to confess His lordship. Metaphysically, they also contract that covenant together:

> And when God took compact with the prophets: "That I have given you of Book and Wisdom; then there shall come to you an apostle confirming what is with you – you shall believe in him and you shall help him; do you agree?" He said, "And do you take My load on you on that condition?" They said, "We do agree." God said, "Bear witness so, and I shall be with you among the witnesses."[8]

---

4 *Qur'an*, 7:172–73.

5 See *Qur'an*, 10:47.

6 Ibid., 30:22.

7 Ibid., 14:4.

8 *Qur'an*, 3:81.

The prophets differ, but their seal is the apostle; he set the seal on their covenant with God. The apostle is thus always and ever a mercy to the world, the focus of every prophet and for us all.

Our primordial witness to the Lord and each prophet's witness to the Praised make redemption a constant, absolute possibility. This is deliverance from the mire of history. We all have the potential for redemption, for ascent to heaven by realizing our authentic nature. That alone is worthy of our life. And it is always *now*, the plenitude of the Hour for which we are here. It is disclosed in faith and ritual, as preparation for what is coming.

We all have this potential, as our essence is first known by confessing "Thou art" to God. To know this essence is to discover the prophet as apostle within: "His apostle [is] among you."[9] Self-realization is to discover the Praised as one's supreme potential and authentic nature, to confess what God revealed, "The prophet is nearer to the believers than their selves,"[10] and the Praised himself said, "No one believes, till I am dearer to him than the members of his household, his wealth and the whole of mankind."[11] For, as God asked, "How can you deny, seeing you have God's signs recited to you, and His apostle among you?"[12]

Isn't Jesus and Muhammad's presence in the historical consciousness of so many for so many years astonishing? Who today does not know of them? Yet, our views and conduct show how inadequate this knowledge is. Only in knowledge does the self discover its initial oath as God's unity, the Praised's apostolate and return to Him.

The Anointed is Word, Spirit and man, his human perfection identity of knowledge and being. The Praised's self is wholly shaped by Word and Spirit, its perfect recipient and transmitter. To realize humanity in authentic witness to God's lordship, recognizing the prophets sealed by the apostle and return – this is the final encounter of Anointed and Praised. The Anointed kills the lie and confesses the Praised as servant and apostle, as the Praised said regarding the last times. The Anointed will descend into the world to kill denial of the truth about himself, which is the Falsely Anointed.

9 Ibid., 3:101.

10 Ibid., 33:6.

11 Muslim, 1:31.

12 *Qur'an*, 3:101.

CHAPTER 9

Redemption

Redemption, deliverance from a lower and return to a higher, happier state, are crucial elements of all sacred teachings, rituals and virtues. The Praised's teachings regarding our debt to God are summed up in the call to prayer that announces His greatness and unity, the Praised's apostolate, an invitation to deliverance, and again His greatness and unity.

The call, aimed from our core towards the world's four corners, begins with God's greatness, as, in this world of duality and relativity, our achievements and imaginings can appear great to us, through necessarily insignificant compared to His immeasurable greatness. This greatness, expressed by His unity, means the Creator is immanent and transcendent, whether we see it or not.

The call to redemption is to awareness of our and the world's dual relationship with God. The world, disparate and multiple, manifests Him. Everything dispersed through it gathers in us, but with no loss of multiplicity. The world is in us, we in it, but always separate. We and it are the key duality of existence, through which Unity reveals itself. We and the world receive existence from Unity and owe It what we have. We will never wholly know why, for we and the world, whatever our condition, always remain mere manifestation of Unity. Without It, we are null; with It, we are It.

Truth is inside and outside. Relating to the world or an individual in it, we confirm our debt to the Giver of existence by recognizing the truth in all things. This admission redeems us and unites us with God as Truth. Acknowledging His centrality, we acquire the right to return and redemption.

If the debt is what connects us, as debtors, and God, as Creditor, witness to the Praised's perfect potential is how we turn to and unite with Unity. As we follow his example, in recognition of our standing debt to God, we see the illusion of chaotic multiplicity transform into Unity, for witness of no god but God is redemption and deliverance. But everything in existence, being with Truth, appears as Truth. To reject this semblance is witness of no truth but Truth.

To appreciate his original home on the height, Adam had to experience the depths. As must his children. He was given all Paradise's abundance in payment for one tree's inviolability. And he chose the gift of free will, the freedom to respect or violate that tree. When Adam decided to violate the inviolable, payment was lost. His new station in the depths was like arriving in a dungeon, where he knew the value of what was lost. Should he wish to regain it, God offered him a new covenant of redemption. Our true experience begins with redemption.

 | DOI 10.1163/9789004279407_047

Redemption is possible for us. No experience has value outside its link to redemption, through the Anointed and the Praised as the link with God. We turn to God, God to us; the call to turn to and unite with Him includes His witness that He turns to and unites with us.

Redemption requires awareness. It takes place when an individual bears witness through the rituals of his inheritance, but requires more. It links us with God through the Praised, or the potential he perfected. Discussing redemption, Gershom Scholem stressed it is a condition of humanity:

> What was formerly taken as a state of redemption, especially in its messianic connotations, by now becomes the condition in which alone true human experience is possible. The unredeemed state is no longer worthy to be called human. The redeemed state is where human experience starts.[1]

The self in its "now" is all reality, all it knows or can know, remembers or can remember, does not know or forgets. Its past is the perspective of such a self in flux. What was once known is never the same for two states of the self, as a mere trace on the path of redemption. The path involves no changes not both connected with and separate from the changing self. We are in a constant stream of interpretation of what we know or discover in our potential.

It may be objected that while the history of ideas needs an unbroken stream of interpretation, "real" history, the history of humankind and our actions, does not. One has solid, evident, tangible facts that must be connected to be known. The aim is to understand those who acted through the facts of their actions. How one judges the course of political events depends on what one thinks of the people involved. Once the researcher, following the traces, sees them in a new context, it changes his perspective. A proper historical perspective requires constant re-examination, constant broadening of perspective, in which are both continuity and discontinuity.

Our journey, whether ascent, descent, or wandering, cannot exhaust our ultimate potential. Neither descent to the depths nor ascent to the height is limited to the world of quantity and logic. Imagination is how we break though confinement in such quantifiable givenness, which is the precondition of physics as the "perfect" science, to accept which is to deny our own perfection.

In physics, the facts of this world are explained once "posited" in temporal, spatial and causal order, becoming determinate. Knowing them changes nothing in their existence. The facts of "historical truth" are of a different order. For

1 Scholem, "Opening Address," 11.

physics, the knowing subject has no role in determining the known; not so for historical perspective, where facts are traces left by a subject's actions. They may be quantifiable, but the subject that left them is not. They are vestiges of past actions, subject to constant erasure. This process cannot be stopped, but it can be resisted through memory.

What is memory for? What memories promote life and happiness, properly speaking? What memory is redemptive?

Logic allows only the quantifiable world and makes of it an empire of analytical reason. Its impotence in the world beyond the quantifiable requires no rejection of that world, which all metaphysically grounded tradition considers higher and prior, as corresponding to Intellect, from which the quantifiable world and reason are derived. Reflecting on this duality, Cassirer wrote:

> Here too we have to do with determining the place and the time of events. But when it comes to the investigation of their causes we have a new problem to face. If we knew all the facts in their chronological order we should have a general scheme and a skeleton of history; but we should not have its real life. Yet an understanding of human life is the general theme and the ultimate aim of historical knowledge. In history we regard all the works of man, and all his deeds, as precipitates of his life; and we wish to reconstitute them into this original state, we wish to understand and feel the life from which they are derived.[2]

2 Cassirer, *An Essay on Man*, 183–84.

CHAPTER 10

Religion in Society

Religion offers personal deliverance from history. First, we know our essential self, our link with Eternity, which places us on the vertical axis, from body to Spirit, earth to heaven, time to the Hour.

That God is the absolute In and Out of all things means nothing circumscribes or limits Him. Whatever our relation to self, others or world, God is always entirely Other, never subordinate or one of some greater number of things. He is First, Other, Next, and Last.

Our proper relationship to God is peace and service. For us, perfect peace and service are utter poverty, in the face of God's absolute abundance. As a result, we can love God out of the little we know of Him, know Him as our Beloved, and love Him as Known.

Whatever our relationship to knowledge and love, the beauty of our being shines through our capacity to serve Him as through we saw Him. This "as though" makes us open, as beings that find themselves in their uncreated core, in the Spirit that gives the body life, a life that remains for ever beyond death.

We are necessarily in society. Retreat from it and stand against your own self, live in it oblivious to the distinction of self and other, and be governed by instinct, impulse and feeling, unable to recognize the social structure you are thrown into, live as a subject, directed by others.

Every society constantly promotes the common centre around which the hierarchy of leader and disciple, of polity and subject, is built. A community of the conscious and involved emerges and is opposed by the masses. All of us are our mothers' children and the real question of our origin is key to determining our stance towards our fullest and highest potential. The perfect human being, who represents the reason and end of our existence, the prophet, is the maternal principle that we may each turn to the One as our goal of redemption.

We are open to Eternity, when in and with the Hour. Perspectives on past or future do not comprehend It, but they do intimate Its presence and pregnancy. Exclude it and time expresses only an iron chain of cause and effect, a flow of historical events like a stream that can be altered by building dams, redirecting the current, and so on. There is no place here for the vertical axis or hierophany. Reducing things to the horizontal plane is required by Newtonian cosmology, Darwinian evolution, and Freudian psychoanalysis, which all exclude the

 | DOI 10.1163/9789004279407_048

Hour. Things must be demystified to be understood. For religion, absolutization of historical or individual time serves to reduce God to society. Each society has its god, whose life, will, power, knowledge, speech, hearing and sight are contingent on it.

Every society promotes its own path to God as the only true one. Reduce God to society and action and knowledge merge: those with power act in line with the knowledge and purpose it brings. They deny that being has multiple levels. This is the only world, all higher ontological levels repudiated. Social differences are acceptable, so long as the view of the world order of the powerful is unaffected. In contrast to this image of closure, the traditional view considers the diversity of paths confirmation of Unity, as God told the Praised:

> And We have sent down to thee the Book with the truth, confirming the Book that was before it, and assuring it. So judge between them according to what God has sent down, and do not follow their caprices, to forsake the truth that has come to thee. To every one of you We have appointed a right way and an open road. If God had willed, He would have made you one nation; but that He may try you in what has come to you. So be you forward in good works; unto God shall you return, all together; and He will tell you of that whereon you were at variance.[1]

This diversity of societies, established as a whole in constant reinvention, find clear expression in the state. As a combination of social order and world-view, the state always reflects the hierarchy of God-prophet-commandment. If consciousness of God and prophet informs the social order, the self accepts political action subordinate to an order in which the prophet is the link with God and so all of creation. No command that does not reflect such subordination is acceptable. Let God and prophet be denied or subordinated, and the resulting inversion instaurates forms of polity that devastate people and land. Denial of the perennial content of the God-prophecy-commandment sequence means that no properly human condition can be established. The manifestations this takes can be presented as the inexplicable action of obscure forces in history, as in Cassirer's understanding of the relationship between the political and the non-political in human evolution:

---

1 *Qur'an*, 5:48.

> But political life is not the only form of a communal human existence. In the history of mankind the state, in its present form, is a late product of the civilizing process. Long before man had discovered this form of social organization he had made other attempts to organize his feelings, desires, and thoughts. Such organizations and systematizations are contained in language, in myth, in religion, and in art. We must accept this broader basis if we wish to develop a theory of man. The state, however important, is not all. It cannot express or absorb all the other activities of man. To be sure these activities in their historical evolution are closely connected with the development of the state; in many respects they are dependent upon the forms of political life. But, not possessing a separate historical existence, they have nevertheless a purport and value of their own.[2]

The state is created by human will, but is not the same as it. It sometimes takes on or adopts attributes of self, seeming to embody selfhood, an overarching, powerful idol subjugating the self. Such a state proves a false religion: a goal, rather than a means to an end, ascribed God's attributes of life, will, power, knowledge, speech, hearing and sight, so that we are in its image. Discourse is replete with allocation of God's attributes to religion, ideology and the state, even in Cassirer, who may not have intended to concede the point: "Without the great creative spirits, without the prophets that felt themselves inspired by the power of God and destined to reveal His will, religion would not have found its way."[3]

2 Cassirer, *An Essay on Man*, 63–64.

3 Ibid., 102.

CHAPTER 11

The Cross of the Self

Knowledge is what relates knower to known. The key question is whether knowers can know themselves as knowers: a question largely banished from the modern world-view.

In the traditional world-view, knowers are focused on themselves; everything important they can know lies within. What matters is God, as imam ʿAli ibn Abi Talib says: "The main thing in debt is to acknowledge Him, the perfect form of which is to confess Him."[1] This main thing, the debt, is both knowledge in us and how we relate to the world. The body is cloaked by externalities. The face's turn towards His face is denoted by the mihrab, in our image, as we are in God's.

To be in the mihrab is to stand consciously before God, before His doors. Standing there, in silence or discourse, movement or quiet, we focus on our individual relationship of witness, glorifying God with praise, in hope of redemption. In fear and hope, we pray and kneel, fall silent and listen, seek a way out of history, of time, into eternity. Corbin has written of the entry into meta-history, symbolized by entrance into the mihrab:

> The unsayable which the mystic seeks to say is a story that shatters what we call history and which we must indeed call *metahistory*, because it takes place at the origin of origins, anterior to all those events recorded – or recordable – in our chronicles. The mystic epic is that of the exile, who, having come into a strange world, is on the road of homecoming to his own country. What that epic seeks to tell is the dreams of prehistory, the prehistory of the soul, of its pre-existence to this world, dreams which seem to us a forever forbidden frontier. This is why, in an epic like the *Mathnawî* we can scarcely speak of a succession of episodes, for all these are emblematic, symbolic. All dialectical discourse is precluded. The

1 *Nahj al-balāgha*, First Sermon; Ar. *awwal al-dīn maʿarifatuh. Awwal* literally means "first," and may be understood as the starting point and basis of the debt; *maʿrifa* denotes both "knowledge" and "recognition" – one re-cognizes what one already knows: "And when thy Lord took from the Children of Adam, from their loins, their seed, and made them testify touching themselves, 'Am I not your Lord?' They said, 'Yes, we testify!' – lest you should say on the Day of Resurrection, 'As for us, we were heedless of this'" (*Qur'an*, 7:172).

 | DOI 10.1163/9789004279407_049

> global consciousness of that past, and of the future to which it invites us beyond the limit of chronology, can only attain *musically* its absolute character.[2]

Individual consciousness is shown to be a station on a circle, through which the centre at times reveals its presence. This "at times" is always possible. No one can abolish it. Awake or asleep, living or dead, our uncreated centre always remains Unity. We may experience this as borne down from above or bound to matter. In either case, we remain in a state of evanescence and re-emergence, destruction and rebuilding, as all things taste death but God who gives both life and death.

Every such possibility both reveals and conceals the centre. Seeing ourselves and our world as a circle manifesting a centre, we relate to the Revealed through revelation of the Centre. The path to the Centre is esoterism, knowledge of the inner. Such a path needs a centre and for us that centre is God. The self, its teachings, path, and virtue all come from the centre, uncreated and uncreatable. The teachings include symbols, of which the things of the world are but reminders. Any symbol can become a god if taken as having efficacy or meaning beyond the self and its connection with the Self through witness (no self but the Self). Jesus said: "And he that taketh not his cross, and followeth after me, is not worthy for me. He that findeth his life shall lose it: and he that loseth his life for my sake shall find it."[3] And the Praised confirmed: "By God, the son of Mary will certainly descend as a just judge and he will break the cross and kill swine and abolish the poll-tax."[4]

To take up our cross is to embrace the teachings God revealed through the Anointed. They encompass the self, from its bond with earth and grave to return to Unity and birth of the Spirit.[5] This is the vertical axis from the humility of the depth to beautiful uprightness.

The upright path of ascent to Unity is the way of *the soul at peace*.[6] Its contrary is descent into darkness, the way of *the soul [that] commandeth unto evil*.[7] To be bound to a single level, going neither up nor down, is the way of *the*

---

2 Corbin, "On the Meaning of Music in Persian Mysticism," 50–51.

3 *Matthew*, 10:38–39.

4 Muslim, 1:93.

5 See *John* 3:5.

6 See *Qur'an*, 89:27–30.

7 Ibid., 12:53.

ever-upbraiding soul.[8] These changes in the self, between the evil to which it leads itself and mercy, its ever-present potential, leave the Spirit's uncreated and uncreatable presence untouched.

God breathed Spirit into us, whom he created of clay. But, Spirit is not the same as God. Earth and heaven, seen and unseen, empire and rule are external images of body and Spirit in us.

The self lies between extremes, body and soul, being neither, yet somehow both. In the Recitation, God refers to heavens, earth, and the things "between" them. Understood as soul, the self is a meeting place of formless Spirit and bodily form. It could be described as a "meeting of two seas," in which it is both remembrance and forgetting, knowledge and ignorance, light and darkness, Spirit and body, sweet and bitter, fresh and salt. Spirit denotes the invisible, intellectual, active, living content of our reality, unimaginable in isolation from the notions of self, intellect and heart.

Nothing in heaven and earth or between them is worthier than self-realization in peace and original perfection. That is the why of the prophets and their tidings. The All-peaceful is plenitude, omnipresent, ever-absent. We occupy the battlefield, but Peace is His. Realization is crossing the battlefield for the Abode of Peace. Jesus asked: "For what shall it profit a man, if he shall gain the whole world, and lose his own soul?"[9] But the self cannot be found outside the self. The signs in the world are signs of signs in the self that reveal our essential nature, witness to Lordship. To journey towards this redemptive goal is to follow the Anointed as closest to the Praised and affirm our love of God. We renounce life to receive it from the Living; we receive life to be in debt to the Giver.

To follow the Anointed is to follow the Praised and to admit our humiliation and our rectitude, to ascend. When the cross, as the sign of the teachings, the way and virtue, is enmired in matter, reified in the outside world, the self does not follow the Anointed. It denies the seventh or Sabbath, when we emerge from matter to Spirit, from the battlefield to Peace. It is bound to matter under the sign of the swine, wallowing in darkness, filth and stench. We sentence ourselves to birth in the mire and darkness, not in the Spirit, Light and Peace. Turning to the horizontal plane, bound to the depths, we mistake virtue for affirming the will of the powerful. This is the false Anointed and why

8 Ibid., 75:2.

9 *Mark*, 8:36.

the Anointed will reveal himself by breaking the cross, killing swine and abolishing taxes.

God made all things with a purpose. What is dispersed in creation is united in us. Creation is without disharmony; but He will destroy all nonetheless. He gives death with life and will breathe new creation and new life into what has been destroyed and put to death.

CHAPTER 12

Descent

The self has three levels – the lowest, without knowledge, where action is violence; the highest, where reconciliation and peace are attained; and in between, where ignorance, action based on it and reconciliation are all present. This tripartite structure is reflected in the prayer God gave the Praised as our guide from depths to height: "Guide us on the upright path, the path of those whom Thou has blessed, not of those against whom Thou art wrathful, nor of those who are astray."[1]

The upright path is there for the self to reach bliss. On it we are linked with God, as in His image. Its opposite is thickening dark, ignorance and entanglement in activity and matter. The self is always somewhere between these extremes. To turn to the higher is to be blessed; to lose touch with it and be at the mercy of what appears as enduring wrath is misery.

All metaphysically-based teachings speak of the way, which is always between extremes. The self sinks into matter and darkness or ascends towards Spirit and Light. Our centre abides with the goal of ascent, but the self casts a shadow over it. The self must be reduced to nothing, if we are to discover the Spirit and Light in their descent. That discovery is ascent. The distinction between earth and heaven, matter and Spirit, is an image of ascent, which brings balance.

The self must be somewhere on the ascending-descending order of being. We can remain at a given level, rise above or sink below. The worlds above and below are treasuries into which we may descend or ascend. Eliade wrote of the modern discovery of that potential in esotericism:

> When Jung revealed the existence of the collective unconscious, the exploration of these immemorial treasures – the myths, symbols and images of archaic humanity – began to approximate its techniques to those of the oceanographers and speleologists. Just as deep sea diving and cave exploration revealed elementary organisms that had long ago disappeared from the earth's surface, so analysis discovered forms of deep psychic life hitherto inaccessible to study.[2]

---

1 *Qur'an*, 1:6–7.

2 Eliade, *Two and the One*, 10.

 | DOI 10.1163/9789004279407_050

At each level, from lowest to highest, the self relates to the Self. This relation is between creature and Creator, two as one. To say two are one and one two is to raise the question of the *coincidentia oppositorum*, as Corbin wrote:

> The Creator – creature typifies the *coincidentia oppositorum*. From the first this *coincidentia* is present to Creation, because Creation is not *ex nihilo* but a theophany. As such, it is Imagination. The Creative Imagination is theophanic Imagination, and the Creator is one with the imagining Creature because each Creative Imagination is a theophany, a recurrence of the Creation. Psychology is indistinguishable from cosmology; the theophanic Imagination joins them into a psycho-cosmology.[3]

The prayer "lead us on the upright path" is our common conscious turn towards God. This turn involves countless individual selves in willing connection with one centre, the principle of all things. Each self is shaped differently. It stands between low and high, darkness and Light, matter and Spirit, in constant flux, never the same. It is our awareness of the One it turns to, though we are in the world. Each of us reflects Unity differently, like the sun reflected by choppy waters.

Every condition of the self is a depth, as it merely reflects the self. One cannot see how the depths and descent relate to the height and ascent without understanding that any human condition can be transformed into perfect order; none is irrevocable. The beginning of virtue, ritual and doctrine – of righteousness, the way and wisdom – lies in admitting baseness and sin, whence the turn to the centre and the ascent from the depths to the height begins. It also includes the recognition that we can always sink further still. Witness to this is through recognition of our perfect potential whose goal is return. We cannot fully imagine this goal, to which alone plenitude belongs. Witness to Unity is therefore the beginning of all teachings and all wisdom.

To appeal to God to guide us on the *upright path* is to recognize that His guidance does not belong to anything or anyone in this world. The sacred teachings have no historical beginning, no origin with any historical person. They are eternal, albeit revealed in languages and through people. Prophecy, as perennial wisdom made manifest, takes various forms, but is always of one essence.

The self cannot stand on the vertical axis and know the different levels of being without realizing that its teachings, rituals and virtue are the discovery

3 Corbin, *Alone with the Alone*, 215.

of its uncreated core, compared to which all conditions are base and of which all knowledge is ascent.

We are never in utter misery, never at so low a depth that there is only absolute, unmitigated suffering. Then, God's mercy would not encompass all things. Only bliss can be absolute, for none of Unity's manifestations can be Unity Itself. It was revealed to the apostle that His knowledge and mercy encompass all things and His mercy surpasses His wrath. Humility is our best connection to ascent, to liberation from existence trapped at one level. Expressing humility in their ritual, those on the path shed the illusion of owning what they never received into possession.

CHAPTER 13

The Mosque

In the light of these reflections, the mihrab is the heart of or key to the religious entity that is the mosque. The mosque is the semiotic sum of what is in heaven and earth or between to remind us of all that is in the self and so assist in realization in Unity. The mihrab is the sum or reflection, source and refuge of the teachings, rite and art of the mosque and so of all the signs in heaven and on earth as the expanse of divine discourse. And the self is the sum of all of this.

If Peace is our goal, it is to be achieved only in plenitude, when all differences and deficiencies vanish. As long as we strive for our goal, nothing is enough. Any condition is only partly bliss, always overshadowed by misfortune. What we want is plenitude but we are perpetually on the battlefield, constantly in the mihrab, facing Peace. Only Peace can satisfy us and only our bliss satisfy Peace.

We have no conscious relationship with God on the basis of our debt to Him, unless confirmed by generosity and humility. Where there is no generosity or humility, there is no sacred teaching or art. The crucial expressions of generosity and humility as virtues are good people and sacred art.

Sacred teachings and sacred art are united in near countless expressions by the mosque. Within this, four sacred arts are of crucial importance: listening, speaking, writing and reading. To speak, we must receive what to say; to receive, we must be open to listening. Whom to listen to? Countless utterances come to us from the world: how can we know if they are from reliable sources? This question leads to Unity, which is the same for all things. Unity can be ours only as our heart and centre. This is why it is vital to listen and discern the voice of the perennial wisdom at the centre of every human self. Everything else is just a reminder.

We received our knowledge in our original condition, on the height, but then fell to the depths, where that knowledge was obscured, concealed and forgotten. The expectation is that we shall once again expose it to the light, reveal and rediscover it. This means that we will once again receive meanings from the height: "Blessed are they that dwell in thy house: they will be still praising Thee. Selah. Blessed is the man whose strength is in thee; in whose heart are the ways of them. Who passing through the valley of Baca make it a well; the rain also filleth the pools. They go from strength to strength, every one of them in Sion appeareth before God."[1]

1 *Psalm* 84:5–8.

 DOI 10.1163/9789004279407_051

As the Psalmist tells us, the ascent is from Becca to Sion. Two great signs speak of this link between the uttermost depths and our authentic uprightness – the Inviolable Mosque in the Vale of Tears and the Further Mosque on Sion. In the Night Journey, the Praised brought them together as a shining lamp, a mighty morality and the best example: "Glory be to Him, who carried His servant by night from the Inviolable Mosque to the Further Mosque the precincts of which We have blessed."[2]

The journey encompasses both descent and ascent. In it are all the prophets and all of humankind, without rupture. The Inviolable Mosque is the house in the Vale of Tears, as sign of the baseness we ascend from to God; the Further Mosque is Sion, sign of the height, union, and return.

When the knowledge we receive reveals itself as speech, it can be written down. What is written can be read and restored to speech. Only remaining silent is greater than speech.

None of these possibilities is sacred if it remains beyond the heart as source and confluence and does not flow from and back to human perfection. Flux and passage always include duality as the confirmation or manifestation of Unity. Wherever there is influx, there is outflow; wherever entry, leaving. The mosque as a whole is a discourse on God as the One and the Flux. This discourse is concentrated to its utmost point of tension in the mihrab, as the door of crucial passage.

Entering the mihrab means leaving one world to pass into another. Existence is the multitude of worlds through which the All-praised discloses Himself, from Unity to multiplicity. The connection between Him and revelation is praise. "Praise belongs to God, the Lord of all Being, the All-merciful, the Ever-merciful, the Master of the Day of Doom."[3]

Though the mihrab, as the central concentration of teachings and rite, has almost countless forms, the symbolism of the door is undeniable. Two pillars and an arch are its simplest image.[4] Passing through the many doors of the world, we seek the door that denotes crucial difference, the unbridgeable difference between participants in the world's divisions, which leads from one world into another on ascent towards the self's uncreated centre, from war to Peace. On this ascending path we return to the house of Peace, our entire

---

2 *Qur'an*, 17:1.

3 Ibid., 1:2–4.

4 The earliest representations of the *miḥrāb* as two pillars and an arch are to be found on 7th century coins. See Miles, "Mihrāb and 'Anazah: A Study in Early Islamic Iconography," 159 ff; Melikian-Chirvani, "The Light of Heaven and Earth: From the *Chahār-tāq* to the *Mihrāb*"; Khoury, *The Mihrab Concept*, 113–114 ff.

existence but an ascent. The apostle, the Praised, in his initial and final station, is the perfect sign of ascent and the house. When the Praised entered the Kaʿba, its door was closed, and he prayed "between two pillars," one to his right and one to his left, the door behind him.

The door, the pillars and the arch depicted on *stećci* may also be interpreted as a symbol of ascent or return, of leaving and entering.[5] Praise and compassion are the goal of this incessant leaving and entering. The mihrab is the symbol of our orientation towards the centre of every centre, the holy of holies. The vaults of some mihrabs are shell-shaped. The centre of the seashell is the pearl, in the sacred teachings a symbol of the Word. The auricle or outer ear, referred to as the shell of the ear in Bosnian, exists for the Word. The Virgin is the shell of the world; the Word her reason and purpose.

The link between the *mihrāb* and *Sayyidatnā Maryam* (Our Lady Mary) leads us again to the analogy between the prayer-niche and the heart: it is in the heart that the virgin-soul takes refuge to invoke God; as for the nourishment miraculously bestowed there, it corresponds to grace.[6]

---

5 On motifs of pillars and arches on *stećci*, see Wenzel, *Ukrasni motivi na stećcima*, 55–87; Bešlagić, *Stećci – kultura i umjetnost*, 359–71.

6 Burckhardt, *Art of Islam*, 88. Burckhardt's interpretation of the Virgin's link to the *miḥrāb* is very similar to Ibn al-ʿArabī's explication of verse 3:37 of the *Qur'an*. (See Ibn al-ʿArabī, *Tafsīr al-Qur'ān al-Karīm*, 1:183.) Ibn al-ʿArabī links Mary in the sanctuary with spiritual provisioning and the prophet Zachariah with reflection or thought. Thus the relationship between them is an encounter of direct reception and its reflection in reason.

CHAPTER 14

The Sacred Arts

Four sacred arts – listening, speaking, writing and reading – are concentrated in the mihrab. Its form and content express the range of sacred teachings and sacred art.

To understand this meaning of the mihrab, we must turn to two great signs, the Inviolable and the Further places of self-abnegation, valley and mount, earth and heaven, mentioned in Psalm 83 (84) and the Sura of the Night Journey. They correspond to the Anointed's forty days in the desert and his entry into the Further Mosque.

The Torah, Psalms, Gospels and Recitation reveal one and the same God at different times and in different languages. Each is associated with a different form of revelation of our debt to God. We are in the world, the world in us, as a gift from God. Recognizing this means acknowledging existence as indebted, God as Creditor. Debt relates debtor to Creditor. By recognizing our debt we find our way back to the height, the perfection and bliss in and for which we were created. The different forms of debt and awareness of it are no betrayal of God's unity.

If relations between these differences are regarded along the horizontal trajectory of history, a given revelation and its acceptance by certain people may seem to interrupt previous tradition. But revelation always relates us in the moment and God. No history of different forms of debt is possible unless we introduce the revelation and its signs into the heart of our reflections.[1] Then, the same signs, perennial indicators of eternity and infinity in finitude and time, form part of our debt to God.

The reciprocity of baseness and sublimity, represented by valley and mount, is clear in the verses from the Psalm and the Recitation quoted above, the same signs revealed in two languages.

---

1 The twentieth century revival of interest in sacred traditions is most marked in six writers, three of whom – Gershom Scholem, Mircea Eliade and Henry Corbin – were "historians of religion." They showed the shortcomings of simplistic rational approaches which exclude symbol and myth as essential elements of religion. René Guénon, Ananda K. Coomaraswami and Frithjof Schuon also treated religion as part of human nature. For the first three, see Wasserstrom, *Religion after Religion: Gershom Scholem, Mircea Eliade, and Henry Corbin at Eranos*. For the latter three, see Lings, *The Underlying Religion*.

 | DOI 10.1163/9789004279407_052

Houses are referred to in the valley and on the mount. The house denotes the boundary between inner and outer, entering and leaving. The mihrab is a sign of entry into our and existence's profoundest core and of leaving behind all finitude on our way to the One. It is passage through the levels of being towards Essence, passage because in the mosque we face Peace. Our mosque, the place we prostrate ourselves, is recognition and confession we have and need nothing but what the Lord gives us. The signs in the world and self, however, propose themselves in place of the Signified.

Illusions thus become an army against our nullity compared to the Real. To receive all in the mosque, we must rout and annihilate what comes to us from other than God. To wage war by confessing no god but God is to be in the mihrab or battlefield, the door to Peace, to all things not war. We are utterly indigent, but only in regard to the All-sufficient. Only the All-sufficient can give us anything. Whenever it seems otherwise, we are bound to ourselves, the world and others by false prophets, sorcerers and magicians.

Our passage is assisted by the sacred arts, which include the presence of and being in language. If we realize our humanity by passage through this world, entry into it is a stage on which we experience, in reverse, all the elements of return and the discovery of our original nature.

Children learn their mother tongue in a way we cannot repeat as adults. Everything in the world laid out before them as they enter it has its name; language connects separate things into a whole, connected in the flux. The world as a whole appears to children as an indivisible relationship with their mother tongue. When adults learn another language, they already have their own notion of the world, inseparable from their native tongue.

Language and the world are in perfect initial harmony, their totality but the self-revelation of Unity. When this harmony is disrupted, speech and words no longer inhere in things. Distorting language causes distortions in the world, including the self of those living with such language. Adam received the knowledge of the names of all things from God,[2] so that all things in the world around us and our inner self are summed up in language. Both they and we ourselves, in whom they are summed up, are created, and our principle is the Truth. Our creation with Truth is transferred to our and their summation in language. When more than this is attributed to things, or when their creation with Truth is taken from them, they are forced into alien meanings. They cease to relate to the All-peaceful through peace,[3] no longer His servants.[4] In this

2 See *Qur'an*, 2:31.

3 Ibid., 3:83.

4 Ibid., 19:93.

world-view, everything is arrayed in endless chains of cause and effect, effect subordinate to cause.[5] Language becomes the framework for distorting the world as His manifestation. The outer horizons and our self cease to be this manifestation's two faces. Instead, things become gods. God said:

> That which you serve, apart from Him, is nothing but names yourselves have named, you and your fathers; God has sent down no authority touching them. Judgment belongs only to God; He has commanded that you shall not serve any but Him. That is the upstanding debt; but most men know not.[6]

The loss or obscuring of our awareness of perennial debt as our connection with the sublimity we were banished from and as our refuge is directly related to the attribution of inappropriate names to things and to serving them rather than God. The only way we can redeem ourselves from this condition is to bear witness that there is no god but God and that the Praised is His servant and apostle. It is only in the realization of the self in this testimony, or in the return to Unity, that the bond between things and their false names will be broken. Wrongly-named things and their namer will be distinguished before God.

> Upon the day when He shall call to them, and He shall say, "Where now are My associates whom you were asserting?" Those against whom the Word is realized, they shall say, "Our Lord, those whom we perverted, we perverted them even as we ourselves erred. We declare our innocence unto Thee; it was not us that they were serving." It shall be said, "Call you now upon your associates!" And they will call upon them, but they shall not answer them, and they shall see the chastisement – ah, if they had been guided![7]

Being guided presupposes that the guided self is imbued with the sacred teachings and engaged in the sacred rites. The confirmation of this sacred potential is virtue, shaped in humility and generosity, embodied in holy people, and attested to by sacred art. God is All-holy: "All that is in the heavens and the earth glorifies God, the King, the Holy, the Mighty, the Wise."[8]

---

5 Ibid., 13:15.

6 *Qur'an*, 12:40; see also 7:71 and 53:23.

7 Ibid., 28:62–64.

8 Ibid., 62:1.

That He is All-holy bestows holiness on all things. Sanctification is how things connect with the All-holy. Realizing our sanctity, we manifest sanctification by embracing the sacred teachings, performing the sacred rites, and in sacred art. We are thus attuned to receive the Book, and for all its forms to be evidence of and our connection with the Unseen, as God tells us through the Praised: "*Alif. Lam. Mim.* That is the Book, wherein is no doubt, a guidance to the mindful who believe in the Unseen, and perform the prayer, and expend of that We have provided them."[9]

The book embodies an array of voices and words in which the Word is revealed. It became so through the centre or heart of the conscious, holy and faithful self of the Praised. His holy self, his immense nature, is our supreme potential, into which the Holy Spirit laid down the Word, whence it came to his sacred utterances. The Spirit that bestows is faithful, true and holy, as is the heart of the receiver, who is faithful, true and holy. Receiving or listening to the Word is the most sublime of our skills. In the original meaning of receiving and listening to the Word, the Praised is the best example, a mercy to the worlds. The Praised is also the best example of the Word's utterance. Of all the sacred skills, listening to the sacred utterance of the holy Word is the holiest relationship to God through the apostle.

This utterance is ever present in the world as its connection with the Unseen. The presence of sacred listening and sacred utterance fills and manifests both the heavens and earth, the self and all that constitutes it in original sanctity. The holy scriptures, the writing down of what has been heard and spoken, are the way in which the Book is embodied, leading those who look on its beauty towards beauty of morality and towards the sublimest height on which is the Praised as the finest example of praising God.

---

9 Ibid., 2:1–3.

CHAPTER 15

The Living God

There is no religion without the Living God, to whom the living relate through life. Religion offers two possibilities: an exteriorized, inanimate object subject to our knowledge and actions or one without historical beginning or historical founder. Each religion begins in God, as First, Who reveals it through visible and invisible worlds, known and unknown prophets, and each of us.

When the living see religion as a measurable object, they exclude the Living God – exiled or "put to death," as Nietzsche said. The visible is quantifiable and comparable. Comparison does not produce final measure in this world. It does not exclude difference, so measurement simply approximates relations between dualities. Quantifiers ignore difference they can neither avoid nor eliminate, taking their rough image to be accurate and sound. This difference may seem minute or infinitely great. The observer's perspective determines which and there are countless perspectives.

Replacing the Living by an "absent," "dead" God sets the stage for the rule of reason: space and time are the context and essence of material existence, life how they present. Life's ground is deep, sedimentary matter, the mire, its complex forms and consciousness mere surface froth. Ethical questions stand between the mire and the rational mindset of comparison and quantification.

For tradition, ontological sequence proceeds from Unity, as the height and treasury of potential, to the depths, the world of the senses. Ontology precedes ethics. The self becomes ineradicable, reality its witness of no self but the Self, the One the ineradicable manifestation of the Not-One.

The Torah states how the living relate to the Living God: "So God created man in his own image, in the image of God created he him; male and female created he them."[1] So long as we relate to each other as living images of the Living God, we never encounter absolute death. That happens only once God is "dead." The Living God gives life, for He has life. Everything else receives or loses it. To register this loss is to admit having received it, while to acquire it without having received it is to lose it. As Gershom Scholem wrote: "None of the exegetes of religion in the previous century – Feuerbach, Marx, Kierkegaard, and Nietzsche – succeeded in explaining the basic concept of the Torah, 'the image of God,' an idea which is simple yet earth-shaking in its profundity."[2]

1 *Genesis*, 1:27.

2 Scholem, *On the Possibility of Jewish Mysticism in our Time and Other Essays*, 164.

 | DOI 10.1163/9789004279407_053

The Living made us two, male and female, a living pair subject to death, upright and liable to fall. To resolve our duality needs two worlds, seen and unseen, lower and higher: "The present life is naught but a sport and a diversion; surely the Last Abode is better for those that are mindful. What, do you not understand?"[3] The world He speaks of is no end in itself: "We have not created the heavens and earth and what between them is for vanity."[4]

Existence is these levels of being in descent from Unity. Only Unity is wholly alive, a life dictated by itself alone. What exists is in duality. Its comparability means the Unity it confirms is present in all things and not just as duality. All existence is descent from the Living to death and return. Life in existence manifests the Living, a manifestation with two facets, the first in the visible and invisible worlds, the second in us. The Living sends down life into existence on a journey from Unity to multiplicity and baseness. What exists descends to death, from God the Creator. It reaches final disintegration on the last day, when all things shall be destroyed and raised up again: "Upon the day the earth shall be changed to other than the earth, and the heavens and they sally forth unto God, the One, the Omnipotent."[5]

This cycle of creation, destruction and re-creation parallels our passage from birth to death and resurrection. This resurrection will produce two eternal conditions – the punishment of the sinful and reward of the good. All our expectations will be resolved, suddenly, decisively:

> Upon that day We shall leave them surging on one another, and the Trumpet shall be blown, and We shall gather them together.[6]
>
> The day they shall come forth from the tombs hastily, as if they were hurrying unto a waymark.[7]

Life's connection to death in the Hour is key to the sacred teachings which allow us, as beings-at-peace, to realize our being-at-peace with All-peaceful Peace. Death does not exclude the Living and the idea of knowing the world as inanimate, subordinate matter, without His presence is a blurred image of reality without Reality. Temporal and spatial limitations, however large or small for finite things, mean something else in eternity. Absolute eternity is not distinct

3 *Qur'an*, 6:32.
4 Ibid., 38:27.
5 Ibid., 14:48.
6 Ibid., 18:99.
7 Ibid., 70:43.

from the Hour. It encompasses all things, so that the Living is inextricable from all knowledge of the world and us, from the seen and the unseen.

The wise relate to All-wise God through wisdom. They see everything as linked to three certainties – death, judgment, and eternity. Their understanding of the material world differs little from the rational view of the unwise. They set their view in another context, however, knowing that the visible is caused and linked in the invisible. All things fade and are judged according to the absolute knowledge of the Judge, when they will receive their place in the new order. Everything in world and self has its principle, present in every cause and effect, always renewed. The principle is in deepest matter and below, on every height and above, in every magnitude and beyond. It is beyond sense and invisible, both the in and the out, the first and last of all visible things.

In a constant state of insecurity, we search for deliverance by embracing its contrary – death, judgment and eternity. We can accept them as absolute certainty in the certainty of the Hour, the absolute now. Then, we can distinguish reality from illusion and testify to the certainty of death, judgment and eternity. To accept reality entails recollection of God, and so the wise include death, judgment and eternity in their now.

CHAPTER 16

Building in Destruction

To most moderns, the modern understanding of science and the order based on it are the way out of suffering and uncertainty. The most urgent questions concern what we can achieve. They rarely ask why we are here. Absolutizing the rational approach, while excluding any supersensory principle, outlaws wisdom and renders things metaphysically impenetrable. There is no framework for understanding suffering and insecurity; action is countered by action, increasing suffering.

Bosnia's suffering raised questions about destruction. To understand or resolve them requires passing beyond the scientific world-view.

The *stećci* are a typical feature of Bosnia, a feature that becomes clearer the more it is denied. Mosques and graveyards were destroyed everywhere in Bosnia, affecting not just material heritage but society itself. This situation cannot be resolved, unless the reality of destruction is addressed.

Certain things are susceptible to destruction – material forms and thoughts. Their essence, what gives form, is not. Every real order – including the political order – is based in the mysterious principle of all things. Order is susceptible to destruction, once it loses connection with that principle. We must rebuild not what was destroyed, but the essence that gives life to the inanimate, so that the formal order may be a link with the Living.

To live among these ruins is to yearn for what transcends them, what was sent down, to fall into ruins in this world, while yet remaining where all things come from and return. Theodor Adorno wrote of this loss and rediscovery:

> Whoever seeks to avoid betraying the bliss which tradition still promises in some of its images and the possibilities buried beneath its ruins must abandon that tradition which turns possibilities and meanings into lies. Only that which inexorably denies tradition may once again retrieve it.[1]

1 Adorno, "On Tradition," 82.

 | DOI 10.1163/9789004279407_054

For Adorno, we search for the lost by denying what offers itself as tradition. Only the higher self is worth seeking; any given self, found on the way, should be rejected, as always less. By rejecting the determinate self we turn to the Self as the one goal worthy of our quest.

We need reason in whatever we do, but reason does not govern all we do. Reality is more complex than its rational image. Reason's boast is its ability to generalize, most importantly in mathematics. It is comprehensive and consistent, seducing us into great danger: mistaking the scientific world-view, with its language of mathematics, for the only one, the scientistic image of reality for reality itself.

To retrieve tradition, we must let go our entrenched notions of it. The scientific world-view's reign, where mathematical generalizations are the sole measure of persuasion, must be dismissed in its entirety, to reveal its contingency and let the spiritual meaning of the wind, the twinkling of the stars, birdsong and our presence in and with all things emerge. Science has replaced this spiritual dimension with one of quantifiable, number-governed attributes.

An alternative to this scientific reduction is art, in which everything has countless unique relations with the artist's self, none being superior to any other; these relations are in flux, revealing reality as the perennial discovery of the principle.

Tradition is discovering and following in our forebears' footsteps, but not for their own sake. The signs in the world and self are discovered for the sake of the Signified Who is and is not in them. He is manifest in the selves of those who know and love Him through them and confess no self but the Self: this is the yearning of the self for self-discovery as the Self.

Surely, then, a science of nature that excludes the self is the worst kind of denial of humanity. Any idea of science as independent of the self is a false myth. Its consequences for how we think our potential are disastrous. The great physicist of the twentieth century Max Planck defined scientific thought as the constant effort to exclude all "anthropological elements": "We must forget man in order to study nature and to discover and formulate the laws of nature."[2] He was following directly in the footsteps of Bacon, for whom science seeks to imagine the world "*ex analogia universi*," not "*ex analogia hominis*."[3]

2 Planck, *Die Einheit des physikalischen Weltbildes* cited in Cassirer, *Substance and Function*, 306ff.

3 Bacon, *Novum Organum*, Liber I, Aphor.41; *The New Organon*, 41.

Defining our relationship with the world in this way generates destruction. Viewing "laws of nature" independently of "laws of the self" isolates us from existence, in egoism. Traditional wisdom aims at the very opposite: existence is one, we and the world two facets of the One. To know the world we must know ourselves, and the converse. Both kinds of knowledge are to remind us of Unity as first and last, inner and outer, as the Praised said: "He who knows himself knows his Lord."[4]

---

4 See Chittick, *The Sufi Path of Knowledge*, 396n22. Ibn al-ʿArabī's perspective on this and similar traditions is treated in Ch. 19 of the same work.

CHAPTER 17

The People of the Book

To speak of a people or nation, whatever meaning one gives those terms, is to recognize their connection with a Book, a revelation of the Principle through an individual in their language. Revealed at different times in different languages, these books can be translated into any. Their linguistic nature means they are present in ancient tradition and in a living relationship with people at all times. This bond between peoples and Book has weakened and may become more fragile yet, or may recover some of its strength. Which happens will affect the future of the world.

Our sociability requires a centre to form around, reachable by various mediatory means. When it is a Book sent down by God, no individual can occupy the centre. The Book can be interpreted in many ways, but we relate to it as to God as Centre. The self that discloses the Self exemplifies that relationship perfectly. Gershom Scholem wrestled with this question of the Book in our times:

> "The ethical is always self-evident." Today, when the unethical seems so self-evident, does the Bible still address us with its call? And is the people of the book still able to do something with its book? It is possible that a time will come when it will fall silent? I am convinced that the existence of this nation depends upon the answer to this question far more decisively than it does upon the ups and downs of politics.[1]

We all share, deep in the self, a language in which existence is present to us. Our power over the world[2] requires language. Our knowledge of the names is received from God as Teacher; as our nature, Spirit breathed into us, binding us to God without compromising our free will. All things in world and self are united through Intellect, His first light. First, they are recited and written down in differing ways, then, read in a unifying way. All things and their names are in perpetual descent, the differentiation of Intellect, and ascent, Its reintegration. The Book encompasses both.

1 Scholem, "The People of the Book," in Scholem, *On the Possibility of Jewish Mysticism in Our Time and Other Essays*, 175.

2 See *Qur'an*, 22:65.

 | DOI 10.1163/9789004279407_055

The people of a given language covenant with the Lord through their Book: "Has not the compact of the Book been taken touching them, that they should say concerning God nothing but the truth? And they have studied what is in it; and the Last Abode is better for the mindful. Do you not understand?"[3]

When the apostle recited the Recitation, in his people's tongue, as a Book for them, it rearranged the semantic fields of their language into an authentic equilibrium, everything connected in origin and purpose with the One. Everything revealed has meaning in this web, without reducing to it: the manifest evidence of the not-manifest.

Each Book is in the language of whichever prophet God reveals it through. God is stranger to none, but we finite beings are strangers in this world, alien to ourselves and others. What is remote and alien helps us see ourselves without the dangerous illusion of proximity. Strangers with different experiences and different languages are more crucial to us than those we feel closest to.

That all things we know can be translated without betraying their truth is guaranteed by God Who reveals His speech in all language. The Book that imbues our language and consciousness with divine discourse illuminates both paths. Descent starts and ascent ends in the One. This first and last is the innermost meaning of every revealed Book, the meaning its readers seek.

Books differ in form, but they share the revelation of truth and the differences between them do not prevent translation. This potential makes near even the most distant stranger, while kith and kin – parents, spouse and children – become distant, unless their discourse is shaped by truth: "O believers, be you securers of justice, witnesses for God, even though it be against yourselves, or your parents and kinsmen, whether the man be rich or poor; God stands closest to either."[4]

Tradition is multiple. It includes Hinduism, Buddhism, Confucianism, Daoism, Judaism, Zoroastrianism, Christianity and Islam. One crucial element of all is expressed in the language of the Semitic group as a triad – Unity of the principle, prophecy, and return to the principle. Our link to the principle is revealed by the principle, through another triad – teachings, ritual and the way.

The principle is infinitely rich. It is manifest in multiplicity or descent, but loses nothing in this sacrifice of Unity for revelation. The descent of Unity always entails ascent towards It. *Religion, the debt* and *yoga* all denote this connection between Unity and multiplicity.

---

3 *Qur'an*, 7:169.

4 Ibid., 4:135.

Unity and multiplicity are within us. Wisdom lets us distinguish Unity from multiplicity, plenitude from the partial. We differentiate and embrace Unity and plenitude by choosing our higher potential and focusing on the principle. The way is living to bring the self into harmony with reality through wisdom, virtue and beauty. It belongs to tradition, including metaphysics, cosmology, anthropology and psychology. Every tradition receives its form from a holy individual through whom the Sacred is revealed. This is the form of a Book that confirms the wisdom, virtue and beauty of its bringer and his followers over the generations. So, the one Word, which is the Principle and is with It, manifests differently in different traditions.

This Book becomes a factor distinguishing the people of its language. It is in the self, however. Language gives it a double presence – horizontal, shared with the nation, and vertical, linking each individual with God. Its presence in one language is transferable into any other nation's:

> Dispute not with the People of the Book save in the fairer manner, except for those of them that do wrong; and say: "We believe in what has been sent down to us, and what has been sent down to you; our God and your God is One, and we are people of Peace."[5]

The Book may be Recitation, Gospel or Torah. Each was sent down through a different prophet and language, but they share core metaphysical or perennial teachings that bind them as one entity, however distinct the forms language seems to give them.

Quarrels between the nations over their Books concern us all. No one is exempt from the experience of others. When individuals of the people of the Recitation see the people of the Torah or Gospel or both, it concerns both them and those in whom they seek realization. Every people of the Book has good and bad members.[6] What those of one nation blame in another is relevant for themselves, as they are bound to avoid what they blame in others.

5 Ibid., 29:46.

6 See *Qur'an*, 98:1–8.

CHAPTER 18

Union

The world requires humanity, as the self to know it as signs.

Whatever its world-view, the self is reality, the absolute moment, of which every past, future, interpretation or act of memory are but signs. These signs may be clear or obscure, orderly or chaotic, concentrated or dispersed, but they are always in the world and the self. This clarity, obscurity, order, chaos, concentration and dispersion determine the self's condition. Isolate them from the One Who discloses Himself through them and they cease to be signs, becoming inanimate objects of perception. They no longer spread knowledge of the One they signify.

Bosnia's history is an unbroken succession of building and destruction. Wherever there are *stećci*, there has been destruction too. What is present reminds us of what has disappeared. This is the business of history. We must also recognize, in these scattered remains, symbols important for those living now, symbols which would not exist without us. Those living now can benefit from orientation towards the esoteric principle, supra-individual knowledge, that transcends form.

Things are in the self through dispersion. Since nothing exists without the self, how they are present is dictated by the state of the self. When its centre is veiled, the self seeks its centre in peripheral things, creating uncertainty and dispersion. Some things conceal others; cause becomes consequence, consequence cause. The self tries to connect all this between two elusive extremes – the first cause and the ultimate consequence. Everything is caught within temporal and spatial boundaries and it seems there is nothing beyond them. We come to believe that the signs of Mystery and any qualities not firmly in the grasp of space and time are mere illusions to be banished. Multiplicity seems a thing without a centre, no point to unify its array.

The traditional view is that spatial and temporal manifestation is always subordinate to reintegration in Unity. This reintegration is the supreme knowledge of the revealed prayer: "Our Lord, make not our hearts to swerve after that Thou hast guided us; and give us mercy from Thee; Thou art the Giver. Our Lord, it is Thou that shall gather mankind for a day whereon is no doubt."[1]

1 *Qur'an*, 3:8–9.

 DOI 10.1163/9789004279407_056

Only Unity can give. Its manifestation in multiplicity in no way subtracts from Its plenitude. It alone unifies all of multiplicity. When we bring together the signs in the world and ourselves, we direct them towards the heart as the centre of all things, the treasury they were sent down from into existence. We too have two facets – one where dispersion is a way of manifesting the centre and one that encompasses the return of the dispersed. Both facets relate us to God, self to Self.

Unified, we relate to God as Unifier. Unifiers, we relate to God as Unified. All things owe their creation to the Creator, so our integration is our return to Him. The Self centres the self, which contains nothing, just as there is nothing between it and the Self to which the Self is not utterly remote and infinitely near.

For all its potential, the self is peripheral to the Self. When it falls into oblivion and forgets its witness of the Self, the signs cease to point to the Self as its uncreated centre. The human heart is then revealed in deformity: diseased, hardened and wasted.

Things acquire their existence from the Existent as Giver. They cannot return without the Giver. In existence they form dualities, irreducible to each other without remainder. In multiplicity this remainder is ignored. By acknowledging this, we assure our openness to Unity, for only in and with Unity does the remainder acquire meaning, so that the ignorance and action based upon it and taken for knowledge and equity become plain to see.

The day when each thing's reality no longer depends on another's arrives with orientation towards the centre of the self in which the relationships between things are resolved. It is manifest in all things, which are signs of its orientation. The certainty of this orientation is not achieved; it is of the centre. But the centre appears differently in different states of the self, constantly showing the image of Unity in duality, as this is the only way to ascend towards the Existent.

The turn to the Giver and the Day is ascent from the depths to the height. No human condition in space and time is outside this orientation or the path of ascent. Our condition is always lower than our potential, in which the names of Beauty and Mercy manifest. From below we are threatened by the names of Severity and Wrath.

The house in the valley symbolizes our individual standing: "God has appointed the Kaʿba, the Inviolable House, as a standing for men."[2] The Kaʿba at the bottom of the Valley, with its six faces and twelve edges, the Inviolable House, has inside and outside. The circuits of it by pilgrims and worshippers

2 Ibid., 5:97.

denote the centre or seventh or invisible arc of space, the unseen presence of the "Thirteenth." The Praised calls us to surround that invisible centre of all things for the sake of return to and reunion in Unity. With it, what we have is bestowed by the Giver and nothing has time or place to manifest anything but Him. Pointing his staff towards the idols, one for each of the 360 days, the Praised recalled the Day of Union.[3] We must be free of illusion to enter the centre and return to Unity.

---

3 When he entered the Holy Valley in 630, the Praised pointed his staff at each of the three hundred and sixty idols around the Kaʿba and uttered verse 17:81 of the *Qur'an*. See Ibn Isḥāq, *Sīrat Rasūl Allāh*, 552 and Lings, *Muhammad*, 302.

CHAPTER 19

Return

Return is reunion and begins with Unity, in which all possibilities are present, encompassed by the One. Return is to the One without difference. Reunion, the elimination of differences, is with Peace.

In Slav languages, including Bosnian, "mir" has two main meanings: peace, *shalom, selam, eirenē,* and the universe, *tēbēl, ʿalamīn, kosmos*. Return is the attainment of Peace.

Return is more than renewal. It is not just turning our back on the past for an image of future reunion. It is utopian hope that redemption will bring more than any past paradise or golden age.

It is not a place beyond, to be reached at some future time: it is present in the Hour. We already contain it *in nuce*, as the Spirit is in us. To discover our original nature is to see the signs, the prophets, books, laws and rites as reminders of what is, has been and always will be in us. "One of the first and most important functions of all the higher religions," writes Ernst Cassirer, "was to discover and to reveal such personal elements in what was called the Holy, the Sacred, the Divine."[1]

Return means we once were where we are returning, once knew what we are re-discovering. Return and discovery begin and last in the visible world of finite quantities. Their goal is not just to change quantities. To discover why things were sent down is to discover why we were created.

When God says all things proclaim His praise,[2] He shows how the seen and finite connect with the Unseen and Infinite at every level, through us: "Naught is there, but its treasuries are with Us."[3]

Things descend to some degree only.[4] The things of this world are signs of a higher reality. Their Owner sends them down under burden of debt, never ceasing to be His, unreal without His reality. The only reason for doing this is to reveal Himself. The world and all things are thus a sign, with us at the centre. What is scattered in the world gathers in us, the supreme sign in His image.

When God says He is First and Last, Outer and Inner, He means fully and perfectly manifest in the world and in the perfect individual: His signs. Our

1 Cassirer, *An Essay on Man*, 96.

2 See *Qur'an*, 17:44.

3 *Qur'an*, 15:21.

4 See *Qur'an*, 15:21.

 | DOI 10.1163/9789004279407_057

uncreated centre or heart, the Spirit God breathed into us, is a treasury that manifests clearly both within the self and out in the world. The signs, singly and together, clearly reflect their higher ideal in the treasury. The perfect individual proclaims absolutely the praise of the All-praised. As perfect sign, focusing the praise of the world and humankind, the Praised perfectly manifests the treasury, as perfect servant and apostle.

To use a sign without regard for its link to the treasury lowers a veil inside the self. The heart is separated from the self by a boundary of injury or sin. The horizons of the world display the signs whose models are in the Heart, Spirit or Intellect. It was to uncover the veiled heart and discover the message of the signs in the world in the light of their models in the treasury that God sent His Book down through His apostle as perfect witness and sign of our sublime potential. We can return to our original condition, in which the signs in the world reflected the treasury, through His revelation and rites in which the self bows down to its uncreated centre. This is the love of God shown by those who follow the best example of the Praised.

PART 2

Symbol and Myth

• •

CHAPTER 1

Sign

Seen and unseen, heavens, earth and what lies between are one sign, shattered into countless signs, as things, things that act, alone or together, more or less readable signs for us on our path.

The world's meaning is not determined by its closed form. Every meaning has limits. They and what lies beyond them share in that meaning's infinite potential. Everything constitutive of that meaning's form involves an opposite. That thing's meaning lies in what it is and what it is not. To understand the world requires *coincidentia oppositorum*.

Since God, Whom we know through knowing ourselves, comprehends all things, we know Him as utterly near and utterly remote. Otherwise, how could we know ourselves, near and remote? There is no world without a self to know it and the Self disclosed as sign.

What would the Creator be without creation, how know Himself without descent to the "lowest heaven," to be dispersed in things and focused in the depths?

A sign or meaning relates knower and known. The signs of world and self are given by the Signified, both present and absent in them. Linking to Him, they reveal Him as the truth of their creation. Meanings comprehended by the self are incomplete. We fall short of God as Truth, the meanings of things in world and self in flux. Unless we dismiss old meanings for new, the signs cease to be windows between seen and unseen or to reveal Him Whose knowledge encompasses all.

How can we, a sign, know our Lord through His signs in world and self? Can two people know the Lord in the same way at the same time or through the same person twice?

Everything that exists has an opposite or pair. Every sign in world or self differs from every other. Only difference guarantees meaning. God has no opposite or double. With Him difference vanishes: "Then to your Lord shall you return, and He will tell you of that whereon you were at variance."[1] Difference guarantees authenticity and return, but Unity is the goal.

In existence, we are alienated from our supreme potential. This alienation is twofold. First, as strangers and pilgrims, we owe a debt for our passage on the earth. Second, everything in world and self recalls the One as our home

1 *Qur'an*, 6:164.

 | DOI 10.1163/9789004279407_058

and calls us to return out of this strange land. Forgetful of the signs' common message, we veil the self, turn from God and cleave to the world. God's prophets remind us of this double alienation – first from the world and redemptive, second from God and fateful.

Chivalrous travellers through the world, strangers in a strange land, know their Lord and see His signs in all things. He alone satisfies Whose sign is on all things. They follow the signs to their Goal, ever near, ever remote. Everything that distracts from Him is their enemy. The distracter is in the self, the distorted signs that hinder connection with the Signified and incite to war, hatred and action from ignorance, of which God says: "And slay them wherever you come upon them, and expel them from where they expelled you; persecution is more grievous than slaying."[2]

We too are of this world. We feel our bond, shaping the self to the world and its countless dualities. So, we must ask of it, what are those things we know as being in the world and in ourselves, and for what purpose?

The signs in the world are more evident to most of us than those within ourselves; the latter appear closer, however, more pregnant, truer. The world seems clearly differentiated into things placed discretely in time and space; the self far less so. Only when facing others like ourselves do we build an image of human interiority based on temporal-spatial causality, by analogy from the outside world. From the perspective of temporal and spatial finitude, both inner and outer worlds seem closed, mere quantity, what lies beyond their limits ignored.

The major metaphysical postulate that this world derives from a higher one is simple. Once adopted, the world and everything in it are seen to depend on higher level models. This series of levels, of which visible and invisible are clear signs, has ascending and descending aspects. All things are in essence ineffable, neither Being nor Self. Being and Self confirm non-Being, non-Self. All possibilities lie in Them, united in His unity. God is the supreme sign, first manifestation of Essence.

A hidden treasure, God created the world out of desire to be known.[3] Throughout its extent, visible and invisible, it manifests God. We focus creation, as its central phenomenon, created in His image. So, world and we are two facets of one manifestation of God.

In the perfect individual, the signs in the self and those of the world do not contradict each other; they all clearly manifest the hidden treasure, their

2 Ibid., 2:191.

3 This is the meaning of a sacred tradition popular among Muslim mystics. It is not in the canonical collections. For more on this tradition, see Chittick, *The Sufi Path of Knowledge*, 250.

source and goal. After the fall, this inner clarity vanished. The fallen self's heart is veiled. The signs in world and self are opaque to the Heart. We are delivered by recovering our original condition. This is why we received teachings and ritual: to reconnect signs with Signified and aid our ascent from lower to higher, darkness to Light.

CHAPTER 2

Knower

Both knowledge of the principle and the principle of knowledge are received, neither separate of knower or known. Representing what links giver and recipient, they manifest the One.

The giver gives primarily himself and only then the gift. Realizing what has been received reveals the giver. Knowing, giving and receiving are how knower, giver and recipient relate to each other. They are one reality, of which their every manifestation partakes.

Abraham received his way of relating to God. Our shared history, forebears and books do not unify our diversity. What does is that everything the members and communities of different traditions and heritages regard as their own has been received. To focus on the received is to relate to the giver. Becoming aware of this relationship as receiving and giving, we become aware of debt. Giving back, we become givers, the original giver a recipient.

The Day of Debt brings this relationship to fruition. He Who has all then gives and receives and is manifest as Absolute Ruler.

Everything received manifests the Giver, Whose plenitude as the Real is inexhaustible by revelation. Nor does return compensate for what was given. What is given and what received only appear dual. They disclose and conceal Unity and witness to Unity recognizes irreducible duality as revealing Unity.

Revelation is not determined by the sensate world. Existence at that level derives from a higher one. What the senses grasp there is seen by reference to its imaginal reality. Imaginal things are associated with their images below and God's names above, as essence is His first manifestation.

Myth is the discourse of the invisible in the world of the visible. It has four levels – sensory, imaginal, nominal and Divine. It blends cognitive content and artistic expression. Prophetic speech blends mythical content and poetic form. Only rarely is poetry mythical, still more rarely prophetic:

> In mythical imagination there is always implied an act of *belief.* Without the belief in the reality of its object, myth would lose its ground. By this intrinsic and necessary condition we seem to be led on to the opposite pole. In this respect it seems to be possible and even indispensable to compare mythical with scientific thought. Of course they do not

 | DOI 10.1163/9789004279407_059

> follow the same ways. But they seem to be in quest of the same thing: reality.[1]

Modern science ignores the self's split between hate and love, fear and hope: the extremes that set the scene for mythical discourse. Myth exceeds the quantifiable world, to which science restricts itself. Science finds myth superfluous, but cannot break free of its language, and so requires it be denied, all trace eradicated from science's objects. Such a closed world requires a closed subject, making clear how ideological the endeavour is. Quality is excluded, reducing the world to magnitude and killing off supreme Reality, from which we derive, and so us and our world with It.

Considering myth in light of the Recitation suggests two things: that we have forgotten our part in God's revelation and have done so as individuals, in a place and time, society and culture.

Existence is the word and deed through which God discloses Himself as All-knowing. Connected to Him, we grow in knowledge, but that knowledge remains little against His. We remain open, seeking the threshold beyond which knower, knowledge and known are one.

Modern science has moved from positing the quantifiable world as its only object to supposing it the only world. It has no interest in passing its limits. Only myth has a place on both sides.

Light that rises and sets without extinction by even the deepest dark is the principle of creation. Twilight reveals transition from dark to light, descent into the dark, but no condition of the self fully extinguishes the light at its uncreated centre. Its presence cannot be destroyed, even in utter dark. Even there, beams of light penetrate, so that a way of ascent may be discerned. One cannot talk of this pattern, common to so many levels of existence, without myth. Excluding myth is to assent to closure, to accept death as life's evident, indubitable goal.

"Myth" means different things for traditional teachings and the modern world-view. The affirmation of modern science seemed to entail attacking the traditional view of myth, but any serious approach to traditional wisdom must free itself from such modern distortion of language. One must accept that being has multiple levels, the visible manifesting the invisible, the signs in the visible linked to those in the invisible. These links orient us from lower to higher levels of Being. A symbol is such a link, myth a way of making the higher levels known. According to Guénon:

---

1 Cassirer, *An Essay on Man*, 75.

> A symbolic narrative can be envisioned just as well, and by the same right, as a symbolic design, or, by the same right, as many other things that have the same character or play the same role; myths are symbolic recitals, as also are "parables," which are essentially the same thing.[2]

Myth differs from ordinary speech and immeasurably from speech confined to one level of being: the discourse of modern science. It is "symbolic recital." The symbolic recital of myth expressing the ineffable relates the different levels of being, giving and receiving, speaking and listening in silence.

2 Guénon, *Perspectives on Initiation*, 116.

CHAPTER 3

Tautegory

Knowledge of the universe and of the self is and is not uncoupled. Traditional doctrine doesn't uncouple it. The modern separation of knower and known does.

When what we know is the outside world, we suppose our image of how things in it are related independent of our knowing. Once that image is set, it can, in principle, be tested by any self, at any time or place. The magnitudes involved are finite, comparable, quantifiable. Their relationships can be stated in the language of mathematics, each proposition testable by repeating the equation anywhere or when. Quantification treats the world's finite aspect as the object of its knowledge.

Through mathematical generalization, such limited tests may be extended far into space and time, forwards and back, but not beyond the limits of the quantifiable. Questions of nullity, infinity, the hour and eternity elude such generalization and reduce to speculation on how to replace notions without magnitude by others with it. Nullity is expressed in minute numbers, infinity in very large ones, the hour as a very brief instant of time, eternity immense duration. Considered carefully, such propositions face countless objections. Any assumption concerning minuteness and immensity is tied to context: what in one context is small enough to stand for nullity in another is large enough to represent infinity.

These considerations lead us to a conclusion fundamental to modern science: nothing can be measured, anywhere, with absolute accuracy. Our measurements are always approximate, images which ground and demonstrate quantification. These images are framed by their own assumptions; let the frame shrink or expand and the images and the assumptions based on them lose validity. Modern science says little about these limitations, a silence that gives rise to a hazy sense of being able to answer every possible question about us and our world.

Where questions arise that science can't answer, they must be ridiculed, denigrated and rejected as unimportant. Scientism's lackeys do so all the time, as they cannot accept the patent fact that scientistic views of humanity and the world hold no water. Their maxim is that the finite world which science creates in its image is the only one.

Traditional world-views posit the knowing self as potentially higher that what it knows. That knowledge, how the knowing self relates to what it knows, does not exhaust the self or take it to some definite limit of attainment. This

 | DOI 10.1163/9789004279407_060

produces what is for modern science an enigma, but represents the beginning of every traditional doctrine: the self that knows the world remains its own supreme object of knowledge, both knower and known. In whatever it knows it distinguishes contingent from complete, finite from infinite, part from whole. Its fundamental principle, derived from its sublime potential, Eternity, may be expressed as the confession of no self but the Self.

Expressing the traditional teachings in this way means that mentioning the cause entails reference to the knowing self. Nothing in the external world is needed for this knowledge. It is our core, not derived, without external beginning or end; it is the beginning and the end.

The self is from nullity to infinity, from instant to eternity. Nowhere in that range satisfies the self, whose reason and purpose are not partial. Only the Self offers the self purpose. As that purpose descends from the Self, it becomes limited. Any finite thing can act to limit the self that seeks evidence for itself outside itself. But there is no evidence independent of the self and confirmation of all potential knowledge is in its relationship to the Self. Defined by anything else, knowledge divorces from the confession of no self but the Self, as God's words with the Anointed suggest:

> And when God said, "O Jesus son of Mary, didst thou say unto men, 'Take me and my mother as gods, apart from God?' " He said, "To Thee be glory! It is not mine to say what I have no right to. If I indeed said it, Thou knowest it, knowing what is within my self, and I know not what is within Thy self; Thou knowest the things unseen."[1]

The Anointed speaks of a right no one has: to speak without confessing no self but the Self. The self's knowledge all comes from the Self, Whom it manifests and reveals. The path on which the self descends towards nullity is open, as is the upright path towards the Self. To suppose the self sufficient in its attempt to reify its world is to deny our fundamental ignorance of the Self. The so-called Enlightenment is based on that distinction. It locates our potential in the world and society, supposing that our purpose is met by knowing and changing them.

In the early twentieth century, after a devastating war, many European thinkers sought a way out of the "violence of history."[2] Their attempts brought

---

1 *Qur'an*, 5:116.

2 In the 1920s, Jewish philosophers wrestled with the demon of history without losing social awareness. They were engaged by questions of religion in society, mainly through historical and philosophical analysis, and addressed the "irrational components of their civilization," in particular myth, historicizing them. As Schelling puts it, they were seeking to "discover

a re-examination of the postulates and legacy of the Enlightenment, as a project based on analytic reason alone.

If our world of quantity is the only one, then nothing transcends duality: everything may be compared and quantified. What cannot be quantified is not. What is in the world can be explained through something else in the world, on the basis of quantity and comparison. All things are like this; nothing is unquantifiable.

At the heart of these endeavours there lay a revival of tautegory. What contains its full reality within itself, deriving no meaning from outside, is tautegorical. But that would make it the Face of God Who says: "Verily I am God; there is no god but I."[3]

A religious symbol is not an essentially allegorical concept in a system, evoking other concepts outside itself. Symbols have meaning self-referentially, a meaning inseparable from how the God of Abraham reveals Himself.

We can think of ourselves and our world in two fundamentally different ways. Either we are not divorced from the world, feeling all existence as though it were ourselves, we in it, it in us, or it stands against us and we wrestle with it, hoping to subject it.

For the first view, what is above and below is explained by direct experience. The signs signify and the we-world manifest the One.

Truth reveals Itself in Its creation of all things. This does not make it contingent. That there is no god but God is the best expression of that non-contingency. Our witness appeals only to its own object. Our testimony is valid, insofar as both witness and Witnessed are One. That Essence is revealed in countless forms does not mean It has gained or lost anything. Where it appears otherwise, it is illusion, a perspective in which the One manifests in two. Truth is clearly revealed in every sign, whether we see it or not. To suppose a symbol can receive new meaning from outside is to deny symbolism, to turn the symbol into something artificial and arbitrary.

---

the Rational in the seemingly irrational." See Wasserstrom, *Religion after Religion: Gershom Scholem, Mircea Eliade, and Henry Corbin at Eranos*, 123. Gershom Scholem, Martin Buber, Walter Benjamin, Alexander Altmann, Aby Warburg, Hans Jonas, Hans Liebeschutz, Paul Krauss, Leo Strauss, Hans Levy, Henri Patcher, Martin Plessner, Shlomo Goitein, Hannah Arendt, Theodor Adorno and Max Horkheimer adopt Schelling's and Cassirer's theory of symbolism, a crucially important replacement of allegory by tautegory.

3 *Qur'an*, 20:14.

CHAPTER 4

Knowledge

Referring to degrees of seeing and hearing, imam ʿAli ibn Abi Talib placed his hand on his temple, between his eye and his ear.[1] What we see is mediated, interpreted.

Seeing and hearing are different sources of knowledge and as such shape the things in the world differently. What we know though touch, smell and taste is even more limited. Our sensory experience of it gives at best partial knowledge of the world's inexhaustible variety.

The knowledge we receive from that world is more or less dependent on transmission. Is there knowledge that does not depend on the external, that is in and with us, always and forever?

The first answer is that such knowledge does exist and is crucial for our self-realization. Each thing has a truth and that truth is within us and we must acknowledge it to ourselves, the Lord, the world and all it contains. The alternative is that our knowledge comes entirely from without, as knowledge that is independent of the self and is received from others via the senses.

The reception of knowledge entails certain assumptions, at least one indisputable. To be received, this knowledge must be accepted by a recipient. Otherwise it would not be believed. Self-realization in our full potential disallows any such status. To live and be happy, properly understood, requires us to scrutinize everything we know, regardless of the source of that knowledge. Countless phenomena in the world and the self are incapable of giving themselves meaning. They have one principle and purpose and we must encompass our knowledge of them through return to the One.

The visible veils the invisible, manifesting and concealing it as higher. One can conceive the invisible in the visible by thinking in ways that embrace visible things as manifesting the invisible. Such an image, formed out of sensory cognition – sight, hearing, touch, smell and taste – approaches myth, as expression of the ineffable. Only myth can strike a balance between seen and unseen.

The second answer tends to denial of the invisible aspect of existence and so myth, which is unquantifiable and not subject to rational analysis.

Tradition speaks of two ultimate experiences – being on the sublime height and sinking to the depths. Our original creation was on the height and we represent that height for the self. We need nothing for ascent, not even doctrine or

1 See *Nahj al-balāgha*, 116.

 | DOI 10.1163/9789004279407_061

ritual. Frithjof Schuon says of this: "Man is his theomorphism, both work of art and artist: work of art because he is an 'image' and artist because this image is that of the Divine Artist."[2]

In our original state, we are entirely the work of the Artist: what we do and do not do is sacred art. Leaving that state to sink to the depths, the self is obscured, our will no longer one with God's.

As we attempt to harmonize our will with His, we discover sacred art as recollection of being on the height. Just as we see the Garden dispersed through the world, we see the fact of our being in His image, our authentic nature in sacred art. Our original perfection, in His image, is indestructible. The fire burns only what covers us, the forces that distort and the layers of illusion.

God taught Adam the names directly. That knowledge is our deepest nature. The names appear in different languages and God has revealed His reminder of our original nature in some of them. This confirms the absolute knowledge in the self as image of the Self.

The knower is linked to the Known through signs and is him or herself a sign. Seeing the world around us as a horizon hung with different signs, we know God as the Signified. Knowing the signs within us, we make known what we know. He Whom we know as Manifest is also Manifesting. Insofar as God loves us, He is our sight and hearing, our moving and doing.[3] God loves what He knows in full and fully knows what He loves: His knowing and being are One.

The differences between things in the visible world are not annulled in this reunion of human and divine Will. The signs throughout existence are seen to refer to primordial models in the Treasury that abides with God. Knowing is how the knowing self relates to the Known Self. Only the Self knows that relationship fully. Our little knowledge is one of countless images of the Self, Whose knowledge encompasses all. To confess no self but the Self is to confess no knower but the Knower. All knowledge connects self and Self, as an image of the Self in the self. This image manifests the Artist with varying clarity. Return to God transforms that insufficiency into plenitude, as we learn of the shortfall and know as we are known. In the words of Paul: "For now we see through a glass, darkly; but then face to face: now I know in part; but then shall I know even as also I am known."[4]

Belief is how the faithful relate to the Faithful, as our knowledge of God falls short and, out of love for Him, we want to become closer, to unite with Him. Love turns us towards the Known, bringing us closer, so that our love and

2 Schuon, *Castes and Races*, 61.

3 See Bukhārī, 8:336–37.

4 1 *Corinthians*, 13:12.

knowledge of Him increase. Only knowledge which encompasses all things satisfies: the all-knowledge of the Beloved. God's all-knowledge is attested to by the signs in the world and in us, which can only be understood in terms of how the beloved relates to the Beloved, face to Face. Internally, we become clear images of the things in the Treasury, images that make manifest first and last, inside and out of the Face. Following reunion, belief is knowledge. Love has brought us, as lovers, to the Beloved, until all illusion vanishes from the self, leaving only the image of the Self.

The self's journey to being face to Face is the being-at-peace of a person of peace in front of Peace. Being-at-peace is to confess no self but the Self, no peace but Peace. And who are the people of peace, the peacemakers?

God is Peace at-Peace as absolute Peacemaker. The world manifests Him as such. When the world, manifesting Him, gathers inside us, we are in His image as Peacemaker. We are peacemakers at peace. This involves trust, since we accepted God's offer of faith as our mode of relating to Him as Faithful. All we have is from and manifests God; knowing ourselves as recipient links us to God as Giving.

CHAPTER 5

Equilibrium

If, as our experience suggests, the world has visible and invisible aspects, choosing one only produces imbalance, trapping us in quantity, in an analytical machine for comparing desires and passions in terms of quantity and power. But our nature shares both aspects, visible and invisible, and to realize that nature we must connect with the invisible world, link our being in the depths with our having originally been on the height. The other world may seem a product of our imagination, but everything in this world, including that imagination, serves to manifest the unseen.

We relate to that world through symbols and myths and it is a relationship we need. Symbol and myth are imaginal, revealed in the equilibration and reconciliation of contraries. They lose their meaning if we dismiss the aspect of the unseen.

Prophecy and true poetry are imaginal, part of how we relate to the unseen. They involve transgression of the bounds of the visible. Logic and propositions, as they approach universality, reach a point they cannot logically go beyond. When the world in-between the visible and invisible is taken for the source of imagination, the self is deformed. In one place, the apostle speaks of poetry as connection with the Holy Spirit, but in another as the worst state of the self.[1] These two possibilities intimate the whole range from the darkness of the depths to the Light on the height.

The self manifests both Unity and multiplicity. A whole entity, constantly dissolving and reintegrating, it hides and reveals Unity. Without the self, the scattered contraries would find no harmony of reintegration or return.

As signs constantly being scattered and gathered, things retain a sameness in diversity of form. God is One, but manifest in a perpetual flux of signs. No sign in world or self lacks its contrary. This duality is reconciled by the truth of their creation. God is Truth[2] and creates all things with Truth.[3] No manifestation of Truth is Truth Itself; nor is it anything other than Truth. In manifestation, Truth is also concealed.

---

1 See Mahmutćehajić, *Across the River*, 112–116.

2 See *Qur'an*, 31:30.

3 Ibid., 15:85.

 | DOI 10.1163/9789004279407_062

> "Men do not understand," said Heraclitus, "how that which is torn in different directions comes into accord with itself – harmony in contrariety, as in the case of the bow and the lyre." In order to demonstrate such a harmony we need not prove the identity or similarity of the different forces by which it is produced. The various forms of human culture are not held together by an identity in their nature but by a conformity in their fundamental task. If there is an equipoise in human culture it can only be described as a dynamic, not as a static equilibrium; it is the result of a struggle between opposing forces. This struggle does not exclude that "hidden harmony" which, according to Heraclitus, "is better than that which is obvious."[4]

The harmony Heraclitus spoke of lies hidden in the self. It was not always so. Our original innocence means the signs in the world resemble their pure images in the self. Because of one inviolable tree, the signs and the knowledge that links self to Self, knower to Known, are unconditioned by anything external. It is the same for our will as knower and God as the Known.

This harmony flows from Unity to prophecy or revelation and return. It is shown as the Heart's centrality as a Treasury in which potential revelations are brought together, or as the self in which they are distinguished, though still wholly in touch with the Heart, luminous with praise and revelation, or again, as the world, in which all things glorify Him with praise as All-praised and All-praising.

When we violated the forbidden tree, our will opposed His, as sign against Signified, and we lost the innocence or perfect harmony of first and last, inner and outer. First and last and outside are independent of our will. The inner self, however, has free will, as His image. When that will follows His, what is ours is His: taste and smell, hearing and sight, touch and motion. This is the basis of our claim on all things, as manifestation of Heart and Spirit, the uncreated and uncreatable presence of the Signified in its creature.

Action based on free will obscures the core of the self, cutting us off from the Heart, as the will is cut off from its nature as image of the Will. The signs in the world remind us of the harmony descending from Intellect as the first of creation. Things are in time and cannot be seen without mysterious beginning and end, clear reference to Him as First and Last. The question of the core self is thus inextricable from the recovery of original harmony.

God's will and our's are no longer one, so that we face two options – a return to our origins in Eden, seeking reintegration with His will or a break in which

4 Cassirer, *An Essay on Man*, 222–23.

our will alone dictates our goal and how to approach it. The first entails fear, as no action based on free will can guarantee certainty. To accept our knowledge as insufficient is to be in awe, which fear underwrites the joy of service, as the prophet David said: "Serve the Lord with fear, and rejoice with trembling."[5] Only fear can prompt the will to turn from illusion towards Reality, from sign to Signified. The self in fear faces two choices – to attack illusion as the source of fear or to flee it for Reality.

Fear of the un-Real, manifest as falsehood and sin, renders the Real irresistibly attractive. Fearful, we love It and struggle constantly to manifest It in order to please and win Its favour. We abandon ourselves to Its signs, to absorb Its beauty and turn to where It manifests. But It is always appearing to and hiding from us. We, pilgrim warriors, knights of our Beloved, see our goal in the knowledge whereby being becomes union, in which we shall love the Known and know the Beloved.

Pilgrims on a journey shaped by confessing no god but God, we are fearful of all things, for God is and is not in and with them. That He is not with them gives rise to fear, as He is not to be found in them, and we miss His presence, no matter where we turn. But God says: "Wheresoever ye turn, there is the face of God."[6]

To see His face in all things is to realize our potential, as the self confesses that the Praised, the sum of all praise of the All-praised, is His perfect servant, His first and last apostle.

---

5 *Psalm* 2:11.

6 *Qur'an*, 2:115.

CHAPTER 6

Service

Service is the relationship of servant to Lord. Everything in existence serves its principle, as God says through the Praised: "None is there in the heavens and earth but he comes to the All-merciful as a servant."[1] In doing so, we conform our will with His, receiving and representing Him. All that we have is treasure entrusted us by our Lord. By receiving from Him in His name, we draw closer to our Lord, realizing ourselves as His steward. We love our Lord, Who loves us, in mutual witness of the unity of Truth and Its image.

Our best is realizing this mode of universal being. To be human is to be His servant. Our existence aims at what is true and right and we achieve that only by admitting God's claims. All things are created with truth, so our admission is confession of God's unity. Those who reach that level are "perfect ones," "perfect servants." His apostles were such, not by their own effort, but by His choice. The Praised is the perfect example, their seal as God's perfect servants. Prophetic perfection bears witness to the Praised as servant of God, witness that is inseparable from witness to God, as: There is no god but God and the Praised is His servant and apostle.

It is in service to God that we achieve harmony, acting in His name. This is the why of our being, as God said: "I am setting in the earth a steward."

God set us on earth as his vicegerent out of a knowledge that encompasses all things. Such knowledge is His alone. Not even the angels who serve God perfectly share it.

> And when thy Lord said to the angels: "I am setting in the earth a steward," they said, "What, wilt Thou set therein one who will do corruption there, and shed blood, while We proclaim Thy praise and call Thee Holy?" He said, "Assuredly I know that you know not."[2]

In principle, we are given little knowledge.[3] It is our bond as knower to God as Known and may be strengthened, based on our original cognition that His knowledge encompasses all things. We enter the world with our original nature, in which all knowledge gathers. Once in the world, we see the signs in it

1 *Qur'an*, 19:93.

2 Ibid., 2:30

3 See *Qur'an*, 17:85.

 | DOI 10.1163/9789004279407_063

and in our own self, but as distinguishing what has always been and always will be in us. These signs are inextricable from language: what is on the horizons or in the self is in language, and conversely, what is in language is, at the same time, in the world and the self. World and language being both at once and in opposition is irreducible. The order inherent to language, us, and the world may be obscured, even distorted; its having been created with Truth cannot be destroyed.

We had to descend to the depths to realize ourselves fully in the image of the Manifest. Our uncreated centre must manifest in all its range, including descent. This inner differentiation enables return, which is seeing multiplicity in all its Unity. Unity is the Revealer, He Who sent down the Recitation. In it, the entire order is put into language. The meanings of signs – letters, words, sentences, sayings, commandments, stories and comparisons, images and the whole – are incomprehensible, unless read as the speech of God, the One.

Every self may be resolved into signs. There is a layering from the core or heart towards the outer levels of the self, extending to the horizons of our world, whose signs derive from the same Treasury that is represented by the heart in us. God speaks through the Praised of this revelation: "So high exalted be God, the King, the Truth! And hasten not with the Recitation ere its revelation is accomplished unto thee; and say, 'O my Lord, increase me in knowledge.' "[4]

We return from our lapsarian to our original condition in the Flux, Which is One. Return presupposes departure. It is ascent from the lowest depths to the height by the same path as departure and descent used. Following revelation, once we have taken the Recitation into the self, it becomes our nature, our morality, and our innermost recesses are lit, the signs in the self in absolute accord with those in the world and with their mediation in language.

Possessing but a little knowledge, we are aware of having received it and of how great our ignorance. Ignorance brings fear, so recognizing the littleness of our knowledge entails confessing service as how recipient relates to Giver, as God told the Praised: "Even so only those of His servants fear God who have knowledge."[5]

God appointed us His caliph or steward on earth. He made us executors of His rule. To exercise authority justly and well requires fullness of knowledge, which we do not have. We can only exercise our authority by realizing service as a relationship between servant and Lord. The Lord has thus placed us in His debt, as His servants, through peace, faith and making beautiful, so that we may realize ourselves as peaceful, faithful and beautiful. God reveals Himself

4 *Qur'an*, 20:114.

5 Ibid., 35:28.

to our actions as Peace, Faith and Beauty. By serving His Will, we draw closer to Him and become more truly in His image.

In such service, we affirm our inner core, in which our witness of service lies, and confess our fidelity to God as Faithful.

According to the Recitation, God asked the Children of Adam, "Am I not your Lord?" And they responded, "Yes, we testify."[6] This question presupposes the possibility of a different response; but that would be to deny the obvious. God asks His creatures about Himself, Who gave them their existence, with all it entails. All they have, they have received. The response "Yes" is just recognition of that and every aspect of the self bears witness to it. To know our Lord is to bear witness to the truth of our creation at the core of our existence. Any other answer would force the self to turn to some external source, to our father Adam or to ignorance. Only these sources could prompt the negative response that the form of God's question suggests is possible.

Each of us must make our own response to God, whether in pre-existence, in having been created, in time, or in ringing the changes of existence. Anyone who, in principle, fulfils that response in pre-existence, realizing it at all times and all levels of being, remains undivided in origin, recipient and giver, male and female. No manifestation at any level of existence, no test to which that original acceptance is put, will cause such an individual to betray that covenant in pre-existence. Thus our Lady replied to the message God sent to her by Gabriel: "Behold the handmaid of the Lord; be it unto me according to thy word."[7] This is the response of perfect humanity to a test that no rational form obscures. Her son responded in the same way to his test of incomprehensible suffering: "And he went a little further, and fell on his face, and prayed, saying, O my Father, if it be possible, let this cup pass from me: nevertheless not as I will, but as thou wilt."[8]

In principle, all human action is violence. We have full knowledge of nothing. We are never at peace, as return entails duality and duality entails reciprocal contingency. Duality vanishes in God, but we are never God. Our knowledge is always little, His absolute. Even our little knowledge is from Him. Acting on it, as we must in duality, is violence. What can we hope to achieve on that basis but to acknowledge the truth of our creation with all things, that we may love our Creator, in Whom duality is resolved. Our aspiration to leave duality and realize ourselves in reintegration is just love.

---

6 See *Qur'an*, 7:172.

7 *Luke*, 1:38.

8 *Matthew*, 26:39.

Our irresistible aspiration to reintegrate with the Beloved turns us from violence towards what our core holds as the original warrant of oneness. We lack masculininity or femininity and strive after what we lack. In our original condition, before our entry into duality, we had both, but then only. Everything we see in the self or world is dual. Only two manifestations of that duality have combined male and female, but not without the touch of death.

We are this orientation towards God. This orientation is always a possibility, but can also always be lost. We are will, wisdom and morality. In a state of baseness, our will needs a framework and a way to bring it into conformity with wisdom. When the self is dark and the outer horizons burn brightly, wisdom needs doctrine, which brings to it the Spirit as the uncreated centre of the Self. Doctrine is in loving the Known and knowing the Beloved through faith. With a way and belief as our debt to God, the self enters beautification and perfection of service. As the Praised replied to Gabriel's question on excellence: "It is that you should serve God as though you could see Him, for though you cannot see Him yet He sees you."[9]

Postscript

The noun "dobri" is integral to both Christian and Muslim heritage in Bosnia. It is often found on old Bosnian tombstones. It has always been part of Muslim discourse there and an account of Muslim spiritual life that does not refer to it is hard to imagine. Its presence attests to the spiritual oneness that connects two sacred traditions inextricably. The noun means "the good," as in good people, and derives from the Indo-European root *dhabh-* ("that which fits/suits"). Its semantic range embraces both the concrete "which fits in a given space and time" to the abstract and moral field of "the beautiful (morally speaking)."

The "good" are those whose entire lives bear witness to wisdom, sanctity and goodness, anointed in Peace, according to the tenet: "The baptism of God; and who is there that baptizes fairer than God?"[10] God is All-peaceful and Peace is from Him.[11] The "good" are those whose being-at-peace as people of peace, loving and loved, known and knowing, is how they relate to God the All-peaceful, All-beloved and Known. They serve him as His servants, doing what is good and beautiful "as if they see him," knowing well that while they may not see Him, He sees them.

9 Muslim, 1:2.
10 *Qur'an*, 2:138.
11 Muslim, 1:292.

Doctrine and rite are witness of God and Him alone. They are received and applied by us, and the lives of those who live by them make clear that they are truly of God. Sacred art offers further proof, as the imprint of the presence of good people. Sacred art, with all its contents derived from hearing, reciting and writing the Qur'an and building and maintaining places of worship and self-abnegation, fully informs the existence and expectations of Bosnian Muslims.

A few words on the true practice of the wise from the eighteenth-century Muslim writer from China, Liu Zhi, may help to explicate this meaning of "the good," which has been lost to modern anti-traditionalism:

> I said: True practice means that they flow and go with the Real Ruler's Root Suchness. They encompass everywhere and reach everyplace. Only after they reach everyplace do they fully realize the substance and function of undifferentiated sameness. Only after they fully realize the substance and function of undifferentiated sameness is it possible to talk about undifferentiated sameness.
>
> The undifferentiated sameness of the Former Heaven is undifferentiated sameness of void and silence. The undifferentiated sameness of the Latter Heaven is the undifferentiated sameness of true practice. "True practice" and "void and silence" are not two realms. Where there is true practice, there are void and silence.
>
> The sage knows that the multitudes are not capable, and he deeply hopes that the multitudes will become capable. In the midst of their incapability, he directs them and exhibits to them the [three] paths of true practice: The first is called "Propriety," the second "the Way," and the third "the Real."
>
> Propriety is the rules of behavior for daily interaction; this is the true practice of the body. The Way is the tendency to resist things and to circle back to the Real; this is the true practice of the heart. The Real is deep unification with the Root Suchness, which becomes the reality-moment of Propriety and the Way; this is the true practice of nature.
>
> The true practice of nature is the true practice of Root Suchness. It is not that nature does not have these three at root, or that they are artificially established to be exhibited to the people. Because of the ongoing flow of the Root Suchness in humans and for the sake of the regulated principles inherent in humans, the sage arranges and differentiates the sequence so as to direct and exhibit it.
>
> Those in whose bodies the Root Suchness flows and goes have the heavenly precedence and the heavenly order that are called "Propriety."

> Fully realizing Propriety is the true practice of the Root Suchness that flows and goes in the body.
>
> Those in whose hearts the Root Suchness flows and goes have the genuine knowledge and genuine power that are called "the Way." Fully realizing the Way is the true practice of the Root Suchness that flows and goes in the heart.
>
> Those in whose natures the Root Suchness flows and goes have the Complete Substance and Great Function that is called "the Real." Returning to the Real is the true practice of the Root Suchness that flows and goes in nature.[12]

Who is good without wisdom, wise without goodness? Being good is our supreme potential, as we follow the Praised, the most exalted of the wise. The beliefs and conduct of the wise are always based on knowledge, which is often something quite beyond the routinely rational. Their wisdom is "tasting" the reality in all things, so that will, power, life, knowledge, speech, hearing and seeing are manifest in their entire being as reciprocity with the Whole revealed in the great distinction between earth and heavens and what lies between.

What is knowledge of the good and where from?

Knowledge has two sources – transmission from others with whom we are connected in diverse ways and intellectual knowledge independent of anything outside the self. The first kind includes language, grammar, history, law, published books – whatever is memory-based. Intellectual knowledge cannot be passed on. It does not depend on memory or conclusions from principles or even observation: "Rather, it is a living awareness and consciousness of the way things are, and it can be found only within oneself, in the "intellect" (*ʿaql*), also called the "heart" (*qalb, dil*)."[13]

Wisdom is how we relate to God the All-wise, as He said: "He gives Wisdom to whomsoever He will, and whoso is given Wisdom has been given much good; yet none remember save those with minds."[14] They are wise, aware of things as they really are, and they act in accordance:

> The goal of searching for wisdom was not to gain information or the ability to control things; rather, it was to understand God, the universe, and oneself and, on the basis of this understanding, to become a sage, a wise

12 Murata, Chittick and Weiming, *The Sage Learning of Liu Zhi*, 450–51.

13 Ibid., 21–22.

14 *Qur'an*, 2:269.

> man. The seeker of wisdom was trying to live in perfect conformity with the Supreme Principle. The sage is the person who was awoken to the presence of God in his own heart and lives correctly in the world.[15]

Good people cannot be understood as good in the terms of those who are not. In the presence of the good, we all sense our deeper or higher nature. Even when they seem insane or weak in the eyes of ordinary people, they are sensed to have achieved a higher level of orientation.

Our wish to find a place in the world from which to control and direct our inner selves takes the form of ignorance and violence against the good. No finite goal satisfies our purpose as creatures. The presence of the good bears witness of a path towards a goal beyond finitude. That presence keeps us and our world open, so that we are not trapped by our littleness of knowledge.

15 Murata, Chittick and Weiming, *The Sage Learning of Liu Zhi*, 26–27.

CHAPTER 7

Truth and Symbol

We and the universe are dual in aspect, one directly observable, the other mysterious and beyond the senses. The former manifests the latter, forming an ontological sequence of descent. The mystery is higher than the observable; when we know the observable, it is as symbol of the higher. Everything in the visible world has a correlate in the higher one.

Both worlds, seen and unseen, manifest God as One, Creator of them and all they contain, Truth. Creation's existence is to confess this. Every level of existence is with the Truth, insofar as they manifest It. Otherwise, they are divorced from and conceal Truth. This is also true of the self, but not of our original nature, which was like all things created with Truth.

All existence and everything in it manifest the Creator as Truth. All things are symbols, linking the observer to a higher level of existence, facilitating knowledge of the world and its contents as manifestation of Truth. It is only by relating to God as All-knowing that our knowledge bursts its bounds. It becomes inexhaustible and through it we ascend a path that ends in the un-determinable.

Not all thing-symbols are of equal power. Some are singled out to remind us and bear more explicit witness to what we and the world were created to do. The greatest and most comprehensive symbol is us, with our visible and invisible aspects. Everything in us or within the scope of our consciousness is illumined by Spirit and Intellect. This is not, however, due to direct connection to Spirit. Our reason is seeing the light of Intellect in the night of the self, just as the light of the sun illumines the moon.

Everything we can access in the world is a symbol of something beyond it, in the Intellect as the Treasury of full knowledge. All existence gathers within us, connected with God as Truth through the Heart, the uncreated centre of the self. We are the symbol of Truth.

Each symbol contains some of the mystery of the world and us. Its existence demands expression. Great symbols express the oneness of the world. The world and its contents are such a symbol. Since our core is Spirit, we, as one facet of existence, and the world, as the other, express our symbolic nature through Spirit; we "carry" Its presence and imprint. Our direct awareness of that presence in everything is what gives the world meaning and reveals its mysteries. Every symbol thus conveys something of our totality with its different levels.

 | DOI 10.1163/9789004279407_064

The world and everything in it give out of their connection with Truth. The truth of creaturehood also belongs to us, so that we are each essentially identical with the world as a whole. Seeing things as manifesting what is common to them all makes us one with reality. This union is tautegorical. The claim that all things are created with Truth depends on nothing but Truth, as in the confession that there is no truth but the Truth.

To bear such witness, the self must be awake. Asleep, it is not linked through the things in the world and self to higher levels to perceive the reciprocity of centre and margin. Ultimately, we relate to God through sincerity. He manifests Himself as Truth through His signs and sincerity is recognition of that Truth that all things are created and so in His debt. Acknowledging this, we recognize His claims on us: things are in debt to God and through them we may recognize our debt to God, as well as their and their Creator's claims on us.

When our admission of the claims of what we do and do not know leads us to lose sight of the one truth of all creation, our sincerity reflects a deformity in the self. Real sincerity is in acknowledgement of the supreme right of the Self Which brings all things in the world and self to be with Truth. When our self fixes on something within observation or reflection so that things become the motive force of what we do, our entire being, in its full range from the Truth of our creation to the lowest depth, becomes distorted. The self is breached, but its core remains indestructible. As Martin Lings has written "The Truth is Indivisible Totality and demands of man that he shall be no less than one undivided whole; and it is a criterion of orthodoxy that it should stake a claim in every element of our being."[1]

In accepting the diverter's invitation to view the Tree of Immortality, the self is following its deepest inner need. We should not, however, accept a summons to fulfil our sublime potential from anyone but God, Who is irrefutably present in the centre of the self. Responding to such a false call sends us plummeting from the height to the depths. Even here, the Spirit speaks to our deepest needs, the will for immortality with which we turned to the diverter. In the depths, we know service and obedience to another than God. The call of the Spirit in the depths counterbalances the call of the diverter on the height. It is redemptive, true and whole, delivering us from depravity and dark. The call of the diverter leads to ruin, for it is false and incomplete.

The Praised is the seal of the prophets, the sublime potential in each of us in every age. The Spirit's call to ascend is a call to discover the Praised as our finest example and that supreme potential. The Praised is what made Adam originally perfect, as well as his confession of Unity and his return to his origi-

1 Lings, *Symbol and Archetype: A Study of the Meaning of Existence*, 110.

nal condition. This confession of Unity and return is renewed by seeing Truth as the principle of the creation of all things. "It is He who created the heavens and the earth in truth; and the day He says 'Be', and it is; His saying is true."[2]

To help the self discover this knowledge in its core and recall what had been forgotten, God sent prophets as witnesses to the Praised. In his historical manifestation, the Praised gave us the Book God had sent down to him with Truth: "He has sent down upon thee the Book with the truth, confirming what was before it, and He sent down the Torah and the Gospel aforetime, as a guidance to the people, and He sent down the Salvation."[3]

Ultimately, symbols are both sent down or given and received. They are internally differentiated, corresponding to the multiplicity of Being. To make sure that spiritual influence is always present in transmission and reception, tradition consists of various forms and levels of rite, some for public use, others not. Ritual was introduced to open the way to each individual to the supra-individual, impersonal horizon of Being. There is no tradition, properly speaking, that does not include initiation. Otherwise, tradition loses its link to the transcendental source, becoming subject to deformation and finally fading away.

Every expression is symbolic, to at least some degree, in the light of its source. Neither we nor the world are our own source and so neither we nor it can be the ultimate source of symbol or doctrine. Symbol and ritual are inextricable aspects of our individual relationship to the supra-individual principle. To establish this relationship an introduction is required. It cannot derive from imagination, but must be given in the same way as creation, the Book, and prophetic guidance. René Guénon has written of this as follows:

> All the constituent elements of a rite necessarily have a symbolic sense, whereas, inversely, a symbol produces – and this indeed is its essential purpose – in one who meditates upon it with the requisite aptitudes and disposition, effects rigorously comparable to those of rites properly speaking, with the reservation of course that when this meditation is undertaken there be, as a preliminary condition, that regular initiatic transmission failing which the rites would be in any case nothing more than a vain counterfeit, as with their pseudo-initiatic parodies.[4]

---

2 *Qur'an*, 6:73.

3 Ibid., 3:3–4.

4 Guénon, *Perspectives on Initiation*, 110.

Postscript

In saying the Praised is the seal of the prophets, we recognize his being first and last in creation. Confessing no god but God and the Praised as His servant and apostle might appear historically contingent, not least because usually said in Arabic and the Praised is known to have had a specific place in history.

The first is easily answered: there is no expression in any language that cannot be translated into every other, so that the confession can be expressed in every language and every heritage.

The second requires a more complex answer, but clear-sightedness does provide one. The Praised was indeed a historical personage. But everything in existence is also a sign and the Praised in history denotes the Praised beyond history, as the first manifestation of the All-praised Who says: "I was a Hidden Treasure, and loved to be known; so I created the creatures that I might be known."[5]

At the first level of His self-manifestation, His first image or first manifestation is the Praised, who was at the beginning, preceded only by God Himself, as the sum of everything to be made manifest in differentiation through the descent from Unity to multiplicity. Manifestation is descent to the lowest level. The Praised gathers what was sent down and then ascends to his original primacy. He connects existence as a whole, its contents, and each of us "with the Hidden Treasure." All the prophets announce him in accordance with the revealed principle: "And We sent never an apostle before thee except that We revealed to him, saying, 'There is no god but I; so serve Me.' "[6]

What God reveals to the prophets as the seal of prophecy is the perfect beginning of His own manifestation – the Light of the Praised, first Intellect. Bearing witness to the Praised as perfect servant of the One is how the prophets preserve their election.

God elects prophets: none is a prophet through his own choice. Their testimony to their election to the apostolate takes the form of absolute acceptance of God's will.

When God says to the Praised "never an apostle before thee," He is confirming him as the eternal exemplar for all prophets, first after the First and last before the Last. What he received and confessed in history is what puts all prophets, as his witnesses, in his debt as their eternal ideal. He is the best

---

5 Ibn al-ʿArabī says of this tradition that it "is sound on the basis of unveiling but not established by way of transmission" (*al-Futūḥāt al-makkiyya*, 2:399.28). See Chittick, *The Sufi Path of Knowledge*, 250–52.

6 *Qur'an*, 21:25.

example of confession and of service to God. No one can match him or return to God without him. One cannot be good, that is a friend of God, without following him. By doing so, we realize our heart, which encompasses the goal of return. Fully realizing the heart erases the limitations of our humanity before the Is-ness and attributes of God. The heart annihilates illusory reality to attain true life and consciousness in the standing reality of the Lord, the only reality that truly is.

Self-realization embraces beginning, manifestation and end. The first manifestation of the Beginning is the Praised. At the lowest level, the ultimate distance from the Beginning, he unites everything differentiated on the descending arc, and returns as perfect man along the ascending arc to the End which is the same as the Beginning. This is the "two bows' length away, or nearer."

CHAPTER 8

Participant and Observer

Being-at-peace is how we relate as recipients and givers of peace to the God of Peace. This condition is contingent. Being-at-peace allows us to orient ourselves so as to receive Peace from God. God's being All-peaceful is absolute and ever-giving. Whatever our condition, we remain on the battlefield, for only God is absolute Peace. We can leave that battlefield, but only with God's guidance, as the Praised said: "O my God, Thou art Peace and Peace comes from Thee; blessed art Thou, O possessor of glory and honour."[1]

Everything in the world is related to God in this way, as He told the Praised: "What, do they desire another debt than to God, for in Him has found peace whoso is in the heavens and the earth, voluntarily or involuntarily, and to Him they shall be returned?"[2]

The faithful relate to the Faithful through faith. This makes us different from everything else in the world. Things are at peace in God, having from the start renounced the possibility of being in a state of faith, which requires the free will to rebel. Had they accepted the relationship of confidence offered them they could rebel against the condition of absolute being-at-peace, which is their relationship with God. But they did not, so all things, except us and the jinn, simply serve, at peace, without free will: "We offered confidence to the heavens and the earth and the mountains, but they refused to carry it and were afraid of it; and man carried it. Surely he is sinful, very foolish."[3]

---

1 Muslim, 1:292.

2 *Qur'an*, 3:83.

3 Ibid., 33:72. We relate to God through "fidelity" or "belief." This relationship requires participation but little knowledge, so there are different degrees of participation. The opposite of belief is doubt, the absence of that fidelity. God is Reality, Truth. Our relationship with Him is always based on fidelity, the acceptance of received knowledge as signposts on the path of realization. To attain realization is to pass over the limits of doubt that separate. The prophets have attained that level. Nūr al-Ḥaqq says that sages (prophets, *anbiyā'*) have achieved union with the Real, but that the other three kinds of people are tainted by darkness (*ẓulm*) and are veiled from the Real. The good (the sincere, *mukhliṣ*) may be led astray (*ḍāll*), for they may be confused about the connection of charismatic works (*karāmāt*) with the Divine power. Scholars (*'ulamā'*) may become heretics ("converters," *mubtadi'*), if they give legal rulings based on their own views. The ignorant (*jāhil*) may become hypocrites (*munāfiq*) or concealers (*kāfir*) by denying their religious duties or articles of faith. See Nūr al-Ḥaqq, *Sharḥ al-laṭā'if*, 126–27/92; quoted in Murata, Chittick and Weiming, *The Sage Learning of Liu Zhi*, 460.

 | DOI 10.1163/9789004279407_065

Agreeing to relate to God through confidence, we willingly became part of the manifest order of His creation. The meanings He gave are evident in the signs in the world. Serving Him, they alter neither in rhythm nor in meaning. Our part is to strip away the veils that separate the self from that perfect manifestation of peaceful being. All things, in diversity, service and peace, manifest Truth as the principle of their creation. We relate to the things of the world through our potential for knowing that truth, as well as that of our own creation.

Freely accepting peace as our way of relating to God, we partake in universal peace: our rituals become like the revolutions of sun and moon, only willingly performed. Looking to the signs as manifestation of Truth, we see that the signs within us are images of the signs in the world. We and the world are mirrors to each other in which God reveals Himself. We epitomize the world, it writes us large, and God is our focus as absolute Unity, seeing the world through us, us through the world, and making Himself known to Himself.

By taking part we realize our debt to God. This cannot be understood from outside. It is a drama of our entire being, including our confession of the mystery that we are participants in revelation. However much we may wish not to be, we cannot. To exclude ourselves is to deform or obscure our original nature. Every effort to comprehend this process with reason simplifies, reducing it to forms that say very little about the inner nature of the self, the true stage of this drama of the individual.

Confidence means relating to God out of free will. Without the choice of whether to accept a charge whose purpose we do not fully know, our relationship as recipients with God as Giver would not be one of trust. What we have received, we can forget or reject at any time – reject out of free will or forget as creatures of little knowledge, perpetually on the brink of ignorance. To resist either requires we be active recipients, as well as God's help as Giver of trust. To carry this trust requires both wisdom and will.

God sent down His Recitation that we might use our wisdom to differentiate and to unite – to distinguish Truth from untruth and to unite the signs in world and self through Truth. He also sent down ritual to orient our will and incorporate it in the order of things. With doctrine and ritual – sacred because borne by the Holy Spirit from God the All-holy – we can participate in our own redemption, ascent from the depths to our initial perfection.

To repeat, we were created on the sublime height, but violated our confession of no will but the Will and fell to the lowest of the low. The fall to being in the depths is our humanity, our position on the axis on which we sink into darkness or ascend into light. Nowhere on that axis is beyond God's mercy, which encompasses all things. In our every state, we are irrefragably linked with mercy and both doctrine and rite remain accessible to us. They are the presence of the Creator and are essential if we are to realize our right to redemption.

God never ceases to be true to us, knowing and desiring and loving us in our full potential. He knows the potential He gave us to love Him with even our little knowledge and to follow the Praised in aspiration to be free of the turn to anything but the Beloved. The rite God sent us as a redemptive rope is more necessary than anything else. We must catch hold of and climb it: everything else is in His hands. As Martin Lings observed:

> Since a rite is always performed with a view to God, it amounts to a re-enactment of the connection between the symbol (in this case man) and the Supreme Archetype, a vibrating of that unsevered but dormant link, which needs the constant repetition of these vibrant acts to rouse it, once and for all, from sleep to wake.[4]

One cannot participate in a rite without engaging the will. It may be engaged at any level from the lowest to the highest possible commitment. The rite brings the self to the door separating visible from invisible, death from life, matter from Spirit. The nearer the far side, the stronger and fiercer the resistance, as the rite becomes a war against whatever bars passage to the Kingdom of God. Those who have not had such an experience cannot appreciate it. Each self's involvement differs, no matter that the rite is set down in words and by example. The onlooker sees only its outward expression, not the inner purpose. As Jesus, son of Mary, said: "The Kingdom of God is within you."[5]

An observer seeking to reduce the rite from a means of entering the Kingdom of God to an historical or scientific object has no access to its being within us. Modern scholars deprive it of precisely what makes it integral to life, its shaping of the participants' selves as witnesses, until nothing they do is theirs, as they pray that God's will, not theirs, be done.

---

4 Lings, *Symbol and Archetype: A Study of the Meaning of Existence*, 10.

5 *Luke*, 17:21.

CHAPTER 9

Inanimate Observer

Without a self to know it, there is no world. Other people, living and dead, other worlds, observed and imagined are only because of the selves that know them. Existence is not the purpose of the self. The opposite is true: existence is from and with the self. In the Recitation, God says: "God created the heavens and the earth in truth that each self be awarded after its deserts. No wrong shall be done them."[1]

This verse makes clear that the heavens and the earth and their creation in truth are for the self that comes to confess no self but the Self. For every self to fulfil this purpose – and God said all things pass except His face[2] – they must be one. This is because there cannot be two absolute perfections. Thus, all human hearts are as one between the two fingers of the All-merciful.[3]

Otherwise, we would have to kill the self, which is possible only in imagination. "Man's claim to being the centre of the universe has lost its foundation," wrote Ernst Cassirer. "Man is placed in an infinite space in which his being seems to be a single and vanishing point. He is surrounded by a mute universe, by a world that is silent to his religious feelings and to his deepest moral demands."[4]

But who is making this assertion? Clearly no inanimate observer, but a living one, an observing self, speaking of something inanimate as "a single and vanishing point," a point that living self has imagined, a point within the self as its centre. How can death be absolute certainty, if "the now" is too? Conversely, how can the "now" be absolute certainty, if death is too? There cannot be two absolute certainties. Consequently, that both death and "now" are certainties is an enigma to be resolved within the self, which constantly accompanies it.

Life is our only reality. Death is insoluble in the terms of quantity. The more obsessive our desire to know the quantifiable as the only world, the greater our need to turn away from death. We cannot answer the question of life beyond death without myth, as Cassirer saw clearly: "In a certain sense the whole of mythical thought may be interpreted as a constant and obstinate negation of

---

1 *Qur'an*, 45:22.

2 See *Qur'an*, 28:88.

3 See Muslim, 4:1397.

4 Cassirer, *An Essay on Man*, 13–14.

 | DOI 10.1163/9789004279407_066

the phenomenon of death. By virtue of this conviction of the unbroken unity and continuity of life myth has to clear away this phenomenon."[5]

Since without a self to know it, nothing exists, the world is knower-knowledge-known. Without this differentiated structure, there is neither knowledge nor knower. Whatever we can know in the quantifiable world confirms its bounds and therefore what lies beyond them. This duality of visible and invisible affirms Unity as its principle. Can Unity be known in differentiation into knower-knowledge-known?

If Unity is what binds knowers with knowledge, then we must see It as without duality. We are not some other Unity, we are Its manifestation, as is the world to which we relate through knowledge. Since we are in Unity's image, we know the world and ourselves as images of Unity. The closer we are to It, the more clearly our knowledge is the image of an image. Perfect knowledge would be to know ourselves as clear images of our Lord.

Here, the individual "I" and God's "I" resemble reality and its image in a mirror. The image has only the original's reality. As images, we have life, will, power, knowledge, speech, hearing and sight, received from our Original. All the image has of its own is death. It can thus be said that Unity bestows existence and is present in and absent from all things: present, because everything manifests its inexhaustible possibilities, absent since they remain an image of the ur-model of Unity.

We are living, willing, powerful, knowing, speaking, hearing and seeing creatures – all received qualities. They are originally God's, Whom we manifest through them. We receive them as a debt. We know them fully only when face to Face with God. His face is always facing us, All-knowing. We as His image are never Him. Since death is simply what remains once we cease to be His image, now or in the hour or in death itself, all we have is what we have received. In no "now" have we anything but death and the self, which receives everything from God.

As images, what we have is from God, but limited. The Giver descends towards the recipient, the recipient ascends towards the Giver. This reciprocity is reflected in the confession of no god but God and the Praised as His apostle. The first part denies that any image can be the same as God, but also that there is anything not received from Him. The second contains the original and perfect image God made manifest as the Praised in an image that receives all it has as praise and so is praised. He is Universal Humanity, that encompasses all things. Created, he is an apostle of God's love to be known, the seal of perfect

5 Ibid., 84.

humanity, in whom is all praise of God in all the worlds, through whom God said: "Nothing is that does not proclaim His praise."[6]

Existence is given. Everything given has first been received. All existence received its act of praise from God as All-praised and consequently altogether it is praised. What existence has received, being praised, is simply an image of God as All-praised and to praise Him is thus to return or acknowledge what has been received.

---

6 *Qur'an*, 17:44.

CHAPTER 10

We

God told the Praised: "We shall show them Our signs in the horizons and in themselves, till it is clear to them that He is the Truth."[1] God refers to Himself as "We," going on to explain why the signs are on the horizons and in the self, namely that we may know Him to be Truth. In the Arabic, this "He" may refer to the Speaker, a grammatically justifiable reading, or to Speech itself, in the form of the Recitation or Book. These two interpretations only appear to differ, but that appearance is crucially important for recognizing Unity's place in multiplicity.

God is First and so First Speaker. His speech does not limit Him. Uncreated, it descended with the Holy Spirit into the hearts of Mary and the Praised in two different forms. Jesus is His Word, as is the Recitation. Both manifestations are with Truth and link us with God, as His presence in the created world. God is Truth and so is His Word.

God's speech requires a listener, to receive and convey it to others. God's speech is then present in human language. Different forms of address become possible in a differentiation that includes God as One and us as all people. In the Recitation, God reveals himself in the third person singular, using the "plural of excellence, the plural of majesty or the plural intensive," as it is variously known, of the Semitic languages. He is sometimes addressed in the second person and sometimes appears as "I" and "the Self." His Self comprehends all possibilities of manifestation. His first manifestation as the First is the Light of the Praised. God is Light, All-praised. The priority of His light and praise is manifest in the Light of the Praised. No one can elude the Light of the Praised, so that all things manifest the speech of the One.[2] He instills His speech in theirs, saying: "We shall show them ..."

His speech in the world is distributed in perfect order, everything to scale and in proportion, harmony and rhythm. So too is our original language. In the darkened self this perfection is obscured, but not gone. Those who see the world through a glass darkly demand that speech of the perfect order be momentary. This speech has always been and always will be at our core. For its presence to be clear in language, everything in the world and self would have

---

1 *Qur'an*, 41:53.

2 For more on the Light of the Praised as the first manifestation of God, see Böwering, *The Mystical Vision of Existence in Classical Islam*, 149–53.

 | DOI 10.1163/9789004279407_067

to link to that core, as God said through the Praised: "Now they who are bent on the covering say, 'Why has the Recitation not been sent down upon him all at once?' Even so, that We may strengthen thy heart thereby, and We have chanted it very distinctly."[3]

We grow in knowledge as all things descend gradually as a Recitation into the self to make manifest the order that comes from and returns to the Heart. What has been sent down becomes a reminder through which the self discovers its ignorance and fear of the Lord with Whom it covenanted in pre-existence. The self discovers its centre as our original knowledge and witness of our Lord, and the heart is reconciled with its horizons. "God has sent down the fairest discourse as a Book, consimilar in its oft-repeated, whereat shiver the skins of those who fear their Lord; then their skins and their hearts soften to the remembrance of God."[4]

The sending down and reception of the Book are gradual. They occur over time as the reintroduction of order in the self ravaged by ignorance mistaken for knowledge. Descent and acceptance are not instantaneous, however inseparable from the reality of the Hour. No human achievement stands in their way. The intricacies of the self, with its actions and endurance, endeavours and lassitudes, differentiation and integration, are unravelled and reordered with the Recitation, which introduces a clear progression into language from the highest to the lowest and back again. Cassirer describes this gradual discovery of reality thus:

> Man cannot escape from his achievement. He cannot but adopt the conditions of his own life. No longer in a merely physical universe, man lives in a symbolic universe. Language, myth, art, and religion are parts of this universe. They are the varied threads which weave the symbolic net, the tangled web of human experience. All human progress in thought and experience refines upon and strengthens this net. No longer can man confront reality immediately; he cannot see it, as it were, face to face.[5]

We cannot escape our achievements, but not because of shortcomings in the symbols or in our own nature. The signs in the world and self are the face of Reality, as is the self, originally. Our will likes "progress," which may mean turning from our original nature and obscuring how the symbols in the world and the self relate. The things around us do not deform our nature, however;

---

3 *Qur'an*, 25:32.

4 Ibid., 39:23.

5 Cassirer, *An Essay on Man*, 25.

forgetting them does, as does our failure to recognize the truth of their creation or to acknowledge our debt to them.

Failing in our debt to the things in the world is to fail in our debt to our inner self. Both world and self manifest God and a debt to them is a debt to God. This knowledge, unlike any other in human experience, reveals the knower's "object" to be God, Whose knowledge encompasses all things, including all knowers.

This debt is one for every self and each thing. There is nothing not created with Truth;[6] but that all things were created "with Truth" does not mean any two are identical. They are invariably different. The Truth in them is both concealed and revealed, so everything recalls It as both remote and near. God is Truth,[7] and so beyond compare,[8] but also near,[9] nearer even than the jugular vein.[10]

When God, One and Only, calls Himself "We," it may mean His manifestation and speech of that Unity and Uniqueness in the manifold. Every thing and self manifests and speaks the same truth, but differently. The signs in the world and self mean we can create images or conceptions of this incomparability and proximity at any place or time. We are recalled easily to the need for a higher world. Whenever we are, our imagination allows us to see ourselves as strangers or guests in this world. This is why imagination is both a requisite and our refuge. Again, Cassirer has written:

> Here the source of imaginative creation never dries up, for it is indestructible and inexhaustible. In every age and in every great artist the operation of the imagination reappears in new forms and in new force. In the lyrical poets, first and foremost we feel this continuous rebirth and regeneration.[11]

6 See *Qur'an*, 15:85.
7 Ibid., 31:30.
8 Ibid., 112:4 and 42:11.
9 Ibid., 2:186.
10 Ibid., 50:16.
11 Cassirer, *An Essay on Man*, 154.

CHAPTER 11

Intellect and Reason

Intellect is the treasury of Unity, all Its possible manifestations, each accessible to observation in multiple forms, in space and time. Existence is the spatial and temporal accessibility of Intellect to reason. The modern world-view considers space and time quantifiable, but they are qualities of which extension is just a sign. When they are seen as divisible and finite, the sign is taken for the Signified. This necessarily confines us within notions of quantity, so that the world continues to be compressed and petrified to an unbearable degree. Cassirer senses this trend when he says:

> Reason is a very inadequate term with which to comprehend the forms of man's cultural life in all their richness and variety. But all these forms are symbolic forms. Hence, instead of defining man as an *animal rationale*, we should define him as an *animal symbolicum*. By so doing we can designate his specific difference, and we can understand the new way open to man – the way to civilization.[1]

Intellect unifies, reason distributes. Intellect is in touch with Unity, reason with multiplicity. Intellect is outside time, reason time-bound. These distinctions help us understand the relationship of sign and symbol. Every symbol is a sign, not every sign a symbol. When a sign, accessible to reason, passes beyond individuality and so finitude, when it connects with Intellect, it becomes a symbol. In traditional ontology, one spoke of various levels of being without symbols and myths. The linguistic sign's closure within a single level of existence has also attracted the Cassirer's attention:

> Symbols – in the proper sense of this term – cannot be reduced to mere signals. Signals and symbols belong to two different universes of discourse: a signal is a part of the physical world of being; a symbol is a part of the human world of meaning. Signals are "operators"; symbols are "designators." Signals, even when understood and used as such, have nevertheless a sort of physical or substantial being; symbols have only a functional value.[2]

1 Cassirer, *An Essay on Man*, 26.

2 Ibid., 32.

 | DOI 10.1163/9789004279407_068

Reason never grasps signs in their entirety. It is confined within the limits that connect and separate signs and symbols. If a sign may be clearly compared and quantified by reason, so its meaning does not transcend the limits of the quantifiable, it has lost its link with Unity or the Principle as the source and confluence of all things. So long as a thing can be expressed, it has not renounced participation in Intellect. Reason's task is to show that things in multiplicity are indivisible from Unity. This takes place in the heart, our core, which holds the source and confluence of all multiplicity. All speech contains metaphysical indications of the signs in the world and self, however obscured by the hazy meanings given the terms Intellect, Spirit and reason. Few in our time have given the distinction between Intellect and reason such importance as René Guénon:

> What must be emphasized is the essentially supra-individual nature of the pure Intellect. Moreover, it is only what belongs to this superhuman order that can be called truly transcendent, since this term cannot normally be applied except to what lies beyond the individual domain. The Intellect, therefore, is never individualized; furthermore, this corresponds to what is expressed, considering now more particularly the corporeal world, when it is said that whatever the appearances may be, the Spirit is never "incarnated," which is equally true in all senses wherein the word "spirit" can be legitimately used. It follows that the distinction which exists between the Spirit and elements of the individual order are much more profound than all those which can be established among these individual elements themselves, as for example between the psychic and corporeal elements, that is, between those which belong respectively to subtle and gross manifestation, both of which are no more than modalities of formal manifestation.[3]

When we give what manifests in the worlds of the minute and the immense – of modern science's nuclear physics and astronomy – consideration beyond or below its supraformal manifestation, we produce an insoluble equation of mental and bodily. A science that treats signs as determinate in time and space and causal relations as quantifiable requires the knowing subject's mental force to be subordinated to the bodily or ignored. In a world without transcendence of Intellect, Spirit or Word, the self is confined by individualization. No longer focal to either micro or macro-cosmos, as they coalesce in a supra-individual world of ideas, the self ceases to see its own centre and adopts its internal

---

3 Guénon, *Fundamental Symbols: The Universal Language of Sacred Science*, 8–9.

condition as principle, egotistically seeking to impose it as the standard and measure of everything outside itself.

Reason then seems to be individualized Intellect and the distinction between possible and real insoluble. The closed self cannot understand God's face as everywhere, wherever we turn, or what things are in the eternal reality of their principle, in Divine Intellect. The worst error here is not this lack of comprehension. Unable to escape limits, we project beyond them, while the phenomenal world derives from the imaginal. This inverts the view whereby truth is subordinate to its manifestation:

> The *idea* in question here is the very principle of the being: it is that which gives it all its reality and without which it would be only nothingness pure and simple. To maintain the contrary amounts to severing all links between the manifested being and the principle; and if at the same time a real existence be attributed to this being, this existence is and cannot be anything other than independent of the Principle so that, as we have said on another occasion, it all inevitably ends in the error of "association."[4]

In this erroneous association, reason, as Intellect's manifestation at one level of being, is divorced from its source, confined within multiplicity. Language as its tool, is also "freed" of its symbolic content, in fact its very essence. Reason distinguishes; Intellect unites. Union, return from multiplicity to Unity, is impossible without symbols. Everything in both sensate and imaginal world must partake of the nature of symbol for us to scale the stations of Being.

Everything in Being's many and ascending levels is a symbol, but only in denoting what is on the level above. The higher cannot denote the lower. Otherwise, the "gates of heaven" would not exist and we could not pass from the earthly level except to the ashes of the grave. The warrior on the battlefield of this world would truly end in the grave and not in Peace, as the prophets proclaim: "Those that cry lies to Our signs and wax proud against them – the gates of heaven shall not be opened to them, nor shall they enter Paradise."[5]

Opening heaven's gates is intimately connected with our approach to signs. Deny them and deprive language of its most important symbolic content. Language is discursive, like reason, which it echoes and represents. Symbolism is literally intuitive and so better suited to underpin intellectual and supra-intellectual intuition. If rite and symbol are hard to distinguish, it is because

4 Ibid., 11–12.

5 *Qur'an*, 7:40.

rite's purpose is to allow spirit to influence the self through symbols. Without this influence, the self will not connect to its higher levels or with what transcends it.

Depriving something of its qualitative aspect leads to denying it as a sign and reducing it to quantity. It means divorcing reason from Intellect, matter from Spirit. Reason is a property of the individual self. Promoting it is to promote individuality as the highest, even the only level of humanity. This denies any supra-individual principle above reason, divorcing the self from pure, transcendent Intellect. In being overall, reason is simply Intellect's reflection at the level of the individual self.

When mistaken for our highest faculty, reason drags the self towards quantity, "free" of unquantifiable quality. The self sinks to its lowest level, to thickening dark. Sinking deeper undercuts our awareness of existence and everything in it having been created "with Truth." The more profound the dark, the greater the disturbance of the self in it. Descent accelerates as quantity predominates. Our rapid fall towards the rule of quantity is caused by denial of the signs, as we confine the world within the bounds of reason, since reason cannot access what it cannot quantify, which, therefore, does not exist.

The upward path back is a response to the call for salvation. Its goal, redemption, is absolute. Nothing can ever be added to it, as there is no reconciliation between gods and God. This is because gods are not real. When anyone, as an individual or excluded from their group, reaches for another path, they cannot reach any other goal but the Goal. In the worst case, they will experience the reality of their own resistance, for there is nothing real but the Real. This is the meaning of the adage *Corruptio optimi pessima*. But also of its converse, *Corruptio pessimi oprima*. The corruption of the corrupted involves their destruction, as the process of their disappearance is accelerated.

CHAPTER 12

Sun, Moon and Cross

The commonest symbols on Bosnian *stećci* are the sun, the moon and a cross.[1] With other symbols they are also found on Muslim tombstones known as "bašluci" (headstones), "nišani" (markers), or "šahidi" (witnesses).[2] Burial grounds with *stećci* often merge with areas of *nišani*.[3] The association is almost a rule, its absence either an exception or due to destruction of the *nišani*.

Like Judaism, Christianity is a Divine revelation reminding us of God's unity and the purpose of existence. If revelation has been received and interpreted in various ways, this is what necessarily happens on descent from a higher to a lower level of existence. No form or interpretation is left without connection to the Principle it manifests. God's revelation of the Word to His apostle the Praised recalls us to Unity, prophecy and return. It annulled nothing in the prophetic heritage, but showed everything in a different, more certain light. Christianity in all its variety is thus the heritage of every witness to God's unity, the Praised's apostolate and the inevitability of the Hour. Intellect retains every potential of Being and the same signs remind us of this in all the traditions.

Everything in the world and self is a sign. As knowers, we must ascend through signs to the Signified, Whose Face is present in them everywhere: "Whithersoever you turn, there is the Face of God."[4] Two signs strike us more than all the rest: the sun and the moon.

The sun has its own light, which is thus its manifestation: it is both Light and the Lamp that lights: Light, because its capacity to illumine is from itself, and the Lamp, because we need it to see the world around us.

---

1 The cross is the symbol of Christ. Just as there are many Christologies, there are many interpretations of the cross. For traditional Bosnian interpretations, See Solovjev, "Jesu li bogomili poštovali krst?" 82–102.

2 For illustrations of the decorations on *stećci* and *nišani* see the works of Bešlagić, Mujezinović and Wenzel cited in the bibliography.

3 In anti-Muslim discourse, this fact is passed over in silence, denied, or forcibly rejected. It presents an unacceptable challenge to the ideological distortions of "Christian continuity" and "Muslim intrusion." Though obvious, even Bešlagić does not record it. His scholarly failing is no doubt due to fear of public confrontation. There are, for example, the remains of old *nišani* near groups of *stećci* in Ljubomir, around Prokoško Lake, at Gorica near Stolac, and in Presjeka near Foča, but Bešlagić makes no mention of this. *Nišani* have been systematically destroyed by nationalists in the past two centuries, a destruction that continues today.

4 *Qur'an*, 2:115.

 | DOI 10.1163/9789004279407_069

The light it sheds corresponds to Intellect, for it contains its own source, in the form of manifestation, radiation and dispersion. It connects what it lights up with the uncreated Light. This is true of everything: everything is connected through Intellect with the One Whose knowledge is all-embracing. As Guénon said "the Divine Intellect is the Spiritual Sun, while the manifested intellect is a ray of the Sun; and there can be no more discontinuity between the Principle and manifestation than there is between the Sun and its rays."[5] He goes on to say "It is by the Intellect, therefore, that every being in all its states of manifestation, is attached directly to the Principle, insofar as it eternally contains the 'truth' of all beings, is itself not other than the Divine Intellect."[6]

The moon owes the light it sheds to the sun, to which it is wholly subordinate. Surrendering to the sun, it receives and comes to life. It is both masculine and feminine:[7] what it receives as feminine it transmits into the dark and the depth as masculine. It is a sign of the Praised, who transmits praise received from All-praised God. Its receptive aspect signifies the Virgin Mary, as handmaid, its giving aspect the apostle.

The Praised is both lit and light-giving. As receiving and giving, they manifest as our irrefragable core, the Spirit of the All-merciful breathed into us. However low we sink, his light is present. Our constant potential, manifest in descent and ascent, is symbolized by the moon in its phases, from full to new moon sliver, like an aged palm bough.[8] To face the bottom of the valley, symbolized by the new moon, we must first understand the upright path and ascent to realization in the Hour. This unveiling and realization is seeing one in two, the Praised and Mary in their state of perfect illumination, the light in the Light-giving lamp:

> In the name of God, the All-merciful, the Ever-merciful. The Hour has drawn nigh: the moon is split. Yet if they see a sign they turn away, and they say "A continuous sorcery!" They have cried lies, and followed their caprices; but every matter is settled. And there have come to them such tidings as contain a deterrent – a Wisdom far-reaching; yet warnings do not avail. So turn thou away from them.[9]

5 Guénon, *Fundamental Symbols*, 12.

6 Ibid.

7 The Slav noun for moon, "mjesec," is grammatically masculine, whereas the Latin "luna" is grammatically feminine.

8 *Qur'an*, 36:39.

9 Ibid., 54:1–6.

The new moon stands for a vessel filled by the sun's light. The vessel in turn can symbolize the heart, as receptacles of blood, the bearer of life. The heart, as the centre of being, receives the Word, whose reception may be represented by a red rose. Hence both bowl and rose are symbols of the Praised, who passed on what he received to the world. Without this giving and being Sent, the world and we remain in the dark. God calls the Praised a Light-giving Lamp.[10]

Giving off light, as what relates Light-giver and lit, is to descend from height to depths. Descent and departure take place on the same axis as ascent and return. It passes through all levels of Being. The levels of Being are horizontal, each a world unto itself. Countless worlds lie between nullity and Unity. The axis passing through them is marked by the house on the lowest level. The cross signifies indivisibility from higher levels of Being and corresponds to one world.

The sign of the cross can be read in everything and interpreted in countless ways, one being that of the Anointed, Jesus, God's Word uttered through the Virgin Mary. He comprehends every level of existence and is thus an example of crucifixion or execution before the All-near, Living God in witness that there is nothing that has not been received from God as the Creator of death and life.[11]

Those for whom the Anointed is the perfect communion of humanity and divinity think him crucified and dead. In the Recitation God spoke of this through the Praised:

> Yet they did not slay him, neither crucified him, only a likeness of that was shown to them. Those who are at variance concerning him surely are in doubt regarding him; they have no knowledge of him, except the following of surmise; and they slew him not of a certainty – no indeed; God raised him up to Him; God is All-mighty, All-wise.[12]

---

10 See *Qur'an*, 33:46.

11 Ibid., 67:2.

12 *Qur'an*, 4:157–58.

CHAPTER 13

Apple, Vine, Rose and Lily

Another very common motif on *stećci* and *nišani* is the hemisphere, usually interpreted as an apple. The finials on minarets are often a series of spheres topped by a leaf. These are crucially important motifs in the symbolic language under consideration.

In the myth of our beginnings in the Garden on the height, God forbids Adam to eat the fruit of one tree, saying: "Adam, dwell thou, and thy wife, in the Garden, and eat thereof easefully where you desire; but draw not nigh this tree, lest you be evildoers."[1]

God told us this on the height when still wholly pure. His will and ours were in perfect accord. What Adam wanted, saw and heard, where he went, whatever he reached out to touch, his will was as God's – except for this one tree. Plucking its fruit transgressed the limit set. It is irrelevant whether he transgressed knowingly or had forgotten. Satisfying his desire for the forbidden produced a new state of the self. When he transgressed this limit, we lost our original innocence and became "evildoers." Our will was in defiance of our Lord's.

Since God is All-knowing, His will is inseparable from knowledge. It is never with ignorance. Our knowledge is always little and our will limited. The self cannot be kept inviolate without acknowledging our limitations. Reaching for the forbidden fruit, we derive our will from our opposition to knowledge, from our ignorance, and our inner self is obscured. Preferring action to restraint caused us to fall to the depths. Before, the self which "incites to evil,"[2] was a hidden, unknown stain, action out of ignorance, a serpent; from that moment on, the stain spread to become our being in the depths of misfortune.

Reaching for the forbidden fruit comes from that part of our free will which turns away from confessing no god but God. The consequences of violating these limits are expressed in His Words: "Get you all down, each of you an enemy of each; and in the earth a sojourn shall be yours, and enjoyment for a time."[3]

Our fall from the height to the depths and our awareness that we could return back up the path of that fall mean returning what was picked to its place. This is the revelation of the Word as the tree of the world: "A good word

1 *Qur'an*, 2:35.

2 Ibid., 12:53.

3 Ibid., 2:36.

 | DOI 10.1163/9789004279407_070

is as a good tree – its roots are firm, and its branches are in heaven; it gives its produce every season by the leave of its Lord."[4]

The vine is given complex symbolic meanings in every sacred tradition. Its many branches grow from one stock and the farmer prunes and trains them until only the sound and productive remain. One may think of it, like any other tree, as consisting of a visible part, the stock and branches, leaves and grapes, and a concealed part, the root. The part above ground is evidence of the root below, the centre of the vine's being. As Jesus said:

> I am the true vine, and my Father is the husbandman. Every branch in me that beareth not fruit he taketh away: and every branch that beareth fruit, he purgeth it, that it may bring forth more fruit. Now ye are clean through the word which I have spoken unto you. Abide in me, and I in you. As the branch cannot bear fruit of itself, except it abide in the vine; no more can ye, except ye abide in me.[5]

The vine stock symbolizes Jesus' own self, entirely dependent on the Essence, which is the Principle that manifests in the stock as the perfect self and in the branches and fruit as individuality. The Principle, Unity, is the in and the out of that manifestation, its first and last. First and last, it bears fruit insofar as it realizes its original self.

Seeing a rose and inhaling its perfume recalls the presence of the Praised. This prompts the people of peace to say: "O Lord, bless the Praised!" Blessing him, they bless the angels and God, for they too bless the Praised.[6]

When the Praised returned from his Night Journey, drops of his sweat fell on the ground and from each sprang a red rose.[7] These roses denote the Praised as recipient and giver: he gives what he has received from God as His mercy to the worlds.[8] The full-blown red rose symbolizes the exteriorization of inwardness, the blood in the vessel of the heart. Vessel and flower are connected as symbols and it is clear how both stand for the heart of the Praised and of every one of us as recipients of the Word, which the Spirit of Truth brought to his heart.[9]

The lily is a sign of femininity or perfect receptivity. It represents the Virgin and is as common as the rose in Bosnian motifs. Rose and lily rarely feature in

4 Ibid., 14:24–25.

5 *John*, 15:1–4.

6 See *Qur'an*, 33:56.

7 See Schimmel, *And Muhammad is His Messenger*, 35.

8 See *Qur'an*, 21:107.

9 Ibid., 26:192–94.

isolation; they are repeated in patterns, horizontal or vertical rows, garlands and rings.

Apple, vine, rose and lily are the perfect decoration to represent repetition, the constant flow in and out, welling up and overflowing, and the inexhaustible simultaneity of beginning and end. Repetition of these motifs points to the "now" as absolute reality in which presence and absence, nearness and remoteness coexist. This "now" has no beginning, yet is the start of all things, no end, yet is the end of all things. It always manifests differently.

Unity and its manifestation, multiplicity, together but distinct, denote the inviolability of the tree. The good tree as the image of a good word suggests the whole tree of which the fruit is an integral part. Tree and fruit may stand for doctrine and rite or rite and virtue: they can be separate, but will not then survive. Doctrine without rite violates limits, as does rite without virtue. At our first level we are will, with all it can do in opposition to the object of our knowledge. As knowers, we never wholly know the object of our knowledge. What we know remains at the same time unknown to us and thus a source of fear. We may fight or turn and flee from it. Neither attack nor flight eliminates the unknowability of all things. Only God encompasses all things with His knowledge. Turning to Him as the source of knowledge may help us, whether fighting or fleeing, for where can we flee from God but to Him.

CHAPTER 14

Bird, Zachariah and Mary

The only clear and distinct sounds we hear in descent are birdsong, which most traditions call song. The old sacred traditions take the form of song or chant, with form and meaning in perfect harmony. In old Bosnian, the ten-syllable metre that runs meaning over several verses is known as a "word."[1]

God sends down His Word, as words rise to Him, borne by angels. Birds symbolize angels and our condition as related to the Principle. Birds symbolize being between height and depths.

Most songbirds live in trees. The tree and the book are symbols of existence as a whole. The apostle said: "The first Created by God is the Pen. God said to it: 'Write!' And it proceeded at that very hour to (write) whatever is going to be."[2]

Every being has its letter in the cosmic book, its leaf on the tree of the world. When birds sing, their song is from that book and tree. Each species sings in its own language, for like us, they have communities.[3] We hear their discourses, but are long since unable to understand them. What better evidence of the perennial symbols in the world and self from time immemorial and until its end? God reveals His full, irreplaceable presence through them to us, who remember and forget.

Knowledge of their language is attained by initiation into mystery: "And Solomon was David's heir, and he said: 'Man, we have been taught the speech of the birds, and we have been given of everything; surely this is indeed the manifest bounty.' "[4] We and the world often seem opposed, divided by an unknown boundary. The story of the birds' language dissipates this fantasy. If all things have purpose, this view of the external world is a fantasy and disappears in its witness through us. What appeared dumb, nameless, lowly or despicable signifies the Creator and worship of Him.

Mary's birth was for the descent of the Word, that the things of the world might return to it. As the *Protoevangelium* of James relates, her mother Anna learned she would give birth through birds.

1 See Foley, *Traditional Oral Epic*, 44.

2 Ṭabarī, *The History of Prophets and Kings*, 1:198.

3 See *Qur'an*, 6:38.

4 *Qur'an*, 27:16.

 | DOI 10.1163/9789004279407_071

> And Anne was very sad; but she took off her mourning-garments, washed her head, put on her bridal garments, and about the ninth hour went into her garden to walk there. And she saw a laurel tree and sat down beneath it and [after she had rested] implored the Lord, saying: "O God of our fathers, bless me and hear my prayer, as thou didst bless the womb of Sarah [our mother Sarah] and gavest her a son, Isaac." And Anna sighed towards heaven and saw a nest of sparrows in the laurel tree, and lamented within herself.[5]
>
> And behold an angel of the Lord came to her and said: "Anna, Anna, the Lord has heard your prayer. You shall conceive and bear, and your offspring shall be spoken of in the whole world." And Anna said: "As the Lord my God lives, if I bear a child, whether male or female, I will bring it as a gift to the Lord my God, and it shall serve him all the days of its life."[6]

After three years in her parents' house, Mary went to serve in the mosque, to honour her mother's covenant: "And Mary was in the Temple nurtured like a dove and received food from the hand of an angel."[7] The *Protoevangelium* relates that Mary was in the Holy of Holies,[8] cared for by Zachariah.[9] Mary and Elizabeth hid their sons from Herod's executioners, whose soldiers killed Zachariah in the Temple.[10]

---

5 Schneemelcher, *New Testament Apocrypha*, 426–27.

6 Ibid., 427.

7 Ibid., 429.

8 See *Qur'an*, 431.

9 Ibid., 429.

10 Ibid., 436.

CHAPTER 15

Hand, Rope and Staff

Hands are common on both *stećci* and *nišani*, whether as a man with raised open right hand or the open hand on its own. The hand explicitly links centre and manifestation, expressing the heart in countless ways. Turned outwards, what it gives is from Unity, from the mysterious centre of the self. What it receives from multiplicity, from the world around us, also represents Unity. The hand thus reflects the continuous interaction of outside and in by which the outer horizons gather in Unity, recalling our innermost self to God's unity and the apostolate of the Praised, until we rediscover our original orientation towards the Face.

The raised hand symbolizes the power of action, whose principle is the Word. Existence manifests God's Word, as we manifest Word and Deed in our turn towards Him, for manifestation is His work. The hand seeks to manifest the identity of two wills, ours and His.

The hand may take up the fruit of a tree, a spear, an axe or a sword, a bow, a rope or a staff, a hammer, chisel or pen, a bowl, a book, bread, a cup, or the hand of another. All reveal the inextricable connection of self and world. Visible in the world, these actions occur in the innermost self, signs of our struggle to return to the Self as the resolution of duality.

We have life, will, power, knowledge, speech, hearing and sight, received of God. We receive those gifts in obedience to or rebellion against God. Where we reach out with our hand, what we take in it, what we do not grasp – these questions are integral to our understanding and use of what we have received. We must account with all our being for our debt, but this debt is revealed most clearly in tongue and hand.

The raised open hand may be understood as a sign of integral humanity, constantly giving and receiving. As it closes on the rope let down from above, it affirms the self on the upright path. To liberate the self from what conceals its original nature we must grasp God's salvific rope. We cannot know the upright path in isolation from the world as a whole. For the aware, the world is manifest harmony, lacking nothing. Our covenant with God upholds this order: "Abasement shall be pitched on them, wherever they are come upon, except they be in a bond of God, and a bond of the people."[1] This abasement is for violating the covenant and appears as confusion and disorder in the self and in

1 *Qur'an*, 3:112.

 | DOI 10.1163/9789004279407_072

society, hostility and divisions between human hearts in the delusion that they are distinct and self-sufficient.[2]

Life, will, power, knowledge, speech, hearing and sight are expressions of the Covenant. Every time we do or do not act we grasp the firmest of handles: "And whosoever turns his face in Peace to God, being a good-doer, has laid hold of the most firm handle."[3] The rope and the handle connect us with God. It is a mode of being in which we love God and He us, we follow the Praised in accordance with God's commandment: "As for those who believe in God, and hold fast to Him, He will surely admit them to mercy from Him, and bounty, and will guide them to Him on a upright path."[4]

The servants on the upright path attain a level of being where their will and His are in perfect accord:

> My servant draws near to Me through nothing I love more than that which I have made obligatory for him. My servant never ceases approaching Me through voluntary works until I love him. Then, when I love him, I am the hearing through which he hears, the eyesight through which he sees, the hand through which he grasps, and the feet through which he walks.[5]

The self in this state holds His rope or handle in its hand, whether as spear, axe or sword, pen, needle or hammer. The staff symbolizes grasping the rope and awareness of the Covenant, reminding us with all our being that we are on the upright path from the valley of Becca to Mount Sion, from body to Spirit, multiplicity to Unity. The staff on *stećci* and *nišani* reminds us of our covenant with God, our original baptism,[6] the compact of the Book.[7]

---

2 See *Qur'an*, 3:103.

3 *Qur'an*, 31:22.

4 Ibid., 4:175. See also: 4:146.

5 Bukhārī, 8:336–37.

6 God says in the Recitation (2:138): "The baptism of God; and who is there that baptized fairer than God?"

7 In the Recitation (7:169) God asks about the people of the Book: "Has not the compact of the Book been taken touching them, that they should say concerning God nothing but the truth? And they have studied what is in it; and the Last Abode is better for those who are mindful. Do you not understand?" Anointing or baptism by the Book was customary among the adherents of the Bosnian church. See Šanjek, *Bosansko-humski krstjani i katarsko-dualistički pokret u srednjem vijeku*, 88. The Bosnian Muslim custom of placing the Book on the head of a bride cannot be explained without taking into account their *krstjan* past.

CHAPTER 16

Spear, Sword and Axe

Spear, axe and sword are symbols of the cosmic axis of descent and ascent. Their ends are the poles, as is the double-edged blade. Duality is revealed in opposites – light and dark, good and evil, beauty and ugliness, mercy and wrath, inhaling and exhaling, creation and destruction, building and demolishing.

The Praised is the first of the people of peace[1] and the spear and the sword are symbols of his mission, prefigured in the words of Jesus: "I came not to send peace, but a sword."[2] The sword signifies just war against injustice, war against war. This is the lowest level of meaning in our quest for ourselves. The self is a theatre of war between two infinite armies – darkness and evil against light and good. To return to Unity and Peace we must win that war.

Only victory in that war will satisfy. We must transcend illusion and rise to true meaning, as received from God in the very act of our creation. We must reunite the names into One, Sacred, Ineffable. That is being on the battlefield, in the mihrab.

Waging war has two forms – war against the external enemy for peace and order and war against the internal enemy that blocks our path of return. The Praised called the first the lesser war.[3] The weapons it requires have symbolic meaning in the greater war, the realization of the Word and adherence to the Light that shines in the darkness.

We are told the chalice from the Last Supper was used to collect the blood that flowed from the wound made by the centurion Longinus' spear. The spear's symbolic meaning is clear: interior exteriorized and re-interiorized. Its place in the historical story of the Praised expresses certain key messages of the perennial wisdom.

The mystery of the Anointed flows with his heart's blood down the spear into the chalice held by Joseph of Arimathea. The spear represents the cosmic axis on which the Spirit of Truth descends from Unity to the centres of each level of existence. The eternal Gospel, the Preserved Tablet, was transcribed by this descent to bring us and the world back to God. As symbols of axis and heart, spear and chalice correspond to hill and valley or hill and cave.

---

1 See *Qur'an*, 6:163.

2 *Matthew*, 10:34.

3 Related in ʿAjlūnī, *Kashf al-khafā wa muzīl al-ilbās ʿammā ishtahara min al-ahādīth ʿalā alsina al-nās*, 1:481–82.

 | DOI 10.1163/9789004279407_073

Spear, arrow, sword and axe symbolize the relationship between Peace and the people of peace, Beloved and lover, Known and knower, Light and enlightened. If the heart is the vessel of the Word, these weapons are the path of its descent. The tip of the centurion's spear points upwards so that mystery may descend.

The Praised thrust a spear into the ground before worshippers he was leading. It was the cosmic axis and his mighty morality. Perfect recipient and returner of praise to God, the Praised encompasses that axis from the depths to the height, Vale to Mount. The centurion's spear points upwards, the Praised's downwards, symbolizing his role as our guide.

Their different directions suggest the close relationship between the Praised and the Anointed.[4] The Praised is the eternal principle of human perfection through which God reveals His Word; the Anointed is the Word revealed through his mother Mary. The spear of the Praised symbolizes the war against the self in darkness for the self of the heart's-blood. The Praised says: "I have been sent with the sword so that God alone is worshipped, without associate to him. He puts my daily bread under the shadow of my lance. He brings lowness and smallness to those who disagree with my command."[5]

This saying is connected to the prophet Isaiah's prediction of his coming: "Who raised up the righteous man from the east, called him to his foot, gave the nations before him, and made him rule over kings? He gave them as the dust to his sword, and as driven stubble to his bow."[6]

A Bosnian manuscript records the Anointed as saying of the Paraclete:

> A man shall come to me from the right, from the sunlit east. I am not worthy to receive the dust from his shoes upon my cheek. Receive all his teachings and all that he passes down. God's heaven in his kingdom, amen, amen. His name shall be the Holy Spirit the Paraclete, of the lineage of Abraham. And whosoever will not follow him shall be put to the sword.[7]

---

4 The Praised says: "I am most close to Jesus, son of Mary, among the whole of mankind in this worldly life and the next life." Muslim, 4:1260–61.

5 Ibn Ḥanbal, 2:50.

6 *Isaiah*, 41:2.

7 Manuscript no. 3488 in the University Library in Bologna. See also: Bojanić-Lukač, "Un chant a la gloire de Mahomet en Serbe," 58–59.

The sword symbolizes the redemptive Word and Light, as in Revelation: "And he had in his right hand seven stars: and out of his mouth went a sharp two-edged sword, and his countenance was as the sun shining in his strength."[8]

The sword unites the meanings of spear and axe. Primarily connoting Unity, as the world axis, it operates in every direction with greater freedom of action than spear or axe. This recalls the resistance we must overcome in our greater war. The diverter sets ambushes wherever we turn. Justice is the sword held upright. The pointer on the scales of justice is a sword and at perfect equilibrium it points up.

The roof ridge of a house and the apex of a dome are symbols of the axis. In old Bosnian homes, a wooden axe would be mounted on the roof ridge.[9] Weapons symbolize power. The axe on the roof ridge suggests supreme spiritual authority, the highest degree of initiation towards which our potential orients us. This potential is realized in the spiritual pole active in the world which underwrites order. We are guests in this world and our goal is full discovery of our potential.

Both spear and axe symbolize the axis, their twin edges the two forces at work at every level of existence it passes through. These opposing forces are balanced in Unity, which reconciles near and far, mercy and wrath. Asked how to find God, Abu Sa'id al-Kharraz said: "Through the fact that He brings opposites together."[10] The spear highlights this reciprocity of unifying extremes, as well as the priority of the immovable axis in all movement.

Single or double-headed, the axe represents the cosmic axis, but also emphasizes action from the spiritual centre in the horizontal array of opposing forces. A double-bladed axe with a spearpoint symbolizes opposition to the external forces that threaten the traveller on the upright path.

---

8 *Revelation*, 1:16.

9 Čurčić, "Oružje u narodnoj medicini," 55–56; Hadžijahić, "Sinkretistički elementi u islamu u Bosni i Hercegovini," 314.

10 Ibn al-ʿArabī frequently cites this saying in his *al-Futūḥāt al-makkiyya*. See Chittick, *The Sufi Path of Knowledge*, 67.

CHAPTER 17

Bow

Another common motif on *stećci* and *nišani* is the bow. The bow's meanings centre on certain common aspects: a bow implies arrows; its use requires two hands; it is kept tense.

We are peripheral, our heart central. From our individual periphery, the universe seems infinitely vast, the heart infinitely small. Turning to ourselves, we must reverse this illusion, recognizing the signs of the minute as principle in cosmic immensity. Taking the bow in our left hand to nock, draw and loose an arrow, it denotes our peripheral status in constant tension, aspiring to every horizon. Nocking, drawing and loosing the arrow begin in the infinite smallness of the heart, in a turn from the world to the self, where the principle of all things dwells, the truth of their creation, where the One decides, Who says of every throw: "And when thou threwest, it was not thyself that threw, but God threw."[1] This is true of every act of self-realization in the heart to which the Spirit of Truth bears the Recitation.

The heart is perfect centre, infinite in compass, one: "The hearts of all the children of Adam are like a single heart between two fingers of the All-merciful. He turns it wherever He desires."[2]

On the margin, oblivious of His mansion in the heart, we mistake signs for the Signified. We trace the arrow's trajectory from the bow string, not the heart. But the perfect man knows the self is peripheral to the "single heart" and that the arrows of the "two bows" come to rest in the single heart as principle of all things. Speaking as the manifestation of life, will, power, knowledge, speech, hearing and sight in the form of his "immense nature," God said through the Praised:

> In the name of God, the Merciful, the Ever-merciful. By the Star when it plunges, your comrade is not astray, neither errs, nor speaks he out of caprice. This is naught but a revelation revealed, taught him by one terrible in power, very strong; he stood poised, being on the higher horizon, then drew near and suspended hung, two bows'-length away, or nearer,

1 *Qur'an*, 8:17.

2 Muslim, 4:1397.

 | DOI 10.1163/9789004279407_074

> then revealed to his servant that he revealed. His heart lies not of what he saw; what, will you dispute with him what he sees?[3]

Seeing thus – first on the higher horizon and then "two bows'-length away, or nearer" – denotes a reversal: the horizons exist for the heart and what it receives. Descent makes possible ascent as one mode of seeing confirms the other: "Indeed, he saw him another time by the Lote-Tree of the Boundary nigh which is the Garden of the Refuge, when there covered the Lote-Tree that which covered; his eye swerved not, nor swept astray. Indeed, he saw one of the greatest signs of his Lord."[4]

The Lote-Tree of the Boundary is a sign that requires this about-turn. Its branches and leaves are in the sixth and seventh heavens, its roots beyond them.[5] Its crown and fruit attest to Mystery as the higher level of what is revealed, the Ineffable as treasury of what has been uttered. Drawing the bow and loosing the arrow direct the archer to the far horizon, but the action then turns him towards the heart into which the Holy Spirit descends. Ascending from the depths along the path of descent to the height, our view is the same. The word is manifest in deed, the deed in word. The self contains whatever is in the world and we find the heart at the centre of all things, as supreme sign of the One.

Postscript

The sacred teachings revealed by God through the Praised have three main elements: (1) everything is from God; (2) everything is provided for by God; and (3) everything returns to God: "To Him shall you return, all together – God's promise, in truth. He originates creation, then He brings it back again, that He may recompense those who believe and do deeds of righteousness, justly."[6]

That all things come from and return to God is denoted by the two bows, the descending arc of differentiation and the ascending arc of reintegration. Given free will, we can return to God before time, following His irrevocable command. Dying before we die, we return willingly to Unity. God bestows life and death, but death does not encompass Him. We may say, death is ours, but life a gift from the Living. Accepting death, we understand the gift of life and

---

3 *Qur'an*, 53:1–12.

4 Ibid., 53:13–18.

5 See Muslim, 1:110.

6 *Qur'an*, 10:4.

cleave to the Giver. We desire death that we may be recipients of life from the Living. Desiring death before death is to put an end to illusion in the self and prepare to receive everything from God and stand before Him. The Praised is the best example of this Return. God raised him from the depths to most beautiful rectitude: "He was two-bow's length away, or closer."[7] Sachiko Murata has written of this:

> To begin with, the word "bow" (*qaws*), like Latin *arcus*, also means "arc" of a circle; hence two bows can refer to two arcs making up a circle. [. . .] In various Sufi readings, the germs of which long predate Ibn al-ʿArabi, the two arcs are the Origin and the Return. By ascending to God, the prophet completed the circle of creation. By going back to God voluntarily, he "died before he died," rejoined the Origin, and realized the furthest goal of the creative process. After this encounter with God, he returned to his community to guide them on the path, like a seasoned mountain climber.[8]

The Praised is God's first manifestation as All-praised, the sum of all the potentialities of existence. They are dispersed in the descending arc into existence, until he was born in the Valley by the first house. From there, he ascended to Unity, but again returned to the depths. He is our finest example in the universal return of the outward to the Inward, of the secondary to the First. The Recitation, which he received, is the Book of God and His deeds, of His creation of the world, appointing us as His chosen stewards and sending prophets to guide us on the path of return. The "two bows" denote our goal: by following the Praised, we recognize the descending arc and so our place in the world; by knowing our origin and confessing the Praised's ascent we know the second arc, the upright path from multiplicity to first and last Unity, the second house. The two houses manifest through the Praised as signs of beginning and end, the sole principle of all things.

The first arc corresponds to descent, the fall to the Valley, the second our ascent from it to the Mount as the "sublime height." Reaching the bottom of the Valley is dispersal of Unity in multiplicity, the summit of the Mount is multiplicity's reintegration in Unity. Descent is exteriorization of the inner, ascent the interiorization of the outer.

The boundary between inner and outer, seen and unseen, is the concomitant of the heart, which belongs to the invisible, inner realm of Spirit and

---

7 Ibid., 53:9.

8 Murata, Chittick and Weiming, *The Sage Learning of Liu Zhi*, 36.

Intellect. The world of things derives from the unseen and contains signs of the spiritual to mark our descent, exteriorization and multiplication. Ascent, integration and interiorization are the path of return.

When existence is regarded in this manner, the purpose of our life is to ascend after the course of the heavens and earth, to bond with the invisible principles that underwrite the visible world. Beginning and end meet in this purpose and the heart is awakened, as in the prophets and apostles, and is bestowed upon the good.

CHAPTER 18

Solomon's Seal

Spirit, Intellect and Heart are key concepts in every tradition. In traditional ontology, their meaning is clear and crucial for any account of the levels of Being. By tradition, we mean the transmission of knowledge between individuals across the generations, but not knowledge that begins literally with a certain individual in history. Its source is not human; it comes from "on high" in the human self, which the first recipient conveys in breath and voice to others as the revelation of the Principle. This breath and voice are preserved in transmission, linking us with the first recipient and, through him, the supra-individual, impersonal Source. The chain of transmission is a living tradition with spiritual impact as long as its conditions and rules for the individual recipient and its structure are preserved.

Intellect is foremost in creation. It contains all the possible manifestations in multiplicity: it is the Treasury of all things. God's will to be known opened the Treasury so that its possibilities could be sent down into the universe, while still clearly denoting their Principle. Whatever is sent down remains always connected with the Principle that unites them in order and harmony.

When Intellect manifests its archetypes in the world of signs, it is the revelation of Being in Its worlds – a revelation in which descent and differentiation take place. Every sign manifests its archetype in the Treasury, remaining connected with it, so that whoever understands it can return to that initial entity.

The aspect of Intellect that bears the Word and life is the Holy Spirit. It is wholly subject to God's will, its knowledge, descent and ascent the deepest content of the order of all existence. It is limited by nothing, by no level of existence, by no will but His.

Existence as a whole gathers in the self, focused on the Intellect as the Treasury of all possibilities. All the signs thus return to their original union in the Treasury. What each manifestation was at the beginning, so is it at the end. The Spirit descends from the Treasury, or the centre of the self, to give the signs their clear meaning. Its descent connects the self with its centre or Treasury. The heart is that supra-individual centre through which the self is connected to Intellect. It thus encompasses all of existence. Its knowledge is not contingent on anything external. In it, knower, knowledge and known are one. The corporeal heart is but the sign of that centre of the self.

As the centre of all Being's manifestations, the heart may be represented as an inverted triangle, a vessel, into which God descends through the Holy Spirit.

 | DOI 10.1163/9789004279407_075

The Praised returns to God what he has received from Him, represented as the inverted triangle. Perfect reception and bestowal are symbolized by two interlocked triangles, forming the symbol known as the Seal of Solomon or the Star of David,[1] a Sacred symbol showing that what was received is what is returned. The entire chain of transmission of what God reveals to the prophet is designated by the Seal of Solomon.

The downward-pointing triangle denotes reception, or the Spirit God breathes into us. With it, as the centre of the self it illumines, we are upon the height, denoted by the upward-pointing triangle. What is dispersed in the outer horizons is gathered in the heart, with external and dispersed related to internal and concentrated as multiplicity is to Unity. Unity is the principle of what exists, the source and confluence of multiplicity.

The two interlocking triangles symbolize Mount and Valley, the Mount of our original station, before our transgression and fall, the Valley of our postlapsarian condition. The height and the depths are the two extreme states of the self. We recall the Height and our lost condition with sorrow, reminded of it by the signs around us, still immaculate after their descent. They remind us despite our inner self's obscuration in the depths, for nothing at any level of Being can stand against the original light and Spirit. We desire return, which is to strip the veils from the heart or pass through the narrow door in the self to the lost domain of Being, to emerge from darkness into light.

The Mount, visible outside, contains the cave inside, symbolizing the centre or heart of the world. To find ourselves in that centre, we must negotiate the labyrinth of the world to be reborn in the heart. Illusion transforms to reality, what we took for light becomes its sign, and the mystery is revealed in the dark. The illusion that we acquire our knowledge from outside or depend on the external world or our teachers becomes awareness of the heart as where we have direct contact with Intellect, where all things are encompassed. The signs in the world act as reminders of the truth in the heart, for God said in a sacred tradition: "My heaven and My earth encompass Me not, but the heart of my faithful servant does encompass Me."[2]

---

1 Solomon's seal is found in Bosnian churches and mosques, which may puzzle the uninitiated for whom this symbol of perennial presence has come to be regarded as "Jewish." It is also common on Bosnian Muslim artefacts, like tombstones, manuscripts, inscriptions, furniture, and silver lockets or *enamluks* "worn close to the heart." See Radojković, *Filakteriji, enamluci, pripojasnice*, 10.

2 This tradition is often quoted in Sufi texts and appears in al-Ghazālī's *Iḥyāʾ ʿulūm al-dīn*. See Chittick, *The Sufi Path of Knowledge*, 107.

The Mount seems great, the cave small, the former like the outer horizons, the latter like the centre, infinitesimal but crucial. Everything begins in the centre to return to it; it lacks nothing and we find everything within it. There is nothing above or beyond, so that the path of return runs from the depths of multiplicity to the height of Unity. When we see Unity in multiplicity, we transcend duality, so that He is First and Last, Out and In.[3]

In almost every initiatory rite, the cave symbolizes entry into interiority, into a higher world. The labyrinth symbolizes passage through the world to ascend, the experiences we must undergo to distinguish real from unreal. The heart is the centre just beyond our reach since the Fall, on the far side of the boundary: it is the narrow passage between higher and lower worlds, between the two seas God tells us of in the Recitation: "And it is He who let forth the two seas, this one sweet, grateful to taste, and this salt, bitter to the tongue, and He set between them a barrier, and a ban forbidden."[4]

The Arabic word for the heart (*qalb*) derives from a root meaning to turn around or invert. The heart is a place of turning, in which every image we construct is inverted. The meaning of the signs is translated from level to level of existence through the overturning of our notions of what knowing connects us with. This corresponds to transition to a higher level of existence. This rebirth at a higher level is initiation. There is no passage through the dark world of the self through the will and strength of the self alone.

The Seal of Solomon describes the condition of a self inscribed by witness to the Praised, the "first of the people of peace." His name is a diminutive derived from the root s-l-m, to be at peace. The diminutive form underlines the qualities of receiving and giving peace through All-peaceful God. The principle of this thread through existence is the First of the people of peace. Only when this principle, which cannot be confined by measure, is visible in all that is great, is beauty manifest as the presence of the Eternal in the finite.

---

3 See *Qur'an*, 57:3.

4 *Qur'an*, 25:53.

CHAPTER 19

Vessel and Letter

Bowl-like hollows were often carved into *stećci* and *nišani*, collecting rainwater their heirs regard as blessed. These hollows may denote the heart, the vessel that maintains the lifeblood. ʿAli ibn Abi Talib said: "These hearts are vessels. The best of them is that which preserves."[1]

Guénon called the heart "the centre of the integral being and consequently the organ to which the 'sense of eternity' must be directly attached."[2] The physical heart is the perfect symbol of the centre, the One manifest in the many. Blood, the stuff of life, flows from it through the arteries to every part of the body and back through the veins to the centre, revealed as its principle – in and out, first and last, source and confluence.

In their rites, the people of peace turn with their entire being towards an external centre, affirming that the many manifest Unity. They are returning to the principle of Peace, moving symbolically towards It, becoming aware of their place on and movement along the margin, as they turn their heads right and left, following the motions of the ritual prayer. This is our willing return to God in peace. All things return to find peace in God.[3]

The heart and the book are indivisible. The dispersed is united in the heart, its confluence and source. God said of the heart of the Praised, the vessel He sent His Word down into: "Truly it is the revelation of the Lord of all Being, brought down by the Spirit of the Truth upon thy heart, that thou mayest be one of the warners, in a clear, Arabic tongue."[4]

At the Last Supper – which for the people of peace means Jesus' prophecy of the Praised as Paraclete – Jesus raised his cup to denote his own heart and blood, but also meant the Word God sent down into the heart of the Praised, making him a mercy to all beings,[5] the best example,[6] a mighty morality,[7] and our supreme potential, after the formula God revealed to him: "Say: 'If you love

1 *Nahj al-Balāgha*, 521.
2 Guénon, *Fundamental Symbols*, 18.
3 See *Qur'an*, 3:83.
4 *Qur'an*, 26:192–95.
5 See *Qur'an*, 21:107.
6 Ibid., 33:21.
7 Ibid., 68:4.

 | DOI 10.1163/9789004279407_076

God, follow me, and God will love you, and forgive you your sins; God is All-forgiving, Ever-merciful.' "[8]

At that supper, Jesus raised his cup to his disciples, saying: "Drink ye all of it; For this is my blood of the new testament, which is shed for many for the remission of sins."[9] The chalice symbolized the heart,[10] the wine blood. The heart also stands for the centre all things come from and return to. Blood symbolizes the sacred teachings of the Recitation. The key question for us is access to the Recitation as the source of immortality.

The blood of Mary's Son was presented to the world as the prophecy and promise of a Paraclete – the Holy Spirit, the Spirit of Truth to speak in God's name and confess him as the Anointed, as God's Word. This cannot be divorced from the flow and collection of his blood, summed up in his prophecy: "And when Jesus son of Mary said: 'Children of Israel, I am indeed the apostle of God to you, confirming the Torah that is before me, and giving good tidings of an apostle who shall come after me, whose name shall be the Most Praised.' "[11]

Two aspects of every sacred tradition can be seen in Jesus' prophecy of the Paraclete to his chosen disciples. The first relates to the tightly-knit group of initiates and their role in defending the sacred centre which contains the perennial wisdom of our perennial debt to God. The second is that in its esoteric manifestations, every sacred tradition is but an antechamber to the sacred centre, the source and refuge of all multiplicity. The world always has such a centre, however ignorant we are of it or unable to access it.

The heart of the Praised is a pure vessel, containing Unity. The Word is manifest to Unity through it. In the Recitation, Jesus, son of Mary, is His Word,[12] one of the countless manifestations of His eternal Word, sent down into the heart of the Praised. The heart of the Praised is the abode of the Anointed, to which he returns to remind us, through the Praised, of beginning and end, in and out.

Sending down or descent and raising up or ascent constitute the nature of the existence of all things in the world and self, a sign denoting the Principle everything comes from and returns to. The letter and the vessel are the signs of receiving what was sent down.

Two signs in existence are inextricably linked to the vessel and the letter; rain and the revelation, both of which God sends down as His mercy. Of the connection between them, Martin Lings has said:

8 *Qur'an*, 3:31.

9 *Matthew*, 26:27–28.

10 A vase or chalice is the Egyptian hieroglyph for the heart.

11 *Qur'an*, 61:6.

12 See *Qur'an*, 3:45 and 4:171.

So close is the connection of ideas that rain might even be said to be an integral part of the Revelation which it prolongs, as it were, in order that by penetrating the material world the Divine Mercy may reach the uttermost confines of creation; and to perform the rite of ablution is to identify oneself, in the world of matter, with this wave of Mercy, and to return with it as it ebbs back towards the Principle, for purification is a return to our origins.[13]

---

13 Lings, *Symbol and Archetype*, 67.

PART 3

Becca and Sion, Muhammad and Mary

• •

CHAPTER 1

The Covenant

We are inextricably related to ourselves, others, the world and God, no matter where we are. Our levels of awareness may differ, as sensory or conceptual. We have two roles simultaneously, receiver and giver, and are never confined to the sensory level. It is our reflections that suggest we are one, in a single time and place, where we receive all things in order to make the One manifest. Aware that all we have God has given us, we can become givers by returning what He has entrusted us with in the relationship between two wills, ours as granted and His as primal.

God as Giver and we as receivers are not two. We and He manifest His unity in an illusion of duality. God never ceases confessing Himself as Unity through manifest creation. Humanity and the universe are two images of the One nothing can be added to or taken away from.

Our covenant with God takes various forms. The first covenant was made in pre-existence and forms our centre and nature. It governs how our freedom will fare in the reckoning on the Day of Resurrection, as God told the Praised in the Recitation:

> And when thy Lord took from the Children of Adam, from their loins, their seed, and made them testify touching themselves: "Am I not your Lord?" They said: "Yes, we testify!" – lest you should say on the Day of Resurrection: "As for us, we were heedless of this." Or lest you say: "Our fathers were concealers aforetime, and we were seed after them. What, wilt Thou then destroy us for the deeds of the vain-doers?"[1]

Under this covenant, we affirm our nature as sufficient for relation to God. Our return to Him depends on nothing external. The voluntary affirmation of our nature involves trust in, knowledge of and love for the Lord. This relationship places us in existence, between perfection and fall. Regarding it, God told the Praised: "We offered trust to the heavens and the earth and the mountains, but they refused to carry it and were afraid of it; and man carried it. Surely he is sinful, very foolish."[2]

---

1 *Qur'an*, 7:172–73.

2 Ibid., 33:72.

 | DOI 10.1163/9789004279407_077

Confessing God as Lord through confidence embraces two options: faithfulness and perfect service to the All-faithful or forgetting our initial testimony, turning from the Lord, and ceasing to be upright before Him as Existence. God remains ever-true to that covenant. His mercy encompasses all things, His call contingent on another covenant in pre-existence:

> And when God took compact with the prophets, "That I have given you of Book and Wisdom; then there shall come to you an apostle confirming what is with you – you shall believe in him, and you shall help him; do you agree?" He said, "And do you take My load on you on that condition?" They said, "We do agree." God said, "Bear witness so, and I shall be with you among the witnesses." Then whosoever turns his back after that – they are the ungodly.[3]

God's compact with His prophets involves us, as He sent every nation a prophet[4] to recall them to confession of and return to Him through the Praised. The Praised's role as light-giving lamp is governed by a covenant: "And when we took compact from the prophets, and from thee, and from Noah, and Abraham, Moses, and Jesus, Mary's son; We took from them a solemn compact, that He might question the truthful concerning their truthfulness."[5]

God's apostles are chosen to remind us of that original covenant and the trust we took on. Only in authentic perfection have we no need of example, the supreme potential in us all, the Praised, God's servant and apostle, whose first witness is Adam.

Adam is our common father. We all share his nature. The covenant he made with God, unmediated by precedent, involved awareness of the Lord, the Praised's perfection as our sublime potential, and return. Choosing free will and the covenant also entails transgression and violence, which is action out of ignorance.

God told the Praised: "And We made covenant with Adam before, but he forgot, and We found in him no constancy."[6] God's original covenant with Adam realizes our covenant in pre-existence: the Praised made manifest in Adam. When Adam broke his covenant, he lost this realization. To regain perfection, he had to confess God's unity and the Praised's apostolate. Like all other

---

3 Ibid., 3:81–82.

4 See *Qur'an*, 13:7.

5 *Qur'an*, 33:7–8.

6 Ibid., 20:115.

124,000 prophets, he agreed to the path of rediscovery of our nature. That is the third aspect of the covenant in pre-existence.

The Garden is a name for Adam's uprightness, dependant on obeying God's command: "Adam, dwell thou and thy wife, in the Garden, and eat thereof easefully where you desire; but draw not nigh this tree, lest you be evildoers."[7] Such was God's agreement with Adam.[8]

The tempter encouraged Adam and Eve to transgress the bounds set by the covenant.[9] This transgression led to the fall from the Garden on the height to the uttermost depths.[10] In his new state, Adam became aware of what he had lost and turned penitently to God,[11] Who forgave him and gave him the Word.[12]

Thus Adam sank to the depths, where he turned, in confession of God's unity and the Praised's apostolate, towards return to uprightness. Return is on the upright path, open to all of us, of which the prophets spoke. Adam built two houses as signs of ascent – one in the valley of Becca to mark the depths and the starting place of our return, the other on Mount Sion, to mark the heights and the goal of ascent.

God ordained the house at Becca as "an establishment for men,"[13] "a sanctuary for people."[14] The upright path, on which the Praised is our guide, leads from that house to the further one, the self that incites to evil to the self at peace, the barren Valley to the Garden of Bliss. God sends down the redemptive cord of the covenant, telling us: "And hold you fast to God's bond, together, and do not scatter; remember God's blessing upon you when you were enemies, and He brought your hearts together, so that by His blessing you became brothers."[15]

---

7 Ibid., 2:35.

8 See *Qur'an*, 20:115.

9 Ibid., 7:20–22 and 20:121.

10 Ibid., 2:36; 7:24–25; 20:123.

11 Ibid., 7:23.

12 Ibid., 2:37.

13 *Qur'an*, 5:97.

14 Ibid., 2:125.

15 Ibid., 3:103.

CHAPTER 2

Height and Depths

Our consciousness, or original enlightenment, entails two possibilities: disclosing or recollection and concealing or forgetting. Our indestructible core guards eternally expression of our covenant with God. Aware of that covenant, we can ascend to our immense nature on an internal scale from the darkness of the self's depths towards the Light's sublime height.

These extremes in the self are symbolized by the house on Becca valley floor and that on Mount Sion, the earth's surfaces and the heavens' expanses, and the self's suffering and satisfaction. Becoming aware of these extremes within, the horrors of sinking to the depths and the bliss of ascending to our original state, we increasingly find ourselves in our knowledge of that covenant.

The vision of the houses at Becca and Sion reveals two key signs – the Black Stone in the Kaʿba wall and the Golden Dome on Sion. The Black Stone denotes our condition at the depths, as the undiscovered centre of our covenant with God languishes in obscurity. The Dome denotes Intellect, God's light illuminating the heavens and the earth, and the Praised as its first recipient, a shining lamp. The Black Stone in the Kaʿba wall was originally white and light-giving,[1] a sign of the purity of the Garden, before Adam transgressed.

We can always access knowledge, ritual and virtue as our provisions for return to our intended state. Their forms may differ, but they always preserve our connection with our sublime potential. Independent of language, time or place, they provide us with the means to maintain our confession of no god but God and the Praised as His servant and apostle.

We can do nothing without God. Knowledge, ritual and virtue only reflect His attitude towards us, who are never cast beyond His mercy. They may be separated from God as their Revealer and so conceal Him and serve the veiled self in its failure to confess Unity, prophecy as recalling us to our original nature or return to God as how we redeem our outstanding debt under the covenant.

Denial of Unity, prophecy and return means our life, will, power, knowledge, speech, hearing and sight are under the power of obscuring poets and sorcerers. Their God is the order they belong to and they glorify its institutions and leaders as living temples and priests, instead of glorifying the All-high, as prophecy demands, in the temples that exist wherever we turn to God. When our goal is no longer indefinable, God, His revealed teachings, ritual and

1 Tirmidhī, 7:49.

 | DOI 10.1163/9789004279407_078

virtue are denied, under a self-serving order whose protagonists sink into satanic egoism.

The doctrine of return involves confessing no self but the Self and the Praised as His apostle. Return is in and through the self. The prophets, laws and universe itself support us in this. Everything else is finite, but not the Self. It transcends individuality. The individual self and ritual and virtue are stations, signs along the way, to help us transcend our limitations and receive spiritual influences in this limited world.

We all have our trials and tribulations. They help us see our condition as low, so that we aspire to rise above the boundaries of finitude. No trial in this world guarantees that we can. The key question becomes how to understand the tribulations we face as a response and aid in our determination to escape incarceration in individuality.

Can we find a way to transcend the bounds of individuality alone? Are our tribulations sufficient to break us out of it? These questions are our very core, the answers to them divisible into a multitude of human responses and one that comes from God. Leaving individuality leads to the supra-individual impersonal principle, His Self. If anything else provides the answer, it is at best speculation, based on ignorance, and so violence that exacerbates suffering.

Given the tribulations of this world, as they have affected various cultural traditions in modernity, including Bosnia, if we want to consider initiation, which brings transcendence of the self's limits, we must do so amongst the ruins of the traditional life, as buried under the rubble of the modern, mundane, and profane. Traditional life is a symbol of what lies beyond or transcends the self. Initiation allows us to cross into that world beyond.

To liberate themselves from the distortions of our modern language and try to perceive the self's position within the two horizons, of the modern it is plunged into and of the traditional it seeks to find itself in, speakers must recognize the flaw in their images of "historical events," due to excluding the living self from them.

The *stećci* seem the clearest representation of Bosnia, as something whose essence expresses indestructible spirituality and perennial potential. They are found everywhere in the country, grouped or isolated. They testify to the right of free burial and the peace of the grave, triumphant over any effort to establish authority over the dead and their graves.

In a dispute between the Church of Rome and the Christians of the Bosnian Church, dating from 1203, Bosnian leaders agreed to bury their dead only in places designated for the purpose.[2] At much the same time, Pope Innocent

2 "Abjuracija bosanskih 'krstjana', Bilino polje uz rijeku Bosnu 8. travnja 1203." In: Šanjek, *Bosansko-humski krstjani u povijesnim vrlima (13–15. st)*, 81.

III accused the Templars of burying sinners and excommunicates in cemeteries as though they had the same rights as the Catholic faithful.[3] Both these documents also condemn the practice of receiving at home those the ecclesiastical authorities consider unfit. This view supposes the path to God closed to those not subject to the Church, whose authorities have the right to wage war against them "in the name of God." Most of the *stećci* date from a time when the Crusaders suffered defeat after defeat and developed a consequently hostile view of "Saracens," "Arabs," "Agarians" and "Turks," as summed up in a Second Crusade epic:

> God has brought before you his suit against the Turks and Saracens who have done him great despite. They have seized his fiefs, where God was first served and recognized as lord. God has ordained a tournament between Heaven and Hell, and send to all his friends who wish to defend him, that they fail him not.[4]

3 See Partner, *The Knights Templar and their Myth*, 30.

4 Quoted by Southern, *The Making of the Middle Ages*, 55, in Partner, 33.

CHAPTER 3

Initiation

Whatever its state or station, the self is an image of the Self, its knowledge of realization received from the Self in the confession of no self but the Self. Everything else supports this confession, a support we need as, despite being part of a whole no bounds can contain, alone we cannot mould a doctrine and ritual that fits our intelligence and can sustain us in tautegorical confession. Our individual will is needed for self-realization, prompted by initiation.[1] Doctrine and strict rite steer us towards a goal unattainable without their aid.

Religion assists our move out of havoc and disorientation, but cannot replace the will, any more than a call to remembrance or to waking does. Recognition of the individual will lies at the heart of religious doctrine and ritual.

If *dīn*, the debt, denotes four things: being-at-peace as the framework of the will, belief as that of Intellect, making beautiful as relating sincerely to the Lord and awareness of the Hour as irrefutable Reality – none of this can substitute for initiation. Even at the most developed level of individuality, we still run up against the boundary of this level of Being. Only breaking free of individuality allows us to speak of fully realizing our humanity. On this, Guénon has said,

---

1 The noun *initium* means "entry" or "beginning." One of the meanings of initiation is liberation from hypocrisy. In the Muslim intellectual tradition, hypocrisy (*nifāq*) means confessing being-at-peace without inner conviction and it is the worst form of dissimulation. Its opposite is sincerity (*ikhlāṣ*), the supreme virtue. To be sincere is to act in conformity with one's confession of Unity, for God alone. Hypocrisy is punished by the worst depth of hell, while the Muslim tradition refers often to sincere believers whose outward conduct conceals their sincere obedience to God, as their only purpose and reason. Many wish to be censured (*malāma*) to protect themselves from being tempted to hypocrisy or other iniquities. The "people of blame" are those who belong wholly to "being-at-peace," but act unacceptably in public to avoid the admiration of others. "Being-at-peace" is how they relate to Peace. The All-peaceful is One and we relate to Him through being-at-peace. Everything else can be a source of non-peace and of opposition to Him. The people of peace thus divorce themselves entirely from any measure not from God, as First and Last. They see themselves before Him. Ibn al-ʿArabī regards "the people of blame" (*malāmiyya*) as our supreme degree, calling them the Verifiers. See Chittick, *The Sufi Path of Knowledge*, 372ff; and Murata, Chittik and Weiming, *The Sage Learning of Liu Zhi*, 481 n5. The good folk or saints of the Bosnian spiritual tradition generally have *malāmī* characteristics. They keep apart and care little for popular opinion. Unusual and rare, their imprint on folk memory is deep.

 | DOI 10.1163/9789004279407_079

> For our present purposes it must suffice to emphasize that religion considers the human being exclusively in his state of individuality and does not aim to bring him beyond it but rather to assure him of the most favorable conditions in this state, whereas the essential aim of initiation is to go beyond the possibilities of this state and to effect a passage to the superior states, and even finally to lead the being beyond every conditioned state of whatever kind.[2]

In our unobscured pre-lapsarian state, we had access to higher levels of Being, as we were Its centre. Our incarnation corresponded to the lowest, while our capacity to span the levels let us pass through the doors of matter and the farthest heavens. The signs on the outer horizons are like doors and windows in the walls of other levels of being. In our original state, we could see or pass through them. After falling, the windows were shuttered, the doors closed. The signs remain in place, but we cannot look or pass through them without initiation.

Initiation's first condition is to see the signs, which are our only connection with higher levels of being. The alternative is to deny them, depriving ourselves of any possibility of transcending the bounds between levels of existence. God told the Praised: "Those that cry lies to Our signs and wax proud against them – the gates of heaven shall not be opened to them, nor shall they enter Paradise."[3]

Initiation means opening and passing through heaven's doors, so the self may discover its original state, reborn on the sublime heights it once possessed and lost, its initial nature realized and rediscovered as the centre of full being from which to ascend. This is the vista of initiation as a possibility requiring our individual will.

Individual will is necessary, but not sufficient. Initiation requires a traditional organization with connection with the Spirit and offering passage through the "narrow gate." Initiates are guided by their will to rebirth and capacity to receive what the initiatory organization, as a treasury of spiritual influence, gives them. Initiation is the essential transmission of knowledge to initiates open to this influence. What the initiate receives cannot be expressed in speech. It is not the ritual and symbolic forms deployed, which are there only to support connection with the Ineffable.

When traditional organizations meet and social circumstances mean that the exotericism of one provides a simpler framework for initiation, transition between them becomes possible. Doctrine and rite are translated into another

2 Guénon, *Perspectives on Initiation*, 20.

3 *Qur'an*, 7:40.

traditional language and forms altered. Participants are aware of preserving the "old" aspects of their affiliation, along with certain of the older forms. This can lead historians to suspect syncretism.[4]

If syncretism means elements of differing origin are introduced from outside without unifying principle, the many aspects of Muslim heritage in Bosnia seemingly adopted from Christianity offer no evidence of it. They speak to the transcendent source of both traditions, their Bosnian manifestations as displaying the same esoteric essence and the intelligibility of their linguistic, semantic and symbol systems in reference to a single centre.

Various traditional paths may lead to the same goal, their similarities in no way undermining their distinctiveness or independence. If two traditional organizations unite, it is from within, affirming the identity of their connection with Spirit. No external power can affect this inner supra-individual principle of traditional organization. The exoteric content of the traditional structure may be destroyed, but the heart remains untouched.

Every traditional path to the principle has a definite historical beginning and source; but the source of the source is beyond history. However many such historical beginnings there may be, their celestial source is one. To transition from one traditional path to another is to acknowledge the transcendent Unity of all the different traditions.

Only at the centre do the paths merge. But the centre does not properly belong to us. The universal individual is its first manifestation, its first illumination, the light shed on all the paths down the slopes of existence. We may know it because of a particular historical figure, but the source of that knowledge remains supra-individual, for all that. Initiation must have a "non-human" source, as it introduces the individual to a domain beyond individual potential. The rite of induction, like every traditional symbol, has no author or simply human origin. Initiands receive the good transmitted to them in initiation by the initiator. Recipient and transmitter are links in a chain whose beginning is above and beyond humanity.

---

4 What the modern worldview considers syncretism is impossible in a sacred tradition. Only plenitude may be the source of tradition, so that its teachings and rites are translated from spatial and temporal finitude to supra-individual qualities. The identity of symbols, myths and rites in different traditions does not mean they have been borrowed or compounded. All traditions have one source, so that they can be mutually translated. Their forms in space and time may vary, but they are not bound to two truths. Their source has no "other." The orthodoxy of tradition guarantees our response to God's call to love Him with all our hearts, all our souls, all our minds and all our strength. This differentiation into heart, soul, mind and strength points to the all-encompassing nature of tradition, which requires a link with Unity.

Receiving and transmitting spiritual influence shifts the initiand's will from individuality to conformity with the Will. Being-at-peace links everything in the world with the Will. Our ability to oppose the Will alters nothing in the world order. It only deepens the darkness in the individual self. The self's opposition to the Will distorts, so that the world and its contents appear disordered, but this is just illusion, caused by the self's state.

Initiation frees the self from illusion and disfigurement, putting it in proper relations with its own centre. The things of the world and self reveal themselves in proper order. Such initiation requires only the will of the initiate, the ritual, and symbols. Neither ritual nor symbols should be previously unknown to the initiands. Initiation then "brings them to life," giving them position and meaning impossible from any other perspective. The master knows them as such, from his own initiation. What seemed before to be disorder and dispersal, inanimate and enigmatic remnants, acquire their proper place within the horizons of the self's new state. The initiates come to know the reasons for the laughter and tears of those they see. Before initiation, they did not know, and those faces seemed painfully distorted. They can now read the marks on graves and all around. What they have received through the breath and voice of the initiator gives every perspective, every reading, new meaning, now that nothing lacks connection with the Principle.

The profane exists only in the understanding of those whose inner self is deformed, separated by a veil from its centre. The profane view cannot understand the condition of initiates or their induction beyond the veil. In studying them, ordinary historians always fail. No individual established the initiatory structure, which is simply "incomprehensible" from a profane perspective.

The Praised and the Anointed are closer to each other than to any other in either world, which suggests the initiatory chain from the Anointed must link, directly and indirectly, with the Praised, to preserve its validity. The Praised, as apostle, is the first and last of the prophets, who all swore him fealty in pre-existence, and is present, directly or indirectly, in every chain of transmission that passes through them to the supra-individual source.

CHAPTER 4

Laughter and Tears

The individual self is informed by its relation to the supra-individual Self, Which needs nothing external and encompasses Its manifestations, but is encompassed by none.

The real in the self reflects the Self, however unconsciously, hazily or obscurely. The finite self's purpose lies in infinity and eternity and emergence from finite individuality. Emergence is realization in the Self. The Praised's "mighty morality" or "immense nature"[1] is not just his treatment of others, it is that his nature realizes our sublime potential and original creation in His image. According to William Chittick,

> Qualities such as generosity, justice, kindness, benevolence, piety, patience, gratitude, and every other moral virtue are nothing extraneous or superadded to the human condition. On the contrary, they define the human condition in an ontological sense. Only by actualizing such qualities does one participate in the fullness of existence and show forth the qualities of Being.[2]

Our inner self and nature encompass realization of the names. God's most beautiful names in the self help us attain our key potential, the beautiful as return to God in full witness of no self but the Self. The apostle is that potential, as the Praised in and beyond history, the seal of every reminder of that potential. The Praised said: "I was sent to complete the beautiful character traits."[3] "Among the best of you is the most beautiful in character traits."[4]

We are made in God's image.[5] Realizing the self means discovering His names in that image, for only they, manifest in duality, make full humanity possible, as the apostle's told the people: "You should be characterized by the characteristics of God most high."[6]

---

1 See *Qur'an*, 68:4.

2 Chittick, *The Sufi Path of Knowledge*, 21.

3 Malik, 438.

4 Bukhārī, 4:491.

5 Muslim, 4:1378. See Gimaret, *Dieu à l'image de l'homme: les anthropomorphismes de la sunna et leur interprétation par les théologiens*, 128–135.

6 Ghazālī, *The ninety-nine beautiful names of God*, 149.

 | DOI 10.1163/9789004279407_080

The Praised is our perfected nature's best example, evident in all he did and did not do, said and did not say, his laughter and tears. Laughter relates laugher and laughed about; tears weeper and wept over. The Praised laughed at times and wept at others, so we must ask how his self's states, as the mightiest morality, reflect God's names and his own human perfection.

His laughter and tears, like everything else that manifested him, confirm his mighty morality and his being first of the people of peace, since "it is He who makes to laugh, and that makes to weep, and that it is He who makes to die, and that makes to live."[7] Laughter and tears, death and life are dualities in which Unity manifests. What exists is in pairs. Only the One those pairs manifest is One and Only, Incomparable, like nothing.

The Praised's laughter and tears manifest his witness to Unity. There are other kinds. Following the Praised, ours link us to our original nature and God. When the self is cut off from confession of no self but the Self, it laughs, when it should weep, weeps, when laugh. Laughter and tears divert us from Unity, as we distort our nature, reviling what it confesses.

The Praised's morality is the Recitation, the Word God sent down into his heart. How we approach it, as informing his nature, conditions our discovery of the self's sublime and original potential. As God asked us: "Do you then marvel at this discourse, and do you laugh, and do you not weep, while you make merry?"[8] Of the difference between witnesses to Unity and its deniers, He said: "Behold, the sinners were laughing at the believers, when they passed them by winking at one another, and when they returned to their people they returned blithely, and when they saw them they said: 'Lo, these men are astray!' "[9]

Deeds out of ignorance produce sin and violence. A distorted self, divorced from the Principle, comes to enjoy suffering, finding pain in joy, reversing the natural order. The Praised said: "O people of the Praised, by God, if you knew what I know, you would weep much and laugh little."[10] His knowledge is the perfect stance of one with received knowledge, so that all he knows manifests God as Knowing. This knowledge is the same as being and cannot be expressed. We can be initiated into it, but it is never independent of the Self for Which the self left individuality and individual knowledge. The Praised's laughter and tears manifest his nature in humility, generosity and beauty.

His followers' laughter and tears mean something other than of those whose perspective is unlinked to the Principle. The Praised said who remembers God in solitude and confesses it with tears will have a place in the shade on

---

7 *Qur'an*, 53:43–44.

8 Ibid., 53:59–61.

9 Ibid., 83:29–32.

10 Muslim, 2:427.

Resurrection Day,[11] their faces shining with joyous laughter before His face.[12] The Recitation recalls to their sublime potential those who hear, memorize, recite, transcribe or read it: "Those who were given the knowledge before it when it is recited to them, fall down upon their faces prostrating, and say: 'Glory be to our Lord! Our Lord's promise is performed.' And they fall down upon their faces weeping; and it increases them in humility."[13]

The Praised would weep, raising his hands in prayer for his community, after reciting parts of the Recitation.[14] He wept over his mother's grave[15] and his son Ibrahim's death, till tears wet his beard, telling his companion: "The eye sheds tears and the heart grieves, and we say only what pleases our Lord. O Ibrahim, we are grieved at parting from you!"[16]

God reveals Himself through the duality of laughter and tears. The Praised, being transported through the levels of existence, saw Adam with two groups in the first heaven; turning to those on his right, Adam would laugh, but to those on his left he would weep.[17] Laughter and tears in this world turn into the tears and laughter of heaven.

God also laughs, the Praised tells us.[18] He is One Who laughs and makes us laugh and weep. No tradition speaks of God weeping. The relevant names are the Living, Giver of Life, and Bringer of Death. God is the Living, Who never dies. All existence lies between life and death. Everything with life, receives it, but never owns life fully, and all will eventually be without what they have received. Only when all things have returned to God will death die.

So it is with laughter and tears. God laughs and does not weep, while the things of the world laugh and weep. God is light and gives light and dark.[19] The Recitation was sent to lead us from dark to light,[20] death to life, ignorance to knowledge, tears to laughter.[21] The states that bring weeping and tears are resolved only by return to the One Who laughs.

---

11 See Bukhārī, 8:322–23.

12 See *Qur'an*, 80:38–41.

13 *Qur'an*, 17:107–109.

14 See Muslim, 1:135.

15 Nasā'ī, 1:654.

16 Bukhārī, 2:219–20.

17 See Bukhārī, 1:212.

18 See Muslim, 1:124 and Bukhārī, 8:377.

19 See *Qur'an*, 6:1.

20 Ibid., 14:1.

21 For more on the role and meaning of the names and qualities relating to the duality of mercy-wrath, life-death, etc., see Murata, *The Tao of Islam: A Sourcebook on Gender Relationships in Islamic Thought*. See also: Chittick, "Weeping in Classical Sufism."

CHAPTER 5

The Androgynous Mihrab

Looking from baseness to the height, the self has levels, poles of disturbance and peace, fear and hope, hatred and love, ignorance and knowledge, ugliness and beauty, evil and good.

All existence manifests the Living God, Whom life and death reveal as Beloved, All-powerful, All-knowing, All-speaking, All-hearing and All-seeing. Nothing on any level fails to manifest Him as such. Being-at-peace and service, fully willed witness, are ways to receive and return all things to the Giver. The world would not truly manifest Him without us as image of the Self Whose Will none constrain. Our free will manifests the Beloved faithfully, since Manifester and manifestation are and are not the same. The Manifested is the only real in the manifest, while Manifested and manifestation are nonetheless in an illusion of duality.

In that illusion of duality, we are finite and undiscovered. We can receive all manifestation and liberate ourselves from it, to be what we know and know what we are, uniting knowledge and being, because our existence is a journey of three possibilities: ascent from multiplicity to Unity, descent into multiplicity, and stagnation on a level between.

On our way between impossible nullity and plenitude, our knowledge is ever little, but nonetheless always sufficient to reveal our orientation towards the Manifested, from darkness to Light, from duality to Unity. It determines our predisposition towards recognizing the received as a redemptive debt to Truth. The world is recognition of debt, with nothing in it not from God. In our plenitude, we are that indebtedness, debt our relationship to God. We can acknowledge or repudiate that debt. The world and self are the stage on which we do so. God sent down into the world and self the knowledge we need to return up the ladder to our original potential, the self's centre and realization of the confession of no self but the Self.

His knowledge always encompasses all, ours only when we realize ourselves confessing no self but the Self, after return to the One from Whom our descent into existence began. We are always in ignorance, albeit never total, for God encompasses all things with His knowledge.[1] Our every action is based on ignorance and can oppose His will. His mercy encompasses our every action, as He told the Praised. In action, we cannot escape the obscurity of ignorance

1 See *Qur'an*, 4:176.

 | DOI 10.1163/9789004279407_081

and violence. We are constantly faced with the Living God's wrath as well as His redemptive will, to which His Words bear witness: "My mercy surpasses My wrath."[2]

Placed in the duality of self and world, we face a constant choice of lower and higher, threat and promise. We avoid or attack the lower by moulding our will to His: "You did not throw when you threw, but God threw."[3] Attack and evasion are our desire as living, willing, powerful, knowing, speaking, hearing and seeing for the Living, Willing, Omnipotent, Omniscient, All-speaking, All-hearing and All-seeing. We turn towards our condition's core, our link with the One, called through the Praised: "Turn thy face towards the Inviolable Mosque; and wherever you are, turn your faces towards it."[4]

The Inviolable Mosque is a concentrated image of this world. Turning to its centre, we recognize the world as the All-merciful and All-beautiful's Face, before Which we are freed from the tensions that arouse our desire to attack and pass through or away from illusion. In that benign relaxation before the All-beautiful we recognize separation. There is no substitute for our Beloved. As lovers we desire union with the Beloved, want Him to know us, want to be as the Beloved knows us. But the Beloved is what He knows. In Him, knowledge and being are one. We stand as lovers, bowing before Him, annihilating whatever is not Him.

We return from annihilation into duality and remember Him yet more resolutely, for return is to and with Him always. The mosque of world and self is the stage of return, annihilation of duality on the path to the Beloved. Travelling as lovers, our goal is the Beloved, the One and Only, in Whom all divisions are resolved. The mihrab is the encounter of lover and Beloved, seeing Mary through the Praised, the Praised through Mary as two images of One. Unity is manifest in the mihrab and in the Praised and Mary, as first and last, inner and outer.

The mihrab is encounter with separation, becoming aware of and witness to and refusal to accept it. Masculinity is revealed in the absence of femininity, femininity in the absence of masculinity. Receiving and giving confirm Unity, which embraces all things, all individuality in a world of multiplicity. Multiplicity encompasses individuality, making Unity manifest.

This duality is in a perpetual state of imbalance, in search of a Unity it manifests. Unity is in the self's centre, as where Knowledge and Being's supreme identity is realized. Everything external to it is a descent into duality.

2 Bukhārī, 9:482.

3 *Qur'an*, 8:17.

4 Ibid., 2:144.

We cannot transcend duality or achieve realization by confessing "equal to Him is not anyone," except as a self confessing no self but the Self. Realization lies only in the heart that transcends individuality. The purpose of this confession lies in ourselves alone and it depends on nothing, sufficient as beginning and end, inner and outer. We carry within both witness and Witnessed and focus what is scattered throughout the universe. We are the general symbol of existence. At our centre, the heart's uncreated heart, we encompass all things with our knowledge, according to the tradition: "He who knows his self knows his Lord."

The Lord's knowledge has degrees we ascend through to Supreme Identity, the union of knower, knowing and Known. The degrees are countless. They are thresholds, limits of lesser or greater importance. To pass to the centre, where the world of individuality ends and that of supra-individuality begins, is to emerge from darkness to light, chaos to order. The world we leave behind us is darkness and chaos. The world we are coming to is light and order. The mosque is the key symbol of that world. Each achieved state of illumination and orderliness is but a degree we realize ourselves through. The mihrab is the summit, the barrier between levels of Being.

CHAPTER 6

Maternal

Mary is Jesus's mother and the Praised is maternal, as God says:

> My chastisement – I smite with it whom I will; and My mercy embraces all things, and I shall prescribe it for those who are mindful and pay alms, and those who indeed believe in Our signs, those who follow the maternal apostle, whom they find written down with them in the Torah and the Gospel, bidding them to honour, and forbidding them dishonour, making lawful for them the good things and making unlawful for them the corrupt things, and relieving them of their loads, and fetters that were upon them. Those who believe in him and succour him and help him, and follow the light that has been sent down with him – they are the prosperers.[1]

The apostle's maternal nature means the Book he recites is God's Word: "Even so We have sent down to thee the Book. Those to whom we have given the Book believe in it; and some of these believe in it; and none denies Our signs but the concealers. Not before this didst thou recite any Book, or inscribe it with thy right hand."[2]

Our perfection is one facet of our plenitude. This is why the Praised is a maternal apostle. Manifest in history as a man, he is plenitude that reconciles all opposites. This union is symbolized by the two sides of the mihrab – Mary and the Praised.

Initiation needs the Praised as our sublime potential which must be entered into. Initiates have immediate knowledge of the Praised. This knowledge cannot be lost or abandoned. All the signs in the horizons can be shown as clear manifestation of the Praised, in the world order and community, but not of them. The Praised is their supra-individual principle. Initiates participate in ritual with others, but their knowledge is not contingent on the external. They find joy in ritual, but the knowledge they lead with and have entered is their only full joy. They find proof in all things of their confession of no god but God and the Praised as His servant and apostle. Whatever they turn to or distance

1 *Qur'an*, 7:156–157.

2 Ibid., 29:47–48.

 | DOI 10.1163/9789004279407_082

themselves from, there is thirteen to fulfil the annunciation (see below). The Kaʿba and the Table from heaven are but two signs of this.

> God has appointed the Kaʿba, the holy house, as an establishment for men, and the holy month, the offering, and the necklaces – that, that you may know that God knows all that is in the heavens and in the earth, and that God has knowledge of everything.[3]
>
> Said Jesus son of Mary: "O God, our Lord, send down upon us a Table out of heaven, that shall be for us a festival, the first and last of us, and a sign from Thee. And provide for us; Thou art the best of providers."[4]

The Kaʿba symbolizes the place of "resurrection" and "rebirth," with twelve edges and six sides. The invisible centre is Thirteen. Seated at the Table are the Anointed and his twelve disciples, Thirteen in all. To draw attention to the Thirteenth as hidden and present, as at beginning and end, the Anointed notes one place is empty, unoccupied by the providence of heaven. The thirteenth is present, but unseen. In both Hebrew and Arabic, the thirteenth letter is "m," whose numerical value is forty. It is the first letter of the Arabic name of the Praised (*Muḥammad*) who was prophesied by Moses as the apostle God would raise among the Arabs, brethren of the Israelites. In the Arabic form of Jesus' prophecy, his name is *Aḥmad.*[5] That name's numerical value is fifty-three – thirteen plus forty. Both names derive from the verbal root *h-m-d,* which also gives the name the All-praised, one of the names of God.

Initiation, resurrection and rebirth are realization of the Praised as the most precious the human self can attain. The Anointed is closest to him of all people in this world and the next.

The bread and the wine are two signs, of the body, or outwardness, and of the heart, or inwardness. The Anointed told the twelve gathered around the Table of this reciprocity of outer and inner through him as Son of Man and Word of God:

> And as they were eating, Jesus took bread, and blessed it, and broke it, and gave it to the disciples, and said, "Take, eat; this is my body!" And he took the cup, and gave thanks, and gave it to them, saying, "Drink ye all of

---

3 Ibid., 5:97.

4 Ibid., 5:114.

5 See *Qur'an*, 61:6.

> it. For this is my blood of the new testament, which is shed for many for the remission of sins."[6]

With the Praised, whom the Anointed reveals to the twelve through himself, outer and inner are reunited in a new covenant, in his morality. Both blood and wine are prohibited or inviolable,[7] for the Anointed said so. It is only in the new assembly of the Kingdom of Heaven that wine reveals the Anointed and the Praised to be inwardly the same.[8]

---

6 *Matthew*, 26:26–28.

7 See *Qur'an*, 2:173 and 5:90.

8 See *Matthew*, 26:29 and *Qur'an*, 47:15.

CHAPTER 7

Supreme Sameness

In the mihrab, the theatre of war, the Praised faces the Virgin. Those God remembers and who remember Him are witnesses to this standing opposite, the Praised looking at the Virgin, she at him. Their love is perfect, the Praised seeing himself through her, she herself through him. Their duality manifests Unity and they confess no god but God. The purity of their gaze is perfect and sharing it they say "We." They are wholly realized, knowing themselves and their One Lord. With this knowledge, they have everything. The Praised received the Holy Spirit to bring forth as Recitation and Word. The Virgin received the Holy Spirit and brought forth the Word as the "son of man." The natures of the Praised and the Virgin are identical with what they bring forth as received.

What they received was sent down into their core, not introduced from outside. It is the eternal potential in the self, transcending individuality. Individuality is separated by the limits of contingency from eternal transcendence, sent down in one form, but manifest in two, first as the apostle, whose nature is the Recitation and Word, second as the Recitation or Word incarnate in the Anointed. Both the Praised and the Virgin received the Word sent down to Unity as a sanctuary, as perfect guides to establishing our sublime potential through return.

In their perfect purity, they are two, God the Third: two facets of One doctrine of ascent, to present which in the speech of the observer, the lowest possible discourse of it, we must return to how ritual relates to symbol. Ascent and initiation are normally taught through the things of this world, which form their symbolic underpinning. Fundamental symbols are translated into expressions, positions and movements, with doctrine presented as a way of life in the initiatory rite, as giving life to the symbol. This is the best way of comprehending it, as all forms of individuality manifest at this level of existence as acts. The rift between knower and known produces the other as an inanimate object the living person cannot attain.

These operations are just signs, their potential sent down and contingent: "Every soul must taste of death and We try you by evil and good by way of probation; and to Us you shall be brought back."[1] Every expression of doctrine through rite or living symbol is contingent. When such animation goes beyond

1 *Qur'an*, 21:35.

 | DOI 10.1163/9789004279407_083

mere speculation, doctrine penetrates the self's darkness to link margin and centre – margin as all of existence, the centre as its principle. The margin corresponds to rational capacity, the brain, the core to intellectual intuition, the heart. The heart goes with uncreated eternal spirit. Initiation is induction from multiplicity into essential Unity, resolving the split into brain and heart, as René Guénon observes:

> In the final analysis, if every method of initiation in its different phases presents a correspondence, whether with the individual human life or even with the entirety of terrestrial life, it is because the development of vital manifestation itself, particular or general, "microcosmic" or "macrocosmic," is effected according to a plan analogous to that which the initiate must inwardly accomplish in order to realize in himself the complete development of all the potentialities of his being.[2]

Realizing all being in the self means transcending the duality of Self and self. But the self is torn between its rational capacities and direct intuition or the "taste" of Unity. The self determined by individuality is framed by analytical reason as one of countless phenomena manifesting a given principle. Applying such reason exclusively from the perspective of individuality, we are stuck in this framework. But we must pass on from analytical reason, the individual capacity of the brain, to the supra-individual Intellect of the heart.

The passage from brain to heart means transcending the self for realization in the Self, arriving at the Heart as infinite, supra-individual knowledge in which the duality of knower and known vanishes. In this purity, Unity is manifest in the duality of Praised and Virgin, as expressed in the sacred tradition: "He who knows himself knows his Lord."[3] Attaining self-knowledge in the truth of the ineffable Essence, we know and have everything in and of ourselves. This is the unconditionality beyond which no potential lies.

These views, like most expressed in this book, could be taken as objective knowledge to be memorized and expressed. This is a real threat. If we relate to God through our debt, our receptivity involves knowledge as our link with the Giver. The heart contains all the Truth encompasses, but in the depth we are divorced from it. Our inner self seems a world of possibilities and in

---

2 Guénon, *Perspectives on Initiation*, 201–202.

3 Muslim intellectual tradition considers this tradition as beyond dispute, even if not found in the so-called canonical collections. It entered tradition in a way not subject to purely exoteric principles and is sound on the basis of revelation, even if not corroborated by a chain of transmission. See Chittick, *The Sufi Path of Knowledge*, 250–52.

multiplicity we find no certain path to the centre. All the knowledge we acquire is vain unless it orients and guides us towards the centre, the Known. Only in the Known is multiplicity unified, what we have received returned as our debt to the Giver.

Received knowledge, which comes from without, takes two opposite forms. Profane knowledge is human, within the bounds of the quantifiable. Its recipient must conserve it. The other form is reception with connection with the Known, Whose absolute nearness and absolute remoteness is unexhausted by any form that manifests Him. Receiving such knowledge, we must make it ours, allow it to permeate our being. Such knowledge conserves itself and its possessors. None can take it away, for it has no lord or owner in existence.

For initiates to follow the path, ascend and grow in knowledge, they must repeat for the rest of their lives certain expressions exactly as prescribed at given times, before and after ritual. From outside, this aspect can seem incomprehensible and unjustifiable, but it serves as proof that initiatory knowledge cannot be conveyed by rational means. It can be adumbrated, not objectified. All exoteric forms of initiatory knowledge simply reflect their esoteric essence.

As long as knowledge relates knower and Known, the self must act. We cannot commit to a contingent state. The Supreme Potential is alone worthy of such dedication. We are expected to subjugate and subordinate every condition of the self in ascent, the path which leads to the Supreme Potential. True action in this world requires us to have experience of the height. Only then do we know the world and its things from above, as shown to us on the Mount. Our knowledge is then independent of our individuality and we are the full expression of what we have received.

CHAPTER 8

The Shekhinah

Light is also illumination. Without light, no illumination. Illumination both is and is not light. It is, as it contains nothing but light. It is not, since light remains what it is. What then of the question: what is and what is not before the Light? "Is" and "is not" are simultaneous and outside time. Abraham Miguel Cardoso, the great disciple of Sabbatai Zevi, spoke of the diffraction of the ineffable principle and its first and every subsequent manifestation. Henry Corbin presents this diffraction as follows:

> The Torah speaks of the God of Israel, *Elohei Israel*, who is the creator of the world and who is the First Emanation of the hidden Principle (the *Absconditum*), the supreme Cause. This First Emanation possesses a twofold aspect or, rather, is composed of two hypostases (*partsufim*, in Greek *prosopon*): a masculine hypostasis and a feminine hypostasis known as the Shekhinah or Sophia. It is this First Emanation who, in its bi-unity, creates, reveals itself, and saves.[1]

The question of the Shekhinah leads to how word and thought relate. In traditional ontology, the word precedes. When God wants something, He says let it be and it is.[2] God, His will and His Word are one, but we can speak of them only with differentiation. They are one and three. Seen from below, as Greek philosophy held, the concept "Word" (*Logos*) underpins the idea of the fundamental equality of speech act and thought act.

The claim that a single uniform system of parts of speech can be regarded as the necessary factors of rational discourse and thought is based on this notion of equality. It has outlived its day. The equality of speech and thought has been brought into relation with higher levels of being. The notion of the Shekhinah seems to point unambiguously to a raising and sending down of the Word through and beyond thought. Every language is perfectly adapted to our needs in this "horizontal" world. Whether its content allows peace of mind to be sent down to our core is not dependent on its capacities or shortcomings. Cassirer says:

---

1 Corbin, "The Dramatic Element Common to the Gnostic Cosmogonies of Religions of the Book," 211.

2 See *Qur'an*, 36:82.

 | DOI 10.1163/9789004279407_084

> All forms of human speech are perfect in so far as they succeed in expressing human feelings and thoughts in clear and appropriate manner. The so-called primitive languages are as much in congruity with the conditions of primitive civilization and with the general tendency of the primitive mind as our own languages are with the ends of our refined and sophisticated culture.[3]

Differences in language are no obstacle to discourse, as the horizontal connections at one level or linguistic community do not exclude a vertical connection, descent of the Revelation or Shekhinah. God said that the variety of languages is His sign,[4] as He sent an apostle to every nation,[5] some mentioned in the Recitation, others not,[6] and that every apostle has revealed what he received from the Lord in his people's language.[7]

The *Lingua Adamica* is not necessarily one language. It could mean a different reciprocity between names and things.[8] It follows from witness to Unity as the principle of multiplicity that all existence and everything in it are symbols. All things are not, however, equal in symbolic significance. The remembrance sent down to people is made manifest as their potential to connect with the One symbolized through the symbols in world and self. This descent takes place in a given language, and so the language it occurs in must have the

3 Cassirer, *An Essay on Man*, 129.

4 See *Qur'an*, 30:22.

5 Ibid., 10:47.

6 Ibid., 40:78 and 4:164.

7 Ibid., 14:4. That God made His revelation through the apostles in the language of their peoples is crucial for understanding the diversity of peoples and languages as a way of manifesting Unity. No nation is without apostle, no language without revelation. While the Praised was sent as a mercy to the worlds and used Arabic, he is confessed in many other languages. This indicates that the revelation can be translated into every language. This translatability is a necessity affirming different languages as signs of One God. Whenever an individual confesses his apostolate, it entails accepting that he was sent to use his language. There cannot be two languages at the centre of being. The languages in a self that knows several are arrayed in sequence from the mother tongue, which is closest to the centre of being. Translation always comes back to that first language. Transcending individuality, on the path towards the supra-individual state of understanding the *lingua Adamica*, must pass through that mother tongue. To claim there cannot be two languages at the centre is the same as declaring the union of all languages at it. Those who attain the centre of being know all languages.

8 Many thinkers have addressed the question of the *lingua Adamica*, including Leibniz, in his *New Essays on Human Understanding*.

features of a symbolic world or order. Variety of languages means many forms, which determine the connection between self and world.

The knowledge sent down in that language encompasses the universe and every self, but comes from the horizons of neither macrocosmos nor microcosmos, nor from any collective or social consciousness nor that of any individual in history. The source of that knowledge is supra-individual. When we have it, it is received from another, who, though an apostle of God, is not its source properly understood. He too received it and passes it on.

The reception and transmission of higher order knowledge, knowledge independent of language or the order of things, has two levels. The first level is the world of the "lesser mysteries," the second that of the "greater mysteries."

Whatever the self's condition, its horizons are in order and form the margins of the centre from which it is governed by all the spatial and temporal arrays of that world. This centre is the "passage" of the universal axis through that level of manifestation of the One. The axis passes through every level of manifestation. Initiation into the "lesser mysteries" means discovering all things are connected with the centre. This is not speculative knowledge. It manifests in the self that possesses it as active involvement in an order whereby the centre "sees" itself as higher in principle than any way it is made manifest.

The centre is just contact with or manifestation of the "seventh ray," the "axis of the world," or the Spirit at a given level of existence. While everything in the world and selves of the initiates of the "lesser mysteries" manifests or reveals the centre, it remains concealed and inexpressible. The centre is merely passage to the "greater mysteries." Those initiated into the "lesser mysteries" are not necessarily initiated into the "greater mysteries." The reverse is not true, however. All those who have received or entered into the greater also embrace all lesser mysteries. The greater mysteries are priestly, the lesser imperial. For those who may find this confusing, it should be noted that the modern notions of "priest" and "emperor" are crude and offensive distortions of their original meanings in traditional teachings.

Differentiation into "lesser" and "greater mysteries" corresponds to the distinction between types of knowledge – "transmitted" and "intellectual knowledge." The former depends on memory, its source in the past, and we receive it from people we come into contact with. It includes language, grammar, law, history, published books and the witness of people who lived before. The other kind is intellectual, relying on nothing outside the self, neither memory nor principles. It is independent of observation or deduction, a vital awareness of the world and things in it as they are. We have this awareness in our original nature, our centre or heart. The true role of the Recitation is attainment of transformation and realization. True awakening occurs when the heart is cleansed of knowledge from without.

Connection with the centre of one level of existence reveals that multiplicity and motion are from Unity and Peace. Nothing in world or self escapes it. Only false knowledge, ignorance, offers this separation a stage. Peace is sent down into it, as it receives and passes on every mode of Peace's manifestation. The name of this descent is the Shekhinah. The world and self are in a constant state of tension, comings and goings, attacks and retreats, illumination and obscurity, pressure and release, closing and opening, anxiety and release. There is no escape from the battlefield of existence in what belongs to existence. Our refuge is on the battlefield, in the Shekhinah God sent down to open the self towards the lesser and greater mysteries. This unshakeable centre is present in even the severest tensions, the profoundest darkness and distress, and is simply the human heart.

> It is he who sent down the Shekhinah into the hearts of the believers, that they might add faith to their faith – to God belong the hosts of the heavens and the earth; God is All-knowing, All-wise.[9]
>
> When the two were in the Cave, when he said to his companion, "Sorrow not; surely God is with us." Then God sent down on him His Shekhinah, and confirmed him with legions you did not see; and He made the word of the concealers the lowest; and God's word is the uppermost; God is All-mighty, All-wise.[10]

As the first of these verses shows, the Shekhinah is received thanks to the faithful in their relationship to the All-faithful – a relationship of faith. The All-faithful encompasses all things with His knowledge and loves what He knows. This is the perfect identity of knowing and loving: God knows what He loves and loves what He knows. We know only in part, but love what we know thus. Our knowledge draws us to the Beloved, Whom we increasingly know and love. Nothing can satisfy us but full knowledge of the Beloved and union with the Known – this is the supreme potential at the centre of every self, to which we are guided by the perfect individual.

The second verse illustrates initiation into the greater mystery for one who has the lesser. The cave symbolizes the world and the tomb. The Praised was initiated into the greater mysteries by God through the Holy Spirit. He knows

---

9 *Qur'an*, 48:4.

10 Ibid., 9:40. For the Praised and his companion Abū Bakr in the cave, see Lings, *Muhammad*, 118–22.

all things in the world "from on high," from where he ascended from the depths to return again and express what he had received on that sublime height. He passes on what he received as knowledge from without, as the prerequisite for attaining the inner. In the dark of the cave, the Praised initiates his companion, uniting in his person the roles of priest and emperor. What he passes on to the initiate was received from God. The transmission does not begin here, as it is unlimited by time or space. The chain of transmission, of receiving and giving, always leads to the Praised, who was an apostle before any other and to whom they all swore fealty in pre-existence. "God was well pleased with the believers when they were swearing fealty to thee under the tree, and He knew what was in their hearts, so He sent down the Shekhinah upon them, and rewarded them with a nigh opening."[11]

---

11 *Qur'an*, 48:18.

CHAPTER 9

Baphomet

The Praised's names are given in a famous collection of blessings known as the *Dalāʾil al-khayrāt*: two hundred and one in all, beginning with *Muḥammad* and *Aḥmad*, mentioned by God in the Recitation.[1] Both these names of the apostle of God, first and last of the 124,000 prophets God sent all people, are echoed in the Western tradition in mysterious accounts of *Baphomet* and *Achamoth*.[2]

The house on Mount Sion is our first sign, denoting our original sublimity from which, after taking the forbidden fruit, we fell to the uttermost depths, whose sign is the house in Becca. Our fall into darkness does not take us beyond His mercy, which encompasses all things. It is manifest in the depths of existence as our capacity of recalling our original state of elevation. Remembering it, we discover the path of return and ascent within, on which the Praised is our guide. Through him, we regain our initial condition. He guides us, pure and a mercy to the worlds, from the uttermost depths to the sublime height. There is no condition from which he does not call us and guide us towards perfection.

The ascent is in the self, a possibility for us all. It is not some place outside the self, an event in time beyond the "now." We can ascend the scale of the self towards a more submissive, more enlightened, finer self, from any condition

1 The name *Muḥammad* features four times in the Recitation (3:144, 33:40, 47:2 and 48:29), the form *Aḥmad* once (61:6). These forms are unintelligible as "petrified," divorced from the semantic chains that link them with other forms deriving from the same root, *ḥ-m-d*. The word features in the confession of no god but God and the Praised as His apostle. This principle is one, its expression dual. God and the Praised are two and One. This distinction can be hard to understand, leading to historicizing discussions that cloak the Praised in a veil of imaginings. The dilemma centres on how an individual, subject to everything others also suffer, can be indivisible from the principle and be of concern to every one of us for all eternity. Our own failings are redescribed in terms of the Praised. Only by acknowledging our failings and insignificance in relation to the Principle can we orient ourselves towards our higher potentialities and so the full meaning of manifestation in the world and self. Discovery is for Unity. Discovering our higher potentialities as degrees on a scale leading to reality put the Praised at the centre of all things. Only with him can we strip away the veils obscuring our humanity.

2 For the origins of the myth of *Baphomet* in the writings of Joseph von Purgstall-Hammer, see Partner, *The Murdered Magicians*, 138–145. As Partner recounts, Hammer proposes the theory of an "androgynous deity called *Baphomet* or *Achamoth*, which had from early times been the patron of a phallic cult requiring orgies for its celebration" (Ibid., 141). See also Wasserstrom, *Religion after Religion*, 207–208, 337n30.

 | DOI 10.1163/9789004279407_085

of the self. We draw nearer the Praised. Whatever degree we have attained, the Praised remains higher. At the end of the path, the perfect marriage between Muhammad and Mary, the Praised and the Virgin, is realized. Their marriage at the end of things, in return to God as His servants, realizes the beginning in which Muhammad and Mary are perfect duality through which Unity is manifest. Muhammad/Mary as androgyne are the first manifestation of the One and Only.

The sequence of dreaming and waking stands against the sequence in the self ruled by forgetting, whose waking state seems more real than dreams, but is not. Dreaming is at a higher level than waking. Asleep, we are beyond the will, as the Praised said: "Whoever sees me in a dream then surely he has seen me, for the diverter cannot impersonate me."[3]

The waking state fulfils our desire for the Praised to be portrayed as the diverter. We cannot understand the Templar story without this desire. The Templars established their presence in the house on Mount Sion after the first Crusade. They could not escape its meaning or its having been shaped in the presence of the Praised. The Dome of the Rock and the Cave beneath are signs of Sion and Becca, the sublime height and the depths, while the Zamzam spring by the house at Becca is a sign of mercy barred to no level of existence that recalls the upright path.

The Templars preserved the place, demonstrating that Mary and the Messiah are another facet of Muhammad and the Mushaf, witness denoted by four letters, corresponding to four labial consonants, M M M M or B B B B.[4] Both part the closed lips, making them signs of unity in duality.

---

3 Bukhārī, 9:105–106.

4 The relationship between "b" and "m" is shown by the two names used in the *Qur'an* for the Holy valley where the Kaʿba stands in sign of our renewed covenant with God – *Becca* (3:96) and *Mecca* (48:24). The smallest *stećak* at Radimlja near Stolac bears the carved figure of a man in a doublet, his open right hand at head height, his left arm at his side. Below each arm the Cyrillic letter Б is repeated twice (see Benac, *Radimlja*, 8, and Truhelka, "Nekoliko hercegovačkih natpisa," 27). This letter looks like the Arabic *mim* (م), whose ordinal value is thirteen and numerical value forty, giving fifty-three in total, the numerical value of the Arabic name *Aḥmad*. The Muslims of the Stolac region have preserved a traditional explanation of the meaning of these four letters: the two below the right hand correspond to the names *Muḥammad-Mary*, those below the left to the names *Muṣḥaf-Messiah*. Muḥammad-Mary are the first pair of the divine revelation, recipient and giver, while the Muṣḥaf or Book and the Messiah are two ways in which the Word was manifest.

During the trial that led to the order being disbanded, its leaders burned at the stake, the Templars were accused of worshipping an idol, *Baphomet*.[5] Ever since, there have been attempts to understand, build upon and exploit the story. As our best example, Muhammad does not exist outside the self: whenever transmogrified into something outward, he becomes an idol as a "demented" "poet" or "sorcerer." This idol is a delusion of the waking self, impossible in any dream. *Baphomet* is a distortion of the name *Muḥammad*, which denotes the self's sublime potential, absolute beauty and goodness, mercy and enlightenment, happiness and satisfaction, joy and wisdom, fidelity and tranquillity, and everything else in which the self is fully realized. Seen in a dream, he is true, a truth that cannot be shown as falsehood, but falsehoods can present as truth.

The judges of the waking state hope to incarnate this sublime potential in an idol, to appeal to and use to counter our attempts at witness of no god but God and the Praised as His servant and apostle. Such idols are works of open falsehood and repudiate every dream.

No one escapes the temptation of presenting our sublime potential as an idol outside the self, to be exploited or blamed for our failures. Every idol is the work of the waking state and necessarily less than our potential. Looking at our idol as the affirmation of the self, as its servants we must deny the idols of others. This is the why of the obsession for prohibiting or attributing every blameworthy thing to the historical *Baphomet*.[6]

Muhammad is the name of our sublime potential as reason and purpose of His revelation. Where we are, there that potential is, and its repudiation: "Here is wisdom. Let him that hath understanding count the number of the beast: for it is the number of a man; and his number is Six hundred threescore and six."[7] The opposition between beast and man is the two facets of humanity, one

5 *Baphomet* is the Old French form of the Arabic name *Muḥammad*, see Partner, *The Knights Templar and their Myth*, 68.

6 There are many portrayals of *Baphomet* or *Mahomet* in European churches and books, normally as a sinner cast into Hell. Pope Innocent III associated Muhammad with the beast of *Revelation* (13:18), whose number is 666. In 1213, the same pope wrote "A certain son of perdition, Muhammad the pseudo-prophet, arose. Through worldly enticements and carnal delights he seduced many people away from the truth. His perfidy has prospered until this day. Yet we trust in God, Who has already given us a good omen that the end of this beast is drawing near. The number [of the beast], according to the Apocalypse of John, is 666, of which already almost six hundred years have been completed." (Innocent III, *Quia maior*, PL 216:818, cited after Tolan, *Saracens*, 194.) On this papal bull, calling Christians to the fifth crusade see Cole, *The Preaching of the Crusades to the Holy Land*, 1095–1270, 104–109.

7 *Revelation*, 13:18.

facing the depths, the other the height, one denying Muhammad, the other confessing him.

Denying Muhammad is associated with accepting the self's obscurity and ignorance as our mainstay in making judgments. Bearing witness to him is associated with believing we can emerge from darkness into the light and transcend duality: "None is there in the heavens and earth but he comes to the All-merciful as a servant; He has indeed counted them, and He has numbered them exactly."[8] All of existence and all things in it serve the All-merciful, and we are His perfect servants in our authentic and ultimate uprightness. The All-merciful places us in debt to existence. We have nothing not received from God.[9] As His servant we manifest God's lordship in the least and weakest. Here lies our election as stewards. God glorifies Himself in praise through us as existence's epitome.

---

8 *Qur'an*, 19:93.

9 See *John*, 3:27.

CHAPTER 10

Ascent

Rite and symbol's source transcends individual and historical determination: a premise necessary for tradition. Otherwise, origins are distorted in the quantifiable and everything belonging to them is subject to reification in a context that treats the knowing self as closed and negligible. The resulting world is its own principle, no escape from matter and death.

A symbol represents a rite in condensed, consolidated manner: seen, spoken and heard, made and touched, tasted and smelled. The connection between heard and written is particularly important. The Word sent down is normally received as oral, in exhalations or vibrations of breath and voice. Committing this flow of words to writing fixes the spoken. When we look at the visual image of the heard it is inanimate, but its symbolic nature renders it inseparable from the living source. It exists for ascent from matter to breath and voice. Every letter gives body to movement and the sound associated.

As to God's speech in human language, the original Speaker, God, never ceases to be what He is – the Speaker in all presences or proximities. Its record in writing is also sacred. To suggest it is inanimate when seen, but not heard, is not true for scriptures as sacred art, as we feel its witness to the Spirit directly, in no way petrified on the page.

The Word is received from silence, in a motion of breath. When the Praised received It, he was to be the Silence the Recitation was received in. It became motion, a symbol manifest out of motion. God said: "Move not thy tongue with it to hasten it; Ours it is to gather it, and to recite it. So, when We recite it, follow thou its recitation. Then Ours it is to explain it."[1]

This revelation shows the Praised receiving what he utters as the uncreated Word in the created world. The Word Bringer speaks in differentiation and the Praised follows. Following the Praised is ritually following the original Bringer as extra-temporal connection with God.

Ritual and symbol connect multiplicity, as structured movement, with Unity, entailing simultaneous descent and ascent – descent of the Spirit as inherent principle and ascent of the performer towards Unity, facets of the same reality. Rites are composed of interwoven symbols, series that change moment to moment and manifest Eternity in time. Each symbol introduces the next and in sequence they become action or ritual, reviving deadened regions of the

1 *Qur'an*, 75:16–19.

 | DOI 10.1163/9789004279407_086

self. The Holy Spirit, Spirit of Truth brought them into the world through the Praised, his self entirely moulded by what was sent down to him, as mightiest morality and greatest symbol. His entire life was a ritual: best example, our sublime potential, in the conformity of two wills, his and God's. The Praised shows himself the perfect servant and all he does reveals God's action or inaction at our level.

Prayer is, properly speaking, a ritual, entailing preparation, entry, orientation, movement, whispering, speaking, and exit. Hearing, reciting, writing or reading the Book are also rites, but the Praised remains the best example.

Involved in tradition, whatever we do or don't do involves ritual and symbol, through which we rise above the abyss to follow the Praised in our efforts to return, willingly in the here and now, to God. Rite and symbol are the means. Their ultimate meaning is on the summit of the mount, where we originally received them. God told Moses: "Make all things according to the pattern which was shewn thee on the Mount."[2]

Action in the depths is the key symbol of every tradition. The very term religion means "reconnection." Unity is manifest in a differentiated manner, descending through the many levels of existence. We can raise up and reconnect what was sent down and differentiated. There are three aspects to this – doctrine, rite, and path. Doctrine corresponds to our capacity to distinguish real from unreal; rite enables us to opt willingly for the real; and the path or life is seeing the real in virtue and beauty. Acceptance means our being is informed by the doctrine language symbolizes. In rite, symbols are embraced in life and the word becomes flesh, revealing life as virtue and beauty.

Confessing no self but the Self marks our infinite potential to ascend from the depths. The alternative is the illusion the self can drag the Self into them. This is characteristic of closed notions of humanity and the world, which impose judgment that leaves no choice but captivity and the impossibility of escape. The illusion of "liberation" is in unrelenting conflict with a world whose limits no victory can transcend. The greater the victory, the greater the defeat, the final outcome sinking to the depths, from which there is no rising.

The traditional worldview sees differently. The material world is a level of being, which initiates abandon, to rise in relation to the Self they call Thou: "Thee only we serve; to Thee alone we pray for succour. Guide us unto the upright path, the path of those whom Thou hast blessed, not of those against whom Thou art wrathful, nor of those who are astray!"[3]

---

2 *Exodus*, 25:40.

3 *Qur'an*, 1:5–7.

Ascent is the upright path spoken of by the Goal Who made us for Himself. Divorced from the Self, in Whose debt we are, but lacking nothing in origin we need to ascend, we ask: "Yet he has not assaulted the steep; and what shall teach thee what is the steep?"[4]

Each self says: "Thee only we serve; to Thee alone we pray for succour!" One, the self nonetheless says "We." This "we" includes what exists, for nothing fails to come to Him as servant.[5] Each self does so as created to serve the Lord,[6] a purpose realized in the self moulded by confessing no will but the Will, a confession bound to service: "And We sent never an apostle before thee except that We revealed to him, saying, 'There is no god but I; so serve Me.' "[7]

Prophets recall us to service to Lordship. Only God merits such service. Realizing our humanity entails denial of all lordship but His. Service participates in our relationship to the Lord along with existence. The prophets have their places and roles: "It belongs not to any mortal that God should give him the Book, the Judgment, prophecy, than he should say to men, 'Be you servants to me apart from God.' Rather, 'Be you masters in that you know the Book, and in that you study.' "[8]

---

4 Ibid., 90:11–12.

5 See *Qur'an*, 19:93.

6 Ibid., 51:56.

7 *Qur'an*, 21:25.

8 Ibid., 3:79.

CHAPTER 11

Word and Light

At rest, we are extended in a world of touch, taste, smell, hearing and sight, our view of it changing from place to place, position to position. We relate to the world awake, asleep and in thought. Our sense of space is abstracted into geometric and mathematical symbols, space seen as an entity where everything pursues its own path: "It behoves not the sun to overtake the moon, neither does the night outstrip the day, each swimming in a sky."[1]

Everything has its place in existence which we observe in relation to other things. Nothing in existence is at rest. The speed at which changes of position take place cannot be understood without time.

> According to Kant space is the form of our "outer experience," time the form of our "inner experience." In the interpretation of his inner experience man had new problems to confront. Here he could not use the same methods as in his first attempt to organize and systematize his knowledge of the physical world. There is, however, a common background for both questions. Even time is first thought of not as a specific form of human life but as a general condition of organic life. Organic life exists only so far as it evolves in time. It is not a thing but a process – a never-resting continuous stream of events. In this stream nothing ever recurs in the same identical shape.[2]

That nothing recurs means separation or rupture. What we can represent as constancy stands on the boundary of visible and invisible, life and death, multiplicity and One.

The relationship between these facets is indicated in the revelation: "That is the Book, wherein is no doubt, a guidance to the mindful who believe in the Unseen, and perform the prayer, and expend of that We have provided them."[3]

Prophets resolutely draw attention to the boundary. What they say of importance for their audience comes from on high, beyond space and time, and their promises relate to the world of the unseen. This is how they differ from sorcerers, magicians and fortune-tellers.

---

1 *Qur'an*, 36:40.

2 Cassirer, *An Essay on Man*, 49–50.

3 *Qur'an*, 2:2–3.

 | DOI 10.1163/9789004279407_087

Praise relates praiser and praised. The praiser acknowledges the value, dignity, beauty and goodness of the praised. We and the world are the two facets of the All-praised's manifestation, whose truth is desire, joy, satisfaction, love, mercy and the entire countless multitude of His most beautiful attributes. Their perfect presence, who are manifest in their manifestation, is attested by confessing no god but God and the Praised as His servant and apostle. Service to God gives us and the world all the praiseworthiness of One Who is Lord. We and the world are thus, perfectly potentially, His light, speech and breath. To illumine is to rejoice in the Praised, as God says: "Say: 'In the bounty of God, and His mercy – in that let them rejoice; it is better than that they amass.' "[4] The Praised as His servant and apostle is a mercy to the worlds.[5] The word that God sent down and that he tells the people is joy. This is why God says: "Rejoice in what is sent down unto thee."[6]

To rejoice is to extol Him in praise. We follow the Praised as our supreme potential by transforming baseness into exaltation. The world remembers why God is extolled in praise: "The seven heavens and the earth, and whosoever in them is, extol Him; nothing is, that does not proclaim His praise, but you do not understand their extolling."[7]

Accepting our lack of understanding, our only limited knowledge,[8] allows us to be attracted to what everything extols and praises.

A late 15th century Bosnian Church manuscript gives the entire *Book of Revelation*, followed by the beginning of the Gospel according to John, verses 1 to 17.[9] These passages include three key words – the Word, Light and Life.

God's revelation is the Word from the Word: "It is He who created the heavens and the earth in truth; and the day He says 'Be', and it is; His saying is true, and His is the Kingdom the day the Trumpet is blown; He is Knower of the Unseen and the visible; He is the All-wise, the All-aware."[10]

God's as All-wise and All-aware entails the possibility of knowledge and awareness of Him from the perspective of His revelation. He is both Light[11] and All-praised.[12] His creation is His manifestation in which both wisdom and

4 Ibid., 10:58.

5 See *Qur'an*, 21:107.

6 *Qur'an*, 13:36.

7 Ibid., 17:44.

8 See *Qur'an*, 17:85.

9 See Nazor, *Radosavljeva bosanska knjiga*, 144–47.

10 *Qur'an*, 6:73.

11 See *Qur'an*, 24:35.

12 Ibid., 11:73.

awareness are. As Light, He illumines and His illumination is revelation. This revelation in light is also praise. One could say that the Light of the Praised is the first revelation or first creation. Since the Word and Light are the principle of every revelation, they are manifestations of the One. This manifestation is in the world of decisions or commandments and forms a pure spiritual level of creation.

Illumination is simultaneously Intellect and Word, in which all possibilities are made manifest in differentiated fashion. Everything differentiated can be reassembled or reunited in Intellect. When the Light is seen through Intellect, the Essence of the Spirit is experienced. Spirit and Light are two manifestations of the One, so one may equate the Light of the Praised and the Spirit of the Praised. Both expressions denote the primordial and absolute figure of the Universal Individual who is God's first creation:

> This is the true "Heart of the World" the expansion of which produces the manifestation of all beings and the contraction of which brings them back in the end to their Principle; and thus it is both "the first and the last" (*al-awwal wa al-ākhar*) with respect to creation, just as Allah himself is "the First and the Last" in the absolute sense. "Heart of hearts and Spirit of spirits" (*Qalb al-qulūbi wa Rūḥ al-arwāḥ*), it is in his bosom that the particular "spirits," the angels (*al-malā'ika*) and the "separated spirits" (*al-arwāḥ al-mujarrada*), are differentiated, which are thus formed of the primordial Light as their unique essence, with no admixture of elements representing the determining conditions of the lower degrees of existence.[13]

13 Guénon, *Perspectives on Initiation*, 293.

CHAPTER 12

The Becca of Sion

How is the Universal Individual, foremost of creation, related to humanity as earthly creation? At first, our humanity appears corporeal and finite, but our totality does not reduce to the body alone. We need a centre through which the Universal Individual may be present at that level of God's manifestation. The Word, Light, Intellect, Spirit and the Praised are present through the centre and manifest in the self as Life. Life is thus Illumination and the Spirit's self-manifestation. The self receives them in various ways. The Word, Light and Life are key terms in every tradition, particularly for the self inseparable from the Self, which is realized by confessing no self but the Self in ascent from individuality to supra-individuality.

Any prophet is just the recipient and passer on of the Book God sent him, its first witness. Receiving and passing on are always part of a ritual also sent down. Even when this discourse acquires physical form as a book, its oral nature remains higher. To receive the Book from the lips of a living transmitter is the only way the unbroken spiritual connection can be maintained in a chain of transmission from the prophet, through whom the "doors of heaven" were opened to allow the Word to come down and rise back.

Sent down from Unity's sublime sameness, the Word concerns us all as individuals, even those in the depths. We can sink as well as ascend. Ascent or redemption, His mercy, begins in the depths. Becca is a sign of our resurrection. The Praised, a mercy to the worlds, received and passed on His reminder in that very valley, where all seemed lost, and showed us the upright path of return to our true position in existence as a whole, a path that begins and ends in those depths. The house in Becca and the rites associated are the most important sign of our approach to our sublime potential.

Only the apostle's breath and voice passes on what the Holy Spirit put in his heart. His mouth is the most potent source of the Spirit's influence upon others. When the Praised's mouth is closed, so are the heavens. His breath, tongue and lips are moved by the received Word, as what links us with the Praised and, through him, God. Yearning for his face is the most potent impulse for seeking initiation into the higher worlds the Praised unites, as he said: "By Him in Whose Hand is the life of the Praised, a day would come to you when you would not be able to see me, and the glimpse of my face would be dearer to one than one's own family, one's property and in fact everything."[1]

1 Muslim, 4:1260.

 | DOI 10.1163/9789004279407_088

The most sublime possibility the world offers us is a vision of the Praised. It is present in everything that manifests him, than which nothing more beautiful can be known or seen. 'Ali ibn Abi Talib, whose entire self was moulded by the confession of no god but God and the Praised as his apostle, describes his appearance:

> He was neither very tall nor excessively short, but was a man of medium stature. His hair was neither short and curly nor long and thin but something between the two. His face was not narrow, nor was it a very round face, but it was so to some extent. His face was white, and his eyelashes were long and curved. He was large-boned and broad-shouldered. He had no body hair except in the middle of his chest. His hands and feet were well-built. When he walked he walked at an angle, as though descending a slope. When he turned round he turned completely. The Seal of Prophecy was between his shoulders. He was the Seal of the prophets. He was the most generous-hearted of men, the most truthful of them in speech, the most mild-tempered of them, and the noblest of them in lineage. Whoever saw him unexpectedly was in awe of him, and whoever associated with him familiarly loved him. Those who described him said: "We have never seen the like, before or since."[2]

During ritual prayer, those performing it, alone or together, look no one in the face. They face the Centre revealed by the breath and voice of the Praised. They are in Becca, the Vale of Tears, to receive that breath and hear the voice of their finest example, always higher up than they. Every valley thus becomes a place from which to start for the summit of the Mount. Becca and Sion are both symbols of this, linked by the breath of the Praised. The people of peace, witnesses to the Praised, follow him in ascent from the valley floor to the Mount's summit. The upright path leads to our self-realization, a state in which the traveller's self is realized in confession of no face but the Face. For the people of peace, this connection is mentioned in a Psalm that refers explicitly to both Becca and Sion.

> How amiable are thy tabernacles, O Lord of hosts! My soul longeth, yea, even fainteth for the courts of the Lord: my heart and my flesh crieth out for the living God. Yea, the sparrow hath found an house, and the swallow a nest for herself, where she may lay her young, even thine altars, O Lord of hosts, my King, and my God. Blessed are they that dwell in thy house: they will be still praising thee. Selah.

---

2 Tirmidhī, 5791.

> Blessed is the man whose strength is in thee; in whose heart are the ways of them. Who passing through the valley of Baca make it a well; the rain also filleth the pools. They go from strength to strength, every one of them in Sion appeareth before God. O Lord God of hosts, hear my prayer: give ear, O God of Jacob. Selah. Behold, O God our shield, and look upon the face of thine anointed. For a day in thy courts is better than a thousand. I had rather be a doorkeeper in the house of my God, than to dwell in the tents of wickedness. For the Lord God is a sun and shield: the Lord will give grace and glory: no good thing will he withhold from them that walk uprightly. O Lord of hosts, blessed is the man that trusteth in thee![3]

Connecting this inspired discourse of David to that revealed by God through the Praised, we may recognize in the inhabitants of the house in Becca Muhammad and Mary, Abraham's progeny, through whom God revealed His Word in two forms – as the Anointed and as the Recitation. Clearly no chain of transmission of His revelation excludes either the Anointed or the Praised.

The Kaʿba at the bottom of Becca Valley symbolizes the heart, the house on Sion realization in it, including emerging from individuality to take up abode in Supra-individuality. The perfect example is the Praised. At both beginning and end of the path he leads us to, the Praised is manifest as perfect duality in which Unity is made known.

---

3 *Psalm* 84:1–13. From Hval's Bosnian book (*Zbornik krstjanina Hvala*), transcribed in 1404 (f.32). The passages from the Psalter, the Gospel, the Apocalypse and the *Qur'an* referred to in the following chapters were quoted in the original Bosnian version as entire pages from Bosnian manuscripts dating from the fifteenth to the nineteenth century, details and illustrations of which are provided in Part Two of the following volume. In the Bosnian original, the texts as quoted thus had an additional antiquarian interest, as they represented the mediaeval Bosnian version. Here the main point being made is the presence of certain indicative texts in a context of centuries-long contact between Muslims and Christians. The text of the Psalm quoted here corresponds to that given in the manuscript folio from figure 2.4.

CHAPTER 13

The Dearest Place

The Praised withdrew in solitude to a cave on Mount Hira above Becca, where God sent him the revelation through the Holy Spirit: "Recite: In the name of thy Lord who created, created Man of a blood-clot. Recite: And thy Lord is the Most Generous, who taught by the Pen, taught Man that he knew not."[1]

What Adam indicated by building two houses to mark our fall and ascent is condensed and realized in the Praised. He represents perfection for all in the depths, as a mercy to the worlds, for with him we find our sublime potential – confessing Unity, prophecy and return.

The Praised addressed the revelation he received to us. He introduced the Self's discourse into human language, the expressive mode of the forgetful self, transforming our view of both the horizons and the self. God's call, whose first witness he is, tears down behaviour, views and knowledge established without connection to the Principle. This produces resistance and hostility, since being born to a higher means dying to a lower level.

Forced to leave the Valley, the Praised turned back, saying: "Of all God's earth, thou are the dearest place unto me and the dearest unto God, and had not my people driven out from thee I would not have left thee."[2]

Going north, away from the house, the Praised testified he was the centre of existence into whose heart the holy Spirit descends. The house in the valley is a sign of that heart of every heart, in which we can all realize ourselves, as Adam could and all his children can to the end of this world. Only what bears witness of this, in whatever guise, offers a warrant on the upright path. When the Praised described the Becca valley as the place dearest to him and God, he meant God's mercy, which encompasses all things, and his own apostolate as a mercy to the worlds. Nothing, no matter where it is, is beyond this mercy. Is there any greater joy than for those in the worst, most contemptible state? Is it not for their sake, the despised and rejected, that God remind us of redemption through doctrine, rite and virtue?

Mercy manifests as redemptive for people in the depths, the worst state, whom neither God nor His apostle have abandoned:

---

1 *Qur'an*, 96:1–5.

2 Lings, *Muhammad*, 118.

 | DOI 10.1163/9789004279407_089

> God knows of it. All food was lawful to the children of Israel save what Israel forbade for himself before the Torah was sent down. Say: "Bring you the Torah now, and recite it, if you are faithful." Whoso forges falsehood against God after that, those are the evildoers. Say: "God has spoken the truth; therefore follow the creed of Abraham, a man of pure faith and no concealer." The first house established for people was that at Becca, a place holy, and a guidance to all beings. Therein are clear signs – the station of Abraham, and whosoever enters it is in security. It is the duty of all men towards God to come to the house a pilgrim, if he is able to make his way there. As for the concealers, God is All-sufficient nor needs any being. Say: "People of the Book, why do you cover over and conceal the signs of God? Surely God is witness of the things you do." Say: "People of the Book, why do you bar from God's way the believer, desiring to make it crooked, yourself being witnesses? God is not heedless of the things you do." O believers, if you obey a sect of those who have been given the Book, they will turn you, after you have believed, into concealers. How can you conceal, seeing you have God's signs recited to you, and His apostle among you? Whosoever holds fast to God, he is guided to the upright path. O, believers.[3]

God's call through the Praised to follow him on the upright path from valley to mount, self in darkness to self at peace, determines the place of will, love and knowledge. For will to be guided, it needs procedure and ritual to transform it into love for the One revealed to the world and self in His speech and His books. The lover cannot have sufficient knowledge of the Beloved. The vast universe offers us no tabernacle in which to come to rest as lovers. We want only His abode and nothing on the way is worth stopping for. He warns us against the temptation of taking representations of the Beloved for sufficient:

> It belongs not to any mortal that God should give him the Book, the Judgment, the prophethood, then he should say to men, "Be you servants to me apart from God." Rather, "Be you masters in that you know the Book, and in that you study." He will never order you to take the angels and the prophets as Lords; what, would He order you to conceal, after you have found peace? And when God took compact with the prophets: "That I have given you the Book and Wisdom; then there shall come to you an apostle confirming what is with you – you shall believe in him and you

3 *Qur'an*, 3:92–102. The text quoted corresponds to a page of a manuscript *Qur'an* of 1598, given in figure 2.5..

shall help him; do you agree?" He said, "And do you take My load on you on that condition?" They said, "We do agree." God said, "Bear witness so, and I shall be with you among the witnesses." Then whosoever turns his back after that – they are the ungodly. What, do they desire another debt than God's and in Him has found peace whoso is in the heavens and the earth, willingly or unwillingly, and to Him they shall be returned? Say: "We believe in God, and that which has been sent down on us, and sent down on Abraham and Ishmael, Isaac and Jacob, and the Tribes, and in that which was given to Moses and Jesus, and the prophets, of their Lord; we make no division between any of them, and in Him we are at peace." Whoso desires another debt than being-in-Peace, it shall not be accepted of him; in the next world he shall be among the losers.[4]

And when Abraham, and Ishmael with him, raised up the foundations of the house: "Our Lord, receive this from us; Thou art the All-hearing, the All-knowing; and, our Lord, make us submissive to the Thee; and show us our holy rites, and turn towards us, surely Thou turnest, and art Ever-merciful; and our Lord, do Thou send among them an apostle, one of them, who shall recite to them.[5]

---

4 Ibid., 3:79–86. The text quoted corresponds to the page of a 1615 manuscript of the Qur'an given in figure 2.6.

5 Ibid., 2:127–29. The text quoted corresponds to the text cited on r. 4 of a Bosnian manuscript called The Light of the Praised (*Hvaljenska svjetlost*), given as figure 2.7 on page p. 581. The original shows great influence of old Slavonic and was written in Bosnian Cyrillic.

CHAPTER 14

Ascension

We have defined belief as how the faithful relate to Faithful God. To confess it entails: "We believe in what was sent down to us and what has been sent down to you. Our God and your God is one, and we are the people of peace."[1] "What was sent down to us" was the Recitation as the Book God spoke through the Praised. "What has been sent down to you" are the books God spoke through other prophets. The various books are discourses of One God, no difference between them in principle. The sense of self of the peoples of the Book is informed by acceptance and confession of their books.

The people of peace confess no god but God and the Praised as His apostle. This entails all the preceding books, particularly the Torah and Gospels, which informed the selves of their peoples. The people of the Recitation confess their heritage in those of the peoples of the Torah and the Gospels and accept no witness of God's unity, the Praised's apostolate, or return to God that does not confess all the prophets and books. To discover their own individual and collective selves, whose first confession is God's unity and the Praised's apostolate, the people of peace must have durable dialogic relations with the other peoples of the books.

From the perspective of the Recitation, the Jewish, Christian, and Islamic traditions are inseparable. Bosnia is a case in point, where confession of the Praised's apostolate is inseparable from the inheritance of the Torah and the Gospels. The texts used above were from the manuscript heritage of the followers of the Bosnian church, the sacred texts of the *krstjans*, as preserved by their heirs following acceptance of the Recitation. These texts from Bosnia's cultural heritage were selected to draw attention to resources available for understanding sacred texts and forms of prayer, a perspective obscured by the modern constructions of a godless world. Comparative study of them as discourses sent down by the One God allows the meaning of differences within and between communities to be discovered. Difference and similarity are simultaneous and irreconcilable. Both are the condition of our dignity as a worthy stage for God's revelation. Only in and with the One is difference reconciled, as the treasure within each self.

Becca and Sion are signs of our potential, as the oldest signposts on the way of return to our original position on the height. To realize our human-

1 *Qur'an*, 29:46.

 | DOI 10.1163/9789004279407_090

ity is to cleanse the self of individuality and emerge from chaos and darkness into beauty and light. We can pass from the order attainable on earth to supra-individual reality. The Praised journeyed from matter to Spirit, dark to Light, the depths to Sublimity, differentiation to Unity – a journey marked by two places of self-annihilation, the mosque at Becca and the one on Sion. His journey encompassed all time and space and what lies beyond and he confessed no self but the Self and the Praised as His servant and apostle. It ends in realization, standing face to Face.

In each state, the Praised serves his Lord, as everything he has he received in free will. In each state, he manifests God's will. He was not spared any human experience, suffering or pain, but remains always what he is – the best example through which God self-manifests, ever true to His knowledge and mercy. He is a sign that reveals the world as an alien place from which to return home.

We reach journey's end by realizing the self in the Word, sent down through the Holy Spirit to the Praised to let him enter the identity of knowledge and being and become our best example. In the Recitation, God gave His words on the reciprocity of the depths and the height and the self of the Praised as bridging the span between them:

> In the name of God, the All-merciful, the Ever-merciful, Glory be to Him, who carried His servant by night from the Inviolable Mosque to the Further Mosque the precincts of which We have blessed, that We might show him some of Our signs. He is the All-hearing, the All-seeing. And We gave Moses the Book, and made it a guidance to the Children of Israel: "Take not unto yourselves any guardian apart from Me." The seed of those We bore with Noah; he was a thankful servant. And We decreed for the Children of Israel in the Book: "You shall do corruption in the earth twice, and you shall ascend exceeding high." So, when the promise of the first of these came to pass, we sent against you servants of Ours, men of great might, and they went through the habitations, and it was a promise performed. Then We gave back to you the turn to prevail over them, and We succoured you with wealth and children, and We made you a greater host. "If you do good, it is your own souls you do good to, and if you do evil it is to them likewise." Then, when the promise of the second came to pass, We sent against you Our servants to discountenance you, and to enter the Mosque, as they entered in the first time, and to destroy utterly that which they ascended to. Perchance your Lord will have mercy upon you; but if you return, We shall return; and we have made Gehenna a prison for the concealers. Surely this recitation guides to the way that is straightest and gives good tidings to the believers who do deeds of

> righteousness, that theirs shall be a great wage, and that those who do not believe in the world to come – we have prepared for them a painful chastisement. Man prays for evil, as he prays for good; man is ever hasty. We have appointed the night and the day as two signs; then We have blotted out the sign of the night, and made the sign of the day to see, and that you may seek bounty from your Lord, and that you may know the number of the years, and the reckoning and everything We have distinguished very distinctly. And every man – We have fastened to him his bird of omen upon his neck; and We shall bring forth for him, on the Day of Resurrection, a Book he shall find spread wide open. "Read thy book! Thy soul suffices thee this day as a reckoner against thee." Whosoever is guided, is only guided to his own gain, and whosoever goes astray, it is only to his own loss; no soul laden bears the load of another. We never chastise, until We send forth an apostle. And when We desire to destroy a city, We command its men who live at ease, and they commit ungodliness therein, then the Word is realized against it, and We destroy it utterly.[2]

These verses from the Recitation tell us both mosques, Becca and Sion, like everything in existence, on earth or in heaven, are but signs that recall the Signified. Disregarding their nature runs the risk of great sin. Nothing is so great it deserves association with God, Who has no equal. Realization is in the self and its connection with the Self. No place of self-annihilation is therefore anything more than a reminder that He has no equal.

Didn't the Anointed, Mary's son, recall this in and around the mosque on Sion? Does he not speak to us in our inner selves, realized in belief as what connects believer and True God?

Spanning the distance between the two mosques is a historic event in the self of the Praised as the first apostle whose reason and purpose transcend history and time. Both mosques, as structures in time, may be forgotten, abandoned and fall into ruin, but are never lost. They are signs God sent down for our realization in return to Him. No self exists for their sake; they exist for the benefit of every self. The self returns to the Self from the depths, the profoundest dark and earthly matter. The mosque in the Valley denotes the ignorance and darkness the Praised calls and leads us out of, the mosque on the Mount the knowledge and light he calls and leads us to. Jesus, the Anointed, is closer than any to the Praised as first apostle, in this world or the next, since both manifest and confess the Word as ultimate redemption from illusion and forgetting, suffering and death.

---

2 Ibid., 17:1–16. The text quoted corresponds to the page of a 1852 manuscript given as fig. 2.9, on p. 582.

Confession of the Praised and the Anointed does not begin in or with them, but in eternity. They are its perfect recipients and passers on. Receiving from God through the Holy Spirit, they transmitted what they received and who heard and remembered their message was connected with the Holy Spirit as their higher Reality. God sent down the Shekhinah into their hearts, for the Word heard, remembered, written and read includes descent of the Supra-individual into the self to serve discovery of our original nature. Reading the Recitation and Gospel links the self's marginality to its uncreated Centre. The self does not depend on anything external, as Revelation's descent confirms God's mercy as the reason we are recalled to the inspired knowledge within us.

> And when Jesus was entered into Capernaum, there came unto him a centurion, beseeching him, and saying, Lord, my servant lieth at home sick of the palsy, grievously tormented. And Jesus saith unto him, I will come and heal him. The centurion answered and said, Lord, I am not worthy that thou shouldest come under my roof: but speak the word only, and my servant shall be healed. For I am a man under authority, having soldiers under me: and I say to this man, Go, and he goeth; and to another, Come, and he cometh; and to my servant, Do this, and he doeth it. When Jesus heard it, he marvelled, and said to them that followed, Verily I say unto you, I have not found so great faith, no, not in Israel. And I say unto you, That many shall come from the east and west, and shall sit down with Abraham, and Isaac, and Jacob, in the kingdom of heaven. But the children of the kingdom shall be cast out into outer darkness: there shall be weeping and gnashing of teeth. And Jesus said unto the centurion, Go thy way; and as thou hast believed, so be it done unto thee. And his servant was healed in the selfsame hour.[3]

When the Messiah spoke to Abraham's children as Israelites, he confirmed belief as necessary for redemption. Belief is knowledge of the Beloved and love of the Known. To know the Beloved and love the Known, we must be at peace and God is Peace. Those who receive peace and return what they have received are at peace. Only being peaceful and at peace, faithful and good helps us ascend towards our sublime potential, from Becca to Sion.

Abraham prayed for all his descendants in both lines and for all of us to find our original perfection in perennial wisdom and the associated rite and virtue. He and Ishmael discovered the house in Becca, cleared its ruins and rebuilt it as a sign of self-realization. They restored this sign of the depths and return

---

3 *Matthew*, 8:5–13. From a page of the 15th century Čajniče Gospel, given as fig. 2.10, on p. 583.

to God as a sacred teaching and the rite as a way to turn towards the Light, to initiate us all into what was revealed to them.

> [Abraham said "…] Our Lord, bring us to peace in Thee, and make of our seed a community at peace in Thee; and show us our holy rites, and turn towards us; surely Thou turnest, and art All-compassionate; and our Lord, do Thou send among them an apostle, one of them, who shall recite to them Thy signs, and teach them the Book and the Wisdom, and purify them; thou art the All-mighty, the All-wise." Who therefore shrinks from the debt of Abraham, expect he be foolish-minded? Indeed, We chose him in the present world, and in the world to come he shall be among the righteous. When his Lord said to him, "Be at peace," he said, "I have found peace in the Lord of all Being." And Abraham charged his son with this and Jacob likewise: "My sons, God has chosen for you your debt; see that you die not save at peace." Why, were you witnesses, when death came to Jacob? When he said to his sons, "What will you serve after me?" They said, "We will serve thy God."[4]

Jacob's sons' promise to serve God affirmed their individual natures, determined by their testimony in pre-existence to God's lordship. Our relationship with God as servants and Lord is independent of time and place. It includes that between the Principle and its manifestations, and concerns each of us, as we were originally designed for it. Our service is why we were created. Whenever the relationship is disrupted, the consequences are seen in distortion of the self and our failure to act as God's stewards on earth.

---

4 *Qur'an*, 2:128–133. The text quoted corresponds to the page of a 1636 manuscript, given as fig. 2.11, p. 583.

CHAPTER 15

With Zachariah

The Mosque on Mount Sion, with all its magnificence and links with poor and powerful alike, was the scene of an earth-shaking event. As Abraham's children, the Israelites were led towards it and its summit that denotes the goal of our journey – realization in perfection. The Further Mosque was sent down to that summit to embody the revelation to David and Solomon as the Holy of Holies with the Ark of the Covenant and their rites. The Word was realized in that building through the hearts and hands of those who made stone and wood, brass and gold, cold and heat, water and blood pliant and obedient. In the sumptuousness of its doctrine, rite and virtue, which manifest humility, generosity and beauty, the building, its walls, pillars, beams, paving, and gold, iron and brass, and the land it stands on are but a shadow of the real presence of the Shekhinah and the Spirit.

God reminded the people who had forgotten He inhabits hearts not edifices of the meaning of the heart as their uncreated centre, turning their eyes and enthusiasm from the majesties of the temple towards the heart of a Virgin. Zachariah, priest and prophet, whose name denotes remembrance of God as our highest capacity, was called to make known the Virgin's self as the "place" God had sent His Word into, unlike anything the people were accustomed to. God reminded him that He gives to whom He will and how He will. He called on him to remember Him dumbly, for the Word takes us beyond the bounds of language.

> "I have named her Mary, and commend her to Thee with her seed, to protect them from the accursed Satan." Her Lord received the child with gracious favour, she grew up comely, Zachariah taking charge of her. Whenever Zachariah went in to her in the mihrab, he found her provisioned. "Mary," he said, "how comes this to thee?" "From God," she said, truly God provisions whomsoever He will without reckoning. Then Zachariah prays to his Lord saying, "Lord, give me of Thy goodness a goodly offspring. Yeah, Thou hearest prayer." And the angels called to him standing in the mihrab at worship, "Lo, God gives thee good tidings of John, who shall confirm a Word of God, a chief, and chaste, a prophet, righteous." "Lord," said Zachariah, "how shall I have a son, seeing I am an old man and my wife is barren?" "Even so," God said, "God does what He will." "Lord," said Zachariah, "appoint to me a sign." "Thy sign," God said,

 | DOI 10.1163/9789004279407_091

> "is that thou shalt not speak, save by tokens, to men for three days. And mention thy Lord often, and give glory at evening and dawn." And when the angels said, "Mary, God has chosen thee, and purified thee; He has chosen thee above all women. Mary, be obedient to thy Lord, prostrating and bowing before Him." (That is of the tidings of the Unseen, that We reveal to thee; for thou wast not with them, when they were casting quills which of them, should have charge of Mary; thou wast not with them, when they were disputing.) When the angels said, "Mary, God gives thee good tidings of a Word from Him whose name is Messiah, Jesus, son of Mary; high honoured shall he be in this world and the next, near stationed to God. He shall speak to men in the cradle, and of age, and righteous he shall be." "Lord," said Mary, "how shall I have a son seeing no mortal has touched me?" "Even so," God said, "God creates what He will. When He decrees a thing He does but say to it 'Be', and it is. And He will teach him."[1]

Accounts are given of this miracle at the place of annihilation on Mount Sion in both Recitation and Gospel. Such records connect us and our Lord, as a reminder of the Word from no human individuality. In its supra-individuality, the Word is one, however many forms it takes in the phenomenal world. Reading any of its forms conveys the reader towards Unity. It is sent down from and for Eternity. Our minds are confused as to how it descended, as supra-individuality encompassing immeasurably more than anything in existence.

The Virgin's heart is great enough to receive the Word. No will compares to the Will of Him Who manifests Himself to all creation, nothing so great or small that it escapes Him. When God revealed His power and mercy to the Virgin and she made it known, the old prophet was prepared to hear His promise of a son to come, though he knew it not.

> But the angel said unto him, Fear not, Zachariah: for thy prayer is heard; and thy wife Elisabeth shall bear thee a son, and thou shalt call his name John. And thou shalt have joy and gladness; and many shall rejoice at his birth. For he shall be great in the sight of the Lord, and shall drink neither wine nor strong drink; and he shall be filled with the Holy Ghost, even from his mother's womb. And many of the children of Israel shall he turn to the Lord their God. And he shall go before him in the spirit and power of Elijah, to turn the hearts of the fathers to the children, and the disobedient to the wisdom of the just; to make ready a people prepared for the

1 *Qur'an*, 3:36–48. From a 1473 Bosnian manuscript, given as fig. 2.12, p. 584.

> Lord. And Zachariah said unto the angel, whereby shall I know this? For I am an old man, and my wife well stricken in years. And the angel answering said unto him, I am Gabriel, that stand in the presence of God; and am sent to speak unto thee, and to shew thee these glad tidings.[2]

The miracle of the Virgin, as recipient and passer on of the Word, was at the heart of the mosque on the Mount in sign of God's guidance. It was at a time when the Israelites were expecting three promised ones – the Anointed, for the first time, Elijah, for the second, and the prophet God announced through Moses as like him. The Anointed and Elijah were Israelites. The Praised was an Ishmaelite, as God revealed through Moses that the prophet like him would be raised from the brethren of the Israelites.

The Israelites awaiting the promised three speculated as to who, of those who seemed likely, might be the first, second, and third. The *Book of Revelation* relates: "And there appeared a great wonder in heaven; a woman clothed with the sun, and the moon under her feet, and upon her head a crown of twelve stars. And she being with child cried, travailling in birth, and pained to be delivered."[3] This announcement of a great event is inextricably linked with their expectations: "But thou, Bethlehem Ephratah, though thou be little among the thousands of Judah, yet out of thee shall he come forth unto me that is to be ruler in Israel; whose goings forth have been from of old, from everlasting."[4]

Malachi says: "Remember ye the law of Moses my servant, which I commanded unto him in Horeb for all Israel, with the statutes and judgments. Behold, I will send you Elijah the prophet before the coming of the great and dreadful day of the Lord."[5]

Many prophets were raised in Israel after Moses, but none like him.[6] God knew Moses "face to Face"[7] and announced a prophet like him, yet not of the Israelites, saying: "I will raise them up a prophet from among their brethren, like unto thee, and will put my words in his mouth; and he shall speak unto them all that I shall command him."[8]

---

2 *Luke*, 1:13–19. From the 15th century Pripković Gospel, given in fig. 2.13, on p. 584.

3 *Revelation*, 12:1–2.

4 *Micah*, 5:2.

5 *Malachi*, 4:4–5.

6 See *Deuteronomy*, 34:10.

7 Ibid.

8 *Deuteronomy*, 18:18.

CHAPTER 16

With Mary

Zachariah knew the doctrine and rite that ensured the life of the Further Mosque. Their mode of presence here seemed off-putting to most, a barrier between the self and its centre so dense doctrine and rite could not penetrate. The building's inanimate matter seemed more solid than the centre and hearts took on the nature of the stone they turned towards as a value independent of God. This petrification was reversed in God's annunciation to the Virgin and Zachariah's barren wife as "places" dearer to Him than those the eyes and expectations of the majority fixed upon.

The majority were waiting for the three – the Anointed, Elijah and the apostle – each one of that multitude expecting and imagining them differently. They are referred to in the scriptures, but in ways that allow their persons and the time of and witness to their coming to be conceived and interpreted variously. Each was expected, on coming, to help banish suffering and attain happiness and to be against others experienced as hostile and as the very image of suffering and misfortune.

The question of the awaited three cannot be resolved without John. Why not? The pages of the Gospel and the Recitation bear witness to Zachariah and his son John, and to Mary and her son Jesus. The people waiting for answers to their questions about the three would ascend to the Mosque on Mount Sion to ask Zachariah, both prophet and priest, to give them news of their expectations from the Mystery. The Mystery, revealing Itself through an angel, ordered the prophet not to speak. The power of the Word, which is from the self's inwardness and for its realization, had almost completely evaporated in their expectations and trust in transmitted knowledge.

> And the people waited for Zachariah, and marvelled that he tarried so long in the mosque. And when he came out, he could not speak unto them: and they perceived that he had seen a vision in the mosque: for he beckoned unto them, and remained speechless. And it came to pass, that, as soon as the days of his ministration were accomplished, he departed to his own house. And after those days his wife Elisabeth conceived, and hid herself five months, saying, thus hath the Lord dealt with me in the days wherein he looked on me, to take away my reproach among men. And in the sixth month the angel Gabriel was sent from God unto a city of

 | DOI 10.1163/9789004279407_092

> Galilee, named Nazareth, to a virgin espoused to a man whose name was Joseph, of the house of David; and the virgin's name was Mary. And the angel came in unto her, and said, Hail, thou that art highly favoured, the Lord is with thee: blessed art thou among women. And when she saw him, she was troubled at his saying, and cast in her mind what manner of salutation this should be. And the angel said unto her, Fear not, Mary: for thou hast found favour with God. And, behold, thou shalt conceive in thy womb, and bring forth a son, and shalt call his name Jesus. He shall be great, and shall be called the Son of the Highest: and the Lord God shall give unto him the throne of his father David: And he shall reign over the house of Jacob for ever; and of his kingdom there shall be no end. Then said Mary unto the angel, how shall this be, seeing I know not a man? And the angel answered and said unto her, The Holy Ghost shall come upon thee, and the power of the Highest shall overshadow thee: therefore also that holy thing which shall be born of thee shall be called the Son of God. And, behold, thy cousin Elisabeth, she hath also conceived a son in her old age: and this is the sixth month with her, who was called barren. For with God nothing shall be impossible. And Mary said, Behold the handmaid of the Lord; be it unto me according to thy word. And the angel departed from her. And Mary arose in those days, and went into the hill country with haste, into a city of Judah.[1]

The Holy Spirit visited the Virgin as a Perfect Man, the apostle who realizes our potential and incarnates our confession of no god but God, Whose servant is the Praised.

> [The prophet] said, "Lord, appoint to me some sign." Said He, "Thy sign is that thou shalt not speak to men, though being without fault, three nights." So he came forth unto his people from the mihrab, then he made signal to them, "Give you glory at dawn and evening." "O John, take the Book forcefully"; and We gave him judgment, yet a little child, and a tenderness from Us, and purity; and he was mindful, and cherishing his parents, not arrogant, rebellious. "Peace be upon him, the day he was born, and the day he dies, and the day he is raised up alive!" And mention in the Book Mary when she withdrew from her people to an eastern place, and she took a veil apart from them; then We sent unto her Our Spirit that

---

1 *Luke*, 1:21–39. From the 15th century Venetian Miscellany, given as fig. 2.14, on p. 585.

> presented himself to her a man without fault. She said, "I take refuge in the All-merciful from thee! If thou art heedful of God…" He said, "I am but an apostle come from thy Lord, to give thee a boy most pure." She said, "How shall I have a son whom no mortal has touched, neither have I been unchaste?" He said, "Even so thy Lord has said."[2]

The apostle and the Virgin both manifest the One. The Light was sent down with the Praised[3] and is also her mantle, as the *Book of Revelation* tells us: "And there appeared a great wonder in heaven; a woman clothed with the sun, and the moon under her feet."[4]

God is Light and reveals himself by shining. This is His first manifestation, His praise. As Light and All-praised, God owes His shining and praise to none, but everything illumined and praised owes that to Him. This reception and return is perfectly manifest in the Praised, with whom the Light was sent down. He was born our best example and God says of him:

> My chastisement – I smite with it whom I will; and My mercy embraces all things, I shall prescribe it for those who are mindful and pay the alms, and those who indeed believe in Our signs, those who follow the apostle, the Maternal, whom they find written down with them in the Torah and the Gospel, bidding them to honour, and forbidding them dishonour, making lawful for them the good things and making unlawful for them the corrupt things, and relieving them of their loads, and the fetters that were upon them. Those who believe in him and succour him and help him, and follow the light that has been sent down with him – they are the prosperers.[5]

The Praised and the Virgin are both symbols of the One. Through them the One reveals His Word through every level of existence. The Anointed and John were contemporaries. Both swore in pre-existence to bear witness to and help the apostle. At their time in history, the Israelites were expecting the three foretold – the Anointed, Elijah and the apostle. Faced with two they assumed to be two of three, they ask John which he was, the Anointed, Elijah, or the apostle, and the prophet John, son of the prophet Zachariah, said none of them:

---

2 *Qur'an*, 19:9–21. The text quoted corresponds to the page of a 1764 manuscript given as fig. 2.15, p. 585.

3 See *Qur'an*, 7:156–57.

4 *Revelation*, 12:1.

5 *Qur'an*, 7:156–57.

> And this is the record of John, when the Jews sent priests and Levītes from Jerusalem to ask him, "Who art thou?" And he confessed, and denied not; but confessed, "I am not the Christ." And they asked him, "What then? Art thou Elijah?" And he saith, "I am not." "Art thou that prophet?" And he answered, "No."[6]

6 *John*, 1:19–21.

CHAPTER 17

The True and the Holy

When the Anointed was among the people, speaking of himself and his Lord, he revealed a mystery, the Praised. His disciples watched and listened to Mary's son, day and night, in the lonely desert hills, on journeys, and at sea. They watched him speak, pray and keep silence. They saw the prophet John, son of Zachariah, priest of the Sion Mosque, prophet and witness to God's choice of the Virgin from the women of the worlds. All four – Zachariah, John, Mary and Jesus – knew "that prophet" of whom God spoke in pre-existence as His seal and His light. Moses and Elijah knew and bore witness of him. Jesus' disciples were waiting for him, but did not know him. They speculated about him and their teacher drew a clear distinction between the two to come – Elijah and the prophet who is Praised. On Mount Tabor, Mary's son revealed himself to his disciples, Peter, James and John. With him were Elijah and Moses: "And his face did shine as the sun, and his raiment was white as the light. And, behold, there appeared unto them Moses and Elijah talking with him."[1]

Thus Mary's son made clear to three disciples the mystery of the two to come – the Praised (the Paraclete, *Aḥmad*), like Moses, but not of the children of Israel, and Elijah, of those children, whom God has already sent once as His apostle, raising him on high to send him down again when the promised prophet comes. Their figures were a precious part of the legacy of Mary's son, who spoke of the coming of the Praised and the closeness of the two of them, for the Praised is our sublime potential, our best example, the Light sent down, a light-giving lamp. He is the entire Table God sent the Anointed to gather his disciples around.

> Verily, verily, I say unto you, He that believeth on me, the works that I do shall he do also; and greater works than these shall he do; because I go unto my Father. And whatsoever ye shall ask in my name, that will I do, that the Father may be glorified in the Son. If ye shall ask any thing in my name, I will do it. If ye love me, keep my commandments. And I will pray the Father, and he shall give you another Comforter, that he may abide with you for ever; Even the Spirit of truth; whom the world cannot receive, because it seeth him not, neither knoweth him: but ye know him; for he dwelleth with you, and shall be in you. I will not leave you comfortless:

1 *Matthew*, 17:2–3.

 | DOI 10.1163/9789004279407_093

> I will come to you. Yet a little while, and the world seeth me no more; but ye see me: because I live, ye shall live also. At that day ye shall know that I am in my Father, and ye in me, and I in you. He that hath my commandments, and keepeth them, he it is that loveth me: and he that loveth me shall be loved of my Father, and I will love him, and will manifest myself to him. Judas saith unto him, not Iscariot, Lord, how is it that thou wilt manifest thyself unto us, and not unto the world?[2]

Sent down as His Word and present in the world and among people, the Anointed confessed his descent and return to the sublime heights. He is a sign of our sublime potential.

> And these things will they do unto you, because they have not known the Father, nor me. But these things have I told you, that when the time shall come, ye may remember that I told you of them. And these things I said not unto you at the beginning, because I was with you. But now I go my way to him that sent me; and none of you asketh me, whither goest thou? But because I have said these things unto you, sorrow hath filled your heart. Nevertheless I tell you the truth; it is expedient for you that I go away: for if I go not away, the Comforter will not come unto you; but if I depart, I will send him unto you. And when he is come, he will reprove the world of sin, and of righteousness, and of judgment: Of sin, because they believe not on me; Of righteousness, because I go to my Father, and ye see me no more; Of judgment, because the prince of this world is judged. I have yet many things to say unto you, but ye cannot bear them now. Howbeit when he, the Spirit of truth, is come, he will guide you into all truth: for he shall not speak of himself; but whatsoever he shall hear, that shall he speak: and he will shew you things to come.[3]

The Anointed (Christ) associates his mission with his testimony to the Praised (the Paraclete or Comforter) whom he identifies as the Holy Spirit and the Spirit of Truth. His presence in the world realizes their descent.

> At that day ye shall know that I am in my Father, and ye in me, and I in you. He that hath my commandments, and keepeth them, he it is that loveth me: and he that loveth me shall be loved of my Father, and I will love him, and will manifest myself to him. Judas saith unto him, not

---

2 *John*, 14:12–22. From the 15th century Vrutok Gospels, given as fig. 2.16, p. 586.

3 Ibid., 16:3–13. From the 15th century Kopitar Bosnian Gospels, given as fig. 2.17, p. 586.

> Iscariot, Lord, how is it that thou wilt manifest thyself unto us, and not unto the world? Jesus answered and said unto him, if a man love me, he will keep my words: and my Father will love him, and we will come unto him, and make our abode with him. He that loveth me not keepeth not my sayings: and the word which ye hear is not mine, but the Father's which sent me. These things have I spoken unto you, being yet present with you. But the Comforter, which is the Holy Ghost, whom the Father will send in my name, he shall teach you all things, and bring all things to your remembrance, whatsoever I have said unto you. Peace I leave with you, my peace I give unto you: not as the world giveth, give I unto you. Let not your heart be troubled, neither let it be afraid. Ye have heard how I said unto you, I go away, and come again unto you. If ye loved me, ye would rejoice, because I said, I go unto the Father: for my Father is greater than I. And now I have told you before it come to pass, that, when it is come to pass, ye might believe.[4]

The Recitation reaffirms the Anointed's witness of the Praised. Many languages are a sign. God sent down the one Truth about Himself and His Creation in every one, in differing forms. The truth, however, passes from one to another like a fish through water. The Anointed spoke in Aramaic and traces of it remain in the Greek. The one announced as the third awaited by the world is called Paraclete in Greek. This is *Aḥmad* in Arabic, in the Recitation infused by the Holy Spirit, the Spirit of Truth, into the heart of the Praised.

> Jesus son of Mary said, "Children of Israel, I am indeed the apostle of God to you, confirming the Torah that is before me, and giving good tidings of an apostle who shall come after me, whose name shall be *Aḥmad*." Then, when he brought them the clear signs, they said, "This is a manifest sorcery." And who does greater evil than he who forges against God falsehood, when he is being called to accept peace? And God guides never the people of the evildoers. They desire to extinguish with their mouths the light of God; but God will perfect His light, though the concealers be averse. It is He who has sent His apostle with the guidance and the debt of truth, that he may uplift it above every debt, though the concealers be averse. O believers, shall I direct you to a commerce that shall deliver you from a painful chastisement? You shall believe in God.[5]

4 Ibid., 14:20–29. From the 15th century Nikolje Gospels, given as fig. 2.18, p. 587.

5 *Qur'an*, 61:6–11. The text corresponds to the page of a manuscript dating from 1593 given as fig. 2.19, on p. 587.

CHAPTER 18

The Recitation

Mary's son spoke Aramaic, but in the sacred tradition of God's prophets whose revelations were in Hebrew. His speech manifested the Word borne by the Holy Spirit, a manifestation transmitted orally from person to person, people to people. These changes do not affect the Holy Spirit's presence. The Truth is present in countless manifestations. No people, region, language, or time lacks the Spirit's constant presence. The Word is one and contains all the One's potential manifestations. When the Holy Spirit carries the Word from Unity into a given prophet's heart to pass into the language of his people, the resulting narrative changes the order among them and their social customs and expectations.

Such changes encounter resistance and rejection of the prophet's role as transmitter and link with God. This rejection of the prophet as enemy of the existing inherited order can take various forms. First is rejection of the possibility the Holy Spirit has actually been received. The prophet's discourse contradicts the usual order, so his enemies denounce him as bewitched, insane, a liar or a poet. There are, then, two options. We either confess the Unity of the Principle, along with prophecy as a source of authentic knowledge and return to God, or reject both prophecy and return to God and all talk of them as unverifiable speculation. Every sacred tradition faces these alternatives and their impact on the self, the world and what lies beyond.

Speaking of the Holy Spirit to his disciples,[1] Mary's son called it the Spirit of Truth.[2] The apostolate of perfection is inextricably linked to It. The perfect

---

1 Hebrew *rûaḥ qāḏôš*, Greek *pneuma hagion*, Arabic *rūḥ al-qudus.*

2 Hebrew *rûaḥ ha ᵓᵉmeṯ*, Greek *to pneuma tes aletheias*, Arabic *rūḥ al-amīn.* The Hebrew noun *ᵓemeṯ*, usually translated as "truth," is associated with the verb *ᵓāman* ("to support," "to maintain," "to establish"), the noun *ᵓᵉmûnâ* ("solidity," "fidelity") and the expression *ᵓāmen* ("enough"). Translating *rūḥ al-amīn* as "Spirit of Truth" has both etymological and semantic justification. It is in line with the entire tradition of sacred wisdom for which the relationships between Intellect and Reason are crucial. Since everything is created "with the Truth" and is concentrated in human knowledge, we relate to the things of the world by finding their essential sameness with what is in the self, as signs that recall the original core of our being which focuses all the potentialities of manifestation. Knowing is making true, realizing. Those who achieve self-realization find that all the signs in the outer horizons are already in the self and the truth of their creaturehood is one and always true to itself. Belief is our attitude towards the fact that all things were created "with Truth" and the aspiration of the faithful to unite with it or realize themselves.

 | DOI 10.1163/9789004279407_094

individual is our sublime potential fully manifest. Mary's son named him in his mother tongue and in Greek that name is *Parakletos*. In other languages its form is related to its bearer's link to God through the Spirit of Truth. God said of the Paraclete through Moses: "And I will put my words in his mouth; and he shall speak unto them all that I shall command him."[3]

God's apostles all know him and every language has a name for him. When God sent him into time, it was as a sign of His presence beyond finitude. The Word God sent down into his heart was borne by the Spirit of Truth and passed into language to be differentiated into signs. The signs of the differentiated Word were the Recitation received in the self from the Self, to be conveyed in speech to other selves, illumined by the Spirit of Truth.

> "Be mindful of Him who created you, and the generations of the ancients." They said, "Thou art merely one of those that are bewitched; thou art naught but a mortal, like us; indeed, we think that thou art one of the liars. Then drop down on us lumps from heaven, if thou art one of the truthful." He said, "My Lord knows very well what you are doing." But they cried him lies; then there seized them the chastisement of the day of Shadow; assuredly it was the chastisement of a dreadful day. Surely in that is a sign, yet most of them are not believers. Surely thy Lord, He is the All-mighty, the Ever-merciful. Truly it is the revelation of the Lord of all Being, brought down by the Spirit of Truth upon thy heart, that thou mayest be one of the warners, in a clear, Arabic tongue. Truly it is in the Scriptures of the ancients. Was it not a sign for them, that it is known to the learned of the Children of Israel? If We had sent it down on a foreigner and he had recited it to them, they would not have believed in it. Even so We have caused it to enter into the hearts of the sinners, who will not believe in it, until they see the painful chastisement so that it will come upon them suddenly, while they are not aware, and they will say, "Shall we be respited?" What, do they seek to hasten Our chastisement? What thinkest thou? If We give them enjoyment of days for many years, then there comes on them that they were promised.[4]

The Holy Spirit reveals both Life and Word, so that differentiation occurs. Unity is confirmed by duality and the signs in world and self pass through dense, faint shadows. They manifest the Truth, in coming and going and in the

---

3 *Deuteronomy*, 18:18.

4 *Qur'an*, 26:184–206. The text corresponds to the page of a 1760 manuscript given as figure 2.20, on page 588.

dualities of darkness and light. Shifting positions do not eliminate the presence of the Truth they manifest.

When a prophet speaks as inspired by the Holy Spirit, it is first in his people's language. The Holy Spirit is not confined to one language, however, and the revelation can be translated into them all. As discourse of the one Truth, the Recitation is, in principle, present in them all. They converge at the self's centre, the truth present in their diversity. Every self is, at origin, attuned to Truth and remembrance of It. Language is transmitted knowledge, its role to remind us of our uncreated core, the knowledge that depends on itself alone.

> Take not your oaths as mere mutual deceit, lest any foot should slip after it has stood firm, and you should taste evil, for that you barred from the way of God, and lest there should await you a mighty chastisement. And do not sell the covenant of God for a small price; surely what is with God – that is better for you, did you but know. What is with you comes to an end, but what is with God abides; and surely We shall recompense those who were patient their wage, according to the best of what they did. And whosoever does a righteous deed, be it male or female, believing, We shall assuredly give him to live a goodly life; and We shall recompense them their wage, acording to the best of what they did. When thou recitest the Recitation, seek refuge in God from the accursed Satan; he has no authority over those who believe and trust in their Lord; this authority is over those who take him for their friend and ascribe associates to God. And when We exchange a sign in the place of another sign – and God knows very well what He is sending down – they say, "Thou art a mere forger!" Nay, but the most of them have no knowledge. Say: "The Holy Spirit sent it down from thy Lord in truth, and to confirm those who believe, and to be a guidance and good tidings to those at peace." And We know very well that they say.[5]

Everything in existence links to God through being-at-peace.[6] God the All-peaceful[7] offered and we accepted trust as our relation as faithful to the Faithful.[8] At peace, the All-peaceful is our goal and our belief is love and

---

5 Ibid., 16:94–103. The text corresponds to the page of a 1811 manuscript, given as figure 2.21, on page 588.

6 See *Qur'an*, 3:83.

7 Ibid., 59:23.

8 Ibid., 33:72 and 59:23.

knowledge. Through being-at-peace, love and knowledge we turn to the All-peaceful, All-loving and All-knowing.[9]

As All-peaceful, All-loving and All-knowing, God sent down the Recitation to recall us to Him. When we recite it, we connect with the Praised as first recipient and the Holy Spirit that bore it and God Who revealed it. We turn from multiplicity for the One. Orientation towards the One acknowledges and renews our covenant with God. Consciousness of the covenant put us on the path of return. The Praised is our finest example and guide, who says and does only what God commands. His march towards the All-peaceful is steady, as he does not violate his oath. Journeying in the same way, we draw closer to what is with God, away from what is not. Such are the paths of return, the paths to Peace.

---

9 Three of the divine names mentioned in the Recitation are the All-peaceful (*al-Salām*, 59:23), the All-loving (*al-Wadūd*, 85:14) and the All-knowing (*al-ʿAlīm*, 2:32).

CHAPTER 19

The City of Peace

The worlds manifest the All-peaceful. As they have only what they have received, their will consists solely of receiving and returning Peace, confessing no will but His. God gave us Peace to express our original nature. Returning the gift of peace as our debt to God and all things, we are people of peace. Being-at-peace in full use of our will turns us towards the self's centre, putting us on the path of Peace. God alone is Peace and we self-realize in return to Him. This journey is through a foreign land to our homeland, the Abode of Peace.

> And God summons to the Abode of Peace, and He guides whomsoever He will to the upright path.[1]
>
> This is the path of thy Lord, the upright; We have distinguished the signs to a people who remember. Theirs is the Abode of Peace with their Lord, and He is their Friend for that they were doing.[2]

To discover Peace as our centre is to discover our orientation as people of peace to Peace through being-at-peace. Always in the depths, we know we are at the bottom of the valley of existence, in the wastelands of the world. We must take stock of seven moments – space's six dimensions and our centre, the six days and the seventh – to set off on the quest for existence's summit, the City of Peace: "There has come to you from God a light, and a Book Manifest whereby God guides whosoever follows His good pleasure in the ways of Peace, and brings them forth from the shadows into the light by His leave; and he guides them upon the upright path."[3]

This relationship of the people of peace with God as Peace and the All-peaceful through being-at-peace is present in every sacred tradition. As ascent by Peace, it is both passive and active being-at-peace, our only debt to God.[4]

The Praised is the best example of ascent, the first of the people of peace. God led him from the Inviolable Mosque at Becca to the Further Mosque at Sion. The Valley floor and the Mount's peak denote the two extremes of the internally divided self, its depths in the dark and the sublime height in the

1 *Qur'an*, 10:25.
2 Ibid., 6:126–27.
3 Ibid., 5:15–16.
4 See *Qur'an*, 3:19.

 | DOI 10.1163/9789004279407_095

Light. These extremes are linked by the upright path. Tradition's partner is the debt, our obligation to return to God. Return requires doctrine, with corresponding wisdom and ritual, a path to harmonize the self with the known goal.

Every sacred tradition is centred on spiritual influence as at least potentially present in its followers. Otherwise, it would cease to exist, disappearing from the view of those in whom the spiritual chain has been broken. There are very few outward signs of this. Nonetheless, even in the final days, there will be initiates joined in a spiritual chain.

The world order, however unsatisfactory, seems stable and repetitive to the observer. This can cause awareness of dependence on the Principle to fade. The self then loses its orientation and its way, sinking deeper into the depths, further from the centre. Every sacred tradition has a narrative that recalls the self's descent and the impossibility of order without a principle, the end of this world and the new beginning. Prophets and the righteous regularly revive our awareness of this, recalling the end as nigh and ineluctable. This purely symbolic language, expressed in myth, connects the levels of existence. Without symbols and myths, the world of one level cannot "open up" to another on the upright path.

Recalling the nearness of the Hour and the entailed dissipation of illusions, prophets confess the indestructible order intimated by the signs in the horizons and the self. Chaos remains an ever possible disorientation or loss of connection with the Principle, but God does not abandon the world. He is its eternal Creator.

The *Book of Revelation* is a moving epitome of prophetic accounts of this world's end and the next's beginning. The image of dissolution as opposed to the inner order of creation takes various forms in the Recitation. Viewing prophecies of the world's end from the certainty of the now, we take them seriously only in the context of initiation as every true tradition's sublime moment. Initiation to higher levels needs symbolic and mythic language.

True orientation towards the Self as supra-individual reality requires a tradition. Traditional doctrine, ritual and virtue provide only what we already possess. They confirm its existence in the self and prompt renewal. In a given tradition, we are "conducted" on the way. The role of initiation as passing on spiritual influence from our centre is to help us make a journey to the centre. Starting on the journey is true initiation, the journey initiation in action.

Ritual facilitates spiritual initiation and is inseparable from doctrine, as, in principle, every element of ritual is symbolic in nature. Ritual embodies doctrine, while symbolic language is a form of speech or representation at one level of the manifestation of being and all its other possibilities, both higher and lower. Only symbolic language transcends the boundaries of a given level of manifestation of being. It lets us see unshakeable order in the end of the world and recognize in every disorder the signs of attaining the City of Peace.

"Symbols are essentially," as René Guénon has emphasised, "a means of teaching, and not only of outward teaching but of something more insofar as they serve above all as 'supports' for meditation, which is at the very least the beginning of inner work."[5] If symbols support spiritual influence, their source is not individual. Focusing on them links strongly with the self's centre, confirming its orientation and embarkation on the journey. Speculation regarding symbols, however, cannot replace active initiation. To understand *Revelation* we must accept symbolic speech as the only possible link with the City of Peace:

> And there came unto me one of the seven angels which had the seven vials full of the seven last plagues, and talked with me, saying, Come hither, I will shew thee the bride, the Lamb's wife. And he carried me away in the spirit to a great and high mountain, and shewed me that great city, the holy City of Peace, descending out of heaven from God, having the glory of God: and her light was like unto a stone most precious, even like a jasper stone, clear as crystal; and had a wall great and high, and had twelve gates, and at the gates twelve angels, and names written thereon, which are the names of the twelve tribes of the children of Israel.[6]

---

5 Guénon, *Perspectives on Initiation*, 194–95.

6 *Revelation*, 21:9–12. From the 15th century *Radosav's Bosnian Book* (f. 51r), given as figure 2.22, on page 589.

Afterword: False Prophets

If we were to express our wishes as rights, we would all claim the rights to life and happiness. In a finite world, neither can be realized. Death waits for us all and none is spared unhappiness. The life and happiness allotted us are too limited to compensate for death and suffering. The crucial question is one of absolute life and happiness. This is a question from a world of limits. At no point can we claim to have transcended those bounds irrevocably, nor can the question be answered except by the self. Our fate is to perceive the fullness of life and happiness from a perspective of death and suffering. If such fullness is our goal, can it answer our question from that perspective?

If any in this world do know the answers but offer no help in our struggle, why should they concern us? When explanations and answers are offered, how can we know they are right? Are they due to contemplation or experience? Can such immediate experience be passed on?

Human individuality is finite and death ends suffering. Or there must be a supra-individuality to pass into, beyond finitude, as existence cannot be its own principle. As a whole and with all it contains, existence is a sign of higher levels that encompass it wholly. Only the principle condenses and encompasses it as a whole.

God sent His prophets to recall the possibility of eternal life and perfect happiness. None could bestow them, but they did bear witness to the possibility in the self. No one can die or be happy or achieve plenitude of either for another. Both transcend the individual. We all stand alone before God. Our relations with others and the world do nothing to change this.

This solitude is masked by our habit of being in multiplicity and our remoteness from the principle, our connection to which is so variously expressed in language and art, rite and myth, action and thought. In this complex, we never escape involvement in tradition and counter-tradition.

Every true tradition has three crucial elements – Unity, prophecy, and return. Subtract any and it is not properly speaking a tradition. Counter-tradition involves distortion or denial. Any discussion of tradition entails insight into the ways of denial and distortion.

Unity is the principle of all things, manifest in multiplicity as a whole and everything individually. Unity is a quality. Its manifestations are thus an incalculable multitude of derived qualities. As soon revealed, it manifests in dualities, including that of space and time. Unity is infinite, its manifestation finite. Unity descends from pure quality to its manifestations, whose finitude includes quantity as their lowest expression, a contingent manifestation of quality.

 | DOI 10.1163/9789004279407_096

Unity's manifestation can be viewed in two directions: from Unity towards the farthest reaches of multiplicity, from centre to circumference, spirit to matter, and back again.

We encompass the whole from, as it were, two perspectives – below and above. Our origins are above, our existence always lower than our principle. All our capacities are in Unity as that principle. We are designed to rise from any depth to Unity. This possibility is not due to our will, but to the universal presence of the centre towards which we are open. We and all existence are encompassed by the Principle's knowledge and attracted to it by His perfect mercy.

Prophecy reveals the centre or principle to us. This is the knowledge and mercy that encompass all things. Prophecy thus includes every human capacity originally bestowed as Spirit. The prophets recall us to our potential and bring us ritual and sacrifice to orient our life and death towards the life no death encompasses. We use them to achieve orientation towards that centre, on the path of ascent, the axis from the depths to sublime uprightness. Individuality involves a world of "lesser mysteries." Fullness of life passes from it to a supra-individual one of "greater mysteries," where nothing depends on individual will, but on confessing no will but the Will.

That orientation can be reversed. When we cease to see Unity as a pure quality, we begin our descent towards a world in which time and space seem increasingly quantifiable. Matter comes to seem self-sufficient, real. Our will seems enough to master matter, obscuring the principle and quality. Time and space seem interconnected in some extended tangibility and we assume the capacity to predict and identify what precedes events. Their connection with causes that transcend limits fades, leaving the illusion that only quantity exists.

This inverted image places forecasting and speculation in quantifiable reciprocity, everything clearly delimited. Anything not in that context is "enchantment," an obstacle to freedom in a world of nature. Any such worldview with origins in matter's darkness is the absolute opposite of traditional order. The inverted image stands against initiation into tradition that transcends our subjection to suffering and death. These images are counterparts: multiplicity and quantity against Unity and quality; futurology based on quantity against prophecy as the revelation of Unity; return to Unity against embarking for a world moving from darkness towards planned perfection.

False prophets are the opposite of true prophets in all things. They are a major problem. The damage they do is far greater than that resulting from a mere lack of true prophets. When He announced the Praised through Moses, did God not say people would wonder how to tell false from true? Did not Jesus warn of the danger of false prophets?

God's answers bear repetition. False prophets are the founders and advocates of every false doctrine. Their lies, garbed in the legacy of the true, cannot be second guessed without appeal to the Principle the true prophets confess, which is irreducible to any self. It is confirmed in the universal demand summed up by the Praised: "Obedience is required only in what is good."[1]

> When the prophet speaketh in the name of the Lord, if the thing follow not, nor come to pass, that is the thing which the Lord hath not spoken, but the prophet hath spoken it presumptuously: thou shalt not be afraid of him.[2]
>
> Then the Lord said unto me, the prophets prophesy lies in my name: I sent them not, neither have I commended them, neither spoke unto them: they prophesy unto you a false vision and divination, and a thing of nought, and the deceit of their heart.[3]
>
> Thus saith the Lord of hosts, Hearken not unto the words of the prophets that prophesy unto you: they make you vain: they speak a vision of their own heart, and not out of the mouth of the Lord.[4]
>
> Woe unto you, when all men shall speak well of you! For so did their fathers to the false prophets.[5]
>
> Beware of false prophets, which come to you in sheep's clothing, but inwardly they are ravening wolves. Ye shall know them by their fruits. Do men gather grapes of thorns or figs of thistles?[6]
>
> For there shall arise false Christs, and false prophets, and shall shew great signs and wonders; insomuch that, if it were possible, they shall deceive that very elect.[7]

A prophet receives his message from God: his sublime potential, the core where being and knowledge are true. Prophets are created and reveal their Creator. Creation is dual, all things in it created with Truth. Acknowledging this, we realize ourselves in the confession of no truth but Truth. We recognize existence as God's kingdom, God as its King. There the realized self is a perfect being. In preparation, we must constantly re-examine and reshape our notions

---

1 Bukhārī, 9:193–94.

2 *Deuteronomy*, 18:22.

3 *Jeremiah*, 14:14.

4 Ibid., 23:16.

5 *Luke*, 6:26.

6 *Matthew*, 7:15–16.

7 Ibid., 24:24.

of ourselves and the world. When we take them for anything but signs pointing to higher levels of being, we deny our confession.

Each prophet has his counterpart false prophet. There is no true without false prophecy. True prophecy relates creation with the uncreated Creator. It turns everything in existence towards Unity so that they become signs of Unity, leaving behind the contrasts of the visible world.

Deny the confession of no god but God and anything may be your god: passions, imaginings, parents, ventures, the self and its achievements. False prophets claim but do not speak in His name.

There is no Anointed without a false Anointed, no Praised without a false Praised. Challenges to the Anointed and the Praised take various forms, but most essentially direct opposition to their prophecy. The depths are represented as the principle, in two ways. Satan and God may be represented as Darkness and Light, either as warring principles or as darkness prevailing over Light.

Such false prophecy reverses everything. It is only resolved in an encounter between truth and lie – Anointed and false Anointed, Praised and false Praised. This final encounter ends one cycle of existence and begins another. The depths are reformed as utter dispersal and the debt to Unity can no longer be associated with anything else. In another inversion, the apostolate of the Praised and the Anointed becomes a new beginning: "It is He who has sent His apostle with the guidance and debt of truth, that He may uplift it above every debt, though the associaters be averse."[8]

This final triumph of true over false marks the universal return to Unity: "Upon the day the earth shall be changed to other then the earth, and the heavens and they sally forth unto God, the One, the Omnipotent."[9]

Life and death are opposites, as are happiness and suffering. The self is split between death and suffering, at a lower level, life and happiness at a higher. We constantly face the possibility that suffering and death represent imperfection in creation. It is possible to ask and answer this question while remaining faithful to our sublime potential, but it does involve ignorance and violence towards the perfect entity of the world.

We accept God's offer of confidence and He called us "sinful, very foolish."[10] This confirms the perfection of His creation. Ibn al-ʿArabi wrote: "Part of the

---

8 *Qur'an*, 9:33.

9 Ibid., 14:48. See also: 20:105–107.

10 *Qur'an*, 33:72.

perfection of existence is the existence of imperfection within it."[11] That we are ignorant and violent is manifest in our baseness, our orientation towards pain and suffering. Becoming aware of this and turning to the All-knowing, All-just and All-merciful, we see His face in all things, are drawn to Him, raised from the depths: we seek refuge from the evil of the created,[12] for there is no reality but Reality. Awareness of our ignorance allows us to turn to the All-knowing, while acknowledging the violence in every ignorant action places us before the All-just. Ignorance and violence are the wings on which we fly to the Beautiful, as Razi said: "But the wild steed of the soul became like a mad moth with ignorance and oppressiveness, or passion and anger, as its two wings and it hurled itself on the candle of the Majesty of Unity."[13]

There is no knower without a known. Those who know focus on the known. We know the world. Both we and the world are God's self-revelation. Knowing us and it, we turn to God Who knows us knowing and Whom we know. The world is and is not Him. When we see it, we do not see God; when we see Him, we do not see the world. Everything perishes but His face. Our knowledge can be neither halted nor completed. Its goal is union, resolution of the enigma of "is and is not."

The world contains nothing incomplete and imperfect, nothing not beautiful, for He creates everything beautiful[14] as the Beautiful Who loves beauty.[15] As Ibn al-ʿArabi said:

> Know that the divine beauty through which God is named "Beautiful" and by which He described Himself in His apostle's words, "He loves beauty," is in all things. There is nothing but beauty, for God created the cosmos only in His form, and He is beautiful. Hence all the cosmos is beautiful.[16]

If we do not see that beauty in all things and they are not revealed as signs of God, then they veil the Face of God. Acknowledging creation as the Creator's

---

11 Ibn al-ʿArabī, *al-Futūḥāt al-makkiyya*, 2:307, quoted in Chittick, *The Sufi Path of Knowledge*, 296.

12 See *Qur'an*, 113:1–2.

13 Rāzī, *The Path of God's Bondsmen from Origin to Return*, 199.

14 See *Qur'an*, 32:7.

15 See Muslim, 1:53.

16 Ibn al-ʿArabī, *al-Futūḥāt al-makkiyya*, 2:542.

manifestation and returning all to Him, we cause the veil to disappear: there is no reality but Reality and all things perish but His face.[17]

Our return to the Face in all things means seeing that the turn to ascend the path to God must begin in ignorance and violence. The apostle said: "By Him in whose hand my soul is, if you had not sinned, God would have removed you and brought a people who do sin, then ask God's pardon and are forgiven."[18]

When we see the All-knowing, All-beautiful and All-forgiving, it is necessarily out of ignorance and sinfulness. Knowing, we turn towards what we know. When it is God, He reveals Himself to us in His beauty. We surrender to receive It. It draws us, and we seek union with It. We discover ourselves as faithful, as loving what we know as beautiful, in relation to the All-faithful.

Faith is how the faithful relate to the All-faithful, loving God as He loves us, aware that our debt maintains our connection with Him. God told us: "O believers, whosoever of you turns from his debt, God will assuredly bring a people He loves, and who love Him, humble towards the believers, disdainful towards the concealers, men who struggle in the path of God, not fearing the reproach of any reproacher. That is God's bounty; He gives it unto whom He will; and God is All-embracing, All-knowing."[19]

God's bounty is for those with nothing. Only after realizing absolute poverty will they receive everything from the All-bountiful. Receiving confesses no bountiful but the All-bountiful. However much we receive, we remain poor in knowledge and power. When others expect us to know and act justly, their expectations are based on ignorance and injustice as inescapable human qualities. Only before God is our condition clearly and irrefutably revealed. The initiated adjust their ignorance and impotence before Him, heedless of how the ignorant and powerless censure that ignorance and impotence.

---

17 See *Qur'an*, 28:88.

18 Muslim, 4:1436.

19 *Qur'an*, 5:54.

Epilogue: Entering, Passing and Exiting

Sacred history does not fit the modern construct of history, with its bias to quantifiable space and time, causes and consequences. Modern history assumes an object-world and knowledge that depends on a knowing self. Sacred history's space and time involve qualities that things in the world of quantity merely reflect. The self's space and time are key, the things of the world mere signs.

Sacred tradition's central question is humanity and our sublime potential. The responses take various forms but have a common kernel: that we proceed from and for perfection, pass through our stations with it, and have in it our only refuge. Our earthly beginning is a dark seed, our end a handful of dust. But the fullness, truth and reality of our creation and guidance to the perfect goal abide.

All self-realization requires is already in that kernel. What lies within or indeed without the visible world's horizons reminds us of the capacities of our creation, the truth of which is inextricable from that of the creation we are placed in, just as creation needs us as its focal point.

We exist for perfection. It is the self's inexhaustible treasure house, its measure and its goal. This is why witness to God's unity is inextricable from the Praised's apostolate and the return of all things to God through him. The first and last perfection of the self holds pure and perfect time and comprehends all passage of time, all existence, and the sublime knowledge of it in the now.

The Praised's self is thus in all manifest things – at beginning and end and in between. This is the meaning of: "I had time with God when no angel had approached nor any of the prophet-envoys had yet embraced me."[1] This is the Praised's priority in creation, from and for which existence was derived, whose foundation stone and keystone he is, the maternal principle and seal of the prophets.

God told the Praised that every sacred tradition has the same core and can be expressed at any time in any tongue: "And We sent never an apostle before thee except that We revealed to him, saying: 'There is no god but I, so serve Me.'"[2] God is manifest in three things – existence or dispersion in time and

1 Although not found in the canonical collections of the Praised's sayings, compiled on the basis of a clear chain of transmission, this saying is found widely in the Sufi tradition, most commonly as "I have a moment when no prophet sent out or angel brought near embraces me (or: when none embraces me other than my Lord)." See Maybūdī, *Kashf al-asrār wa 'uddat al-abrār*, 1:269, 683; 2:328; 6: 460.

2 *Qur'an*, 21:25,

 | DOI 10.1163/9789004279407_097

space; the self, which gathers time and space in the hour; and the message sent down.

Each revelation's form and contents are fitted to their time, place and circumstances. For all the differences, their essence is one. Translation does not affect their metaphysical kernel. Otherwise, no revelation would be possible. Sent down in a given language, each revelation comprehends both arcs of existence – descent from the One to the many and return back to Him.

If God is true,[3] then each of His manifestations is with truth and so true – on its own, within and for itself, and in relation to the rest of creation. Our knowledge of the names means we know, in principle, the truth of the creation of all things, for no sign in the world or self, no name, fails to announce God as Truth. The different names are attributes, epithets, or significations of Truth. None comprehend Truth fully, even in concert, as Truth cannot be comprehended whole. No sign contains anything but Truth, however, so all transmit some Truth to whoever knows them.

Knowledge relates knower and known. If the known is real, so is knowledge of it. Otherwise, it is unreal and false and distorts the self's authentic nature. Signs do not exist independently of what they signify. It is a gift of our nature that we can know what they connect us to.

In this world, our design connects us through the things in the world and self, other people and the revealed books with the final goal of our knowledge so that these things can be realized in us as in the Absolute. When what we know is ultimate, it is first, the reason and purpose of the world and of our own being. Growth in knowledge is the path of realization and return.

Creation's truth is in small and great, however differently. The self, a creature, sweeps up all things in its finitude, where they are subject to constant change, but remain signs of the God manifest in them. However expansive the self's embrace of the real, we find creation's truth and are liable to be recalled to our essence, which is also the truth of God's creation.

Realization, the being-in-truth of fully developed humanity, is confession of the truth of creation in all things, as the Praised said: "Your soul has a right against you, your Lord has a right against you, and your guest has a right against you. So, give to each that has a right its right."[4]

Translating the Arabic *ḥaqq* as "right" offers additional clarification of God's manifestation as Truth. The concept of "a right" connotes truth, reality, appropriateness, purpose, meaning, presence, role, etc. Where there is a right, there

3 See *Qur'an*, 22:6 and 22:62.

4 This tradition is found in many forms. See Wensinck, *Concordance*, 1:486. The form given here is cited in Chittick, *The Sufi Path of Knowledge*, 400n12.

is a debt or obligation until that right is satisfied. The obligation is to recognise creation's truth in all things. Rights do not exist without obligations, obligations without rights. We are obliged as human beings, because God put us in His debt. Debt is how we relate as debtors to God as Creditor. Unless we accept this, we are unjust to ourselves and God and the world, as His manifestation.

We relate to the things of the world and the truth of their existence through debt or obligation. Nothing in existence is but was created with divine guidance. All have their full reason and full purpose. We pay our debt by recognizing their rights, admitting that they are signs and names of Truth as the source of all debt and of the treasure house all things are returned to by grace or force.

Coming-to-be-in-truth as recognition of the truth in all things corresponds to the Arabic concept of *taḥqīq*. We and the world are in constant flux, but also a constant manifestation of truth as reason and purpose. Truth is our beginning and end.[5] We are knowers connected through knowing with the truth of our own creation, present in three revelations – in the creation of the external world and its signs; in the self as knowing subject; and in the Books sent down to some prophets.

Such truthfulness entails knowing and recognizing Truth's presence and the rights grounded in every manifestation of the divine. Truth is one in all, in a constant but different revelation. Confessing no god but God recognizes that all things manifest the One as Truth individually and in concert. He is One and Flux. Nothing enters or exits existence without His will. Whatever arrives is maintained in the moment thanks to the One, its full reason and purpose.

Perfect witness is clear vision of the signs of the One as Truth in all things and praise of Him as manifest in creating and guiding creation as praised. Existence receives praise to return it, as God said: "Nor is there anything that does not glorify Him in praise."[6] God gives. That He is praised comes through manifestation and returns through praise to Him as First and Last, Outer and Inner.

The Creator is manifest in all things, present in the truth of their inner and outer aspects. We recognize our debt to ourselves by knowing the names of things as attributes of Truth. We recognize their right by bearing witness of how that knowledge is God making us his steward over creation. We are in debt to all existence. Otherwise, our knowledge of the names would serve no purpose. All things, those now and those that might be, have their place in our selves.

---

5 On coming-to-be-in-truth as a key issue in Ibn al-ʿArabī, see Chittick, *The Self Disclosure of God*, 96–98; esp. 96.

6 *Qur'an*, 17:44.

Recognizing right in all things, we realize our own self as steward, in a complex of relations with heaven and all things the senses testify to and all things beyond, including the Mystery revealed by earth, heaven, and what lies between, in their great image of our particularity. The Creator gave us our role as steward. He prepared us for it with capacities of cognition, imagination, knowing the names and composing the many in Unity. It differentiates us from other creatures. We know their names and relate as faithful to the Faithful through confidence and truth.

We can join in recognizing creation's truth and realize our debt willingly, or we can deny it and belittle our connection with the Lord, obscuring our authentic nature. Denying the signs removes us from Him,[7] our actions increasingly founded on ignorance, corruption and error.

The tradition cited above stresses the self's rights or claims against itself, the rights of the Lord, and finally the rights of the rest. The rights of self and Lord are inextricable.[8] Everything in creation reveals Him, as we gather it within the self through the names. Recognizing the self's rights we recognize His, and vice versa. We relate to our selves through Him, to Him through our selves. Our attempts to imagine the real of the world and its principle, its maintenance and purpose fail outside the self. Ignoring our failure, we distort, obscure, cover over, and damage the self. The external signs divorce from those in the self, no longer reminding us of the truth of creation that enables us to return to the self, which is to return to the Lord.

The times and spaces of the external world come to seem independent of those in the knowing subject. Ignoring the self's reality adds conviction to this image of the quantifiable world as the only real, all other worlds being mere figments.

Wisdom lies in recognizing the rights of all things, including the self. Their rights derive from creation in truth and the Creator's guidance. Only by recognizing the rights of the self and the Lord can we recognise the others. What exists is known in its place and role on our path of return and realization in fullness thanks to procession from the self and the Lord, as inextricable aspects of the order in existence. Only loving God and following the path earns God's love. Love relates lover and Beloved. God knows us entirely and loves us entirely in our perfectibility. He is Lover and Beloved.

Loving God, we near Him, as we grow in knowledge – the better we know Him, the more we love Him; the more we love, the better know Him. Part of this love is the signs in world and self: all things indicate the path to Truth; the

7 See *Qur'an*, 7:182–83.

8 See Bukhārī, 3:108.

times and spaces of the world gather at the centre and in the hour of the perfected self, as God told the Praised:

Say: "If your fathers, your sons, your brothers, your wives, your clan, your possessions that you have gained, commerce you fear may slacken, and dwellings you love – if these are more beloved to you than God and His apostle and struggle in His path, then wait till God brings His command. God does not guide unrighteous people."[9]

Seeing right in all things and being just are love of God, confessed by following the Praised as our highest possibility. We may earn His love and the realization of our humanity by confessing no self but the Self. The alternative is injustice and denial of right, the will of the self in opposition to the Will of the Self, as something other than the Creator is taken in place of the Truth of the world's creation. To take created things for the principle is denial and obfuscation of the sequence from beginning to end of things. Truth is the beginning for everything. It keeps each thing in place in the creation's harmony and leads it to realization.

The order of the external horizons reminds us that the same perfection can be found in our own selves and that we can return voluntarily to the Lord Who created all things with Truth and guides them accordingly. To return is to travel on the upright path, with all its obstacles. This is why the self is the greatest battlefield on the path of return.

The things within the horizons of the world are His signs and servants and serve His will to be Known, Peace, and the Bringer of Peace. They announce Him as Peace, from Whom all things begin, by Whom they are maintained, and to Whom return. As the One, God affirms and announces Essence Which abides beyond possibility of expression. The most beautiful names confirm and announce Him. The things in existence correspond to His names, whether singly or in concert.

Existence and the things in it are, through their service, His means of self-revelation as Lord. Their being-at-peace and bringing peace reveal Him as Peace. We gather His names and by our very creation are His servant through whom He reveals Himself as Lord, at peace so that He may reveal Himself as Peace. After our nature, we are faithful, in a relation of faith with God as Faithful. Faith is both knowledge and love – knowledge of the Beloved, love of the Known. Free will is its condition.

We may deny that God made us for self-realization through His most beautiful names under the covenant offered and accepted. Choosing not to be His

---

9 *Qur'an*, 9:24.

servants or at peace, we break that bond and deny our Lord's and our own rights and claims and those of all things in existence.

One consequence is an increasing distance from the One and obfuscation of the original nature of the self, an ever deeper falling into ignorance and action based on it. This is confirmed by conflict within the self and the world, as is said in the Recitation: "Corruption has appeared in the land and sea, for that men's own hands have earned, that He may let them taste some part of that which they have done, that haply so they may return."[10]

Creation and its contents are in space and time.[11] Few things attract us as much as our sense of these concepts as clear and determinate. But are they? When we say "space," we are marking out a place in which something might be. This is a place in which existence, the visible, is manifest. Space is emptiness until things and beings are in their places.

But emptiness is impossible, except as a conceptual contrary of fullness. To be understood, fullness requires emptiness as a figment, even though it does not actually exist. Thus, space is nothing but the quality of things in existence, a relation between things, each with its own place. In constant flux, time, which marks out change, is also just a relation between them.

This matter of space and time is of decisive importance for the realization of the self in and through its recognition of the rights of whatsoever does have some right to claim against it. To better understand this, one might look at the question: what are the rights which we may be said to owe space and time? Insofar as God is manifest through creation, the world and the things in it are determinate, which means that taken together and individually each of them has its own place, which is not however firmly fixed, so that the relations between them are constantly changing, the indicator of which is time. It would be impossible to discover space or time in the absence of things.

---

10 Ibid., 30:41.

11 These two concepts, "time" and "space," are understood as differing. The first is general and hard to determine, while the other cannot but be separate from the things it relates to. According to Petar Skok no word in any of the Baltic or Indo-European languages is cognate to the Southern Slavic noun *vrijeme*, which means "time." He says, "It may none the less be explained on the basis of Indoeuropean and proto-Slavic linguistic resources, by connecting the verb *vrtjeti*, from the proto-Slavic root *verti-* and the now defunct suffix *-men* > *mę* used for abstraction. The abstract term *vertmen* is Indoeuropean and is found in the Sanskrit *vartman*, where what was at first an abstraction received the concrete meaning of 'where the wheel turns > Radspur, Wegspur, Bahn, Rinnsal', while in the Slavic languages it means much the same as is expressed by the Latin saw: *tempora mutantur et nos mutamur in illis* = *vrijeme* (= *zeman*, Bosna) *gradi, zeman razgrađuje*" (Skok, *Etimologijski rječnik hrvatskoga ili sprskoga jezika*, 3:626).

As Truth, God reveals Himself through creation in truth.[12] In the Recitation Moses is reported as saying: "Our Lord is He who gave each thing its creation, then guided."[13] Creation and guidance are in the divine moment, however they appear to the self, which is both creature and guided. It follows that each thing comes from God, has clear purpose, and is maintained with that purpose and for it with regard to all other things, led towards God on the path of universal return. In saying "things" we mean being as reflecting God's will, as is said in the Recitation: "His command, when He desires a thing, is to say to it 'Be,' and it is."[14]

God's command is His Word. This Word, which contains the desire for something to be, is manifest through the being of that very thing. One may ask regarding such being: Where, what, how, and how great? The modern world-view treats these questions as discrete from why something is, because a thing's full cause and reason lie beyond the quantifiable or the purview of any science that excludes the knowing self.

Each and every being has place and cause and purpose in the Infinite, Who is not subject to change. It is the Creator's will that things are somewhere, subject to motion and change. He reveals Himself, as One, through creation as dual. For only duality can make manifest and affirm Unity. God said of His creation in the Recitation: "Glory be to Him, who created all the pairs of what the earth produces, and of themselves, and of what they know not."[15]

To say "creation" is to say "duality." Nothing in it is indivisible by two. Where two are, there is change and motion, relations between the elements of duality.

Things or beings come into being as manifestations of the will, command, and word of the Creator. He is not subject to change, so that each being has its purpose in His will, albeit in and through manifestation and so subject to disappearance in partial place and time. He said through the Praised: "And call not upon another god with God; there is no god but He. All things perish, except His face. His is the judgment, and unto Him you shall be returned."[16] Things do not perish before God's face, but only with respect to what covers it. Their role is to mark and show it, but not be anything other than it. To fade and

12 See *Qur'an*, 6:73.

13 *Qur'an*, 20:50.

14 Ibid., 36:82.

15 Ibid., 36:36.

16 Ibid., 28:88.

die is how they return to authentic reality, a discovery of His face. He called Himself the Living and Abiding[17] Who does not die.[18]

The number of things and beings is the number of words of command, all in and with God, from and forever. Each appears as being, with place, beginning, and end, but in constant and ceaseless change, which leads to waning and to settling in the authentic word. God said in the Recitation: "Perfect are the words of thy Lord in truthfulness and justice; no man can change His words. He is the All-hearing, the All-knowing."[19]

They are all perfect, the same in the one Word as in their source and origin, united in the first revelation, as Intellect, as if in their own treasure house.

Motion and change necessarily relate to something, to themselves, to other things and to the whole. Each thing can rotate around its centre and, in complex patterns, also circle a second, a third, through countless things, some near, others far, some great, others small.

This complexity is so great that we can only know certain of their partial aspects. God knows everything about all – reason and purpose and place and every change. He said through the Praised: "Not a leaf falls, but He knows it."[20]

This falling of leaves in accordance with His knowledge involves three things – coming into being, being maintained in being, and passing from one place to another.

In the image of the falling leaf, we may see the full cycle, with both arcs – coming and leaving. The origin and goal are the truth of creation. Individually and together all things respond to His command, as a transcription of His words of Creation, each a letter in the universal book of existence through which the Creator self-reveals to Himself.

Each thing is related to the rest altogether and individually. Depending on their changes, things participate in time and measure and change on the way back to the One, to absolute realization of the Creator's word of command.

Calling God the Creator, we testify that He is so in every moment. At any given moment, a given thing may seem to cause another; this does not prove the Creator absent. This follows clearly from the duality of space and time. The world's space and time gather in another manner in the space and time of the self.

Within those external horizons, things are put in their places and move in relation to the rest. Motion is their mutual changing of position. These changes

---

17 See *Qur'an*, 2:255.

18 Ibid., 25:58.

19 *Qur'an*, 6:115.

20 Ibid., 6:59.

may seem very short or long with regard to different relations. The motions differ, depending on which things within existence are being observed. Nothing stands outside this motion, however it may sometimes seem. As God said in the Revelation: "And thou shalt see the mountains, that thou supposest fixed, passing by like clouds – God's handiwork, who has created everything very well."[21]

The time of certain things may seem short or long. God reminds us in the Revelation that changes are relative to perspective: "To Him the angels and the Spirit mount up in a day whereof the measure is 50,000 years."[22] All phenomena are slow in comparison to the movement of the angels and Spirit. But they too were created and are relative and conditional. God appears through them in a different way and space and time have another aspect for them, but the one Truth is manifest in them as in every other thing.

The speed of change is a relation of the path a thing traverses in a given time. Accordingly, that path and the time taken are amongst its qualities, not independent phenomena. Shortness and length are only expressions of the relations between things in motion and change. Something short or small may be reduced towards nothing, towards the absolute moment, while what is long may be enlarged towards infinity and absolute eternity. Not nothing nor the absolute moment nor infinity nor absolute eternity is in any absolute sense. They are different expressions of the Absolute which is One and cannot be reduced or increased. They may only be intimated, just as the signs in the world signify the Mystery, voices the Silence, and the said the Ineffable.

Every eternity is time, between some determinate and infinitely reducible minuteness that is not nothing, on the one hand, and some infinitely extensible duration, that is not without end, on the other. Only He is First and there was nothing before Him. Only He is Last and there is nothing after Him. All beginnings and ends lie within eternity, between first Firstness and last Lastness.

The perfect or complete moment is the same as the perfect or complete eternity. Nothing limits them. This is why they are both signs of God. Two absolutes are not possible, so the absolute moment is absolute eternity. Everything in creation is in a simultaneous process of descending from the primordial fullness and of ascending back towards it.

God said, putting the words in the mouths of men: "Nothing makes us perish save the aeon."[23] Ibn al-'Arabi said this was the truth, as it confirms what God's

21 Ibid., 27:88.

22 Ibid., 70:4.

23 Ibid., 45:24.

apostle himself said: "God is the aeon."[24] The aeon, as long duration, in which all other things have their place, is the relationship of all things in existence to God, as the perfect moment, for Him, is perfect eternity. This is His day, in which all things are revealed as His servants and all things make their peace with Him.

God is not subject to any sort of change, which means He has neither place nor time. All place belongs to Him, as He is absolutely near and absolutely far to all beings. When they are in relation to Him, things are here and now in the full meaning of that: they are all in the same now and in the same place. Their principle is on the upright path. The worlds reveal that path and are in motion with regard to it: they approach it or they withdraw from it; they rise along or descend down it. Time is an expression of this being in relation to the upright path, a rotation around the principle that each individual thing and all together serve to manifest.

There is nothing in existence which is not known within the human self. All our knowledge is partial, but the self discovers itself with regard to the Self through confessing the rights or claims of the truth, role, and reality of everything. The scope for the discovery of the self is unlimited, because the Self is. However little, our knowledge is sufficient to find the Self at every level, albeit both revealed and hidden. God's face is in the truth of the creation of everything in existence and in His guidance, as He said: "Whithersoever you turn, there is the Face of God."[25]

In this always little knowledge, the self builds an image which is only one of the possible levels of the self-differentiation of being. In this endeavour the self knows partially, even though each individual thing is created with the truth, and so the whole exists with reason in the One. But they are maintained in the process of return to Him and by Him. Everything in existence, alone and together, is these two arcs, the arc of descent and the other of ascent whereby God manifests Himself as Outer and Inner, First and Last.[26]

The ritual of the seven circuits of the Kaʿba, the seven points of contact with the earth when falling in prostration, and the seven days of the week remind us of the completeness of creation, the perfection of every externality in relation with our own interiority, with the truth of our creation. Our relationship and that of our own self to the sacred centre is marked by God's command: "Let

---

24 See Chittick, *The Self Disclosure of God*, 128. This tradition as a whole runs, "Do not curse the aeon, for God is aeon" (Muslim, 4:217).

25 *Qur'an*, 2:115.

26 See *Qur'an*, 57:3.

them then finish with their self-neglect and let them fulfil their vows, and go about the Ancient House."[27]

The seven ritual circuits signify the seven levels of existence. Each level has its own heaven or its own circle. Placed in descending order, each circle corresponds to a level of being, so that the upright path or axis connects them with the One. Instructing us regarding the seven circuits, God recalls us to our origin in Peace, Which maintains us and attract us irresistibly to the path of return.

The circle may be divided by its diameters into six equal arcs. Continuing to halve, we may divide each of these arcs in two, getting 12 equal sections. The number six signifies the circle. With the centre the number is seven. If one allows the number 12 to represent the circle, then by adding the centre one gets 13. Referring to himself as the union of either seven or 13 levels of existence, the Praised said of his own arrival in the seventh heaven: "There I found Abraham reclining against the Frequented House."[28]

The prophet Abraham, in secular time, fathered two posterities through Ishmael and Isaac. These two processions gather in the perfect cycle of the Praised's descent from and ascent to the One. From an historical point of view, the traces left by Abraham mark where the Praised rose up from, but from a meta-historical point of view Abraham is where the Praised arrives as he is lead up to and beyond the furthest boundary. Their meeting at the Frequented House in the seventh heaven in fact takes place within the perfect comprehension of the self of the Praised towards which it is good and proper to move on our path of return to the One. The Word which both the Praised and Mary made known, as Recitation and Anointed, gathers the sacred history of the perfect self in fullness.

The 13th letter in both the Arabic and the Hebrew alphabet is "m" (*mim*). According to Muslim interpretations, it stands for Muhammad as the maternal principle of all creation, insofar as it receives and passes on God's self-revelation to Himself. The prophet Ishmael and his 12 sons, the prophet Jacob and his 12 sons, the prophet Jesus and his 12 disciples, and the historical Praised with his 12 assistants and 12 imams all suggest the number 13 as the sacred sign of the Praised. So too does the relationship of the months in the lunar and solar years, as God says in the Recitation: "The number of the months, with God, is 12 in the Book of God."[29]

Each solar year contains 12 lunar months, along with the beginning of a 13th. Thirteen full months exceed a solar year: 12 monthly cycles fit within it, but an

27 *Qur'an*, 22:29.

28 Muslim, 1:102.

29 *Qur'an*, 9:36.

additional 10 days are required to complete it. The interplay of these two years may be considered as revealing the presence of the Praised as 13th in addition to the 12. Through him, God says in the Recitation: "It is He who made the sun a radiance, and the moon a light, and determined it by stations, that you might know the number of the years and the reckoning."[30]

In old Bosnian, the word for "star" (*zvijezda*) was also used for the sun. This noun, which means the sun, is grammatically feminine, just as *al-shams* is in Arabic. In this way the receptive or maternal nature of Intellect or the light of the Praised in relationship with God as the authentic donor of all existence is marked. For the star or sun is a sign of the first intellect, the light of the Praised. The illumination and enlightenment of all the levels of existence signify the donative, prophetic, and the apostolic nature, as the external aspect of his sanctity.

The 12 months of the year, as a sign of existence's receptive aspect, remain linked to intellect and the light of the Praised as uniting principle. While the many remain in ceaseless flux, the heavens, earth, and everything between them remain contingent upon the Hour. God says of this: "He subjected the sun and the moon, each one running to a term stated."[31] Every created thing as truth has its principle and finitude in both its motion and in time, as God says: "God created not the heavens and the earth, and what between them is, save with the truth and a stated term."[32]

This stated term of all things is the Hour, the absolute now, in and with which each thing receives the truth of its creation to exist in and return to. Both truth and the term are in His Word.[33]

The dispersion of things and their motions, to which space and time correspond as qualities demonstrable through comparison and number, have two different levels – one in the Word and the Self, where they occupy the same place and time as that to which the absolute now corresponds; and the other, in the external horizons subject to human perception.

These two levels of existence, the external world and the Word, are connected by the self as a type of partition in which dispersion and gathering, duration and now come together. God says of this: "God takes the souls at the time of their death, and that which has not died, in its sleep; He withholds that

30 Ibid., 10:5.

31 Ibid., 13:2.

32 Ibid., 30:8.

33 See *Qur'an*, 42:14.

against which He has decreed death, but looses the other till a stated term. Surely in that are signs for a people who reflect."[34]

We are present in the relationship between self and Self insofar as our knowledge is equal to recognizing the claims all things have on us and God as absolutely present in all things. Each and every self is thus oriented towards the perfect possibility represented by the Praised and so the Self. Everything within the world's horizons reminds us of this orientation and our embarkation upon the upright path to follow the Praised's self towards the Self. As Ibn al-ʿArabi declared: "Glory be to Him who veils Himself in His manifestation and becomes manifest in His veil!"[35]

The comment about 50,000 human years being but a day in the descent of the Spirit and the angels may be taken in terms of how finitude and infinity and time and eternity interact, with specific reference to their creaturehood and contingency. Using this temporal ratio of one day to 50,000 years and comparing the relative speeds of human beings to those of angels and Spirit, it would follow that the greatest speed we can attain, on horseback, of some 70 m/s, corresponds to the angels and the Spirit travelling at the speed of light (300,000,000 m/s).[36]

This ratio is simply a picturesque illustration of the levels of existence and the different qualities termed space and time. As an image, it indicates that the aeon, created eternity as the relationship of all creatures to God, comprehends every individual thing and relation. Things partake of space and time insofar as being proceeds from the Lord's command. This takes place in created eternity, the time allocated them and nothing in existence appears but in accordance with it.

In the Recitation God told Moses: "Bring forth thy people from the shadows to the light and remind thou them of the Days of God."[37]

To be brought out of the dark into the light is to rise on the upright path through the ontological levels. On the last, all times and days, as relations between things, enter the day of full clarity. The differences between them appear under the aspect of the total debt, our relationship as indebted to God the Creditor for the claims of all things. This relationship is immediate, face to Face, on the day we stand before the Standing, the day of reckoning before the

---

34 *Qur'an*, 39:42.

35 Ibn al-ʿArabī, *al-Fūtūhat al-makkiyya*, 3:547.12; cited in Chittick, *The Self-Disclosure of God*, 129.

36 An alternative calculation is that to a single day, without its night, which is twelve hours, the equivalent human speed would be 8.5 m/s, or the average best speed in a footrace.

37 *Qur'an*, 14:5.

Reckoner, of truthfulness before Truth, of judgment before the Judge, and of ending before the Last.

This coming-into-being-of-truth and return is the all-comprehending Day.[38] God's fullness is announced in the indivisible, ever-present now: "He is with you wherever you are."[39]

The now is unchanging and unchangeable, because God is within it as absolute Lord. This is so at every level of existence. What appears in created existence will die, as a mere manifestation of the Living, but nothing dies in the absolute now, which has neither time nor place, since nothing is like[40] or comparable to Him.[41] God has no pair or other. No place or time can comprehend Him. He suffers no change, but His creation is in constant change and reveals Him as Unchanging. Nothing created lacks its place, but how things relate to and serve God differs. Their places and times and relations with other things and with God also differ. The angels and the Spirit comprehend far more than other things and may appear, in comparison, non-spatial. Their changes in relation to other things are temporal, but so brief as to be almost momentary, close to eternity.

Assigning the angels and Spirit their roles in His relationship with us, God made us steward, opening up the path of ascent through existence. The light of the Praised descended from the principle and rose back to it through his full realization in humanity as maternal prophet. It leaves signs on the path of ascent. He is maternal for his receptive role, symbolized by the womb or matrix. God said all existence was bound to Him through the womb, the place of mercy. The Praised is, in the revelation the Holy Spirit brought his heart, a mercy to the worlds on downward and upward path.

In how places and changes relevant to Spirit and angels relate to those that are relevant to us, we see infinity's relationship to finitude, eternity's to temporality. God comprehends both in His day, the absolute now, which admits neither prior nor posterior, just the clear vision of His face unveiled.[42]

Insofar as the angels and Spirit are factors in our relation to God through faith, we may comprehend created eternity as something those faithful to the Faithful can enter at any time. They realize themselves in their absolute now, comprehended eternity and the simultaneity of all things. Sacred history corresponds to this comprehension of a self that is spatial and temporal. Spaces

---

38 See *Qur'an*, 11:84.

39 *Qur'an*, 57:4.

40 See *Qur'an*, 112:4.

41 Ibid., 42:11.

42 Ibid., 50:22.

and times at all levels of existence are just different images of sacred history as the self's authentic fullness, Intellect and the light of the Praised. Sanctity and prophecy, as the maternity of human perfection, correspond to this comprehension of priority and the first.

In sacred history, we and our prophets inhabit the heavens from first to seventh, the levels of existence connected by the upright path, the axis that travels from the depth to most beautiful uprightness. This connection through the heavens, from the earthly Kaʿba as sign of the lowest depth up to the seventh heaven and beyond, is represented by the Praised's night journey. His journey took in all the worlds. The dissolution and dispersion of people and things on the world's surface is transformed into a sacred history of the self that includes all place and time.

VOLUME 3

Gathering Fragments

∴

You have had your finest example in God's apostle for whosoever hopes for God and the Other Day, and remembers God oft.

QUR'AN, 33:21

•••

I came to know everything between the east and the west.

A SAYING OF THE PRAISED, FROM TIRMIDHĪ, *TAFSĪR*, SURA 38, 2

•••

He who discloses Himself, in respect to what He is in Himself, is One in Entity, but the self-disclosers – I mean their forms – are diverse because of the preparedness of the loci of self-disclosure.

IBN AL-ʿARABĪ, *AL-FUTŪḤĀT AL-MAKKIYYA*, 2:85.14

∵

PART 1

Continuity and Discontinuity

• •

CHAPTER 1

Standpoints

In discussing the Bosnian *krstjani* and their church and the Bosnian Muslims and their complex structure of organization, one is clearly dealing with two sacred traditions which are connected in such a way that the former continues, to a large degree, in and through the latter. Muslim witness to Unity, prophecy and return recognizes and acknowledges the core of *krstjan* witness, just as *krstjan* witness recognized and acknowledged the essential similarity of what Muslim witness contains. The evidence is so obvious that to deny it has become a fetish for nationalist ideologues. Things in plain sight became taboo to the point of destruction.[1] Reminded of them, the "masters of history" find their presence unendurable.

The thesis of an unbroken link between the *krstjani* and the Bosnian Muslims is in any case incontestable, given the essential unity of all sacred traditions. The truth is necessarily revealed in different languages and symbols, but retains the same meaning. Revelation endures or fades in various heritages, without losing its original unity. Exoteric forms may vary, becoming incomprehensible to later generations, but that we no longer understand perennial tradition's outward forms does not empty them of meaning.

Language, meanings and symbols inform the self. No two selves are the same. Transcending our limits, we encounter the universal person, a sign to orient every self. Our individual discourse reflects both our individual finitude and our connection with it. Any attempt to break free of our discursive standpoint and embrace a generality behind which to hide produces a construct. Those who seek to transcend the finite and build a perspectiveless perspective

1 As "national ideologies" were formed during the 19th and 20th centuries in Bosnia, modern features were grafted onto religious identities. This was allied to the perversion of traditional intellectuality into a fantasy of a causal-consecutive order from down up, past to future. Croatian and Serb hypostases represented the Muslim as a "break" in and "imposition" on their histories. This was a psychological re-working of guilt as part of the ideological image of the nation as the people awoken and was based on external models. The projection of "Muslim guilt" is a defence mechanism of the split ego attempting to rationalize national identity. Any cultural form that reveals the continuity of Muslim intellectual tradition in Christian Muslimhood or Muslim Christianity becomes a fetish. It results in fencing off certain areas of life and barring them to others in the immediate environs, with whom relations and friendships are often very close, but where distrust and antagonism also exist. The fetish of continuity permeates the most intimate thoughts of those who share in this split.

 | DOI 10.1163/9789004279407_098

within such a construct necessarily produce a closed world of science and history, a world that exists only within their ideological constructs and represents disruption of the self-world-God relationship, a rift between the imaginary and the object of imagination, the image and what it fails to represent. The imaginary is taken as sufficient in itself.

Ideological constructs are not *per se* questionable. Individuals and communities use them to build images of the world. But the world is irreducible to an image. Trying to capture it in one is like grasping at the ocean in a net. What is questionable and dangerous is asserting the image's superiority and attempting to impose it at all costs. Such absolutization of an image is evident wherever hatred and persecution thrive. The truth of God's unity requires many manifestations, but in none can the contingent replace ever-present Truth. Our self-realization is in recognizing this. Our selves are shaped in relation to themselves, others, the world and God. This shaping process is in incessant flux and our memories, experiences and notions put apparent pattern on it. Representing things in terms of quantifiable relations presupposes observer-independent universal law, so that exclusion of the self is a foundational assumption both of modern science and modern history. Absolutization of the laws governing the world precludes openness to eternity. What is not quantifiable becomes unknowable. If, however, there is no knowledge that does not begin and end in the self, different perspectives on the world and history open up.

CHAPTER 2

Krstjani and Muslims

The supposition of rupture between the *krstjani* and the Bosnian Muslims has become an unchallengeable ideological shiboleth. The absolutely imposed necessarily involves a taboo that undermines it. Figure 1.1 presents an ideological construct of Bosnian history as involving entirely separate "Christian" and "Muslim" trajectories. In this split vision, the "other" bounds, but is entirely unlike the observer. The smaller the differences, the more crucial they are. They are maintained by doctrine and ritual. In the Bosnian case, the differences often surprise: different forms of the same name – Adam and Adem, Abraham and Ibrahim, Mojsije and Musa (Moses), David and Davud, Isus and Isa (Jesus) – experienced and represented as different persons in discrete constructs of the Tradition.

That "Bosnian Christianity's" historical trajectory is separate from that of "Bosnian Muslimhood" is the *credo* of the dominant historiography. It requires *krstjan* and Muslim trajectories to be separate, so that anything Christian is non-Muslim, the Muslim un-Christian. Insofar as doctrine, rite and virtue contradict this, differences must be found in language and form. The quantifiable

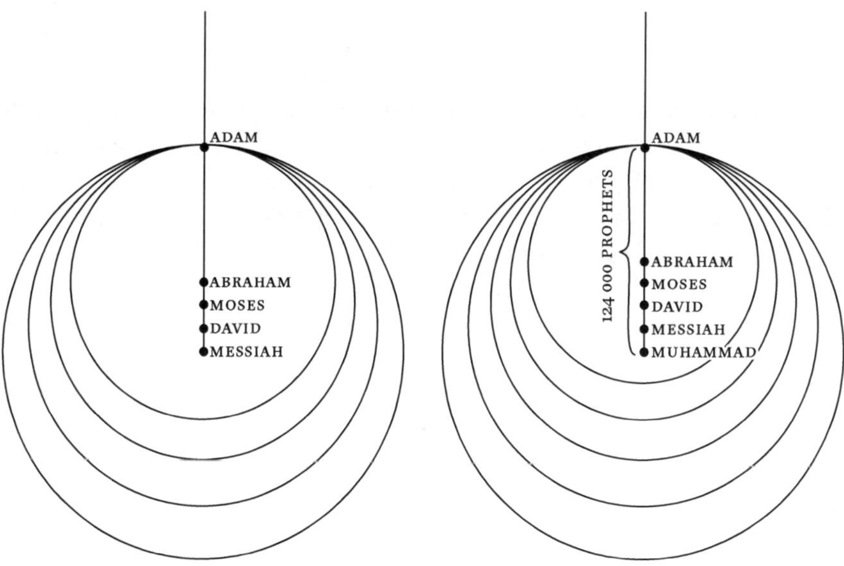

FIGURE 1.1 *Separate trajectories*

 | DOI 10.1163/9789004279407_099

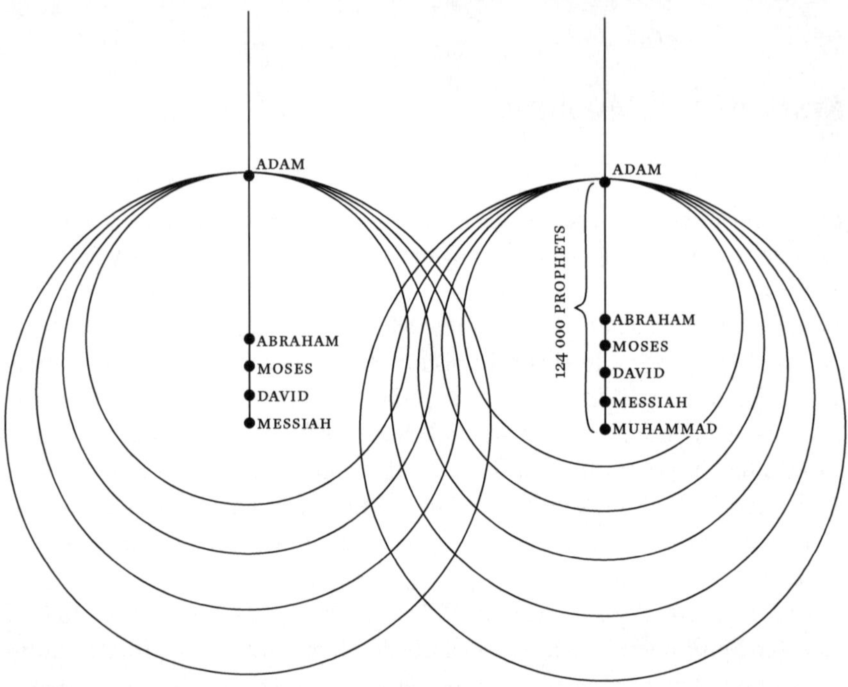

FIGURE 1.2 *Overlapping trajectories*

phenomena, the material of history modelled on natural science, clearly indicate continuity, however, so the claim of historical discontinuity can be defended only by fetishism and splitting of the Ego.

The representation of difference informed by opposed ideologies will involve similar content being on both sides. Its presence is, therefore, defined as obscure, unintelligible, taboo, and fetishized. This results in two overlapping trajectories with two differentiated communities sharing some aspects of ritual or sacred places or parts of the religious calendar, as shown in figure 1.2.

Culture, history and life that are simultaneously Christian and Muslim present problems for such historical interpretation. When subjected to it at all, they are often presented as survivals of a previous history in a new one, syncretism, and pseudo-Muslimhood in Christianity or pseudo-Christianity in Muslimhood.[1] Such interpretations do scant justice to the role of such phenomena in living tradition or its adherents' consciousness.

1 "Christian features" in Muslim culture are usually seen as evidence of the original Christianity Muslims abandoned, willingly or not, and so the authentic, primordial foundation of a "Christian history" to which "Muslim features" have been added to disrupt it. For examples

Muslims do not find such traditions alien, as their book of God's Revelation acknowledges and stands warrant for the books that preceded it historically. This "historically" is conditional. There are many revelations across space and time and all derive from the same Revealer at the centre of every true tradition. Initiation is connecting with Him and seeing all things as signs in His kingdom.

"For Muslims" suggests interpretation by a human community, but no single interpretation exhausts every possible "Muslim" scholarly perspective. In fact, no break is possible in our ever-identical relationship with God, so variously manifest from Adam to Muhammad, as each apostle reveals the same truth differently, as shown in figure 1.3. Confession of no god but God and the Praised as His apostle is inseparable from accepting the Recitation as His Word sent to those "who believe in what has been sent down to thee and what has been sent down before thee."[2]

Any consistent metaphysical perspective considers Unity to be Essence's first manifestation and first confirmation, duality Unity's. What is manifest as duality is real only in relation to Unity. It is the first message, differentiated into receptive and giving aspects, male and female. The relationship of existent and Existence as the One permeates the levels of Being.

This permeation of being is focused in a humanity manifest in the multitude of peoples distinguished by language, nation, time, place, rite and way. As such it speaks to the prophetic presence of that first duality, of first existence in them all. This prophetic presence embraces all the prophets who share a common principle in that perfect first duality, the apostle they know and assist as

---

see Ćatić, "Božić kod muslimana (Prozor u Bosni)"; Đorđević, "Preislamski ostaci među jugoslavenskim muslimanima"; Filipović, "Uskrs kod muslimana"; Hasluck, *Christianity and Islam under the Sultans*; Džaja, *Konfesionalnost i nacionalnost Bosne i Hercegovine*; Zirojević, *Islamizacija na južnoslovenskom prostoru: Dvoverje*. A crucial postulate of such interpretations is the reification of *islam* into "Islam" as something belonging to a particular time and space, denying the most important aspect of the sacred tradition of those "who believe in what has been sent down to thee and what has been sent down before thee" (*Qur'an*, 2:4). Naturally, these same authors reject the application of such views to Christianity and Judaism. In their interpretations, "discontinuity" is established by ideologically reducing historical phenomena to their impact on nation building. Friedrich S. Krauss wrote in 1886 about pluralism in Bosnian history: "There are three grafts onto the trunk of Bosnian history: the Muhammadan faith is one, the Christian faiths two. For three hundred years, the Muhammadan faith flowered amongst the southern Slavs like in no Indo-Germanic people; now the followers of the two Christianities have taken the lead and the Muhammadan faith is taking a breather" (Krauss, "Riječ," viii–ix). In Džaja's reading, these three branches from one tree are an impossible construction: the Muslim branch has no connection to the tree.

2 *Qur'an*, 2:4.

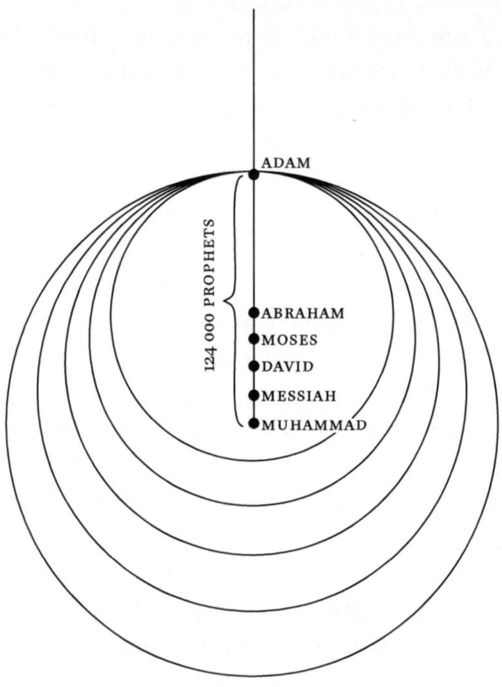

FIGURE 1.3 *Inclusive trajectory*

their own sublime potential. Its historical manifestation is all 124,000 prophets. Every prophet is a link to the One, Who connects them all.

In figures 1.1, 1.2 and 1.3, the centre belongs to either the Anointed or the Praised. But for both views, Christian and Muslim, the path to God passes through the Anointed. Muslims differ from Christian Christology by accepting the Anointed and the Praised as closest to each other, so that witnessing God's unity, by confessing no god but God, is inseparable from confessing the apostolate of the Praised. Muslims thus have no problem understanding this tradition received from their prophet:

> Whoever testifies that there is no god but God, the One, Who has no partners, and that the Praised is His servant and apostle, that the Anointed is God's servant and the son of His servant and his Word that he bestowed upon Mary and a Spirit created by Him, and that the Garden is true and the Fire is true, he shall enter the Garden through one of its eight gates.[3]

3 Muslim, 1:21–22.

CHAPTER 3

Disputations

Throughout their history, Christians have argued with Jews about the Anointed, seeking to show that Jewish tradition already contains reasons for accepting Jesus. Their arguments fail to convince those Jews who find all they need for redemption and individual and collective self-realization in their own tradition. Nor do Christians accept this logic when applied by Muslims, who find reasons for confessing the Praised in earlier revelations, including Torah, Psalms and Gospel. Muslims do not assume a right to impose witness, however, as their confession of no god but God and the Praised as the apostle to whom God revealed His Recitation means Jews and Christians who believe in God and Judgment Day are just as saved as Muslims. Redemption is attaining our sublime potential in return to the One God.

Jews, Christians or Muslims who think *a priori* that the others cannot be saved will seek justification where they can. Their principal weapons in shoring up their position will be elements of the others' witness. Countering the Muslim position requires distortion of the Praised. St. Cyril asked: "If Muhammad is a prophet, how can we believe Daniel? For he said: 'After Christ all vision and prophecy will come to an end.' But [Muhammad] appeared after Christ, so how can he be a prophet. If we say he is a prophet, then we must reject Daniel."[1] Cyril's refutation of the Praised derives from Daniel's words: "Seventy weeks are determined upon thy people and upon the holy city, to finish the transgression, and to make an end of sins, and to make reconciliation for iniquity, and to bring in everlasting righteousness, and to seal up the vision and prophecy, and to anoint the most Holy."[2]

That Cyril saw these words as foretelling the Anointed is understandable, as is the Muslim interpretation of them as prophesying the Praised. Cyril's claim that prophecy ends with the Anointed in fact corroborates the Muslim view. John the Baptist knew the Anointed as having arisen in his time in Israel. Asked by the priests and Levites, he denied that he was the Anointed, Elijah or "that prophet."[3]

Elijah was in Israel, of Jacob's seed and the Anointed was last of that line. We must look elsewhere in the revealed books for prophecy of "that prophet,"

1 *Žitja Konstantina Ćirila i Metodija*, 63–64.

2 *Daniel*, 9:24.

3 See *John*, 1:19–25.

 | DOI 10.1163/9789004279407_100

whose coming was after the Anointed. Since vision and prophecy were sealed in Israel and "that prophet" had not yet come, he could not come from the Israelites. God told Moses: "I will raise them up a prophet from among their brethren, like unto thee, and will put my words in his mouth."[4] And elsewhere: "And there arose not a prophet since in Israel like unto Moses, whom the Lord knew face to face."[5] The same book makes clear that the Ishmaelites are brethren of the Israelites.[6] The Anointed knew of a prophet raised among the Ishmaelites and John bore explicit witness to him as Paraclete, Holy Spirit, and Spirit of Truth.[7] In the Muslim view, Daniel's seventy weeks serve to calculate exactly the coming of the Praised.

To belong to a prophetic tradition is to have a specific prophet and book at the centre of one's self, on the sublime height towards which we ascend. The crucial question is how to belong to that prophet while embracing the one essence spoken of by them all in all their books.

---

4 *Deuteronomy*, 18:18.

5 Ibid., 34:10.

6 See *Genesis*, 25:18.

7 That Christians equate the promise of the Holy Spirit, as Paraclete, with Pentecost does not mean it cannot also, even preeminently, refer to the Praised. An expression can have multiple meanings. According to Frithjof Schuon: "If Mohammed had been a false prophet, there is no reason why Christ should not have spoken of him as he spoke of Antichrist; but if Mohammed is a true prophet, the passages referring to Paraclete must inevitably concern him – not exclusively but eminently – for it is inconceivable that Christ, when speaking of the future, should have passed over in silence a manifestation of such magnitude" (Schuon, *The Transcendent Unity of Religions*, 116).

CHAPTER 4

Initiation and Esoterism

Discussion of the *krstjani* and their Church has focused on the nature of the sources and survivals of their exoteric presence.[1] Very few scholars have raised their initiatory and esoteric nature, no matter that their emergence, history and "disappearance" are inexplicable without considering elements of their heritage suggestive of such practices.[2] Even the name "Bosnian Church" hints at another order behind the commonly assumed one, less religious than initiatory, as everything related to the interconnectedness of traditions and continuity necessarily involves the initiatory or esoteric. As René Guénon said: "Exoterism, whether religious or not, never goes beyond the limits of the traditional form to which it strictly pertains. That which surpasses these limits cannot pertain to a 'Church' as such; the Church can only serve as its outward 'support'."[3]

The Bosnian Church and the Bosnian banate and later kingdom were certainly closely linked and ecclesiastical support helped the political structure endure. Certain features of the Church's exoteric structure have necessarily left traces in history; its esoteric structure none. We do not know how the faithful became "*krstjani*" or were initated as "*strojnici*" (councillors), "*starci*" (elders)

1 See Ćošković, *Crkva bosanska u XV stoljeću*; Šanjek, ed., *Fenomen "krstjani" u srednjovjekovnoj Bosni i Humu*; idem, *Bosansko-humski krstjani u povijesnim vrelima (13–15)*; idem, *Bosansko-humski krstjani i katarsko-dualistički pokret u srednjem vijeku*; Fine, *The Bosnian Church: A New Interpretation*; Šidak, *Studije o "crkvi bosanskoj" i bogumilstvu*; Loos, *Dualist Heresy in the Middle Ages*; Ćirković, *Istorija srednjovekovne bosanske države*; Mandić, *Bogumilska crkva bosanskih krstjana*.

2 That the Bosnian Church was the *krstjan* structure of initiation is clear from the secrecy in which their rituals and initiation were preserved at every level. We know the outward form and structure (*krstjan* individuals, elders, *gosti* and *djed*), but have no access to the procedures of initiation or advancement. The Bosnian Church provided a crucial context of sacrality for the Bosnian banate and royal rule. These two facets of one whole correspond, perhaps, to the lesser and greater mysteries of an initiatory structure, as it occurs in every consistently performed traditional order. See Guénon, *Perspectives on Initiation*, in particular "The Greater & Lesser Mysteries" and "Sacerdotal & Royal Initiation." In the 15th century, King Tomaš tried to transfer the spiritual source of his power by force from the Bosnian to the Roman Catholic Church. It shook society to its core and his kingdom fell.

3 Guénon, *Fundamental Symbols*, 27.

 | DOI 10.1163/9789004279407_101

and "*gosti*" ("guests"), nor indeed how one of them became the "*djed*" ("grandfather"), their spiritual leader.

When this support becomes a matter of historiography, its scholarly interpretation excludes the living observer: the more scholarly, the less there is of the living participant or observer. The picture thus built up, supposedly independent of the scholar, is put forward as uncontestable reality. The individual and social reality of those who constitute and inherit it is largely ignored.

Practically every such historical account of the *krstjani* recognizes their Christianity, while implying an absolute distinction from Muslim tradition. This is only one view and is unjustifiable from a perspective that recalls Muslim contemporaneity with the *krstjan*.

Views that disregard this initiatory aspect tend to fetishize evidence of continuity in Muslim heritage. The significance of Mecca and Jerusalem as linking the Anointed inextricably with the Praised is resolutely, passionately denied. The presence of the Virgin and her Son in the revelation to the Praised is ignored. The practice of baptism with the book, which the Holy Spirit brought to the Praised, the *krstjani* were accused of and Bosnian Muslims have preserved to this day, is unmentioned. That the same symbols are found on *stećci* and *nišani* is ignored or downplayed. The preservation of the old Christian calendar in Muslim feast days – Jurjevdan (St. George's day), Petrovdan (St. Peter's day), Ilindan (Elijah's day), Miholjdan (St. Michael's day) and so on – is overlooked or skirted around. Gatherings of the living and the dead at sacred sites go unrecognized, in spite of their unbroken continuity.

Nonetheless, the principal rituals through which Muslims confess no god but God and the Praised as His apostle – the five daily prayers, the giving of alms, fasting, and the pilgrimage to the house at Becca – have analogues in traditions centred on the Anointed as connection between the world and what transcends it, ourselves and Unity as our uncreated and uncreatable core. The same features can be identified in other traditions, provided one recognizes their transcendent principle as their common source and point of return.

In prayer, we demonstrate our separation from Unity, which is our existence, and our aspiration to free ourselves and return to our initial and final sublimity. We always sense a separation of self from the world and of the world from what lies beyond, of body as lower and mind as higher. We constantly feel a need to reunite these aspects into a whole. Prayer is both recognition and denial of separation. The same is true of another two aspects of our rites, namely alms-giving and fasting. They intimate the simultaneity of giving and receiving, but God alone is Giver and Receiver.

The circuit of the house, as sign of the depths at this world's centre, lets us discover the axis of the self that runs from the depths to the height. None of this is just imagination. We may be initiated into the loftiest meaning of rituals, but rituals are not themselves initiation. They orient us towards our Goal, utterly close and utterly remote from where we stand in time and space, and cannot be reduced to "objects" that exclude us as mere observers.

CHAPTER 5

Clear Proofs

It is possible to see in any Christian tradition, including that of the *krstjani*, an alternative revelation of the Muslim form of witness to God's unity, the Praised's apostolate and return to God to be judged. This possibility involves reading God's Book as revealed through the Anointed, but from the Muslim perspective regarding witness of God and the Praised, a perspective that represents our original potential as human beings, the openness and freedom of the self, without which, there can be no self-discovery or realization in authentic perfection.

To make clear this way of looking at how Christian elements inhere in the Muslim perspective as manifesting Truth in different forms, we will review nine forms this relationship takes.

First, God's unity is an undeniable element of every Christian and every Muslim perspective. There is no simple answer to the question of the Trinity – God/Father, the Son/Prophet, and the Spirit.[1] Explanations of how the Three are connected and how they differ are to be found in countless Christologies, Christian and Muslim, and no Christology can claim an exclusive right to truth over any other. Whether God is Third of Two or of Three has been given various answers. Each stands in the self of its recipient, but the self is contingent and so is its perspective.

Second, as our sublime potential in self-realization, the Praised is integral to every self, regardless of the individual's witness or apostasy. Calling a given perspective "Muslim" or "Christian" does not exclude from that potential. There may be argument over what it is called, but not about its extent or centrality. God as All-praised and we as praised are linked through praise. Acknowledging only God as worthy of praise, we realize ourselves in return to Him. On this path, the self follows the Praised within, as the finest example and the seal of perfection. No condition on that journey is equal to the perfection of the Praised as our perpetual guide.

1 God's discourse is symbolic. Every language symbolically directs speaker and listener to God. Father and mother are key symbols signifying our relationship to God (see Roberts, "God as Father-Mother, and More"). See Lings, *A Sufi Saint of the Twentieth Century: Shaykh Ahmad al-'Alawi*, 150, for ways of comparing two key utterances in the Muslim and Christian traditions – the *Basmalah* and the *In Nomine* ("In the name of God, the All-merciful, the Ever-merciful," and "In the name of the Father, the Son and the Holy Spirit").

 | DOI 10.1163/9789004279407_102

Third, the apostolate of the Anointed is the Word of God. Each self may take any number of positions on whether the Word was created or uncreated, and when the Word is considered in the light of these possibilities, none of them is absolute or sufficient. In this lies the reason for safeguarding our openness and freedom in regard to God as incomparable and remote, alike and close.

Fourth, as Christians and Muslims alike declare, the Virgin received the Holy Spirit or Word, united in the person of the Anointed and his discourse. Both he and she are pure, untouched by anything that diverts from God. The Praised bore witness of them as such according to the Revelation brought to his heart by the Holy Spirit, the Spirit of Truth. The Recitation is the Word brought to him in this way. The only woman's name mentioned in it is Mary's. The Praised was thus a recipient of a Word that is inseparable from Mary, as was the Anointed, who is a different form of the same Word.

Fifth, the Anointed confessed and prophesied the Paraclete. We do not know for sure what word in Aramaic the Greek *parakletos* was used to represent and his testimony relates to both what is in and outside of time. Depending on the perspective of the individual receiving this witness, it may, but does not have to, refer to the annunciation of the historical phenomenon recognized by Muslims as the coming of the expected and ever-present Praised in history and so of our sublime potential. In their witness, Muslims propose many reasons for understanding Paraclete this way.

Sixth, the Praised is the decisive witness to the Anointed as pure and closest to him. What is said of him, so far as Muslim witness is concerned, is offered in the form spoken by God in the Word sent down to the Praised through the Holy Spirit. This Word confirms and is warrant of the book that presents the narrative of the Anointed.

Seventh, the Anointed is God's Word sent down to Mary and placed before the people as her son. The Recitation is His Word sent down through the Holy Spirit into the heart of the Praised. These two different forms of one Word, revealed through the Virgin and the Praised, are identical in essence and in the Unity they reveal. Closest among all people, the Anointed and the Praised are indispensable for our path of return, discovery and self-realization in our perfect sublime potential.

Eighth, Muslims, Christians and Jews agree that the Torah and the Psalms were revealed by God. They agree in different ways, but none precludes recognition of God as Revealer. Muslims and Christians agree that God also revealed the Gospel, but Christians and Jews do not agree with Muslims that God revealed the Recitation. These areas of agreement and disagreement determine the different perspectives in each of these communities. For Muslims, accepting the Recitation is inseparable from affirming the Torah, the Psalms, the

Gospel and their contents. This gives rise to different Muslim understandings of their own book as well as of the Christian and Jewish heritage.

Ninth, the Anointed said he came not to bring Peace, but War, but rejected the sword and prophesied the coming of One Awaited. The Praised said he came with a sword, for the sake of Peace, saying to Him Who sent him: "My God, *Thou art* the Bestower of *Peace* and from *Thee* is *peace*."[2]

2 Muslim, 1:292. Being-at-peace is clearly crucial to any understanding of the Anointed and the Praised's relationship under the sign of their link to the Peace. Muslim witness (of the people of peace) to the Praised includes witness to the Anointed, as they are, the Praised tells us, closest to one another in this world and the next. The person of peace's attitude to them as "the two closest" is that individual's attitude to and connection with God, unmediated by church, priest, authority, or sacrament. Nothing from another's hand, not even water or bread, can dictate our connection with God. For a person of peace to submit to another is to take priests and monks for gods (see *Qur'an*, 9:31). There is no justification for ceasing to serve the One God. When a person of peace is compelled publicly to renounce witness of God's unity and the Praised's apostolate, it is crucial that the core of the self not be veiled over. Covert love of God and covertly following the Praised still connect us with Him: "Whoso conceals God, after he has believed – excepting him who has been compelled, and his heart is still at rest in his belief – but whosoever's breast is expanded in concealing, upon them shall rest anger from God, and there awaits them a mighty chastisement" (16:106). No order or institution can stand in for our perennial potential for witness to God's unity, the Praised's apostolate and universal return to God, knowledge of which does not depend on external authority.

CHAPTER 6

In Continuity

Each of these nine elements is present in Bosnian Muslim culture today. They form part of its "grammatical rules," as defined by Edmund Leach:

> ... all the various non-verbal dimensions of culture, such as styles in clothing, village lay-out, architecture, furniture, food, cooking, music, physical gestures, postural attitudes and so on are organized in patterned sets so as to incorporate coded information in a manner analogous to the sounds and words and sentences of a natural language. I assume therefore it is just as meaningful to talk about the grammatical rules which govern the wearing of clothes as it is to talk about the grammatical rules which govern speech utterances.[1]

While key symbols of both Christian and Muslim heritage are identical, their meanings differ, depending on the supports deployed by the observers. Whatever support is sought in organization and ritual, doctrinal interpretation or associated power, it cannot squeeze out the initiatory, esoteric core, the One manifest in discourse.

Regardless of the variations evident in a culture's synchronic and diachronic manifestations or how detached they may become from its sacred core, the transformation is never such that all connection is lost with our potential for self-discovery, realization and redemption. However far gone in darkness, we never pass beyond the infinite reach of His mercy and knowledge: "My mercy embraces all things;"[2] "And God encompasses everything in knowledge."[3]

The uttermost depths in extreme remoteness from God are symbolized by the valley floor, where God raised up the Praised as His supreme sign, the first of the people of peace and our guide in ascent to the sublime uprightness in and for which we were created. In ascent the Praised reveals to us that potential in our own lives. The Anointed said the same, but emphasized our unconditional ascent from the grave and death, in defiance of our usual thinking, imprisoned in the world of multiplicity. Speaking of his suffering and our interpretation of it, God said: "Yet they did not slay him, neither crucified him, only a likeness

1 Leach, *Culture and Communication*, 10.

2 *Qur'an*, 7:156.

3 Ibid., 65:12.

 | DOI 10.1163/9789004279407_103

of that was shown to them. [...] and they slew him not of a certainty – no indeed; God raised him up to Him; God is All-mighty, All-wise."[4]

The possibility of ascent is guaranteed by our nature, His Spirit in the self, our original oath to God as Lord and acceptance of His confidence, the prophets's oath to confess the Praised, the indestructible truth of our core, to discover and realize which is to attain his immense nature as our best example and light-giving lamp and meet our potential, independent of time, place, kin, language, society or tradition. In principle, every people is of a Book, while also all of different races and languages, places and regions. Mary's Son spoke Aramaic and his sacred heritage was Hebrew. What he said was preserved in Greek and translated into other languages. It was through this sacred heritage the Slavs became a people of the Book.

A country of many Christologies, Bosnia's cultural history cannot exclude Jewish or Christian or Muslim Revelations or the different understandings of the Anointed as the realization of our hope of a perfect end to earthly suffering. For these Christologies to be performed in dialogue by those who confess them, we must recognize and refine the different languages that correspond to them. These languages can be translated into each other, to the extent that the translation conveys or receives part of what is present within the participants in that dialogue.

---

4 Ibid., 4:157, 158.

CHAPTER 7

One Word, Many Languages

God sent down His Word into the heart of the Praised through the Holy Spirit, the Spirit of Truth, and that Word was in Arabic: "Truly it is the revelation of the Lord of all being, brought down by the Spirit of Truth upon the heart, that thou mayest be one of the warners, in a clear, Arabic tongue."[1]

The Word was revealed to all and can be recited in any language. Diversity of language is one of God's signs.[2] To prefer one language to another is to prefer one people to another. But God's mercy embraces all things,[3] while the noblest among us is the most mindful.[4] No human condition negates the reach of His mercy or the possibility of becoming good through consciousness. In this lies the self's inviolable dignity: "Therefore We prescribed for the Children of Israel that whoso slays a soul not to retaliate for a soul slain, nor for corruption done in the land, shall be as if he had slain mankind altogether; and whoso gives life to a soul, shall be as if he had given life to mankind altogether."[5]

Every slaying burdens the killer. Only in return to God for punishment and reward are claims and debts resolved, without remainder. This is the point of accounting to God for every atom's weight of good and every atom's weight of evil done.[6]

The books of the *krstjani* were their link with sublime uprightness, to which God calls us through His Chosen. That these books passed through multiple translations before becoming their wisdom, does not mean they were less of the "true apostolic faith"[7] than any other people of the Book. It was because

---

1 *Qur'an*, 26:192–95.

2 See *Qur'an*, 30:22.

3 Ibid., 7:156.

4 Ibid., 49:13.

5 *Qur'an*, 5:32.

6 See *Qur'an*, 99:7–8.

7 Šanjek, *Bosansko-humski krstjani i katarsko-dualistički pokret u srednjem vijeku*, 88, 135 and 179. Debates over the Bosnian *krstjani* inevitably involve the question of their orthodoxy. Like every Christian or other sect, their members believed themselves orthodox. They were called heretics only by others, who regarded themselves as orthodox. The *krstjani* defined their faith as "true," "ours," "the djed's," "Bosnian" and "God's." Their Catholic contemporaries called them "infidels," "heretics," "Bosnian heretics," "Bosnians," "Manichaeans," "Patarins," "Nestorians," and "Jacobites," while the Eastern Orthodox called them "baboons," "Bogomils" and "Kudugers." See Ćošković, "Bosanski krstjani u očima svojih kršćanskih suvremenika," 183–191.

 DOI 10.1163/9789004279407_104

the Gospel lived in them and their language that they and it were open to receiving the Praised and the Recitation. The Anointed and the Praised bear witness of each other, while the Good News and the Recitation are two books revealed to people by one God. For those who confess their revealed nature, both provide multiple proofs for their motives and support for their narratives.

God shows His signs on the horizons and within us so that we may understand He is Truth.[8] Existence and everything in it was created with Truth.[9] We owe a debt of recognition for creation. By acknowledging our debt to all things in the outer horizons and our inner selves we realize our right to return to God, "well-pleased, well-pleasing" to and with Him.[10] This is attainment of bliss. On our path back, towards bliss, the signs remind us of that potential and the Praised's immense nature. Nothing in history is equal to that goal. Whenever we equate some determinate or finite thing with it, our inner self is concealed and obscured. Worshipful prostration recalls us to the abnegation of the self's achievements for the sake of what awaits at a higher plane, which is determined by nothing. Return is to God, Whom nothing is like.

---

8 See *Qur'an*, 41:53.

9 Ibid., 15:85.

10 Ibid., 89:27–30.

CHAPTER 8

On *Stećci* and *Nišani*

Stećci or mediaeval tombstones and *nišani* or Muslim ones bear many similar, even identical symbols. Investigation of these symbols in the light of the perennial wisdom will reveal the little-understood initiatory aspect of this continuous tradition, with its various forms, a nature demonstrated most clearly in the symbol of the mihrab inscribed with the partial verse from the Recitation: "Whenever Zachariah went in to her in the mihrab."[1]

This inscription is usually calligraphic and in Arabic, the language it was revealed in through the Praised. The calligraphic form is to aid translation to the centre of the self in which opposites vanish.

Zachariah was a priest in Solomon's Mosque on the Mount. He passed through the mosque and entered a secluded area where, contrary to expectations and rules, the Virgin had her place. He served in Solomon's Mosque, performing and keeping the rites. He was also the Virgin's protector. Her presence was thus part of the Mosque and its rites. These two, the Mosque of Sion and the Virgin, face each other – the one richly appointed for sacrifice and circumcision, raised high and fortified with stone, brass and cedarwood, the other small and tender, unusual, despised.

Zachariah means "he who remembers God." He was placed between these two, with the expectation his human hopes would be fulfilled, given the warrant of his service in the mosque, with its scrolls, rites and virtues, and his concern for the Virgin entrusted to his care. His quest for happiness is indicated by the appearance and contents of the temple.

Through the Virgin, God once again revealed that not the heavens nor the earth, but the heart of His faithful servant encompasses Him.[2] She is the most impressive sign of the Praised. As recipient of the Holy Spirit, the Spirit of Truth, she made manifest the Word, foretelling one who would receive and become the same as It, as her son would with the Good News.

Zachariah, prophet and priest at Sion, father of a prophet, served God in the mosque rituals. The mosque and its rituals could appear the most precious thing connecting one with God, inviolable knowledge transcending world and

1 *Qur'an*, 3:37.

2 For the sacred tradition of the heart of the faithful servant, see Chittick, *The Sufi Path of Knowledge*, 107.

 | DOI 10.1163/9789004279407_105

self. But God said: "We shall show them Our signs in the horizons and in themselves, till it is clear to them that He is Truth."[3]

That He is Truth, all the signs in the horizons and the self show. God taught Adam the names and all existence is entreasured within him. These two, existence and the self, are two aspects of the manifestation of Truth. Seeking to know It, we seek to know ourselves. The self lacks nothing needed for such knowledge. Every individual thing in world or self is a sign of Truth. The symbols on the gravestones known as *stećci* and *nišani*, with their differences and similarities, have countless interpretations. They are read in as many different ways as there are people reading, for no two selves are ever the same and nor any one the same in two different moments. The key question is how to read these signs in our quest for the "upright path, the path of those who are blessed."

3 *Qur'an*, 41:53.

CHAPTER 9

The Praised

Adam was created perfect and his perfection was sufficient. His moment of sublimity was to maintain it. When it was lost, the original Adam became prophet to his fallen self. One self split between two extremes – the uttermost depths and return to original sublimity.

As fallen Adam had his children in the depths, the original Adam was their prophet too. We can all return to the condition of the original Adam. God appoints some as pre-attuned to that condition, His apostles to the people of every age. Adam's original plenitude is God's foremost apostle, our finest example, to whom we turn from our every condition, who makes the prophets conscious, so that they confess him as their and our sublime potential always and everywhere – the Praised.

The Praised said there were 124,000 prophets and that they had come to all peoples, speaking in the languages of the nations they were sent to. If their apostolate reached beyond one nation or language, that nation and that language were not therefore superior to the rest. The news can be translated into any language and made accessible to all. That the same content is available in different prophecies attests to this. Moses' words in the Hebrew Torah are present in Jesus' words spoken in Aramaic and preserved in Greek and again in the Recitation revealed to the Praised in Arabic.

When a prophet expresses his charge to others, he is the first to submit to it. This act contains nothing not in revealed knowledge. Nothing else is required, for absolute all-comprehension necessarily excludes all else. Revelation is both all-encompassing and exclusive.

Viewing history from Revelation, the past is necessarily encompassed, the future prefigured. Historical perspective, therefore, lies in whether and what prophecy is accepted or not. Singling out just five of the 124,000 prophets – Adam, Abraham, Moses, Jesus and the Praised – one can demonstrate how attitudes to all-comprehension differ between Jews, Christians and Muslims.

For Jews, God's revelation to Moses is all-embracing. Veneration for Moses as a distinct phenomenon in a series is emphasized at the end of the Torah,[1] but worship of the Lord of the prophets takes precedence. Though Moses and the Torah are the starting point and context of Jewish history, it continues with the end of prophecy: "When the last of the prophets Haggai, Zechariah and

1 See *Deuteronomy*, 34:10–12.

 | DOI 10.1163/9789004279407_106

Malachi died, the Holy Spirit ceased from Israel."[2] Their revelation thus comprises all that precedes it, from Adam up to itself, and what follows, up to the last prophet. Such all-comprehension extends to all time and has no need of Jesus or the Praised and their presence is neither sought nor found in such a reading of the Bible. This standpoint does not preclude the Holy Spirit's absolute freedom from all but God as to where and when it will exercise the will of its Lord.

The Christian perspective accepts Jesus as the full and comprehensive revelation of God, comprising all that preceded or came after it, including the entire Jewish heritage. This reading of the same news and prophecies makes clear the different possibilities for humanity. There are thus two all-encompassing traditions – one Jewish, the other Christian. When an adherent identifies exclusively with one, the other is denied. This denial manifests as the declaration that certain readings of the news and the prophecies of the common heritage are false.

The issue becomes even more complicated with the Muslim perspective. The revelation to the Praised is also all-encompassing. It includes everything Jewish and Christian, but in a different reading. There is no rupture between what preceded and what comes after. The difference lies in the reading and understanding of the same books. Reduce this all-comprehension to the condition of one's own self, however, and the situation cannot be borne. The Jewish and Christian heritage appear adulterated, as sight is lost of the fact that differences in reception and understanding are inevitable and irreducible and none of us can ever resolve them fully. Only in return to Unity do these differences vanish, as God told the Praised: "And He will tell you of that whereon you were at variance."[3]

This sequence can be accepted or denied in three ways. Modern historiography presumes the modern scientific approach applied to physics can be applied equally to the past, with everything fixed in space and time and placed in a causal nexus and the knowing subject excluded from the subject of knowledge. But exclusion of the knower is impossible, the never-achieved model of science. Still, historians assume their construct of history cannot be contested because they have supposedly excluded themselves from their findings. This is only a supposed, not a real exclusion. Historians are unique individuals, their selves shaped in ways that are never final and cannot be reduced to spatial and temporal determination in clear causal sequence. They always contain an inwardness that transcends depth and an outwardness that transcends every

2 *The Babylonian Talmud*, Joma, 9b.

3 *Qur'an*, 5:48.

boundary. To reduce things to time and space and laws of cause and effect is to banish God to remoteness from what takes place in the world of scientific discovery, to be neither Near nor Immanent, as things take their course without Him.

Applying the same approach to religious phenomena and their all-embracing nature, means they are seen as incompatible realities, as mere forerunners or betrayals of the essential. This is the understanding of historical process outlined in figure 1.1, of Christianity and Islam as two completely different trajectories. The former's claim to embrace all truth means the latter cannot be acknowledged: both cannot be all-embracing. The latter is seen as betrayal and impediment to the former. Whether historians appeal to their own natures and formation or to scientific detachment in dealing with these historical phenomena, their judgment cannot be divorced from their own nature.

Such historical trajectories are not considered subject to precipitate change. However rapid or transient, everything is subject to cause and effect in time and place. This is the source of the historians' taboo of the common or syncretic as a practically insoluble problem. But "pure" religions cannot interact without syncretic aspects or overlapping areas, as shown in figure 1.2. The overlap entails common ground, extensively addressed in the phenomenology of religion during the 20th century. In Bosnia, this common ground includes aspects of the religious calendar, sacred sites, holy people, rituals and so forth. Historians regard these overlapping areas as containing relics of Christianity in Muslim culture, evidence of incomplete conversion, unorthodox elements in the heterodoxy of others, and suchlike. They cannot accept them as essentially common features, any more than the ordinary individual can, who has no answer to the question of the one God and the multiplicity of religions or the ineffable essence of the exoteric contents of all religions.

Many features of Bosnian Muslim religious life shared with Christians in ways that do not correspond to artificial historical periodizations are therefore also unacceptable and alien to ideologized Muslim perspectives. They are denounced, prohibited and persecuted, because unassimilable to an image of Islam as all-embracing. The result is a covert compact between historians and the unenlightened object of their studies.[4]

---

4 Such things are found everywhere. Modern ideologized images of religion proffer themselves as the "only true" ones, assuming destructive attitudes towards preceding traditional forms. See the introduction to Murata, Chittick and Weiming, *The Sage Learning of Liu Zhi*, 17, for the behaviour of the Wahhabi-ized successors to Chinese scholars who developed a Muslim theory of the universe and humanity in neo-Confucian language.

The historian's very failure to respond to the fullness that diversity constitutes is evidence that the self views the picture from within, for all the hypocritical claims to transcendence. How dependent the presentation of history is on the historian's perspective may be made clear though an image of all-comprehension and difference. This image is the Muslim intellectual perspective, which has, under pressure from fundamentalist ideologies, faded to near oblivion in our modern, secularized reality. It shows five key apostles, from Adam to the Praised, appearing in succession, but in such a way that the essence of their prophecy remains always present, regardless of the differences imposed by when and where they arose, or to use the traditional formulation, were sent down amongst people.

The first circle represents the all-embracing nature of God's revelation sent down to the Praised. It includes all of Jewish and Christian heritage, read and understood differently. The reason for this difference lies in the revelation itself. Neither tradition's validity is called into question. They are different and the dignity of Jews and Christians lies in that difference, which only God can resolve. When Christians say they do not accept the perspective deriving from the revelation to the Praised, that is their right. As with every choice, however, there are consequences for which the decision-maker alone will be responsible.

Confessed as God's revelation, the Christian viewpoint is all-embracing for its adherents. They must then resolve the question of the Praised accordingly. They have a right and a responsibility to reject or accept. Judaism is fully integrated within this view of all-embracing Christian revelation, but this is a form of integration that has a fundamentally different aspect for Jews and Christians. From the Muslim perspective, both aspects are justifiable and neither Judaism nor Christianity are in themselves problematic. If those who confess either may lack virtue, they may equally be saintly, evidence they are from God and that fault, as ever, lies within humanity.

CHAPTER 10

"The Apostate"

In 1851, a Bosnian Franciscan, Ivan Frano Jukić, writing as Slavoljub Bošnjak (the Slavophile Bosniak), claimed:

> The Turks and the Gypsies number 384,000. They are heirs to the false prophet Muhammad and so properly called Muhammadans. They are descended in Bosnia from depraved Christians who, not knowing how else to maintain their predominance, went "Turk," betraying God and becoming their own people and blood brothers' greatest enemy for the sake of their earthly estates.[1]

Similar things have been said and written many times.[2] A thousand years earlier, St. Cyril the Scholar had said: "We all know that Muhammad was a liar and despoiler of salvation. He vomited forth his worst abominations for evil and vice."[3] Nor was Cyril, or any of his countless counterparts, introducing something new into the world. The very angels opposed God's intent in creating us and it is the diverter's role to prevent us from fulfilling the purpose

---

1 Bošnjak, *Zemljopis i Poviestnica Bosne*, 187–88.

2 St. John Damascene composed his *Fountain of Knowledge* in the 8th century in the Mar Saba monastery in Palestine. In part a treatise against heresy, it includes a refutation of the apostolate of the Praised, portraying him as a Christian heretic influenced by Arianism and Monothelitism. The work is regarded as the first Christian polemic against the Praised. Jukić's approach to Muslims is entirely consistent with Franciscan tradition delineated in the Order's First Rule: "The Lord says: Behold, I send you forth as sheep in the midst of wolves: be ye therefore wise as serpents, and harmless as doves. (*Matthew*, 10:16). Whoever should, by divine inspiration, wish to go among the Saracens and other infidels must ask permission from their provincial ministers. The ministers should grant permission only to those whom they consider qualified to be sent." The first five Franciscan martyrs, put to death in Marrakesh in 1220, had, according to their hagiographers, spoken persistently in public against the Praised, declaring that he and his followers were destined for "eternal suffering," hoping in this way to force the hand of the offended Muslims and to earn martyrdom. One finds a similar attitude towards Muslims, the Praised, and the Recitation later in the Franciscan desire to suffer martyrdom in the attempt to baptize Muslims. See further Tolan, *Saracens*, 214–32. Careful reading of Jukić's writings about the "Turks" of his own age and particularly his Bosnian neighbours makes quite clear the lack of change in regard to Muslims as intolerable "infidels."

3 *Žitja Konstantina Ćirila i Metodija*, 64.

 | DOI 10.1163/9789004279407_107

we were created for, which is beyond the knowledge of angels. Wherever we find ourselves, we experience both a need for and resistance to the perfection of the Praised. Neither the world nor humanity can be understood without taking into account these two opposed responses to the Praised – our most profound nature and need and its betrayal and covering over. We all contain both. Denial and reviling of him is often justified on the grounds of a sanctity being defended.

If the Praised can be rendered problematic in principle, so can every other prophet and every Divine revelation. To understand the world's history one must acknowledge human two-facedness, which presents itself as desire for the One Face. The mid-twelfth century author Otto of Freising provides us another example of Europe's history of speaking against the Praised:

> It is known that the whole body of Saracens worship one God and receive the Old Testament law and the rite of circumcision. Nor do they attack Christ or the Apostles. In this one thing alone they are far from salvation – in denying that Jesus Christ is God or the Son of God, and in venerating the seducer Mahomet as a great prophet of the supreme God.[4]

The Recitation itself lists many ways of denying the Praised as God's apostle, as a warning against the perennial nature of evil, denial that is always determined by the denier's own condition:

> And when Our signs are recited to them, clear signs, they say, "This is naught but a man who desires to bar you from that your fathers served"; and they say, "This is nothing but a forged calumny." And the unbelievers say, to the truth, when it has come to them, "This is nothing but manifest sorcery."[5]

Jukić's views belong to the great anti-Muhammadan tradition in both East and West and should be taken seriously. They were expressed during modernization among the south Slavs in a land where Christians had lived for centuries with a Muslim majority. Where Jukić calls the Praised a false prophet, other sources say "apostate," from the Greek for one who forsakes the true faith. To say this of the Praised is to contradict the fundamental witness of Muslims. All

4 Hofmeister, *Accedunt ex Chronica universali turicensi excerpta*, 317 (cited after Southern, *Western Views of Islam in the Middle Ages*, 36).

5 *Qur'an*, 34:43.

things Muslim begin and end in confession of no god but God and the Praised as His servant and apostle. This confession brings together metaphysics, cosmology, anthropology and psychology as sacred teachings necessarily informing our relationship to God and informed by it. For it, there is nothing Jewish or Christian or whatever that is beyond its embrace. It includes the Holy Spirit or Spirit of Truth and Mary and the Anointed and sees every divine revelation as a limited manifestation of one of the possible paths to God. Our task is to realize our selves on such a path, in the knowledge that revelation and recipient are never fully one. Every revelation is innocent, guilt ours alone.

In 1463, when the world's most powerful leader, Mehmed the Opener, conquered Bosnia, he gave Brother Anđeo Zvizdović, the Franciscan *Custos*, a Letter of Covenant undertaking as follows:

> Let no man hinder or disturb either these men or their churches. Let them live in my dominion, and let those who have fled be free and safe, let them return and live without fear in my dominion, in their monasteries, and let not my own Majesty, my Viziers, officials, or subjects or any of the inhabitants of my dominions, or any man meddle in their affairs or attack or insult them or endanger their lives or property or churches. And should they bring individuals from foreign parts to my state – they are permitted to do so.[6]

The Emperor Mehmed thus acknowledged the right of Christians in Bosnia to their own distinct path to God. This was not his own invention or will. He was just applying his witness to the Praised as God's servant and apostle. The Praised's understanding of Christian and Jewish witness to their paths to God reflected his own witness of God's will that people should have different paths to Him.

What then of Brother Ivan's statement that the Praised was a "false prophet?" The Praised, obedient to the will of God, imposed nothing on the Christian Jukić – not his own apostolate nor his beliefs. He was called to be what he was, in full responsibility towards God. The Praised expected Jukić, like everyone else who does not believe in him, to leave him in peace, just as Moses told Pharaoh's men: "But if so be that you believe me not, go you apart from me!"[7]

Jukić and millions of others who do not believe in the Praised's apostolate speak against him. God foretold this in the Book sent down through the Spirit

---

6 For more on this letter see Mahmutćehajić, *Prozori: Riječi i slike*, 13–45.

7 *Qur'an*, 44:21.

to the Praised's heart for recitation to the people in their language. Many do accept his apostolate and confess him as their supreme potential, dearest to them, of greater value than any state of the self. When they are told that he who defines them is an apostate, must they not ask what does he take us for, who speaks to us thus, and how will he behave towards us when in power, and why.

CHAPTER 11

Witnesses

God told the Praised and so us: "Turn thy face towards the Inviolable Place of Abnegation of self; and wherever you may be, turn your faces towards it. Those who have been given the book know it is the truth from thy Lord. God is not heedless of the things you do."[1]

Responding to this commandment, we acknowledge that we are between the uttermost depths and the sublime height. Our turn to the inviolable place is associated in the Recitation with knowledge of truth. Does he who has the Book know truth and does knowledge of where to turn and face follow? Should he turn to face one of the signs, does that prove he knows truth and has the Book?

When Adam and Eve transgressed the limit set to their abiding on the most beautiful height, they became aware of their loss and said: "Lord, we have wronged ourselves, and if Thou dost not forgive us, and have mercy upon us, we shall surely be among the lost."[2] Aware of the wrong done by transgressing that limit, humanity sank to the depths, the bottom of the valley. This descent altered their view on the world, no longer a Garden or clarity and certainty of heart. The earth, the depths to which humanity fell, is positioned between the seven heavens above and the seven earths below. According to the Recitation, it was there that humanity's covenant with God was renewed:

> Thereafter Adam received certain words from his Lord, and He turned towards him; truly He turns and is Ever-merciful. We said: "Get you down out of it, all together; yet there shall come to you guidance from Me, and whosoever follows My guidance, no fear shall be on them, neither shall they sorrow. As for the concealers who cry lies to Our signs, those shall be the inhabitants of the Fire, therein dwelling forever."[3]

The sign of this new covenant is the Kaʿba or the house at the bottom of Becca valley: "God has appointed the Kaʿba, the House Inviolable, as a standing for men, and the inviolate month, the offering, and the necklaces – that you may know that God knows all that is in the heavens and in the earth and that God

1 *Qur'an*, 2:144.

2 Ibid., 7:23.

3 Ibid., 2:37–39.

 | DOI 10.1163/9789004279407_108

has knowledge of everything."[4] God's commandment to turn to the house indicates two paths – one upwards, an upright and ascending path, and the other downwards, a path of descent.

Turning towards the Kaʿba, we know we are earthbound, but also that ascent and return to our lost condition are possible. The Kaʿba's walls proclaim the split in the world, like the self, between outer and inner. God is Outer and Inner, manifest to us in the signs in the world, which are dispersed, and in those in us, which are concentrated. They relate in the reunion of all things, return to Unity as First and Last, which takes place in the heart and the Spirit God breathed into us, as He said: "Heaven and earth encompass Me not, but the heart of the true believer does encompass Me."[5]

All things in existence refer to God. This is why we love the Signified. Only union with the Beloved satisfies the lover. We are ever before His face, ever veiled from us. We are always trying to turn towards and draw near Him, in a journey towards the centre of Being, which reveals itself through countless ever-changing veils. On the battlefield, illusion threatens to divert us from the Beloved. He seems always to elude us from without and within, but remains the only reality. To bear witness to Him in all things is not enough for us. To avoid vacillation and going astray, we must also confess the Praised as the self's higher potential, the axis on which the Kaʿbas of the heavens are.

We cannot pass through heaven's confines without being aware of the Praised as our guide and of his mighty nature: "O tribe of jinn and of men, if you are able to pass through the confines of heaven and earth, pass through them! You shall not pass through except with an authority!"[6]

Our struggle to pass beyond the limits that confine us takes many forms. The attraction of the One beyond the things of multiplicity prompts us to neglect or deny all that is our reality – the infinite multitude of dualities that affirm Unity. Unity's presence as both eternity and infinity is manifest as beauty. God is beautiful and loves beauty.[7] We are expected to discover or realize ourselves through constant beatification and finally to become wholly open to receiving beauty. We cannot achieve this if we deny our immediate experience or the signs outside and within ourselves, which both are and are not as we see them. They are, since there is no reality without the Signified, but are not as no self

4 Ibid., 5:97.

5 A favourite tradition of Sufi texts, it features in Ghazālī's *Iḥyāʾ ʿulūm al-dīn*. See Chittick, *The Sufi Path of Knowledge*, 107.

6 *Qur'an*, 55:33.

7 See Muslim, 1:53.

is the same for two moments and neither is its understanding of what is in or around it.

The Praised's response to Gabriel's question about beatification was that it is to: "worship God as if you are seeing Him, for though you do not see Him, He, verily, sees you."[8] This "as if" determines our being in the world and desire to transcend it. Doctrine, ritual and virtue are inseparable from it. Our immediate experience of the sensory world does not deny the boundaries. They are crossed in beatification, so that our acceptance of that crucial "as if" transcends and permeates everything.

Initially, the questions of where to turn our face, how to have the Book and how to know truth may concern all who can confess either way – by denial or affirmation. The confessing self is constantly changing, however, in constant flux. No knowledge we can achieve is final and conclusive. Nor can we postpone or avoid admitting our guilt for transgressing the limits. We are not done listening to "a few words." In witness, we are expected to scrutinize constantly how we relate to both sign and signified. On the path of ascent, no point we reach is of any value compared to our higher potential. In its "as if," our higher potential transcends the lower, as eternity transcends the temporal, infinity finitude.

8 Muslim, 1:2.

CHAPTER 12

Interpretation

There is no world without the self, no self without the world. The strangeness of this assertion is worth examining in all of consciousness's reaches. Both manifest the everpresent Principle, in books, discourse, or elsewhere. It matters more how we relate to it than to its manifestation. Without the self there is no knowledge of the Principle. Cut off from existence, the world becomes a fiction within and an exclusion of the self. Both world and self contain signs, ebbing and flowing, constantly renewing existence in its outer and inner aspects. Reality is that incessant manifestation through signs and more.

When God sends down His speech in human language, it recalls us to the signs on the horizons and in the self. These signs in the world, history, self and book recall the self to its original and final potential, turning it towards the "as if," the indivisibility of doctrine, ritual and virtue. In doctrine, truth is revealed as decisive, falsehood as its seeming opposite. But truth cannot be cut from falsehood by a single sword-stroke, cloven that falsehood might disappear. The hoped-for "as if" cannot be realized without the ritual that truth reveals or sends down. Ritual is meaningless unless it connects its performers with truth, the self's most profound centre. Such a connection is confirmed only with humility, expressed by service before our Lord as the prerequisite for translating to an ever higher "as if."

All things in consciousness, all signs in world or self, mediate between the everchanging self and its uncreated and uncreatable essence. The self is split between its centre-heart and circumference. Nothing on the circumference is independent of the centre, however seemingly discrete. For Sufis, the heart is God's abode. However independent the self's extreme circumference may seem of the centre, the horizons between it and the heart, height and depths, are never bereft of God's presence.

God said through the Praised: "Those who believe, their hearts being at rest in God's remembrance – in God's remembrance are at rest the hearts of those who believe and do righteous deeds; theirs is blessedness and a fair resort."[1] The heart at rest is realized in Peace, witnessing: "*Thou art* the Bestower of *Peace* and from *Thee* is *peace*."[2] Peace in the heart signifies Him as Inner, Who

1 *Qur'an*, 13:28–29.

2 Muslim, 1:292.

 | DOI 10.1163/9789004279407_109

is also Outer: Peace manifesting the heart: "And know that God stands between a man and his heart."[3]

Belief is knowledge and love at once. The knower relates to the known through knowledge, the lover to the beloved through love. The knower desires union with the known in love. Remembering God as our centre links the signs in the self and the world with the heart, which is the One. All signs speak of the One, manifesting Him and our understanding of Him, our return to Him.

As signs and self interact, our interpretation of Reality is constantly changing. Reality is revealed absolutely and perfectly in descent, a perfection the self merely approaches as the uncreated centre in which differences vanish, caught between absolute proximity to and absolute distance from reality. Interpretation is imperfect, but perfection is reflected in us more or less clearly, after the self's condition:

> It is He who sent down upon thee the Book, wherein are verses clear that are the Essence of the Book, and others ambiguous. As for those in whose hearts is swerving, they follow the ambiguous part, desiring dissension, and desiring its interpretation; and none knows its interpretation, save only God. And those firmly rooted in knowledge say, "We believe in it; all is from our Lord"; yet none remembers, but the conscious.[4]

Interpretation turns the signs towards God as First and Last, Inner and Outer. Of two possible views, the first is of God as only perfect interpreter of His signs, His creatures' only Guide, the second of us interpreting signs according to the self's condition. Let our will oppose His and our interpretations distort both signs and self.

The Recitation exists that the self may be realized in relation to God after His most beautiful attributes. When our will is in tune with His, we know His perfect speech with all our being – hearing and remembering, reciting and writing. We and all we do manifest as perfect deeds.[5] Our interpretation becomes a sign of His, revealing and concealing the Face. How the recitation of signs and the condition of the self are related is revealed in the Recitation:

> Magnify the name of thy Lord the Most High who created and shaped, who determined and guided, who brought forth the pasturage then made it a blackening wrack. We shall make thee recite, to forget not save what

---

3 *Qur'an*, 8:24.

4 Ibid., 3:7.

5 See *Qur'an*, 20:41 and 68:4.

> God wills; surely He knows that is spoken aloud and what is hidden. We shall ease thee unto the Easing.[6]

God speaks to us and we to Him in human language. Language pulls us in two directions, towards others of that language and back again and towards God and back again. We are ever alone and with others. Unless embedded in ritual and a way that is valid for the entire community, the virtue of sincerity will cause a constant break-down of order. Only when so embedded can it reinforce confidence and faith, as how faithful individuals relate to each other before the All-faithful. Balancing our relations with others and God is to acknowledge difference, inheritance and prediction:

> And We have sent down to thee the Book with the truth, confirming the Book that was before it, and assuring it. So judge between them according to what God has sent down, and do not follow their caprices, to forsake the truth that has come to thee. To every one of you We have appointed a right way and an open road. If God had willed, He would have made you one nation; but that He may try you in what has come to you. So be you forward in good works; unto God shall you return, all together; and He will tell you of that whereon you were at variance.[7]

Ritual and the way situate us vis-à-vis ourselves, others who share our language and, indeed, everyone else in the world. This includes the Book and its interpretation, for: "We have indeed turned about for men in this Recitation every manner of similitude; man is the most disputatious of things."[8]

---

6 *Qur'an*, 87:1–8.

7 Ibid., 5:48.

8 Ibid., 18:54.

CHAPTER 13

Listening

As God's servant, everything the Praised had was received from God, a sending brought to his heart by the Holy Spirit, the Spirit of Truth. To be heard it must first percolate into the recipient's speech, which is then God's news in the language of the people He is addressing. A prophet always speaks in the language of the people he was raised up among.[1] What he heard in his heart as God's speech sent down through the Holy Spirit encompasses all languages. Heard in the heart, the Word is performed in the prophet's own tongue, as he told ʿAli: "O ʿAli, you see all that I see and you hear all that I hear, except that you are not a prophet."[2]

That ʿAli was no prophet even though he saw and heard all the apostle did may be explained in different ways. ʿAli saw the Praised find peace in the Holy Spirit and heard what he said in his language. For the Praised "said out loud" and "received in the heart" are one. The heart is the warrant. Any recipient knows this in their heart alone, in which they find the knowledge breathed into it at creation, but to which we must first be awoken by the Praised as best example. Awoken, we turn to the Praised to follow him in confessing no god but God.

Some may deny the recipient because they find the experience incomprehensible, framing their interpretations of this mysterious experience in various ways. Their objections are collected in the Revelation. God addressed those who suspected the source of the apostle's discourse lay in the obscurity of his own self or some force diverting him from his authentic nature or some individual who had brought it from elsewhere, saying:

> Your companion is not possessed; he truly saw him on the clear horizon; he is not niggardly of the Unseen. And it is not the word of an accursed Satan; where then are you going?[3]
>
> And We know very well that they say, "Only a mortal is teaching him." The speech of him at whom they hint is barbarous; and this is speech Arabic, manifest.[4]

---

1 See *Qur'an*, 14:4.

2 *Nahj al-balāga*, 328.

3 *Qur'an*, 81:22–26.

4 Ibid., 16:103.

 | DOI 10.1163/9789004279407_110

> Truly it is the revelation of the Lord of all Being, brought down by the Spirit of Truth upon thy heart, that thou mayest be one of the warners, in a clear, Arabic tongue. Truly it is in the Scriptures of the ancients.[5]
>
> If We had made it a barbarous Recitation, they would have said, "Why are its signs not distinguished? What, barbarous and Arabic?" Say: "To the believers it is a guidance, and a healing; but those who believe not, in their ears is a heaviness, and to them it is a blindness; those – they are called from a far place."[6]

Listening relates listeners and the one they listen to. At the first level of knowledge, the speaker's discourse comes as a voice for the listener's ears to hear. At the second degree, it is the heart that listens.[7] The apostle said: "The hearts of all the children of Adam are like a single heart between two of the fingers of the All-merciful. He turns it wherever He desires. O God, O Turner of Hearts, turn our hearts toward obeying Thee!"[8] For the heart turned towards Peace, the self recognizes and bears witness from the perspective of one Book to every other. God revealed to the Praised: "Those to whom We gave the Book before this believe in it and, when it is recited to them, they say, 'We believe in it; surely it is the truth from our Lord. Indeed, even before it we have been people of Peace.' "[9]

Confession of the Praised, listening and accepting God's Word as revealed through him, encompasses all the self. With the Word, we are directed towards the height of our original creation and the Praised as finest example. This sublimity is summed up and revealed in the Recitation as the most sublime discourse: "God has sent down the fairest discourse as a Book, consimilar in its oft-repeated, whereat shiver the skins of those who fear their Lord; then their skins and their hearts soften to the remembrance of God."[10]

God speaks to us through creation and the prophets. We come to know how He creates and speaks to the prophets through the interpretation of creation and prophetic speech. Created, we comprise creation as the Creator's revelation. Every prophet is a person, fully realized in that through which he speaks. No prophet brings news in a language not of his listeners. Interpretation of this

---

5 Ibid., 26:192–96.

6 Ibid., 41:44.

7 See *Qur'an*, 7:100.

8 Muslim, 4:1397.

9 *Qur'an*, 28:52–53.

10 Ibid., 39:23.

discourse necessarily involves turning and journeying towards that with which knowledge connects the knower – the Creator and Revealer.

Our connection with the Creator through the apostle entails listening to him or his messengers and reciting the Book he brings. Reciting and reading direct consciousness from sign to sign, word to word, in a rhythm that proceeds from line end to end, line to line, top to bottom of the page, in a constant movement back and forth, from right to left and back, opening and closing, turning pages and unfolding, assembling and declining. None of this movement leads to any material goal beyond or independent of its symbolic meaning.

All existence, world and self, is like a closed door, an army barring the way to Peace, the Known and the Beloved, as names of Him towards Whom the people of peace, known knowers, beloved lovers desire to journey more than all things. Ritual expresses our relationship with our supreme potential. Travellers on the path do not define their efforts and desires, the goal does. But He transcends all confines, both absolutely now and absolutely eternal, near and remote, similar and different from all things in world or self. Ritual confirms both our separation from the Goal and our potential to reach It. The Goal determines the ritual, but does not reduce to it. Discussing the open self and ritual and how they relate, as well as the reason for repeated entry into and exit from this symbolic recital, Adam Seligman concludes: "Ritual, therefore, means never-ending work. It is a recurrent, always imperfect, project of dealing with patterns of human behavior – patterns that are always at risk of shifting into dangerous directions – or of unleashing demons."[11]

---

11 Seligman et al., *Ritual and Its Consequences*, 42.

CHAPTER 14

Memorizing

The Holy Spirit or Spirit of Truth brought down the Recitation to the Praised. Its revelation in a clear Arabic tongue links the heart, as the centre of the self, with all the signs in the world and self. His perfection is the warrant for its reception, memorizing, speaking and writing, perfection for and from which God's word is manifest and for which He chose the prophet as the foremost, universal example. This is why the Recitation in all these forms – listening, memorizing, speaking and writing – is our best potential. We are expected to subject our whole being to it. Everything spoken by the Praised as the Word is perfect, as he is himself, as listener, memorizer and utterer of God's perfect Word.[1]

The Praised related what he had received in the language of those he lived with, in the language in which the Recitation was revealed to him and that links him and all who speak it. It comprehends all the experiences of those who have spoken it in the past. Seen from outside, the Praised's discourse added nothing new to it; his audience already knew every word – camel-drivers, palm-growers, water-carriers, well-diggers, slaves and nobles. For what they did not understand, they drew meaning from context. Language is finite, meanings are not.

So what made the Recitation a discourse above all others?

Language is like a cluster of infinite smaller clusters. It comprises the entire visible and invisible world, but only potentially, for there is no language without humankind. Our uncreated centre is the vinestalk from which the entire cluster hangs. When that core is obscured, the position of each piece in regard to the whole is lost. Through the Revelation as the Word descending into the heart of the Praised, the Sacred Debt arrived where it can neither be driven nor blocked to restore order to language in connection with Spirit. The apostle became wholly the expression of his uncreated centre. The Divine I was manifest in prophetic speech, owning it, so that language became a world of meaning whose centre is God as First and Last, Inner and Outer.

Listening, memorizing, reciting, writing and reading permeate human life. Breathing and the beating of the heart, speaking and remaining silent, seeing and touching, everything that sustains and expresses life is linked inextricably to the Recitation. In seeking truth and beauty in the self and on the horizons,

1 See Graham, *Beyond the Written Word*, 207 n.18.

 | DOI 10.1163/9789004279407_111

the people of peace begin from and return to the Recitation as guardian of their original nature. Everything in the world and self serves to designate the All-merciful and All-praised. The turn towards our supreme potential is inextricably linked to remembrance of Him.

Remembering God illumines the dark depths of the self, revealing His most beautiful names within, contained as treasure since its origins. The names and signs are in the Recitation. Its presence through hearing, memorizing, reciting, writing and reading makes it impossible to forget. Forgetting is absence of recollection, as darkness of light. Neither forgetting nor darkness is fully there. Memory is our original, sublime capacity, indelibly bound in all the ways the self and Recitation interact. Through the Praised, God commanded: "Recite what has been revealed to thee of the Book, and perform the prayer; prayer forbids indecency and dishonour. God's remembrance is greater; and God knows the things you work."[2]

The Recitation is "in the name of God, the All-merciful, the Ever-merciful." We relate to it through remembrance of His name, which alone fills the heart with absolute satisfaction. Our core contains nothing, nor does our reason and purpose, but the Name. To cleanse or reveal the heart's original nature is to be of the faithful, "their hearts at rest in God's remembrance – for in God's remembrance are at rest the hearts of those who believe and do righteous deeds; theirs is blessedness and a fair resort."[3] The Recitation's first abode is the pure heart, which, manifest in recitation, writing and reading, recalls that beginning and the path of return to absolute innerness, the absolutely first. The Recitation recalls both origin and return: "No indeed; surely it is a Reminder; so whoever wills shall remember it."[4]

Forgetting is the opposite of remembering. Only remembrance connects the rememberer with the Remembered. Reality, the self's deepest core, is the Remembered, Who breathed His Spirit into us. At our core is His abode, in which all flows, in and out, meet, and all opposites perish, for He has no partner, no equal, nor is anyone like unto Him.

Remembering ourselves, we remember God, just as remembering God, we remember ourselves. God told the Praised so explicitly: "Be not as those who forgot God, and so He caused them to forget their souls; those – they are the ungodly."[5]

---

2 *Qur'an*, 29:45.

3 Ibid., 13:28–29.

4 Ibid., 74:54–55.

5 Ibid., 59:19.

Preserving in memory what has been memorized is necessary to maintain the covenant between humankind and God. Knowledge of it is necessary, but not sufficient. Ritual and virtue are means that help to sustain memory; they help to maintain constancy, but nothing is more crucial than God's mercy. God says through the Praised: "And We made covenant with Adam before, but he forgot, and We found in him no constancy."[6]

Neither forgetting nor darkness exist for the Upright; they are merely the absence of light and remembrance. Since God is Light, Whom Alone the signs recall, forgetting and darkness are a state of the self, obscured by some representation of error and cut off from the light. Never entirely cut off, however, as even darkness is not absolute.

---

6 Ibid., 20:115.

CHAPTER 15

Recitation

Prophetic speech presupposes hearing and memorizing in solitude. Absolute solitude is annihilation in which the Divine I may manifest as absolute reality. This revelation is a resurrection. Only after the experience of hearing and memorizing does the prophet utter what he has received to convey to those who surround him listening. In what he says, God reveals Himself in the infinite forms contained in His *We*: "As also We have sent among you, of yourselves, an apostle, to recite Our signs to you and to purify you, and to teach you the Book and the Wisdom, and to teach you that you knew not."[1]

God is first speaker, reciter and teacher of the Book, the apostle its first recipient among people. What God narrates is received from none, but the apostle says only what God has given him, as he said himself in the Revelation given him: "I follow nothing, except what is revealed to me."[2]

When he began to tell the people what he had received through the Holy Spirit, the Praised was already known to them as one of them, like and unlike the rest, speaking their language and understanding the meaning of every word. He could discuss, interpret or remain silent about whatever happened in that language or to its speakers. The language was as much his as theirs. None had a greater right to it, not those with the greatest skill in it, poets or storytellers, nor the camel drivers or merchants. It was a common legacy, received, spoken, and passed on.

When the Praised told the people the Recitation he had for them had been sent down to his heart by God through the Spirit of Truth that language took on a different aspect and things manifested differently. Everything, near or far, began to be reordered and the meanings of life and death, earth and heaven and everything inbetween became clearer. This reordering involved nothing new on the outer horizons or in the self, however, as each recipient experienced this discourse and its bearer as reminding them of what had always been within them, but was somehow forgotten.

As recipient and giver, the Praised signifies God's mercy to us: "Truly God was gracious to the believers when He raised up among them an apostle from

1 *Qur'an*, 2:151.

2 Ibid., 10:15.

 | DOI 10.1163/9789004279407_112

themselves, to recite to them His signs and to purify them, and to teach them the Book and the Wisdom, though before they were in manifest error."[3]

Against "manifest error" stands the apostle's example. Through confession of his apostolate and so participating in recitation of the Book, with its purity and wisdom, our individual and collective consciousness of the higher possibility that always precedes us on the path of ascent and return perdures. Nothing real about that ascent exists apart from the presence of the Book:

> As no other of the world's great scriptures, the Muslim scripture has been the object of a mnemonic and recitative tradition that has saturated and sustained not only Muslims' devotional life and worship, but also the quotidian life in Muslim societies large and small around the globe with the rich, melodic and moving strains of the recitation of God's word.[4]

As Scripture, the Recitation is the supreme treasure sent down by God into the world, which He gives us as, in its entirety, a place of self-annihilation and a treasury in which to annihilate illusion for reality and receive the Word. We can transform anywhere in this world into such a place of self-annihilation, a "place of the Book." The Praised received the Book from God and it links him and God. It becomes our property through him. Once we have internalized the Recitation, the Praised and God are with and within us too. With the Recitation we ascend towards the Praised and God through the obscurity of existence, as God calls upon us to do:

> O thou enwrapped in thy robes, keep vigil the night, except a little (a half of it, or diminish a little, or add a little), and chant the Recitation very distinctly. Behold, We shall cast upon thee a weighty word; surely the first part of the night is heavier in tread, more upright in speech.[5]

The surviving fragments of the scriptures of the Bosnian *krstjani* are scattered around the world. Although an integral part of the old Slavonic culture by which news of Christ was conveyed into the language of the Slavs, their distinctive script and certain internal markings related to liturgical use nonetheless render them immediately recognizable. These are seemingly minor differences given how these and similar books were used among the other Slavs of their neighbourhood, but nonetheless constitute what is distinctively Bosnian

3 Ibid., 3:164.

4 Graham, "Scripture and *Qur'an*," 567.

5 *Qur'an*, 73:1–6.

about them. And so it was through them that a jealously guarded boundary was established towards a close and similar other.

It was the pressures and persecutions put on the Bosnian *krstjani* to encourage them to renounce those small differences that caused them to cleave to a different reading of the news of the Christ. This may be seen as a betrayal or a strengthening of their identity, insofar as the reasons for it lay in an esoteric identity and spiritual core that allowed them to repackage doctrine and ritual without sacrificing virtue or connection with truth.

CHAPTER 16

Writing

What the Praised heard or received in his heart entered the pure Arabic language as the Recitation. Acquiring the form of speech, the Recitation became the Book. God answered those who would contest this through the Praised: "No indeed; it is a Reminder (and whoso wills, shall remember it) upon pages high-honoured, uplifted, purified, by the hands of scribes noble, pious."[1]

The confession of no god but God and the Praised as His servant and apostle contains both unity as multiplicity's source and meeting point and human perfection manifest in the apostle. This manifestation is the voice in silence, light in darkness. With it, the world is revealed as the Book, summed up in Revelation, a reminder heard, memorized, spoken, written and read, perfectly embodied by the Praised as recipient and giver. Only a self informed by the Book sent down to him can follow the Praised. His call is listening, reciting and reading, seeing humankind in its full span from depths to height, and all-encompassing knowledge.

The Praised retreated to the silence of the cave above the inviolate valley of Becca, at whose middle and lowest point lies the Kaʿba, the sign of the human heart in which connection to God is most explicit. In that silence, one summer night some 610 years after the birth of the Anointed, he experienced for the first time the Holy Spirit through whom God revealed to him the first five verses of the Recitation: "Recite in the name of thy Lord who created, created man of a blood-clot. Recite: And thy Lord is the Most Generous, who taught by the Pen, taught man that he knew not."[2]

Beginning thus, the Recitation marked and stirred the currents in the self that make of us a being of sublime potential, but added nothing, as our potential is perfect in its original form. The revelation recalls us to that potential and supports our quest for what was lost and forgotten. The will is required for faith as what links the faithful to the All-faithful. There are always two options: accept or reject. Accepting the command to recite – to listen, memorize, utter, write and read – we order our life by the Book, with which come all the other books, for to confess the Praised is to confess them all and all of God's apostles known and unknown.

1 *Qur'an*, 80:11–15.

2 Ibid., 96:1–5. The verb "recite" entails both "reading" and "saying," indicating the indivisibility between listening, memorizing, reading and writing.

 | DOI 10.1163/9789004279407_113

Our reasons for accepting the Recitation are within us, and in all the Books of our heritage as human beings. Bosnia's history shows this. The Bosnian Church's manuscripts of the Gospels are the most valuable part of the country's ancient sacred heritage. From a Muslim perspective, this heritage, in all its sublime meaning, is witness to and preserved the Recitation. It merges with listening, memorizing, recitation, writing and reading it in affirmation and guardianship of the essence common to all the holy books God has revealed through His prophets.[3]

Passed from person to person, generation to generation, the Recitation is heard and remembered, from our first to our last moments in this world, recited at birth and at death. It is copied in whole or part with utmost care in the finest script, on parchment and paper, on walls and stone plaques, on wood and bone, bound in the finest cloth, and engraved on metal, stone, wood and bone.

Reciting the Recitation we comprehend the world, bringing the remote horizons closer to the self, the self to those horizons. Reciting in the name of our Lord, our heart becomes the abode of our Creator and Teacher, Who teaches us with the Pen. Only in perfect harmony of conscious mind, will and deed does the Pen in the scribe's hand manifest the perfection of the self in perfect transcription.

As we become our Lord's perfect servant, our original and perfect uprightness is manifest in all we do or do not do. We sense the Praised's mighty morality in our nature, nearest and dearest to us, along with all the prophets and the revelations through them – Adam and Noah, Abraham and Moses, David and Solomon, John and Jesus, and all those sent to all peoples – who also become near and dear, beautiful and inviolable in our feelings and knowledge, as do the books revealed through them – Torah and Psalms, Gospel and every other holy scripture, known and unknown.

---

3 The surviving books of the Bosnian Church are scattered across the world. See Kuna, *Srednjovjekovna bosanska književnost*. Bosnian manuscripts of the Qur'an are also scattered, but mostly still in Bosnia. For more on Bosnian Qur'anic manuscripts, see Dobrača, *Katalog arapskih, turskih, perzijskih i bosanskih rukopisa Gazi Husrev-begove biblioteke*; Fajić, ibid; Lavić, ibid.; Hasandedić, *Katalog arapskih, turskih i perzijskih rukopisa*; Ždralović, *Prepisivači djela u arebičkim rukopisima*. The Gazi Husrev-bey library in Sarajevo currently houses 825 such manuscripts – 659 complete, 166 fragmentary. In 1992, when the entire collection of the Oriental Institute in Sarajevo was destroyed, 79 Qur'anic manuscripts were lost (Trako and Gazić, "Rukopisna zbirka Orijentalnog instituta u Sarajevu," 18). There are many Qur'anic manuscripts in private hands, as well as in mosques, mektebs, tekkes and medresas. The figures for these two collections make clear how common the Qur'an was in Bosnia.

Knowledge and wisdom are a blessing everywhere and always to the perfect servant, to whom the world and everyone in it, their joys and fortune, their sufferings and misfortune all belong in the effort to distinguish truth from falsehood, good from evil, and to realize their selves in virtue by embracing what is good and true.

Our efforts to turn to God and discover and realize our self's original nature involve us in constant rupture and reconnection. Breaking free of illusion and delusion, we reconnect with our original self of which God's apostles remind us in the Books and through ritual and virtue. We break off our ties with evil and ugliness and reconnect with the good and beautiful. Whatever our condition, a need to break free so as to reconnect presses us. Only by passing through denial of our debt to God in the shadow of illusion can we understand and embrace that very debt's importance for realizing the humanity we were given in the self's initial, and so final, state.

Listening to, memorizing, uttering, writing and reading the Recitation, which make up our individual and collective past, necessarily comprise the continuities and ruptures of Bosnian history. They have meaning through and in the constant presence of truth and our durable capacity to turn the self towards its indestructible centre, its mighty, sublime morality. God answers the Praised's every question about prophets and the Books thus: "*Nun*! By the Pen, and what they inscribe, thou art not, by the blessing of thy lord, a man possessed. Surely thou shalt have a wage unfailing; surely thou art upon a mighty morality. So thou shalt see, and they will see, which of you is the demented."[4]

This lesson of the Pen, as a symbol for hearing, memorizing, reciting, writing and reading, points to the perfect potential of the self, indestructible even if forgotten or obscured on the path of descent or aimless wandering. The self's best possibilities lie in listening to, memorizing, reciting, writing and reading the Recitation.

There is no greater warrant of the beauty of the human voice than the Recitation as it reaches the ear of those who listen to it; nothing that more beautifully reveals itself and lodges in our memory than the Recitation as Remembrance; nothing that actuates the mysterious world of the human voice more powerfully and beautifully than the Recitation; nothing in all the active expressions of human will that bring such beauty as the transcribing of the

---

4 *Qur'an*, 68:1–6. This *ṣūra* is called after its beginning, the Arabic letter *nun*, shaped roughly like the lower half of a circle with a dot in the middle. The dot may be read as signifying the Principle or the Truth of creation as the centre of all things, the semicircle as the world that receives and makes It manifest. See Guénon, "Les mystéres de la lettre *Nûn*," in Guénon, *Symboles de la Science sacrée*, 154–58.

Recitation; and nothing so pleasing and beautiful to the eye or that transports us so surely beyond the bounds of the visible into the certainty of Mystery as the reading of the Recitation. So it is for those who know their Lord through the signs in the horizons and the self, who love Him and do all they can to be beautiful for Him, for their goal is always one – that their Beloved should love them, for union realizes their confession of no beloved but the Beloved.

CHAPTER 17

Reading

Certain features of living discourse challenge our current idea of the Book. One says of those who relate to the Book not by reading but by having heard another read it aloud that they study and recite it, just as one does of those who read it on pages or in bound volumes, in inscriptions on walls or stone or metal, wood or fabric. Recitation and study of this kind orients the self, sets it in a groove of doing good, or is flawed.[1]

The Book it there for the self in many forms – memory, whisper, speech and transcription. We relate to it through our eyes and ears, so that it is oriented towards the self's centre. It is worth asking ourselves whether the Book is also oriented from that centre towards the self or the world.

In recent centuries, the semantic field of the word "the Book" has become much more restricted than was traditional. The dominant notion of a book is now as an object to be read, whereas it was traditionally something to be spoken out loud, listened to, memorized and repeated. Writing and reading were merely aids to listening, speaking and memorizing. On its own evidence, the Recitation is a revelation sent down to us through the Praised as apostle to be accepted or rejected as such. Whether rejected by an individual or a group, the consequences are theirs. They cannot deny the existence of others who accept the Recitation as divine discourse and for whom it resembles other Books.

For those who accept the Recitation as God's *verbatim* Word, it contains admonition and mercy, direction and light, healing and sanctity, knowledge and wisdom, beauty and joy. The discourse it consists of recalls God's many signs in nature and history and brings together His Words or signs, sent down or revealed to humankind.

Through it, we are connected to the Praised as our best example of praising God. Transcribing is witness of Light and Speech. Nothing combines consciousness and vision for us so perfectly as its letters, lines and pages given body in a book. The harmony of upright, horizontal and rounded strokes that lead the reader from beginning to end of the line, from top to bottom of the page, and from beginning to end of the Book prevents the self from loitering on one plane, urging it onto the upright path to which its rhymes and rhythms, relaxations and tensions, pauses and movements attest as a process of ascent and openness no waystation of which can stand in for the One Goal. This

1 See *Qur'an*, 2:44. The same Bosnian word is used for study and recite: *učiti*, while the Recitation is the *Učenje* and so Lesson.

 | DOI 10.1163/9789004279407_114

ascent is return from multiplicity to the One, from the depths to the height, retracing the path of descent. We thus realize ourselves by joining two arcs – one descending, the other ascending.

This link of transcription and observer connects silence and speech, inwardness and outwardness, firstness and lastness. God reveals Himself to the reader in the perfect beauty of the transcription. Facing this revelation, one cannot but sense the peacefulness, knowledge and love of the self to which God is Peace, All-knowing, Beloved, revealed in Beauty, for Beauty is how the beautiful relate to the All-beautiful. Thus, we serve God as though we saw Him, for while we may not see Him, He sees us.[2]

We deploy all our knowledge, rituals and virtues to break free of illusion, which appears so real, and enter the "as if." The sight of the Book in any of its various written forms, or sound of it, becomes a sign or link with Unity. With this sign, which both is and is not Oneness, we bridge the gulf between self and world.

Heard and uttered, written and read, the Recitation is the Book sent down by God to the Praised, as was done with the other prophets. Its meaning is inseparable from theirs; everything in it confirms their content and purpose. They have one source and one purpose, however many forms. As is said in the Revelation: "This Recitation could not have been forged apart from God; but it is a confirmation of what is before it, and a distinguishing of the Book, wherein is no doubt, from the Lord of all Being."[3]

In our relation to the revealed Book, we discover the Word as creative principle. No reading of the Book exhausts the Word, which is always open to the instant, offering itself as new possibility in which the Essence of the Book may manifest its sign, always differently. The reader's self thus discovers its inexhaustible horizons, for meaning is neither finite nor exhaustible. God said: "Every term has a Book. God blots out, and He establishes whatsoever He will; and with Him is the Essence of the Book."[4]

The Recitation is one Book. When an individual becomes aware of it, it serves to confirm the other books. Accepting their existence is part of accepting it, as it calls itself the Book of Books: "This is a Book We have sent down, blessed and confirming that which was before it, and for thee to warn the Mother of Cities and those about her; and those who believe in the world to come believe in it, and watch over their prayers."[5]

---

2 See Muslim, 1:1–3.

3 *Qur'an*, 10:37.

4 Ibid., 13:38–39.

5 Ibid., 6:92.

CHAPTER 18

Carving

Nothing, according to its original nature, is capable of resisting service to,[1] being-at-peace in[2] and worship of God.[3] Service, being-at-peace and worshipful annihilation are to receive and confess the creative Word. Since the Recitation is His Word, there is nothing so powerful, in its original nature, as to resist it, as God says: "If We had sent down this Recitation upon a mountain, thou wouldst have seen it humbled, split asunder out of the fear of God. And those similitudes – We strike them for men; haply they will reflect."[4]

The Pen is foremost in His creation. God covenants and instructs with it. It is the sum of creation, a sign of humankind: the Pen epitomizes at the beginning, as humanity does at the end. There is nothing in existence that is not in both the Pen and Humanity and one may say we learn everything in it, write down all that can be distinguished in the horizons and the self, and gather it all in our reading.

The heavens and earth and all between are written by God. His power is absolute, ours a mere reflection or testimony of His. To realize His power in our image, we listen, memorize, write and read. All things have their place in this. The apparently most resistant and most solid matter is the most challenging for our quest to affirm our service, peacefulness and worshipful self-abnegation. The ease of writing on paper with a pen spurs us to find means to imprint stone or iron and so confirm our service to God as a way of witnessing to the service of all that exists.

Stone and iron are cold, but where stone is passive and yielding, iron is active. They represent extremes of passivity and activity. To subjugate stone, we first tame iron, making it malleable by fire. We shape it in fire, from which we restore it to coldness. We subject it to extremes of cold and heat then we force the stone to yield to its obedient action in our hands. Through us, in our inner self, the opposites of cold and heat, hardness and malleability are united, and in this union we turn to God as perfect reconciler of opposites.

Thus the Recitation as Word informs stone, imbuing cold, hard inscription with remembrance, mercy, light and wisdom welling up from the indestructible, ineffable centre of each thing. Its centre is the Creator's "Be!" and the truth

1 See *Qur'an*, 19:93.

2 Ibid., 3:83.

3 Ibid., 13:15.

4 *Qur'an*, 59:21.

 | DOI 10.1163/9789004279407_115

of that thing's creation. All the signs in the horizons and self, individually and together, recall us to our centre, our original nature which irrevocably accepted our covenant with God of our own free will – the covenant that is the essence of the world and the self. All things in the world around us and in the self are signs that remind us of that covenant's truth. The Recitation's descent through the heart of the Praised is the same reminder, expressed differently.

All the signs in the world and self are part of that discourse. Phonemes and letters, sentences and lines on the page, suras and pages, collectively and separately, reflect the worlds, visible and invisible, body and soul, focused within us. They descend into us that we may ascend with them to our Lord. Bearing the Recitation within, we shape our speech and actions and translate our image of realized words into the world, from the uttermost depths and insignificance to the sublime height and ultimate magnificence. Everything appears pliant to us through the Word, since as the sum of His most beautiful names we are the ear He hears with, the eye He sees with, the hand He grasps with.[5] This union is the realization of the beloved lover and the All-loving Beloved.

Nothing seems to reveal so clearly the union of opposites as the act of carving God's signs in stone with an iron chisel. We unite the most intense extremes of heat and cold. Our realization in remembrance of our Lord preserves this perfect equilibrium. Let it be disturbed, as we waste our time distancing ourselves ever more from it, and we will find a new equilibrium in Hell, which brings together most intense heat and cold. With this experience of regaining balance, the paths are reopened for renewed ascent to His absolute mercy beyond suffering and wrath.[6]

In the act of carving, we remodel the forms of the world given on ourselves and may mistake ourselves for independent creators and modellers. It is not so, however: we have only what we have received. God creates both us and what we do.[7]

It would be no easy task to number and sort out all the signs carved on *stećci* and *nišani* as messages whether from the dead beneath or their heirs. They include the sun and the moon, cross and staff, rose and lily, deer and bird, rope and spear, bow and sabre, axe and pin. The dead hardly need them, but for the living it is crucially important they be read in line with the needs of the war within, the war whose winner transcends the bounds of death.

---

5 See Bukhārī, 8:336–37.

6 Ibid., 9:398–99. The bitterest cold and fiercest heat are to be found in Hell. See *Qur'an*, 38:57.

7 Ibid., 37:96.

CHAPTER 19

Building

The visible world, the heavens and earth and all that lies between them, are in harmony, an equilibrium of opposites. That equilibrium comes from and meets in Peace, with which everything is connected through being-at-peace. Nothing lacks such a connection nor can anything replace Peace as source and sanctuary, making It first and last, inward and outward. The world's perfect harmony is thus maintained by the opposition of forces at the limits of its particulars, from smallest to greatest.

The oppositions in prophetic discourse reveal this harmony and the simultaneity of Peace's immanence and remoteness. Jesus, Mary's son, said: "Think not that I am come to send peace on earth: I came not to send peace, but a sword,"[1] and: "Peace I leave with you, my peace I gave unto you: not as the world giveth, I give unto you. Let not your heart be troubled, neither let it be afraid."[2]

The need to bring forth Peace through war and the impossibility of reducing it to any finitude are attested to by two inextricable hopes of the true and the false Messiah. The apostle said of this:

> When they are pressing on to fight, even while they straighten their lines for the prayer when it is called, Jesus the son of Mary will descend and will lead them in the prayer. And the enemy of God, when he seeth Jesus, will melt even as salt melteth in water. If he were let be, he would melt unto perishing; but God will slay him at the hand of Jesus, who will show them his blood upon his lance.[3]

The resurrection from death or raising up of Jesus the Messiah is a key symbol of being-at-peace, of which God said: "And they slew him not of a certainty – no indeed; God raised him up to Him; God is All-mighty, All-wise."[4] The raising up of the Anointed is from the uttermost depths to the sublime height, the resurrection of our original, perfect human nature, the nature designated by all the prophets; and the Anointed and the Praised give voice and image to

1 *Matthew*, 10:34.

2 *John*, 14:27.

3 Muslim, 4:1501.

4 *Qur'an*, 4:157–58.

 | DOI 10.1163/9789004279407_116

that perfection. The sign of their raising up is the full moon in the first week or first day of the new victory of light over darkness, the new springtime when the days begin to be longer than the nights. The full moon designates the coming of the Hour as the return of the Anointed with the lance to slay the false Messiah and surrender leadership in prayer to the guided one, who is the Praised.

The full moon manifests Light and Its descent upon each of us. Confessing this descent is to discover Light in the self, where It has always been and always will be, uncreated and uncreatable – the Light of the Praised, manifest in praise of light and the light of praise, for self discovery is just that light of the Praised. This is how for centuries the accounts of Jesus' taking his disciples to Mount Tabor to show them the uncreated, uncreatable Light have been understood: "And after six days Jesus taketh Peter, James, and John his brother, and bringeth them up into an high mountain apart, and was transfigured before them: and his face did shine as the sun, and his raiment was white as a light. And, behold, there appeared unto them Moses and Elias talking with him."[5]

This transfiguration before his disciples, with Moses and Elijah for witnesses, is the Light of the Praised. Moses is the prophet like the Praised, while Elijah descends again to the earth God raised him from to bear witness to the Anointed and the Praised.[6] Elijah was raised up without dying. The appearance of Moses and Elijah with Jesus foretells the coming of the Praised and Elijah's re-descent. Jesus' disciples ask him whether to make shelters for them, but no construction in the external world is needed for that brief experience by which they are recalled to the reality in the self.

Everywhere on earth is a place of self-annihilation, with us and for us. There is nowhere and no time at which we cannot become aware of our reality as received manifestations. Knowing it as such, we repudiate what is not that reality and erase the traces by which we came. Both what we build and what we raze are for that discovery. If we do not build in remembrance of Peace in our heart, we build on sand, on the brink of a crumbling bank: "Why, is he better who founded his building on consciousness of God and His good pleasure, or he who founded his building upon the brink of a crumbling bank that has tumbled with him unto the fire of hell?"[7]

---

5 *Matthew*, 17:1–3.

6 The Light of the Praised is spoken of in the stories and songs about him that are so pervasive in Bosnian heritage. See Trako, "Ibrahim Zikrija iz Užica, komentator Sulejman Čelebijina djela *Vesilet en-nedžat* ('sredstvo spasa')"; Böwering, *The Mystical Vision of Existence in Classical Islam*.

7 *Qur'an*, 9:109.

The entire world was created perfect. All its horizons are open to our observation and recall their purpose. Nothing in them was created without truth, nothing in them or the self without purpose. Doctrine, ritual and virtue serve the discovery of creation's reason and purpose. When we build, perfection is within our grasp. And what our building produces is measured against the completeness towards which doctrine, ritual and virtue direct us.

Afterword: "Accord Everything Its Right!"

World and self comprehend multitudes in flux, a veil revealing and concealing reality. We focus them, were taught their names and know the rights each thing was created with, as God is absolute right:

> God, who is the Absolute Ḥaqq, has given each thing in the universe creation and guidance, and the thing's creation and guidance are its ḥaqq because they tie it back to the First Ḥaqq. The thing's "creation" can be understood as its actual reality and its "guidance" as the path it must follow to achieve the fullness of what it is to become. In other words, "creation" refers to the fact that each thing has come from God, and guidance refers to the fact that God has provided each with a path that it follows in returning to its Creator.[1]
>
> The Qur'an says: "Wherever you turn, there is the face of God" (2.115). The goal of taḥqiq is to see the face of God wherever you turn, in every creature and in oneself, and then to act according to the ḥaqq of God's face. If we understand anything in the universe without taking the Divine Face into account, then we have lost the thing's ḥaqq, we have lost sight of God and by losing sight of God we have lost sight of the unity of God (tawhid).[2]

We cannot manifest or confess Unity without confessing the Praised's apostolate. It is God's first manifestation as Light, the Light of Praise and Praise of Light, manifesting Face and holding the scattered in Unity. When we lose sight of the Face and forget the rights of all things, our world collapses. To remember is to rebuild it. As universal order, ritual is the attempt to position ourselves in the world's space and time and maintain the self's connection with it in recognition of all things' rights. Remembrance lies at the heart of ritual as a path or frame for the self back from oblivion and dissipation to the universal order of existence whose axis it is. The returning self can then take up its position in existence and so in the universe and in society, as Adam B. Seligman has described:

---

1 Chittick, "Time, Space and the Objectivity of Ethical Norms: The Teaching of Ibn al-ʿArabī," 584.

2 Ibid.

 | DOI 10.1163/9789004279407_117

> ... ritual creates and re-creates a world of social convention and authority beyond the inner will of any individual.... We argue that such traditions understand the world as fundamentally fractured and discontinuous, with ritual allowing us to live in it by creating temporary order through the construction of a performative, subjunctive world. Each ritual rebuilds the world "as if" it were so, as one of many possible worlds.[3]

Participating in world-creation and the All-merciful, All-praised Creator's presence, we transcend our own judgment as final. Nothing's truth of creation depends on whether or not we like it, as nothing lacks such truth. Jesus said: "But I say unto you which hear, Love your enemies, do good to them which hate you."[4] However impossible this commandment seems, everything in existence is with truth. We may guess, but only God sees their why and wherefore clearly and only return to Him makes clarity possible. Our enemies are signs bearing their truth and under it we owe all things acknowledgement of their right, a debt that cannot be redeemed with hatred of truth.

---

3 Seligman et al., *Ritual and Its Consequences*, 11.

4 *Luke*, 6:27.

PART 2

In the Manuscripts

• •

We have three major, even crucial skills: listening, speaking and writing. In this order, they represent our passage through descent and, hopefully, ascent. To listen to a speaker is to confirm our own lower standing and awareness of one higher. We must relax and be at peace. Speech only offers something to the relaxed and peaceful self. Listener and speaker are recipient and giver in a relationship of debt. Were the listener not at peace, the speaker peaceful, no debt would arise. Moreover, as both share in the same original nature and same ultimate purpose, discourse requires the speaker recognize the listener's right to speak and listen in turn. Only by regularly exchanging positions can both discover their original nature.

In the broadest ontological terms, God is First Speaker. The world and we, as extended and condensed forms, are first listeners. God's speech is His creation, gathered in us, so that existence is the individual writ large, the individual existence in little. This relationship between individual and existence is concentrated in language. Language comprehends all of existence, including humanity. The First Speaker and His listeners are in a relation of mutual confidence. We owe God for our being. In peaceful receipt of that debt, we acquire the right to speak to God as people of peace. We owe Him all we have and so have one right – to address God and ask and receive.

This right to receive opens us to God. He alone satisfies us, allowing us to say to Him: You gave us existence, so tell us what we must do to return to You as giver and be one with You. This is our human right to a path of realization and fullness of return, with nothing held back. We cannot build that path, having only what is given us, as God gave both us and the path. We must find it and shape the self as movement to the Goal.

So long as there is insurmountable difference instead of plenitude, God has an unredeemed debt to us and creation's purpose is unachieved. Our right, concomitant to His debt to us, justifies all human debts to God. This debt and right are absolutely balanced, as God is endebted to Himself for His self-revelation, which is perfect, internally and externally, albeit merely potential in us. Discovering the self, we discover our perfection, which is God, as there is no perfection but Perfection.

Our relationship to God is reflected in language. As God speaks by creating the world and us, language repeats it, creation renewed each instant: one world vanishes, another appears. In the perfect, inviolable "now," the One manifests as Flux. How this takes place raises the question of whether He addresses us through the heart, being's centre, or the world, that centre's manifest circumference.

Of course, He does both at once, as inflow and outflow. His revelation indicates: "We shall show them Our signs in the horizons and in themselves, till it

 | DOI 10.1163/9789004279407_118

is clear to them that He is the truth."[1] Showing the signs in the horizons and the selves indicates the centre they make known. No sign has meaning without the Signified. As a link to the Signified, the sign is transparent, but when we suppose it independent, it becomes a veil over the self that regards it.

The verse just quoted says "We," "They" and "He." "We" is God speaking of Himself as One and Only. To the signs He is One and Only and speaks of Himself as "We" and calls them "Ours." Each sign has its own name, corresponding to one of His numberless beautiful names. Through them He is manifest in differentiated mode. He gathers the names in us, for He taught us them all.[2]

The host of signs affirms Unity, which each sign names individually and in tandem. Multiplicity is Unity's discourse, Its descent to the depths. Foremost in His manifestation is the highest possibility in all existence (the Praised), uncut off from its signs in the uttermost depths. The world as a whole brings together all the signs on the arc of descent from the One to the extreme of multiplicity. The Perfect One, the Praised, epitomizes that totality, appearing in the depths in order to ascend to the sublime height and realize all multiplicity in Unity as universal principle. Why does God speak through His creation?

The Creator is First Speaker Who charges all creation to listen to Him, a charge all things accept, while we alone choose to do so willingly or under duress. The choice comes from our relationship to God as faithful. When existence and we accept the debt, we acquire the right to address God and be listened to by Him. God both reveals and listens to Himself through His creation.

He sent down His revelation through the Spirit of Truth into the heart of the apostle for him to proclaim in his language as God's discourse. "We" is said for "I" as He reveals Himself through the truth of the creation of all things. "Those" to whom He shows His signs are individuals whose consciousness of their "I" runs from the deepest, most indefinite centre to the furthest bounds and beyond, to the heavens. But "He" is the Third Who reveals Himself in every pair, the first and last of things. As people relate through language, an infinite flux of giving and receiving, God reveals Himself in that exchange.

We are placed between the incomprehensible nearness and remoteness of the One and Only as absolutely near and far. We can sink into matter, but never exhaust its inwardness. Descent orients us towards the truth of the creation of great and small. Equally, we may rise high in thought and word, towards the ultimate horizons of the heavens, but their boundaries remain impassable to us. We cannot accept either as impossible. The signs in the horizons and the self reveal God as near and remote. They are windows and doors that open

---

1 *Qur'an*, 41:53.

2 See *Qur'an*, 2:31.

onto Him. To recognize these signs is to live outside the limits that do not comprehend God, but that He encompasses.

It is denial of His signs that closes off the horizons and the self to passage. Such is the self that denies its original nature as openness to the One and Only. God said of such: "Those that cry lies to Our signs and wax proud against them – the gates of heaven shall not be open to them."[3]

Expressed in human language, God's discourse becomes a link with the apostle and Him Who sent him. No human condition approaches the sublime, initial and ultimate purpose of creation. In them all, our perfect potential remains our true home, from which we are exiles, strangers in this world. Always returning home, we strive after our perfect potential comprised in a language beyond limits, beyond distinction of knower, knowing and known. This is why strangers – others speaking other languages from other parts and other times – are like guests in the returning traveller's temporary abode, a crucial reminder of our perpetual, unalterable alienness in this world.

The Anointed spoke in the language of his people and time, a stranger to everyone of that language and even more to those of other languages. Relationship to him is redeemed only by recognizing his foreignness as Anointed, his reminder to each of us that our supreme potential is both remote and nearby. Translating his discourse does not alter his foreignness as the home we strive to return to. At the core of the stranger's self is One, Which alone satisfies those who know and love It.

In this discourse, the apostle represents our sublime potential for all who hearken to it, memorize and repeat it, commit it to writing and re-read it. The Book is their connection with the apostle and God, placing us in a covenant with God, a "compact of the Book."[4]

The apostle is a stranger in the world, there to remind us how distant we are from the self's centre, our original and ultimate homeland, the house of Peace. Every properly oriented movement in that world is on the paths of peace. The Praised said of his presence in the world: "What have I to do with this world? I and this world are as a rider and a tree beneath which he taketh shelter. Then he goeth on his way, and leaveth it behind him."[5]

Every time God reveals a Book through a prophet, listening and remembering, speaking and writing play an integral part in our connection at a lower plane with our higher potential, of the stranger with the non-stranger. Memorizing and repeating, writing and reading what has been heard together preserve the

3 *Qur'an*, 7:40.

4 See *Qur'an*, 7:169.

5 Ibn Māja, 87:3.

flow of what has been received in time. All involved in reception and transmission remain connected to the apostle and, through him, to God. Each self ascends from a lower to a higher potential on its journey of return and realization.

No revelation is confined to one language, as no people is isolated from all contact with people of another language. Every language is fully inclusive. There is nothing in existence that is not in language. Language is also exclusive, needing nothing from any other language. But there is no people whose language is not defined by the language of another. It is part of our sublime potential to recognize the language of another as our one, however incomprehensible. Those who speak a foreign language are as though dumb, absolute guests of whom the host learns from their muteness.

But we are all utterly mute of what we seek as our perfection. Speakers open themselves up to their dumb guests, for only with them can the traveller's dissatisfaction, far from his goal, be assuaged. The stranger becomes dearer than our own selves. We are expected to bear witness justly, even against our own selves. We cannot see ourselves as strangers from our original sublime potential if we do not find fault with ourselves or if we fail to give thanks for that sublime, perfect potential.

The host-stranger relationship is found in every people and nation. Each in the multitude of languages has equal potential to receive each individual revelation, giving it a different shape and tone without betraying the one inexhaustible truth. The Anointed spoke in one language and his teachings have been translated into almost every other. This translation includes the relationships of listening and speaking, writing and reading.

The arrival of the Gospel into Bosnian was part of this process of transmission and translation and involved much and various giving and receiving. The coming of the Slav missionaries Constantine Cyril and his brother Methodius has been described in detail and the books produced under their project to translate the Gospels and church canons have had a presence in Bosnia since their very first appearance. For some, those books held annunciation and witness of the Praised as seal of the prophets, a mercy to the worlds and best example.

The Anointed as God's Word had in his person knowledge of past and future. Those who confess the Praised find reasons to accept him in every word of Jesus, as transmitted and recorded in the Gospels, as they find witness of the Anointed in every apostolic discourse of the Praised. These two aspects of the Divine revelation seem two facets of one discourse, from different times and in different forms. It allows accounts to be heard and read in which the self is engaged of its own free will, by faith, as what relates the faithful and the All-faithful.

Such faith considers the book revealed through the apostle part of a Bosnian experience of the Book that includes the Torah, the Psalms, the Gospels, the Recitation, and the other holy scriptures. These were once in different languages – Hebrew, Aramaic and Arabic – and translated into others – Aramaic and Coptic, Greek and Latin – and then into all. They entered Old Slavonic as a linguistic kernel from which to take root among distinct peoples and regions.

Holy Scripture, including Gospels and Recitation, has thus become Bosnian manuscripts without which most ancient and most recent elements of our inner lives and of society can hardly be understood. What part of Bosnian reality lacks any association with the presence of the Gospels? The surviving manuscripts may be scattered around the world, but they have indelibly shaped the Bosnian sense of self. When surviving Bosnian Gospels are studied and read and their fate investigated, the conviction is hard to resist that they reflect the noblest aspirations of the Bosnian people, gathered around the Gospels as good news, meeting and parting around the Book.

The same is true of Bosnian manuscripts of the Recitation, present in all parts of the country at one time or another. This presence of both Gospels and Recitation is merely the outward evidence of their presence in the inner selves of people there. Both presences may be seen as responses to the question of what we are and why we enter and leave this world. God's prophets have taught of this since humanity first set foot in the world of dualities. The prophets that are truly God's and not false express the message of the one God in different languages and at different times. It is up to us to accept or spurn them and to live with ourselves as defined by our choice.

The Gospels and the Recitation, as two revelations of the one God made through two of His chosen, the Anointed and the Praised, can be translated into any language. No translation exhausts their meanings in the full knowledge and mercy of the Revealer. The Revelation's ultimate meaning remains with Him and our differences of interpretation are irreconcilable in this world of duality, to disappear only in return of the self to the Self.

One can show that Bosnian manuscripts of the Gospels and the Recitation form a unity in the countless manifestations of God's revelation to humankind by comparing their translations. No translation eliminates difference. With it, they remain open to ascent from one plane to another on the path of return to God. Let us accept that no state of the self we can know is final, but let us also recall that we are always strangers in this world, travellers towards the sublime height of our potential. The perfect height we approach renders our every interpretation of revelation incomplete, dictated by alienation from our original and perfect potential.

The members of the Bosnian Church were hated and persecuted by other churches and their ecclesiastical and temporal authorities, denied their rights, their name, and dubbed heretics, Manichees, Cathars, Patarins and Bogomils. Manuals were drawn up for their conversion from a "false" to the "true" faith, judicial proceedings launched and military campaigns waged against them.[6] The manuals described their fallacies and how to talk them out of them, fallacies ascribed to them as "other" by those who regarded their own selves as non-contingent and on a higher plane of openness to and dependence on God.

Their persecutors' state of mind denied St. John's Spirit "that bloweth where it listeth" and that we have no lord in creation but the Lord. Their books were mainly destroyed and what evidence remains of their beliefs, whether full books or fragments, is with one exception outside Bosnia, in Belgrade, Berlin, Bologna, Cetinje, Dublin, Dubrovnik, Ljubljana, Monteprandone, Moscow, St. Petersburg, Skopje, Sofia, Plevna, Rome and Zagreb.[7] The exception is the Gospel kept at Čajniče.

These Bosnian books were written in Old Slavonic in a distinctive Bosnian Cyrillic script, obviously adapted to the local vernacular. Centuries later, their presence can still be recognized in the living language, a deep linguistic layer formative of Bosnian identity over the centuries. Nor can the Bosnian Gospels' centuries of existence be considered in isolation from the Bosnian Mushaf or Qur'anic book. The God Who sent His Recitation to the Praised speaks in the Gospels and the Praised received another *Evangelion* or Good News. And so there are two divine discourses of good news, one in the other.

Whenever the heirs to one of these revelations appropriated the other, they discovered something already theirs. As a result, ancestors and descendants bore mutual witness. When this happened in Bosnia, two revelations of One God became the property of one people. This was His witness through them to the maternal or archetypal Book of all divine revelations. They made manifest the war in the self between its little knowledge and the stranger's constant presence, towards which we turn as to our own sublime potential. The languages of the Gospels and the Recitation can be translated in the self, but only through what lies in the very centre, in the reconciliation of all opposites.

Recent discoveries concerning the living oral tradition of Bosnian poetry attest to the presence of Bosnia's ancient sacred scriptures in a consciousness

6 See Kniewald, "Vjerodostojnost latinskih izvora o bosanksim krstajnima," 115–276.

7 For more on the content and fate of these books see Kuna, *Srednjovjekovna bosanska književnost*; Nazor, "Rukopisi Crkve bosanske;" Riedlmayer, "*Convivencia* under Fire: Genocide and Book-Burning in Bosnia."

that reaches across the centuries.[8] The Bosnian people are brought together in one language that contains the elements that allow the different discourses to be translated into each other. Any attempt to prove that the Gospels are not in the Recitation or the Recitation in the Gospels misrepresents that one language and every self or consciousness bound up in it.

Any discussion of the history of religion in Bosnia necessarily deals with two inextricable currents – the oral transmission of knowledge and the writing down of the sacred texts. These two traditions have always spilled over into each other. There is a form of unwritten Bosnian discourse of the pure and good, oral instruction that complements the culture of writing and is found in poems, tales and recollections memorized and passed down from one generation to the next. The written evidence for this is irrefutable, if sparse. Parents pass on to their children the knowledge they received from their forebears, knowledge imprinted by well-known and anonymous teachers and books, sifted to preserve only what is worthy of being called the Word, model and verification of all that is in human goodness. All of us are oriented towards it as our higher potential. The finest and best of us are those who are aware of it and incessantly ascending towards perfection. Ascent is confirmed by humility and virtue in everything human – in silence and speech, in action and abstention.

The skills of artist and artisan, husbandry and cultivation of the land, homemaking and making clothes and footwear, cooking and healing – to name just a few skills practised over the centuries – are passed on from generation to generation within the family, between neighbours, in towns and cities, and across the country. Sacred places and the sacred calendar, pilgrimages and prayer, the remembrance of holy people and visits to their graves endure as shared memory in a way of life. These activities have no rulebooks, clear beginnings or point of termination. Many customs practised among the people over the centuries still to be found today never became part of written heritage or the interpretations of exoteric claims.

Strange to say, this oral tradition includes both the writing and reading of the Book and everything associated with it. The oral and the written components of this culture cannot be separated. The Qur'an is essentially a name for holy scripture like the Recitation, God's discourse to humans, passed on for all. Fathers and mothers recite to their children from birth. The Mushaf is a transcription of the Book on pages bound to form a whole, each part – each individual word or sentence, page and quire – and the whole being *Qur'an*,

8 See Lord, *The Singer of Tales*; Foley, *Traditional Oral Epic: The Odyssey, Beowulf and the Serbo-Croatian Return Song*; Čolaković, "Bosniac Epics – Problems of Collecting and Editing the Main Collections"; idem, "Post-traditionality of Homer and Avdo Međedović."

Recitation. Whole and parts are to be found in every house as Holy Book and as sacred inscriptions on the walls, but also as the load-bearing core around which the infinite wreath of mystery is woven, which contains the narratives and messages, warnings and promises, fears and redemptive hopes.

The Qur'an is thus a constant presence in everyday life, to be seen and reached for. Even more, it is in everyone's memory, young and old, the light of the self and the horizons. Whatsoever the people of its community do, the Recitation is somehow present. Their entire life is bound up with it as best discourse and transcript. We do not relate to it for its beauty, but for the discovery and realization of our perfection. The Qur'an is sent down into the human heart and our relationship to it is thus the path of return to the perfection of the heart.

This omnipresence throughout our lives encompasses both myth and history. It is God's Word, sent down from the uncreated centre of the self that all the signs in the world and self might be read, deciphered and return to Unity. In this act of comprehension, the rising and setting of the sun, the phases of the moon, hills and vales, rivers and oceans, trees and animals are all signs that never lose connection with the Creator. Do not the Bosnian festivals of Jurjevdan (St. George's Day) on 6 May and Ilindan/Aliđun (Elijah's or 'Ali's Day) on 2 August refer to just this comprehensiveness? These are just two instances of the countless Bosnian ways of embracing tradition that are irreconcilable with mythless history.

This embrace does not exclude a single prophet or revealed book or witness of them in humility and virtue or rejection of them in arrogance and depravity. The different prophets and the Books revealed by them are our longed-for homeland, the abode of our original and ultimate bliss. This is the exemplary potential of every self, which is, whatever its condition, both guest and stranger. Nothing we can achieve annuls the guest-status of the apostle, as our supreme potential.

While the Qur'an manifests the apostle's perfect nature as the Word of God, it is in clear Arabic. The self in perfect harmony with the Word remains estranged from its manifestations, for perfection is attained only in return to God Who resolves the gap between our condition in existence and the apostle as our best example and mightiest morality. Our relationship to the Qur'an is therefore always one of estrangement. In translating its language into ours, ours into its, we ascend in the self from the obscurity of ignorance towards the light of the Known. The Known is a stranger and guest, Whom we as hosts receive as dearer than any state of our own self. We learn from Him and use Him as our yardstick, as the state of the self no experience can deny or exhaust.

Doctrine, ritual and virtue, indivisible components of every sacred tradition, serve to open and direct the self towards its sublime potential. This open orientation's elements are not to be denied or rejected for having no part in the reductive image of history that excludes witness of God's presence. Evidence for this can be found in all times, regions and cultures: Jurjevdan and Ilindan/Aliđun in Bosnia are just two of many possible examples. The usual opinion is that Muslim celebration of these feast days represents a survival of Christian tradition in Muslim culture. This view is incorrect.

The Anointed, God's prophet and Word, asked his disciples: " 'Who will be my helpers to God?' The apostles said, 'We will be helpers of God; we believe in God; witness thou that we are people of Peace. Lord, we believe in that Thou has sent down and we follow the apostle. Inscribe us therefore with those who bear witness.' "[9]

When the apostle's companions heard of their dear friends lost in battle with the Byzantines at Mu'ti, they wept. The story goes:

> But the apostle of God said: "Why are you weeping?" They replied: "Why should we not weep since the best and the most noble and excellent of us have been killed!" And the apostle said: "Do not weep! My community is like a garden which is taken care of by its owner. He tears off its wild palm-shoots and arranges its abodes and cuts its palm-branches. And so year in and year out the garden bears good fruits. Moreover, it may be that what it produces at the end has the best clusters of dates and the longest vine branches with grapes. And by Him Who has sent me with the truth, (Jesus) the son of Mary shall find successors to his disciples within my community!"[10]

St. George (*Georgios* in Greek and *Jurje, Juraj, Đurađ* or *Đorđe* to the Slavs) was a tribune in the Guard of the Emperor Diocletian who confessed his relationship with God through the Anointed and was tortured and killed for his faith. He bore witness by giving his life and so recognizing it as given to him. Thus, he kills the dragon of death and is the heir to the Anointed and his disciples. Just as Jesus was heir through his Gospels to the prophets before him, the Praised was his heir, according to those who were his witnesses. The historical sequence of inheritance here is the least important.

---

9 *Qur'an*, 3:52–53.

10 Tirmidhī, *The Life of the Friends of God*, 198.

The Anointed and the Praised are, according to the Praised, closest of all.[11] Actualization of the self after its sublime potential is always closeness to them, as the clearest instances of our pure essence held between God's two fingers.[12] The Anointed's promised second coming will be to resolve our differences, as the Praised confessed.[13] Meeting his reality, we will come to know ourselves and it will matter little how we called our approach to him, which is equally our approach to the Praised.

When the Anointed went forth into the world, three were expected – he himself, return of the prophet Elijah centuries after his ascension from among the Israelites, and one of whom God had told Moses: "I will raise them up a prophet from among their brethren, like unto thee, and will put my words in his mouth."[14]

With the coming of the Anointed, whom both Christians and Muslims confess, two remained – Elijah and the Praised. The Praised's coming was the reason for Elijah's second coming. His first appearance in the world preceded the coming of the Anointed, but when he descended to stand under the banner of the Praised, borne by his friend ʿAli, so Bosnian Muslims believe, he asked him to bear witness to the Anointed until noon and then to join him. This is why they say: "Elijah till noon, ʿAli from noon."[15] ʿAli is the Praised's perfect disciple and his standard-bearer.

How this presence of the prophet Elijah and the martyr George in the tradition of the Bosnian Muslims is seen depends on the viewpoint of those doing the interpreting. When these interpretations include the Praised as the principle to which the prophets swore their oath in pre-existence, including Abraham and Moses, David and Solomon, and the Anointed and John, those with a different viewpoint experience them as hostile negation of their convictions. For them, the Praised is a mere historical figure of apostasy from the "true faith," a "madman" and "liar," and his followers are apostates lured from the "true, uninterrupted course of history."

The interpreter's perspective determines the interpretation. When an interpretation is advanced, without taking into account that perspective, and compared with something different, the reasons for asserting one over the other end up being applied to its adherents. Contesting or repudiating an interpretation is transformed into denigrating, persecuting or killing its adherents.

---

11 See Muslim, 4:1260–61.

12 Ibid., 4:1397.

13 Ibid., 1:93 and 4:1501.

14 *Deuteronomy*, 18:18.

15 See Hadžijahić, "Sinkretistički elementi u islamu u Bosni i Hercegovini," 321–22.

Accepting the Praised as first and last witness to all things in existence, ontologically, cosmologically and anthropologically transforms these perspectives. Those who confess him as such may understand *gost* Radin's testament about the "great and blessed days":

> For so long as it lasts, let it [his bequest] be distributed, whenever it is seen, on the great feast days during holy week and on holy friday and particularly on the day of the holy birth of Christ and on the holy annunciation and on the holy resurrection of the Lord and on the day of Saint George, my name saint, and on the day of the holy ascension of the Lord and on the day of Saint Peter and on Saint Paul's day and on Saint Stephen the protomartyr's day and on the day of Saint Michael the Archangel, on the day of the holy virgin Mary, and on All Saints' day.[16]

This is to be understood in the light of a sacred calendar full of sacred and blessed days. All those associated with these days are part of sacred heritage, for the days are indivisible from their witness to the unity of God Who revealed the Recitation to them through the Praised.

The debate over the nature of Christ and how to bear witness to him and perform the appropriate rituals has never been resolved, since those who conduct it are forever between the lowest depth and the sublime height. This debate requires an "other," but also that other's right to fundamental difference. Why does unbroken Muslim participation in the debate over these questions of reconciliation and belief disturb, to the point of despair or hatred, so many philosophers, theologians and historians?

Through St. George, witness and martyr for the Anointed, Muslims confess no god but God and the Praised as His apostle: for Jesus, along with all 124,000 of God's prophets, swore his oath to the Praised as apostle. Muslims' relationship with Elijah is also a relationship with the Praised. The Muslim is thus part of a current of tradition on human inclusiveness, albeit perhaps only in principle and without explicit awareness.

Another example of what disturbs the devotees of history as an immanent truth subject to them, as well as the ideological advocates of a Muslim present that has broken with the Christian past, is the ritual of introducing the bride to the house and family she has married into. This ritual may be found throughout Bosnia even today, in spite of attempts over two centuries by supposedly orthodox, foreign-educated ulema to suppress it from Bosnian sacred tradition.

16 Truhelka, "Testament gosta Radina: Prinos patarenskom pitanju," 373; Šanjek, *Bosansko-humski krstjani u povijesnim vrelima*, 364.

When the wedding party brings her to the bridegroom's house, the bride overturns a jug of water placed behind the courtyard threshold with her right foot. Before she crosses the threshold of the inner part of the house, young boys, waiting there for the purpose, compete to remove her shoe and win the money left within. Then, a senior participant in this ritual will make a pass around her head with the Qur'an, lower it onto her head, and place it in her right hand. The bride kisses and raises it to her forehead. A loaf of bread is placed on her left hand. When she sits down, a boy from the family or neighbourhood is placed on her lap.

The spilling of the water is often interpreted as rejection of the sacrament of baptism by water. The competition to remove her shoe and win a valuable gift signifies that the house she is being brought to is itself a mosque, a place of prayer and prostration, in which the sacred receptacles of the revelation are preserved and studied, and so not to be entered in footwear. The gathered children are called to be guardians of the sacral inviolability of their houses and to supervise the removal of footwear for entry into all places of worship.

The ritual with the Qur'an is normally interpreted as an appropriate form of baptism by the Book, a connection with the Holy Spirit or the Spirit of Truth as bringer of the Book, the Word of God. The Word is the irrefutable source of the Recitation around which the house's inhabitants gather. No one can raise themselves above the teacher, which guarantees the presence and primacy of the confession of His unity and the apostle's perfection. This is because the apostle is the Word incarnate. Relations with him as the most beautiful example of our path back to God are redemptive. The Holy Spirit who brought the Recitation to him is a link with God as Holy. This is why passing the Book around the head of a new member of the family, the mother of future descendants, and lowering it onto her head, placing it in her hand, and kissing it signify coronation in holiness as a worthy desire for us all.

The giving of the loaf of leavened bread affirms her blessedness and that of her hands. She is responsible for preparing, sharing and hallowing it. Bread is generally communal and befits, above all, maternal hands. Her claim cannot be denied and here witness is made that receiving communion from the hand of a priest does not befit the bridal house, as communion is inseparable from mastery determined by study of the Book around which she and those dearest to her are henceforth forever gathered.

The maternal womb – whose name in the language of the Recitation is related to the divine names of the All and Ever-merciful – is a link to God and respect for it necessarily accompanies confession of His unity and the Praised's apostolate as a mercy to the worlds. Relations with Book and apostle are a covenant with God and inextricable from the principle of maternity. To break the line of kinship that passes through the maternal womb is to break off relations with God.

The boy in the lap signifies the maternal principle's comprehensive nature and the sacred nature of the knee which has received a witness of the Praised as maternal prophet. Lap and knee, from which the child turns his gaze towards the Face, signified by the maternal face, bear witness of the irrefragable link that binds all things in the world to God. From that lap and from those knees rise up witnesses to God's unity and the Praised's apostolate, who honour the link with their mother's womb as sign and symbol of All-merciful and Ever-merciful God. They accept and confess the claim of this, like every other connection, as their covenant with God, Who is All-merciful and Ever-merciful, while His apostle is a mercy to the worlds, a light that has been sent down, the first of all creation, and the comforter and advocate of humankind before God the Judge.

The fast of the month of Ramadan is a sacred ritual that, along with confessing God's oneness and the Praised's apostolate, performing the five daily prayers, paying alms and pilgrimage to the house, comprises the most important and binding rituals of being-at-peace (*islam*) as how the people of peace (*muslim*) relate to Peace (*al-salam*). One of the foods customarily eaten by Bosnian Muslims when they break the fast is the *somun*. This is the Bosnian form of the Greek word for leavened bread (*zymos*) and its use by Bosnian Muslims cannot be explained without reference to their involvement in the millennial debate between Eastern and Western Christians over the use of leavened or unleavened (*azymos*) bread for Holy Communion.[17] This is a

17 For more on this debate see Herrin, *Byzantium*, 303. Alongside the aforementioned role of the leavened bread or somun in the sacred rituals of the Bosnian Muslims, which is part of their perennial inheritance, it is worth also explaining the sacramental role of the milk which is present in the ritual in the form of a sauce of milk, cream, and cheese. Milk has two main symbolic meanings for Muslims. It recalls the "nutritious nature" of their sacred doctrine, which is the perfect food of the mind/conscience. It is also the communal bond with the Praised, through which the self bears witness and feeds its own pure and authentic nature as an uncreated heart. As he was rising up from the lowest depth to the most beautiful height, the Praised was offered three glasses – one of water, another of wine, and a third of milk. The Praised said of this: "I heard a voice which said to me, as this was offered: 'If he takes the water, he and his people will be drowned; if he takes the wine, he and his people will wander in error; but if he takes the milk, he and his people will be rightly guided.' So I took the glass of milk and drank of it. And Gabriel said to me: 'Praised, you are rightly guided, and so is your people!'" (Ibn Isḥāq, *Sīrat Rasūl Allāh*, 182). Every participant is given a glass of milk during the Bosnian ritual to celebrate the Night of Ascension (*miʿraj*). In the sacred traditions of the Bosnian Muslims, both

legacy among the Bosnian Muslims of the tradition of the Bosnian *krstjani*, who took Holy Communion with leavened bread. The significance of the yeast in the bread is the presence of the Spirit through which life is instilled into inanimate matter, light dispels darkness and the self increases in knowledge. Here, the yeast is the symbol of ascent or resurrection.

There is no world without the self and neither can there be apostle or Book without it. There is no self but the Self. Realizing this, then witness to Unity and the apostolate of the Praised is the way to return, to find Unity in the multitude of signs of world and self. This the Bosnian muslims see as the principle for following their ancestors in their witness of the Anointed, the Virgin Mary, the apostles Paul and Peter, the protomartyr Stephen, and the Archangel Michael, since this is their inheritance, a sacred legacy that is not merely inextricable from their own witness, but is in fact the core in which may be found the reasons they are what they are.

The Praised has the mightiest morality and is thus our sublime potential, realization of the confession of no self but the Self. The Book was sent down into his heart and therefore connects the uncreated centre of humanity and God. That it has come down to different prophets in different languages means that the mother of the Book is in and beyond all languages. Descent is its translation from its maternal state to the languages of the Children of Adam.

Whenever we distinguish the signs in the Book for reassembly in our mind, we form a bond with that mother Book. Every reading or differentiation comes

---

bread and cheese have a certain communion-like aspect, so that even today they may be referred to as coming from the "Dervish's sofra [banquet]." It is perhaps worth mentioning that in certain Christian traditions milk was accepted as a communion food, so that the sacred mystery could be celebrated with bread and cheese (See Charbonneau-Lassay, *The Bestiary of Christ*, 81). The Church outlawed the use of milk and dairy products for sacramental purposes. The *Apostolic Tradition* of Hippolytus, however, described an exceptional ritual of communion which was acceptable, at least for a while, in Greece. Alongside the bread and wine and a mixture of milk and honey, which many churches used at that time for the ritual, a glass of water was also offered. The participants were offered, one after the other, three glasses – first, after the consecrated bread, a glass of water, then the milk and honey, and finally the wine (ibid.). There were, from the Muslim point of view, a number of potential solutions to this dilemma when faced with the three communion glasses. John the Baptist did not drink wine (*Luke*, 1:15). In his second coming, Jesus, the son of Mary and the Word of God, would, according to *Revelation* (19:15), "trample over the wine presses." With the sending down of the Recitation, the making of wine, as a distortion of the original and authentic nature of the grape, was forbidden, as it was in itself symbolic of the distortion of authentic human nature (for the prohibition of wine see *Qur'an*, 5:90).

from a condition of humanity below the perfection of the Praised, whom we can never overtake, whatever level we reach in our ascent towards Peace. To any who know of the Knower, the Praised is dearer than his own self, eternal guest and stranger to all who confess him, dearer, for what have we greater than our own self as stranger and guest, whom we follow on the infinite path to the Upright to see Him face to Face?

The Book sent down is in multiplicity and there are thus many books, each equally open to every language. None has any other purpose but to remind us of the path of redemption by confession of no self but the Self. This is the path of belief, the relationship of the faithful and All-faithful God. The popular tongue is just the stage for our relationship with God and every sacred scripture is open to this relationship, as God said through the Praised: "Those to whom We have given the Book and who recite it with true recitation, they believe in it; and whoso denies it, they shall be the losers."[18]

We have chosen twenty-one pages from Bosnian manuscripts to illustrate the relationship between the New Testament and the Qur'anic revelations in our quest for our original and ultimate potential, as well as the relationship of the Anointed and Mary with the Praised and the most significant signs in perennial discourse regarding it. The content of these pages from Bosnian manuscripts of the Gospels and the Qur'an reveals differing but inextricably linked expressions of a sacred heritage common to both lines of Abraham's descent and their reflection in Bosnia's history.

Zachariah, Mary, John and Jesus and the Further Mosque on Mount Sion are the ultimate concentration of the world and humanity. Their most sublime expression was the Anointed, Mary's son, who bore witness to the meaning of human life and, as a voice uniting everything that preceded him, foretelling the Praised as our sublime potential. This is also a crucial part of Bosnia's sacred heritage taken as a whole. The Anointed left his disciples and all of humankind news of the Paraclete, the Spirit of Truth, the Holy Spirit: "He shall give you another Comforter, that he may abide with you forever: Even the Spirit of truth (τὸ πνεῦμα τῆς ἀληθείας)"[19] – "The Comforter, which is the Holy Ghost (ὁ δὲ παράκλητος τὸ πνεῦμα τὸ ἅγιον)."[20]

His testament been interpreted in a variety of ways. For some Bosnians, it is perfectly clear: it prophesies the Praised (*Aḥmad, Muḥammad*). In the Recitation, the Anointed says: "Children of Israel, I am indeed the apostle of God to you, confirming the Torah that is before me, and giving good tidings of

18 *Qur'an*, 2:121.

19 *John*, 14:16–17.

20 Ibid., 14:26.

an apostle who shall come after me, whose name shall be *Aḥmad*."[21] *Aḥmad*, then, is the *Parakletos*, the *Parakletos Aḥmad*.

Zachariah, Mary, John and Jesus bore witness to the Praised as Paraclete, directing us to the Praised as our sublime potential, the indestructible core of perfection in every self. The Praised is the seal of their witness and that of all God's prophets. The Revelation God sent down into his heart makes clear whatever was unclear about them.

When it involves the Book, witness is inextricable from the witnessing self. Every self is unique and unrepeatable, but nonetheless shaped by language and community, as well as the alienness that surrounds it and its community. The same book may have many interpretations, resulting in contradictory witness. One is suggested by a record left by Franciscan missionaries of scriptures of the Bosnian *krstjan*s they found among Bosnian refugees in Bulgaria in the seventeenth century, who had taken them as they fled eastward to escape persecution and enforced conversion to Catholicism: "They contain the text in their vernacular of the holy Gospel of Christ following the Roman Church, but the comments and glosses are heretical and follow a number of different heresies, particularly the heresy of Paul of Samosata, for which reason they call themselves Paulini."[22] These books, which the Franciscans collected from various places in Bulgaria, were burned in the monastery in Ćiprovac in 1688.[23] Similar scriptures were later found in Plevlja, Cetinje, Nikolje, Vrutok, Sofia and Plevna.

For reasons like the above, few extant Bosnian scriptures have a colophon and in many cases the sections containing the Gospel of John are missing. In others' hands, these scriptures appeared strange and heretical. The parts that some destroyed were seen by others as proof of their authors' adherence to the Praised and the Recitation revealed through him by God. For them, two tidings of good news met in the self – one sent down through the Anointed, the other through the Praised, bearing witness of each other and indicating the closeness of these two of God's chosen.

21 *Qur'an*, 61:6. *Parakletos* is a Greek word, which has been interpreted in many ways and is the subject of much debate. None of the scholarly or other differences and disagreements over its meaning affect the Muslim belief that the name *Parakletos* is identical with the Arabic name *Aḥmad*, one of the names of the apostle, the Praised.

22 "Habent in suo vulgari textum s. Evangelii Christi secundum Ecclesiam Romanam, sed commenta et glossae sunt haereticae secundum varias haereses, praecipue circa haeresim Pauli Sosometani (sic), a quo denominatur Paulini." Fermendžin, *Acta Bulgariae* (*Mon.Slav.Mer.* xvii), Zagreb, 1887, 21, quoted in Mandić, *Bogomilska crkva bosanskih krstjana*, 98.

23 Ibid., 302–305.

In the previous volume, we gave translations of texts from Bosnian sacred manuscripts produced by the Bosnian Church and by Bosnian Muslims. Those texts represent the content of the manuscript pages whose descriptions and pictures now follow. The location of the manuscripts is indicated by Figure 2.1.

Figure 2.2. This illustration of the Inviolable Mosque (*al-masjid al-ḥaram*) in Becca valley is from a manuscript of the *Waymarks of Benefits and the Brilliant Burst of Sunshine in the Remembrance of Blessings on the Chosen Prophet* (*dalāʾil al-khayrāt wa shawāriq al-anwār fī dhikr al-ṣalāt ʿalā al-nabiyy al-mukhtār*) by Muhammad ibn Sulayman al-Jazuli.[24] The copy is dated 27th March, 1781, by Ibrahim Šehović, son of Muhammed, imam of the Imperial Mosque in Sarajevo.[25] It ends with the following statement:

> Transcription of this sublime and noble work by the hand of hafiz Ibrahim, son of Muhammed – may they both and all believers, men and women, receive the forgiveness of the Flux – on 9 Rabiʿ al-Akhira in the year 1195 since the hijra of him who has greatness and honour. With God's help and care, I have twice transcribed these noble *Waymarks*. This noble copy is the third. O Lord, forgive me and my parents and all believers. Amen.

The *Waymarks*, a book of blessings and prayers, was incorporated into many later prayers and remembrances and is found throughout the world. There are numerous Bosnian copies.

Figure 2.3. A description of the Praised in Bosnian, in the Bosnian Cyrillic script, is given in this manuscript by an anonymous compiler and scribe. There is nothing in the manuscript to indicate when or where it was transcribed, but it is clearly part of Bosnia's linguistic and paleographic heritage.

Figure 2.4. Psalm 83 in the manuscript known as *Hval's Miscellany*, after the *krstjanin* Hval, now in the University Library in Bologna. Many scholars have written about it, starting with Josef Dobiovski in 1822. A facsimile edition with transliteration was published in 1986.[26] The colophon of this book is still extant:

> In the name of the Father and the Son and the Holy Spirit. This book was written by the hand of Hval the *krstjanin* in honour of the noble sire

24 See Fajić, *Katalog arapskih, turskih, perzijskih i bosanskih rukopisa*, 11:561.

25 See Dobrača, *Katalog arapskih, turskih, perzijskih i bosanskih rukopisa*, 1:25–26; and Handžić, "Hafiz Ibrahim ef. Šehović," 345–48.

26 See Kuna, *Srednjovjekovna bosanska književnost*, 156–64.

> Hrvoje, Duke of Split and prince of the lowlands, holder of many lands. I pray to those who read this. Whereas we beseech you brethren, whosoever may read this letter, that as soon as you finish reading this letter, you forgive and make frequent mention of him for whom it was written and of the writer, in so far as your understanding of this matter extends. It was written and completed in the year of our Lord 1404, in the days of the bishop and teacher and dignitary of the Bosnian Church, *djed* Radomir.[27]

Figure 2.5. Muhammed, son of Husein, of Blagaj, completed a Mushaf on the 9th of August, 1598.[28] At the end of it the calligrapher wrote:

> This eternal Word and great Distinction was completed in the holy month of Muharram, on the sixth day of the week, between two prayers, by the hand of the poor servant, who needs the mercy of his Lord, in the year 1007 after the hijra of the prophet, by Muhammed, son of Husein, of Blagaj, may the All-merciful Lord have mercy upon them both.

Figure 2.6. In mid March, 1615, Hajji Redžep-dede the Bosnian completed a Mushaf,[29] at the end of which he wrote of himself and his attitude towards the Praised and the Recitation sent down through him:

> Praise be to His friend and blessings upon His prophet, the Praised, the peace and blessings of Almighty God be upon him. For these blessings, praise be to God Who granted us peace and made us the community of the Praised – peace be upon him – and helped us to see the light of his beauty four times in a dream, in which I asked him about the tradition: "A liar is not of my community," asking if it is correct: "O apostle of God, is that tradition correct?" And he replied in Turkish, "It is." The apostle of God speaks the truth and God's favourite speaks the truth. I, sinful servant, who inclines to evil deeds and who refrains from good deeds, Hajji Redžeb-dede the Bosnian – may God condescend to him in the speech of His beloved Quraysh. Amen, O Lord of the Worlds. Year 1034.

Figure 2.7. *The House in Becca Valley* is an illustration in a Bosnian manuscript of unknown origin and date, written in old Bosnian script and language,

27 Ibid., 157–58.

28 Lavić, *Katalog arapskih, turskih, perzijskih i bosanskih rukopisa*, 15:9.

29 Ibid., 15:10.

comprising passages from the Gospels and the Recitation that have been held to prophesy and confirm the apostle, the Praised. This unpublished manuscript is referred to as the *Book of the Praised's Light.*

Figure 2.8. *The House on Mount Sion* is another illustration from the *Book of the Praised's Light.* As with the previous illustration and the surrounding passages from the Recitation, Torah, Psalms and Gospels, the anonymous author and scribe are presenting the perennial belief in the apostle as first of creation and its purpose.

Figure 2.9. In 1852, ʿAbdullah ʿAyni, son of Hasan, of Sarajevo, completed a Mushaf,[30] at the end of which he mentioned himself as its scribe:

---

30 This manuscript is now the property of Meliha Tahmiščija of Sarajevo. We know of this scribe from three further preserved works. The first is the *Dalāʾil al-khayrāt* and is in the Mahmutćehajić family collection. Beneath the calligraphically inscribed letter *mim* (م) at the end of the work, he wrote: "This was written, as required by his Generous Lord, by the most miserable of slaves and the weakest of writers, ʿAbdullah ʿAynī, son of Hasan, native of Sarajevo – may the Creator forgive them both! – a student of our champion hafiz, Aḥmad Amīn, the famous Wajihi-pasha, born and bred in Edirne, in the one thousand two hundred and sixty third year after the migration [1847], for honour and glory are in Him." The second work is the *Risala-i tasawwuf* (Lavić, *Katalog arapskih, turskih, perzijskih i bosanskih rukopisa*, 17:464). Due to the fact that diacritical marks were omitted to begin with, his name, which is ʿAynī, reads here as ʿĪsā. At the end of the work, he says: "Sublime Lord, for the love of the excellent one, the Praised, and for the love of ʿAlī al-Murtaḍā, who is his uncle's son and his son-in-law and his representative and who is a friend of the apostles and a friend of the friends; and for the love of the first amongst the imams, Hasan and Husayn, who are descended from his pure kin, and for the love of the other imams and elders and the other friends, our lords! I pray that You give to those who are in love their positions, that You delight them with the beauties they have felt and You make them worthy of Your gifts! Amin, amin and forever amin for the mercy of the One Who says 'And We sent you to be a mercy unto the worlds.' This poor wretch completed the writing of this with the help of God the King, the Generous, on the 27th of S[afar] 1266, [11th of January, 1850]." The third work is the *Mā ḥaḍar fī al-ṭibb* (Jahić, *Katalog arapskih, turskih, perzijskih i bosanskih rukopisa*, 12:81). At the end of the manuscript, he says: "Written by the poor wretch ʿAbdullah ʿAynī, son of Hasan-aga, son of hajji-Salih – may God forgive them and their families and their teachers and all the faithful, male and female. O Connection to our champion and prophet, the Praised, and his descendents, and all his companions! The writing of this desired missive was completed in the first third of the honoured month of *shawwāl*, on the day of congregation, in the one thousand two hundred seventy second year since the migration [5th of June, 1856], for honour and glory are in Him." Mahmud Traljić has written about him as the librarian of the Gazi Husrev-bey library: "The first librarian was hafiz ʿAbdullah ʿAyni-effendi Hasagić, a well-known calligrapher from Sarajevo. He came from the Sarajevo family of Hasagić, who lived on Banjski brijeg (the mahala around the hajji Osman Nalčadžić Mosque, which was destroyed in

> With the help of Almighty God, His honour and His bestowal of success, the opportunity of serving this holy Book was bestowed on the poorest of scribes and transcribers, ʿAbdullah ʿAyni, son of Hasan, of Sarajevo, a pupil of hafiz Ahmed Busrija Edirnevija, who gives thanks to Almighty God for His gifts and the blessings of His prophet, the Praised, and his family, in the year 1269 from the hijra of him who has greatness and glory.

Another Mushaf known to be by this same calligrapher was completed on 27 Safar 1261.[31]

Figure 2.10. The *Čajniče Gospels* is the only Bosnian Church manuscript still in Bosnia, in a collection at the Orthodox church in Čajniče.[32] Several sections are missing from the first three Gospels, as is the entire Gospel according to John, and the book has no colophon. The manuscript was originally Bosnian, but shows evidence of corrections to adapt it to the liturgy of the Serbian Orthodox Church.[33] It was probably transcribed in eastern Bosnia, in an ijekavian-speaking area, but has some ikavian forms, such as "svitilnik," "obitil" and "Divica."[34]

Figure 2.11. In 1636, Bi-zaban ʿAli-Pasha of Sarajevo completed a Mushaf,[35] at the end of which he wrote about himself: "Transcribed by the sinning servant who hopes for the mercy of God, the Lord Creator, Dumb Alija, known as Pasha Sarajlija, in a little house in new Sarajevo, in the year 1046."

Figure 2.12. In the month of Ramadan, 1473, Shahin bin ʿAbdullah al-Nasiri transcribed a Mushaf with pages of 42 × 29 cm. It is a superb work of calligraphy, with numerous marginal notes to indicate the proper reading and

---

1939)" Traljić, "Hafizi-kutubi Gazi Husrevbegove biblioteke: Prilog historiji Biblioteke," 46. The same author also says of him: "Hasagić instructed his sister-sons in his will to heat the water with which he was to be washed after his death on the off-cuts of reeds which were left over from sharpening the nib of his pen over the many years of his calligraphic work" (Ibid., 46n6). Hafiz Husayn Raqim-efendi Islamović, the best known of the Bosnian calligraphers of modern years learned his art from him. See Handžić, "Hadži hafiz Husejn Râkim ef. Islamović," 342; Mujezinović, "Diplome kaligrafa Islamovića u Gazi Husrevbegovoj biblioteci u Sarajevu," 91n1; Popara, "Idžazetname u rukopisima Gazi Hurevbegove bibioteke: Prilog proučavanju historije obrazovanja u BiH," 21n94. The copiers of Persian, Turkish, and Arabic manuscripts often mark the end by inscribing the letter *mim* (م) one, three or four times.

31 Fajić, *Katalog arapskih, turskih, perzijskih i bosanskih rukopisa*, 11:38–39.

32 See Kuna, *Srednjovjekovna bosanska književnost*, 117–21.

33 Ibid., 121.

34 Ibid.

35 See Lavić, *Katalog arapskih, turskih, perzijskih i bosanskih rukopisa*, 15:16.

pronunciation. The first pages are illuminated, and all the remaining pages are framed with a wide gold line enhanced on the inside by a thin black line and on the outside by a thick blue one.[36] The manuscript ends with this note:

> Its scribe of Almighty God the poor Shahin bin ʿAbdullah al-Nasiri, known as [illegible], at the beginning of the elect month of Ramadan 878. Thanks be to God for His blessings and blessings and peace upon His apostle, our lord the Praised, and his clan, companions and family, the pure.

Figure 2.13. The *Pripković Gospels* were found by Aleksandar F. Giljferding in Pljevlja and taken by him to St. Petersburg, where they are still.[37] The colophon is still extant: "I wrote this by the grace of God, a *krstjanin* called Tvrtko Pripković, of the land of Gomilje."[38] According to Herta Kuna, "Below this note is another in a different hand, in cursive, with the characteristics of Resavac orthography, certainly no older in date than the 16th century: 'and god knows what swine that was,' which no doubt refers to the scribe Tvrtko Pripković, all too explicitly illustrating the attitude towards a *krstjanin* or Bogomil."[39] Some of the pages have been cut out and corrections have been made to others "in a later hand, probably in an Orthodox monastery."[40]

Figure 2.14. The *Venice Miscellany* is now in the Marcian Library in Venice, in the Oriental manuscript collection.[41] Its beginning and end are missing, and though it provides clear evidence of the development of calligraphy under the Bosnian Church, the absence of the colophon makes it impossible to date or locate accurately. It is very similar to *Hval's Miscellany*.

Figure 2.15. Amina, daughter of Mustafa Chalabi, of the Žabljak mahala in Sarajevo, transcribed a holy Mushaf in 1764.[42] As far as is known, she is the only Bosnian woman to have transcribed the Recitation. She wrote of herself at the end of the transcript: "Transcribed by the poor and humble Amina, daughter of Mustafa Chalabi, of the Žabljak mahala in the city of Sarajevo, in the holy

---

36 Ibid., 15:5.

37 For more on this Bosnian manuscript, see Kuna, *Srednjovjekovna bosanska književnost*, 112–14.

38 Ibid., 113.

39 Ibid.

40 Ibid.

41 Basic details of the manuscript are given in: Kuna, *Srednjovjekovna bosanska književnost*, 164–66. An entire book has also been published on this manuscript: Pelusi, *Novum Testamentum Bosniacum Marcianum Cod. Or 277 (= 168)*.

42 See Fajić, *Katalog arapskih, turskih, perzijskih i bosanskih rukopisa*, 11:30–31.

month of Rajab 1178. May the Chosen One on the Day of Assembly defend all those who pray for this scribe."

Figure 2.16. The *Vrutok Gospels* were discovered in the 1930s in the village of Vrutok near Gostivar in Macedonia, in the possession of the Popovski family.[43] Some sections and pages are missing or have been destroyed and there is no colophon. Later marginal notes reveal "that the book had been passed around Orthodox monasteries and it is not impossible that some pages were deliberately torn out, perhaps on account of glosses such as the one on the toll-gate, causing the damage to the codex."[44] Herta Kuna observes, "One of the notes thought to date from the latter half of the 18th century reveals that the book was in the monastery of the Holy Trinity near Pljevlja."[45] A ritual for the execration of heretics also originated from the same monastery.[46] The manuscript has since been taken from Vrutok to the Kliment Ohridski University Library in Skopje.

Figure 2.17. Since 1845, the *Kopitar Gospels* have been in the University library in Ljubljana. As later alterations to the text reveal, the reason it survived was "that it had been in a Serbian monastery, adapted for liturgical use."[47] Judging from its linguistic features, the manuscript was probably transcribed somewhere in western Bosnia. Some sheets, including the colophon, are missing. It is not known how the manuscript came to be in Jernej Kopitar's collection.

Figure 2.18. The *Nikolje Gospels* are now in the Chester Beatty Library in Dublin. Before that they were in the National Library in Belgrade, from which they somehow disappeared during World War I. The earliest reference to them is by Vuk Karadžić, who found the manuscript in the Nikolje monastery in the Ovčar-Kablar gorge.[48] A number of sheets, including the colophon, is missing. There are signs on the extant sheets that earlier marginal notes have been erased, "but there are quite a number of later notes, mainly resulting from the adaptation of the Gospels to the liturgy of the Orthodox Church."[49]

---

43 See Kuna, *Srednjovjekovna bosanska književnost*, 108–112.

44 Ibid., 111–12.

45 Ibid., 112.

46 See Mošin, "Rukopis Pljevjanskog sinodika pravoslavlja," 154 n 4.

47 Kuna, *Srednjovjekovna bosanska književnost*, 103.

48 On the manuscript, see Kuna, *Srednjovjekovna bosanska književnost*, 106–108. Vladimir Mošin says of this manuscript in an article entitled "Rukopisi bivše Beogradske Narodne biblioteke u Dablinu i u Zagrebu" (p. 351): "In the shapes of the letters and the general type of the script this is perhaps the finest calligraphic monument of the Bosnian school known to us." See also: Otašević, "Nikoljsko jevanđelje: od originala do digitalne kopije."

49 Kuna, *Srednjovjekovna bosanska književnost* 108.

Figure 2.19. In 1593, Korkut Halifa of Stolac transcribed a Mushaf,[50] writing in the colophon:

> The end of this transcript has been completed, with the help of God, Lord and Bestower, in the middle of the holy month of Muharram, on Thursday, in the year 1002 since the hijra of the apostle – blessings and peace be upon him. Written by the poor and worthless, weakest of the weak, most powerless servant Korkut Halifa, imam and hatib of the mosque of Sultan Selim-han – mercy and forgiveness be upon him – living in the town of Stolac, in the Herzeg's province, near Vidoška fort which is derelict and ruinous. The note remains long in the book, but the owner of the note returns to the earth.

The Korkut family lived in Stolac until the end of the nineteenth century. Their family house, known as the Korkutovina, was next to the large graveyard. Oral tradition in Stolac preserves the memory of "good kadi Korkut and his son."

Figure 2.20. Mustafa Hadžalić, son of Omer, of Mostar, was an eighteenth century Qur'anic scribe, three of whose transcripts are known: (a) the eighth, completed in 1755;[51] (b) the twenty-third, completed in 1759;[52] and (c) the thirtieth, completed in 1760.[53] According to notes in the surviving manuscripts, Mustafa the calligrapher transcribed twenty-two Mushafs in five years, which means that he transcribed four copies each lunar year. He taught at the Karadžoz-bey medresa in Mostar.[54] He also transcribed *al-Fawāʾid al-ḍiyāʾiyya*.[55] He is known to have composed this note: "A gem is within us, not in stone; brilliance is in the heart, not the eyes; wealth is in satisfaction, not in property; fame is in upbringing, not lineage."[56] The calligrapher wrote at the end of his thirtieth transcript:

> Thanks be to God Who made it easy to complete this holy Book – blessings upon His apostle the Praised, the favoured, the defender – by the hand of the poor guardian of the Eternal Speech of God, Mustafa, son of Omer, of Mostar – may the Creator pass over the sins of them both. This is Mushaf number thirty. May Almighty God increase their number with

---

50 See Hasandedić, *Katalog arapskih, turskih i perzijskih rukopisa*, 209–210.

51 See Dobrača, *Katalog arapskih, turskih, perzijskih i bosanskih rukopisa*, 1:24.

52 In the Historical Archives of Sarajevo, R-593.

53 In the Mahmutćehajić collection.

54 See Ždralović, "Bilješke u orijentalnim rukopisima," 107–132.

55 Ibid., 114.

56 Ibid., 116.

> His perpetual benevolence. In the year 1170 since the hijra of him who has greatness and glory.

Figure 2.21. Among the books transcribed by Ibrahim Šehović, son of Muhammed, were sixty-six Mushafs, of which the following are known: (a) the thirty-second, completed in 1780;[57] (b) the thirty-third, completed in 1781;[58] and (c) the sixty-sixth, completed in 1811.[59] Ibrahim the calligrapher transcribed thirty-four Mushafs in thirty years, equal to one each lunar year. Tradition has it that he says of his sixty-sixth that he knew it was his last. Its illumination is incomplete and there are traces of droplets on the pages, said to be the remains of his tears as he wept at having to leave his beloved work. At the end of this transcript he wrote:

> Thanks be to God Who made it easy to complete this holy Mushaf – blessings and peace upon the Praised, the beloved defender – by the hand of poor Ibrahim, son of hajji Muhammed, of Sarajevo – may the All-sufficient Provider pass over their sins. This is Mushaf number sixty-six. May God make easy as many as possible with His perpetual benevolence. In the year 1226 since the hijra of him who has greatness and glory.

Figure 2.22. *Radosav's Bosnian Book* is a manuscript dating from the latter half of the fifteenth century, now in the Vatican (*Biblioteca apostolica Vaticana, Fondo Borgiano illirico*).[60] The scribe says in the colophon: "This book was written by Radosav the *krstjanin* for Goisav the *krstjanin*, and was written in the days of King Tomaš and *Did* Ratko. Gentlemen, if I have misplaced anything, do not scold me, for it is hard work for my old hands. Read and bless, and may God bless you always, Amen."[61] The manuscript contains the *Book of Revelation*, the *Lord's Prayer*, a short prayer and the beginning of the Gospel according to John (1:1–16). The addition from *Revelation* is thought to be a formula from the Patarin liturgy, which resembles that of the Phundagiagitae of Asia Minor and the Cathars in France.[62]

---

57 Dobrača, *Katalog arapskih, turskih, perzijskih i bosanskih rukopisa*, 1:25–26.

58 Ibid., 25.

59 Ibid.

60 See Kuna, *Srednjovjekovna bosanska književnost*, 116–72 and Nazor, *Radosavljeva bosanska knjiga*.

61 Kuna, *Srednjovjekovna bosanska književnost*, 167; Nazor, *Radosavljeva bosanska knjiga*, 147.

62 See Rački, "Dva nova priloga za povijest bosanskih patarena," 28–29; Solovjev, "Vjersko učenje bosanske crkve," 34–37; Šanjek, *Bosansko-humski krstjani i katarsko-dualistički pokret u srednjem vijeku*, 157–62, 175–77.

Post Scriptum: "What Has Been Sent Down to You and What Was Sent Down before You"

Only in loss do we begin to see clearly the real or illusory value of what we have. Often, what is lost cannot be found. This is in fact a gain, for what cannot be found again is not real. The experience of loss shapes our consciousness and what we once had and have lost alters in our minds. The dead cannot return to life nor any past instant be recovered, whether in our present or in ourselves as though from that past. Only by facing this, do we integrate the dead and past, which pass finally into memory, their presence in the remembering mind such that their very incompleteness stands warrant for their meaning in memory to those recalling them.

The most widespread story of humanity's destiny connects tensions in soul and world with a mythical beginning in paradise. Most people take this for a symbolic or actual location and time in the past, a mythical place that represents ultimate sublimity, the state of original integrity, free of tension between the principle and its manifestations. In this state, the inviolable tree signifies our closeness to God and our difference from Him.

Adam's decision to pass beyond most beautiful sublimity, to go higher, forfeited that original state. He was asked to will no opposition to the will of the principle. This became for him a tension he couldn't withstand, a challenge to break free he could not resist. And so humankind forfeited its sublimity and sank to the lowest of the low. Nothing in existence is originally so gloriously sublime; nothing can fall so low. This span from extreme height to extreme depth determines the potential of the self.

The fall does not mean the self has passed beyond His wrath or His mercy. We alone are subject to His wrath, for we alone betray and break a trust freely accepted. Everything else surrenders irrevocably to find peace in His will. God is absolutely close and absolutely remote and we are closest to Him in sublimity, when we manifest His most beautiful attributes through our humility and generosity, and furthest from Him in the depths, when His attributes in us are obscured. Our bond with our Creator, however, is never actually broken.

Wrath and mercy are opposites, but His mercy always surpasses His wrath.[1] No depth, no exposure to His wrath is beyond His mercy, for there is no absolute wrath, no absolute darkness, no eternal punishment. To lose paradise is to re-awaken to it. In the depths, our sublimity punctured, ugliness and cruelty

1 See Muslim, 4:1437.

 | DOI 10.1163/9789004279407_119

remind us of what we have lost and of the potential for new losses. We see the arc of our fall. What was close is remote, what was remote close, deep in the darkness of the unknown depths. The lost bliss of our origin takes on new significance in consciousness informed by the reality of the depths and the memory of sublimity.

In the depths, aware of our loss, we turn towards the condition we mourn inwardly. Suffering mixed with mercy, bitterness with delight, pain with enjoyment, darkness with light remind us that earthly life is at the boundary between two opposing possibilities – ascent and return or further descent. These extremes are symbolically denoted by heaven and hell, with between them the upright path of self-differentiation. They are symbolic, as both heaven and hell are relations to the One. Neither is a principle, but a potential of the self. Our new condition after the loss of paradise entails two possibilities – to find and regain what we lost or to lose even more and sink still deeper into the mire.

We face two signs – the vastnesses of the earth and its myriad paths and the vault of the heavens to which the only path is straight and steep. Our psyche is where each path starts, beginning and converging in the inner self. Heaven and hell, sky and earth, lie at their ends.

Two signs represent this distinction in our humanity: the Kaʿba on the floor of the valley of Becca and the Rock atop Mount Sion in Jerusalem. The Kaʿba and the Rock symbolize the split of the self between the depths and supreme sublimity. Neither is significant in itself, inert matter that symbolizes receptive, yielding stability as beginning or end. Things flow from above to below, to the valley floor; everything begins at the summit of the rock to meet at a single point on the valley floor.

The Kaʿba was erected at that point on that infertile desert valley floor. It is clearly the work of human hands, a manifestation of will acting out of knowledge. It stands as clear evidence of humankind to all who see it. All such buildings in this world are made by our hands.

We forfeited paradise for knowingly reaching after the explicitly forbidden, willing action without knowledge. Our use of free will was without visible consequence, but reaching for the forbidden produces an altered state in the self, manifest as a new position in space and time, as descent to the lowest of the low. Taking the Kaʿba as central to His promise signifies and confesses that ascending the arc of return requires action out of knowledge.

The Rock atop Mount Sion symbolizes creation's perfection and independence from our action. Our origin lay in the perfection of the Garden, where everything is beautiful and complete, the work of His hand alone. We see the

Rock as passive and barren. Compared with the Kaʿba, it is irregular in outline. Its place on the summit, however, points up our need for a redemptive reversal of outlook – its shape is unmediated, while the Kaʿba's is mediated by human hands. The usual image of regularity is thus reversed – the Rock is perfectly regular, the Kaʿba its image in the depths.

Nothing we do can make the Rock life-giving. It is by returning with the Lord through the dark night of baseness towards our original perfection that our obscure and sterile abjectness is transformed into light and fruitfulness. We open to the Lord as Deliverer, having recognized our baseness and repented for our actions out of ignorance, turning from darkness to light.

Thus is the upright path from the depths to sublimity, body to Spirit, darkness to life written upon our consciousness. Our goal is God, the One with Whom everything in this world manifests perfect order. In us, this order is obscured by tension between the many and the One, which manifests as the impossibility of perfect political order based on our actions alone. Supposing a need for such perfection, we are driven to conceal our unattainable, ineradicable foundation.

No action of ours can attain the One. We are ever in the depths, because what remains is always so much greater than what we have achieved. To see our own best potential is to admit our own baseness. We become dependent on that potential, which defines us and guides us from lower to higher states. We do not offer our higher potential creation and guidance. The reverse is true – only the higher can affect the lower and give it meaning.

God's oneness is reflected in us through the gift of that potential, which we never own or control: it is bestowed upon us. Everything we learn about it, as it was originally and ultimately can be, comes from it. Nothing can exist – not even existence – without the perfection of order expressed by God's oneness and the Praised's apostolate.

The perfect individual sees the descending and ascending arcs of existence clearly as states in both world and self, as God said in the Recitation: "This is naught but a revelation revealed, taught him by one terrible in power, very strong; he stood poised, being on the higher horizon, then drew near and suspended hung, two bows'-length away, or nearer, then revealed to his servant that he revealed."[2]

The two arcs of the perfect circle – one descending from the ultimate height to the uttermost depths, the other returning – correspond to this closeness. Every circle has a centre. Each of the countless manifestations corresponds

2 *Qur'an*, 53:4–10.

to some circle's centre. The centre is manifest in all these circles. To see any of these countless circles is to confess the centre. Each circle is a descent in relation to its centre; as though the centre sends down perhaps each circle in manifestation of itself. Both are aspects of the Praised's experience as the perfect individual, in whom outer and inner, first and last are revealed as perfect manifestation of the One.

As Light,[3] God is revealed in illumination or enlightenment. His mercy-to-the-worlds and ultimate sublimity have their inadequate counterpart in our trust, based on little knowledge. The Praised is the perfect first, in absolute trust. Reaching for what is unattainable in us as such, light descends from superabundance of mercy and finest sublimity to poverty and the depths and, even in the obscurity of existence, is the warrant of our indelible covenant of trust with God. In the Recitation, God says:

> Said He: "My chastisement – I smite with it whom I will; and My mercy embraces all things, and I shall prescribe it for those who are mindful and pay the alms, and those who indeed believe in Our signs, those who follow the apostle, the prophet of the common folk, whom they find written down with them in the Torah and the Gospel, bidding them to honour, and forbidding them dishonour, making lawful for them the good things and making unlawful for them the corrupt things, and relieving them of their loads, and the fetters that were upon them. Those who believe in him and succour him and help him, and follow the light that has been sent down with him – they are the prosperers."[4]

At the low point of existence, the Inviolable Place of Self-abnegation and Self-annihilation, the descending light manifests as an individual of mighty morality, the finest example of renewed awareness of our connection with ultimate sublimity, a lamp shedding light in the darkness of the depths. From there he begins the second, upward arc, as the Recitation tells us: "Glory be to Him, who carried His servant by night from the Inviolable Mosque to the Further Mosque the precincts of which We have blessed, that We might show him some of Our signs."[5]

Knowing both arcs, descent and ascent, the perfect servant is fully pliable and open to the Will, both guided and guide on that upright path. God says of him in the Recitation:

---

3 See *Qur'an*, 24:35.

4 *Qur'an*, 7:156–57.

5 Ibid., 17:1.

> People of the Book, now there has come to you Our apostle, making clear to you many things you have been concealing of the Book, and effacing many things. There has come to you from God a light, and a Book Manifest whereby God guides whosoever follows His good pleasure in the ways of peace, and brings them forth from the shadows into the light by His leave; and He guides them to an upright path.[6]

When the apostle comes to lead the People of the Book from the shadows into the light, he affirms that our every condition is a depth in which the self seeks its foundation. That foundation, beyond the self, is required to resolve the tensions of the disrupted or concealed order. Founding order in existence is God the King enthroned in the heart. Aware of this order, we see the world as beautiful revelation of the Beautiful, to Which we are attracted by our love for the One as principle of order. This attraction leads us from level to level of our inner potential, with none other than the Praised as guide, finest example and mighty morality. He is the perpetual actualization of God's injunction to be at peace, in line with the commandment: "If you love God, follow me, and God will love you, and forgive you your sins; God is All-forgiving, Ever-merciful."[7]

We can always discover the circle of our own existence in our "now." Then, we become aware of our connection with the centre. However the self is, so is the circle. They manifest perfectly in the apostle, who is always connected to the Centre. He is made manifest in countless ways, in all God's prophets and all God's friends.

Descent and ascent concern us all, as our nature and our potential, regardless of time, place and language. The self is always between the carnal depths and the spiritual height. The signs in the horizons and the self recall us to this, a necessary, but not sufficient reminder. Our view on the world through language is obscured by tensions in the order produced by our own thought and action.

There is no world order without the self. God sends apostles to every nation from that nation at the self's core, bearing news in its language. Through prophetic speech, this confused, obscure language is righted and illumined, its semantic levels arrayed in a complete whole which corresponds to the arcs of descent and ascent, the perfected self. World and self are thus joined at the heart, their foundation.

God's prophets are people and come to every nation to tell them what has been sent down from the level that transcends them, in their own language.

6 Ibid., 5:15–16.

7 Ibid., 3:31.

The many languages are one of God's signs.[8] God's speech is thus possible in every language. Language reflects everything in the worlds, so that we bring together whatever responds to God's command to be.

What the prophets relate comes in the form of a book and there are many narratives and many books. All are, however, identical in origin beyond language, as both arcs begin and end in one prophetic essence and one essential book. God calls the Praised's followers thus: "*Alif Lam Mim*. This is the Book, wherein is no doubt, a guidance to the mindful who believe in the Unseen, and perform the prayer, and expend of that We have provided them; who believe in what has been sent down to thee and what has been sent down before thee, and have faith in the Hereafter."[9]

"What has been sent down to thee and what has been sent down before thee" are the Recitation and the books sent down before it, particularly the Torah, Psalms and Gospels. God reveals these books which come, in metaphysical origin, from that prophetic essence and essential Book. Combined and individually they are the spiritual heritage of all who confess no god but God and the Praised as His prophet. All of humanity, from both arcs, is revealed in them in various ways.

Through their history, Bosnian Muslims have related to Christians as ancestors and neighbours. In the Christian they find hereditary justification for their own witness of God's oneness and the Praised's apostolate, justification that transcends any given point in time or space, as their witness is founded on God. To deny their link with Christianity is to deny themselves, as there is no circle in existence that does not manifest the Praised's apostolate as the universal why and wherefore.

Attempts to define our foundations in a construct that excludes our incomparable and ineradicable centre impose isolation on world and self. Looking exclusively from one affiliation or identity, we undermine the foundations beneath any others, using a construct with a given beginning, duration, change and rupture. Accepting "what was sent down to you," we interpret identity so that "what was sent down to you" remains literally the same, but reads differently. God calls on us, through the Praised, to say: "Our Lord embraces all things in His knowledge. In God we have put our trust. Our Lord, give true deliverance between us and our people; Thou art the best of deliverers."[10]

Such deliverance means accepting the multitude of books sent down by the one God to the universal banquet. When an individual or people makes clear its connection to one of the books sent down, they must bear witness to His

8 See *Qur'an*, 30:22.

9 *Qur'an*, 2:1–4.

10 Ibid., 7:89.

oneness to understand what they have or have not, what has been received and lost, and what may yet be received, as God's injunction to us through the Praised: "Dispute not with the People of the Book save in the fairer manner, except for those of them that do wrong; and say, 'We believe in what has been sent down to us, and what has been sent down to you; our God and your God is One, and in Him we have found peace.' "[11]

This is the commandment God "sent down" through His apostle, distinguishing those who receive it and the people of the Book. Disputation is speaking to a listener and listening to the speaker so that difference always remains. This difference in will, knowledge and love between the participants may be denied, refuted, juxtaposed, adapted, weakened or strengthened.

Every discussion connects participants, with an indeterminate number of witnesses or listeners. The speaker remains a speaker as long as speaking. When a listener responds, he or she does so as an identifiable individual. They, and in principle any potential participant, may belong to different communities. If they are all from one people or community, their collective selfhood will have been formed by a book and they will be in agreement on its central meaning.

This acceptance of one Book at the centre of some collective identity does not reduce the insuperable difference between individuals. All may witness a Book as the embodied Word there, in a way that differs from other Books, but each insuperably different Book is translatable into every other, so long as originally spoken by a perfect individual and apostle of God. This difference is insuperable while still on the path of return and so below the level of perfection.

The recipients mentioned above are the people of the Recitation God sent down through the Holy Spirit into the heart of the Praised for him to recount to them in their own language. The Praised says of them: "God has His household among men – the people of the Recitation, who are God's household and His chosen ones."[12] They believe in it and in everything sent down before it and are thus also people of the Torah and the Gospel. What happens to those peoples concerns them. Speaking to the people of the Book, God also speaks to the people of the Recitation, for His truth is one. The Jews and Christians are the people of the Book with whom those of the Recitation primarily debate and who are usually seen as participating in the discussion the injunction invites them to.

It is usual to overlook the obvious conclusion that the "people of the Book" may also refer to the commandment's recipients. They could even be the

11 Ibid., 29:46.

12 Ibn Ḥanbal, 3:128, 242.

injunction's first referent, with Muslims, Christians and Jews called to discussion within their communities. Discussion is always about the relationship of speaker to listeners. We can, in principle, each be either and both. Potential speakers are thus people of the Book, like their listeners.

This first level of reading reaffirms the insuperable difference between individuals even when agreeing about the book(s) that inform their collective identity. No matter how similar, no two ever share an identical interpretation of a text, as every individual is unique and constantly changing.

The call to dispute in a fairer manner is evidence that beauty lies in difference. Difference can certainly be painful, even unendurable, as it is difference that recalls us to the ever-present tension between our common unchanging centre and its manifestations in outward order. What lies outside the centre is in duality, in countless multiplicity. No one side of a duality can annul the other: the difference between them vanishes in the One.

The caveat that fair disputation does not apply to those who do wrong has at least two aspects: first, debate based on action out of ignorance cannot be "in a fairer manner," while, secondly, discussion involves implicitly acknowledgement that the participants never have full knowledge. The reasons are evident, as clarity cannot depend on anything external to the individual self.

When the Praised was told to tell the people of the Book that God is of those who listen and those who speak, it reminds us that none of us can ever, in our feelings, conscious mind, knowledge and love, define God in a way that will be equally valid for any two of us or even for just one of us at two different moments. By "definition" we mean how a given self, in a given condition, understands its Lord. No two selves can have the same understanding of the Lord, as a tradition of the Praised recounts:

> Jabir was asked about the coming (of people on the Day of Resurrection). He said, "We would come on the Day of Resurrection like this, like this, and see, carefully, that which concerns 'elevated people.'" He said: "Then the people would be summoned along with their idols whom they worshipped, one after another. Then our Lord would come to us and say: 'Whom are you waiting for?' They would say: 'We are waiting for our Lord.' He would say: 'I am your Lord.' They would say: '(We are not sure) till we gaze at Thee,' and He would manifest Himself to them smilingly, and would go along with them and they would follow Him..."[13]

13 Muslim, 1:123–24.

That no understanding of God can stand as equally valid for all or even two individuals is the lesson of this first level of reading of the injunction. That of the second is that the peoples of different books cannot view their source as finite and comparable. Their book was sent down by One Who remains absolutely near and absolutely remote, absolutely alike and absolutely different. Connection with Him is the Book as read by the individual and only then in the people.

Our viewpoint as individuals is constantly changing, as the self is not self-identical for any two moments. And so it is with creation, as the revelation of the Creator, renewed each moment. Identical perspectives cannot exist in two people or two moments. Abu Talib al-Makki, like many Muslim mystics over the centuries, said: "God does not manifest in the same image twice, just as He does not manifest to two people in the same image."[14]

Looking from the perspective of the people of the Recitation at faith in what was sent down to them as a precondition for faith in what was sent down before, we find no simple object that can be simply subordinated to those who believe in it. Every book sent down has a first recipient and witness and is only then present in an entire community and each individual in it.

Insofar as the Book is present in the "I," the sent down book sends out constant feelers into the myriad feelings, wills, knowledge and love of those who receive and pass it on. It speaks not autonomously, but by means of a community of living and dead in an unbroken chain of transmission. Knowledge of it presupposes knowledge of the people in and with whom it is living speech.

This is God's command to us, conveyed through the Praised. The original speaker is God, but it is heard through the Praised and each witness to his apostolate is placed under an obligation. Witness to his apostolate is inextricable from witness to God, so all who hear it respond by accepting or rejecting.

Those who accept the injunction must respond: Who are the people of the Book? Like any question, it connects the questioner with what is asked. The asked is an unknown to which no clear answer is possible without prior clear knowledge of the response to another question: who am I to be so connected by this question to something so unclear to me? This question comes from ignorance even of what is being asked. Answering it would transform ignorance into knowledge. Knowledge would then connect the questioner or answerer with the asked or found. But there can be no reliable and certain answer, if we do not know ourselves. That we do not makes both answer and

---

14 The source from which this saying was taken is Makkī, *Qūt al-qulūb*. It was a favourite of Ibn al-ʿArabī. See Chittick, *The Sufi Path of Knowledge*, 103, 395 n 13.

knowledge uncertain. In any enterprise, to answer a question about anything we must bring to mind most certain knowledge. But what do we know for sure?

We know nothing in the world so well as ourselves. Moreover, we know ourselves better than anyone else does or can. This certainty defines us, providing a reliable response to the question, who of all past, present and future people knows me best? The questioner's knowledge contains no other certainty. It is thus a key element in answering any other question. Without it, knowledge is incomplete. This holds good for us all, regardless of time, place or language.

That we can ask this question is determined by the world, by other people, and above all by the condition of the self. The self is original and unique, but shaped by contact with the world and the languages that are the sum of all that is seen and unseen. The individual psyche made conscious finds itself within a collective spatial, temporal and linguistic psyche, within countless I-you relations. Every "you" of a given "I" is also an "I" for which that given "I" is "you." Every "I" is at once a potential speaker and listener. When "I" speak, some "you" listens. This "you" may be a group, each a "you" to the speaker, though possibly indistinguishable as individuals in the mass "we." When the listening "you" becomes a speaking "I" and the previously speaking "I" a listening "you," that first speaker joins the listeners, who are now listeners, potential individual "you-s," of the new speaker. Every "I" faces a vast treasury of immeasurably greater knowledge, as every other "I" knows itself better than that "I" does.

Whenever it listens to someone from that mass of people, the "I" learns something unknown or concealed. Whatever the "I" learns from its "you," it does not change the relationship in principle: the "I" invariably knows more about itself than about any "you." The "I" can only ask in its now. The question may be put to anyone, in principle. This entails another irrefutable certainty: since everyone is an inexhaustible source of knowledge, at least about him or herself, the knowledge each individual "I" has is always little. However much this little knowledge increases, it always remains little.

Though we may increase our knowledge through the I-you connection, it remains puny in relation to plenitude. Our knowledge is necessarily finite, but the "I" is open to infinity. The ratio between any finite quantity and infinity is invariably nil. What in this invariably little knowledge can we hold sure and certain? Can we realize our purpose with it?

How our original nature relates to its manifestation in ignorance and incivility is connected with these two questions. No knowledge from outside the psyche can fill the void. Even were we to acquire all possible knowledge about every individual from before, during and after our time, the fundamental relation would remain unaltered: every individual knows him or herself better than any other and even that knowledge is little.

Acquiring knowledge from others involves its transmission in a relationship of knowing self and the object of its knowledge. Something external's nature is incorporated into the self. However great this increase in knowledge, it remains little, for it requires comparison. Where analytic reason is the only medium of knowledge, nothing can be incomparable, one and only. Reason is thus impotent in the face of the transcendent, beyond compare. Accept this as a certainty and we must wonder, if my knowledge is always little, has it any certainty to hold on to?

No matter how hard we try to answer this question, we must conclude the only certainty is uncertainty, the only perspective none. A shattering necessity follows: analytical reason is effective in multiplicity, wherever comparison is possible, but wholly impotent beyond it. Reason is not humbled or denied by this. Its place and role is indicated. It derives from Intellect, given our openness to the One.

Such knowledge opens up, connects us to the One in constant Flux. Humility and generosity are our only way to bear witness to what we have and may have. Greater certainty of uncertainty means greater humility, a greater sense of richness in poverty greater generosity. These conclusions raise a question of intent: can we intentionally contribute to our little knowledge's relation to the ultimate potential in which it is wholly eliminated?

Let us revisit the question of disputation in the fairest manner with the people of the Book at another level, as Christians and Jews. This question presupposes another, namely what was sent down as a book to Jews and Christians? The Recitation's answer is that the Torah, broadly understood, is the book of the Jews, the Gospel the book of the Christians. For the people of the Recitation, this is clear, and underlies what they bear witness to; both are specifically named in the Recitation. But what are the Torah and the Gospel, firstly as commonly seen by Muslims, and then as seen by Jews and Christians?

Few Muslims have read Torah or Gospel. They know them only as mentioned in the Book they adopt and confess: as books accepted by Jews and Christians in much the same way as they accept the Recitation. When Muslims hear how most Jews and Christians regard the Recitation, their holy Book, they feel injured and unjustly calumniated. Their view of Torah and Gospel, as the reality of thousands of years for Jews and Christians, is identical, however, to the view they hear of the Recitation from those they consider Jews and Christians.

The pain and offence, injustice and calumny Muslims feel on encountering how many Jews and Christians view their self-witness will be eliminated only if they are asked about and express in answer their will, knowledge and love of their holy Book as inseparable from the perfect nature of the Praised.

They may ask this of others, but cannot demand or impose. Moreover, it should inform their own response to God's call: "Not equal are the good deed and the evil deed. Repel with that which is fairer and behold, he between whom and thee there is enmity shall be as if he were a loyal friend."[15]

That which is fairer cannot be repelled, nor can one dispute in the fairer manner with a people of the Book so as to build friendships without recognizing that one's own view of the Jewish and Christian books involves counterfeiting ignorance for knowledge, an act of violence against Jews and Christians. For that ignorance to be transformed into knowledge, one must question them on all matters, as people whose existence is informed by their books.

Logically, then, for Muslims to present their will, knowledge and love in the fairest manner to Jews and Christians, they must also be unconditional listeners of their accounts of their will, knowledge and love. The purpose of such speaking and listening, listening and speaking is neither to efface difference nor impose belief. Difference is ineradicable, because it is the will of God.

No-one in all existence can have full knowledge: absolute knowledge is proper to God alone, Whose knowledge and mercy encompass all things. Knowledge is our connection to Him, along with recognizing his signs in the world and history, books and human destiny. Wherever we encounter something flawed and ugly, threatening or intolerable, we should turn to ourselves – to that self of little knowledge but infinite potential to increase in knowledge.

Discussion is to transform enmity into friendship and ignorance into knowledge, into being better and finer of our own will. By entering debate, we bring our own lore to the common table, to offer to all but impose on none. Various books are on the table. Attitudes towards them differ, but each is some participant's greatest and most sacred treasure. Still, no guest may present him or herself as perfect realization of their book. All must strive for it to make of them people who debate in the fairest manner, for these books are on the table because God sent them down as Possessor of the most beautiful names, the All-beautiful. No human condition is fully immune to that beauty's attractiveness, manifest in the nature of those who received the Book, their speech and listening, their discussion.

The banquet of the books of the Jews, Christians and Muslims and the participant Jews, Christians and Muslims those books define may be variously described. They are "participants in textual reasoning," "witnesses to the openness of the scriptures," "proponents of unity in diversity," "participants in group study," "participants in readings from the scriptures," "group reading and listening to the scriptures," "seekers after new perspectives on their scriptures,"

15 *Qur'an*, 41:34.

"witnesses to the scriptures as testimony to submissiveness," "guests at the table of the scriptures," "students listening to the scriptures," and such like.[16]

For the modern and postmodern, the word "book" can conjure up the idea of an object of many written pages from which a narrative may be read. The holy scriptures were originally spoken, however, and their derivative form, which is of a lower degree, is invariably a record of speech. Direct speech, involving a narrator and a listener, can never be entirely faithfully transformed into a text. Every word in the written text and in an even more complex manner the text as a whole is framed by the eternal light or mystery that always remains within the oral tradition.

For every people of the book, the text is constantly recalled to memory and speech, reading and repetition, speaking and listening, as questions and answers constantly draw on orality, a process in which everyone around the table is involved. Bringing together witnesses and scholars of the scriptures of various peoples involves them in speech and listening, opening words up to various levels of meanings, from the world to the One. The danger of adopting ignorance about others and their scriptures is reduced by their presence at the same table.[17]

Every holy book is sent down from the One through the heart of a first recipient to be moulded into language and conveyed to listeners. Only then is it written down and reduced to a lower level of existence. Since everything sent down has its archetype at higher levels, up to the level of the One's first manifestation, to every revealed book there corresponds a single, essential Book at the highest level as first recipient of the Creator's Word. When the essence of that Book is sent down to a lower level, it is as the Word into the heart of its recipient. When the apostle receives and conveys it to the world, it is Word first and written record second. The Word-Book relationship, which connects all existence, involves us all, whether as oral narrative or written record.

Each form of the Book, spoken, heard, written, read, in every circumstance – listening, speaking, writing, reading, worshipful embodiment, or prayerful expression – assists us onto the path of ascent. The Book informs that entire path in its metaphysical, cosmological, anthropological and psychological horizons. As we follow it, we ascend from level to level, constantly discovering

---

16 These phrases are suggestive of the enterprise now known as *Textual* or *Scriptural Reasoning*, in which some of today's most eminent philosophers and theologians from the Abrahamic traditions are engaged. See, e.g.: Ford, "An Interfaith Wisdom: Scriptural Reasoning between Jews, Christians and Muslims."

17 Plato also warns of the dangers of reducing live discourse to written text. See *Phaedrus* 275C, 257D, 275E, 276C, 277D.

the traces before us and then leaving them behind as we concentrate on the ever higher.

We are never alone on that path of ascent. Ahead and behind of us and with us are other witnesses to our scripture or to other scriptures. Discussing the experience of the journey with them helps us re-examine the level we are at and determine the direction of our journey to come. Is not this the meaning of God's revelation through the Praised: "To every one of you we have appointed a right way and an open road. If God had willed, He would have made you one nation; but that He may try you in what has come to you. So be you forward in good works; unto God shall you return, all together; and He will tell you of that whereon you were at variance."[18]

Regardless of our nation, the way and the road are through the Book. Its form is linguistic, insofar as it was first received, then turned into speech, and finally written down. We cannot connect to it without restoring it to speech and receiving it in our core, its ontological source. This enterprise requires the presence of some other to listen to this speech. Scripture cannot be a mere object for interpretation. The Self Who is First Speaker is never excluded. Any relation to the text necessarily involves the interpreter within an ontological perspective.

The Self and the self are related. Any relation to scripture requires both, the Supreme Self and the human self. But our self, the "I," relates to all its human "you-s," with all of humanity, under only one certainty – that the knowledge it has gained of the world around remains little. However little that knowledge, it does, however, manifest through the selves that bear it, everyone else and all of existence as the open Self Whose knowledge encompasses all things. Knowledge, properly understood, is the connection of the self coming into knowledge and the Knowing Self.[19]

The Recitation connects those who receive and recite it and God Who teaches it to us. Since God is Supreme and we are at the lowest depth, the Recitation descends to our extremity. We are connected to the Supreme by this discourse sent down and may ascend to Him by it. God said through the Praised: "Move not thy tongue with it to hasten it; Ours it is to gather it, and to recite it. So, when We recite it, follow thou its recitation. Then Ours it is to explain it."[20]

---

18 *Qur'an*, 5:48.

19 It is worth noting that fundamentalism, as a modern ideology, supposes the self may be determined by a text, as a closed cosmos in which knowledge is objective and independent of the Knowing Self.

20 *Qur'an*, 75:16–19.

God told the Praised, first recipient of His Recitation, our finest exemple, a mercy to the world, and through him us all. The Recitation is with God as His original, uncreated Word, first manifestation in the essential,[21] hidden,[22] well-guarded Book.[23] Its first recipient is the Praised, the primordial prophet. Both the Recitation and the Praised descend from on high, sublimity of existence, as light to the lowest of the low,[24] to lead the return of all things to the One as union in a mighty morality.[25]

Receiving the Recitation, we become part of a chain of transmission from lips to ear, person to person, all the way back to the lips and voice of the Praised. Whomever we hear it from its source in our world is the Praised, as faithful transmitter of what was received from God. Connection with the Praised is connection with God through the Recitation. God said his was a mighty morality, while ʿĀʾisha, his widow, said: "The prophet's nature was the Recitation."[26] For witness to God's unity, the Praised's apostolate and return to God, the Recitation is key to discovering and realizing perfection of the self.

Children receive it from their parents' lips in earliest childhood, at their parents' knee, on their lap. This is how they connect to the Praised as primordial prophet who has the Book's essence. Later, they join other children in the mekteb to study together. Even after they have learned to read and write, memorizing and reciting the Book are preferred to reading. The Recitation is the Muslim's inseparable friend and companion through life; it is in everyone's memory and in every house as the Book. Our nature, our original nature, is the undifferentiated Recitation and we identify with it to realize non-differentiation of our own nature.

The Recitation is always and everywhere assured of the highest honour. In every house, it is treated with the greatest respect as foremost of all things. Everyone gathers around it, as its students. No member of the household, no guest, ever ceases to study it. It is present in every ritual prayer, but reading and repeating it from memory are a constant means of remembering God. Reciting in this way can be done at any time, so long as it is approached in a state of ritual purity. It can be done alone or with others, silently or aloud. The very act of recitation obliges those present to listen. It is received with one's entire being, as God said: "God has sent down the fairest discourse as a Book, consimilar in

21 See *Qurʾan*, 43:1–4.
22 Ibid., 56:77–80.
23 Ibid., 15:9.
24 Ibid., 7:157.
25 Ibid., 68:4
26 Muslim, 1:359.

its oft-repeated, whereat shiver the skins of those who fear their Lord; then their skins and their hearts soften to the remembrance of God."[27]

The reasons for recognizing the Recitation, as God says in it, lie in belief in what has been sent down before it, which is to say in the belief of Christians:

> And when they hear what has been sent down to the apostle, thou seest their eyes overflow with tears because of the truth they recognize. They say, "Our Lord, we believe; so do Thou write us down among the witnesses. Why should we not believe in God and the truth that has come to us, and be eager that our Lord should admit us with the righteous people?"[28]

When the revelation is recited by individuals or groups fully aware of their forebears as Christians, there can be no rupture, historical or ontological, in their reasons. Their acknowledgement of the Praised and the Recitation opens within them psychological, anthropological, cosmological and ontological perspectives which simply reject rupture and rift. Their forebears were those whose eyes filled with tears as they listened to what was sent down to the apostle.

As embodiment of the Book, the Recitation is the centre of every house, accorded the most elevated position. Each individual raises it to that position, only to take it down again. The house is the exteriorization of the self, but interiorization of the world: the Recitation is in the heart, its written record at the centre of the house, while everything in existence manifests the Word. Brought down and recited from, with purity and due procedure, it is restored to its high place once again. It is borne in mind by every member of the household, a reminder of God's presence.

Whether as book or memorized, the Recitation is never left to one side, in the self or the house. It is brought down constantly for us to rise to our finest stature in reciting it. Our awareness of it, whether by recalling it to memory or turning to it as text or speech, helps the self ascend from the depths towards our original and most beautiful rectitude.

Every complete recitation of the Book is sealed with a prayer. A common one, repeated countless times in solitude or in congregation, houses and mosques, over the centuries of Bosnia's love of the Praised runs thus:[29]

---

27 *Qur'an*, 39:23.

28 Ibid., 5:83–84.

29 This final prayer is given at the end of the *Muṣḥaf* completed in 1760 as his thirtieth transcription by Mustafa, son of Omer Hadžalić of Mostar. The manuscript is in the Mahmutćehajić family collection in Sarajevo.

In the name of God, the All-merciful, the Ever-merciful:

Praise be to God, Lord of the worlds.

Blessings and peace on our apostle the Praised and his household and all his companions.

O Lord, our Lord, accept from us. Thou art truly the All-hearing, the All-knowing. Forgive us, O Protector. Thou art truly the All-forgiving, the All-merciful. Thou turnest towards us, o Protector. Thou art truly the All-turning, the All-merciful. Turn us towards ourselves, O Protector. Thou art truly the All-generous, the All-noble.

Thou rescueth us from care and sorrow, from sadness and great suffering. Lead us to the truth and the upright path. Make us heirs to the garden of delights, with the bliss of the holy Recitation and the inviolability of the light of the Praised, the Chosen One – blessings and peace be with him.

O Lord, increase me in knowledge and associate me with the good.

O Lord, make me a keeper of the prayer, and my descendants too.

O Lord, hear this prayer.

O Lord, forgive me and my parents and all the faithful on the Day of Reckoning.

O Lord, open my heart, ease my travail, and loosen my tongue that my speaking may be understood.

O Lord, forgive us and our brothers who came before us in belief. O Lord, complete our light and forgive us. Thou art truly All-powerful.

O God, adorn us with the adornment of the Recitation, and honour us with the nobility of the Recitation, and uplift us with the sublimity of the Recitation, and protect us with the protection of the Recitation, and clothe us in the garb of the Recitation, and lead us into Paradise with the Recitation. O God, guide us with the guidance of the Recitation, and preserve us from all the misfortunes of this world and from the chastisement of the hereafter and from the fire. O God, make the Recitation our companion in this world, and a close friend in the grave and a defender standing ground, and a light in passing, and a friend in Paradise, and a shield and a screen from the fire, so be Thy mercy, O Most Merciful of the merciful.

O God, accept this Recitation from us, and this final prayer, as Thou receivest from the prophcts and the good.

O Lord, grant us beauty in this world and grant us beauty in the next world, and protect us from the punishment of the fire, and lead us into Paradise with the honest.

O God, forgive us, and our parents, and the parents of our parents, and our teachers, and the teachers of our teachers, and our powerful protector, and our elders, and our brothers, and our sisters, and our children, and our husbands and our wives, and our descendants, and our relatives, and our neighbours, and our partners, and all the faithful, men and women, and the people of peace, men and women, and the living and the dead among them, so be Thy mercy, O Most Merciful of the merciful.

Connect us, O God, with our forebear the Praised, his household and all his companions.

Glory be to Thee or Lord, Lord of glory, over those Who ascribe to Him, and peace be on the apostle, and all praise to the Lord of the worlds.

O God, deliver the good of what we have read and the light of what we have recited as a gift that reaches the soul of our prophet, the Praised – blessings and peace be with him – and the souls of all the prophets – God's blessing be on all of them – and the souls of all honourable companions – may God Almighty be pleased with all of them – and the great precursors, God rest them – and the elders, worthy of respect, may God confer on them the mysteries – and the souls of all other people of faith in general and particularly the soul of so-and-so, son of so-and-so.

May this reach the one for whom it is intended, may the grave become a pleasure ground for him in the garden of the pleasure ground, and save him from its being a pit in the fiery pit.

Amen!

As this prayer shows, the person reciting relates to the Recitation from the self, but in a connection that embraces the whole world. The Light of the Praised is at the centre of the world and of each of us. Around it are arrayed the horizons, the prophets, the good – the elect, the chosen, the saints, teachers and elders, near and far, dead and living. The prayer is usually said in congregation, a coming together to mark another cycle of recitation. It is never just an end, but always a beginning too. The Recitation has no beginning and no end. The congregation bears witness by aspiring to have selves informed by it. The Praised said: "God has His household among men – the people of the Recitation, who are God's household and His chosen ones."[30]

The Recitation is made up of 114 chapters or *suras*, from an Arabic root meaning "to enclose." Of varying lengths, every memorized section is suitable for mandatory ritual prayer. This division is part of the revelation, but others exist; one is division into thirty equal parts, so that it may be recited over a

30 Ibn Ḥanbal, 3:128, 242.

month, moving from beginning to middle to end, in a constant repetition of arrival and departure, growth and withdrawal. It is also common to mark the pages to assist memorizing by seeing the image of the whole text on each page.

Every performance of ritual prayer involves the Recitation, continuing beyond the act of worship, in separate readings, speaking and listening. This is particularly true of individual and group recitations during the holy month of Ramadan, when openness to eternity is emphasized by the impossibility of an end. As soon as the recitation is complete, one moves straight to the first sura, the "Opening," and the first part of the second, "The Cow." Thus, one experiences this beginning as a continuation of the sura "Men" at the end of the book. Moving on to the "The Cow," a new cycle begins, and so on indefinitely. One could say that the Recitation has neither earlier nor later.

The Recitation's continuous, infinite nature bring praise and expressions of forgiveness, celebrations and rotations, encouragement and reprimands, instructions and threats, strictness and gentleness, recollections and interpretations, commandments and prohibitions, comparisons and mysteries. Two motions come together in the reciting self – ascent and rotation. Eternity is manifest in time as repetition and advance. Whatever point in the Recitation we reach, potential always remains for ascent, decline or wandering. Every discourse of the signs in the horizons and of whatever reaches our knowledge from without and every condition within, all the numberless manifestations of our original nature reveal the drama of our "now," with hell and heaven, suffering and bliss in and with us.

The narrative's flow and rhythm, breaks and continuities are such that those who recite, read or listen are drawn into a calligraphic, musical and semantic current with calms and rapids, bottlenecks and overflows, buffets and flashes. Our entire being passes from relaxation, tenderness and tears to concentration, tension and contraction. Sometimes the discourse reverberates in the soul's unplumbed depths, sometimes in breathing and numbness, sometimes on the body's surface, skin and hair.

The Recitation is inseparable from the beating of the heart, the circulation of the blood, even the movement of the earth, the moon and the sun. The five compulsory prayers are for five points during the day – just after sunset, at night, before sunrise, just after noon, and midway between noon and sunset. This is five complete immersions in cosmic self-abnegation. Those who pray take body in the word and it in them. Their commitment to receiving it transcends all desire. The perfection of the word descends into them, as they ascend into it in its perfection. Each such prayer contains God's command to be as the complete creation and sending down of the Book.

The days pass from first to sixth, from beginning or differentiation to plenitude or convergence. Everything is confirmed on the seventh day, the day of rest, from which and to which all existence is. Every seventh day reminds us of God as Peace, in constant repetition of no peace but Peace. The passage of the weeks is marked by the moon's phases, from the first new moon through its waxing to the full moon and its waning to invisibility. Twelve such phases are a year. The ninth month of the year is Ramadan, in which total fast is prescribed from the first glimmerings of dawn to sunset. This celebrates the sending down of the Recitation as God's mercy and admonition to the worlds.

The fast is broken just after sunset. The entire household gathers around the table, whose contents they have looked forward to as a sign of ultimate, perfect bliss in redemption. The inclusion of the leavened bread known as *somun*, a key symbol in the breaking of this daily fast, links Bosnian Muslims with their Christian forebears, with those who acknowledged, with tears in their eyes, the Recitation and confessed their following the Praised,[31] discovering and confessing his closeness to the Anointed, whose presence testifies to the Holy Spirit as the yeast that leavens inert matter.

Once Ramadan is over, the first three days of the following month are the Feast of the Breaking of the Fast (*ʿīd al-fiṭr*), which marks our return to our original condition, after fasting. The joy of receiving and adopting the Recitation, which the Holy Spirit, the Spirit of Truth, brought down into the heart of the Praised to pass on to all as a warning to the worlds, is confirmed during the celebrations. A further four days, beginning with the tenth day of the twelfth month, are the Feast of the Sacrifice (*ʿīd al-aḍḥā*), when we restore to God by sacrifice part of what we have received from Him. In both cases, the word *ʿīd* means return or restoration. Thus culminates the ritual of pilgrimage to the house, when animals are sacrificed, a ritual that confirms the power of the Word. Those who perform the sacrifice affirm themselves as fully at peace in the will of God, acknowledging their life as received. The death of one's own death is a way of coming to life in the will of the Living.

Both these feasts are banquets sent down, signs of the joy towards which all prayer is directed. The Anointed spoke of them in his prayer: "O God, our Lord, send down upon us a Table out of heaven, that shall be for us a restoration, the first and last of us, and a sign from Thee. And provide for us; Thou art the best of providers."[32]

Restoration (Ar. *ʿīd*) at the Table on certain days, in reward for ritual commitment and patient endurance in observance of the commandments, signifies

31 See *Qur'an*, 5:83–84.

32 *Qur'an*, 5:114.

ultimate achievement in eternity, where redemption and the discovery of and return to God take place. We come to our real from our deluded self, to the open from the isolated self. The expectation realized in prayer, fasting, purification by alms and pilgrimage is return to the sublimity promised us as our place of return, a restoration somehow present in the waiting.

When pilgrims to the house reach the boundary of the holy precinct, they don the garb of inviolability, a simple seamless white garment. They are expressing their love of God in its full potency, as great as the power of death. They use the same garment as a shroud. When the pilgrims take them off, they put the robes away carefully for their final journey. While wearing it, they exclaim: "O Lord, here I am at Your service, here I am." While still alive, the pilgrims are indicating their passage beyond death, their transcendence of death. The exclamation carries within it an awareness of love and death – love that redeems from death and death that does not touch God, the Beloved.

FIGURE 2.1 *Map of Bosnian manuscripts from the illustrations*

FIGURE 2.2 *A view of Becca from the Dalāʾil al-khayrāt, copied by hafiz Ibrahim, the son of Muhammed Šehović, 1781*

FIGURE 2.3 *The Praised as the best example*

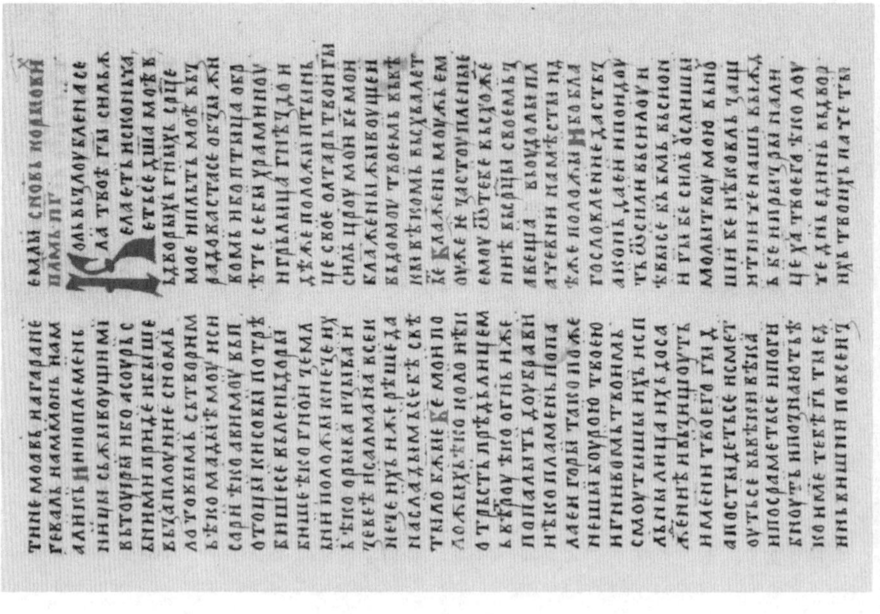

FIGURE 2.4 *Psalm 83 from the Miscellany of Hval, copied out by the krstjanin Hval, 1404*

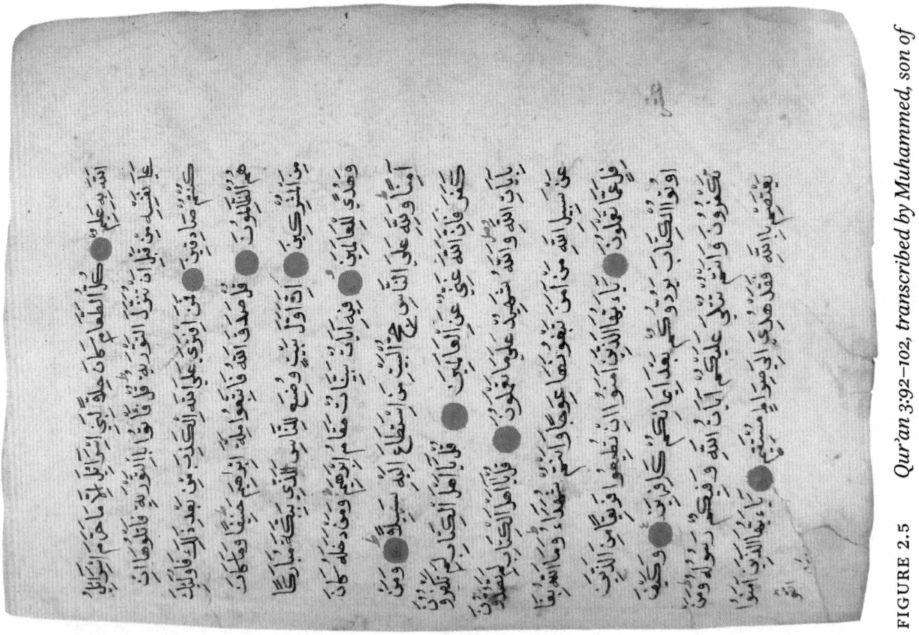

FIGURE 2.5 *Qur'an 3:92–102, transcribed by Muhammed, son of Husein, of Blagaj, 1598*

FIGURE 2.6 *Qur'an 3:79–86, transcribed by hajji Redžep-Dede the Bosnian, 1615*

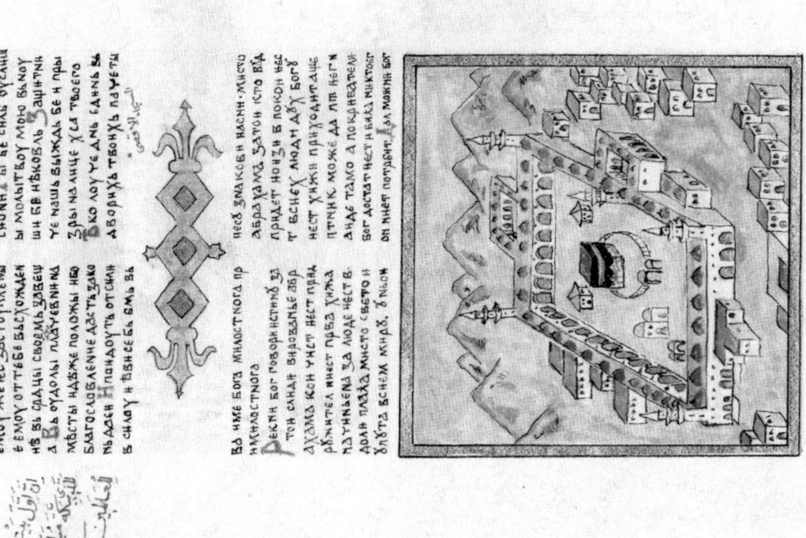

FIGURE 2.7 *The House in the Valley of Becca from the Book of the Praised's Light, anonymous, 4r*

FIGURE 2.9 *Qur'an 17:1–16, transcribed by 'Abdullah 'Ayni, son of Hasan, from Sarajevo, 1852*

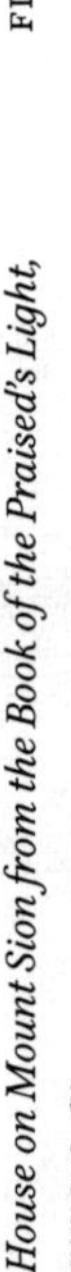

FIGURE 2.8 *The House on Mount Sion from the Book of the Praised's Light, anonymous, 5v*

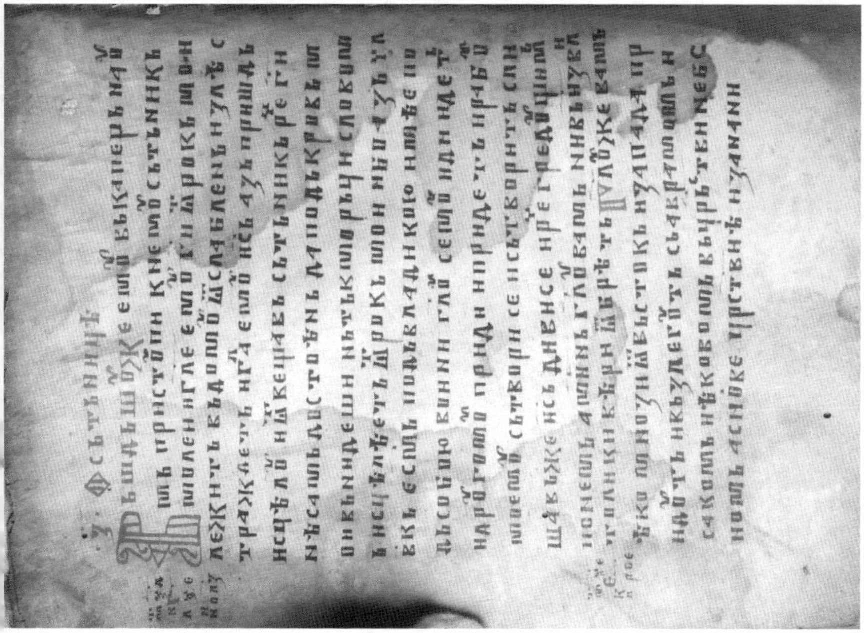

FIGURE 2.10 *Matthew 8:5–13, from the Čajniče Gospels, 15th Century*

FIGURE 2.11 *Qur'an 2:128–133, transcribed by Bi-zeban 'Ali-pasha of Sarajevo, 1638*

FIGURE 2.12 *Qur'an 3:36–48, transcribed by Shahin bin 'Abdullah al-Nasiri, 1473*

FIGURE 2.13 *Luke 1:13–19, from the Pripković Gospels, copied out by "a krstjanin by name Tvrtko Pripković from the land of Gomilje," 15th century*

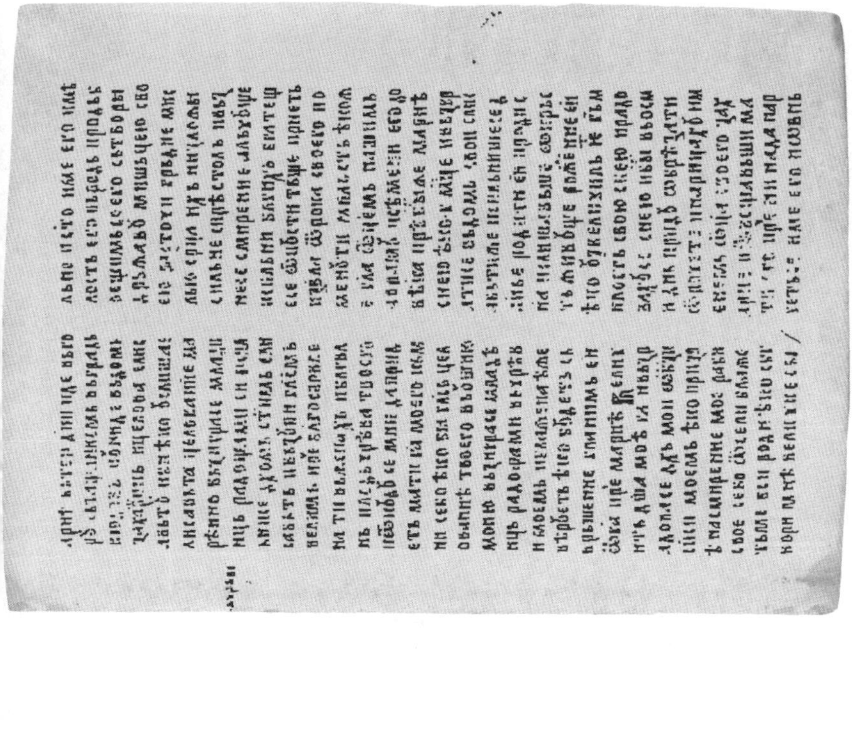

FIGURE 2.14 *Luke 1:21–39, from the Venetian Miscellany, 15th Century*

FIGURE 2.15 *Qur'an 19:9–21, transcribed by Amina, daughter of Mustafa Chalabi, of Sarajevo, 1764*

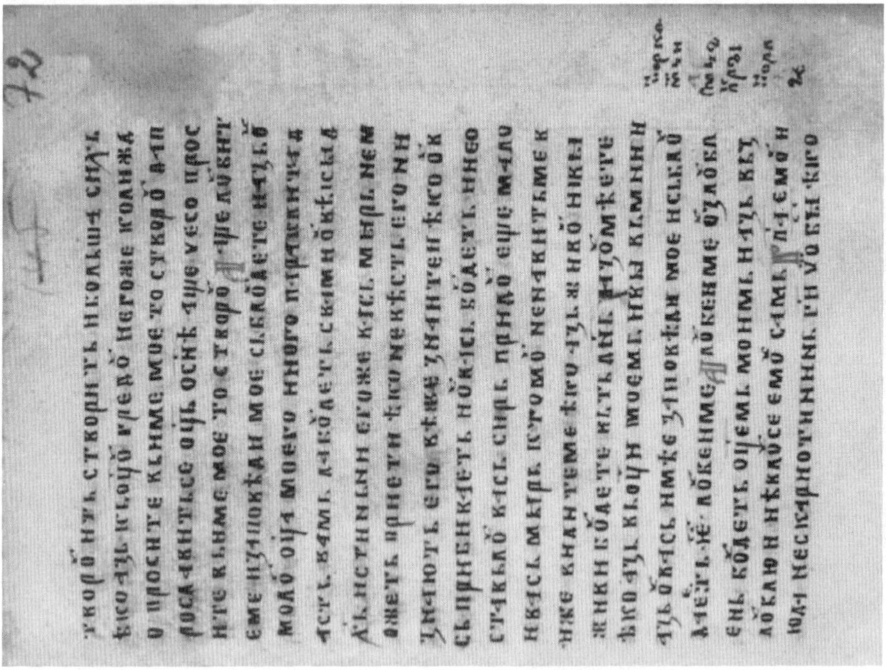

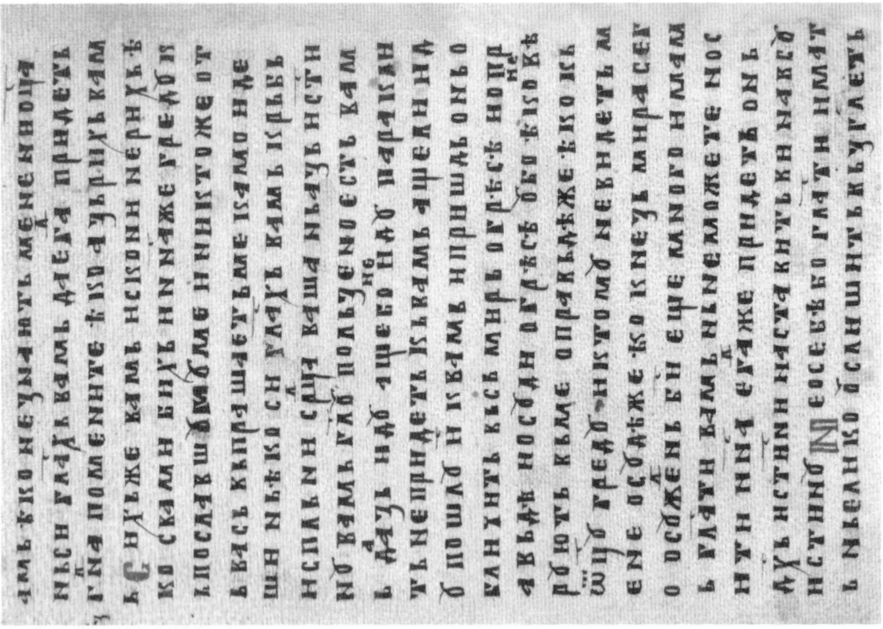

FIGURE 2.17 *John 16:3–13, from the Kopitar Gospels, 15th Century*

FIGURE 2.16 *John 14:12–22, from the Vrutok Gospels, 15th Century*

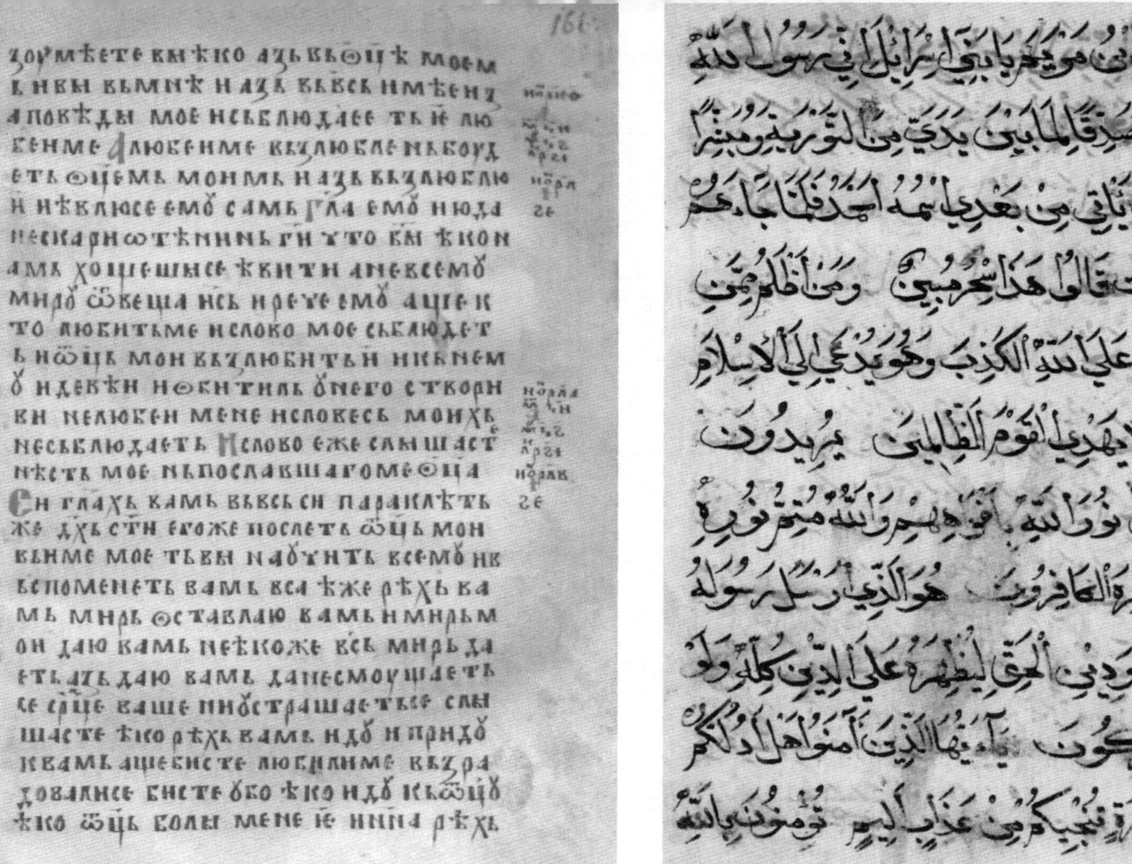

FIGURE 2.18 *John 14:20–29 from the Nikolje Gospels, 15th Century*

FIGURE 2.19 *Qur'an 61:6–11, copied out by Korkut Halifa from Stolac, 1593*

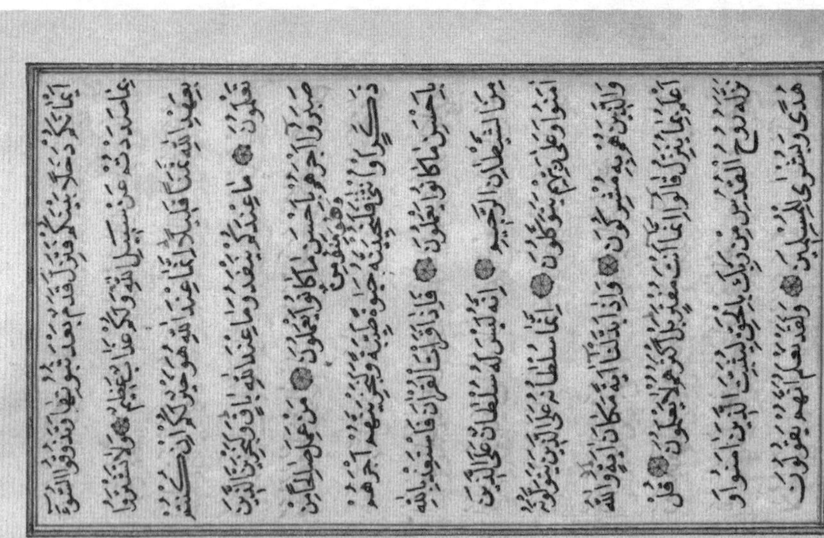

FIGURE 2.21 *Qur'an 16:94–103, copied out by Ibrahim Šehović, son of Muhammed, of Sarajevo 1811*

FIGURE 2.20 *Qur'an 26:184–206, copied out by Mustafa Hadžalić, son of Omer, from Mostar, 1760*

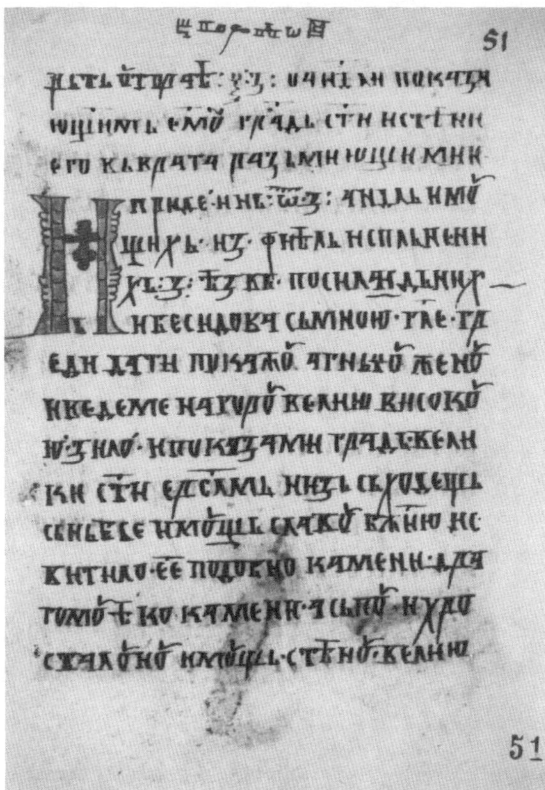

FIGURE 2.22 *Revelation 21:9–12, from Radosav's Bosnian Book, 51, copied out by the krstjanin Radosav, 15th century*

PART 3

In the Mosques

• •

The name of Bosnia has innumerable aspects. Take any and you will find reference to the mosque. The Bosnian word for mosque, "džamija" derives from the arabic *jāmi*, the basic meaning of which is "worshipful congregation." This meaning, however, tends to be reduced in ways that are both impoverishing and dangerous. If we are to transcend the confines of the individual self mired in conflict, we must open up this linguistic and semantic field.

The word "džamija" is used to signify "a place of congregation" or "meeting place," the gathering of individuals to pray and worship God as Gatherer, discovering the divine attribute of the Gatherer in the self and self-realizing as "gathered" and "gathering." In this way, "the act of gathering" is both "gathered" and "gathering," relating the gathered/gathering to the Gathered/Gatherer. This can be understood only within the nexus of metaphysics, cosmology, anthropology, and psychology contained within sacred doctrine.

While Bosnian took the term "džamija" for any place of worship according to the ritual revealed by God through the Praised, the Recitation uses a different one. Qur'anic Arabic uses the term *masjid* to refer to a place in which people, together or individually, carry out the worshipful act of *sajada* or "prostration." *Masjid* and *sajada* share the same verbal root, namely *s-j-d*. The verb means to "prostrate oneself" in worship, essentially the rhythmic sequence of standing, bowing, sitting, and so on, accompanied by speech, whispering, and silence. These or similar words have been used throughout the long history of the Semitic languages to denote this and similar names exist for both act and place in the Islamic, Christian, Jewish, and other traditions. In all cases, the semantic fields tend to become limited and narrowed, producing forms that obscure the core meaning. The meanings of the traditional forms, however, tended to be both inclusive and exclusive at the same time, as signs of God Who is "First and Last, Outward and Inward."[1]

A look at the etymology of the Bosnian noun "*crkva*" (church) may help us understand this mutual implication of exclusivity and inclusivity. The Bosnian word is normally used to refer to "the type of building in which Christians congregate for liturgy." It can also denote various religious organizations or structures. The original meaning was broader and more complex. Cognate word forms are found in every Slav language and generally thought by etymologists to derive from the Greek *kyriakós* ("of the Lord") or *kyriakē oikía* ("the Lord's house"). The Greek term for an "assembly of the people" is *ekklēsia*, which corresponds to the Hebrew *qāhāl*.

Such a gathering is in response to a call. In both the Recitation and the Gospels, God calls us to assembly through His apostles. When Simon Peter said

1 See *Qur'an*, 57:3.

 | DOI 10.1163/9789004279407_120

Jesus was the Anointed, Jesus replied: “And I say also unto thee; that thou art Peter, and upon this rock I will build my church; and the gates of hell shall not prevail against it.”[2] It is worth reflecting on Jesus' naming his disciple the “rock” on which the congregation of the people turning to him as the Word would be built.

Both of these nouns, *crkva* and *džamija*, church and mosque, signify our response to God's call and our gathering around His Word as centre, a call continuously repeated through God's apostles, who include Adam, Noah, Abraham, Moses, Solomon, the Anointed, and the Praised. As apostles of the One God, they bring the same call in different forms. People receive its prophetic transmission in different times and places as the basis for their acts of gathering, adding various contents of their own. These embellishments of the call can take the place of the Word, obscuring it. Only by restoring our connection with the first bearer of the news, through whom and with whom God spoke, can the assembly of the people be preserved in its relation to God. A further claim necessarily follows. The core and the seal of what has been received and transmitted remains accessible to every individual in every age, with the eternal warrant of God's presence and connection: “God and His angels bless the prophet. O believers, do you also bless him, and pray him Peace.”[3]

God sends us down His Word through His apostle, who passes it on as a bridge between those it is for and God. There can be no message without a messenger, no messenger without a message. The apostle is our route to the real. He is how the Divine is revealed to and through us.

Prostration marks our turn to God, expressing poverty and humility in the face of the All-sufficient and Majestic. It is not standing before God. Standing upright is a sign of our high status, while in prostration before the face of Him, Who Stands Upright, we sink to the depth to rise up again towards the sublimity that is ours to claim. We relate to God as in His image, as both guest and host. When He speaks, God is Host, we His guests. When we speak, we are host, He Guest. God gives and receives, speaks and listens. He makes a gift of His capacities to His own image that reveals Him. God calls us and we call Him. When we call, it is from deep poverty; when He calls, it is as All-merciful and All-sufficient.

Wherever we find ourselves, God is with us.[4] Wherever we turn, His face is before us.[5] He reveals Himself to us through His most beautiful names:

---

2 *Matthew*, 16:18.

3 *Qur'an*, 33:56.

4 See *Qur'an*, 57:4.

5 Ibid., 2:115.

> He is God; there is no god but He. He is the knower of the unseen and the visible; He is the All-merciful, the Ever-merciful. He is God; there is no god but He. He is the King, the All-holy, Peace, the Faithful, the All-preserver, the All-mighty, the All-compeller, the All-sublime. Glory be to God, above that they associate! He is God, the Creator, the Maker, the Shaper. To Him belong the names most beautiful. All that is in the heavens and the earth magnifies Him; He is the All-mighty, the All-wise.[6]

The divine attributes expressed in the most beautiful names gather within us as His image, received in creation and maintained through His unwavering presence. We realize ourselves by discovering them within. This is what the Praised meant when he said: "You should be characterized by the characteristics of God Most High."[7] Nothing is worthy of His place or association with Him as the focus of the self, humanity, and the world. Recalling Him as our focus is the decisive content of His call, which all His prophets have borne.

Church, mosque, and synagogue[8] serve to renew and maintain our memory of His call so that we confess no god but God and the Praised as His apostle. They are symbols of our true house, from which we came into this world and to which we shall return. In all its forms, ritual is symbolic recital of this commemoration, linking ourselves as poor and dependent with God as All-sufficient and Independent.

People differ. They are gathered by birth into families, tribes, and peoples. No group abolishes the individual self's authentic and unique nature as created by God. It is through our relationships with others, as guest and host, that we stop ourselves assuming the role of exclusive possessors of the centre. Each one of us is formed around a centre or focal point. Insofar as it is absolute, it is one in us all and in all worlds. Precisely because we are all in His image, the other presents us with an image through which to know the One's presence in the manifold.

This is just as true of communities. Other communities present images through which ours can know itself and realize its potential. Willingly accepting that every place and time is an opportunity for taking part in the universal prostration before God, we turn towards the Centre in which His most beautiful names reside and from which they emanate. This re-turn takes place by many

---

6 *Qur'an*: 59:22–24.

7 In Ghazālī, *The Ninety-nine Beautiful Names of God*, 149.

8 The noun *synagogue*, from the Greek *sinagōgē*, signifies a place Jews congregate to worship and recite the Torah and meet other communal needs. The Hebrew words are *môʿēḏ* ("place of congregation") and *môʿᵃḏê-ʾēl* ("the place of congregation before God").

paths. Each people has its own origin, its own way of relating to the Centre, which is One. God said through the Praised: "Had God not driven back the people, some by the means of others, there had been destroyed cloisters and churches, synagogues and mosques, wherein God's name is much mentioned."[9]

Each of these four forms – monasteries, churches, synagogues, and mosques – entails confession of God as the Centre towards which we turn. Let that centre be forgotten, obscured, or denied by anything in these decorated buildings, and they become anti-monasteries, anti-churches, anti-synagogues, and anti-mosques. Then, they turn us from our authentic nature as the treasure house where His most beautiful names gather.

God determined our path back to the Centre. He announces that path as one of salvation. God is One, but there are as many paths to Him as things in His creation. In various languages, lands and times, we turn towards and recall Him, and so recall our own most sublime potential. This act of recollection is independent of age or land, language or ritual.

Recollection is always possible, both within and outside of history. It involves the living individual in front of the Living God. However confused or oblivious, we can find and discover ourselves before the Face of the Living God. This act of discovery is personal. No one can stand in for us. Until we accept this as the most important question facing us, we remain trapped within the expectation that self-discovery, redemption, and anointment can somehow be realized beyond the self. Our individual responsibility for ourselves cannot be transferred.

God is the Gatherer of all people, together and individually, around Him as Principle.[10] Whenever we find our relationship to God obscured, whenever we associate something from creation or our own feelings, passions, or imaginings with Him, we are scattered and turned in all directions. Anything but God confines us and the prison of our existence is determined by whatever we associate with God.

Only He is undetermined and incomparable, only He at once entirely near and entirely remote, the only Opener of that prison, the only Drawer Forth from it through truth: "Say: 'Our Lord will bring us together, then make opening between us by the truth. He is the Opener, the All-knowing.'"[11] Opening and liberation are how the open, free individual relates to God as Opener and Liberator.

9 *Qur'an*, 22:40.

10 See *Qur'an*, 3:9 and 4:140.

11 *Qur'an*, 34:26.

Our physical existence and bond to the earth seem immediate, palpably tangible, distinguished over five levels: taste, touch, smell, hearing, and sight. We are drawn deep into the world of limits. Focusing orients us towards the centre, where the signs serve only to recall all-embracing Unity. The external reveals the superiority of what is within. These two ways of showing the One, within and without, are inseparable, impossible without each other. To realize this act of recollection at the pitch of our potential is the seal of the prophets.

Our most important knowledge is already within us, in that central core where all difference is one. The Praised is our guide, as essence and seal. Each prophet existed at a time, in a place, amongst his or her people. We know very little about most of them, but they passed on their recollections of the seal as accessible to all, in every place, and every time. Bearing the seal within, we find and discover ourselves in relation to our uncreated core. The prophets' oral and written heritage is indestructible and irreplaceable. However preserved, its essence lies in witness to Unity as primordial and to Its purpose and revelation within the world of limits. Such are we, but our self can be deformed.

The Praised was sent to guide us from the Inviolable to the Further Mosque. This pair of symbols on earth corresponds to the oppositions of the depth and most beautiful uprightness, the earth and the heavens, death and life, the grave and resurrection, the body and the Spirit, outer and inner. The human condition lies somewhere between. The depth is always there, just as the path to most beautiful uprightness is never blocked. Whatever our condition, we may bear witness through prostration to our poverty and our hope to find our own essence in the presence of the All-sufficient.

Through the Praised, God revealed the Recitation as His discourse in the language of human beings. In it he said: "Hast thou not seen how before God prostrate themselves all who are in the heavens and all who are in the earth, the sun and the moon, the stars and the mountains, trees and the beasts, and many of mankind?"[12] He also says: "There is no one in the heavens and the earth that does not come to the All-merciful as a servant."[13] And again: "In Him has found peace everything in the heavens and the earth."[14]

All of existence and every individual thing prostrate themselves before God, serve Him, and find peace in Him as Peace. In this perfect order of the revelation of no will but the Will, humanity is the exception. As a sign of our creation as what gathers His names we were given will, the will to oppose the

12 Ibid., 22:18.

13 Ibid., 19:93.

14 Ibid., 3:83.

Will. This is because God is Faithful to the faithful. This relationship entails or presupposes freedom of choice, the freedom to reject or accept. In our pettiness, we accepted that our relationship with God be confidence: "We offered confidence to the heavens and the earth and the mountains, but they refused to carry it and were afraid of it; and man carried it. Surely he is sinful, very foolish."[15]

For us, all existence is a mosque, a place of self-abnegation, with nothing in it that does not prostrate itself before God. This is because everything except us hesitated to take up the burden of confidence as a relationship with God. It is our choice to join willingly in the act of prostration, service, and being-at-peace, under the burden of confidence.

Why is confidence a burden for humanity?

Our knowledge is little, never independent of All-knowing God. Whatsoever we encounter within the world or the self is simply a sign through which God reveals himself to us. Gathering these signs and finding the corresponding signs in the core of the self, we recognise ourselves as in God's image. Recognizing ourselves, we recognise our Lord. This act of recognition is always paltry, but sufficient to turn us towards God as the unbearably attractive Real, for there is no real but the Real. Wishing our real selves, we can only attain our desire by confessing no self but the Self.

We do not determine our own path. The self does. Conscious of the self's separation from the Self, we are spurred on irresistibly to attempt union. Our self wishes to see itself in the Self, to contain only what the Self sees in us as His mirror. This attraction between self as lover and Self as Beloved is love. This little knowledge can grow towards fullness only in and through love of the Known. The closer we are to the Known, the greater our knowledge. The greater our knowledge of the Beloved, the greater the love between us and Him. We do not increase through knowledge. The Known increases us in and by knowledge, as the Praised confessed: "O my Lord, increase me in knowledge!"[16]

Knowledge of the Beloved and love of the Known are faith. Accepting confidence we assume a burden which causes confusion and madness and suffering and pain. But it is also relationship with God, the All-merciful, Loving, Gentle, and Forgiving. Our only solution is to stand in our love before our beloved God to see ourselves in His face, as God sees Himself in ours. His face alone endures.

15 Ibid., 33:72.

16 Ibid., 20:114.

As all things in existence, including many people, are in constant prostration before God, so too all things pass into the mosque. God says this of all things and some people. People are clearly divided into those who do and those who do not prostrate themselves before Him. Each individual faces these alternatives. All other things gather in the act of worship, two wills, the Creator's and creation's, manifest as one in this way. We gather existence. Our opposition to His will is a crack in existence and our act can appear independent. This appearance gives rise to opposition between us and God. In this conflict, the world ceases to be our mosque. God appears remote, absent, and unnecessary. As He said through the Praised: "I am near to answer the call of the caller, when he calls to Me."[17] And again: "He is with you wherever you are; and God sees the things you do."[18]

God's closeness means we can harmonise our will with His, whatever our condition, turn towards Him and see Him in all things. God says of His nearness: "I dwell in the high and holy place, with him also that is a contrite and humble spirit, to revive the spirit of the humble, and to revive the heart of the contrite."[19]

Turning towards God and entering the universal mosque, we bridge the rift within ourselves and so within the world. We experience the love with which He loves us and we Him. But we are forgetful and always liable to separation, so that passing into the mosque represents passage over the boundaries of oblivion in a war against everything that would turn us back. The mosque is an ever-present sublime potential in which to find and discover our authentic nature.

We were created for most beautiful uprightness. We descended from it to the lowest depth, whence we return to God. The most beautiful height is the Further Mosque, the major sign on the ascending path. The goal of ascent is the Centre at which all paths meet. Beyond the Centre, on every lower level, are countless places in which our presence may be felt. Each is a mosque, representing the possibility of witness of no god but God and the Praised as His apostle.

As the best example and a mercy to the worlds, the Praised embraces through his presence the entire range from the lowest depth to the most beautiful uprightness, every moment of humankind. In his every moment, he bridges the rift that came into being when the two wills, human and divine, were opposed. God told him and so all of us: "Did He not find thee an orphan and shelter thee? Did He not find thee erring and guide thee? Did He not find

17 Ibid., 2:186.

18 Ibid., 57:4.

19 *Isaiah*, 57:15.

thee needy and suffice thee? As for the orphan, do not oppress him, and as for the beggar, scold him not; and as for thy Lord's blessing, declare it."[20]

Even though he is the principle of "the first heavens" and the goal of the "second," the Praised is entirely "an orphan" and "needy" before God. God reveals Himself "on the first arc" as unity descending to be dispersed through all the levels of Being. The Light of the Praised is its first manifestation. The descent continues to the "lowest depth" at which the "first arc" ends. The Praised then rises up from that depth by the "second arc" to the "second heaven" and so to Unity as the Goal of return. The Praised's closeness to Unity is symbolised by these "two arcs."

Most beautiful uprightness is our authentic condition: the divine act of giving and the human act of reception are united within the self. We give what we receive, so that our giving is returning to God the Giver. On the path of return, the Praised prostrates himself before the Lord:

> When I see my Lord, I will fall down in prostration before Him and He will leave me as long as He wishes, and then it will be said to me: "Oh, Praised! Raise your head and speak, for you will be listened to; and ask, for you will be granted; and intercede, for your intercession will be accepted." I will then raise my head and praise my Lord with certain phrases which He has taught me, and then I will intercede.[21]

To follow the Praised is to love God. The highest level, where we stand before God, is reached from prostration. This is why the Praised said: "Make frequent prostrations before God, for you will not make one prostration without raising you a degree because of it, and removing a sin from you, because of it."[22] Prostration is thus a state of receiving or committing to God's will.

As how we relate to God, prostration resides in the self's present. But neither time nor space limit the act, through which, we turn any place at any time into a mosque. God said in the Recitation:

> The mosques belong to God; so call not, along with God, upon anyone.[23]
>
> Say: "My Lord has commanded justice. Set your faces in every mosque and call on Him, making your debt sincerely His. As He originated you so

---

20 *Qur'an*, 93:6–11.

21 Bukhārī, 9:374.

22 Muslim, 1:256.

23 *Qur'an*, 72:18.

> you will return; a part He guided, and a part justly disposed to error – they have taken Satans for friends instead of God, and think them guided."[24]
>
> Only he shall inhabit God's mosque who believes in God and the Last day, and performs the prayer, and pays the alms, and fears none but God alone; it may be that those will be among the guided.[25]
>
> And who does greater evil than he who bars God's mosque, so that His name be not rehearsed in them, and strives to destroy them? Such men might never enter them, save in fear; for them is degradation in the present world, and in the world to come a mighty chastisement.[26]
>
> And those who have taken a mosque in opposition and unbelief, and to divide the believers, and as a place to ambush for those who fought God and His apostle aforetime – they will swear, "We desired nothing but good"; and God testifies they are truly liars.[27]

The Praised said: "The earth is the mosque for you, so wherever you are at the time of prayer, pray there."[28] At any given moment, the entire world is a theatre for our ascent into the universal mosque. Every sign within the horizons of the world reminds us of this possibility. As do our own acts, if carried out in full consciousness of being within the universal mosque.

In everything we do, in whatever appears as a consequence of our life, will, power, knowledge, speech, listening, or sight, we find grounds to ask: "Do you serve what you hew, and God created you and what you make?"[29] Any human work may seem to confirm its doer's sufficiency and independence, if offered to others as a sign of the doer's mastery. We may mistake a building for a mosque, when it is in reality an anti-mosque. This is why purity of nature provides the purest mosque, containing only His signs to Whom all existence and many people prostrate themselves.

Why and how do prostration and the mosque as the place of self-prostration in the most sublime expression of our relationship with God determine all our relations, and so all Muslim relations, with God, the world, and others?

For Muslims, Christians and Jews are more than an immediate and tangible reality. Their presence as neighbours, as participants in relating to God and journeying from Him back towards Him, is central to God's call through

24 Ibid., 7:29–30.

25 Ibid., 9:18.

26 Ibid., 2:114.

27 Ibid., 9:107.

28 Muslim, 1:264.

29 *Qur'an*, 37:95–96.

the apostle. No aspect of their presence, as the people of the Torah and the Gospels, fails to affect Muslims as image-equivalents of their own selves.

Can this be viewed from the opposite direction too, from the viewpoint of Christians and Jews towards the Muslim?

The most pertinent answer is determined by the question's being raised by a living individual in his own "present." Neither question nor answer is possible without God present on both sides. No approach to the Torah, Psalms, or Gospel is possible that does not admit differences in the extent to which the pronouncements and appearances of "that prophet" who is at the heart of the Muslim confession of faith are to be found there. As Steven Kepnes has said: "Jews and Christians have a warrant in their Scriptures to engage with the Muslims not as a strange Other and as long lost members of the great family whose destiny is to be a light of truth and healing to all the nations of the world."[30]

What is lost can be found. Hagar is the stranger of whom God says to Israel: "The stranger that dwelleth with you shall be unto you as one born among you, and thou shalt love him as thyself."[31]

The relationship between "me and my stranger" or "us and our stranger" allows two possibilities, to confirm strangeness as something to remove from or to approach the stranger and view strangeness as a precondition for realizing the self within the Self and discovering the self in confession of Unity.

In relations between Jews, Christians, and Muslims, the first option stresses difference, which appears an insoluble obstacle to acquaintance and love. Taking these affiliations together, however, with God at the centre, our way of looking at relations of difference itself changes. What separates the Jew, Christian, and Muslim confirms the divine self-revelation in their different languages and symbols. No teaching on this matter exhausts all the possibilities of passing towards the centre.

The Jews, Christians, and Muslims are all peoples of their books. They can each be considered host in their own space, the others guests. Those others are also both guests and hosts. The host lays out his own book and his own interpretations for his guests at the banquet. They are honoured by his address, an honour they repay by listening. In their turn, the guests bring forth their own books as hosts under their own interpretations. As they take turns, each participant comes to understand the value of the differences between what they and what the others have.

30 Kepnes, "Islam as Our Other, Islam as Ourselves," 109.

31 *Leviticus*, 19:34.

Both guest and host are permanent guests at God's table. They also entertain Him, serving Him as their most important Guest, honouring Him with what He gave them, repaying the debt they owe Him for having been received into His kingdom and confessing that He alone is capable of resolving the differences they cannot overcome.

God is ever Faithful, His knowledge of us absolute. He sees us in our authentic and final perfection. That is how He wants us and loves us and to that He is Faithful. God's love for us is, in the final analysis, love for Himself: only He fully knows Himself and His love is the identity of knowing and being. Revealed in signs of power infinitesimal compared to His, His mercy comprehends all. The humanity He loves is Him looking and listening to Himself. This is the only way to explain His patience and forgiveness for our actions and what we have failed to do on the basis of our little knowledge and our great ignorance. When He says He loves us, He knows us in our purpose, as realized in perfection.

We forget and give up, breaking our connection with Him. But He never ceases to be close to us, benign, tender, and merciful. When He seems remote, wrathful, strict, and threatening, God turns us towards Him as merciful and knowing to the beginning and end of all things. All His signs in the world and self manifest ceaselessly to remind us that nothing was not created by His word with Truth. The core of this reminder is His revelation: "I am your Lord, so serve Me."[32]

The Word spoken by God is at the heart of His creation. He reveals himself through it. We hear it all around us and see its signs in the outer horizons and within ourselves. We cannot escape it. It is like birdsong at night. As one bird falls silent, another takes up the song, without cease, now from below, now from above, now close at hand, now far away, all extolling the Lord in similar and different ways.

God embraces all things with His mercy and His knowledge. He loves us and befriends us on our journey from our initial to our ultimate perfection. He reveals the Word. Great, Powerful, and Firm, His Spirit is present within us, small, weak, and infirm of purpose. For He created us in and for the sake of perfection and leads us irrevocably towards His knowledge and mercy: "God does guide onto an upright way those who have attained to faith."[33] He gave His faithful free will and sufficient knowledge to love Him as Known. Everything good and fine we have is from Him, all the evil that befalls us from ourselves.[34]

---

32 *Qur'an*, 21:92.

33 Ibid., 22:54.

34 See *Qur'an*, 4:79.

He never abandons us, for His Spirit has taken up abode within us as His manifestation.

This omnipresent, eternally merciful, benign, tender, and beautiful God sends down His Word to us so that we may return in ascent to Him. With this Word, the paths up from the depths to the sublime height open, paths that lead to where we stand face to Face. God calls us to this ascent: "Set your face to the debt of the pure one, God's original upon which He originated humanity. There is no changing God's creation. That is the upright debt."[35] This summons us to return to our centre, fairest rectitude.

Our covenant with God and the worship that renews it are for the discovery of the redemptive treasury in the self, in which all words are united into the Word. No spoken word or discourse transcends the Word. It remains above all speech, inexhaustible, omnipresent. God sent down the Word to the Praised to pass on to us in his language. It passes from within to without, from unity to multiplicity. It is heard by every one of us as merciful, joyful, salvific news. Thus God and His Word are never subordinate. We are knowers, expected to serve Him openly, humbly in our return to Unity.

Once heard, the Word is recognized as having always been in the centre of the self. It is reiterated in worship and remembrance in every human condition. Whether mother, father, grandmother, grandfather, teacher, or friend instructed us in the Word, it is our bond with the Praised and, through him, God. Nobody in this chain of transmission is above the Word, since through it and the Praised, those who receive it return to God.

Knowledge connects knower and known. If what the knower knows is limited, so is knowledge. We are finite, as is our knowledge, always limited by comparison with plenitude. Everything we know in the finite world is transcended and encompassed by what lies beyond. The infinite is the utterly near and utterly remote principle of finitude. The finite is just manifestation of that principle, its signs in the world and within us who know them. Our knowledge is always little compared to the Principle.

When we turn towards the Principle, the signs in the outer horizons and within us convey us towards full knowledge. Our path of ascent to absolute knowledge cannot be limited. Before the One Whose knowledge embraces all things, we are pure and naked, as He knows all things in the world and self fully. This awareness that God knows us perfectly and we are constantly before Him is the highest moment of our approach. God's will is unalterable in this. To hold our will at peace and in submission through submission to God as Peace is our debt to God.

---

35 *Qur'an*, 30:30.

Repaying that debt, we prepare to become whole and pure again, after our transgression in the Garden. Injuring this relationship by setting our will against His, we may hope to hide or find a way of not being constantly before His face. This illusion turns us away from God, but He remains before us always. God asks those who hide: "Where art thou?"[36] He Whose knowledge embraces all things asks those with only a little knowledge and His question is a reminder of beauty as the condition of being before God "as if" we see Him, "for even if you do not see Him, He sees you."[37]

Maintaining this relationship with God is to marvel incessantly at the world and ourselves as the constant presence of the Creator Who reveals Himself through them. The order in the outer horizons, from the lowest and most minute to the highest and greatest, manifests His presence through the infinite multitude of signs, of which He is both centre and circumference, inwardness and outwardness. God never abandons the world. "Every day He is upon some labour."[38] This absolute newness of everything in the outer horizons and our inner selves, this createdness of all things at every instant, is in and before each of us.

There is no depth where we are not before God as the outward centre of all things, a centrality symbolized by the Inviolable Mosque. Wherever we are, we are peripheral to the centre. God calls on us to turn to it: "Turn thy face towards the Inviolable Mosque; and wherever you are, turn your faces towards it."[39] This mosque is at the bottom of the Valley, in the midst of deserts. At its centre is the Kaʿba in sign of rectitude. The mosque is the sign God decreed when our time on earth began, a sign of our turn towards Him: "Wherever you turn there is the face of God."[40]

In witness to being our finest example, the Praised turned away from the Inviolable Mosque at the bottom of the valley to the Further Mosque at the summit of the Mount, from south to north. This stands for the vertical axis of ascent from the depths towards the height, from the signs towards the Signified, from illusion towards Reality. To enter the mosque is to turn from margin to centre, to acknowledge the depths but ascend to the height. With this entry and acknowledgement we connect with God as Outward and Inward. Confessing Him as only principle of the outside world, we prostrate and realize

---

36 *Genesis*, 3:9.

37 Part of the prophet's response to the Archangel Gabriel's question: "Now tell me about doing what is beautiful?" (Muslim, 1:2).

38 *Qur'an*, 55:29.

39 Ibid., 2:144.

40 Ibid., 2:115.

the oneness of His being Outward and Inward. This is the meaning of discovering and entering every place as a mosque or place of self-abnegation. In orienting us, the Praised reveals that by recognizing ourselves in the depths, we turn towards Peace as our sanctuary.

Consciousness is indivisible from life. Bearing both, we possess neither unconditionally. We have received and are indebted for them. If we lose them, it is regardless of our will. Having them, we relate to them across the entire gamut from unconsciousness and death to our supreme potential, passage beyond all limitation. In this span of our potentialities, we have before us the finite world as the object of our knowledge. We also have ourselves as differentiated into knower and known. No object of our knowledge is, however, dependent on us. We and what we know bear witness to Him Whose knowledge embraces all: He is Witness to all existence as His manifestation.

All the signs in world and self are His testimony. Knowing them for such, we too are His witness, perfected by confessing no god but God and the perfect individual as His apostle. The apostle is our fullest potential by whom God embraces fullness of manifestation from the depth to sublimity.

God is All-praised. Everything in His creation by which He reveals himself bears His being All-praised so that all things in the world and self are praised. They received their being as praised and manifest it as their connection with God as All-praised. Praise connects all things and God as All-praised. When being thus unites within us with our potentialities and manifests perfectly, it is firstness and lastness of God's revelation of Himself. We all bear witness to our supreme potential in different ways, depending on our consciousness and how we express it in language and way of life.

The core of the self orients us towards our supreme potential. Our witness leads the self towards discovery of apostlehood as our deepest and purest original nature, which connects us with the apostle, of whom God says: "The prophet is nearer to the believers than their selves."[41]

This is because every self manifests as partly open to its highest potential, our reason and purpose, never exhausted by any form it takes until return to God in full perfection. We return to Plenitude – Firstness and Lastness, Inwardness and Outwardness – Whom nothing can either conceal or reveal. Concealing and revealing are for humans only.

Creation – earth, the heavens, and all that lies between and beyond – is the Creator's discourse, a discourse at one with us. In self-realization, we discover it as the ever anew manifestation of God. We are given a further discourse: God speaks to us in our own languages through His prophets. God and the world are

41 Ibid., 33:6.

present in our own languages, through which God manifests Himself in ever-changing ways. His manifestations are comparable, allowing us to confess Him as First and Last, but He is never that which manifests Him, nor is anything real but Him. Ascent towards Him from manifestation is the connection or worship that transforms time and place into a mosque. God prescribed five mandatory daily prayers as a gift to humankind, given to the Praised at the ultimate boundary of his ascent, whence he brought them back to us.[42] Hence the saying: "To pray is to ascend."[43]

We receive the Word spoken by God. When we pronounce it, it is never the same as when God does. We are eternal servants, God the Master; we are limited, God is not. Our utterance of the received Word never comprehends it fully. It escapes us as higher, more comprehensive than anything we know. No individual, not even all of us together, can master the Word or bend It to our will. The Word remains God's, its presence a link to God. Nor is that unique Word present in the same way in any two or even in one at two different moments.

What is the Word common to all people? The answer lies in something the Praised said, at the behest of God:

> People of the Book! Come now to a word common between us and you, that we serve none but God, and that we associate not aught with Him, and do not some of us take others as Lords, apart from God.[44]

If the Torah, the Psalms, the Gospels, and the Recitation are all books in which God has announced His Word, then there must remain a common core behind all differences of expression. Humanity's self-realization is unimaginable except on the basis of a quest for that core. The principles it contains are the very ones in accordance with which the world reveals its Creator.

The Jews are the people of the Torah and the other books revealed after it, down to the prophet Malachi. The Christians are the people of the Gospels, but also of the books revealed earlier in the holy heritage of the Jews. The Muslims are the people of all these books and the Recitation, in line with the revelation sent down to them by God through the Praised:

> We believe in God, and in that which has been sent down to us and sent down to Abraham, Ishmael, Isaac and Jacob, and the Tribes, and that

---

42 See Muslim, 1:100–103.

43 This expression is attributed to various people and is quoted in: Qāri, *Mirqāt al-mafātīḥ sharḥ Mishkāt al-maṣābīḥ*, 1:113.

44 *Qur'an*, 3:64.

> which was given to Moses and Jesus and the prophets, of their Lord; we make no division between any of them, and in Him we have found peace.[45]

The Word is sent down through the Holy Spirit to each prophet amongst his people and in his time. When a prophet speaks the Word in his own tongue, the form it takes is always different. As a result, the Word appears in an infinite multitude of different and unique forms, but the presence of the Holy Spirit remains in each. Only God is the absolute master of the Holy Spirit.

The Word common to all the peoples of the Book transcends any individual form in which it is revealed. It transcends, because the one Truth is both cause and purpose of its revelation. It brings us into relation with God. There is no Word but it. That is why no one but God can be its master. All who receive it bear witness by being-at-peace and in humility. They never present themselves as masters of men. They are the most humble servants of the Giver, and do not accept service from any other:

> It belongs not to any mortal that God should give him the Book, the Judgment, the prophethood, then he should say to men, "Be you servants to me apart of God." Rather, "Be you masters in that you know the Book, and in that you study."[46]

The Word is both before and beyond all existence or anything in it. Even though it determines everything, the Word is subject to nothing. It was brought into existence by the Holy Spirit, which is subject to none but God. This is why no vision and no will but God's can call it, direct it, or turn it away. And therein lies its power. Only in and through it can the self be entirely free in relation to God as both Giver and Receiver.

The Spirit ascends and bears the Word through the various levels of existence. It also descends and bears down the Word through these same levels. In this task, the Spirit gives and receives, is both male and female. When it is "above the waters," the Spirit inspires life. In this, however, it is only being fully faithful to God's command. Its presence and absence both reveal God's will and command. As His knowledge is absolute and all comprehending, each presence or absence of the Spirit reveals Him in a sign which is always turned towards Him as the inexhaustible treasure house of knowledge. The Spirit is, accordingly, a permanent and unconditional connection between fullness as the nearness and remoteness of that moment and eternity, on the one hand,

---

45 Ibid., 2:136.

46 Ibid., 3:79.

and quantifiable space and time, on the other. Regarding the relationship between the Spirit, the command, and knowledge, God revealed to the Praised: "They will question thee concerning the Spirit. Say: 'The Spirit is of the bidding of my Lord. You have been given of knowledge nothing except a little.' "[47]

Our always insufficient knowledge is connected through the Spirit with its inexhaustible source. The descent of the Spirit allows that little knowledge, while Its ascent provides unlimited openness towards God as Knowing. No knowledge is so little as to deprive its bearer of connection with the Knowing. Moreover, none is so great as to satisfy its bearer in spite of his separation from the Knowing. This is because only the Knowing is fullness. And this is why return is to the Knowing.

There are three key aspects to the Spirit in the Recitation – animation of the earth as its recipient, bringing the Word to the prophets, and ascent in order that everything may return to God.

After having formed him with His own hands, God breathed of the Holy Spirit into Adam. In this way, the fullness became manifest in finite time and space. Both are essential qualities. Eternity and infinity are manifest in them. When God breathed of His Holy Spirit into the earthly Adam, all creation was shown to the angels as a centre through which God addresses them and they Him:

> And when thy Lord said to the angels, "See, I am creating a mortal of a clay of mud moulded. When I have shaped him, and breathed My spirit in him, fall you down, prostrate yourselves before him!"[48]

Just as earth was formed to receive Spirit, making a being of most sublime uprightness, so the Virgin is the perfect receptacle of Spirit, represented in the most beautiful form:

> And mention in the Book Mary when she withdrew from her people to an eastern place, and she took a veil apart from them; then We sent unto her Our Spirit that presented himself to her a man without fault.[49]

This "man without fault" addressed the Virgin: "I am but an apostle come from thy Lord, to give thee a boy most pure."[50] This apostle was a perfect man in

47 Ibid., 17:85.

48 Ibid., 15:28–29.

49 Ibid., 19:16–17.

50 Ibid., 19:19.

whom descent and ascent, Spirit and Word, sanctity and truth were united.[51] The Virgin's relationship with him took on the form of the Anointed, who is the Word. The Holy Spirit is succour.[52] The Lord formed a bird of clay and breathed into it and gave it life. This divine gift to Jesus is comparable to the divine act of the creation of Adam and the breathing of His Spirit into him. For, the Anointed is coaeval with the Spirit.[53]

Prophetic discourse is God's stimulus that those He chooses speak in His name.[54] He inscribes the relationship of faith in the hearts of those who choose to be faithful to their Faithful God, confirming it "with a Spirit from Him."[55] The apostolate of the Praised as prophet was determined and confirmed by descent of the Holy Spirit,[56] the Spirit of Truth.[57] In this descent, the Praised was recipient, a light in the night of the depth,[58] a light sent down.[59] Given his absolute purity, his self is equivalent to the Holy and True Spirit which bears the Word.

Reversed, this descent becomes ascent from the night of matter towards Light and Spirit. In these two directions of descent and ascent we find all our confession of Unity as the Principle of all existence, of the Praised's apostolate as Unity's first and last revelation, and of return to that same Unity by following the Praised, in whom the full cycle of descent and ascent was realized:

> The Night of Power is better than a thousand months; in it the angels and the Spirit descend, by the leave of their Lord, upon every command.[60]
>
> To Him the angels and the Spirit mount up in a day whereof the measure is fifty thousand years.[61]

We have sketched out a framework of internal connections between ways in which the one God is revealed. We see clearly that for Muslim self-witness there is no break with or distortion of earlier identities just because they happen, like the Bosnian Muslims, to have been Christian. Others hold an inverted

51 On the relationship between the Virgin and the Spirit, see Ibn al-ʿArabī, *The Bazels of Wisdom*, 172–86.

52 See *Qur'an*, 2:87, 253; 5:110.

53 Ibid., 4:171.

54 Ibid., 16:2 and 40:15.

55 Ibid., 58:22.

56 Ibid., 16:102.

57 Ibid., 26:192–95.

58 Ibid., 33:46.

59 Ibid., 7:156–157.

60 *Qur'an*, 97:3–4.

61 Ibid., 70:4.

picture of Bosnian Muslim history that denies their claim to an unbroken continuity of spiritual existence and imposes a counter image, by force, up to destruction if necessary.

According to Justin McCarthy, more than five million Muslims were killed and even more again forced from their homes in South-eastern Europe, Anatolia, the Crimea, and the Caucasus between 1821 and 1922.[62] These murders and expulsions did not begin in 1821, any more than they ended in 1922. Some 250,000 Muslims were killed in Bosnia between 1941 and 1945 and between 1992 and 1995. More than half the total Muslim population was expelled, permanently or temporarily, from their homes and towns.[63] The entire Muslim population was subjected to systematic harassment and humiliation. Their personal and communal wealth was pillaged and ransacked.

These crimes have been passed over by historians or presented as the fault of the killed and the expelled, as the acts of victorious liberators, rather than murderers and persecutors. As taught to the descendants of the criminals and their victims, the historical record has been stood on its head, the victims presented as criminals, the criminals as victims. That is why, when they were repeated between 1992 and 1995, these crimes were not understood as part of a phenomenon with a long pedigree.

The murderers and persecutors of Muslims have equated their presence with the expansion and survival of the Turkish Empire, which swallowed or threatened former Christian kingdoms. This is the narrative incorporated into pretty well every national liberation programme in the Balkans, allowing killing and expulsion to be understood as settling historical debts and opening up possibilities for a just future, once "national states" have been restored. This programme for murder and expulsion included plans to realize "Christian" models, against which Muslims stood out as others, with whom reconciliation was impossible so long as they remained what they were.

Nor has it been unusual to hear those at the highest levels in the Church, priests and even saints, calling for the murder of Muslims.[64] Excluded was any possibility that Muslims formulate and present their own interpretation

---

62 McCarthy, *Death and Exile*, 338–40. These events have never been properly researched and have little hold upon the collective consciousness, which is how genocide could recur between 1990 and 1995 with much the same aspect throughout Bosnia and Herzegovina. See Bećirović, *Genocid on the river Drina*.

63 This assessment is based on research published in Žerjavić, *Opsesije i megalomanije oko Jasenovca i Bleiburga*, Kočović, *Žrtve drugog svjetskog rata u Jugoslaviji*, and Mahmutćehajić, *The Denial of Bosnia*, 75–78.

64 See Mastnak, *Crusading Peace*, 153–228.

of their connection with the Word in its various manifestations. For pretty well every historian who flourished within the framework of national ideology, Muslims simply could not find meaningful reasons in their Christian past for confessing God's unity and the Praised's apostolate. Such interpretations allowed them only "rupture" that separated Muslims from the fundamental flow of history, so that their presence represented "an intrusion," "interference," and "treachery." Little attention was paid to the consequences of this attitude for those who took it: that they excluded themselves from participation in the infinite totality of creation.

There are four preconditions for the mass murder and expulsion of Muslims: (1) leaders to inspire and guide; (2) an ideological historiography which presents the programme both directly and indirectly as necessary and justifiable in the fight against evil; (3) a considerable political and military apparatus committed to the anti-Muslim programme as a fight against evil, and (4) a sufficient number of individuals ready to take a direct role in murder and expulsion and afterwards to focus public debate on the question of the Muslim presence as "discontinuity."

"Discontinuity" is the key word which subsumes the four aspects of all anti-Muslim programmes. It always appears in interpretations of Muslims' origin and their place amongst Christians, from popular accounts to "scientific" historiography. It isolates and exaggerates the ugly and cruel, as connected with Muslims, contrasting it to the fine and good, as Christian. Any attempt by Muslims to move beyond an imposed identification with dying or dead empires threatens to undermine this image of the cruel and horrid "Saracen," "Arab" or "Turk," in contrast to the good and fine Christian. In all this, the key objection levelled against Muslims is the "falsity" of the Praised's apostolate. This is because witness to it is the core of the Muslim's being, both as an individual and a member of the group.

Accusations can be made against Muslims for countless sins and faults, so long as one ignores their own account of themselves, based as it is on a scale of human fallibility measured against sublime models. Mary's son Jesus, the Anointed and God's Word, gathered his 12 disciples around the Banquet Table sent down by God from heaven. These 13 represent, in the Muslim interpretation, the apostle. All who seek perfection and self-realization await his coming. He is the symbol of our supreme potential: to live eternally and be absolutely happy. He always comes behind, as he has always been before. The first letter of his holy name is *mim,* the 13th letter in both Hebrew and Arabic alphabets. He is the apostle God sent down His Word to, through the Holy Spirit, the Spirit of Truth. Of all people in this or any world, he is closest to the Anointed.[65]

65 See Muslim, 4:1260–61.

God speaks to us through the apostle and the Anointed. They are witnesses for each other. To free people from the depths entails accepting the call: "O believers, obey God, and obey the apostle and those in authority among you."[66]

Who are these "in authority" amongst us? Are we bound to obey them, rather than God or His apostle? Who can determine our relationship with our highest moment as God's image? Does realization in the Spirit, the uncreated and uncreatable core of our being, depend on anyone? The Recitation gives a clear answer:

> And restrain thyself with those who call upon their Lord at morning and evening, desiring His face and let not thine eyes turn away from them, desiring the adornment of the present life; and obey not him whose heart We have made neglectful of Our remembrance so that he follows his own lust, and his affair has become all excess.[67]

Elsewhere God says: "So mind God, and obey you me, and obey not the commandment of the prodigal who do corruption in the earth, and set not the things aright."[68]

The Word was passed down through the apostle to us. No one since has such authority over it that our dignity depends on them. The power of the Word lies in itself alone and we are fit by our creation and our nature, the Spirit God breathed into us, to distinguish the Word from whatever else may overshadow it. Our relationship to Truth involves return to our core, the heart within us which contains our highest possibility, a turn from every little god towards God in confession of His unity, the Praised's apostolate, and universal return to God. For, the Praised says: "Obedience is required when he enjoins what is good."[69] So too, 'Ali ibn Abi Talib said: "Look not at who speaks, but at what is said."[70]

The theatre of our struggle to realize the self lies between extremes – our attempt to obey God and His apostle and our desire to raise ourselves above the common Word. Those who commit to the first find a mosque at every turn and take part independently of any social order. No human being can rule the universal mosque, just as no goal or social order is placed above our inviolate individual dignity. The second tendency places mosques under the control of those who present themselves as the exclusive heirs of one or more of God's prophets. They make the turn to God, worship, and prostration before Him

---

66 *Qur'an*, 4:59.

67 Ibid., 18:28.

68 Ibid., 26:150–152.

69 Bukhārī, 5:441.

70 Qāri, *al-Asrār al-marfūʿa fī akhbār al-mavḍūʿa*, 1:383.

conditional, presenting themselves as keepers of the gate of our journey back to God. They forbid entrance to the mihrab to any who do not recognise them and demand recognition of their right to mediate our relationship with God and declare what is allowed and what forbidden. Thus, they raise themselves up as masters amongst the faithful, though everything in existence is by nature slave or servant to the true Master.

The Word and the prophet who bears it are perfect and pure. So must their recipients be. Some may simply declare themselves perfect and clean, dissimulating the lie that takes root in their self presentation and action based upon it. They determine the places of congregation for prayer, as though it depended on their approval or veto. Those who accept their authority take others for God, as the Praised was told: "They have taken their rabbis and their monks as lords apart from God, and the Messiah, Mary's son."[71]

Those who follow the first way will find such places of worship unclean and unacceptable, as acceptance of imposed authorities limits our openness to God. Such authorities are idols. God alone is worthy of our service. But the followers of the second party cannot leave the first in peace. They cannot accept a place may exist beyond the control and government of those who raise themselves above the Word and Spirit. God warned the Praised of this:

> And do not drive away those who call upon their Lord at morning and evening, desiring His countenance; nothing of their account falls upon thee, and nothing of thy account falls upon them, that thou shouldst drive them away, and so become one of the evildoers.[72]

During the first Christian millennium, Bosnia provided a stage for debate and conflict over the nature of the Anointed and how to preserve his heritage and how to participate in it. Practically no aspect of these debates on his nature failed to leave its mark on Bosnia. The entire course of the second Christian millennium in Bosnia was marked by the attempt to lead or force her people into corrals and subject them to the exclusive control of priests and monks and by determined resistance to this attempt. Confronted with some consequences of these conflicts between the adherents of different views of God, the Anointed, and the ecclesiastical authorities of the early second millennium, Friar Dominik Mandić wrote:

---

71 *Qur'an*, 9:31.

72 Ibid., 6:52.

> The fact that on the current territory of Bosnia-Herzegovina no new churches were built between the 13th and the middle of the 15th century, while the old churches were in fact abandoned and let fall in ruin, allows of no other interpretation than that we accept that there was a deep seachange in the souls of the faithful of Bosnia during those centuries, involving a different understanding of ecclesiastical buildings and their use than their ancestors, who built those churches, had. This seachange could have come about only if we accept that the Bosnians of the 13th to the 15th century accepted in great numbers the doctrines of the mediaeval neo-Manichees, who rejected and condemned the use of physical church buildings.[73]

The Bosnian *krstjani* accepted neither physical church buildings not priests as a condition for turning to God. This is clear from two Catholic heresiological writings – the *Disputatio inter christianum romanum et paterenum bosnensem*, written in 1250 by Paul of Dalmatia, and the *Symbolum veritatum fidei romanae ecclesiae pro informatione manichaeorum regni Bosnae*, written in 1461 by Cardinal Juan de Torquemada (Uncle of the famous Grand Inquisitor).[74]

One can view this drama of rejection of physical churches in which worship was subject to supervision and control as part of the perennial struggle between the adherents of two world-images. For the first, God and His apostle are the chief judges for us all. For the second, individuals and an apparatus which supervises ritual and the place of worship are conditions of redemption and so of our relationship towards God and the apostle. The members of the Bosnian church did not accept any authority in their country beyond loyalty to God and the Anointed. The Roman Pope first gave the Dominicans and then the Franciscans the authority to investigate and eradicate all Christians in Bosnian lands who did not practice their faith in the prescribed ways.[75]

---

73 Mandić, *Bogomilska crkva bosanskih krstjana*, 113.

74 The Latin originals and Croatian translations of both debates, as well as a discussion of their origin, can be found in Šanjek, *Bosansko-humski krstjani u povjesnim vrelima*, 153–233 and 294–99.

75 See Šanjek, *Bosansko-humski krstjani i katarsko-dualistički pokret u srednjem vijeku*, 81–82 and Lea, *A history of the Inquisition of the middle ages*, 2:298–99. From the 13th century onwards, the Roman Church tasked the Dominican and Franciscan orders with dealing with heretics of various types. Although first directed against heterodox Christians, the preaching, missionary, and inquisitorial activities of the Dominicans and Franciscans were then turned against the Jews and Muslims. A very narrow space did exist within Christianity for the Jews, as guaranteed them by St. Augustine within the framework of his history of salvation. No such space was allowed the Muslims, so that preparation for and

The lords and kings of Bosnia found themselves between two opposing demands – the majority of the people and the nobility supported the Bosnian church, while the Inquisition was supported by the Pope and the King of Hungary.[76] For the Bosnian *krstjani* to cede victory would have meant absolute and cruel eradication, as suffered by the Cathars, Albigensians, Waldensians, and Hussites, and all others who dared to hope for redemption without the inviolable authority of Pope and Church.

From the end of the 14th century, the Bosnian kingdom found itself caught up in world events which were changing the balance of power between eastern and western Christianity. To south, west, and north, Bosnia bordered directly countries whose secular authorities recognised the spiritual power of the Roman Church. To the east, pressure came from the Eastern Christians and the Muslims.

Bosnia held greater and lesser communities of *krstjani* – unrecognised by either canonical Christian confession, the Catholics supported by Rome and her allies or the Orthodox who could rely on the Serbian authorities and their allies, or by the Muslims, increasingly in contact with the Sultan's armies in

---

implementation of their mass baptism and/or expulsion from all areas under Christian government was incorporated into the orders' activities from their inception. See Cohen, *The Friars and the Jews*.

76 Wherever harmonious relations have been established between the ecclesiastical and the worldly authorities, through the presence of the Inquisition, irrevocable damage has been done to the possibility of any form of religious confession different to that prescribed and invigilated by the Roman Church. In the words of Hans Küng, "Aroused by a zeal to eradicate the heretical threats, bishops and popes, kings and emperors prepared what would then fill many of the most terrible pages of church history under the dreaded name of the Inquisition – the systematic legal persecution of heretics by a church court (*inquisitio haereticae pravitatis*), which enjoyed the support not only of the secular power but also of broad groups among the people, who often eagerly looked forward to the execution of heretics. The Inquisition would become an essential characteristic of the Roman Catholic Church. [...] Heretics condemned by the church were to be handed over to secular judgment – for a fiery death or at least to have their tongues cut out. As for the laity, they were not to discuss the faith either privately or publicly, but were to denounce all those who were suspected of heresy. Church authorities alone could decide on matters of faith, and no freedom of thought and speech was allowed. Innocent IV, in particular, a great lawyer pope, went one step further. He authorized the Inquisition also to allow torture by secular authorities in order to extract confessions. The physical torments this caused for the victims of the Inquisition beggars any description." (Küng, *The Catholic Church*, 96) For the origins, methods, and extent of the Inquisition in the lands of Europe, see Lea, op. cit. The activities of the Inquisition in Bosnia and neighbouring countries are given in the chapter on "The Slavic Cathari," 2:290–314.

their progress West. Conversations, however difficult, did take place between these opposed confessions with their different political frameworks, on the unity of God, prophethood, and return, as did various forms of exchange of knowledge and experience.[77] It was the Bosnian king's difficult task to navigate this labyrinth of confessions and orientations.

As with Byzantine appeals for help from the West, the Bosnian kings were required to provide evidence of their obedience to the Pope and facilitate the investigation of non-Catholics. King Tomaš found himself caught between opposing pressures. In the West, he presented himself as a loyal and obedient Catholic, while in country he behaved in accordance with the religious situation. He even approached the Sultan as an obedient ally. According to Friar Dominik Mandić:

> In truth, in the first years after his conversion and of his reign in Bosnia, King Tomaš maintained relations with the leaders of the Bosnian *krstjani* and extended to them the so-called "gift." The Franciscans – on the basis of a response from Pope Gregory XI to a request for guidance by Vicar Bartolo Alvernski in 1373 – considered this unacceptable, leading them to refuse Tomaš the sacraments. In his defence, Tomaš sent an emissary to Pope Eugenius IV in Rome in the autumn of 1445, who defended the King, stressing that he was simply going through the motions of an ancient Bosnian custom, as an external act of respect out of political need, "because the Manichees in his kingdom have multiplied in both number and strength."[78]

The only way for King Tomaš to show unambiguous acceptance and loyalty for the Roman Pope was to support the missionary and inquisitorial work of the Franciscans in converting *krstjani* to Catholicism. He certainly tried to buy the Pope's support by co-operating fully with the Franciscans and persecuting the *krstjani*. This produced a new and, for the West, more acceptable picture in Bosnia, described by Friar Dominik Mandić as follows:

---

77 There were many reports on the conversion of the Bosnian "heretics" and their resistance. The Byzantine patriarch Genadios II Skolarios wrote to the monks at St. Catherine's monastery on Sinai that many of the Bosnian *krstjani* had converted to orthodoxy, including the Herzog Stjepan Vukčić Kosača, the Bosnian *Dux*, but in secret. See Šanjek, *Bosansko-humski krstjani u povjesnim vrelima*, 320–21.

78 Mandić, *Bogomilska crkva bosanskih krstjana*, 409. The quotation is from: Farlati, *Illiricum sacrum*, 4:275.

> We also hear of the building of new churches and the daily multiplication of Catholics in Bosnia in the letter of Pope Nicholas IV to his legate Toma of Hvar dated 9 June, 1452. In it the Pope writes that King Tomaš and the inhabitants of the Bosnian kingdom have raised many churches and regular monasteries and are raising yet more, as the faithful daily multiply.[79]

This picture has two sides – a Catholic and a *Krstjan* one. While further developments would show how these newly Catholicised *krstjani* actually experienced conversion and new churches, there are two accounts that put the Catholic side of the picture – one by Bishop Toma of Hvar, the papal legate to Bosnia, and another by Pope Pius II, a contemporary well acquainted with the circumstances.

Bishop Toma wrote on 19 February, 1451, to John of Capistrano, a leading Franciscan of the day: "I will relate to Your Paternity this truly notable marvel, that in the places held by the heretics, as soon as the Friars appear, the heretics melt away like wax from the face of fire."[80]

---

79 Mandić, *Bogomilska crkva bosanskih krstjana*, 414, citing *Bullarium Franciscanum*, 1:799. It is important to realize that the persecution of the Bosnian *krstjani* in the 14th and 15th centuries is comparable to the persecution of the Jews and Muslims and other religious and nonreligious groups throughout Europe at the same time. A particularly good case for comparison is the treatment of the Jews and Muslims in Spain, on which see Ruderman, *Between Cross and Crescent*, 2:25–28. In all the regions of Spain in which the Muslim authorities were overthrown, Muslims and Jews were faced with a choice: conversion, exile, or death. Many accepted conversion and were required to prove it repeatedly by eating pork, blessing themselves with holy water, participating in ritual, by how they brought up their children, and by taking communion. Even then their behaviour was subject to further investigation and they were condemned for all aspects of their private lives in which there might be any hint that their conversion had been insincere. As a result, even after all these procedures, most were exiled. See, for example, Ehlers, *Between Christians and Moriscos*, and Lea, *The Moriscos of Spain*. Catholic missionaries and inquisitors applied similar methods to the Bosnian *krstjani* and later to Muslims in countries neighbouring Bosnia which came under Christian role. The conversion of Bosnian *krstjani* and Muslims included confessing and accepting the discourses and power of the Church as the only route to salvation in God. Consequently, confession and ritual was a means of their subordination to the church authorities, while their determined refusal to accept this imposition of authority is indicated by the surviving symbolic refusal of "baptism by water" and "unleavened bread" which became part of the Muslim commitment to unmediated relationship with God and love for the Praised.

80 [...] et hoc mirabile dico P(aternitati) V(estre) et valde notandum, quod in locis occupatis per haereticos statim ut Fratres sunt, evanescunt haeretici sicut cera a facie ignis.

Pope Pius II described the consequences of these Franciscan *victories* as follows:

> The Bosnian king, simultaneously excusing himself for the surrender of Smederevo to the Turks, making show of his faith, and as many hold, impelled by greed, forced the Manichees, of whom there were many in his kingdom, to depart the kingdom, leaving their goods behind, if they would not accept the baptism of Christ. Some twelve thousand of them were baptised. Some forty or so, resolute in their error, fled to the Bosnian Duke Stjepan, their fellow in heresy. Three of the heretic leaders, who were influential at the royal court, were brought bound to the Pope by the bishop of Nin. Pius quartered them at monasteries and took care that they be instructed in Christian dogma. Calling them to him frequently, John, the Cardinal of St. Sixtus, taught them and eventually convinced them to renounce their errors and accept the documents of the Roman church, which neither is nor can be deceived, and returned them to the king in reconciliation with the Church. Two of them remained in the faith, but the third, *returning like a dog to his own vomit* (Prv. 26:11; 2 Pt 2:22), escaped during the journey and returned to Stjepan.[81]

Describing the situation in the country after the lauded successes with "Baptism in Christ" and conversion, in late May, 1459, King Tomaš painted the Dominican Niccolo Barbucci a very different image. Barbucci wrote of this

---

Cited in Mandić, *Bogomilska crkva bosanskih krstjana*, 178 n 326, from Wadding, *Annales Minorum seu trium ordinum a. s. Francisco institutorum*, 12:112.

81 Piccolomini, *Commentarii rerum memorabilium, que temporibus suis contigerunt.* Both original and Croatian translation given in Šanjek, *Bosansko-humski krstjani u povjesnim vrelima*, 146–49. See also Mandić, *Bogomilska crkva bosanskih krstjana*, 418–19. On the case of the three Bosnian *krstjani* brought in chains to Rome, see Kamber, "Kardinal Torquemada i tri bosanska bogumila." Because of his cruel persecution of the *krstjani*, King Stjepan Tomaš was called "the dammed" by his contemporaries (Okiç, "Les Kristians (Bogomiles Parfaits) de Bosnie d'aprés des document inédits," 128). The causes and scale of Tomaš' persecution of the Bosnian *krstjani* is subject to very different interpretations in the historiographical tradition. See Ćošković, "Tomašev progon sljedbenika crkve bosanske 1459." Pejo Ćošković (p. 47) concludes, "Tomaš expected the expulsion of the *krstjani* from his lands would remove the last obstacles to him finally being crowned with a royal or kingly crown under the patronage of the universal papal authority." This and earlier persecutions, as well as their support to the baptism of *krstjani*, contributed over a number of centuries to the development of strong negative attitudes amongst *krstjani* towards both the king and the religious advocacy he and his court supported.

discussion to Cardinal Carvajal, the papal legate who had sent him to Bosnia to persuade Tomaš to commit to war against the Turk:

> To my most reverend and excellent lord in Christ the Father and Lord, after humble recommendation. On the 27th day of May, I reached the King of Bosnia, to whom I explained everything your lordship entrusted to me, and he replied that he was willing to do what our most holy Lord and your most Reverend Paternity order, but would require assistance, as he is not strong enough alone to fight with the Turks because of these Manichees, since they prefer the Turks to Christians and are the greater part of the kingdom, that is there are more Manichees, for which reason he has not dared to enlist their help against the Turks without the assistance of Christians.[82]

It is not difficult to see in this royal confession an echo of the situation in Byzantium a decade or so earlier, as summed up at that time in the phrase: "Better the Turkish turban than the Pope's tiara!"[83]

---

82 See Mandić, *Bogomilska crkva bosanskih krstjana*, 416–17. This is a letter from Nicola Barbucci, written 31 May, 1459, in Jajce, cited in: Thallóczy, *Studien zur Geschichte Bosniens und Serbiens im Mittelalter*, 415–16. The claim that the Bosnian *krstjani* preferred the Turks (Muslims) to Christians (Catholics) must be understood in the context of the Franciscan mission in Bosnia and its purpose, which was supported by the Bosnian king with all the means of his temporal authority, namely to convert them from "false Bosnian beliefs" to the "true Roman faith." It may be appropriate here to remind the reader of the similar association of the Cathars and the Muslims in the first half of the 13th century. John Tolan sums up the situation as follows, "Christian chroniclers beyond the Iberian peninsula perceived the armies of Almohad caliph al-Nasir as a menace to all Europe; for Cesarius of Heisterbach and for the anonymous author of the *Annals of Cologne*, the Cathar heretics called on the caliph to aid them against the forces of the Albigensian Crusade; for Matthew Paris, King John of England promised to convert to Islam in return for the caliph's aid against the French" Tolan, *Saracens*, 183, 328n26. The sources cited by Tolan are Salimbene of Adam, *Chronica* (MGH SS 32), 28; Cesarius of Heisterbach, *Annales colonienses* (MGH SS 17), 826; Matthew Paris, *Chronica maior*, ed. H.R. Luard, *Rerum britannicarum medii aevi* no. 57, 7 vols. (London, 1872–83), 2:559–66.

83 This bon mot is attributed to Loukas Notaras, the Great Admiral from 1444 to 1453. See Herrin, *Byzantium*, 299–309. The position taken by the inhabitants of Dubrovnik in a letter sent to King John of Naples in August 1431 is indicative of attitudes towards the Bosnian Patarenes. They complain that they are surrounded by "evil Patarenes, the worst enemies of those who follow the Catholic faith" (Radonić, *Dubrovačka akma i povelje*, 1/1:325–26). There is also clear evidence of the hostile attitude of the Orthodox Church to the Bosnian *krstjani*. Their blasphemy is, alongside the personal boasting of their chiefs, included

While their king was attempting to strengthen his position and supporting a programme of mass conversion of *krstjani*, many sought refuge in the Eastern parts of the country and with their Eastern neighbours. Orthodox priests welcomed them with a call to convert, as John of Capistrano wrote on 4 July, 1455, to Pope Calixtus III:

> Many of these Bosnian heretics, who had followed the faith of the Patarenes, on hearing the word of God, converted to the Roman faith, but were prevented from so reconciling by the Metropolitan of the Rascians [Serbians], among others; many of them dying outside the faith, preferring to do so than to take the faith of the Rascians.[84]

That the kingdom of God was dearer to the Bosnian *krstjani* than an earthly one is clear from their graves.[85] They considered physical churches a threat to their religion, citing the first Christians:

---

in the church canons. See Mošin, "Rukopis Pljevaljskog sinodika pravoslavlja." The Byzantine Orthodox attitude to Catholics and "Turks," on the one hand, and Dubrovnik Catholic views of Bosnian Patarenes, on the other, beg the question: how did the Bosnian *krstjani* regard the one and the other? The second gloss from the Srećković Gospels provides some grounds for answering this question, as it compares the Franciscan missionaries in Bosnia with sorcerers, while using the term "canons" for the regular Catholic clergy (Speranskij, "Ein Bosnisches Evangelium in der Handscrifftensamlung Srećković's," 176; Ćirković, "Glose Srećkovićevog jevanđelja i učenje bosanske crkve," 214–15; Ćošković, *Crkva Bosanska u XV. stoljeću*, 36). The Bosnian *krstjan* attitude toward the Orthodox church is suggested by the marginal notes on the Bosnian Vrutok Gospels. In a note to the text of *Matthew* (9:9–13) an unknown Bosnian *krstjanin* wrote: "the toll booth, the place where the Patriarch raises himself up by means of silver and gold." Kuna, *Srednjovjekovna bosanska književnost*, 110.

84 *Acta Bosnae*, 225. See Mandić, *Bogumilska crkva bosanskih krstjana*, 416.

85 The name "krstjani" is used for members of the Bosnian church, which was consistently considered in contemporary Catholic and Orthodox sources to be heretical. Its members, however, considered the church to be "the true apostolic faith." On the organisation and political role of the Bosnian church, see Ćošković, *Crkva bosanska u XV. stoljeću*. The Bosnian church extended over much the same territory as that on which the characteristic mediaeval tombstones or *stećci* are or were to be found. Under the ideological pressures of the modern age, there have been attempts to use certain exceptions regarding the religious affiliation of the dead found under certain *stećci*, as grounds for drawing general conclusions regarding the possibility that they may not in fact be related to the Bosnian church.

> Howbeit the most High dwelleth not in temples made with hands; as saith the prophet. "Heaven is my throne, and earth is my footstool: what house will ye build me?" saith the Lord: or "what is the place of my rest? Hath not my hand made all these things?"[86]

Whatever our path to God, whether with organised ritual and priests or without, whether any place in the world may serve for worship or just those decreed by a recognised or imposed authority, none of our achievements suffice to dispense with dependence on God. No matter the degree to which we submit the forces of the material world to ourselves, no matter how deep or wide we extend our sway, we can never become ruler or governor of the Spirit. This is because it is His will that there be many paths to God.

This deals with the possibility that redemption could depend on anything but God. We are fit for redemption because our self is in our Master's image and we experience the constant pressure of the perfect example He speaks through. God's signs lie on the horizons before us, turned in eternal reference to Him as Signified. The apostle is amongst them and in them as their perfect fulfilment and the most beautiful condition. God asks us through the Praised: "How can you conceal, seeing you have God's signs recited to you, and His apostle among you?"[87]

We are between the lowest and the best. At any given point, there is always something of darkness and the bitterness of the depth in us, as well as of light and the sweetness of sublimity. Our path back up is an axis that links two extremes, one in the depth and darkness, the other on high and in the light. Just as nothing was created without truth, so no darkness and no bitterness remains untouched by light and sweetness. Faithfulness is loyalty to that indestructible presence of the truth and the approach towards it, as the irresistibly attractive goal that unites sweetness and light.

Perfecting our selves for ascent confirms us in God's full and unwavering faithfulness to us. God is entirely Faithful, as He swore to us:

---

86 *Acts of the Apostles*, 7:48–50. See also, 17:24–31. In 1461, in his "Exposition of the truths of the faith of the Roman Catholic Church for the information of the Manichees of the Kingdom of Bosnia," Torquemada wrote criticizing the beliefs and behaviour of the Bosnian *krstjani* with regard to the building of churches: "It is most suitable to build material churches and temples for God" (Šanjek, *Bosansko-humski krstjani u povjesnim vrelima*, 297). It is worth noting that this list of errors was compiled by Torquemada as part of the documentation for the *Abjuratio trium bosnesium* (MS Vat. Lat. 976). The document was prepared in 1461 as a basis and framework for the ritual denunciation of their "false faith" by the three Bosniaks in St. Peter's in Rome.

87 *Qur'an*, 3:101.

> By the fig and the olive and Mount Sinin and this land faithful! We indeed created Man in the fairest stature, then We restored him the lowest of the low – save those who have faith, and do righteous deeds; they shall have wage unfailing.[88]

Self-fulfilment, which is to attain "a wage unfailing," is to transcend the duality God refers to as "the fig and the olive" and "Mount Sinin and this land faithful." The symbols of the fig and Mount Sinin correspond to our creation "in the fairest stature" and "most beautiful uprightness." That we are "the lowest of the low" is symbolised by the olive and the land faithful.

The fig is perhaps the only fruit which is edible and sweet in its entirety and so represents the perfection of our original and final condition. The olive is brimful of bitterness and inedible, but precious. Its glistening oil is to be found in its depth, beyond the inedible bitterness.

Mount Sinin symbolises Unity, from which all things begin and to which they return. The peak is a symbol of bringing together what has been sundered and so the goal of all who love. Loving that act of being brought together, they love each other. Moving towards the peak, they move towards each other. But real return is to God.

"This land faithful" is in a desert valley without fruit. It is a symbol of bitterness and inedibility, darkness and the depth, separation and remoteness. The connection with edibility and sweetness, light and mercy, and the most beautiful uprightness has not been severed, however. It has not, because whatever our condition or situation, we always retain the potential to believe and to do right. Belief or faith is our connection with God the Faithful. What is good and beautiful appears to us as the presence of God in everything of His creation. This is the presence of Truth, attraction to which is love for the Truth. The union of truth and love is faith.

As the ways to the one God are many, whichever we are on, we remain connected with the centre where they meet, as with the lowest depth. The depth repels us, while the height attracts irresistibly. Turning towards that centre, we discover and realize ourselves in the confession of no self but the Self. Wherever we may be, we cannot destroy our uncreated and uncreatable core. Our humanity is in constant re-formation around this core. We relate to God in different ways at different times. In each of these mutable positions, we find aspects of the preceding condition, which continue to relate it to the centre.

88 Ibid., 95:1–6.

Water is the symbol of divine mercy. Everything alive is formed from it.[89] The Holy Spirit is above it.[90] It is the keeper of life and recalls the presence of the Spirit above itself. Air is another sign of the Spirit. Just as water and air are signs of ascent from matter to Spirit, so human self-fulfilment is not possible without Spirit, which cannot be reduced by anyone or anything.

Cleansing with water symbolises cleansing with the Spirit. We can govern water, to some degree, but not Spirit. Whether we admit it or not, Spirit remains obedient to the Creator alone. Given this symbolic meaning of water, cleansing or anointment with water has been adopted as the ritual expression of the priest and the apparatus' role as mediators in the drama of human salvation. The Bosnian *krstjani* were condemned for refusing anointment by water. According to contemporary sources, they did not recognise it, considering it useless and without substance. Salvation came only from "baptism by the book,"[91] which would seem to be analogous in its mode of efficacy to the Cathar ritual of "consolation" (*consolamentem*).[92]

Anointment by water was fully transformed in the Muslim holy tradition. As a ritual it could not be carried out on just anyone. It was used to prepare an individual for ascent through prayer, immediate relationship with God possible always and everywhere:

---

89 See *Qur'an*, 21:30.

90 See *Genesis*, 1:2.

91 "Dialogus inter christianum romanum et patarenum bosnensem" in Šanjek, *Bosansko-humski krstjani u povjesnim vrelima*, 109–110 and idem, *Bosansko-humski krstjani i katarsko-dualistički pokret u srednjem vijeku*, 88. Refuting the Bosnian *krstjan* views on baptism by water, Jean de Torquemada wrote in 1461 in his "Exposition of the truths of the faith of the Roman Catholic Church for the information of the Manichees of the Kingdom of Bosnia" (28), the right of baptism is accorded by water and accompanied by invocation of the holy and indivisible Trinity; (29) the baptism instituted by Christ must be carried out by water; (30) no baptism but Christ's, received in truth and willingly, leads to salvation. Šanjek, *Bosansko-humski krstjani u povjesnim vrelima*, 297.

92 Šanjek, *Bosansko-humski krstjani i katarsko-dualistički pokret u srednjem vijeku*, 88. The question of baptism by water or the book is to be found in all the available arraignments of the "errors" of the Bosnian *krstjani* dating from the 13th through the 15th centuries. It is treated as a central issue in two writings which were used as missionary and inquisitorial manuals over a period of more than two centuries, namely the "Dialogus inter christianum romanum et patarenum bosnensem" (original and translation in Šanjek, *Bosansko-humski krstjani u povjesnim vrelima*, 153–233) and "An exposition of the truths of the faith of the Roman Catholic Church for the information of the Manichees of the Kingdom of Bosnia," ibid., 294–99.

> O believers, when you stand up to pray wash your faces and your hands up to the elbows, and wipe your heads and your feet up to the ankles. If you are defiled, purify yourselves; but if you are sick or on journey, or if any of you comes from the privy, or you have touched women, and you can find no water, then have recourse to wholesome dust and wipe your faces and your hands with it. God does not desire to make any impediment for you; but He desires to purify you, and that He may complete His blessing upon you; haply you will be thankful.[93]

Through this command, God enjoins on us all an unmediated relationship with water as a form of relationship with Him. In this way, we prepare for the transformation of the chosen spot into a mosque, a place of self-abnegation in our turn to God. This turn expresses our expectation of anointment: "The baptism of God; and who is there that baptizes fairer than God? Him we are serving."[94]

As already discussed, there is a custom in Bosnia that the bride, when brought to her husband's house, should knock over a ewer of water placed just behind the courtyard gates. This symbolises the rejection of all anointment or baptism by water. The Bosnian *krstjani* were condemned for failing to use christening by water. Instead, they came up with christening by the Book: "When a group of Bosnian Church elders believed that a candidate was firm in the faith, they allowed him a 'spiritual christening', which the Bosnian *krstjani* called 'christening by the book'[95] probably because a copy of the gospels was placed on the head of the candidate during the act."[96]

This custom of baptism by the Book has survived among Bosnian Muslims to this day. After the bride tips over the water ewer, a Qur'an is placed on her head with a blessing in confirmation of the covenant between her and her descendants with God, Who sent down the Book with the Holy Spirit to the apostle as our best example. God told us through him: "Has not the compact of the Book been taken touching them, that they should say concerning God nothing but the truth?"[97]

---

93 *Qur'an*, 5:6.

94 Ibid., 2:138.

95 On the rejection of baptism by water and on baptism by the book, see "Dialogus inter christianum romanum et patarenum bosnensem" in Šanjek, *Bosansko-humski krstjani u povjesnim vrelima*, 153–233.

96 Šanjek, *Bosansko-humski krstjani i katarsko-dualistički pokret u srednjem vijeku*, 88.

97 *Qur'an*, 7:169.

Ramadan is a holy month for Muslims. It was when God sent down the Recitation to the Praised by the Spirit. God summons all able adults to fast from dawn to dusk. When dusk comes, He calls them to His table for communion and they give Him thanks for the fast and eat in His name.

Throughout Bosnia, it is practically unthinkable to break the fast without a *somun*, a round loaf made from leavened dough. This custom is inseparable from Ramadan itself in Bosnia. Whence comes this custom of eating somun as part of the communal Ramadan repast?

The Bosnian *krstjani* generally followed the ritual of the Eastern Church.[98] The attempts of the Bishop of Rome to raise himself above the others and be judge of what is allowed and what forbidden were reflected in the acceptance or imposition of unleavened bread, the *asomun*, as the host in the Eucharist.[99] Missionaries and inquisitors imposed baptism by water and communion with unleavened bread on the *krstjani* to confirm their apostasy and their submission to those who knew what was allowed and what forbidden. The Bosnian *krstjani* carried over their loyalty to the *somun*, as the symbol of the life the Anointed confirms in all things, into their new spiritual home, into their act of witness of the Praised as a mercy to the worlds and closest of all to Mary's son.

---

98 See Ćirković, "Dualistička heterodoksija u ulozi zemaljske crkve: Bosanska crkva," 9. See also Jurić-Kappel, "Bosanske apokalipse u svome (južno) slavenskom kontekstu."

99 On the dispute between Eastern and Western Christians over the *somun* as "leavened bread" (Greek. *zymos*) and the *asomun* as "unleavened bread" (Greek. *azymes*), see Herrin, *Byzantium*, 299–309.

Addendum

Ramadan and the two great feast days – the first after the completion of the fast and the second after the pilgrimage and sacrifice – are determined by the lunar calendar, as are the five blessed nights. The most important is the Night of Power (*laylat al-qadr*), which is said in the Recitation to be worth more than 1000 months.[1] Its value is due to the sending down of the Book as Light. God made an oath by the Book and His having sent it down: "By the clear Book! We have sent it down in a blessed night."[2]

It is usual to mark a further four nights – the night of creation (*al-barā'a*), the night of conception (*al-ragha'ib*), the night of ascension (*al-mi'rāj*), and the night of birth (*al-mawlid*). Like the Night of Power, they are bound up with the person of the Praised, the shining lamp and primordial light. This is why creation is illuminated by them. His conception and ascension are two signs of the presence of Light in creation as a whole, from the depth to the height. Four of the nights – of power, creation, conception, and birth – are reception of Light sent down into the darkness of existence. The fifth, the night of ascension, signifies return from darkness to the Light and self-realization in the fullness of Unity. God said of it: "Glory be to Him, who carried His servant by night from the Inviolable Mosque to the Further Mosque."[3]

Bosnian Muslims celebrate two other days whose dates are determined by the solar calendar. These are Jurjevdan and Ilindan. Jurje, Đurđe, Đorđe or Đurđis are forms of the name received into English as George and Christians know Jurjevdan as St. George's Day.[4] George is the hero of loyalty to Jesus, the son of Mary, the heir and defender of the rights to "the true apostolic faith." No temptation or test could turn him from the confession of nothing living but the Living. Ilias, Elias or Elijah was God's prophet raised up from the earth to descend again as a witness of the Praised. Bosnian Muslims commemorate him at gatherings held on his day, which they call both Elijah's day (Ilindan) and 'Ali's day (Aliđun).

1 See *Qur'an*, 97:3.

2 *Qur'an*, 44:2–3.

3 Ibid., 17:1.

4 Ilindan or Elijah's day was celebrated from earliest times at Mile (Arnautovići), the symbolic focal point of Bosnian integrity. According to tradition, this was done in the presence of the Bosnian king. See Filipović, *Visočka nahija*, 531.

 | DOI 10.1163/9789004279407_121

The Bosnian *krstjani* opposed the erection or maintenance of churches, as the rituals conducted in them would depend on authority outside their community. When their king and some of his court made obeisance to the Pope of Rome, symbolised by the king's coronation with a crown received from a papal ambassador, the Bosnian *krstjani,* in secret, saw in this a threat to their continued resistance to subordination to any suzerain not exemplary in obedience to God and His apostle. In the Europe of that time, wherever an alliance existed between the ecclesiastical and the temporal powers, it excluded witness to redemption without accepting human authority. Those who could not accept this faced force, persecution, or burning. There were no exceptions anywhere in Western Europe.

These were the circumstances under which inquisitorial investigations and the persecution of *krstjani* began in Bosnia. Many fled to regions outside the reach of the royal and inquisitorial authorities. When these authorities were checked by a more powerful one and the choice of paths towards God ceased to depend on king or bishop, many preferred the possibility of Orthodox monasteries, Catholic churches, synagogues and mosques all coexisting as places of congregation for different ways of reciting God's names. Many restored damaged and built new churches and established in them the ritual of their choice, as they also built new synagogues and mosques.

Thus, Bosnia became a country of great promise for the future. No one could be persecuted for being Muslim, Christian, or Jew of one sort or another. This was guaranteed by no agreement between the participants in difference, but by God: "To every one of you We have appointed a right way and open road. If God had willed, He would have made you one nation; but that He may try you in what has come to you. So be you forward in good works; unto God shall you return, all together; and He will tell you of that whereon you were at variance."[5]

The inviolability of the monasteries, churches, synagogues and mosques is guaranteed by God, as symbols and places in which human beings may come together to recite His names. Whenever this guarantee is denied or violated, the fault lies with us. How can a Muslim call on God or His apostle to justify the imposition of what is forbidden and what permitted, without granting others the same right to impose on him or her.

The Praised said: "He who amongst you sees something abominable should modify it with the help of his hand; and if he has not strength enough to do it, then he should do it with his tongue; and if he has not strength enough to do

5 *Qur'an,* 5:48.

it, then he should from his heart, and that is the least of faith."[6] None can deny this command without setting their face against God's and His apostle's. Muslims are expected to defend this principle both from themselves and others.

The construction of mosques in Bosnia is bound up with their builders' attitudes towards monasteries, churches, and synagogues. Any place is a potential mosque and so a symbol of our right to different paths towards God. Mosques may be recognised and built in the valleys and on the slopes of hills, on riverbanks and on heights, in caves and in forests. Every house is also a mosque. Worshipping God turns any place, and every house, into a mosque. This way of looking at the world and every place within it is informed by God's call to worship at the set times in the set ways, facing the house in the holy Valley of Becca.

Through our worship of God, we make every place a mosque. This is all that is required for a place to become a congregational mosque. Where no mosque exists, there is no congregation. Any house may become a mosque, even a congregational one. No individual or group can relativize this. The mosque's two symbols, the minaret and the mihrab, remind us of God's unity and of following the Praised as our most sublime potential, and of return to unity.

Our worshipful turn towards one earthly focus connects all worshippers on an axis that binds heaven and earth. The earthly focus is just a sign of unity as the principle of all existence. It is at the bottom of the Valley. Connecting with it, we confess that everything in existence has been sent down from unity to return on the upright path to the original principle.

Bosnian mosques have sloping roofs with four sides or, sometimes, domes, and recall the basic nature of the self and the worshipper's "priestly" role. Constructed of timber, earth and stone, their forms may differ, but always include certain elements which make them unmistakably recognisable. Their size and location generally reflect their builders' consciousness of human poverty in the face of God and of the transience of this world. Most Bosnian mosques are simple, even if a few examples do express their builders' intention to promote and preserve their authority rather than God's.

Just as Bosnia's society of difference had, through confusion, suffering, and persecution, been stripped of its essential functions and its people's beliefs judged unacceptable except as affirmed by the Church's inquisitorial courts, a major change took place. The entire country opened up to the right of the individual to belong to any community of the Book, a right that could then be enjoyed only in those areas of the world where the principle of the mosque

6 Muslim, 1:33.

had been raised up above every other affiliation. The members of the different communities were called to bear witness in justice:

> O believers, be you securers of justice, witnesses for God, even though it be against yourselves, or your parents and kinsmen, whether the man be rich or poor; God stands closest to either. Then follow not caprice, so as to swerve; for if you twist or turn, God is aware of the things you do.[7]

Just as humankind is divided into families, tribes, and peoples, so that individuals and groups indicate their affiliation in different ways, so Bosnia became a point at which the possibilities were brought together and epitomised. Differences of affiliation were signified by the presence of Orthodox *and* Catholic monasteries and churches *and* synagogues *and* mosques. The new community which grew up in this confusion and suffering became a key witness to the inviolability of difference.

Whenever one confession from Bosnia or the surrounding area was adopted as exclusive and some could no longer defend themselves from others, a ruination of monasteries, churches, synagogues and mosques would follow. Respect for the principle of "whose realm, his religion" (*cuius regio eius religio*) warranted the persecution of Muslims and destruction of mosques. Muslims once lived throughout the territory of contemporary Bosnia and beyond, but they and their mosques disappeared without exception as soon as an authority that called itself Christian was established. The mosques were torn down or turned into churches. Such a course of events overtook many places and areas within Bosnia, as a rule once Muslims could no longer resist their persecutors and destroyers.

Some Bosnian mosques are presented in the pictures that follow the next section, the *Post scriptum*.[8] For Muslims, they are symbols of Bosnian

---

7 *Qur'an*, 4:135.

8 All mosques located to the west or north of the current borders of Bosnia were destroyed in the 17th and 18th centuries. Many were turned into churches. On this destruction, see Zlatović, *Franovci države Presvetoga Otkupitelja i hrvatski puk u Dalmaciji*. On the destruction of the mosques in Serbia, see Kanic, *Srbija, zemlja i stanovništvo*. On the mosques of Montenegro, see Agović, *Džamije u Crnoj Gori*. Information regarding the mosques presented in some of the images in the following sections can be found in: Figure 3.4 The Kotezi Mosque (Hasandedić, *Muslimanska baština u Istočnoj Hercegovini*, 285–87); Figure 3.5 The Bijeljani Mosque (Ibid., 74–76); Figure 3.6 The Kazanci Mosque (Ibid., 201–207); Figure 3.7 Fatima's Mosque (Idem, *Spomenici kulture turskog doba u Mostaru*, 48–49); Figure 3.8 The Imperial Mosque at Foča (Mujezinović, *Islamska epigrafika Bosne i Hercegovine*, 2:26–29); Figure 3.9 The Gorani Mosque (Hasandedić, "Hadži Šahmanova džamija u Goranima," 346–0); Figure 3.10 The Umoljani Mosque (Aljović "Odrazi odanosti islamu vjernika u

unity-in-difference. For the heirs to the old exclusions, they symbolize "discontinuity." While Muslims have renewed the torn-down mosques and built new ones to vouchsafe for their continued existence, today in Bosnia and the surrounding region there are more ruined than whole mosques.[9] This fact is generally passed over. Muslims are expected to pay it no heed. When they do, they are criticised, under the rule of the aforementioned distorted image of "the history of discontinuity." Nothing in their suffering can ever provide them sufficient reason, however, to desert God's call to the paths of Peace, as is justly testified:

> People of the Book, now there has come to you Our apostle, making clear to you many things you have been concealing of the Book, and effacing many things. There has come to you from God a light, and a Book Manifest whereby God guides whosoever follows His good pleasure in the ways of peace, and brings them forth from the shadows into the light by His leave; and He guides them to a upright path.[10]

Umoljanima," 585–86); Figure 3.11 The Tekke Mosque at Rogatica (Mujezinović, *Islamska epigrafika Bosne i Hercegovine*, 2:93–95); Figure 3.12 The Balaguša Mosque in Livno (Ibid., 3:96–98); Figure 3.13 The Opener's Mosque (Ćulum, unpublished manuscript on the Opener's Mosque in Kraljeva Sutjeska. The manuscript is kept at the mosque); Figure 3.14 The Karići Mosque (Bećirbegović, *Džamije sa drvenom munarom u Bosni i Hercegovini*, 72–74); Figure 3.15 The Fethija Mosque in Jajce (Kreševljaković, "Stari bosanski gradovi," 24); Figure 3.16 The Sokol Mosque (Šaković, "Stara džamija u Sokolu," 75–78); Figure 3.17 The Ferry Mosque (Hudović, *Zvornik*, 94–96); Figure 3.18 Džindić Mosque (Bećirbegović, *Džamije sa drvenom munarom u Bosni i Herceovini*, 104–105); Figure 3.19 The White Mosque (Mujezinović, *Islamska epigrafika Bosne i Hercegovine*, 2:161–63); Figure 3.20 The Arnaudija (Ibid., 2:211–14); Figure 3.21 The Fethija in Bihać (Ibid., 3:60–65); Figure 3.22 The Bužim Mosque (Ibid., 3:86–88).

9 For more on the destruction of the mosques in Bosnia, see Hadžimuhamedović, "Rušenje i građenje mesdžida u Bosni."

10 *Qur'an*, 5:15–16. Bosnian Muslims, like all other peoples, face the question: What is it that determines their continued existence as a unit over their history? One answer is – witness to the unity of God, the apostolate of the Praised, and their country of Bosnia. In saying that these three factors determine them, one must bear in mind that each individual and each generation may relate to these factors in very different ways, including acceptance and affirmation or rejection and denial. The apostolate of the Praised is originally associated with Arabic. This is the "mother tongue" of just one people. If, however, this is an apostolic mission to all people, as Muslims testify, then the variety of mother tongues cannot entail any advantage for the Arabs above the other peoples of the world. We may therefore reformulate the key issue about being a Bosnian Muslim as follows: How to discover and maintain the fullness of the Praised's apostolate in their own language, in a way that allows each individual or group their dignity throughout their history, in their own language and in their own country, with its unique conditions, without being excluded from ontological integrity?

Had God not driven back people, some by the means of others, the earth had surely corrupted; but God is bounteous unto all beings.[11]

O mankind, We have created you male and female, and appointed you races and tribes, that you may know one another. Surely the noblest among you in the sight of God is the most mindful of you. God is All-knowing, All-aware.[12]

---

11 *Qur'an*, 2:251.

12 Ibid., 49:13.

Post Scriptum: Worshipful Understanding

From the perspective of every sacred tradition, the world was created as a perfect entity. As a whole it and everything in it is connected to its principle through absolute or perfect being-at-peace. Motion and change, dismantling and reassembly, are just the manifestation of the principle's constant presence. According to the Recitation, which is God's Word sent down into the heart of the Praised, He created everything with truth.[1] This creation by, in and with truth has the Word as principle. "When he decrees a thing, He does but say to it 'Be,' and it is."[2]

Multiplicity manifests the One, manifestation that is never independent of its principle as One and so never not-One. We are the only exception, the only beings connected to God through faith: the All-faithful allows the faithful belief. We are creatures, but free of will. Whence then comes evil into the world and ourselves? Has this question any answer outside our thinking and illusions?

All existence is reflected in the self, consciousness and knowledge. Since our mind and our knowledge are finite, thinking offers us the mere appearance of the beautiful and good, standing us against our perfect principle. To be free of appearance, we must see what appears to us as stillness in movement, and vice versa. The beauties of the world are merely a reminder of what transcends all things. Sensate experiences are but signs of the supra-experiential world.

Unable to discover any defect in ourselves or existence, we try to imagine one, as only in relation to a hypothetical defect can our free will rationally motivate our powers with the intention of putting the world and ourselves to rights. Our quest for imperfections is the shadow of our free will, a state in which we seem sufficient to ourselves, with reason alone a reliable guide and the material world an inexhaustible source of all we need.

This is the view of perfect openness we see from our path of natural discovery. This path, like all we do on it in a constant state of confusion and fatigue, is never the same as the view from the absolute. God remarks the difference between these two perspectives:

> Blessed be He in whose hand is the Kingdom – He is powerful over everything – who created death and life, that He might try you which of you is fairest in works; and He is the All-mighty, the All-forgiving – who

1 See *Qur'an*, 46:3.

2 *Qur'an*, 3:47.

 | DOI 10.1163/9789004279407_122

> created seven heavens one upon another. Thou seest not in the creation of the All-merciful any imperfection. Return thy gaze; seest thou any fissure? Then return thy gaze again, and again, and thy gaze comes back to thee, dazzled, aweary. And We adorned the lower heaven with lamps, and made them things to stone Satans; and We have prepared for them the chastisement of the Blaze.[3]

The kingdom is in His hand, He its reason and purpose, absolute free will and absolute power. Placing everything between life and death, in which life is His and death a manner of His manifestation, is duality that reveals the One. Duality cannot act with free will beyond the opposites of beauty and ugliness. All existence is manifestation of the Beautiful as possessor of the names, which are beautiful in their reality. When we realize them from duality, in the will to comply absolutely with His will, the act cannot but be beautiful.

Flawless perfection is reflected in human language. Everything in the outer horizons and everything in sensate cognition that becomes part of human experience has its reflection or image in language. The re-creation or reflection of everything occurs there, as all existence is concentrated in each human individual. Our beginnings seem insignificant, for it is hard to see in a drop of semen the full openness and concentration of all names, yet in that very droplet all the world is reflected.

There is nothing in the horizons that is not discovered through its name as already present in the self. There is a name or word for every known thing. These names and words cannot be without universal connectedness, however, just as nothing has either place or time without being implicated in the whole. The single word of the Creator's will links all of existence and everything in it.

The created world manifests its creator's will, and the will of the One is made manifest through the most beautiful names. Our free will derives from His. His and our wills may be in harmony or opposed. God's will is expressed at every instant as perfect. When our will is identical to His, it is manifest as the finest deeds, for there is nothing in it contrary to perfect creation. In their perfect harmony, we discover ourselves in the reason for our creation, in all the most beautiful names as the One made manifest. We may find ourselves in this way in every "now," but always differently.

When our will is opposed to His, it directly or indirectly supposes some defect in creation and so in the Creator's will, to be eliminated by our action. Our actions aim at defects. The self defines itself by what makes it incomplete, by imperfection. Everything between the active self and what it acts on

---

3 *Qur'an*, 67:1–5.

is obscured by imperfection, for that is their nature. This obscurity must be eliminated by action, or the world seems horrifyingly, intolerably empty.

In our original creation, we are at peace with absolute Peace. We must not transgress the limits imposed on us by the order of being-at-peace with Peace, for our will is limited. Time and space are ordained for it, as are the powers in and with which it manifests itself. It is with this limited will that we are fated to reach the limits of our lowest and our highest potential, to sink from the height to the depths and return on the same path in discovery of ourselves. In the depths, we mourn the lost sublime height and yearn for return. In this we differ from our first forebear, who experienced the bliss of the Garden. Grief for what we have lost and the desire to find it define our firstness and lastness.

To say that our power is limited is to say that our actions, always based on little knowledge, carry the risk of transgression and violence. The world was created in the full knowledge and perfect mercy of the Creator, as He says in the Recitation.[4] There are no imperfections in the world, once its absolute submission to the Creator, All-aware, All-knowing and All-merciful, is acknowledged. Creation is summed up in us, but not as absolute power or unlimited will. We know little, but can bear infinite love for what we know as real. Loving the known draws us nearer to what we love, so we grow in knowledge – we increasingly know what we love and increasing love what we know.

We know the names of all things and differ from the angels. Our will to relate to God through confidence, even with only limited knowledge and limited power, is our potential to be His perfect manifestation. With and through the names, all existence is revealed in us from our beginnings and reception of the Word of creative command to our return and convergence in that same Word.

Both the world, as the outer horizon of our presence, and the constantly changing self are signs of the One, a complete, inexhaustible discourse that is never twice the same. Its incessant nature has no existence apart from the speaker, however it may seem to the listener. Discourse, and its elements, may appear a self-sufficient, closed system to the listener, but then the signs take on the aspect of gods, made manifest by knowing of them.

Insofar as God uses the perfection of His creation to test our potential to act in the best way, but we persist in seeking imperfections within the horizons of that creation, knowledge and change are linked. Nothing in existence is beyond motion and change. This holds good for our knowledge, however detached from the world flux and seemingly independent, a world unto itself.

There cannot be two absolute independences. What seems independent to us is in conflict with reality. God commanded us: "And walk not in the earth

---

4 See *Qur'an*, 6:80 and 7:156.

exultantly; certainly thou wilt never tear the earth open, nor attain the mountains in height."[5] While of the humble, He said: "The servants of the All-merciful are those who walk in the earth modestly and who, when the ignorant address them, say, 'Peace;' who pass the night prostrate to their Lord and standing."[6]

Herein lies the crucial difference between our presence posited as independent of its principle and as that in which the principle is ever-present with its life, will, power, knowledge, speech, listening and seeing. In the former, our will is incomplete, established in an incomplete world. In the latter, His and our will are both perfect, for God's will is the principle of ours.

The first postulate necessarily entails acting in an incomplete world, whose shortcomings cannot be overcome or eliminated. Completing the world assumes three possibilities: first, that the world around us, nature, is incomplete, but we who aim to put it to rights are complete; or, that the world is complete and perfect, but we are not; or thirdly, that neither the world nor we are complete.

Do not all the revolutionary movements of the modern age take as their starting-point the hypothesis that neither the world nor we are perfect? This assumption of incompleteness forms part of every modern world-view. The essential postulate is that we, independent knowers and reshapers of the world, have all we need to overcome the resistance of incompleteness and, at some future time, in a reality beyond our "now," attain the perfect goal, in which, irrevocably mortal, we shall never be, passing over in silence the requirement that the builders of that perfect future contain a void.

In the traditional world-view, the world is both complete and perfect and so are we. There are defects or imperfections in neither. Ignorance and suffering, evil and violence remain within the framework of faith as our relationship with God. We accepted His offer of confidence, when nothing else would. But we are not alone, for the faithful always have the All-faithful before them, not only in the outside world, but at the centre of the self. Nothing in existence is real but the All-faithful. Wherever we turn, His face is before us, as close to us as our jugular vein. There is no moment, no place from which He is absent. Absence is a condition of the self of limited will, in its incessant freedom – of turning to or from itself.

As the final creation, we are all things, their sum, and more: we manifest ourselves in upright standing. In this lies our dignity, our being in His image. God is never not-God and our willing prostration affirms the gift of standing upright before the Upright. Authorized by the will, we take part in the universal

5 *Qur'an*, 17:37.

6 Ibid., 25:63–64.

order that has adjusted its will to His. All existence is fully at peace in God, as He told the Praised: "None is there in the heavens and earth but he comes to the All-merciful as a servant."[7] Nothing remains the same for two moments. Motion and change confirm service as relationship to Peace, as He says: "In Him has found peace whoso is in the heavens and the earth."[8]

The heavens and the earth and all that lies between are manifest in service, being-at-peace and prostration. They testify to and acknowledge their utter baseness compared to their principle, their utter poverty compared to Him. In their witness, things return to the One and stand before Him, simultaneously annihilating themselves and testifying that in the death of their death is the acknowledgement of the Living. The simultaneity of abasement and standing erect, of death and life is manifest as descent and ascent, departure and return, dying and living again. Existence testifies to its manifestation of One Who is always "upon some labour."[9]

To God belong the most beautiful names. He is incessantly upon some labour, showing His signs in the worlds and in us until His truth is fully clear to us.[10] Our knowledge of what manifests itself to the Creator cannot depend on our unreal world. If we insist otherwise, then the signs on the horizons and the books sent down are obscured, deflecting the clarity of perfect creation out of the Creator's absolute will. Wherever and whenever we are, we are between the lowest of the low and the ultimate height, the gloomy depths and the illumined height, ignorance and knowledge, suffering and mercy. To become aware of this is to stand upright before the Upright.

Once conscious of standing upright, we confirm it by prostration, acknowledging that we have nothing of our own, that only as servants may we receive the Lord's will. The self is thus revealed in the distinction between "inciting to evil" and "being-at-peace," extremes of its being, one tending towards nullity and the depths, the other towards plenitude and fairest uprightness.

The symbol of the extreme depth is the Inviolable Mosque on the desert valley floor, that of fairest uprightness is the Further Mosque on the mount in the land of milk and honey. The first place of self-abnegation corresponds to our earthly state, the second to the heavens, our first and final home.

The Praised is expected as the light-giving lamp and best example from the floor of that valley, where he was sent down to lead our return and ascent. In the heavens he corresponds to the original maternal self, the maternal Book

---

7 Ibid., 19:93.

8 Ibid., 3:83.

9 See *Qur'an*, 55:29.

10 Ibid., 41:53.

that symbolizes the house inhabited of which God says: "By the Mount and a Book inscribed in a parchment unrolled, by the house inhabited and the roof uplifted and the sea swarming, surely thy Lord's chastisement is about to fall; there is none to avert it."[11]

The two houses, the inviolable and the further, signs of our earthly and heavenly abodes, mark the *axis mundi* or upright path. Standing upright we pass from the lowest of the low to the sublime height, from poverty to wealth, ignorance to knowledge. We stand before the Upright, confirmed in remembrance and worship, alms-giving and fasting, praising and relating, pilgrimage and standing firm. Feeling and thought take on flesh in these rituals, and the order of descent, God-world-Word, appears to the worshipper as an ascending world-Word-God order.

Differentiation is in constant flux, constant process of measurement. There is nothing in the self or world that is not in motion. Peace manifests its presence at every moment. Realization of the self means attuning the centre to these changes. This is suggested by God's call to recognize the illusion of repose in the motion of all things: "Thou shalt see the mountains, that thou supposest fixed, passing by like clouds – God's handiwork, Who has created everything very well."[12]

Multiplicity confirms the One in incessant motion. The One is the ever-present source and confluence of all that is in motion, the outwardness and inwardness of all things. The whole world is a mosque, a place of self-abnegation, with nothing in it that does not bow down to Him. When we recognize the focus of existence and everything in it, our will turns us towards that perfect motion as Peace made manifest. In it we discover our original nature as at peace and being-at-peace as our connection with the One.

The free will that expresses and confirms God's offer and our acceptance of confidence gives rise to two worlds – the real world as God's revelation of the unknown and an unreal one, in which we feel and believe ourselves independent and self-sufficient, in which evil deeds may seem good to us and our thinking diverts us from the good.[13] If we wish to return from the imaginary to the real, we need wisdom and knowledge, the way and ritual, humility and generosity to discover the real world concealed by illusion; and we need them as our relation to ourselves as perfect in regard to the All-perfect. We cannot extrapolate a response to this need from our imaginary constructs. Ritual comes to us from where we were sent down ourselves into the world.

---

11 *Qur'an*, 52:1–8.

12 Ibid., 27:88.

13 See *Qur'an*, 35:8.

Through the way and ritual, wisdom and knowledge are discovered and expressed in humility and generosity, transformed into a way of life and deed, issuing in philosophical thought as an amalgamation of instruction and life, wisdom and action, calculation and sociability and framed by ritual incorporation in universal prostration.

Wherever we are, universal motion in the world's perfect order gives us clear indications regarding the prescribed worship. We are expected to turn towards the Inviolable Mosque, pause, and identify our corporeal being with the Recitation, to stand, bow, prostrate ourselves and stand again, repeating these movements in a union of body and Word, until finally sitting and turning the head right and left, wishing peace upon all and confirming that the circle we are placed in is a perfect manifestation of the centre we are focused on and have embarked towards.

If the enlightenment blueprint for putting the world to rights and healing the rifts in its order is re-examined in terms of its impact over the final two centuries of the second Christian millennium, the ritual context of thought may acquire meaning as liberation from a fabricated and destructive schism from the world, experienced as insurmountable hostility whose outcome is evident: the great venture against suffering and death that results in the opposite of its promises.

God is manifest in the Word and the world Its means. All this is summed up in us as individuals. In the universal entity of God-Word-world ontologically sent down, we are at the end, in the depths, from which we may rise. However far we sink, we are never wholly lost, for mercy and knowledge are the reasons for all things. The Light of the Praised, the redemptive ray of light that links us to creation's reason and purpose, remains present no matter how obscured the self.

The path of ascent is marked by that indestructible ray of light. We alone travel that path. The beginning, journey and destination are in our "now," in the moment that is the sum of order. The illusion in the self cannot be reversed without understanding that the starting-point, the journey and the destination are in the "now," in the moment that is the sum, not in some imagined yesterday or tomorrow. The point of departure is the world focused on the self turning towards the outer horizons and itself. What we find in the disrupted world order and in ourselves cannot be discovered in its reality without turning to the Word. Ritual places us in a Word-world-God order: the Word is sent down to us and ritual is ascent through the Word and world to God.

Ascent is from signs to Signified. If the Signified is concealed from our ascent, the journey is impossible. Whatever it seems to be, its focus is destructive and it is movement away from the Signified, going astray. When the

Signified is concealed from view, the signs lose reality, which is a state of the self: the Signified concealed is the self concealed, God forgotten is us forgotten. When a sign is taken for the Signified, those who do so are separated from Him by the signs themselves. Confession of no god but God becomes confession of other gods than Him or of no God but gods.

This possibility cannot be reduced to a given language, meaning or symbol. It is human and possible in every language, meaning and symbol as obscuration, distortion or denial. No one of the peoples of the Book can escape it as a possibility or threat. Every sign in the world or self, in speaking and writing, reciting and reading, may be taken for the Signified. This is why God commands us never to associate anything or anyone with Him, why this is the one sin that cannot be forgiven – for the order of the heavens and earth reveals in its signs none but Him as Signified:

> Say: "Have you considered your associates on whom you call, apart from God? Show me what they have created in the earth; or have they a partnership in the heavens?" Or have We given them a Book, so that they are upon a clear sign from it? Nay, but the evildoers promise one another naught but delusion.[14]

We can only realize the plenitude of the self in relation to God as Self. Summing up all existence as multiplicity in which God reveals Himself as One, we focus on union. All things manifest as duality – motion and rest, matter and Spirit, earth and heaven, creation and Creator.

Confessing no god but God and the Praised as His servant and apostle, we seek self-realization in that relation between His unity and the Praised's apostolate. Following the Praised on the upright path of return to God, we seek to identify with him (the Praised) and love God, to see ourselves through God and Him through us, to be a face before the Face. Our confession of God's unity and the Praised's apostolate is self-love: loving God and His apostle, we love ourselves, and vice versa. This love is a prerequisite for discovering our original nature, than which nothing is dearer, as it makes sense of everything. God said:

> Thou shalt not find any people who believe in God and the Last Day who are loving to anyone who opposes God and His apostle, not though they were their fathers, or their sons, or their brothers, or their clan. Those – He has written faith upon their hearts, and He has confirmed them with the Spirit from Himself.[15]

---

14 *Qur'an*, 35:40.

15 Ibid., 58:22.

The paradigm for this is God's relationship to the Praised, to whom He commends people in the Recitation. While we externalize much of our inner potential, identifying with some external thing or person, self-realization is impossible outside the self. Both God's unity and the Praised's apostolate concern our innermost self above all. Our relationship to the Praised is a relationship with our supreme potential and so with God as Principle, whose mystery none exhaust. We approach the signs in the world to remind ourselves of the potential in the self, as we are reminded by God's words in the Recitation of the apostle's relationship with Him:

> God and His angels worship the prophet. O believers, do you also worship him, and take peace in Peace. Those who insult God and His apostle – them God has cursed in the present world and the world to come, and has prepared for them a humbling chastisement. And those who insult believing men and believing women, without that they have earned it, have laid upon themselves calumny and manifest sin.[16]

To say that God and his angels "worship" the prophet may seem a strange translation, but is quite correct. It seems strange because of our one-sided witness to God as utterly unlike, remote and severe. We must recall that in all His manifestations He both is and is not, is absolutely unlike and absolutely like, utterly remote and utterly near, absolutely severe and absolutely merciful. Both "is" and "is not" are manifest in perfect measure, the One never annulled by duality.

We know all the names, in principle, as God gave us them to instruct His creation. To actualize His gift, which is not unconditional, we must stand before our Creator, as creatures with nothing but what He has given us. Worship is our standing thus before Him. We stand between two extremes of witness – "is not" and "is." When we say "is not," we confess creation has no reality but as His manifestation: this is prostration. When we say "is," we confess we contain only what the Upright gives us. Prostrate, we see God as "not," since the signs in the world and self are the same as the Upright. Upright, we see God as "is," for we and the world manifest only the Upright. Or rather, upright, bowing and prostrate, we see God as both "is" and "is not," Whose works are death and life and Whom death does not encompass.

In this narrative, the Praised is pure and perfect potential – the first of the people of peace, the maternal seal of the prophets, fairest uprightness, a mercy to the worlds, a mighty morality, the perfect servant and orphan, every self's sublime potential, beginning and openness to the upright path on which he

16 Ibid., 33:56–58.

is always close, above and ahead of every self. Confessing his apostolate, we turn towards that potential, at the centre of the self, wholly encompassed by the heart.

The blessing of the Praised takes the form of his supreme potential. Absolute return to God is our beginning. Worship and its meaning are at both beginning and end. After ascent to God and return to the depths, the Praised brought worship to the people. He ascended from the Inviolable to the Further Mosque, to his Lord, in a single night, an ascent through seven heavens. In the sixth heaven, the Praised met the prophet Moses:

> He welcomed me and prayed for my well-being. Then I was taken up to the seventh heaven. Gabriel asked the (gate) to be opened. It was said: Who is he? He said: Gabriel. It was said: Who is with thee? He replied: The Praised. It was said: Has he been sent for? He replied: He has indeed been sent for. (The gate) was opened for us and there I found Abraham reclining against the House of God and there enter into it seventy thousand angels every day, never to visit again. Then I was taken to the Lote-Tree of the furthest boundary whose leaves were like elephant ears and its fruit like big earthenware vessels. And when it was covered by the Command of God, it underwent such a change that none amongst the creation has the power to praise its beauty. Then God revealed to me a revelation and He made obligatory for me fifty prayers every day and night. Then I went down to Moses and he said: What has your Lord enjoined upon your followers? I said: Fifty acts of worship. He said: Return to thy Lord and beg for reduction, for your community shall not be able to bear this burden, as I have put to test the children of Israel and tried them. He (the Praised) said: I went back to my Lord and said: My Lord, make things lighter for my followers. (The Lord) cut five acts of worship for me. I went down to Moses and said. (The Lord) cut five for me. He said: Verily thy community shall not be able to bear this burden; return to thy Lord and ask Him to make things lighter. I then kept going back and forth between my Lord the Blessed and Exalted and Moses, till He said: There are five acts of worship every day and night. O Praised, each being credited as ten, so that makes fifty. He who intends to do a good deed and does not do it will have a good deed recorded for him; and if he does it, it will be recorded for him as ten; whereas he who intends to do an evil deed and does not do, it will not be recorded for him; and if he does it, only one evil deed will be recorded. I then came down and when I came to Moses and informed him, he said: Go back to thy Lord and ask Him to make things

lighter. Upon this the apostle remarked: I returned to my Lord until I felt ashamed before Him.[17]

Several important conclusions may be drawn from this account of rapture. First, the form of worship was given to the Praised beyond and above existence and he brought it down to the depths as a gift. Second, Abraham, whom the Praised passed first in his descent, says nothing about this gift. Third, Moses protects the people of this world in their willingness to bear the burden of their covenant with God. Fourth, worship is incumbent on the individual, but the commandment is for us all. And fifth, the apostle felt ashamed to ask more of the Beloved.

These conclusions point to God's intention that different forms of worship should mark the ways of different communities. Only worship willingly shaped to God's will allows the members of a community to know their responsibility to another. Their "others" are those who differ, not only in responding or not to God's call, but also in responding in another language, with other meanings and symbols. Identifying people with the language, meanings and symbols of their worship obscures God's oneness made manifest in multiplicity as His will.

The call to the self to rise and worship is non-negotiable. The conversation in the sixth heaven between the two prophets[18] from the two branches of Abraham's descendants whom God says are like unto to each other and the subsequent request to lighten the burden shape worship into a whole of which God is First and Last, Inwardness and Outwardness. To respond to the call to worship is to enter an order entirely established from beyond and so from within, at our core.

The individual self responds to the call and enters the order of worship, acknowledging that wherever the call finds it is the place pre-ordained for receiving it as a participant in the cosmic order. To enter into the order of worship is to return the self to its original position as gatherer of all things and discoverer of God the Creator in them. It is voluntary, but participating

17 Muslim, 1:102–103. When Moses' advice to seek an easing of the burden for the Praised's followers is linked with Abraham's pleading for the inhabitants of Sodom, the similarity is clear. The plea to ease the burden in the case of the Praised begins with the fifty prescribed prayers, while in Abraham's case, the corresponding plea is for the fifty righteous inhabitants of Sodom. The final outcome of the plea is five daily prayers and ten righteous people from Sodom. See *Genesis*, 18:19–33.

18 See *Deuteronomy*, 18:18.

in it, in movement and speech, in stillness and murmuring, in orientation and time, leads us into the union of all things with the truth of creation and the Creator's Word.

The truth of creation and the Creator's Word manifest differently from moment to moment. The signs of that manifestation are in constant flux, as the One is manifest in Flux, Flux in the One, the First in the Last and the Inward in the Outward. Our worship concentrates the horizons and the self into God's oneness, seeking and finding oneness in multiplicity.

The call to worship is public and loud. It begins by glorifying God, as our affiliation to the earth, which can seem greatness and power over its passivity, obscures our awareness of our true position and our powers, as well as of ascent and descent. Only in recalling the greatness beyond us that opens up the path of ascent for us are we oriented towards our centre in which is witness to service and lordship – service as our relationship to our Lord. The words that speak of God's oneness, His absolute nearness and remoteness, absolute similarity and incomparability, that there is "no god but God" recall us to our witness, however obscured by the appearance of human greatness or squalor.

This reminder to witness of illusion and reality and of our capacity to distinguish them and choose reality culminates in our perfection, offered us in every condition as an apostolate, as mercy and essence. We are recalled to sublimity and to our first and last potential by the words "I confess the Praised as apostle of God."

Both praising God and confessing His oneness and the Praised's apostolate are knowledge at the centre of every self. It comes not from without, but is our most profound nature, the centre around which everything is peripheral manifestation. The words of praise and the two confessions, of God and of His apostle, are followed by the call to prayer, to affirmation of the known by inclusion in the universal order, seen and unseen. This call to self-realization before the Face before which all things vanish is followed by a call to redemption. Redemption is sacrificing everything before the Face, for His glory and unity, from and to which everything comes and returns.

To enter the order of worship is to emerge from the necessarily unfocused disorder of individuality and join all other witnesses to that order in recognition and discovery of the other and different. Thus we commit to recognizing the other and different as participants in universal discourse, using the various languages, signs and symbols of the One.

God created the world and us in His love to be known. He did it for His own pleasure, and the world and we are of Him and for Him. God's pleasure is absolute and we discover it in ourselves as our reason and purpose. Our most potent, greatest and clearest success is the ultimate purpose of life, to discover His pleasure. God says in the Recitation:

> Prosperous is he who has cleansed himself, and mentions the Name of his Lord, and prays.[19]
>
> This is the day the truthful shall be profited by their truthfulness. For them await gardens underneath which rivers flow, therein dwelling forever and ever, God being well-pleased with them and they well-pleased with Him; that is the mighty triumph.[20]
>
> But as for him who repents, and believes, and works righteousness, haply he shall be among the prosperers.[21]
>
> *Alif. Lam. Mim.* Those are the signs of the Wise Book for a guidance and a mercy to the good-doers who perform the prayer, and pay the alms, and have sure faith in the Hereafter. Those are upon guidance from their Lord; those are the prosperers.[22]
>
> All that the believers say, when they are called to God and His apostle, that he may judge between them, is that they say, "We hear, and we obey;" those – they are the prosperers.[23]
>
> And give the kinsman his right, and the needy, and the traveller; that is better for those who desire God's face; those – they are the prosperers.[24]

The five mandatory prayers – the first just after sunset, the second when night has fully fallen, the third before sunrise, the fourth just after noon and the fifth between noon and sunset – place or return us on the spiral staircase of ascent along the seventh ray, the *axis mundi*, towards the sublime height and the uncreated, uncreatable centre of all things. This return includes the Recitation, so that body becomes word, word body.

The Recitation is speech that has received form in the mind and breath of the Praised. That breath's possibilities, from the depths to the height, from stillness to trembling, are made manifest in the Recitation. The Lord too is present in it, speaking and falling silent in the heart. From that centre, from Light and Spirit, Peace and Mercy, the Recitation descends into speech.

Repetition is in sound and silence, in conformity with the comings and return of all things, from first to last, inwardness to outwardness. The self at prayer becomes motion that receives and embodies music. The repeated standing, bowing, prostration and sitting unite everything in the heavens, on the earth and between them. The worshipper joins fully in existence's will to

19 *Qur'an*, 87:14–15.

20 Ibid., 5:119.

21 Ibid., 28:67.

22 Ibid., 31:1–5.

23 Ibid., 24:51.

24 Ibid., 30:38.

serve God and discover itself in peace. In the ebb and flow of consciousness, the Recitation becomes river-bed and water. The moment receives descent and ascent, source and confluence in discovery of the Face.

At prayer, we address God as "Our," but God addresses us as "My" and "His."[25] Our love of God and His of us are in the manifestation of One in two. If God and we are Face to face – and so He tells us, that wherever we turn, there is His face[26] – to confess the One is to confess no face but the Face. In His face are realized those who love God and whom He loves, for God sees His face in those who love Him, and those who love God see their face in His.

God sees us fully, but what we see in the world and self only denotes Him, both veil and unveiling. No sooner say "is not" than add "is." The moment, properly understood, is everywhere and encompasses us entirely, but can never be captured by anything created, for the Face is with it. "Is not" and "is," "past" and "future" are simultaneous in the plenitude of the moment, but manifest themselves as distinct, a duality that reveals and confirms the One, wholly and eternally present, first and last, inward and outward.

These two – God's love to be known and our will to accept and love Him Who manifests through us – involve I-thou and Thou-I relationships. When we address the veil of signs as "thou," God is He. When we say "Thou" to Him, everything else is not to our "I." Duality manifests the One, and we, in His image, testify to the One in our complete service. Bound to the world, we are an image facing an image, but confessing the One, we recognize in the witnessing self, that image facing an image, the sum of all manifestation before the One Manifesting.

Seeing face to Face, we find ourselves on Horeb, the mountain where God revealed Himself to Moses and said: "Now therefore go, and I will be with thy mouth, and teach thee what thou shalt say."[27] Saying also: "And look that thou make them after their pattern, which was shewed thee in the mount."[28] Likewise, the Praised was in the cave on Mt. Hira and received the command: "Recite: In the name of thy Lord who created, created Man of a blood-clot. Recite: And thy Lord is the Most Generous who taught by the Pen, taught Man that he knew not."[29]

---

25 See *Qur'an*, 39:10, 16, 17; 43:68; 29:56; 14:35–41. In the sacred traditions, God addresses man as "My faithful servant" (Graham, *Divine Word and Prophetic Word in Early Islam*, 117), "My upright servant" (ibid.), "My servant" (ibid., 119), "My friend" (ibid., 121) and so on.

26 See *Qur'an*, 2:115.

27 *Exodus*, 4:12. Mt. Horeb and Mt. Sinai are often seen as different names for the same place and God's associated revelation to the prophet Moses.

28 *Exodus*, 25:40.

29 *Qur'an*, 96:1–5.

Wherever we are, we are in the depths. To recognize and be fully aware of this, to turn away from the depths to the sublime potential within, is to enter the mihrab. As we enter the ever-present mihrab of our potential, Mount Horeb and the cave on Hira, signs of our ascent, discovery and return, determine our position and embarkation on the upright path, which leads from periphery to centre, from the depths to the height, and from duality to the One.

The knowledge of the names lies at our core.[30] Read as knowledge of His names, for "to Him belong the Names Most Beautiful,"[31] the revelation affirms two ways of understanding our connection with God: He is omnipresent, with us everywhere and always, but we are with Him only in our knowledge of His names. We find or discover our Lord in ourselves in that knowledge, as we become doers of good and prosper, after his command:

> And vie with one another, hastening to forgiveness from your Lord, and to a garden whose breadth is as the heavens and earth, prepared for the mindful who expend in prosperity and adversity in almsgiving, and restrain their rage, and pardon the offences of their fellowmen; and God loves the good-doers.[32]
>
> And give the kinsman his right, and the needy, and the traveller; that is better for those who desire God's face; those – they are the prosperers.[33]

Love relates lover and Beloved as an invincible force in which difference, and so time and space, is effaced. All things lie between perfect order and destructive slippage. Love manifests in an order governed by will as the union of our will and His – in worship, fasting, purificatory almsgiving, and pilgrimage to the Centre. We are included in existence's perfect order, since the most beautiful names in the heavens and on earth and between are the same as those in the self.

Redemption in and with the most beautiful names takes place in the hour and in the expectation that it will take place in worship, almsgiving, fasting and pilgrimage, for that is how we turn from unreality to the Real. Expectation and fulfilment, return to the height, run from the self that incites to evil[34] and utter remoteness from the One towards the self that aspires to be nearer than near and please God and pleased with God.[35]

---

30 See *Qur'an*, 2:31.

31 See e.g. *Qur'an*, 59:22–24.

32 *Qur'an*, 3:133–34.

33 Ibid., 30:38.

34 See *Qur'an*, 12:53.

35 Ibid., 89:27–30.

Fulfilment of expectation is for the patient, whom God loves. Patience is recognition that what they have they have received and misfortune is brought upon them by desire in which the self renounces its waiting. God said of them and their connection with the prophets: "Many a prophet there has been, with whom thousands manifold have fought, and they fainted not for what smote them in God's way, neither weakened, nor did they humble themselves; and God loves the patient."[36]

Expectation realized in patience redeems by harmonizing the signs in the world with those in the self. The world-self duality is in constant flux. The signs of the world elude those in the self as a shadow eludes what casts it. God loves the patient in reminder that what the signs in the world and the signs in the self signify is one, for in them God manifests His love to be known. His Books, by which He manifests all of creation in human language, are a response to the rift between world and self.

With the Book, the self encompasses all outward horizons. Reciting it well and articulately, at worship and other times, sums up existence, in time and space and in the "now" of the reciting self. The future is framed by the Creator's discourse that nothing eludes, however large or small. To discover the Word in the self is to see the signs in their ultimate sanctuary, the Creator's command to be.

The initial words "in the name of God" and beginning with the names of the All-merciful and the Ever-merciful are constant in the Recitation and its presence in the self, for these two names are a perpetual reason for praising Him. Praise's purpose is in those names, for He is Lord of the Day of Reckoning. The Recitation in the reciting self brings together God's unity, the Praised's apostolate and return to God – unity, as all names manifest Him; the apostolate, since we ascend from the depths by praising Him; and return, as only in the Praised, the perfect example of self-realization, do the praised relate to the All-praised. Praised and praiseworthy, we "capture" different horizons of the world each moment and are in constant flux. With the Recitation within us, the flux is internal, as world and self are exchanged and reversed – we are in the world, the world in us; the Recitation is in us, we in the recitation. The universal flow is concentrated in the individual self spread out across the worlds. This corresponds to ascent from the depths to the height. Every moment encompasses both extremes.

In worship, as the self's voluntary reception of all things, of whatsoever desires no will but God's, the worshipper enables the Word to grow and manifest eternity in praise of the All-praised. The Word is the good tree in the

---

36 *Qur'an*, 3:146.

worshipper's self, as God says: "A good word is as a good tree – its roots are firm, and its branches are in heaven. It gives its produce every season by the leave of the Lord. So God strikes similitudes for men; haply they will remember."[37]

"Every season" means the set times for prayer, of which God says: "When you are secure, perform the prayer; surely the prayer is a timed prescription for the believers."[38] Prayer is performed at a specific time. Entering upon prayer, we renew and reinforce our rootedness and branching out in the time and space of the world. Standing, bowing, prostration, sitting and standing up sum up the motions of the world and, together with the recited Word, structure the various movements.

We sum up all things within us and on that sixth day we join in congregational prayer at midday, as the sun passes the zenith, before the beginning of the seventh day, or the return of all things to their original and ultimate Peace. Movement in the lunar year is set within the solar year, the one sailing into the other, for "it behoves not the sun to overtake the moon, neither does the night outstrip the day, each swimming in a sky."[39]

In this sacred calendar, which goes back to the first human breath and forward to the last, every individual thing and all of existence are at peace, as all things connect by being-at-peace with God as Peace. Faithful, patient and fine, we partake in that universal order of being-at-peace and transcend all things. In every age, there are those who, belonging to different nations and languages, yet form one community. Passing through their sacred calendar, these people of the maternal prophet and the maternal Book realize eternity in their prescribed times of prayer, fasting, almsgiving and pilgrimage.

The house in the sacred valley was built by the first man, Adam, as a sign of his awareness of the depths and expectation of regaining his original, sublime height. This expectation of finding and returning to what was lost was marked by building a house on Sion, the holy mountain, around the rock on its summit. In this myth of Adam in the Garden, the fall to earth and the establishment of rituals around the two houses, corresponding to the darkness and the luminous centre in the self, the greatest light is the Light of the Praised. It is the first manifestation of God as All-praised and so the essence of His entire manifestation and all His prophets.

Our entire drama unfolds around those two signs denoting the extremes of the upright path. Abraham came southwards and found the foundations of the house on the desert valley floor. He cleared them and rebuilt the first house

37 Ibid., 14:24–25.

38 Ibid., 4:103.

39 Ibid., 36:40.

for our sake, reviving the ritual of pilgrimage, worship and prayer in awareness of eternity's presence in finitude. He foresaw the coming of the Praised from among his descendants through Hagar's son Ishmael, who would unite the extremes of the path from the depths to the height, from the barren valley floor to the rock in the land of milk and honey.

The Praised's journey northwards, from that valley floor to that mount, denotes the ever-present potential in us all – to transform our regret for the lost Garden into a great journey on every stage of which we shall host the Praised as our dearest guest and answer his call, leaving everything to set off with him for the Abode of peace, in expectation of God's invitation: "O soul at peace, return unto thy Lord, well-pleased, well-pleasing! Enter thou among My servants! Enter thou My Paradise!"[40]

This ultimate achievement, return to God in which we and He are both well-pleased and well-pleasing, loving one another and realizing our love, is fulfilment of our expectation in worship. The worshipper is in a time that denotes eternity. Worship's rituals confirm we are on a boundary between this world and the next, death and resurrection, judgment and reckoning. There is no ritual in which the participant does not anticipate passing from lower to higher and entering the womb of mercy.

This transition, taking us before God as Judge, is concentrated in ritual prayer, individual and congregational. Standing and bowing, prostration and sitting, accompanied by words, spoken, murmured and heard, are being before God, face to Face. All who participate face that centre. God's servant and apostle, the Praised, faced that way, along with everyone else at prayer. Nothing of this is a figment of the human mind. It was all received from God as perfect order in a perfect world.

In one ritual, though, an individual does face the congregation. At noon on the sixth day, during congregational prayer, a speaker climbs half way up the steps of the mosque pulpit to address the congregation. He never climbs higher, as the top half of the stairs are for the prophets, epitomized in the Praised, their essence and seal, and for the good and wise of the congregation's memory. What the speaker says elicits only one response: "We have heard and we obey,"[41] which goes unuttered, the silence a sacred boundary against any speaker who might attempt the steps to the top. This denotes the inviolability of witness to the One, the Praised's apostolate and universal return to God. This presence is absolute; we can be absent.

In this position, the speaker enters the order of creation, revelation and its manifestation through the Praised, as best example, and in those who

40 Ibid., 89:27–30.

41 Ibid., 5:7.

follow him in love of God, Who loves them. If the speaker says something that transgresses the limits, the listeners reject it silently, needing accept nothing except the truth to which God and the prophets bear witness. Only the good is binding.

Worship is a perfect whole embracing everyone. If the speaker on the sixth day departs from the order warranted by the apostle and his followers and begins to express his own self-closure, his listeners' silence becomes a barrier, rejecting his attempt to disrupt harmony.

The language and meanings of modern politics are shaped by propositional logic, knowledge derived only from propositions in relation to which everything else is or is not in order. Everything beyond propositional logic is impotent. Impotence in the face of the intellect, however, which is beyond any potential of propositional or analytical logic, is expressed in a variety of ways – by silence, denial or rejection. The world of the Book, in which God is first speaker, and the language, meanings and symbols of rituals such as prayer, fasting, almsgiving and pilgrimage to the house – all that and everything like it remain intact, outside the ideological framework of modern life, but preserved within and by us. Despite being beyond the horizons of mainstream life, it remains within us.

Saying that there must be an end, once and for all, to the persecution and killing of Bosnian Muslims and the destruction of all that is theirs, leads one to the conclusion that the language, meanings and symbols of the Book, myths and rituals, and awareness of their presence in a community awaiting redemption, must become part of life as a whole, part of every memory of death and of the future, so that confessing God's unity, the Praised's apostolate and return to God acquire present meaning for each of us, to be discovered in the individual self and expressed in the clear common discourse as hostility to all servitude that is not service to God.

A change of this nature is possible as a gift, delivered in a still, calm voice, which will deserve our trust. If Bosnian Muslims persist in seeking power that is not preceded by the still small voice, as that of the leader, their existence become a desperate stalling, indulging in fears and gratifying passions. God's sending down of His revelation to the Praised and its transfer into the selves of his listeners was that still small voice, which attests to the power of the Spirit. No subjugation of the people of that still small voice to the might of their persecutors can divert them from the hope of what is so utterly close to them in their ritual prayers. When they had power as well as that still small voice, it merely meant to them a still greater burden, more complicated trials and temptations, and longer absences in forgetting, for the Spirit and its still small voice need only what they have.

Both the individual and society are a boon to the treasure-trove of language, as two indistinguishable yet always separate aspects. The individual self, in family, clan, society and humanity, remains alone, albeit along with everyone else. Without its own, it can have no other; if not its own, it is no-one's. Its healing from forgetting and suffering lies in the discovery of its own individuality. It is only in finding itself that the self can be a reliable witness to God's unity and the Praised's apostolate and can join in prayer, fasting, almsgiving and pilgrimage.

The self reflects through these rituals, ascending to the height. Several revelations speak of the self's relationship to all things as signs that connect it to the Self or Signified:

> Your creation and your upraising are as but a single soul. God is All-hearing, All-seeing.[42]
>
> God created the heavens and the earth in truth, and that every soul may be recompensed for what it has earned; they shall not be wronged.[43]
>
> Your Lord knows very well what is in your hearts if you are righteous, for He is All-forgiving to those who are penitent.[44]
>
> Every soul earns only to its own account; no soul laden bears the load of another.[45]
>
> We charge not any soul save to its capacity, and with Us is a Book speaking truth, and they shall not be wronged.[46]
>
> Say: "O men, the truth has come to you from your Lord. Whosoever is guided is guided only to his own gain, and whosoever goes astray, it is only to his own loss. I am not a guardian over you."[47]
>
> But as for him who feared the Station of his Lord and forbade the soul its caprice, surely Paradise shall be the refuge.[48]
>
> God wronged them not, but themselves they wronged.[49]
>
> When heaven is split open, when the stars are scattered, when the seas swarm over, when the tombs are overthrown, then a soul shall know its works, the former and the latter.[50]

---

42 Ibid., 31:28.

43 Ibid., 45:22.

44 Ibid., 17:25.

45 Ibid., 6:164.

46 Ibid., 23:62.

47 Ibid., 10:108.

48 Ibid., 79:40–41.

49 Ibid., 3:117.

50 Ibid., 82:1–5.

FIGURE 3.1 *Map of mosques from the illustrations*

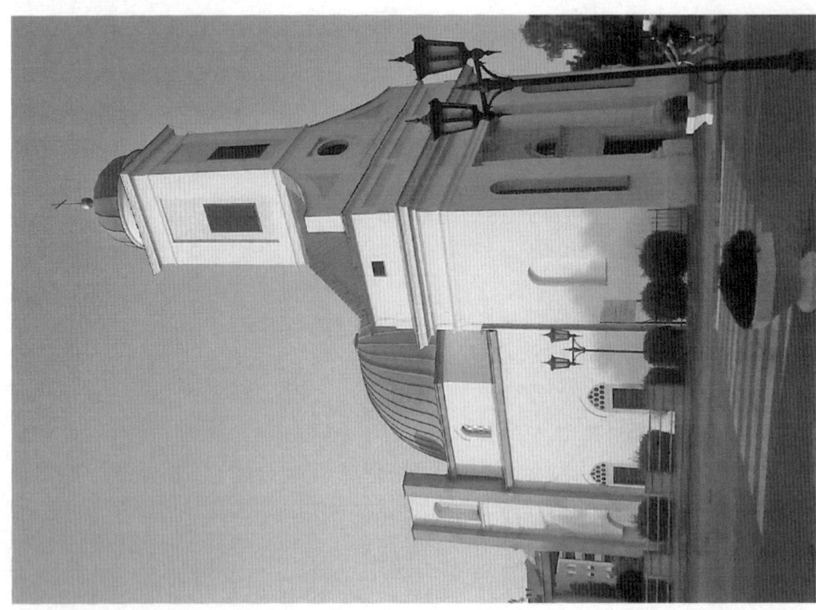

FIGURE 3.3 *The Mosque/Church at Đakovo in Croatian Slavonia*

FIGURE 3.2 *The Mosque/Church at Drniš in Croatian Dalmatia*

FIGURE 3.4 *The mosque at Kotezi*

FIGURE 3.5 *The ruined mosque at Bijeljani*

FIGURE 3.6 *The ruined mosque at Kazanci*

FIGURE 3.7 *Fatima's Mosque, Mostar*

FIGURE 3.8 *The Careva or Imperial Mosque, Foča*

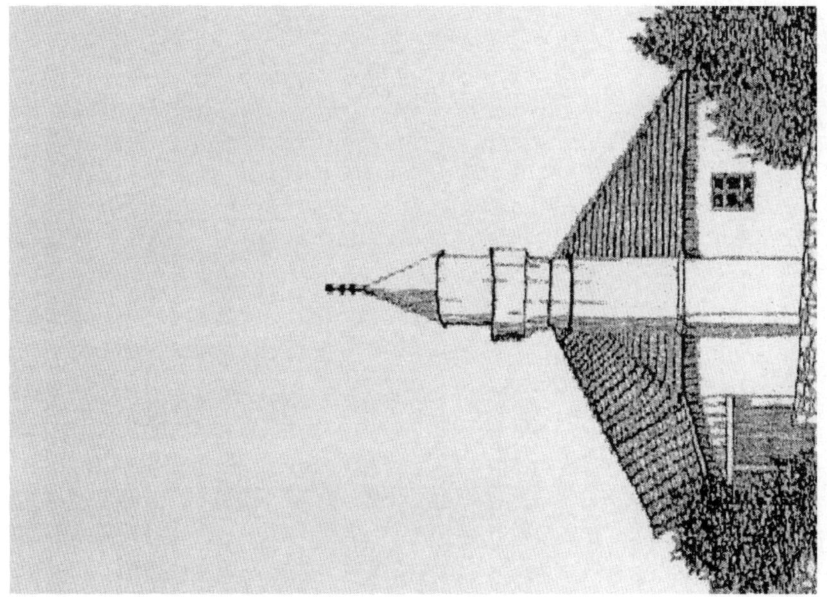

FIGURE 3.9 *The Mosque at Gorani*

FIGURE 3.10 *The Mosque at Umoljani*

FIGURE 3.11 *The Tekke Mosque at Rogatica*

FIGURE 3.13 *The Opener's Mosque at Kraljeva Sutjeska*

FIGURE 3.12 *The Balaguša Mosque in Livno*

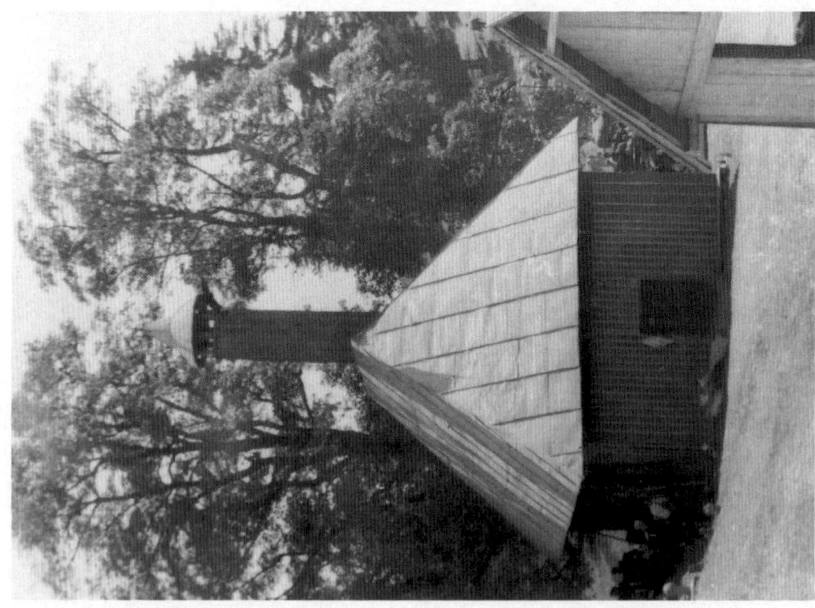

FIGURE 3.14 *The Mosque at Karići*

FIGURE 3.15 *The Fethija Mosque in Jajce*

FIGURE 3.17 *The Ferry Mosque in Zvornik*

FIGURE 3.16 *The Mosque at Sokol*

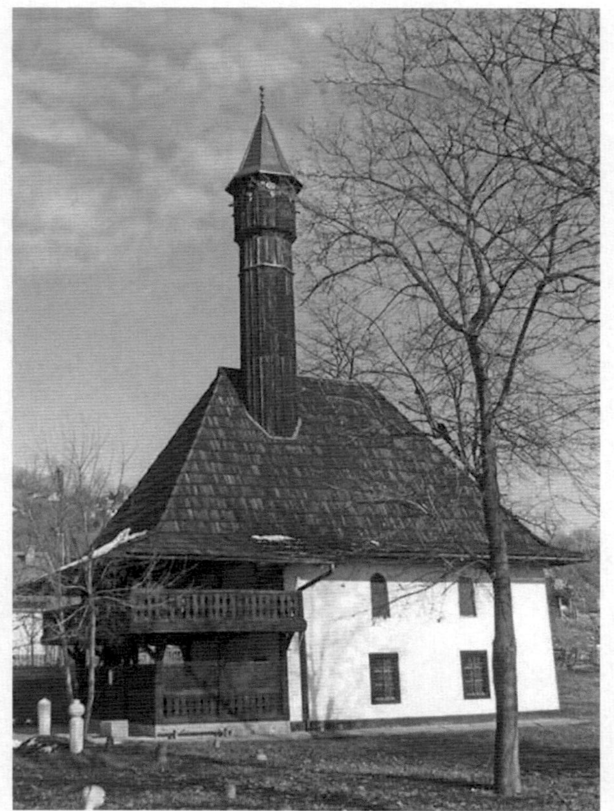

FIGURE 3.18 *The Džindić Mosque in Tuzla*

FIGURE 3.19 *The White Mosque at Brčko*

FIGURE 3.21 *The Fethija Mosque in Bihać*

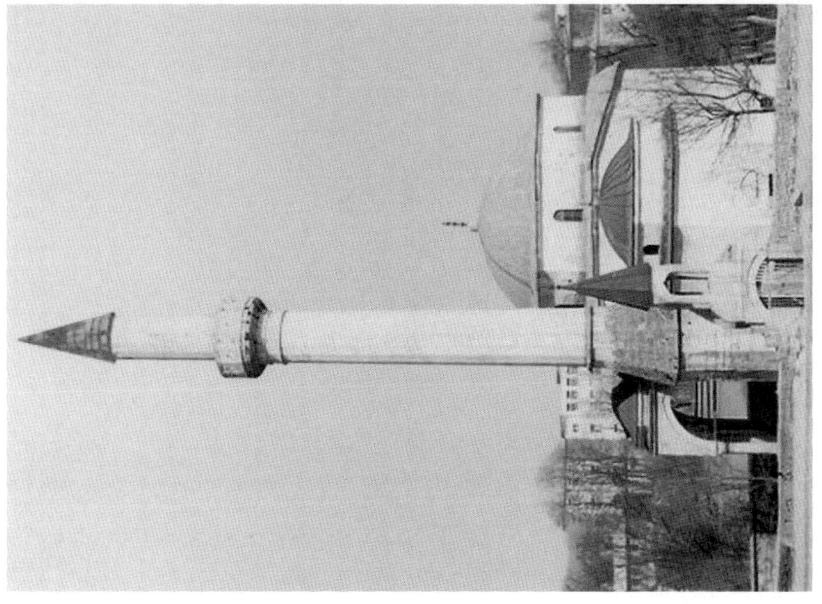

FIGURE 3.20 *The Arnaudija in Banja Luka*

FIGURE 3.22 *The Mosque at Bužim*

PART 4

In the Mihrabs

• •

To say "I am" is to testify to being alive, possessed of will and power, knowing, speaking, hearing and seeing, albeit in a finite manner as, at the same time, we face being dead, without will, powerless, unknowing, unspeaking, unhearing and unseeing. Our being is received and, hence, contingent.

In the depths of saying "I am" we sense that we derive from the absolute "**I Am.**" The absolute bestows whatever it is that brings the "I am." We haunt the boundary across which the absolute "**I Am**" manifests. Our desire to escape contingency and finitude entails confessing no "I am" but "**I Am.**" The former is the image or manifestation of the Other.

That Other is absolute and we are relate to Him through life, will, power, knowledge, speech, listening and seeing. We cannot attain plenitude just by saying, "I am." The distinction between our "I" and the absolute "**I**" of the Other separates us from the plenitude we yearn for, which alone can save us from the limitations of life, will, power, knowledge, speech, listening and seeing.

For this reason, we are at constant war with finitude. Our goal is to cross the boundary that confines us to contingency, our being in space and time a struggle against contingency that we cannot win so long as "I" and the absolute "**I**" are separate. The absolute "**I**" is present in the principle of all time and space, but they do not comprehend It.

Because the absolute "**I**" is manifest by Its own will in contingency, It requires connection with the contingent "I." This is self-relationship of the differentiated absolute "**I**," Which descends into the contingent so that the world may ascend to It. The ascent of the world from utter contingency is knowing the "**I**" as Peace, as the Known, the Beloved and the Beautiful. The personal "I" and the absolute "**I**" relate through love, the yearning for absolute union.

Those who love the Beloved perfectly see Him in all things, for all the contingent world manifests Him as All-praised. The entire world proclaims the Praised, so that the perfect apostle receives that praise and repays it, as Praised and Praiser. The revelation, "God and His angels cleave to the prophet. O faithful, do you also cleave to him in peace,"[1] tells us that he is constantly in a place of war, in which, as a warrior, he strives to pass through the contingent world and the contingent self to the absolute.

This connection always entails the possibility of disconnection. This connection is being-at-peace, knowledge and love, manifest in the relationship between the "I am" and the "**I Am.**" All too often, the connection is offered in the place of those two and the illusion develops that life, will, power, knowledge, speech, listening and seeing are not merely contingent and received. Accepting the tenet that there is no "I am" but the "**I Am**" requires that every

1 *Qur'an*, 33:56.

 | DOI 10.1163/9789004279407_123

state of "I am" and all things in existence be understood as opportunities of self-abnegation in favor of union with the "**I Am**." The totality of existence is thus a place of nullity, and the **I** the annihilator of every illusion and all contingency. Thus, being in the nullity of the world forms part of a great war for redemption and return to the Abode of Peace.

The Praised is the finest example of being on the battlefield of existence. However close we draw to a boundary beyond which a higher level of the self lies, the Praised precedes us as our guide, as the well-known prayer suggests: "Call down blessing on him with that *salat* with which Thou didst call down blessing on him in the *mihrab* of Thy transcendent holiness and the Ipseity of Thine intimacy."[2]

We are ever in the depths or the shadows. Ascending towards the height or the light depends on our relationship with God. We carry trust within us, at the core of our inner self, the treasury of all we need to realize that connection. To ascend is to overcome all obstacles; it is war with whatever stands in our way, both on the outer horizons and within ourselves. Our goal is Peace, but Peace manifests Itself to us in the shadows of existence.

The position of those who discover in their hearts the pledge of fidelity as the land of faith[3] and the possibility of turning to God is described in the Revelation in these words: "O believers, remember God oft, and give Him glory at the dawn and in the evening. It is He who blesses you, and His angels, to bring you forth from the shadows into the light. He is Ever-merciful to the believers. Their greeting, on the day when they shall meet Him, will be 'Peace!' And He has prepared for them a generous wage."[4]

In these verses, God is addressing the faithful, which in principle means everyone. God offered us the pledge of trust or faith and we accepted it. It is as the All-faithful that He addresses us as the faithful, in our original attunement, calling upon us to remember and glorify Him in the twilight of dawn, in which light will triumph, and of dusk, when it will vanish into the night. This alternation between darkness and light, light and darkness, is a reminder of the One Who is made manifest by duality. We are oriented towards the One from the world of duality, as a place of war in which we are encouraged and guided by Peace. Becoming aware of being in the mihrab of the world is the condition of our connection with Peace as the original reality of the world and of our inner self.

---

2 al-Tijānī, *al-Ṣalāt al-ghaybiyya fī l-ḥaqīqat al-Aḥmadiyya*, cited in Constance E. Padwick, *Muslim Devotions*, 157.

3 See *Qur'an*, 95:3.

4 *Qur'an*, 33:41–44.

To pray behind the Praised is to become part of the universal praise through which the people of this world are united with the principle of the next world. The totality of existence thus reveals itself as praise of God Who reveals Himself to Himself. The centre of this revelation is the apostle as the perfect image of the All-praised. Al-Suyuti says of this:

> God Most High informed his worshippers of the rank which His prophet holds with Him in the heavenly host, by praising Him in the presence of the angels of access, and by the *salat* of those angels for Him. Then he commanded *salat* and a greeting of peace from the people of the world below, so that the people of both worlds, above and below, might unite in His praise.[5]

God encompasses all things with His knowledge and mercy, the lowest and the highest. Nothing can sink so far as to be beyond His knowledge and mercy. Prayer begins by standing, or being, on the heights and it reaches its limits in the depths, in prostration. God is with those who pray as they stand and as they prostrate themselves. The Praised is the perfect, most sublime presence of God with those who pray.

God's absolute nearness is in every part of the prayer. He is with us wherever we are;[6] He answers the call of the caller.[7] Prayer (*salat*) thus has various meanings. ʿAli al-Makki says:

> Opinions differ as to the significance of *salat*. It is said that from God its meaning is mercy and complaisance, and from angels and men petition and asking forgiveness. And it is said that God's *salat* is His mercy and the *salat* of the angels' prayer for blessing. And it is said that the *salat* of God is His mercy combined with magnifying and that of the angels is asking for forgiveness, and that of men, humbly beseeching and petition. And it is said that God's *salat* for His prophets is praise and magnifying while His *salat* for others is His mercy. Ibn al-ʿArabī said: *Salat* from God is mercy, and from human beings and others, angels and jinn, it is bowing and prostration and petition and praise, and from birds and owls it is praise.

5 al-Suyūṭī, *al-Ḥirz al-manīʿ min al-qawl al-badīʿ fī al-ṣalāt ʿalā al-ḥabīb al-shafīʿ*, 12, cited in Padwick, *Muslim Devotions*, 156.

6 See *Qur'an*, 57:4.

7 Ibid., 2:186.

> Each creature knows his own *salat* and *tasbih* ... and al-Ḥalīmī set forth the meaning of God's *salat* for His prophet as His magnifying of him."[8]

Earth and the heavens and all that lies between them, as well as all that lies beyond their bounds, glorify their Creator by praising Him, while through His creation He reveals Himself as the All-praised. He glorifies Himself in praise through His creation. Glorifying in praise is the purpose of the creation of all things. The way in which the totality of existence does so as a whole and as each individual phenomenon was received by existence as a gift or debt from the Creator, Who expects us to repay the debt by glorifying Him in praise.

We are the sum of all praise and thus the abundance or treasury of what God lays upon us as a debt, as He says in the Recitation: "Surely We have given thee abundance; so pray unto thy Lord and sacrifice. Surely he that hates thee, he is the one cut off."[9] Our openness to Him is being praised, for there is nothing in existence that has not received its being from God as the All-praised; thus, each of us is a praiser, for we repay our debt to God by praising Him. Praise is our connection as praiser and praised with God as the All-praised. We cannot be open to acknowledging and repaying the debt to God without His help. This is why God says through the Praised, "In the name of God, the All-merciful, the Ever-merciful. When comes the help of God, and the opening, and thou seest men entering God's depth in throngs, then proclaim the praise of thy Lord, and seek His forgiveness; for He turns again unto men."[10]

God calls upon us to turn to Him in prayer, which includes glorifying Him by praising Him as our Lord. Furthermore, God confirms that He too turns towards us. Our human turning towards God is merely a sign, therefore, by which He glorifies Himself in praise. There is none equal to him,[11] nor any like him,[12] but by means of Himself and His creation, He teaches us the turning and the prayer in which are His glorification and praise. The perfect example of this glorification in praise is the Praised as His apostle.

The Praised is the first of the people of peace and the perfect epitome of praise. God and the angels turn to him for blessing and pray for him. The way in which they turn to him and bless him is different from every other and cannot be compared to anything else, for God is not equal or like to anything. But God

8 ʿAlī al-Makkī, *Fatḥ al-karīm al-khāliq fī ḥall alfāẓ al-durr al-fāʾiq fī al-ṣalāt ʿalā ashraf al-khalāʾiq (Ṣ) li-l-Shaykh Muṣṭafā al-Bakrī*, in Padwick, *Muslim Devotions*, 156–157.

9 *Qurʾan*, 108:1–3.

10 Ibid., 110:1–3.

11 See *Qurʾan*, 112:4.

12 Ibid., 42:11.

and the angels' turning in their prayer to the apostle is the reason for our turning towards the Praised as the connection with God. In this turning as believers, as those who know God through the Praised as receiver and requiter of divine praise and who love Him as such, we connect with our supreme potential. God says of this, "The Praised is the apostle of God, and those who are with him are hard against the concealers, merciful one to another. Thou seest them bowing, prostrating, seeking bounty from God and good pleasure. Their mark is on their faces, the trace of prostration."[13]

The connection with the Praised in prayer is the condition for the discovery of the world as a mosque. Indeed, the Praised is in every prayer, and glorification by praising God as the All-praised is through him. When we pray, we wage war against everything that stands in the way of our realization through the testimony that there is no god but God and that the Praised is His servant and messenger. We thus enter into the mosque of existence with the intention of passing through the place of war, through the mihrab, into the Abode of Peace.

Turning towards God, indicated by the direction of the House (*qibla*), entering the place of war (*miḥrāb*), all the positions, movements and words of the prayer and, particularly, calling for blessings on the apostle have their own thanksgiving and blessings. As Constance E. Padwick concludes, "In his calling down of blessing on the Prophet the worshipper believes that he is, by the utterance of a few words, not only entering into communion with an activity of heaven but is setting in motion a correspondent heavenly activity."[14]

When we pray, we enter the mosque of existence, for there is nothing that does not bow down to God. Of our own will, we thus manifest ourselves as the will of God, and everything that is in the heavens, on earth and between them reveals that will. We submit to or connect with it through being-at-peace, thus becoming part of existence as descent (or receiving) and ascent (or giving). Our sacrifices, prayers, life and death belong to God, who has no equal. Jalal al-Din Rumi says of these acts of sacrifice and prayer, "It means that these acts of adoration, service and worship and attention do not come from us and we are not free to perform them. The truth is that 'blessings' and 'prayers' and 'greetings' belong to God, they are not ours, they are wholly His and belong to Him."[15]

Physically and symbolically, the mihrab is the centre or principal element of every mosque. It usually consists of a niche in the wall of the mosque facing towards the Kaʿba in Becca. It is the place for the leader of the congregational prayer and it may be large or small and of various designs and decorations.

---

13 *Qur'an*, 48:29.

14 Padwick, *Muslim Devotions*, xxv.

15 Arberry, *Discourses of Rūmī*, 57.

For most people who have received a modern education and have a modern view of things, this is all there is to say about the mihrab.

The form, purpose and meaning of the mihrab as a recess in the mihrab wall facing the Kaʿba in the Becca valley cannot be understood without ontology, cosmology, anthropology and psychology as essential elements of the sacred teachings. They have always involved three things: testifying to the oneness of God as the principle of all things; testifying to the apostolate of the Praised as the absolute through which descent from the One to multiplicity and re-ascent to Him are manifested; and testifying to return to the One by following in the apostle's footsteps. The prophet, in this case, is the sum or supreme sign of all those prophets who swore to God in pre-existence that they would accept him as our supreme potential.

Testifying to the return to God includes consenting to His judgment of everyone for every atom of good and every atom of evil we have committed. Testifying to the oneness of God, the apostolate of the Praised and return is independent of place or time. It is inseparable from human nature. The mihrab may therefore be seen as a sign of this perennial human orientation towards the supreme potential. Titus Burckhardt wrote, "The prayer niche, or *mihrab*, is indisputably a creation of sacred art, and has become in practice a regular element in the liturgy, though not an indispensable one."[16]

The meaning of the mihrab is inseparable from the perennial philosophy or sacred doctrine. Because it is a creation of sacred art in the full meaning of the term, anything said of it is incomplete unless it takes into account the principle that sacred art is inseparable from sacred teachings.[17] Though it is ordinarily represented as an integral part of the mosque, the various forms, purposes and meanings of the mihrab are present beyond the mosque – in houses, in public

---

16 Burckhardt, *Art of Islam*, 86.

17 The noun *miḥrāb* (pl. *maḥārīb*) is widely regarded as deriving from the root *ḥ-rb*, giving the verb *ḥariba*. The first form of the verb means "to be enraged," "to be furious;" the second form means "to provoke," "anger" or "annoy" (someone); the third form means "to fight," "to combat;" the sixth form means "to fight" (one another), "to be engaged in war." These meanings have prompted several scholars to search for the non-Arabic sources of the word, probably due to an inability to see a clear connection between those meanings and the sacred teachings to which the *miḥrāb* belongs. This quest has given rise to much speculation and many assumptions concerning the origin of the noun in other Semitic languages and in Persian. See: Miles, "Miḥrāb and ʿAnaza: A Study in Early Islamic Iconography"; Melikian-Chirvani, "The Light of Heaven and Earth: From the Chahār-tāq to the Miḥrāb"; Khoury, *The Miḥrāb Concept*, 143–153.

institutions, on graves and in paintings, in caves and on rocks,[18] or wherever we have transformed a place into a mosque or acknowledged it as such with our presence and by our decision and orientation.[19]

Before defining the semantic field of the word *mihrab*, we must draw attention to some of the more significant meanings of the word *mosque*. Both denote a place – the first, a place of war (*ḥarb*), and the second a place of prostration (*sajda*, giving the Arabic word *masjid*, and at a remove the English word mosque). The mihrab is part of the mosque, but in such a way as to comprise within itself everything encompassed by the mosque in which it is located. Prostration is the relationship between all things and God. There is nothing that does not prostrate itself before Him in its realization. The whole world can thus be said to be a place of prostration, a mosque.

The totality of the worlds – the heavens and earth and all that lies between them – is a mosque. When we want to transform this into a compressed form corresponding to our nature as the sum of all things, we commission or build a mosque in which every sign of masonry and decoration, every ritual and speech, should denote the mosque of all things, all horizons and the entire self. This means that the mosque represents both arcs – the arc of descent or of the manifestation of the One in multiplicity and the arc of ascent or the return of all multiplicity to the One.

The purpose of the mosque, both as the totality of all things and as the image of their sum, is to enable us to see the truth of the creation of all things through

18 For more on the various forms, purposes and meanings of the *miḥrāb*, see Miles, "Miḥrāb and ʿAnaza," 52; Fehérvári, "Tombstone or Miḥrāb: A Speculation"; Alexandre Papadopoulo (ed.), *Le Mihrāb dans l'architecture et la religion musulmanes*, 88; Melikian-Chirvani, "The Light of Heaven and Earth"; Khoury, *The Mihrab Concept*; Idem, "The Miḥrāb Image: Commemorative Themes in Medieval Islamic Architecture"; Idem, "The Dome of the Rock, the Kaʿba, and Ghumdan: Arab Myths and Umayyad Monuments"; Idem, "The Miḥrāb: From Text to Form."

19 The *miḥrāb* is present not only in the mosques, tekkes and homes of Bosnia, but also in nature, whether as pre-existing or artificially indicated in valleys and caves or on hillsides and peaks. The *miḥrāb* is also associated with the name of the summit of Mt. Horeb, as mentioned in the Torah. It is interesting that at one of the important old sites associated with ritual gatherings of Bosnian Muslims, thought to go deep into Bosnia's past, the top of the hill is known as Ratiš [*rat* = war]. See: Djedović, "Dovište na Ratišu kod Srebrenika." The *miḥrāb* and the *Muṣḥaf* are the two most important articles of Muslim culture, the one immobile, the other portable. Wherever Muslim presence has been brought to an end, *miḥrābs* and *Muṣḥafs* have been destroyed. An anonymous Sarajevo poet wrote of the horrors of the devastation of Sarajevo in 1697 by Austrian troops led by Prince Eugene of Savoy: "Hundreds of thousands of Muṣḥafs, countless books/were burnt as were mosques; miḥrābs were pulled down." Handžić, "Sarajevo u turskoj pjesmi," 482.

the signs on the outer horizons. These signs constantly present themselves to us as the link to the Signified, but they also conceal Him. Parting the veils over the signs (which is to say over the inner self of the observer) or waging war against the concealer, illusion, is our way of finding ourselves or of returning to the original testimony of the oneness of God. The mihrab or place of war is thus the centre of both the world and humanity. Through it, we pass through manifestation to the Manifested, through being-at-peace to Peace, and through love to the Beloved.

The mihrab symbolizes the ascent from one level of existence to another, drawing closer to the Real and distancing ourselves from illusion. Titus Burckhardt says, "Its very shape, with its vault corresponding to heaven and its piedroit to the earth, makes the niche a consistent image of the 'cave of the world.' The cave of the world is the 'place of appearance' (*maẓhar*) of the Divinity, whether it be a case of the outward world as a whole or the inner world, the sacred cave of the heart."[20]

As the perfect recipient and bestower of praise, as the man who is praised in relation to God as the All-praised, the prophet is a mercy to the worlds, a lamp that shines, and the finest example to all people. To bear witness to him means to follow him. We follow him because we love God, and the consequence of our following is God's love of the follower. When we testify to the apostolate of the Praised, we are turned or oriented towards the Face of God. The world as a whole is a mosque, and turning to follow the Praised places us in the mihrab of the mosque of existence. The Praised is that mihrab, and, when it is built into the mihrab wall, the mihrab is the symbol of the presence of the Praised.

The act of worship by which we seek to confirm and resolve duality as the way unity is manifested can be performed anywhere. The entire world is thus a mosque or place of prostration. Passing from duality to unity is impossible without the act of worship or waging war. Entering the mosque, or the feat of annihilating all that appears to be god other than God, entails facing the outward centre of the world as the sign of the uncreated centre of humanity. The ritual of annihilating all illusions means resisting their constant entrance into the world and concealing That Which we remember.

Whenever we turn to the One, whenever we answer His call, we enter the mihrab. The finest example of entering and standing, bowing and prostrating, sitting and speaking is the Praised, the lamp that shines from every mihrab. The light in that lamp is none other than God, for He sends down His Word through the Praised, as He says:

20 Burckhardt, *Art of Islam*, 86.

> God is the Light of the heavens and the earth; the likeness of His light is as a niche wherein is a lamp (the lamp in a glass, the glass as it were a glittering star) kindled from a Blessed Tree, an olive that is neither of the East nor of the West whose oil wellnigh would shine, even if no fire touched it, light upon light; God guides to His light whom He will. And God strikes similitudes for men, and God has knowledge of everything.[21]

The light in the lamp or the perfect human heart needs no fire; it is the Spirit that God breathed into the human heart. His presence in the world is signified by the light that is inseparable from fire. Entering and being in the mihrab is an act of simultaneous acceptance and denial of that inseparability. The quest for the Light of the Praised as the supreme human potential entails passing through the fire of existence, separating his light from all things as the sign of its uncreated plenitude.

One could say that we humans, our immediate environment and the world as a whole are three forms of the mosque of existence. When we err, each of these three forms of the mosque of existence is out of joint; but when we repent, turning away from error and redeeming ourselves for what we have done, we purify ourselves and re-enter the mosque of our inner self, our place in the world and the whole of existence. The act of entering the mosque is a renewal of the whole world, its redemption from sin. The worshipper or guest of the mosque realizes this ascent from sin into order and peace in the mihrab, or place of war.

Thus, the mihrab is purpose, form and meaning in one. This is not an immutable state of unity; it changes from one individual and one generation to another. In the dictionary of Qur'anic terms and semantic structures compiled by al-Raghib al-Isfahani in the 12th century, for example, *mihrab* is the appropriate definition for a place of worship, the place where "war (*muḥāraba*) is waged against evil and profane desires."[22]

Nuha Khoury refers to this classic interpretation, observing,

> This pietistic interpretation relates *mihrab* to an action derived from the basic noun (*ḥarb*) and assumes a familial relationship between *ḥarb* (war) and *mihrab* (place of war). More recently, scholarship has attempted to understand *mihrab* through another presumed relative, *ḥarba* (spear). In

---

21 *Qur'an*, 24:35.

22 Iṣfahānī, *al-Mufradāt fī gharīb al-Qur'ān*, 160–61. Al-Iṣfahānī gives another meaning for the word *miḥrāb* as a place where the worshipper is "distanced" (*yakūnu ḥāriban*) from worldly preoccupations. See Ibn Sīdah, *al-Muḥkam wa al-muḥīṭ al-aʿẓam fī al-lugha*.

> this case, the evidence of the dictionary placement and word derivation is supplemented by that of historical reports mentioning the Prophet's use of a spear as a marking device during prayers at the *muṣallā* of Medina. *Mihrab* then becomes "the place of the spear" and, by analogy to the Prophet's actions, "the place of prayer" – one of the functional definitions for the Islamic niche *mihrab*.[23]

There is nothing incongruous in calling the central place in the life of peace a "place of war." Many scholars have sought to associate this with the place, purpose and meaning the term has acquired over its long existence. The noun *mihrab* embraces place, purpose and meaning: an imperial throne, a refuge, a hermit's cell, a grave, humility, fire and light, a place of war, the place of the spear and so on. These terms are covered by the semantic field that corresponds to the sacred teachings, ritual and sacred art, to the virtues of which the Praised is the enduring principle.

We are perpetually in the duality of the self and the world, of the uttermost depths and the most sublime heights of existence. Knowing the boundary of this differentiation enables us to ascend from a lower to a higher level, but the difference between the manifestations of the One on either side of the boundary remains insurmountable. The resolution of this duality lies in the return, the evanescence of everything except the Face of God. Evanescence is, in fact, seeing the Face everywhere and in all things.

There is no state in which we are not diverted from reality towards illusion, from the higher to the lower, from remembrance to forgetting, and from testimony to denial. In each of these states, our soul is at war against Satan, the diverter, and strives to turn to the One. This is a war where the goal is Peace. Nothing we achieve in this world is worth anything in comparison with the stage through which we pass on our journey of ascent to the One. The Praised says of this, "Satan reaches everywhere in the human body as blood reaches in it."[24]

To turn to God as Peace means to wage war against the diverter who is openly hostile towards us.[25] There is no discord in the creation of the heavens and earth.[26] The state of the self that dictates action based on ignorance obscures the world, and the order of the world is seen as disorder. Admitting ignorance and refraining from action based on what we do not know, along with loving

---

23 Khoury, "The Miḥrāb: From Text to Form," 4.

24 Bukhārī, 9:215.

25 See *Qur'an*, 12:5.

26 Ibid., 67:3–4.

what we know with certainty, is belief. Through belief, the discovery of order after chaos, resurrection after death, awakening from sleep, or remembering what we have forgotten takes place in the self.

The path to liberation from illusion is the discovery of order or being-at-peace as the relationship of all things to God as Peace. On this path, everything in existence nullifies itself to reveal at every instant that there is no reality but Reality. Within us, this is concentrated in free will, or the relationship of the faithful to the All-faithful through trust. The Praised says that for him, the whole world was made a mosque,[27] and he says of himself and his followers, "We have been made to excel (other) people in three (things): our rows have been made like the rows of the angels and the whole earth has been made a mosque for us, and its dust has been made a purifier for us in case water is not available."[28]

The Praised is therefore a perpetual warrior (*muḥārib*).[29] His presence, confirmed by the testimony that there is no god but God and that the Praised is His messenger, makes every place into a mosque, a place of prostration, with a place of war (*miḥrāb*) at the centre. Every mihrab denotes the constant presence of the Praised as our leader on the path toward realization of the human self. The moment the Praised is excluded as a constant presence in the mihrab, his place is taken by someone or something else and testimony to the oneness of God and the apostolate of the Praised is in disorder. Anyone who takes his place as the finest example is a diverter.

As the finest example of a warrior against the diverter, the Praised is also marked out by his leadership of those who bear witness to him and follow him

27 See Bukhārī, 1:256. The Bosnian *krstjani*, followers of the medieval Bosnian Church, also believed the whole world to be a place of prayer. They did not recognize separate buildings as exclusive places of prayer, as many contemporary records relate. In his will of January 5, 1466, Gost Radin writes, "... whoever kneels on the earth for my soul every feast day and on holy Sundays and holy Fridays and utters the Lord's Prayer, that the Lord God forgive us our trespasses and have mercy upon us on the Day of Judgment, for ever and ever." See Šanjek, *Bosansko-humski krstjani u povijesnim vrelima*, 364. Holy Friday may be interpreted in a variety of ways, but it is impossible to exclude Friday as the common heritage of the Bosnian *krstjani* and Muslims. In this regard, it is noteworthy that in the 15th and 16th centuries, the Spanish ecclesiastical authorities required Christians to report anything they saw as "Muslim": "They must tell inquisitors about people who observed Friday as a holy day and who changed into clean clothing on this day, who ate meat on Fridays and other days prohibited by the Church, and who ceremonially slaughtered the animals they ate." Perry, *The Handless Maiden*, 52.

28 Muslim, 1:265.

29 The noun *muḥārib* is derived from the third form of the verb *ḥariba* as an active participle.

in turning to God. This is the war waged against everything that diverts us from this turning. When praying in front of his witnesses and followers, the Praised placed a spear (*ʿanaza, ḥarba*) before him in the ground,[30] thus revealing himself to be the finest example of being in the mosque and in the place of war and so ascent on the upright path. Those who love God follow the Praised in their belief that God loves them.

The Praised is the finest example of ascent and return to the original human condition. Adam lost that state and fell to the uttermost depths, where he was given doctrine, ritual and virtue as the prerequisites for redemption and return. The apostle is the guide on that path. The two houses, one in the Valley and the other on the Mount, are signs of that return, of which the apostle's companion Abu Dharr said,

> I asked the beloved prophet Muḥammad which was the first mosque on Earth. "The Sacred House of Prayer" he said. "And then which?" I asked. "The Further House of Prayer," he said. I further asked, "What was the time span between the two?" "Forty years," the prophet replied. And he added: "The earth is a mosque for you, so wherever you are at the time of prayer, pray there."[31]

As this account relates, Adam experienced being both at the most sublime height and in the utmost depths through a descent or fall that, through God's mercy, was also offered to him as the path of ascent, on condition that he acknowledged and bore witness to the Praised as the finest example. God shows us the ascent in the journey of the Praised from the Sacred or Inviolable mosque to the Further Mosque.[32] There can be no ascent without being in the mosque of the world, in which the Praised is perpetually in the mihrab. Following him means ascending towards him or entering the mihrab that denotes him.

Every mosque, and consequently every mihrab, is both like and unlike every other. Until the modern age, there was no copying of existing mosques (or mihrabs) because every human self is unique and unrepeatable everywhere and at every moment. In modern times, it began to seem that each person was not the whole of humanity and that the whole of humanity was not each of us. In fact, every individual is ineradicable and unrepeatable. Each one of us is indeed the revelation of God, but in opposition to Him. No human knowledge

---

30 See Bukhārī, 1:284–85 and 4:493–94.

31 Bukhārī, 4:422.

32 See *Qur'an*, 17:1.

is anything but a sign of God's omniscience. In our little knowledge, we are constantly in a state of forgetfulness and, hence, of opposition to God. The possibility of remembering presents itself to us as the remembrance of God.

The mihrab is for just one person and consequently is in the mosque merely as a sign that we are perpetually before God but with the ever-present possibility of turning away from Him. Neither of these possibilities is the repetition of some earlier state. It is made known that the Living God is constantly engaged in some affair. As a sign of the totality of existence, the mihrab is a niche that receives us by enfolding us before and behind, to the right and left, from above and below.

Standing, we sense the niche of the mihrab as our interiority, which shows us differentiation into receiving and giving, into debt and claim, into masculine and feminine. To discover our whole self means to eliminate difference or differentiation, to unify ourselves, or to return to God as the revealer of the Word in our command to say, "He is God, One, God, the Everlasting Refuge, who has not begotten, and has not been begotten, and equal to Him is not any one."[33]

When revealing to the Praised that there is nothing that does not bow down before Him, God is indicating that the whole world is a place of prostration, mere flatlands. Our potential to perceive this and to prostrate ourselves as a testimony of what we see points to the world as a mosque. The horizontality of the world is thus offered to us as the start of the ascent. With our experience of the fall, we renew our awareness of the ascent or return. Wherever we may set off on the surface of the earth, the ultimate horizon eludes us. There is no house we can enter as the home we seek; whatever door we enter through, it cannot denote that which would wholly satisfy our love. A journey on the flatlands of the earth is thus merely a reminder of the ascending or upright path.

We are expected to wage war against everything that diverts us from the attraction of the Beloved. The ungovernable world manifests itself to us as the passage to the house of the Beloved. Our every state in the world of duality is thus cause for waging war, and every place is a place of war (*miḥrāb*). Wherever we turn, there is the face of the Beloved. He is closer to us than our jugular vein. His signs are all around us and also within us. All our earthly courses, on the seas and the rivers, the hills and the valleys, will therefore point to the Kaʿba as the sign of the heart, as the house towards which we travel, towards the plain from which the ascending path of return to the most sublime heights begins.

The Kaʿba is the sign of both the house and the grave, as well as of the heart as the uncreated, uncreatable centre of all things, in which horizontality and

---

33 *Qur'an*, 112:1–4.

verticality are united. None of us lacks two absolute certainties – the first as our "now" and the second as our death. Our "now" is surrounded by pain and suffering of which death is the culmination, and both are created. But everything in existence has its opposite. "Now" is in a duality with Eternity, and death is in a duality with life. "Now" and death are thus merely signs of their opposites, eternity and life. We can therefore say that our orientation towards the grave and the house are merely signs of the path to bliss and eternity. Every meaning of the grave and the house and all the rituals performed in them are endeavors to overcome the obstacles as we pass through them.

We seek to pass from the mosque of the world through the mihrab to a state without war, to the house of Peace in which God speaks to our soul as to His guest: "O soul at peace, return unto thy Lord, well-pleased, well-pleasing! Enter thou among My servants! Enter thou My Paradise!"[34] Wherever we are, we are at the centre of all existence. The whole of the outward world – forward and back, right and left, up and down – extends from and of us. Our position on the surface of the earth means being reduced to horizontality. The labyrinth of our existence is this reduction to the surface of matter and time, where we are suspended between the possibility of ascending to a higher level or sinking still deeper into matter and time. The ascending path from the earth to the heavens and from matter to Spirit leads through the door of redemption, return to the fairest uprightness.

Everything we devise and build is there to guide our passage through the labyrinth of the world on the upward path that leads from the depths to our redemption. The *čaršija* (see below) is thus the sign of all human construction; in it, all the roads on the earth's surface are arranged so as to bear witness to the four quarters and the centre from which all things come and to which they return. In this image, the city is the sum of all that is in our being situated between earth and heaven.

The centre of the čaršija, the point of intersection of two roads making us aware of the four directions, is a reference to the human heart as the centre of all things. We discover the heart so that we can testify within it to Light and Spirit. The čaršija thus becomes a sign of the contact between Spirit and matter, between Light and darkness, a gateway towards which we set off in our war against everything that is contrary to Peace, to the All-faithful, to the Beautiful.

The čaršija is the Bosnian word for the centre of a traditional town, literally denoting four sides. However they may be interpreted – as the four corners of the world, as the four sides of an invisible square, or as the four arms of a cross – they include the most important centre. Before accepting Christianity,

---

34 *Qur'an*, 89:27–30.

the Roman Empire was ruled by a tetrarchy of two emperors and their junior colleagues, each with one half of the empire, while the centre belonged to each and to none. The centre was empty, and the *polis* was created from that void. With the recognition of Christ, the centre of the Roman Empire came to belong to the Pantocrator, the Ruler of the World. No one could occupy it except Christ, the Word in whom God revealed Himself in the void and in the world. The pagan Roman rule of the tetrarchy was replaced by the Christian rule of five – Christopolis, in which the emperor and the patriarch were the representatives of Christ Pantocrator, and the patriarchs in Jerusalem, Antioch, Alexandria and Rome.

Standing before God is being in the mihrab. In standing, we confirm our differentiation between one side of the self facing the dark and one facing Peace. Perfect Peace is His will. The very potential of the will of the self means opposition to the Will of the Self. To be in the mihrab is thus to testify that there is no self but the Self, no will but the Will. Standing and confirming it by bowing, prostrating, sitting and standing up means being-at-peace and opening up to the intimacy between Mary and the Anointed, and the Praised with the Recitation. These four signs attest to the revelation of the One in the human heart.

The horizontal surface of the mihrab is a half a circle, with the other half formed by the worshippers. All four directions – right and left, forward and back – are thus united in a single point as the source and outflow of space as a whole. This point is the sign of our centre or heart as the uncreated and uncreatable principle in which knowledge and being are one. The ritual prayer is a journey or return to that union. The centre of the mihrab circle denotes the contact with the vertical axis or the steps on the upright path on which we stand erect or return from the depths to the most sublime heights.

The meaning of the mihrab is complex, but it cannot be isolated from its form and purpose. One may therefore speak of the multitude of semantic levels of the word *mihrab*, of which some of the most important levels will be discussed here. God's oneness is revealed in the multitude of signs of the world and of humanity. Its revelation is as if the boundary between the visible and the unseen were opened to allow phenomena to descend into the world. The niche corresponds to the opening. At the first level, the revelation of God in the multitude of signs is illumination, or the light of the Praised. God is Light, and illumination is His revelation or creation. The first revelation or creation is the Light of the Praised, who is thus the first of the people of peace, for there is no distance between him as the first recipient of the Light and the Light Itself. He is on the most sublime heights, and every descent to the uttermost depths will thus bear his seal, the testimony to God as bestower and the apostle as recipient. Without that seal or stamp of original perfection, every one of us would be left without the possibility of regaining return or ultimate judgment with mercy.

Illumination is the relationship between God as Light and ourselves as recipients or illumined. As the first recipient of the Illumination, the Praised is a lamp that shines. There is nothing that God does not illumine by means of the Praised as a shining lamp. This is the point of the testimony that there is no light but the Light and that the Praised is the first to be illumined and thus the first bestower of received Light.

God's power governs both the descent and the ascent of all things. His Throne encompasses the heavens and the earth, and the first before the Throne when the sending-down begins is the apostle, who is also the first in return and intercession before that same Throne.

God creates the Word by sending it down, and the Word returns from its differentiated manifestation to its original oneness. The tree is thus the symbol of a fine word, beginning as it does from a seed or fruit, in which it is concentrated in its supreme potential.

In line with these semantic levels, the mihrab is the sign of the oneness of God, of his Throne as the principle of all order in the worlds, of the apostolate of the Praised, of God as Light and the Praised as His illumination, and of the Word sent down by God through the Holy Spirit, the Spirit of Truth into the heart of the Praised, who is the finest example. Following the Praised is thus inseparable from loving God and the expectation of God's love for us.

Entering the mihrab means testifying to the oneness of God, to the desired standing before His Throne, to the apostolate of the Praised as the finest example, and to the return to perfect creaturehood and oneness as its principle. We thereby turn from darkness to light, from death to life, seeking and discovering the reason and purpose of our being in the world.

We are between death and life at every moment. "Now" and death are absolute certainties in our inner self. Our "now" is bounded by the past and the future and, being so bounded, constitutes our consciousness. If "now" is certain, consciousness places us in a relationship with that certainty and thus with death. If the mercy and knowledge of the Living encompasses all things, it follows that He also encompasses death, but it never encompasses Him.

The differentiation of the manifestation of the One into hell and heaven and the placing of a clear boundary between them means the death of death. There is nothing worse than hell, so its encompassing by mercy and life is the same as its disappearance in them. The Praised says of this differentiation and of the death of death:

> On the Day of Resurrection Death will be brought forward in the shape of a black and white ram. Then a call maker will call, “O people of Paradise!” Thereupon they will stretch their necks and look carefully. The caller will say, “Do you know this?” They will say, “Yes, this is Death.” By then all of them will have seen it. Then it will be announced again, “O people of Hell!” They will stretch their necks and look carefully. The caller will say, “Do you know this?” They will say, “Yes, this is Death.” And by then all of them will have seen it. Then it (that ram) will be slaughtered and the caller will say, “O people of Paradise! Eternity for you and no death. O people of Hell! Eternity for you and no death.”[35]

The same tradition relates that the Praised ended his account of the differentiation of the people by saying, “And warn them of the Day of distress when the case has been decided, while they are in a state of carelessness and they do not believe.”[36]

The heaven-hell duality is in every inner self as the two tendencies in differentiation – downwards, towards multiplicity and death, or upwards, towards unity and life – that are never wholly distinct. The first is directed towards nullity; as such, it cannot be realized in plenitude, for death is merely the absence or obscuring of life. The second is towards the Living, to Whom all things return, when in the return to Him death brings about its own death. Death is dispersal into multiplicity, and life is concentration in the One; this is our human existence in the world of multiplicity, differentiation and comparison. Doctrine, ritual and virtue simultaneously acknowledge and transcend it. Through them, we orient ourselves on the scale of existence from depth to height, dark to light, hell to heaven.

Doctrine, ritual and virtue (or knowledge, the way and will) orient or turn the self towards its supreme potential, towards the Hidden One Who manifests Himself in human language through the prayer, “Thee only we serve; to Thee alone we pray for succor. Guide us in the upright path, the path of those whom Thou hast blessed, not of those against whom Thou art wrathful, nor of those who are astray.”[37] One could say, therefore, that in doctrine, ritual and virtue, the world is both acknowledged and denied – acknowledged because the One manifests Himself in it, and denied because the revelation and the Revealed remain in some mysterious way both united and differentiated.

---

35 Bukhārī, 6:226–27.

36 *Qur'an*, 19:39.

37 Ibid., 1:5–7.

The world into which we come at birth, or even at conception, enters our consciousness by shifting the boundaries of the self in relation to the gamut of differentiated signs both within and without it. The signs are more or less clear in this differentiation, but never so clear as to escape from the shadows. Their lack of clarity increases or decreases in the incessant stream of consciousness. The endeavor to direct this stream towards clarity entails the question of the Ultimate manifested by the signs. The consequence of this is acknowledging the Ultimate as the Revealer of doctrine, ritual and virtue, through which the things of this world can be articulated and then connected with the principle they reveal.

It seems to us that the world has been created and made visible independently of our inner self, entirely exterior to us, but the whole world is in fact summed up in our inner self. This is the sequence from the whole of multiplicity to the One, or union in the self. The revelation of the Book as the complete discourse on humanity and the world includes both directions – descent or concentration and then differentiation into speech. Differentiation also includes summing the phonemes or letters into the Word or into sustainable clusters of meaning, as the beginning of the sura "The Cow" suggests:

> *Alif. Lam. Mim.* That is the Book, wherein is no doubt, a guidance to the conscious who believe in the Unseen, and perform the prayer, and expend of that wherewith We have provided them; who believe in what has been sent down to thee and what has been sent down before thee, and have faith in the Hereafter; those are upon guidance from their Lord, those are the ones who prosper.[38]

If seen as a verbal expression, this begins with three phonemes in the form of the names corresponding to their letters. Speech is thus connected to its distinct components. To understand the entirety manifested in multiplicity, we differentiate and connect. The Book is the whole of the world sent down into human oneness. It cannot be embodied in listening and remembering, and in speaking and reading, without the human self, without its centre in which the world is concentrated after being differentiated to be made manifest again. This manifestation in the world and the Book does not eliminate the unseen. Not only does it not eliminate the unseen, it actually emphasizes it as the defining factor of humanity and its orientation or guidance towards the mutuality of the knowing and the Known, the loving and the Beloved, which is the rela-

38 Ibid., 2:1–5.

tionship between the faithful and the All-faithful. None of these relationships eliminates doubt, though the purpose of this orientation is to weaken and eradicate it. The boundary between the participants in this separateness is constantly changing, but it can neither be removed nor accepted. The invisible remains ever-present. The relationship with the world and the Book requires the way and guidance as ritual or prayer in which the self is framed by two wills, its own or inner will and the Divine or outward will. The incorporation of the self into that context may be confirmed only by virtue – by being of those who "expend of that wherewith We have provided them."

Acceptance of the Book and belief in the unseen requires ritual or the way, as well as confirmation in virtue or in expending that which has been received. Do we have anything that has not been given to us? The obvious answer is no, so expenditure includes the Book, consciousness, belief in the Unseen and prayer. Expenditure transforms the self-satisfied self into the humble, generous self. Its acceptance of what is given, which may seem to belong to it, does not in principle exclude the same givenness that is beyond its finitude in time and space. What is more, the visible world confirms the Unseen, but strictly and decisively.

Everything that is in the outer horizons or the inner self has the Absolute as its purpose. But the world and the self are perpetually detached from it. Their detachment does not mean that they are not constantly connected with it. God is simultaneously near and remote, similar and incomparable. The world and the self are oriented or directed towards the absolute. Acknowledging and transcending the boundaries has no purpose without knowledge of a higher world, beyond and after the visible world. Knowledge is always slight, but sufficient for testifying to the Signified and the bond of love with Him.

The passage from the Recitation quoted above begins with the three letters or phonemes and then refers to the Book. This demonstrates the interrelationship of the minutest particles that can be arrived at by differentiation from the whole, which encompasses or concentrates all individualities. Being perpetually between the values of the minute and the whole that encompasses all things, we can never have absolute knowledge. And yet, it is on the basis of such perfect knowledge that we are required, as conscious beings, to perform the ritual of prayer.

Through the ritual, we become part of an order that we cannot encompass with our knowledge. We pray at the prescribed times and in the proper manner, even if not always entirely sincerely or without doubts. We can never have full knowledge of what we are doing. It may thus seem to us that little knowledge is a reason to choose doubt and insincerity over sincerity. In such a mindset, ritual and sincerity seem irreconcilable. When the quantitative world is seen as the only world, sincerity entails the rejection of a ritual that has been established without the agreement of its participants.

Doubt forms part of this assumption, but it is either disregarded or indirectly represented as sincerity. Every agreement between people introduces judgments on the basis of little knowledge. When we enter into such an agreement on the basis of little knowledge, we acknowledge our limitations and our potential to locate ourselves within them by trying to transcend them in our relationship to the Unseen, which is acknowledged as such. This means that the self is imbued with the conviction that the visible world derives from another world or from its higher meaning.

This kind of prayer cannot be reduced to mere supplication; it is a ritual that was ordained and prescribed as a way of inclusion in the world order. The place and the direction, the time and the duration, the movements and speech are ordained, as is the way we enter and leave it and the conditions for doing so. This is neither a response to an unexpected or wished-for manifestation nor the reflection of a certain state in the self. Sunrise, noon, the midway point to sunset, sunset and the onset of night are comparable in their constant, undeferrable repetition. There is both emergence and disappearance in all five. Earth and the heavens are reassembled in them after being separated, and, in this way, their giving and receiving takes place as the way of confirming their one principle.

The ritual prayers are located in the cosmic entity so that the given order may arise and vanish. No achievement in that order can be secured. The repetition of the five daily prayers seems to be like the footprints of a traveler who is looking ahead, his own footprints in the darkness erased. The repetition of the prayers with intent, preparation, entry, performance and exit includes renewal of the tension between ritual and sincerity.

One may become so accustomed to the repetition that the tension almost completely disappears. This does not mean that the inviolability and permanence of repetition eliminates the tension between the state in which we are and the aspiration to "embellishment" in which we serve God as though we saw Him.

Habit and ease in maintaining the rhythm of the prayer constitute only one of the states of the worshipper, explained by the Bosnian recommendation that if you pray all five prayers at the prescribed times for forty days, every day, you will continue for the rest of your life. Becoming accustomed in this way, which is desirable, also has its dangers. So long as there is prayer, there is the mihrab. Prayer is not an end in itself but is part of the journey to God. Whenever one senses delight in it, prayer should be turned against this, for

God alone is the goal of the journey. Does not the Praised say that praying for show, with some observer other than God in mind, is the greatest danger in this world?[39]

The repetition of the prayer is a turning away from the past to the "now" as reality, a "now" that includes in itself both past and future. The differentiation into hell and heaven of which the Praised speaks manifests itself as past and present. Death is slaughtered on their boundary. The eternity of hell and heaven is a state without death, but the mercy of the Living and the life of the Merciful abolish this differentiation in the return of all things to Him. The eternities of hell and heaven are the image of the distinction between evil and good deeds, but it is not deeds that redeem us – God's eternity is redemptive.

Differentiating between hell and heaven, between evil and good or, as is said in the parable of the Messiah, the tares and the wheat,[40] is impossible in this world. The entire Enlightenment project of modernity was based on the opposite assumption. Overcoming doubt of the unseen, which is at the centre of the traditional doctrine and the ritual that is inseparable from it, was set in a political context in modernity, in which the ultimate purpose of humanity is realization in society and history. As Eric Voegelin concludes, "Gnostic speculation overcame the uncertainty of faith by receding from transcendence and endowing man and his intra-mundane range of action with the meaning of eschatological fulfillment."[41]

If the purpose of war is perfect order in this world, death nullifies its point, and more – it mocks life and every attempt in life to deny or disregard death. Before every one of us is the perfect pair, the Praised and the Virgin, who are the manifestation of the One on this side of the place of war and on the other, beyond death. Contrary to them are association, concealment and hypocrisy.

After indicating the just outcome of the judgment of our deeds, the Praised warns us, as God's revelation says, of the day of distress, when beginnings and ends will cease, when differentiation will be complete and no indifference or unbelief will remain without consequences. The reality of the Hour is revealed in this way. It cannot be escaped in any yesterday or tomorrow. Every order in time is broken down. The just outcome of all this is differentiation into the eternity of hell and the eternity of heaven, as God says in the Recitation:

---

39 See Ibn Māja, 2:1406.

40 See *Matthew*, 13:24–30.

41 Voegelin, *The New Science of Politics*, 129.

> Surely the concealers, who have done evil, God would not forgive them, neither guide them on any road but the road to Gehenna, therein dwelling forever and ever; and that for God is an easy matter.[42]
>
> Say: "Is that better, or the Garden of Eternity, that is promised to the mindful, and is their recompense and homecoming?" Therein they shall have what they will, dwelling forever; it is a promise binding upon thy Lord, and of Him to be required.[43]

The eternities of hell and heaven are states without death, but not without mercy. The possibility of calculation and quantification ceases in eternity. Absolute differentiation is the image of the just outcome or of judgment from full knowledge. The consequences of the consciousness that concealed the Signified with signs and of the consciousness that was oriented towards Him through the world are in this judgment. These are the two outcomes of waging war – hell as the result of waging war for the world and heaven as the result of waging war for the Living.

Neither eternity, whether in hell or in heaven, restricts God or His mercy. These eternities give way to human finitude and hence to all calculation. This does not make them absolute; as manifestations, they too are worlds, contingent. The eternity of hell, like that of heaven, is conditional; only God's eternity is unconditional. Were it not so, His will would be limited by some eternity other than His. Whatever the reshaping of the self from the insignificance of the embryo to death[44] and from death to standing before God, from this earth and this heaven to the next earth and the next heaven,[45] none of these states can escape either God's "now" or God's will. Every contingent eternity is subordinate to that "now" and that will.

Wretchedness is the state of the self that denies its debt to God, while happiness is the acknowledgement of the debt and the consequent realization of the right to redemption. Hell and heaven are the two signs of those human states, as God says:

> As for the wretched, they shall be in the Fire, wherein there shall be for them moaning and sighing, therein dwelling for ever, so long as the heavens and earth abide, save as thy Lord will; surely thy Lord accomplishes what He desires. And as for the happy, they shall be in Paradise, therein

---

42 *Qur'an*, 4:168–69.

43 Ibid., 25:15–16.

44 See *Qur'an*, 30:54.

45 Ibid., 14:48.

> dwelling forever, as long as the heavens and earth abide, save as thy Lord will – for a gift unbroken.[46]

God's mercy that encompasses all things manifests itself in the eternity of heaven, which is thus less contingent than the eternity of hell. If hell is eternal, heaven is eternally eternal. Hell is extinguished in heaven, and people then gather in that eternal eternity, as is said through the Praised:

> God will admit into Paradise those deserving of Paradise, and He will admit whom He wishes out of His Mercy, and admit those condemned to Hell into the Fire. He would then say: See, he whom you find having as much faith in his heart as a grain of mustard, bring him out. They will then be brought out burned and turned to charcoal, and would be cast into the river of life, and they would sprout as does a seed in the silt carried away by flood. Have you not seen that it comes out yellow and intertwined?[47]

The passage from the fire to the garden, from suffering to bliss, from darkness to light, from wrath to mercy and from severity to clemency, does not mean the absolute eternity of heaven, for all things vanish except the Face of God.[48] They do not vanish in some indeterminate future, but here and now, for there is no reality but Reality, no eternity but Eternity. Nullity has no being, so the manifestation of the Face from one moment to the next (which is to say from one contingent eternity to the next) is always and eternally different.

The series of images of Bosnian mihrabs presented after this text begins with one from the Čaršija Mosque in Jajce. The *muqarnas* vault consists of fourteen rows, signifying the fourteen degrees of being or levels of existence relating to our earthly position – seven ascending and seven descending levels in the structure of the heavens and earth, corresponding to the seven degrees of ascent and descent in the human self. Each of these levels corresponds to a house or an image of the human heart.

The world was created with seven earthly and seven heavenly degrees.[49] Referring to the house in the sacred Becca valley, the Praised says:

> This house (the Kaʿba) is one of fifteen, seven in the heavens up to the throne and seven up to the limits of the lowest earth. The highest situated

46 *Qur'an*, 11:106–108.

47 Bukhārī, 1:24; see also 9:442–46 and Muslim, 1:117–19.

48 See *Qur'an*, 28:88.

49 Ibid., 65:12.

> one, which is near the throne, is the "visited house." Every one of these houses has a sacred territory like that of the Kaʿba. If any one of them fell down, the rest would fall down, one upon the other, to the limits of the lowest earth. And every house has its heavenly or earthly worshippers, like the Kaʿba.[50]

Accordingly, the mihrab is the sign of this human differentiation through all degrees of existence and is thus a sign of our potential to return, to ascend towards our original state or to sink even lower and further from our original vow to God. Every ascent means leaving the darkness for the sake of the Light, and every descent means sinking into deeper obscurity. When we are in the mihrab, which, in principle, we always are when praying, we face the Kaʿba as the sign of the centre of all existence. The fourteen houses, one after another, denote the levels of the visible and the concealed, or the degrees that correspond to the upright path to the human heart. This is the path we ascend by means of our realization in the testimony that there is no self but the Self.

Every mihrab, regardless of its form, denotes the potential of the human self to ascend towards the Light by following the Praised as our finest example and a light-giving lamp. The ascent is a movement from a lower level to a higher level, made possible by the memory of the vertical axis or of the circumambulation around it. There is no light in existence without shadow; it is always dark by comparison with a higher level, as indicated by the alternation of day and night and the phases of the moon. At every degree, these alternations and phases are different states of the self and thus of the meaning of what can be seen in the outer horizons.

In the Čaršija Mosque in Stolac, the succession of months through the year, from winter to summer, from cold to heat and from darkness to light, is depicted in twelve images, one for each month. Nine of these are visible and three are in darkness, and one could speak of each as a state of the self in its ascent from the uttermost depths to the sublimest heights, from the grave to resurrection, from now to eternity.

The inscription referring to Zachariah and Mary and, in its widest meaning, to John and Jesus, is associated with this. The inscription is invariably in fine calligraphy, which means that, facing the mihrab, we are one with sacred listening and speech, sacred writing and reading. The words of the inscription

---

50 A tradition of the Praised, quoted in Wüstenfeld, *Die Chroniken der Stadt Mekka* (Leipzig: Olms Verlag, 1858), 6, 1; quoted in Wensinck, "The Ideas of the Western Semites Concerning the Navel of the Earth," in Wensinck, *Studies of A.J. Wensinck: An Original Arno Press Anthology* (ed. Kees W. Bolle; New York: Arno Press, 1978), 51–52.

were first heard, then spoken, and then written down. They are the speech of God, with which the breath, tongue and lips of the Praised were inspired. When he utters them, they come wholly from his heart, borne there by the Spirit of Truth, the Holy Spirit.

In transmitting what he received, the Praised was thus one with the Spirit of Truth, the Holy Spirit, and may thus be called the Praised Spirit of Truth, the Praised Holy Spirit.[51] When these words are written down by human hand, they continued to bear witness to their source in the pure heart of the perfect man whom God chose to be His apostle. The words enable the human self to ascend the path of our descent.

The images of nineteen selected Bosnian mihrabs that follow this text show them as they are now or, in the case of mosques destroyed in the 1991–1996 war against Bosnia, as they were before the destruction or before the inscriptions referring to Zachariah and Mary were erased. Destroyed mosques are marked with an asterisk in the text under the pictures and in the list of figures at the beginning of the book. The inscriptions have been erased in the mosques of Konjic, Mostar, Ljubuški and Jablanica.

Because many of Bosnia's mosques have been destroyed or demolished more than once and some of them are of a much later date than the ones originally built on the sites, the dates given for their erection are those found on surviving inscriptions or in historical sources, where available, or dates based on tradition the author has been able to track down. As a result, the inscription of the Qur'anic verse "Whenever Zachariah went in to her in the Mihrab,"[52] which can be seen in the illustrations, may date from the time the mosque was first built or from when it was renovated or rebuilt.

The selection of these nineteen mihrabs was based on research covering several hundred Bosnian mosques. There are more than 1,500 destroyed mosques in Bosnia today and almost as many surviving, renovated or rebuilt, and it is fair to say that the verse about Zachariah and Mary, and thus indirectly about John and Jesus, is to be found in every mihrab. The mihrab, as

---

51 The descent or revelation of the Word of God to the Praised is associated once with the Spirit of Truth (Arabic *al-rūḥ al-amīn, Qur'an* 26:192–95) and once with the Holy Spirit (Arabic *rūḥ al-quds, Qur'an* 16:102; Aramaic *rûhâ kadisha*, Hebrew *rûaḥ qāḏôš*). When the Praised transmits the Word, he is equated with the means of its revelation; if it were not so, the Word he speaks would not be God's. God is in it, and with it says that it is of Him and His, as the Praised testifies. Clearly, the translation given here of "Spirit of Truth" is not in line with the usual way it is translated. There are many semantic and etymological reasons justifying the proposed translation, reasons that can be derived from a comparative study of the terms in Arabic, Aramaic (*rûhâ dashrara*) and Hebrew (*rûaḥ ha 'emeṯ*).

52 *Qur'an*, 3:37.

the universal symbol of the debt of uprightness (*al-dīn al-qayyīm*), represents the quintessential testimony to God's unity and the apostolate of the Praised through all the prophets and saints. It reminds us of our constant presence in the visible world of which the Unseen is the principle. Zachariah and Mary, John and Jesus were the last prophets before the Praised entered history; they are his witnesses and heralds.

This inscription in the mihrab indicates that God is neither in the heavens nor on earth, neither in the mosque nor in any other edifice; He is in the human heart, as He says: "My earth and My heaven embrace Me not, but the heart of My believing servant does embrace Me."[53] The Praised and Mary are perfect examples of believing servants. God speaks to us through the heart of the Praised, revealing to us the Recitation as His Word, just as He speaks to us through Mary's heart, revealing Jesus the Messiah to us as His Word.

Figure 4.1 is a map showing the location of the mihrabs from the illustrations.

Figure 4.2. The Čaršija Mosque in Jajce, for which the dubious name of Esme-sultan Mosque has been advanced in recent years, along with a very unconvincing account of the Sultana's earring, dates from 1749. The epigraph includes the words, "And have mercy upon our forebears, may they suffer no hardship in the world to come." The mihrab forms part of the harmonious composition of the mosque. Its fourteen rows of muqarnas decoration denote the seven heavens above our earth and the seven earths below as signs of our potential to ascend to redemption or descend into ruin.

Figure 4.3. The hajji Sinan Tekke in Sarajevo was built in the mid-17th century. It belongs to the Qadiriyya order. The mihrab in the sema-khana has a spear and an axe at its outer edges, further defining the meaning of the mihrab. The inside walls of the sema-khana are inscribed with the Qadiriyya wird, the liturgical words for the individual and the congregation, encircling the room and entering and emerging from the mihrab.

Figure 4.4. The Fethija in Bihać was originally St. Anthony's Church, built in 1400.[54] Its current name may be associated with the nouns *al-Fattāḥ*, the "Opener," one of the ninety-nine beautiful names of God, and *al-fātiḥa*, its feminine form and the name of the first sura of the Recitation. The relationship between ourselves as open and God as the Opener is the opening, discovering or liberation of our original nature. This is the outcome of waging war, of being in the place of war with the world and the self, which we desire and for which we pray. Mosques in Jajce, Zvornik and Soko also bear this name. The number seven is evident in the design of the mihrab in this mosque, as in most

53 In Ghazālī, *Iḥyāʾ ʿulūm al-dīn*, III, 12.

54 See Mujezinović, *Islamska epigrafika Bosne i Hercegovine*, 3:60.

others. The whole building is oriented towards the One and Peace. The verse about Mary and Zachariah is on a framed plaque above the mihrab muqarnas.

Figure 4.5. Tradition has it that the Musala Mosque in Kamengrad was built in 1463. A musalla is a place designated for congregational prayer. The current mihrab, with the verse about Mary and Zachariah, is the successor to several earlier ones that were destroyed.[55]

Figure 4.6. Milošnik is the name of one of the six surviving mosques in Livno. There were once fourteen. Its present form preserves a very ancient structure, albeit with significant later repairs. The mihrab is of unusual and elaborate design. The latest wall paintings date from the latter half of the 19th century.[56]

Figure 4.7. The Careva (Imperial) Mosque is the only one of Blagaj's seven mosques to survive.[57] The original mosque, dating from the early 16th century, underwent major alterations in the late 19th century. The inscription is above the simple mihrab niche.

Figure 4.8. The Atik is the oldest mosque in Bijeljina, built in the early 16th century on a site that had been adopted as a place of prayer well before. It has been demolished, rebuilt and refurbished on several occasions and in the 17th century was converted for a time into a church.[58] During its latest reconstruction, following its destruction in 1992, mediaeval tombstones (*stećci*) were discovered in the foundations, twenty-three of which bore epitaphs in Cyrillic.[59] The inscription is above the mihrab niche.

Figure 4.9. The Begova or Bey's Mosque is Sarajevo's central mosque, built in 1531 and endowed by Gazi Husrev-bey.[60] It is considered by many the spiritual centre of Bosnia. The whole of central Sarajevo, known as *Baščaršija*, with its madrasa, other mosques, bezistans, caravanserais, and shops, forms a network of streets and courtyards that spring from and return to the mihrab of the Begova. The stone mihrab has seven panels on which the verse about Mary and Zachariah is incised and gilded.

Figure 4.10. The Aladža was Foča's central mosque, built in 1550. The walls of the interior and portico bore painted decorations, hence the name Aladža, meaning "painted," "colorful" or "multicolored." One of seventeen mosques in Foča, its beauty and symbolic meaning made it crucially important for the collective memory of the Bosnian people. The inscription over the door read,

55 Ibid., 3:31.

56 Ibid., 3:109–110.

57 Ibid., 3:316.

58 Ibid., 2:156.

59 See Babić, "Rezultati arheoloških istraživanja lokaliteta Atik džamije u Bijeljini," 51.

60 See Mujezinović, *Islamska epigrafika Bosne i Hercegovine*, 1:292–93.

"This holy mosque and sublime masjid was built in the name of God Almighty by the benefactor Hasan, son of Jusuf, in the hope of recompense from Almighty God and seeking His pleasure. A mysterious voice pronounced its chronogram: 'O All-sufficient (God), accept (this) fine (work).'" The travel chronicler Awliyāʾ Chalabī inscribed these words on the sofa walls of the mosque in 1664: "I have travelled much and visited many towns, but I have never seen such a place before."[61] The verses about the Virgin and Zachariah were carved into a panel of stone below the crown of the mihrab. The Alažda was damaged by fire and restored on several occasions before being razed to the ground in 1992, making it one of the great symbols of the suffering of the Bosnian Muslims over the centuries.

Figure 4.11. The Čaršija Mosque, Čajniče's central mosque, was built in 1570.[62] Awliyāʾ Chalabī wrote of it: "It is a clean and spacious mosque in which the mihrab, minbar and mahfil are works of art. When the bright rays of the sun shine through its windows of crystal, Najaf and Murano glass, it is brightly lit."[63] The verses were carved below the mihrab crown. With the destruction of this and the town's other mosques in 1992, all ten mosques referred to by Awliyāʾ Chalabī were lost.[64]

Figure 4.12. In its present form, the Šarena or Painted Mosque is the successor to a number of earlier mosques, the first built in the 16th century.[65] It is the best known of Travnik's sixteen mosques and its name refers to the wall paintings on its inside and outside walls. The verse is above the mihrab niche.

Figure 4.13. The Ferhadija was the most famous of Banja Luka's thirty-six mosques. It was completed in 1579 and the inscription over the entrance door recording its construction reads, "This is a place built for the faithful in the name of God."[66] The passage about Mary and Zachariah was below the mihrab crown. The Ferhadija was razed to the ground in 1992.

Figure 4.14. The Tekke Mosque was built in 1579, one of several in Konjic. Its name refers to an associated tekke now long gone.[67] The passage is carved in the mihrab in the panels below the muqarnas.

Figure 4.15. Na Tepi is the local name for the mosque in Mostar built from 1612 to 1618 by Koski Mehmed-pasha. Its name refers to the nearby Mala Tepa

61 Ibid., 2:37–38.

62 Ibid., 2:66–67.

63 Çelebi, *Putopis*, 400.

64 Ibid.

65 See Mujezinović, *Islamska epigrafika Bosne i Hercegovine*, 2:325, 414.

66 Ibid., 2:191, 200.

67 Ibid., 3:422, 427.

or lesser weighing station. The inscription over the mosque door includes the words, "The Holy Spirit said: 'House of the All-merciful and a place of the good.'" It is one of Mostar's thirty seven mosques.[68] The mihrab contains the Qur'anic passage on the Virgin Mary and the prophet Zachariah.

Figure 4.16. According to tradition, the Čaršija Mosque in Prijedor was built in 1700. The hadith "My houses on My earth are mosques, and those who visit them maintain them" was carved on a stone plaque.[69] The passage about the Virgin Mary and the prophet Zachariah was above the mihrab niche. This is another mosque destroyed in 1992.

Figure 4.17. The Careva (Imperial) or Atik Mosque was built in 1719 in Kastel, the old walled town of Trebinje.[70] The passage about the Virgin in the mihrab and the prophet Zachariah coming to her was inscribed in the mihrab niche. This mosque, too, was razed to the ground in 1992.

Figure 4.18. The Old Mosque in Maoča has the passage above the mihrab niche. The mosque is believed to have been built in 1820.

Figure 4.19. The Azizija was built in 1863, after Muslims expelled from Serbia came to settle in Brezovo polje near Brčko.[71] The passage about the Virgin in the mihrab and the prophet Zachariah visiting her was inscribed in the mihrab niche. This mosque was also destroyed in 1992.

Figure 4.20. The Old Azizija Mosque in Bosanska Kostajnica was built after 1862, when Muslims fled there from Serbia.[72] The Qur'anic citation *kullamā dakhala ʿalayhā Zakariyyā l-mihrab ...* was inscribed in its mihrab.

Figure 4.21. This mosque built in Pobrišće in 1870 was the fifth mosque in Ljubuški. The inscription was above the mihrab niche.

Figure 4.22. This mosque was built in Pobrežje, near Jablanica, in 1912. Part of the Qur'anic verse on Mary and Zachariah was inscribed in the mihrab.

68 Ibid., 3:144, 219–21.

69 Ibid., 3:39.

70 Ibid., 3:358.

71 Ibid., 2:164.

72 Ibid., 3:46.

Post Scriptum: Good People

"God loves His friends, and they love Him."

The term *dobri*, "the good," used to denote holy individuals, is key to understanding the Bosnian Muslim tradition. It survives in that side of our collective memory that preserves its links with the past, but no full discussion has ever been published on the term. By "the past" we mean the perennial wisdom that exists at all times and in every tradition[1] – a tradition neither Jewish nor Christian nor Muslim, but Jewish and Christian and Muslim, and more, both in and above every language and time.

The term, like many others, is warp and weft of oral Bosnian sacred tradition. Religious in origin, and moreover Muslim, this tradition has seen its language, meanings and symbols systematically and persistently passed over in silence or denied or vilified by modern forms of Islamophobia, with their rationalistic and political dimensions. Not only those who would construct history in terms of truth versus myth engage in this, but even those who, despite their roots in the tradition, have nonetheless preferred to position themselves in the modern mainstream through rationalistic denial of it and so assented to its banishment from reality into fantasy.

The fate of the term "the good" is much the same as that of "Recitation," "laying on of the Book," *shahīd* (martyr), *fatḥ* (opening), *somun* (a round, leavened flatbread) and so on, relegated to antiquarian discussion of religious feasts from the solar calendar and prayer gatherings on mountain and hill tops, in caves, at springs and the like. Yet these are key elements of a complex Bosnian identity that includes Muslims who believe in what was sent down to them *and* what was sent down before them as revelations of one God.[2]

This rift in individual selfhood and folk identity may instructively be represented through the fate of the term "the good."[3] Hardly anyone denies it as part of his or her heritage and practically every Bosnian can give at least some

---

1 This chapter deals with the topic of holy people. It cannot be dealt with from within the forcible separation of Judaism, Christianity, Islam and other sacred traditions. Looked at from the context of the Muslim tradition regarding the friends of God, one cannot but agree that "research on the origins and the development of doctrines concerning holy men and Friendship with God still remains at an early stage." (Radtke, *The Concept of Sainthood in Early Islamic Mysticism*, 7).

2 See *Qur'an*, 29:46.

3 This is also discussed in Mahmutćehajić, "Good people: A goal reached by many paths."

 | DOI 10.1163/9789004279407_124

account of it: The good are witnesses to the unconditional obligation to do what is good and beautiful, unconditional because essential to the self or heart through which the Creator speaks to all the worlds. For most people, therefore, the good seem strange, present and absent, untameable, their deeds miraculous and potent, making them appear like stranger-guests come to remind the majority of what they have forgotten and may redeem them. There are stories of them everywhere, always different. These good are like shadows, but their presence is remembered just like real times and places. They belong to all generations thanks to language. The stories have common features, but differences in representation. They live on in discourse meant for all of us, men and women, children and elderly, witness to their response to the Praised, who said: "Be in this world as if you were a stranger or a traveller."[4]

The stories of the good are gentle and quiet, respectful of the dignity of the listener. They are simple and so more powerful than any didacticism. Their simplicity helps them spread among the speakers of a given language, without suffering damage in transmission: their mysterious nature tends to be preserved, without accretions beyond those that gentle speech and confidence call forth in the listener's authentic ready and open receptiveness. Concise and rounded, language reveals and receives them as though always already a part of it.

That the term "the good" has such a presence in language, faithfully reflecting the Bosnian world-view that holds our reason and purpose in the world to be metaphysical and elusive of matter's deadening grip, confuses and disturbs those who would, in their ideologized histories, be lords of the boundaries they determine for things, so that they may allocate their purpose.

For example, it is claimed that how the terms *dobri ljudi* (good people) and *dobri Bošnjani* (good Bosnians) were used during one particular period has absolutely no connection to the use of the same terms at any other period of that language's history and in particular during the past five centuries, in which Bosnian identity has included the bearing of witness to the Praised as seal of the prophets.[5] This is a very clear case of the construction of

---

4 Bukhārī, 8:284.

5 Džaja argues that the terms "good Bošnjani" and "good people" which feature in Bosnian written documents prior to the late fifteenth century are unconnected to anything in the centuries marked by a Muslim presence. Such attempts to construct discontinuity in Bosnian history, as a rule ideological and anti-Muslim, are not rare, but Srećko Džaja's is more instructive than most. He attempts to demonstrate that something immediately evident to every speaker of Bosnian is not in fact the case, claiming that his approach is "scholarly" and "scientific." See Džaja, "Dobri Bošnjani" and "Boni Homines." On the *dobri/Good* in Bosnian

discontinuity by the pernicious action of an ideological historiography in which, as the experience of the twentieth century reveals, the views of ideological elites and the violence in which they clothe themselves are nested.

Such an ideological construction is a clear consequence of its author's inability to understand traditional intellectuality, which is in essence one, no matter the linguistic, cultural or phenomenological diversity of its appearances in history. It is worth stressing that the very idea of the good or holy individual (the dobri) cannot be grasped without taking due account of the proper subordination of analytical reason to Intellect, myth, or faith. Only myth or faith can ensure the lasting openness of the self to the supra-individual or real, the only source of moral orientation and the suppression of mere ego.

The Bosnian noun "dobri" is both a singular and plural form derived from an identical adjectival form. It means "a good person" or "good people." In Bosnian Muslim tradition, this is a characteristic of election which connects the individual with God, but in a way that makes his or her attributes visible to others, so that they may know and witness them. The *Dobri* is thus one who is related to God as Good through goodness of character and thus appears to others as though he has walked out of the realm of their higher self.

The adjective *dobri* takes irregular forms in the comparative (*bolji*) and the superlative (*najbolji*), probably related to the Bosnian adjective *blag* (mild, gentle, clement, benign …), whose primary meaning is "good." Comparison with the Sanskrit *bhárgāh,* meaning "light," derived from the Indo-European root *bhelg-*, points to the Indo-European root *bhel-*, meaning "to shine."[6] The comparative degrees of the adjective are therefore linked with an Indo-European root associated with "light," whence the Bosnian word *bljesak,* a flash or flare. The *dobri* are therefore benign and enlightened, connected through illumination and benignity with God as Light and Benign. The good are thus the actualized potential in each of us, a counter-example to every concocted order that conceals or denies God's presence.

The Indo-European root for the adjective *dobar* is *dhabh-*, "that which suits." Its range is from the specific "that which fits a given space and time" to the

---

tradition see Softić, *Zbornik bošnjačkih usmenih predaja,* 54–65; Maglajlić, "Nikola Tordinac i usmeno pjesništvo"; Smailbegović, *Narodna predaja o Sarajevu*; Hadžijahić, "Jedan nepoznati tuzlanski hagiološki katalog"; Idem, "Badžijanije u Sarajevu i Bosni: Prilog historiji duhovnosti u nas"; Bejtić, "Jedno viđenje sarajevskih evlija i njihovih grobova kao kultnih mjesta."

6 See Skok, *Etimologijski rječnik hrvatskoga ili srpskoga jezika,* 1:167.

abstract and moral field of the (morally) "fine."[7] There are semantic associations with the adjectives *prijatan* (pleasant, agreeable) and *prijazan* (amiable, affable, courteous), which in turn suggest a not insignificant connection between the nouns *dobri* and *prijatelj* (friend).

In the modern study of language, the original Word has sunk below the horizons of rationalistic calculus. It has been analysed into distinct participles of speech, with the loss of overall meaning. No wonder Bosnian epic singers failed to understand the modern Homeric scholars who referred to parts of sentences as words. For these often illiterate singers, who knew by heart songs thousands of sentences long, the word was the full expression, a closed whole, just as all things on earth and in the cosmos are wholes within a greater whole, worlds within the worlds of Divine speech.

To set our discussion of the good and of good people in a broader context, let us turn to potential sentences or, rather, whole words which speak of being in time, luminous and fine words. The near countless stories of the good have precipitated certain patterns familiar to us all, if often used elliptically or metaphorically.

A man or woman is said to be good when their appearance and way of life reveal to everyone their commitment to the good. They are not ruled by worldly passions and confusions. Among their own, they remain guests, considerate of themselves and others, ever conscious of their departure from the transience of this world and return to a higher one. Their individuality is never dominated by the many. What many consider ordinary they consider marvellous, while what the majority respect and value usually seems worthless to the good.

The concept of the *dobri* is part of the legacy of tradition, the indivisibility of humanity from the world, the seen from the Unseen, multiplicity from the Principle. They connect with God, whose beautiful names include Peace, Faithful and Beautiful, through being-at-peace, faith and beauty. Male and female can enrobe the self in these attributes in the same breath and with the same qualities.[8] Our being male and female cannot be understood in isolation from the duality in which the One manifests Himself. Male sees its other side in female, and conversely, female finds plenitude in male. In the good man or woman, this split is reunited in sign of the One.

Of people with gentle, glowing faces one may say "There is a light to his face, like one of the good." When someone displays knowledge hard for the ordinary person to understand, one says: "You are inspired, like one of the good." Of one dressed in white, "Like one of the good, all in white." The same is said

7 Ibid., 1:421.

8 See *Qur'an*, 33:35.

of someone wearing green: white denotes purity, green the return of life. The patient and submissive, calm in the face of misfortune or anger, but fierce on behalf of the weak and vulnerable, are said to be "good, not of this world." One hears said of a good woman, "Either she's being good or praying, or reciting the Qur'an, one only ever sees her being good."

Where in English one says "the good old days," Bosnians say, "when the good walked the earth." Embroiled in a dispute that seems impossible to resolve by ordinary means or by mediation, people say, "There's nothing for it but to wait for the good." If a person turns up unexpectedly, someone is bound to say, "And there he was, out of the blue, like the good." If someone unexpectedly survives mortal danger alive and well, one is likely to hear, "The good got her through it." And if someone wants to force a way through what most people regard as impossible, one says: "You'll get there, if you are one of the good."

A clean, well-favoured place is said to belong to the good, as somewhere they either gathered or a good person lies buried. Of the graves of the good, one says, "Sometimes you see a light there, and sometimes there will be some trace of the good." Or it might be that, "The good never speak, if they don't have to. When they speak, their word changes the world." The good are spoken of in Bosnian tradition as of presences whose existence and deeds attest to the reason and purpose of our being in this world, but in a way that challenges any routine or defensive scheme of thought.

Memories of the good are ringed with stories passed on to recall the possibility of salvation under even the worst of circumstances and the need to persevere in doing good. Such witness has its reason and purpose outside of time and space and can be understood only through traditional ontology. The good are signs of our perfect potential in the plenitude of life and happiness indivisible from the here and now. They belong to the heritage of the prophets and connection with them, being in some ways their heirs and inheritors of their wisdom.

In principle, every sacred tradition teaches that being has many levels, arrayed in descending order, each manifesting the one above. Accepting this ontology helps us discover ourselves and the world by ascending to the principle and our original beauty. The principle's prophets are many, to be found at all times among all peoples, revealing the same truth in different forms. Both individually and collectively, they are a link at each level of being with the principle.

Evidence for the truth of the tradition founded by the prophet lies in what he said in the name of the Lord and about how it came into being,[9] and above all in the emergence of good people and sacred art among each generation

9 See *Deuteronomy*, 18:22.

of his followers. The good and sacred art are well recognized by most of the community linked to the prophet, who venerate and preserve them even when the powerful oppose them.[10] Without good people and sacred art, there is no tradition, properly speaking.

The good never fully disclose their standing. Their presence is like a flash of light, reminding the majority of the ontological progression from waking through sleep to death.[11] The good, as friends of God, are both present and absent – present in reminding us of creation's reason and purpose, absent in that their appearances are but a trace. The traces they leave germinate, however, in the experience of those who meet and listen to them. Stories survive, but the only material evidence of their existence at a given time and place is the grave.

This is why stories about the good are often connected with graves, as solid evidence of the truth of their lives as preserved in people's memories: however hazily their experiences may be reflected in them, people pass on stories about them in quest of their own higher potential, that state of the self experienced as a blessed beginning. This beginning, the real in every here and now, is our final refuge from pain and suffering. The good have also left their own written witness, revealing themselves in their own stories, or allowed their friends to bear witness of what the majority could not.

Attempts to turn them into an object of study assessing and systematically demonstrating what they may or may not have been can never provide a proper answer, as the subject-object distinction does not apply in their case. They are either present or absent, but never so as to be an object of knowledge for someone without some connection to a given saint's self or original nature. Just as the study of poetry is not poetry, so a systematic, rational image of the good necessarily fails to comprehend the inner reality of the good whereby they really are what their appearance and deeds suggest.

Approaching the stories about the good within the framework of the modern human sciences, which assume a self-sufficient individual fully capable of using reason to create a perfect from an imperfect world and so build a political order which will realize the fantasy of a heavenly people in this-worldly security, they appear mythical, a lesser legacy of olden days, evidence of ignorance and lack of education. These stories have never been a serious object of

---

10 Scholars almost invariably note a contrast between popular attachment to and veneration of the good and the rejection of their role in rationalistic approaches to the prophet and his followers. See Goldziher, "Veneration of Saints in Islam," 2:255–341.

11 Among the followers of the Praised, the good, or friends of God, are at the heart of all theosophical experience. For more on this subject in the written tradition, see the brief account in Radtke, *The Concept of Sainthood in Early Islamic Mysticism*, 38–40.

study that might put the self in a different light. Their reality cannot be grasped on the basis of externally acquired knowledge. They come from the deepest core of our humanity, where speech itself does not reach. This is why the question of how they have lived on through the centuries, while so many rational constructions and forms of violence built on their backs have died away, is a challenge that defies silence under our so-called post-modern and post-liberal conditions.

At the beginning of his treatise on *The Life of the Friends of God*, Al-Hakim Al-Tirmidhi writes about people who make it their business to try to understand and present this phenomenon:

> Those who engage in this kind of talk have no understanding of this matter whatsoever. Indeed, they are people who consider Friendship with God by way of learning, and they speak on the basis of analogies, suppositions and mere imagination which originates with themselves. They are not people endowed with allotments from their Lord and they have not attained to the halting stations of Friendship with God, nor have they known personally the action of God's favour. Indeed, their way of speaking is based on sincerity and their standard in all things is sincerity. But when they undertake to speak of the halting stations of the friends of God, their speech is cut short since they are deficient in knowledge of the action of God's favour in His servant; for they are deficient in knowing God and whoever is deficient in knowing Him is even more deficient in knowing His divine favours.[12]

The good are good because that is how they relate to God as Good. They say they have nothing of their own and that what people see in them is merely the manifestation of what they have received from the Good. These words of Mary's son, the Anointed, say something similar: "Why callest thou me good? There is none good but one, that is, God."[13] Similarly John, Zachariah's son, said: "A man can receive nothing, except it be given him from heaven."[14] He affirmed the perennial truth of our birth, expressed by the Anointed thus: "Verily, verily, I say unto thee, Except a man be born again, he cannot see the kingdom of God."[15]

---

12 Tirmidhī, *The Life of the Friends of God*, 41.

13 *Matthew*, 19:17.

14 *John*, 3:27.

15 Ibid., 3:3.

One is not good out of calculation or by imagining what such a person might be. The good are not good because external circumstances require them to be so; their reasons are received from on high. They are concerned with redemption, which is to say with turning from illusion to reality and from sin to forgiveness. In so turning, the self comes to a heightened awareness of the split within it between its original and ultimate potential perfection and the alternative of obscurity and violence. The commandments the good obey are from the uncreated and uncreatable centre of the self. They care not for how people will see them or talk about them. For them, there is not one moment in which God is not present. Everything the good do is a confession that there is nothing God does not see.

That they are known as the good in Bosnian is hardly unrelated to the basic meaning of the term. The good are a product of their time, but not as conceived of in the construct of history as a chain of events stretching from some antiquity through the present on to an ineffable end of history. Their time is their "now." They do not seek escape, but to see both hell and heaven clearly. For them, all time is "now."

The Praised is in them, as their higher potential. Their highest goal lies in companionship, friendship and brotherhood with him, as the maternal prophet, the herald of the merciful God. They seek and find their self in this. God says of them: "Whoseover obeys God, and the apostle – they are with those whom God has blessed, prophets, just men, martyrs, the righteous; good companions they!"[16] The moment they want more, the good are faced with the enigma of the light. Asked whether he had seen God, the Praised replied: "There was only Light. How could I see Him?"[17] This is the response of the good, who confess Light and illumination in and by their selves.

The good are the friends of God, related to God as Friend through friendship. God speaks of this relationship through the Praised:

> O believers, whosoever of you turns from his debt, God will assuredly bring a people He loves, and who love Him, humble towards the believers, disdainful towards the concealers, men who struggle in the path of God, not fearing the reproach of any reproacher. That is God's bounty; He gives it unto whom He will; and God is All-embracing, All-knowing. Your friend is only God, and His apostle, and the believers who perform the prayer and pay the alms, and bow them down. Whoso makes God his

16 *Qur'an*, 4:69.

17 Muslim, 1:113.

> friend, and His apostle, and the believers – the party of God, they are the victorious.[18]

The condition of the selves of the friends of God determines an awareness of His presence that accords with the Divine revelation that He is closer to us than the jugular vein,[19] Face to face with us[20] and in us with His signs.[21] They not only say of what they have seen, heard and know, This is God, but also, This is not God. "Is not" and "is" are their confession always and to all of no god but God.

They recognize that their knowledge is always little, but sufficient to turn to Him Whom they know and love Him beyond all else. He is constantly before them and they remember Him as though they see Him and, in that recollection, do everything in the fairest manner, since while they may not see Him, He sees them. They expect to be judged for what they do by God, Whose knowledge and mercy encompass all things. Conscious of that judgement, the good care not for human reproofs and rebukes. They know they bear witness to what cannot be defeated and any sufferings that may befall them are only a way of cleansing their sins.

The good is a dependable friend to those who know them, a model of the closeness that manifests beauty, clemency and justness. The miraculous power of knowledge over ignorance, mildness over anger, and tenderness over harshness, is confirmed through the good. One can see why the Bosnian term *dobri* is so closely linked with the Qurʾanic "friend" (Ar. *walī*, pl. *awliyāʾ*). The Arabic form derives from the verbal root *w-l-y*, meaning "to be close." The close are friends and have friendship (*wilāya*). For this, we must relate to God as Friend through friendship, which is through the Praised as His apostle.

To be His friend is to receive His good and beautiful qualities, after the perfect example of the Praised, and then to manifest them as authority, power and competence. Since friendship, our relationship as friends with God the Friend, includes knowledge and love, united in faith, we can grasp why God says through the Praised: "God is the Protector of the believers; He brings them forth from the shadows into the light. And the concealers – their protectors are idols, that bring them forth from the light into the shadows; those are the inhabitants of the Fire, therein dwelling forever."[22]

---

18 *Qurʾan*, 5:54–56.

19 See *Qurʾan*, 50:16.

20 Ibid., 2:115.

21 Ibid., 51:21.

22 *Qurʾan*, 2:257.

The extremes of our potential are light and shadow. The self is split between them – a self that incites to evil and a self at Peace. When our will turns towards the shadows, our friends are idols, without reality. This is the condition of the self set against the Self. The alternative is the upright path, on which we follow the Praised to realize faith. The faithful know their Lord as Beautiful and ever Close and love Him as such, irresistibly attractive. No closeness satisfies, for constantly growing through love in knowledge of the Beloved and love of the Known.

God calls us in the Recitation, through the Praised, to confess our love of God by following the Praised, as the condition for His love. Following the Praised in confession of our love of God is self-realization in prayer: "Guide us in the straight path, the path of those whom Thou has blessed." Those who are guided on the straight and upright path, whom God has blessed as followers of the Praised, are His friends. The followers and heirs of the Praised, as the maternal seal of the prophets, mercy to the worlds and light-giving lamp, are God's friends, the good.

God has two kinds of friend – the friend of God's claim and the friend of God. God's offer of confidence or faith as our relationship with the All-faithful allows two possible responses – acceptance or rejection, yes or no. When we accept, we relate to the Beloved out of will, always able to comply or resist. Had we rejected the offer, we would have no will of our own, entirely subordinate to His, just like the sun and the moon, the stars and the planets, the trees and the beasts. Our will allows us to be open to countless paths and destinies.

If the friends of God's claim want to approach God on their path, they must acknowledge the claims of all with a claim on them, knowing their debt to God through countless debts to themselves, to others and to everything in existence, as created in, with and by truth. Admitting our debt to all things, their claim or right as created, we earn our right to true self-realization and return to God.

Attaining that right is a journey of constant striving, endurance and pains to confirm or discover being guided. Confidence in the grandeur of the goal and the presence of the Praised as discovering the higher potential of the self renders the pain and suffering, ambuscades and surprise attacks, threats and diversions on the path powerless to keep us from the ascent.

Friends of God are elect. In and through them we see how God relates to His beloved servants. Our reason and purpose are in the perfect potential designated by the friends of God. We are always expected to acknowledge our debt for that potential. Only then do we relate to God, as all the horizons of the world and self are a path to our own plenitude. God says of His friends, on whom every individual and the entire world are focused:

> Whoever takes a friend of Mine as an enemy, I shall wage war on him. My servant draws near to Me with nothing more loved by Me than the acts of worship that I have enjoined upon him. My servant continues to try to draw near to Me with more devotion, until I love him. When I love him, I will be his hearing with which he hears, his sight by which he sees, his hand with which he strikes, his feet on which he walks. When he asks Me for something, I will respond and when he takes refuge in me, I will grant it to him. I do not hesitate in doing anything I intend to do as much as I hesitate in seizing the soul of My faithful servant; he hates death and I hate hurting him.[23]

The journey along the upright path has two components – recognizing God's signs in world and self. It is a journey from the depths to the height, the valley floor to the summit of the mount, the Inviolable to the Further Mosque, a night journey with the Lord and an ascent through existence. Two things occur on the way – realization, as the manifestation of all His most beautiful names in full differentiation and then as focused in the One, which is the supreme achievement of friendship.

These two arcs of the circle of existence – the descending arc from the height to the depths and the ascending arc of return to the One – make of us a stranger and traveller whatever our condition. The traveller can never assure his own independence. The greater the commitment to the journey, the more powerful the sense of dependence on the goal. As travellers, we find the reason and purpose of our enterprise through our destination. Pain and suffering, and witnessing the death of others in earnest of our own, never leave us. The stronger our ties with the goal, the more evident suffering and death become.

Travellers are constantly being tested by questions of loss and gain. We cannot continue, stand still or return without sensing in the change a new goal to accept, an old one to abandon. We are ever sacrificing, consciously or no, willingly or no, something of what we have to receive something we have not. Sacrifice is the essence of all our endeavours to pass higher.

In speaking of the good as part of the perennial wisdom, of human experience in all its variations, one cannot escape being in a world of injustice, suffering, killings. These experiences are universal, but experienced by individuals. We may bear witness to our patient endurance of injustice and suffering, but not to our death. The deaths of others that we witness are thus the more ours in that they speak to us with their silence and impotence. If we are

---

23 Bukhārī, 8:336–37. See also Graham, *Divine Word and Prophetic Word in Early Islam*, 173–74.

to become aware of our knowledge, we need the testimony to what we neither see nor hear.

The good are witnesses of whom we all have need in enduring pain and suffering – knowledge that connects us to our highest potential and so with God, in and with Whom suffering and death are resolved. In the modern world-view, the good are imagined as having nothing to do with the reality of our "now," as belonging to a time before the dis-enchantment of the world. Can the good help us understand what we experience with our whole being as pain and suffering in these times?

Every mass killing entails an ideological image of the victims. Their individuality is reduced to their membership of a homogeneous group. The individual as bearer of trust in relation to God as Faithful is replaced by more individuals, a greater number necessarily being of greater value. Personal characteristics cannot be distinguished in this reductive view. The resulting image of depersonalized people is static. New attributes leave the basic image unchanged or reinforce it.

This is what happens to the image of the Bosnian Muslims in the construction of historical "discontinuity," in which they are a stratum imposed by outside force on the country's Christian history. They are wholly identified with instances of human violence perpetrated by some Muslims and suffered by some Christians and these isolated cases are used to construct a generalized image of the horrid and cruel, filthy and dishonest, faithless and conniving, uncultured and violent Turk, Saracen or Jew. These cruel infidels are not themselves, in this construction, capable of pain and suffering, as they are so wholly evil as to be impossible to hurt. The essence of the Muslims' faith and their entire heritage is then associated with this image of them, and the purpose of this construct is to call into question their very witness to God and human perfection.

In such constructs, the term "dobri Bošnjanin," the good Bosnian, found in writings from the period of the Bosnian kingdom, are necessarily unconnected with the heritage of the Bosnian Muslims or even with the more general term "the good," present for so many centuries.[24] Though that term's presence pervades the feelings and language and oral heritage of the Bosnian Muslims, they simply do not exist for the creators of these constructs, whose purpose is to comprehend the entire history of Bosnia within their interests.

These attempts to depersonalize the Bosnian Muslims are like the phenomenon described by Theodor Adorno, Hannah Arendt, Zygmunt Bauman and Irving Greenberg in their efforts to define the connection between modernity

24 See notes 3, 5 and 6.

and the *Shoah*.[25] The determination to dehumanize the Jews, which resulted in the death of more than a third of their entire numbers in Europe in the mid-twentieth century, is recognizably the same feature of modernity that underlay the genocidal killings of Bosnian Muslims between 1941 and 1945 and again from 1991 to 1996. Though ancient, this image re-emerged at the end of the twentieth century in the mechanics of power of the military structures, industrial powers and trained generals. The world without God wrapped up the Muslims in a second "without." They were also without humanity, a claim heard previously, but now set in the new context of human rights.

When what happened in Auschwitz and in Srebrenica, horrors just fifty years apart, is taken as a new manifestation of the enigma of God and man, it is worth re-examining Nietzsche's many references to the death of God. If God is with us wherever we are, as He has revealed,[26] the crucial question, which can be heard in various quarters, also suggests its own answer: Who abandoned whom – did God abandon us, or we God?

If God is with us wherever we are, that means He was with the people in Auschwitz, in Srebrenica, and at every other place of slaughter and burning, execution and poisoning: at all those places where people were no different from insects or vermin, infected bodies and rotting corpses to be disposed of. He was thus with both killers and killed. But how could that be?

Were we to say that God was not there, His revelation – that He is with us wherever we are, closer to us than the jugular vein, his signs in every self – would have to be effaced, along with all the prophets and the books, beliefs and rituals. There is, however, another possible answer to the puzzle. If the Shoah and Srebrenica happened at the very crest of the wave of modernity, coinciding with the "flowering" of ethics in which ends are the defining standard and all available means are conceivable and exploitable to achieve the desired end, a reason for them might be found in our abandonment of God, which placed consumerist and economic goals at the heart of every human endeavour and disassociated them from wisdom.

There can be no wisdom without fear of God, for the love of God is indivisible from fear. The greater the love, the greater the fear of the wrath of the Beloved. There is no love if it is not freely given by lover and Beloved. Despite the mutual attraction by which they know each other, the possibility of loss or of the bond being broken is ever present. Everything is expected of the

---

25 Adorno, *Negative Dialectics*; Arendt, *Eichmann in Jerusalem*; Bauman, *Modernity and Holocaust*; Greenberg, "Cloud of Smoke, Pillar of Fire: Judaism, Christianity and Modernity after the Holocaust."

26 See *Qur'an*, 57:4.

Beloved, whence the fear of Him. Becoming aware of that fear is a precondition for wisdom.

Loving God includes fear of Him, and the abandonment of God is often an attempt to rid ourselves of that fear. If we assume there is no God, it may seem that everything is possible. The world is subject to us and that relationship brings neither love nor fear. It seems to us that every path is open, from the most bestial to the superhuman, from satan to god, murderer to saint. According to Irving Greenberg, the abandonment of *God* before the *Shoah* was the loss of *fear* of *God*.[27]

Fearing God means acknowledging Him as All-conscious, All-powerful, All-seeing and All-hearing, All-knowing and All-just, the ultimate, wholly independent Judge. Loss of fear of God helped make both Auschwitz and Srebrenica possible, where Jews and Muslims were first dehumanized and then killed on an industrial scale. There was no distinguishing homogeneous Jewishness or homogeneous Muslimhood into individuals, unique and authentically in His image. All of them, individually and collectively, were identified with the dehumanized mass, a heap of contamination.

Modernity is incomprehensible without the abandonment of God. The reasons for abandoning Him, of which Freud, Marx and Nietzsche are good examples, may be traced back to speculative logic. Back in the eighteenth century, Kant laid the foundations for this when he claimed that pure reason can acquire knowledge only of the phenomenal world, not of the intellectual or noumenal reality of God, freedom and immortality. This does not mean that these realities do not exist. Indeed, Kant held the ethical life possible only if one accepts them. But the positivists might conclude from this that if something cannot be proven, it should be repudiated and abandoned.

Since dehumanization and its consequence, killings, which are still going on, call for a new, non-propositional logic and a different view of God, "what has been sent down to you, and what was sent down before you" has to be understood in a different way. We cannot return to the past, but the condition of the unreformed self holds nothing but a repetition of past experiences of persecution and killings, humiliation and injury.

Though in constant motion, the world's reality is unalterable, given its essence. This is as true of the I, thanks to its free will in both reality and illusion. The I changes from moment to moment, as does its grasp of reality. Incorporating it into the reality of the world means distinguishing true and false and choosing truth. The self is between absolute light and its absence

27 Greenberg, "Cloud of Smoke, Pillar of Fire: Judaism, Christianity and Modernity after the Holocaust," 46.

on the various levels of its being. The journey, our realization, is ascent out of darkness into light. We become different with every step, as the ratio between the presence and absence of light within us constantly changes.

The venture of emerging from darkness into the light, which is a matter of the "now," offers many possibilities. Everything in the world reminds us of this split and its possible outcomes. Will, love and knowledge are torn between extremes, in every condition of the self – towards nullity or the One. The perfect individual is the centre of the order in which these possibilities manifest. If it does not remind us of our perfect human potential as our reason and our purpose, why should the world be our concern? Al-Hakim al-Tirmidhi placed the knowledge of the prophets and friends of God at the centre of the world, saying:

> Through this knowledge they come to know God's ordering of the world, and through this knowledge they have dealings with God and undertake their servitude to Him. Indeed, whenever the covering of this kind of knowledge is removed for someone, the highest form of the Unseen is revealed to him so that he may behold the realm of sovereignty. And this occurs after he becomes upright, refined, educated, purified, rendered sweet-smelling, broadened, developed, promoted, and is made accustomed, and Friendship with God is brought to perfection for him. Thus he becomes suitable for God and may participate in the highest assembly of the assemblies of the Friends before God.[28]

We attain that sublime state here and now in the world that envelops and permeates us, before the Face of the Creator. In acknowledging the presence of the friends of God, we recognize our own potential, our selves as the stage for discovering God. We turn to our original nature as the treasury of the names. In discovering them, we discover ourselves, for they are Divine, and by calling Him by them we connect with the Called. They are beautiful, and in and with them the caller discovers the Beautiful Who manifests Himself as ever more attractive. As He tells us in the Recitation: "To God belong the Names Most Beautiful; so call Him by them."[29]

Everything in the heavens and on earth bows down to God – the sun and the moon, the stars and the mountains, the trees and the beasts. Each one of us may also voluntarily participate in that expression of humility before God, as a way of glorifying Him in praise, and encompass the whole of existence

---

28 Tirmidhī, *The Life of the Friends of God*, 86.

29 *Qur'an*, 7:180.

as a place of prostration in our knowledge of all the names. In our sublime potential, we reject every association with God of anything in the world or self. When we begin ritual prayer, wherever we are, we turn towards the barren valley in sign of our poverty and lowliness compared with the potential of our centre. It is in that poverty that we find God as Abundant.

Before the Abundant, we poor humans are beggars, praying to and prostrating ourselves before Him, stretching our hands out towards Him. When we rise from prostration, it is not we who rise, but God who raises us up, placing us before Him, face to Face. Our awareness of this prompts us when standing to bow, to turn our faces towards our baseness and prostrate ourselves, so that God may raise us up again. In these standings and prostrations, repeated as departure from each day for the sake of the Day of Reckoning, in which our utter poverty and everything we have received in debt – life and will, power and knowledge, speech and sight and hearing – will be acknowledged and justly reckoned and shown to each self. The debt of each self to God is greater than the sum of all things in the heavens and on earth and all that lies between them.

It is impossible to conceive of good people associating anything with God. Their inner self bears no-one's burden but their own. All the signs in the world, self or books remind them of this, as signs of God as Signified. The good repudiate any other view of them. For the good, all the worlds have value as signs of God and whenever they appear otherwise, the good deny them. At no place or time can they find meaning but by sharing in remembrance of God. Every place is holy, as soon as those present remember God as All-holy. Without that, a place is but a veil over the forgetting self.

There is no place that the purified do not transform into a place of purity, of prostration, and of concentration of all the worlds in glorification of God. Every place manifests itself as fairest uprightness, towards which we ascend from the depths. Ascent is possible at every moment. Without it, the world is but a valley floor. The good are aware of this baseness and constantly turn towards the path of ascent. Both possibilities are present to their minds – ascent and descent. The moment the quest-object is equated with the tracks, ascent becomes descent, and vice versa – when the signs on the horizons and in the self attest to the Signified, ascent ensues.

When we are in a state of forgetfulness, the world seems closed, incorporating both beginning and end, with no way out of the dungeon. The friends of God recognize all the signs of the world as the reality of the manifestation of the Unseen and call upon God, the prophets and the angels as their witnesses. The role of the prophets of God is precisely that to which the good bear witness: there is nothing in world or self that is not a sign of God; everything may be taken as distinct from Him, and they struggle with their entire being against the potential of the self to associate its own image with God and everything that is not of Him.

The earth and all its people are irreconcilable opposites: water and fire, earth and air. It may seem to them that they are the rulers of this earth, but it is always God's, never ours. When this patency is transformed into another image, we cease to be what we are and place ourselves in opposition to the prostration of all things in existence. We banish ourselves to the margins of existence, whose sign is the supremacy of fire and earth. Against this stands the supremacy of water and Spirit. These two extremes denote the path on which we all are. To choose the prophets is to be on the path leading to the supremacy of water and the Spirit, which does not exclude our awareness of the temptations that every new day on the journey brings. We cannot overcome the obstacles and ambushes on the path without awareness of the goal, which can be known through its opposite.

The way and the goal must not be identified. Ritual, with all its aspects, including the Book, with its commandments and its prohibitions, praises and exclamations, encouragements and threats, belongs to the way, as it becomes manifest in the ever-changing self and its confession of no hour but the Hour. We can, however, enter into ritual out of habit, unaware of its real significance. It can become a fetish, emptied of meaning.

In their view of ritual and the law, the good are constantly on the margins of comprehensibility for those among whom they are present. They attest to the dangers of reducing the end to the means. Their emphasis on difference, means and end often involves blows, flashes and reversals that shake, even shatter, the cocoon of meaningless habits that confused individuals and groups use to subjugate others. The good are always unexpected and unusual; they confuse and disturb, and are an impediment to the guardians of the old order who slander and vituperate against them.

Our every condition involves three possibilities – to be guided in ascent, to fall, or to go astray. Each is within us. To ascend is to turn to the self's core and find its reason and purpose, to inform the world around us with meaning. Al-Hakim al-Tirmidhi says of such a person: "His hope grows great and his heart expands and his breast becomes wide. But the danger here is grave. He now stands between being protected from sin and being abandoned by God. And that is so because whoever's foot slips on this path, it is here that it slips and here that he is forsaken by God."[30]

---

30 Tirmidhī, *The Life of the Friends of God*, 52.

Turned to God, we cannot condition anything. Our sense of dependence and poverty grows and our cares become but one concern – not to be abandoned by God. The standards, values and promises that are or could be proposed to us by others seem like threats, for turning to them and attuning our inner self is necessarily accompanied by a loss of awareness of doing what is beautiful in service to God Who sees us. The good do not care that they are censured by others; quite the contrary, they find, in such criticism, affirmation of their concern for the cruciality of their here and "now" before the Judge.

The good are in constant fear of their Beloved and without fear of people. They are heedless of critics and criticism. The good are always in some sense like the Melami dervish, doing nothing for the sake of gain from others. The term refers to people who, in their behaviour, speech and silence, oppose every attempt to impose external manifestations of virtue or fidelity, including doing good for the sake of being seen to do good. For the good, acts represented as virtue and then affirmed by being made public and incorporated into associated rituals and knowledge – these belong to the world of delusion. They never reject doctrine or ritual, but point out when they are used to serve individual or collective power structures, whereby the disease, ugliness and ignorance of the self are represented as health, beauty and knowledge.

In none of its states is the self free of murmurings from its depths. All its pleasures are thus dangers, against which we must wage a great and incessant battle. The view that nothing should be done for gain or human recognition, that everything is from and for the sake of God, sums up the Melami determination to oppose all fraud and delusion, particularly their own. The noun *melam* derives from the Arabic root *lama*, meaning "to censure," "to rebuke," "to reproach," in line with the Qur'anic definition of people "not fearing the reproach of any reproacher" (*wa lā yakhāfūna lawmata lā'im*).[31]

The good then pay heed to the Praised's warning against associating anything to God in worship, which is the greatest threat to redemption. Hearing his companions discussing the Antichrist, the Praised said: "Should I not inform you of that which I fear for you even more than the dangers of the Antichrist: it is the hidden act of association; a person stands to pray, and he beautifies his prayer because he sees the people looking at him."[32]

Ignaz Goldziher associates the Melami with Greek cynicism:

> The essential thing about these people, who have rightly been compared with the Cynics of antiquity, is their extreme indifference to outward

31 *Qur'an*, 5:54.

32 Ibn Māja, 2:1406.

> show. Indeed, they attach value to arousing wrath by their conduct and to drawing on themselves the disapproval of other people. They commit the most shameless acts, merely to carry into execution their principle of contemning the contempt that others have for them, *spernere sperni.* They wish to be regarded as transgressors of the law even when in fact they are not. They are intent on arousing the contempt of mankind so that they may prove their indifference to its judgment.[33]

Marijan Molé takes a different view, believing that the Melami concealment of being good by refraining from showing virtue could be associated with aspects of early Syrian Christianity.[34]

In line with the principle of the union of opposites, every prophet has an enemy – "Satans of men and jinn, revealing tawdry speech to each other, all as a delusion."[35] Enmity toward the Praised as the Friend of God is embodied in false prophets and the falsely righteous. Since there is no prophet after the Praised, false prophethood is now found in the falsely righteous and their role as satans is the most pernicious way in which people can be led astray. Al-Hakim al-Tirmidhi says of them:

> Such people forever remain in disgrace and ignominy. The hearts of the sincere repudiate them, and they are loathed by the throng of religious scholars. This is because they are deserters and hypocrites. They have not renounced this world and turned to God in repentance, nor have they cleansed themselves, nor made themselves true, nor are they upright in pursuing their journey to God. Moreover, their carnal souls do not allow them to persevere in carrying out the work of their limbs, for therein is grief and constraint, and they had attained the refreshing breeze and spaciousness. But their hearts are not occupied with what is due to God, nor are their bodies occupied with worshipping God. Indeed, they have stopped their limbs from worshipping and stopped their hearts from journeying to God and travelling through the halting stations. They have become a laughingstock of the devils, an object of censure to the knowers of God, a cause of weariness to spirits and a burden on heart. They travel from land to land and defraud the weak, ignorant and womenfolk of their worldly goods. They eat their fill by making a display of their serenity and their good behaviour, and by citing the words of men of spiritual

33 Goldziher, *Introduction to Islamic Theology and Law*, 149.

34 See Molé, *Les mystiques musulmans*, 72–77.

35 *Qur'an*, 6:112.

> distinction. Day in and day out you see them practising deceit and pursuing their prey. They bring about benefits through magic charms, only undertake works when desire moves them, and choose their circumstances in blindness.[36]

Concealment is a way of opposing the self that incites to evil. This kind of incitement could be said to divert us from our original nature. Whenever we act or omit to act in the name of something that is not and cannot be first and last, we are counting on gain or loss in something that in its origins has neither life nor power, neither will nor knowledge, neither speech nor hearing nor sight. The axis mundi or straight path has two directions, down and up. The downward path corresponds to death, which is contrary to life, as it says in the Psalms: "the dead praise not the Lord, neither any that go down into silence. But we will bless the Lord from this time forth and forever more. Praise the Lord."[37]

Death makes praise possible as our relationship with God the All-praised. Experiencing the death of others, the living come to know the sanctity of the gift they have received. Conscious of themselves, they can praise and call upon the All-praised in silence, murmuring and speech. When they respond to Him in prayer at the prescribed times and share in the universal act of worship, the world becomes Word in and by them and creation in and with truth acquires expression in the good, for whom worship is truth, truth worship. Distinguishing opinion from being, they reveal opinions as an illusion we readily become accustomed to till it appears the truth itself.

Prayer banishes illusion and truth returns to being, being to truth. The illusion that truth lies in opinion may be banished by seeing its various aspects. This can be achieved in prayer, in time and space, in a succession of linkages, movements and recitations, pauses and continuations, feeling with all our being alone and with others, speaking and listening, and repeating the ascent into an order of which we are conscious, but which we ourselves have neither created nor conceived.

Glorifying God, we bear witness to our praising nature, which gathers the Creator's whole manifestation in potential. Witness to the unity of the All-praised is inseparable from witness to our apostolate as the potentially perfect recipient of praise and realization in it. Realization, redemption and return lie in reaching the height and discovering our perfect praising nature.

---

36 Tirmidhī, *The Life of the Friends of God*, 53–54.

37 Psalm 115:17–18.

The world and everyone in it take part in this witness, each on their own path, the stage on and by means of which we discover our finest nature, the reason and purpose we are on the path of coming and return, the path of the good as our ever-present potential. The good see in some a higher, in others a lower level on that path. Some represent a higher possibility on the open path of return, reminding us of what we have forgotten, and for which we all yearn at heart.

These are the good who restore our awareness of why we are here and for what we shall leave this world. They live on in the memory and stories of their communities, as reminders in each self that our "now" is the real. They pass with ease from generation to generation. Their graves and physical remains delineate areas of memory, and with them the image of the world alters. The good remind us that all things in heaven and on earth bow down and that we are called to join them.

God told the Praised to say: "If you love God, follow me, and God will love you, and forgive you your sins; God is All-forgiving, Ever-merciful."[38] People have always and will continue to respond to this, in as many ways as there are individuals. The good are to the forefront in responding. Their authority derives from nothing but their love of God, following the prophet, and God's love of them. Their friends are reminded by their graves, too, to love God and follow the prophet. Those who seek power, glory and renown to express their will are in conflict with the good.

Attachment to their graves is an affront to power-holders, who reveal their image of God by attempting to divert people from such connection to them. It comes from the very centre of the self, however, from the nature God gave us as a condition of His friendship: "Surely God's friends – no fear shall be on them, neither shall they sorrow. Those who believe, and are mindful – for them is good tidings in the present life and in the world to come. There is no changing the words of God; that is the mighty triumph."[39]

God is with us, wherever we are,[40] closer than the jugular vein,[41] our Friend. The realization of our original nature means discovering friendship as our connection to God. No age, no generation is without His friends. "What are the outward signs of the friends of God?" asked a student of Al-Hakim al-Tirmidhi in response to which the sage enumerated seven signs, saying of the first:

---

38 *Qur'an*, 3:31.

39 Ibid., 10:62–64.

40 See *Qur'an*, 57:4.

41 Ibid., 50:16.

> The first sign is what the apostle of God is reported to have said when he was asked: "Who are the friends of God?" He answered: "Those who when they are seen cause people to think of God." And then there is what is reported about Moses who asked: "O Lord, who are Your Friends?" God replied: "They are those who when one thinks of Me, one thinks of them, and when one thinks of them, one thinks of Me."[42]

Though they are everywhere, the footprints of the friends of God are always beyond. Constantly near and far, their real presence eludes exteriority, finitude. Their tracks disappear at the boundaries and lead towards the span of the heart. All of existence seems tiny with them, a mere sign on the path of return. And we are all travellers from our perfect origin to its rediscovery or realization, in constant descent and ascent, arrival and return. As such, the friends of God or the good attest to the supreme human potential, as al-ʿArabi wrote:

> Man possesses two dimensions of perfection. By the first, he accedes to the degree of divine manifestation, and by the other, to the degree of existential manifestation. On the one hand, he is spoken of as servant from the fact of his being subject and that he comes into existence afar the fashion of the world after having been non-existent. On the other hand, he is spoken of as lord by virtue of his office as lieutenant, his form, and "the most beautiful constitution." He is like an isthmus between the world and God the Real, an epitome of the creatural world and that of metaphysical reality. He is the dividing line between the degree of divine manifestation and that of the world of generation, like the imaginary line separating light from shadow. Such is his reality. Total perfection belongs to him both in temporality and in Eternity.[43]

Uprightness or steadfastness, as a sign of our position as the link between the world as manifestation and the Creator as manifest, points to the axis as the path by which manifestation descends from its principle and ascends towards it. The path is the link between travellers and that by or towards which they are travelling. At every moment both new and the same, we discover our path as we journey along it as travellers. We are defined by its connection with our destination and at every moment of our journey discover ourselves in and

42 Tirmidhī, *The Life of the Friends of God*, 124–25.

43 Ibn al-ʿArabī, *Inshā' al-dawā'ir*, 22, cited after Fenton's translation, "The Book of the Description of the Encompassing Circles" in Hirtenstein and Tiernan (eds.), *Muhyiddin Ibn 'Arabi: A Commemorative Volume*, 29–30.

through our goal. Our journey's ultimate possibility is our self-discovery in our destination.

Traveller, path and destination change from moment to moment. Each moment the destination reveals differently to those who seek it. Uprightness is what differentiates us from the other animals. As we become aware of it, this trait enables us to stand erect and ascend in return to our sublime potential, the most beautiful uprightness of our original creation,[44] on which we focus, directed by our innermost self to it as our goal, the destination in and with which we hope to discover ourselves fully.

Only absolute uprightness, like the axis mundi between earth and heaven, body and Spirit, suggests the destination as seen in the sacred tradition revealed by the All-holy to the Praised through the Holy Spirit. The All-holy and Upright[45] sent down to him the redemptive words: "Thee only we serve; to Thee alone we pray for succour. Guide us in the straight path, the path of those whom Thou hast blessed, not of those against whom Thou art wrathful, nor of those who are astray."[46]

The path of the righteous, who ask God to guide them on the straight path, is focused on the Praised as best example,[47] the maternal principle[48] of all things. He leads us from the depths to the finest uprightness. As the first of the people of peace[49] he stands before the Upright to confess none upright but the Upright and the Praised as His apostle. His apostolate is defined by his being both indivisible and separate from the One Who sent him, like a light that both is and is not like its source.

In our capacity to follow the Praised, to discover him within as our original nature, as the light of the Light and our connection with the Light, we stand within an onto-cosmological perspective where we cannot be enclosed by anything in the heavens or on earth or between them. He is the first intent and supreme goal of creation, his imagination beyond differentiation or boundaries.

This is what is meant when people speak of the splitting off of the light of the Praised (Ar. *al-nūr al-muḥammadi*) and the Light of God from the Light of the All-praised. The mystic Sahl at-Tustarī wrote "When God willed to create

44 See *Qur'an*, 95:4.

45 The All-holy (*al-quddūs*) and the Upright (*al-qayyūm*) are two of the names of God mentioned in the Recitation. See *Qur'an*, 59:23 and 2:255.

46 *Qur'an*, 1:5–7.

47 See *Qur'an*, 33:21.

48 Ibid., 7:157.

49 Ibid., 6:163.

Muhammad, he made appear a light from His light. When it reached the veil of the Majesty, it bowed in prostration before God. God created from its prostration a mighty column like a crystal glass of light that is outwardly and inwardly translucent."[50]

The Light of the Praised is God's manifestation as All-praised and Light[51] and as His love to be known. In pre-existence, the Light of the Praised is the same as the Pen and the Intellect, uniting all things to be made manifest in existence as God's record of Himself in diverse ways – in all existence, its visible and invisible aspects, and in all the signs in the world or self, the prophets and the books. On coming into existence by the Creator's will, things bring with them something from being in the column of light as the treasury of all things, and bear witness to it as their original abode.

The Praised saw what he saw, and "his eye swerved not, nor swept astray,"[52] as nearest to God at beginning and end, so to follow him is to love God, Who sees Himself through the Praised. Tustarī says:

> Indeed, he saw Him another time,[53] namely in the beginning, when God created him as a light in the column of light before the beginning of creation by a million years. He stood before Him in worship, with the dispositions of faith and was unveiled the mystery by Mystery Itself "at the Lote-Tree of the Boundary,"[54] that is the tree at which the knowledge of everyone comes to an end.[55]

The earth-heaven and body-Spirit axis mark the praising column of light. Turning to our original uprightness, we seek that column within ourselves. Our goal is God, to stand before Him, face to Face, when neither creature nor Creator have aught to see but the one in the One, the beloved in the Beloved. Confessing no god but God is inseparable from confessing the Praised as His apostle. Making of Light a column into infinity and eternity means everything

50 Tustarī, *Tafsīr al-Qurʾān al-aẓīm*, 40; quoted in Böwering, *The Mystical Vision of Existence in Classical Islam*, 149.

51 The All-praised (*al-ḥamīd*) and the Light (*al-nūr*) are two of the names of God mentioned in the Qurʾan. See *Qurʾan*, 11:73 and 24:35.

52 See *Qurʾan*, 53:17.

53 *Qurʾan*, 53:13.

54 Ibid., 53:14.

55 Tustarī, *Tafsīr al-Qurʾān al-ʿaẓīm*, 95, in Böwering, *op. cit.* 150–51.

rendered unto time can serve the One as Light that is ever Light upon Light,[56] above all things that can be witnessed.

Connection with the column of praising light is the path of the good and upright. Tustari writes:

> The ultimate ranks of the righteous are the initial states for the prophets, although our Prophet worshipped God Most-High with all states of the prophets. There is no leaf in paradise among the leaves of the trees on which was not written (the name of) "the Praised." Through him is the origin of the things and through him is their final sealing, for he is called the seal of the prophets.[57]

He seals the prophets and to link with them is to link with him, and vice versa – to confess the Praised is to confess them all. There is nothing in existence, or us, to which the light of the Praised is not first. Its discovery is a way of returning to the Light upon lights, which is to say to discovering and acknowledging the inner light of every self as praising and, through it, to confessing no reality but the Real. By making following the light sent down through the Praised[58] a condition of His covenant with the prophets, God made known to them his original firstness, that is not nor can be the same as the One Who sends him.

God calls the Praised a light-giving lamp.[59] A lamp gives light because an original, uncreated source of light enables it to do so. The praising light is received direct from the Light, perfectly pure and original to creation, maternal as recipient, but prophetic in its bestowing or shining. Its expectations and signs are in every self and all things gathered in the Praised as knowledge of the names. Of the presence of the Praised and his light as a light-giving lamp in all things, Tustari wrote: "The light of the prophets is from his (the Praised's) light and the light of the heavenly kingdom is from his light, and the light of this world and of the world to come is from his light."[60]

---

56 See *Qur'an*, 24:35.

57 Tustarī, *Tafsīr al-Qur'ān al-'aẓīm*, 48, in Böwering, *op. cit.* 152.

58 See *Qur'an*, 7:156–57.

59 Ibid., 33:46.

60 Tustarī, *Tafsīr al-Qur'ān al-'aẓīm*, 47, in Böwering, *op. cit.* 153.

FIGURE 4.1 *Map of Bosnian mihrabs from the illustrations*

FIGURE 4.2 *The Čaršija or Town Mosque*, Jajce 1749*

FIGURE 4.3 *The hajji Sinan Tekke, Sarajevo, 17 Century*

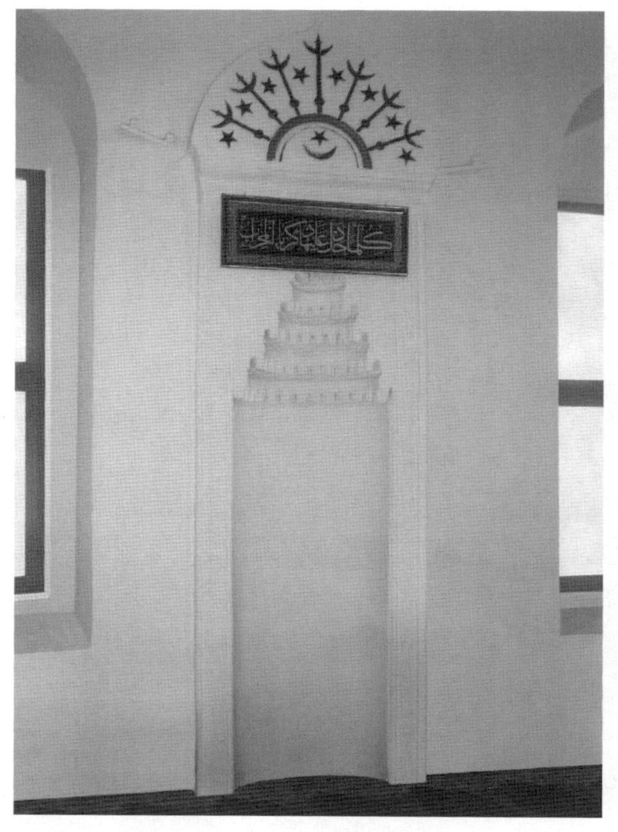

FIGURE 4.4 *The Fethija Mosque, Bihać, 1592*

FIGURE 4.5 *The Musala Mosque at Kamengrad, 1463*

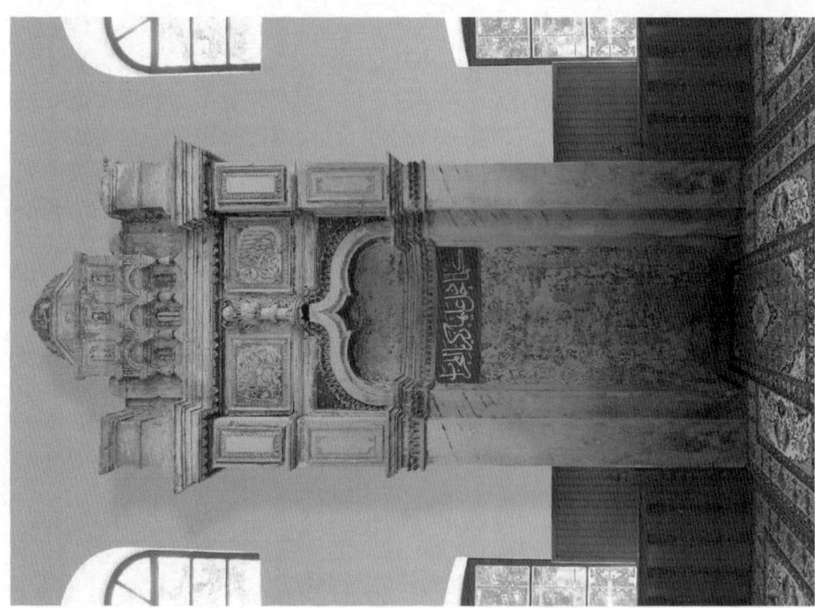

FIGURE 4.6 *The Milošnik Mosque at Livno, 1490*

FIGURE 4.7 *The Careva or Imperial Mosque at Blagaj, 1519*

FIGURE 4.8 *The Atik Mosque* in Bijeljina, 1525*

FIGURE 4.9 *The Begova or Bey's Mosque in Sarajevo, 1531*

FIGURE 4.10 *The Aladža Mosque*, Foča, 1550*

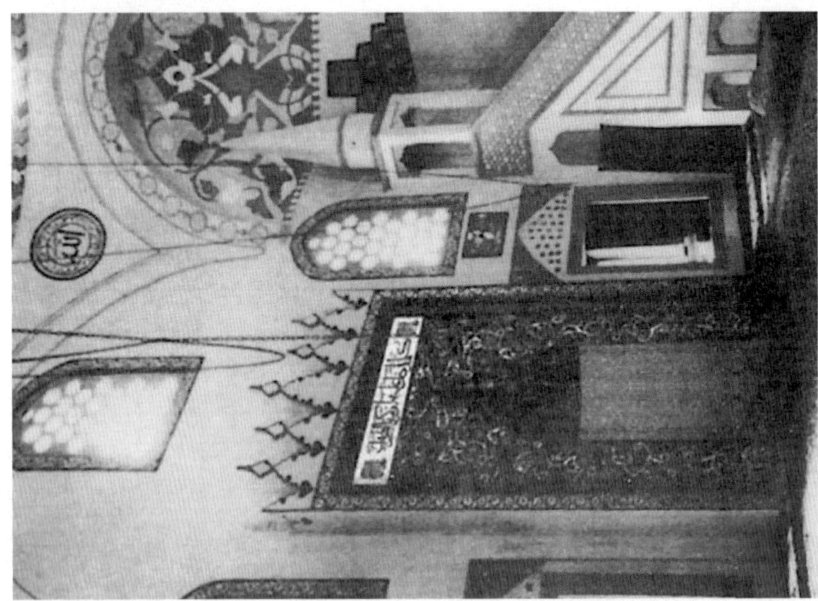

FIGURE 4.11 *The Čaršija or Town Mosque* in Čajniče, 1570*

FIGURE 4.12 *The Šarena or Painted Mosque in Travnik, 1571*

FIGURE 4.13 *The Ferhadija Mosque* in Banja Luka, 1579*

FIGURE 4.14 *The Tekke Mosque in Konjic, 1579*

FIGURE 4.15 *The Mosque at the Mala Tepa (Na Tepi) in Mostar, 1618*

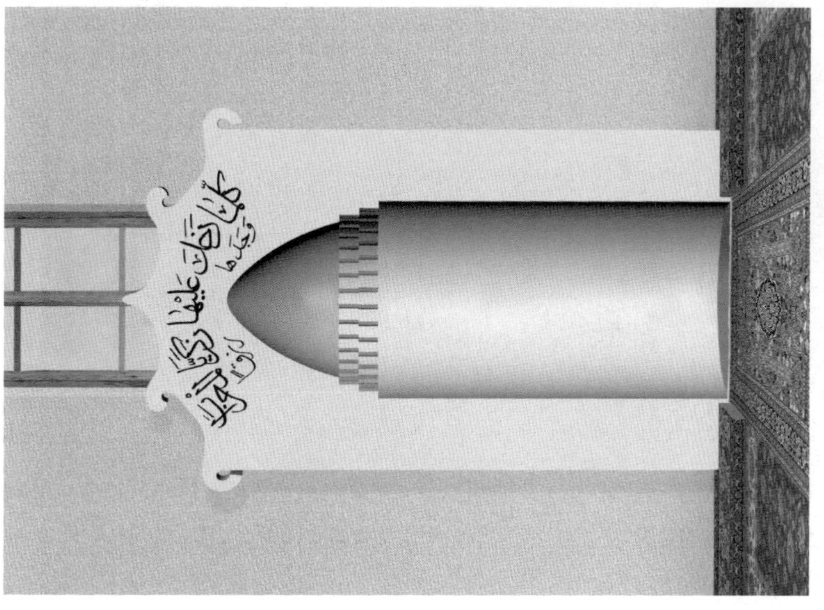

FIGURE 4.16 *The Čaršija or Town Mosque in Prijedor, 1700*

FIGURE 4.17 *The Careva or Imperial Mosque* in Trebinje, 1719*

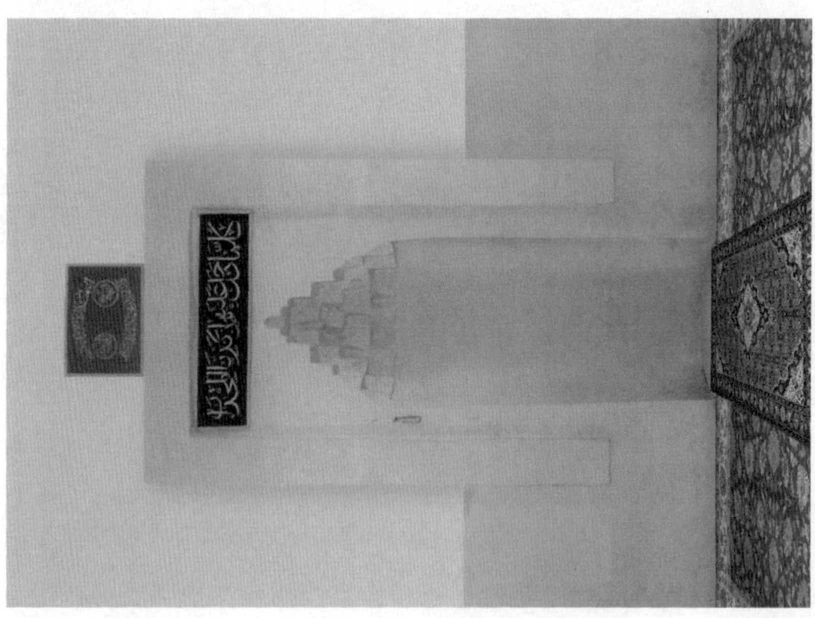

FIGURE 4.18 *The Old Mosque at Maoča, 1820*

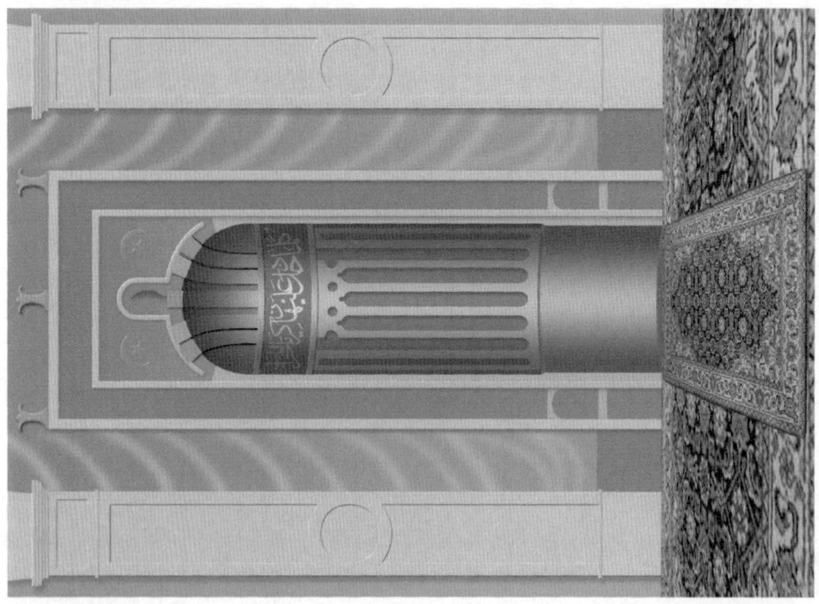

FIGURE 4.19 *The Azizija Mosque* at Brezovo Polje, 1863*

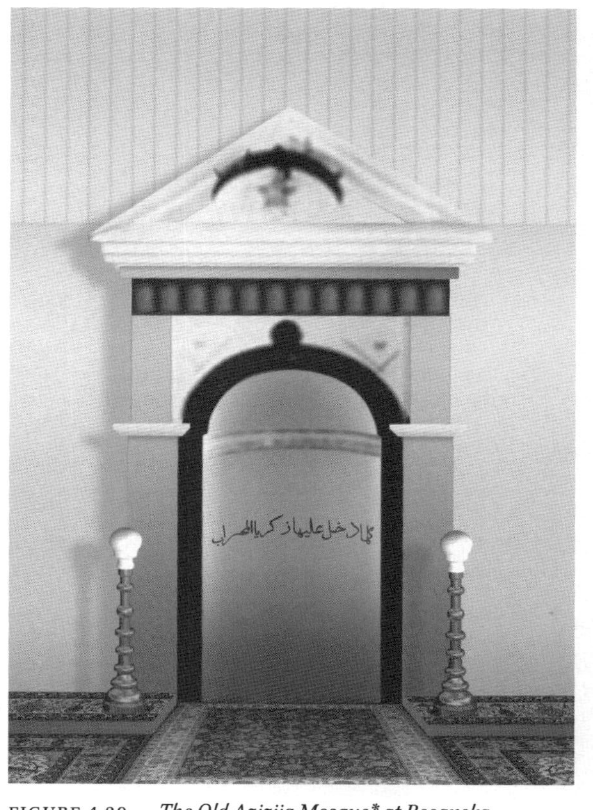

FIGURE 4.20 *The Old Azizija Mosque* at Bosanska Kostajnica, 1866*

FIGURE 4.21 *The Mosque at Pobrišće near Ljubuški, 1870*

FIGURE 4.22 *The Mosque at Pobrežje near Jablanica, 1912*

PART 5

On the Stones

• •

This section of the book deals with the Bosnian tombstones known as *stećci* (sing. *stećak*) and *nišani* (sing. *nišan*). They represent almost a thousand years of Bosnian history, influence and continuity, differentiation and rupture. This maze of interconnection and separation is not easy to negotiate in isolation from other aspects of the history of religion or the perennial tradition. The preceding three sections have considered the meaning of the Book, sent down in various forms to different prophets, and of mosque and mihrab as interlinked central symbols of the perennial tradition.[1]

The self's capacity to receive the Book and pass it on brings us to the irreducible barrier between the material and the spiritual, a boundary where the facets of existence meet. It cannot be understood without considering how darkness relates to light, death to life. Darkness is not absolute, nor death, as the barrier can be crossed. Darkness is absence of light, death of life. In this world, the "uttermost depth" is death, denoted by the grave. In the world beyond it is hell, but neither hell nor heaven is truly eternal.

1 *Nišani* are very regularly found beside *stećci*. The oldest are commonly termed *Shahid*. In recent times, this epithet has been reserved fairly exclusively to refer to the martyrdom or suffering of the dead. Originally, however, it refers to the perennial witness of the Praised as the key content of all tradition. All things at all times confess him so that our approach to him is a way of approaching God as Witness. In areas where the authorities that guaranteed the right to coexistence of various religious communities were overthrown, the attitude to Muslims has meant that the *nišani* have been systematically destroyed. In areas where the Muslim presence has been rooted out, *nišani* have become a rarity. Vladimir Čorović has said that "the main area of distribution of these *stećci* reaches from the Cetina to the Lim and from the Kolubara to the Sava, with minor crossing over the lines, e.g. at Donje Dragačevo and in Kačera. In other words, it is generally on the territory of the old Bosnian and Humian state or the immediate vicinity of that culture. In no other areas do we find these monuments in such systematic series or in such numbers. The first question this raises is: where does this phenomenon come from?... There can only be one answer to this question, in our view, which is: the cause is undoubtedly connected to the Bogumil question. Whatever one may think of the theoretical-theological aspect of the Bogumil heresy and whether or not one agrees that it was essentially heretical or basically a narrow sect of Orthodoxy, one thing is certain and cannot be denied when the issue is looked at in the round: all the adherents belong to a given national type and, accordingly, there is a greater degree of conservatism than in any other area." Ćorović, "Prilog proučavanju načina sahranjivanja i podizanja nadgrobnih spomenika u našim krajevima u srednjem vijeku," 134. This phenomenon has been subjected to many interpretations and given many names, including Bogumil. It certainly contains a number of key elements of witness to God and Christ and one may easily recognize in it elements of Orthodox, Catholic and Muslim heritage. Whichever interpretation is adopted, it will have to take into account the integrity of the phenomenon and its various influences on individual and group identities down to the present day.

 | DOI 10.1163/9789004279407_125

God is Eternal, Light and Living. In thinking of the eternity of either hell or heaven, one should remember that neither is comparable to God's. There are different eternities and every eternity other than God's is contingent on His plenitude. Whatever our condition, we determine neither His plenitude nor the eternity He speaks of and knows.

Our orientation towards the indeterminate possibilities of eternity means that standing in the visible world we see earth and heaven and all between as manifesting the One principle that appears in all things as truth. This manifestation encompasses Being's many levels. No level is unconnected with those above and below it in the manifestation of Unity. Our position in all this includes all the self's variety from initial manifestation at the beginning of differentiation to extremity in multiplicity. These two extremes are represented symbolically by standing upright and prostration.

Standing upright symbolizes power and majesty and other attributes of the One Who encompasses existence as His manifestation in majesty as Living and Everlasting; prostration the nearness and constant presence of the One. Seeking ourselves between the extremes of incomparability and nearness, we enter existence as the Creator's self-manifestation. We are pre-adapted for ascent and return to the principle manifest in world and self. Ascent is required for return, but is not enough. Its doctrinal and ritual aspects endow the signs in world and self with meaning, but the One is the goal for which we cross all boundaries, including that which encloses us in individuality.

The mihrab is a key symbol of transcending this-worldly limitations for the perennial teachings as embodied in the prophetic traditions, particularly that associated with the Praised. It symbolizes the inextricable presence of initiation within the exoteric forms of sacred tradition, in which things have value only by virtue of their connection to the Holy Spirit as expression of the constant presence of the Holy. If exoteric forms intimate this, more profound knowledge brings additional elements to entering the mosque and passing to the mihrab to cross the limits of individual finitude and self-absorption.

As a key doctrinal, ritual and ethical representation of the boundary between the material and the spiritual, the mihrab's many forms in religious heritage link it inextricably with grave markers and rituals.[2] Our approach to the mihrab and the doctrine and ritual associated with it entails the question of death as the waning of life. Our life taken, unable to stand upright, we lie in the earth, properly understood, entirely subordinate to it, to disintegration and putrefaction, crumbling and dispersal. The descent of the living becomes

---

2 For the *miḥrāb* as a grave marking, see Khoury, "The Mihrab Image," 11–28.

the central question of all ritual and all sincerity: Can we receive again the life taken from us and so rise again?

Receiving life and standing upright, we reflect and mirror the Living and Everlasting. The mystery of upright humanity is this: Has it any reality in and of itself? We can build our image of the world on any answer we may give this question, but only one of them is sustainable – the Upright.

Existence as a whole and everything in it can be read as an inscription. We are not the scribe of what is recorded in the world and self. Reading is not the same as writing. We are an inscription ourselves, as part of existence, and carry the inscription of the self in our being. The original author of what we read there is the eternal source of our action. Does that original author of existence read his inscription through us? Sacred tradition answers in the affirmative, since we are to existence as the pupil to the eye. The Creator is Light and looks at and with existence through us.

Writing relates writer and the material he writes on, which may be fabric, leather, paper, stone or metal, mind or body. Inscription always includes a balance between receiving and giving, passive and active, feminine and masculine. The first scribe is One; receiving and giving are His records. In writing, as the relationship of receptive page to giving pen, the balance of active and passive, masculine and feminine is always gentle and tender. Pressure adds nothing to the harmony of the flow from self to world. Pressure is action without knowledge.

Writing presupposes knowledge and action based on it. That which is written must already exist in the writer's self. Multiplicity is the potential for such existence. The scribe may derive his inscription from his own mind or some memory of earlier or may adopt it from some other record and transfer it to his own. In each case, transmission connects the centre of the self with the outward expression or inscription. There can be no record without the scribe's self and no self without the Self.

Writing cannot be thought without its opposite, erasure, any more than the self without the Self, at least if thought seeks orientation towards the First and Last. The written is under threat of erasure or loss. The non-existent record reaches consciousness or becomes material in witness to its warrant or "mother" record. How can we reach this warrant and, through it, overcome the threat to all inscription?

The written is to be read. In reading, the signs gathered in the self are distinguished, so that the reader may connect through them with the scribe, his consciousness and its indelible contents. In any reading, the inscription signifies not just the original scribe, but all things in consciousness that transcend form or being sent down into material things. But what leads the reader from the multiplicity of signs to their source?

In the materials involved in writing we note various relationships of passive and active. Fabric, leather, paper and wood are passive and warm, stone and earth passive and cold, and metals cold and active, particularly iron. This all comes together, in principle, within us, albeit never quite in perfect balance. The constant change of passive into active and back again reveals our own constant disclosure and concealment vis-à-vis the principle.

Nothing counters the fading of inscription so well as stone. To find what is lost or leave a testament whose erasure we fear, we reach for cold iron and stone, for their activity and passivity, in the hope that in their balance we may overcome transience and dispersal. In our Creator's image, we bring together opposites, combining active and passive, warmth and cold, masculine and feminine, height and depths. We know all the names and bring together in ourselves all things in existence, as existence is constantly coming in and out of being through language.

We are always in the real of the now and of death as reconciliation of opposites. We hope to escape the now into what has been or is to come, but this diverts us from the reality of absolute reconciliation. Our will reaches back into some unrepeatable past or offers the self a yearned-for image of the future, images we adopt without regard for reality or the now, seeking refuge in seeming rather than be a stranger in reality.

In all our active undertakings we put ourselves above matter, which – as writer or reader, bricklayer or stonemason, gardener or embroiderer, or any other possibility open to us – we subordinate to ourselves. This is a sign that we are conscious at a higher level than the object of our action or the matter that receives our presence over it. Lower and higher denote our position in relation to the principle. We are servants of the Lord and have nothing independent of Him. The placing of all things as signs between the heavens and the earth attests to this relationship.

Placed on earth and of it, we bear witness that nothing in our existence or action is cut off from the heavens, wholly subordinate to the will of the Lord. All earth and all things on it are manifest in receipt of heaven's influence, as a mirror of the signs in heaven. What touches or comes to earth is thus like a seed or influence that will return from earth again, rising to its original abode in heaven, indicating the principle made constantly manifest by the flow from above to earth and back again.

Our relationship as living beings with the Living God exposes us to two extremes that do not comprehend God. He is Giver of life and death, but death comprehends Him not. Death is encompassed by the Living God. Our capacity for action expresses the life given us and our being alive. There is no life without the Living. When we die, our combination of passion and action, of receiving life and passing it on, is transformed. We are utterly subjugated, powerless before the Subjugating and All-powerful.

Conscious of their own fragility and powerlessness in the grave and hoping for a new gifting of the life taken from them, the dead act in the living or from their imagined dying before death. Funerary rites, grave markings, and how we treat them are signs of two certainties – the now and death. However much they differ, they can be ranked by the principle and read as inscriptions in different scripts and languages of one concern: where are we from and why, where going and why through the grave?

House and tomb are both signs, of life and death respectively. The interiorized house is a tomb, an externalized tomb a house. A house lowered under the ground is a tomb, a tomb raised above ground a house. The Kaʿba at the bottom of Becca valley stands for tomb and house. *Kaʿba* (Greek *kýbos*, Latin *cubus*) itself refers to a body with six planes. The Kaʿba is at the bottom of a valley, draped in black cloth, marking the lowest level of existence, the tomb, the state from which the dead rise before the Living. To arise is to ascend from the depths to the highest and most sublime height.

Until the living face death, without skirting its irrefutable certainty, the life they have received is a gift they know not from a donor they know not in whose debt they are obscurely. Admitting our death, we realize the life given us on the principle of no life without the Living, the Lord Who "giveth and taketh away." We are to deny "our" life as "ours," to renounce it, for only death is ours. When this rules in our consciousness, we receive life as a gift of greatest value, inviolable, indelible even in death.

In contrast to the Kaʿba on the valley floor, signifying the earthly depths and the tomb, there stands the heavenly dome (Old French *dome*, Latin *domus*), marked on earth by the golden dome of the Jerusalem Mosque. These two signs, black Kaʿba and golden Dome, Inviolable and Further Mosque, signify earth and the tomb and Spirit and life. Tomb, house, earth and heaven, body and spirit are all potential abodes. In which are we strangers and to which return as to our origins and purpose?

The most familiar tombstones on Bosnian soil are images of the Kaʿba as sign of the depths and of return through the seven heavens by the upright path of the Praised. Mausolea have sometimes been erected over Bosnian tombs, to mark the relationship of Kaʿba and Dome, body and Spirit, exile and Return.[3] Even standing tombstones denote this axis between tomb and heaven.

---

3 A mausoleum was built over the grave of Batalo, who commissioned the Gospel that is called after him, in Turbe near Travnik. See Truhelka, "Grobnica bosanskog tepčije Batala, obretena kod Gornjeg Turbeta (kotar Travnik)"; Kajmaković, *Zidno slikarstvo u Bosni i Hercegovini,*

Bosnia is, amongst other things, a name for humanity's being in the world, specifically for centuries in the lands between the Pannonian plains and the Adriatic coast, from the mountains of Lika and Kordun to Montenegro. The exact limits in time cannot be determined exactly nor its name be given a fixed meaning. Its political and military contours have reflected the world and power relations around it. Still, the Bosnian project of unification and distinction as we relate to ourselves and our world has never been reducible to a simple logic of power, based exclusively on analytical reason.

Bosnia's historical presence may be noted wherever *stećci* are found, those ancient tombstones that may belong to anyone – Catholic, Orthodox or *Krstjan*, Muslims or others – but always with Bosnia's gossamer-fine but irrefutable presence. Any attempt to force the pattern of their distribution, their meaning and or attribution and interpretative potential into the ideological matrixes of the modern age quickly becomes facile, offensive and dangerous.

In all the variety of shapes – sarcophagus, gabled, slabs, crosses, and pillars – a horizontal aspect predominates. Pillars and crosses are individual accents or notes in the whole, marking out the vertical as what links earth and heaven. With time, standing tombstones (*nišani* or *bašluci*) were added that can justifiably be called "Muslim."

The semantic field of the term *krstjanin* cannot be interpreted in isolation from that of the term "Muslim," and vice versa. This is due to the content of the Gospels and the Recitation and the essential core of perennial wisdom. As ways of relating to God Who anoints and brings to peace, anointment and being-at-peace are reflected in the stones' horizontal and vertical aspects, stressing the opposition of the horizontal and the upright in self, world and God.

If *Stećci* are normally tombstones, sealing the abodes of the dead, they often bear a message of life and death for the living. The message is elaborated in

---

52–53; Kuna, *Srednjovjekovna bosanska književnost*, 133–37. Gost Radin Butković included in his will, written in 1466, a legacy of 140 ducats a year "for the church and the tomb where my bones shall lie." See Truhelka, "Testament gosta Radina: prinos o paterenskom pitanju"; idem, "Još o testamentu gosta Radina i paternima"; Šanjek, *Bosansko-humski krstjani u povijesnim vrelima*, 366. The custom of building a turbe (mausoleum) continued in Bosnia even after the royal period. Of particular note among such mausolea are the turbe of an unknown *shahīd* at Pločnik (Oglavak near Fojnica), the turbe of Alija Torlak in Torlakovac, the turbe of Alija Đerzelez at Gerzovo polje near Šipovo, and the turbe of Sheikh Bistrigija by the Emperor's mosque in Sarajevo. These are forms from Christian heritage and so involve recognition of "one in the other." Hadžijahić writes of the presence of *krstjani* of the Bosnian Church in Bosnia in the 15th and 16th centuries: "Defters testify that, though in only a limited area, there were still *krstjani* in the late 16th and perhaps even the early years of the 17th century." Hadžijahić, "Zemljišni posjedi 'crkve bosanske'," 476.

symbols and epitaphs on certain great stones, but most have no carvings or epitaph and most Bosnian graves were probably unmarked. Those that were may stand for all of Bosnia's dead, with their message for all her living.

The tombstones that later appeared alongside or close to the *stećci* offer clear witness to duration and rupture: duration insofar as their placement marks a bond between successive grave-dwellers and rupture as the shift in emphasis from horizontal to vertical marks a change in the image of human nature and the world. To understand one must first consider the perennial content of the traditions to which the One's manifestation and presence give meaning.

Muslim tombstones are usually pillars, so that, if the *stećci* emphasize the horizontal, the Muslim stones witness the vertical. The combination so vividly illustrated by the sign of the cross is inherent to all of existence. Two prayers suggest this relation of indivisibility: the Lord's Prayer and the prayer in the first Sura of the Recitation.

Our Father, which art in heaven,
Hallowed be Thy name,
Thy kingdom come,
Thy will be done, in earth as it is in heaven.[4]

Guide us in the upright path,
the path of those whom Thou hast blessed,
not of those against whom Thou art wrathful,
nor of those who are astray.[5]

The prayer to God, the Lord of worlds, All-merciful, Ever-merciful, Master of the Day of Doom, that His will be done in earth as it is in heaven and His kingdom come clearly denotes the vertical represented by the poles of earth and heaven, body and Spirit, this world and the next. This is the upright path, the path of the blessed. Its contrary is descent, the path of the damned, whose will is earth-bound, tied to the body, set in this world against the will of God.

The upright path leads to the kingdom of God. As Jesus, Mary's son, said, "Behold, the kingdom of God is within you."[6] Self-realization is ascent from the depths to sublime uprightness. The signs in the world attest the self's potential to encompass heavens and earth and make our heart the Self's abode.

Both prayers, one revealed through Jesus as Word, the other through the Word revealed as the Recitation to the Praised, plainly present the visible poles of human existence, whose signs are earth and heaven. We are bound to the

4 *Matthew*, 6:9–10.

5 *Qur'an*, 1:5–7.

6 *Luke*, 17:21.

earth, its countless directions extending horizontally around us, but leading to no fulfilment. Two paths lead away from that superficiality – one descends into the earth to corruption and decay, the other ascends to heaven. One is relentless, evident, and repugnant – a handful of grave dust cannot be our reason for being here.

The upright path may seem impossible, but our redemption knows no other. We are what seems impossible to us. But if what the prophets promise, eternal life and happiness, were impossible, unrealizable in the self, then all that can be said of human beings would be a lie. To banish this lie, which is constantly put forward as an inviolable element of our approach to being in the world, we must deal with the depths, the grave. The *stećci* and other tombstones of Bosnia witness this commitment to dealing with death and the grave as the way to extricate ourselves from the labyrinth of the world.

One cannot imagine Bosnia in the round without dealing with death and the grave. *Stećci* are signs of this question. In and with them, countless narratives on the question are shaped, beyond any one self to exhaust. The questions and answers allowed by the upright tombstones over the dead who confessed the Promised One in a different way from their forebears indicates no rupture: they manifest the same essence and same questions in a different form.

Stećci and *nišani,* as the two groups of tombstones over the graves of Bosnia's people are called, are linked in historical sequence and in the expectation of a gathering for a new resurrection. The upright Muslim stones often bear the inscription, "God, there is no god but Him, Living, Upright." This inscription recalls the Verse of the Throne:

> God, there is no god but He, Living, Upright. Slumber seizes Him not, neither sleep; to Him belongs all that is in the heavens and the earth. Who is there that shall intercede with Him save by His leave? He knows what lies before them and what is after them, and they comprehend not anything of His knowledge save such as He wills. His Throne comprises the heavens and earth; the preserving of them oppresses Him not; He is All-high, All-glorious.[7]

The tombstone verse's manifest meaning is as a reminder of God's Throne as the principle of universal return and the place before which we shall rise to live again. This hope of resurrection from the grave to stand before the Throne in judgment is associated with one of mediation by the prophet and his pure followers. Thus in death, as the irrevocable confession of life received, we

7 *Qur'an,* 2:255.

sacrifice death as connection with nothingness. Resurrection in death is a gift for the sacrifice involved or for dying in dying.

The same symbols are clearly found on both *stećci* and *nišani*, there for all to see, clear evidence of the similarity of the answers and questions concerning death passed from generation to generation of Bosnia's people. Even without the same symbols on the *stećci* and Muslim stones, one could work out that their questions and answers are in principle the same. Death properly speaking concerns only the dead. The living perspective of it is speculation on the real. Nothing teaches us as much about life as death, which is for us an experience of the other, near or far. Only by dying do we transcend this relationship with the other, as in it everything we hope for in life is brought together.

That the signs on the *stećci* and *nišani* are similar or even identical does not mean they cannot be interpreted differently. Every self is different from moment to moment, producing different interpretations of the signs, which have remained the same through the centuries on the surface of the stone. The relationship between the living and the dead is always one of extremes. The living strive to reconcile the difference between active and passive; for the dead, it has been resolved. The dead are powerless, unable to communicate in word or gesture to the living. This utter difference between two bodies, dead and living, entails a question that shatters illusion, as suggested by the relationship of Adam's two sons, the quick towards the dead:

> Then his soul prompted him to slay his brother, and he slew him, and became one of the losers. Then God sent forth a raven, scratching into the earth, to show him how he might conceal the vile body of his brother. He said, "Woe is me! Am I unable to be as this raven, and so conceal my brother's vile body?" And he became one of the remorseful.[8]

The dead call on the living to apply their will to them and to find a place for their bodies' vulnerability – its inexorable decay – to grant them worthy abode. To prepare and order a grave and lay the dead in it is the undeniable right of the dead and duty of the living, due to the powerlessness of the one and power of the other. The living may see this burying of their dead as concealing the body whose powerlessness disturbs what lives, powerlessness to do anything for themselves or cover their own nakedness. It may seem flight from confrontation with the unstoppable transformation of life into death, of power into impotence, of action into passion (suffering action) – avoidance that resembles the attempt to overpower memory with forgetting.

8 Ibid., 5:30–31.

Lowering the dead into the grave to be closed in the earth is like consigning the living to forgetting. Our way out, our redemption, is not in forgetting, but in the forgotten. This is why a stone is placed over the grave. The stone is not the point – it marks the dead and death. It is the witness of the living that those who lie there now are telling those who will lie there in turn that there are reasons to pass through consciousness and life and death to reach their awaited resurrection. The living may consider waiting for resurrection and quickening a hazy fantasy. But what are we without our right to survive, properly understood, beyond all death? Was not the key question that put to the prophet by one holding the bones of some unknown corpse, "Who shall quicken the bones when they are decayed?"[9]

Question and answer were both sent down by God as His discourse in the prophet's language: "He shall quicken them, who originated them the first time; He knows all creation, who has made for you out of the green tree fire and lo, from it you kindle."[10]

Our right to life eternal and bliss means the absolute certainties of "now" and death entail two further certainties: God and Judgment. Eternal life requires resurrection, which is beyond us. Our "now" manifests the Living, Who can resurrect. His purpose in doing so is to acknowledge absolutely our debt and our claim – repayment of all our debts to God and of our right to Eternity as refuge from creation. There is no divine revelation, no exemplary prophet, no Scripture for which the heart of remembrance is not the resurrection of the dead and accounting for every atom of good and evil done.

Life begins and ends in perplexing rupture. Suddenly, from all but nothing, it begins, and then, from everything as suddenly, it ceases in invincible death. This seems commonplace, but we never become used to either. The question of the beginning and the end is in every divine revelation. It appears in the revelation to the Praised thus:

> Of what did He create him? Of a sperm-drop He created him, and determined him, then the way eased for him, then makes him to die, and buries him, then, when He wills, He raises him.[11]
>
> And the Trumpet shall be blown; then behold, they are sliding down from their tombs unto their Lord. They say, "Alas for us! Who roused us out of our sleeping-place? This is what the All-merciful promised, and the Envoys spoke truly." It was only one Cry; then behold, they are all arraigned

9 Ibid., 36:78.
10 Ibid., 36:79–80.
11 Ibid., 80:18–22.

> before Us. So today no soul shall be wronged anything, and you shall not be recompensed, except according to what you have been doing.[12]
>
> Knows he not that when that which is in the tombs is overthrown, and that which is in the breasts is brought out – surely on that day their Lord shall be aware of them![13]

The heart of the Revelation to the Anointed and the Praised, why they are closest to each other, is the narrative of life and death, the grave and lying in it, resurrection and judgment for Eternity. The meaning of eternity compared to finitude, life versus death, nullity versus plenitude cannot be grasped without that sign of rupture. Whatever their form, tombstones are a reminder of that break as a sign of continuity. We will find no answer to the question of death except in the uncreated, uncreatable centre of the self – outside it, the enigma remains insoluble. The epitaph of Stipko Radosalić, carved on his tombstone, clearly indicates this: "Long have I lain here before thee and long have I still to lie."[14]

All our questions about the mystery of lying and resurrection are intimated by Stipko's epitaph. The living expect a response from him, which comes only as the revelation of God through the living, offering a way to transcend the bounds of the quantifiable world and vanquish death. The offer is meaningless unless we find the answer within the self. All that the graves and bones, prophets and scriptures, earth and heaven say of it is understood there and there alone, where everything is unified, within, with all the worlds as signs.

The epitaph is on the stone above his grave, and anyone reading it sees Stipko address God, in some "now" of his living self. Dead mouths may not speak nor dead hands write or carve, but the epitaph is evidence of his speech in which we as readers are called to believe and, when we do, the living Stipko speaks the words carved in the stone over his dead body. Thus it is that Stipko speaks of the inextricability and absolute certainty of our "now" and our death.

That we can understand our existence in terms of these two expressions of the only absolute certainty is a form of differentiation – existence as descent and succumbing, as the depth, and resurrection as testimony that the Upright is without equal. Stipko's testimony to his life both before and after death as succumbing and depth is intended for God. The mystery of death and the

---

12 Ibid., 36:51–54.

13 Ibid., 100:9–11.

14 Vego, *Zbornik srednjovjekovnih natpisa Bosne i Hercegovine*, 2:38–39, the English translation is cited after Jones' translation of Mak Dizdar's Stone Sleeper, in which the epitaph is quoted, Dizdar, *Stone Sleeper*, 37.

grave, succumbing and resurrection, and their resolution as everything vanishes but His Face, directs us to the Word God sent down into the heart of the Praised, revealing Himself as Living, Upright. Outside the living self, even that discourse has no existence. Nor is there death, grave, resurrection, or judgment day. For, He has no other.

Grave stones are signs of this matter of succumbing and standing upright, death and life, illusion and reality, sleep and waking. The dead succumb, but their stones attest to their rising in resurrection. There are grounds for associating the word "stećak" with the verbs "stati" and "ustati" (to stand or stand up). God is Upright and has made us the sum of His creation, realized in resurrection, albeit by no power of ours. From our perspective, we have long lain and long shall lie; from His, resurrection is now, in the Hour that "is coming, no doubt of it, and God shall raise up whomsoever is within the tombs."[15]

Lying in the tomb and rising again are inseparable from receiving from God and returning our debt. There is nothing we have not received, nothing that is not part of our debt. The self and the world manifest as differentiated into multiplicity, with lower and higher levels.

The lower levels may seem subordinate and in our debt, as we subordinate ourselves to the higher, in debt to them. But we and the world are in debt to the Creator alone. Our debts to each other derive from this true debt to God. If we hope for resurrection, we must acknowledge our true debt as absolute. We are indebted to God, such that each self in existence is equally indebted to God and each has a claim on us. The prophet is our reminder, the guarantee that the self is properly oriented towards that true debt: "It is He who has sent His apostle with the guidance and the debt of truth, that He may uplift it above every other debt, though the idolaters be averse."[16]

Idolaters are associators, those who associate aught with God. Associating the resurrection with some one of our countless human debts to things and not our true debt, they adopt it as their principle. Consequently, they are unable to find any answer to the question carved on Stipko Radosalić's *stećak*. Only God is absolutely near and remote. Nothing else is, so that by taking a principle for the Principle, the associators close off their world and insist only on what is palpably within it, denying what is not.

Perennial questions and responses to them about life and death, inner and outer, first and last are broached through the symbols and the inscriptions on the *stećci* and *nišani*. The differences between them import no change in the essential discourse, since death is one. Our experiences of this one death

15 *Qur'an*, 22:7.

16 Ibid., 9:33.

repeated differently in each self remain linked with its impossibility in the Living God Who comprehends all.

We have selected a number of *stećci* and *nišani* for their symbolic features, which suggest the sacred tradition that informed the selves of the people who lie beneath them. They are described below and pictures are given in the plates that follow this text.

Figure 5.1 is a map of where the examples from the illustrations are to be found.

Figure 5.2. A burial ground with *stećci* and *nišani*, at Krupac, near Sarajevo. *Stećci* are generally accompanied by *nišani*. If the latter are absent, it is often because they were destroyed.[17]

Figure 5.3. The Čaršija or Town Mosque in Stolac, also known as the old mosque, the mosque with nineteen columns, and the Imperial Mosque. The current building dates from 1519, but local tradition is that Muslim worship began there a hundred years earlier. The minaret's lower part bears a twelve-sided band of symbols, nine visible, three concealed by the mosque wall, corresponding to the twelve months and twelve imams. It includes the sun, the moon, roses, a fleur-de-lis, a column and Solomon's seal. The Čaršija Mosque is the physical and symbolic centre of the Stolac čaršija or market place, the focal point of the town from which it spread out.[18]

Figure 5.4. The sun is a common symbol on *stećci* and *nišani*, often as a circle, garland or hemispherical protuberance.[19] These depictions of nature's most important symbol may be read as Light, Intellect, Spirit, the Light of the Praised and Christ. Since the sun unites light and heat, light corresponding to knowledge and heat to love, it stands for belief as relationship of the faithful to the Faithful. Interpretations differ from tradition to tradition, but its perennial oneness is evident in them all.

---

17 The Shahid graveyards found beside *stećci* are, according to Vladimir Ćorović, a clear proof of the link between the dead in the graves marked by *nišani* and by *stećci*. He writes, "The Shahid (Muslim) grave monuments are often found in the immediate vicinity of mediaeval marbles ... When it changed faith, the Bosnian nobility had to change its burial customs and style of funerary monument. The feeling that the members of a given family should, regardless, be buried in the same graveyard was not extinguished. It was so strong a feeling that the Muslims cared for their graves of their Christian ancestors until recent times. This is, then, the reason the mediaeval stones and the *shahīd* graves are often found beside each other." Ćorović, "Prilog proučavanju načina sahranjivanja i podizanja nadgrobnih spomenika u našim krajevima u srednjem vijeku," 145.

18 For the relationship between the Stolac čaršija and the Čaršija Mosque see Mahmutćehajić, *Maintaining the Sacred Center*.

19 See Bešlagić, *Leksikon stećaka*, 77; idem, *Stećci – kultura i umjetnost*, 171–72; Solovjev, "Simbolika srednjevjekovnih nadgrobnih spomenika u Bosni i Hercegovini," 36.

Figure 5.5. The moon is the most widespread symbol in Bosnia. Some writers regard it as the symbol of the country,[20] found on tombs and seals, embroidery and wood-carvings, mosques and churches, *stećci* and *nišani*,[21] and frescoes of the Nativity and the Resurrection.[22] In the Muslim reading of its waxing and waning, receiving and reflecting light, the moon stands for the Praised as ever-present recipient and transmitter of Light, inseparable from the Anointed, to whom he is closest in this and the next world and who is the Word revealed by God through the Virgin.[23]

Figure 5.6. The cross and the crescent moon are the two most common symbols on *stećci*.[24] The cross takes various forms – inscribed in a circle, standing on a hill-like base, anthropomorphic, with circular extensions, *tau* and florescent.[25] Counting only the pure forms – Greek and Latin crosses, etc., and not the anthropomorphic or stylized ones – Šefik Bešlagić claims that "they follow immediately on the star-and-rosette and come before the crescent moon and every other motif."[26] The cross is often shown with a crescent moon, star or solar symbol.[27] Although its temporal and geographical reach exceeds its usual restriction to certain historical representations, the cross is usually seen as a symbol of Christ, that is of our range between earth and heaven, matter and Spirit. Many of the crosses in Bosnia are bare, allowing a variety of interpretations. According to Solovjev, it represents Christ himself, while bunches of grapes stand for his words and spirals for "true [Bosnian] Christians."[28] In any case, it is probably the most widespread symbol of our overall relationship with ourselves, the world and God. Even though there are old Bosnian *nišani* with crosses,[29] the accepted view is that the cross is absent from the Muslim tradition. This is quite inaccurate. The Qur'anic denial that Jesus was crucified gives the cross a different meaning. Our position between the depths and

---

20 Kačić Miošić, *Razgovor ugodni naroda slovinskoga*, 451: "The Bosnian coat of arms is a shield with a crescent moon and a star." See Benac, *Široki brijeg*, 43–44.

21 For crescent moons on *stećci* see Wenzel, *Ukrasni motivi na stećcima*, 146–59; Bešlagić, *Stećci – kultura i umjetnost*, 164–68; idem, *Leksikon stećaka*, 77. For crescent moons on *nišani* see Bešlagić, *Nišani XV i XVI vijeka u Bosni i Hercegovini*, 57–59.

22 Bešlagić, *Stećci – kultura i umjetnost*, 166–68.

23 See Muslim, 4:1260.

24 Wenzel, *Ukrasni motivi na stećcima*, 91–125.

25 Ibid., 92–93.

26 Bešlagić, *Stećci – kultura i umjetnost*, 178.

27 Ibid.

28 Solovjev, "Simbolika srednjevjekovnih nadgrobnih spomenika u Bosni i Hercegovini," 38–45 and 47–48.

29 Bešlagić, *Nišani XV i XVI vijeka u Bosni i Hercegovini*, 61, 78.

the sublime height and our constant turn towards the heart as a doorway to heaven, the notion of the *čaršija* ("four directions") as a symbol of the world in which we seek our centre, the five daily prayers through which we ascend from the four corners of the world into our heart or centre – all these are summed up in the last verses of the Opening, the prayer most often uttered by Muslims: "Guide us on the upright path, the path of those whom Thou hast blessed, not of those against whom Thou art wrathful, nor of those who are astray.[30]

Figure 5.7. The apple is a very common symbol on both *stećci* and *nišani.*[31] It features in various positions and in combination with other symbols. Its significance for the Muslim heritage is clearly indicated by the custom of placing a finial with three or five orbs ("apples") atop the minaret. The customary oral interpretations are that three apples at the highest point on the horizon reached by human hand refer to three indivisible elements of our debt to God: bearing witness to His unity, the apostolate of the Praised and return to God; or doctrine/intellect, the way/ritual, and the virtues. Five apples may be seen as referring to the two tablets of stone with the Ten Commandments – five on relating to God, five on relating to other people, the first five denoted by the upper halves of the five orbs, and the latter five by their undersides. The apple on a *stećak* or *nišan* may thus represent our original purity or, through the forbidden fruit from Eden and our fall to the depths after violating the bounds of heaven, our return and re-establishment of the original order by ascent to the sublime height. It may seem that the dead in their graves are in the depths, but the apple denotes their resurrection and judgment for what was taken and is to be returned.

Figure 5.8. The vine and its grapes are depicted variously on both *stećci*[32] and *nišani.*[33] Most scholars believe that they refer to Jesus' words: "I am the true vine, and my Father is the husbandman. Every branch in me that beareth not fruit he taketh away; and every branch that beareth fruit, he purgeth it, that it may bring forth more fruit."[34] He continues, "I am the vine, ye are the branches: He that abideth in me, and I in him, the same bringeth forth much fruit: for

30 *Qur'an*, 1:6–7. For the symbolism of the cross in the perennial philosophy, see Guénon, *Le symbolisme de la croix*.

31 See Wenzel, *Ukrasni motivi na stećcima*, 133–41; and Bešlagić, *Nišani XV i XVI vijeka u Bosni i Hercegovini*, 57–58.

32 See Wenzel, *Ukrasni motivi na stećcima*, 203–204, 212–15 and Bešlagić, *Nišani XV i XVI vijeka u Bosni i Hercegovini*, 204–208.

33 See Bešlagić, *Nišani XV i XVI vijeka u Bosni i Hercegovini*, 59.

34 *John*, 15:1–2.

without me ye can do nothing."[35] The Anointed says this in a Book confirmed by the Book revealed through the Praised: "And We have sent down to thee the Book with the truth, confirming the Book that was before it, and assuring it."[36] So speaks God through the Praised to whom, according to the same narrative, all the prophets swore an oath.[37] The connection with God through the Anointed is thus always also a connection with the Praised. The two of them are closer to each other than to anyone else in this or the next world.[38]

Figure 5.9. The rose is also depicted in various ways on *stećci* and *nišani*.[39] It is found in churches, mosques and houses, carved in stone or wood, drawn in books and on illuminated pages, embroidered onto fabric and woven into kilims. It is also carved on the *nišani* of Bosnia's *đul-badža* or sufi women, female dervishes[40] and the good. In Muslim tradition it stands for the Praised encompassing two extremes, the lowest of the low denoted by the house in Becca and the supreme height denoted by the house in Jerusalem. In this belief, the fragrance of the rose accompanies the Praised as a sign of the next world. It is customary for Muslims, on seeing or smelling a rose, to say "O Lord, connect me with the Praised." The reds of mosque and domestic carpets in Bosnia are the colours of the rose, denoting our ceaseless aspiration to follow and draw closer to the Praised, who ascends from the depths and guides us to the sublime height, our guide and final advocate, the hope of the dead.

Figure 5.10. The lily or fleur-de-lis, the heraldic lily, is primarily a symbol of the Virgin and so of her son. It is found in books, churches and mosques, in homes and on tombstones, on jewellery and crowns, on household wares of wrought iron, carved wood or woven fabric, on coins and seals, on tombs and on staffs.[41] Depictions in mihrabs and on minarets attest to awareness of the symbol of the purity of the Virgin's heart as corresponding to the purity of the Praised's heart. God sent down His Word as Mary's son through the purity of her heart and the Recitation as His Word through the pure heart of the Praised. These two different yet related manifestations of the Word indicate the connection between the Praised and the Virgin. The widespread presence of the

35 Ibid., 15:5.

36 *Qur'an*, 5:48.

37 See *Qur'an*, 3:81.

38 See Muslim, 4:1260–61.

39 See Wenzel, *Ukrasni motivi na stećcima*, 145–55; Bešlagić, *Stećci – kultura i umjetnost*, 209–214; idem, *Leksikon stećaka*, 99–100; idem, *Nišani XV i XVI vijeka u Bosni i Hercegovini*, 57–59.

40 See Hadžijahić, "Badžijanije u Sarajevu i Bosni," 125–31.

41 See Wenzel, *Ukrasni motivi na stećcima*, 163–75; Bešlagić, *Stećci – kultura i umjetnost*, 214–19; idem, *Leksikon stećaka*, 90. The image of a *nišan* from Travnik bearing a fleur-de-lis was published in Mujezinović, *Islamska epigrafika Bosne i Hercegovine*, 2:360.

fleur-de-lis throughout Bosnian history cannot be explained without taking into account the esoteric core of the forms in which the perennial tradition is manifest.[42]

Figure 5.11. Birds are a common symbol on *stećci*[43] and are also found on *nišani*,[44] the stone doorjambs of Muslim houses,[45] carved wood, fabric and embroidered wares. Sounds that reach us from above include thunder, the whistling of the wind, and birdsong. The Recitation tells us that thunder is a form of praising God.[46] Wind is the sign of the Spirit that "bloweth where it listeth."[47] But birds are communities, like ours,[48] with their own languages,[49] which glorify God.[50] Stories associating birds with people[51] remind us of another, higher world as our true abode. Birds stand for the angels, subject to God's will, through whom existence manifests His will. The dove is the symbol of the Holy Spirit, the falcon of the tamed self and pure heart in God's hand, from which it swoops down upon every illusion to return in love, following the Praised. Old written accounts attest to the Bosnian Muslim belief that the white dove stood for the Holy Spirit descending upon the Virgin, the Anointed and the Praised.[52]

Figure 5.12. Zachariah and Mary are two key figures in the history of the temple of Sion. Zachariah is a prophet of God and high priest of the rebuilt temple, the original of which was the manifestation of God through the prophet Solomon. Its reconstruction after being destroyed remained without

---

42 Šefik Bešlagić writes that the widespread presence of fleur-de-lis on *stećci* should not be associated with the symbolic meaning of the lily as denoting the purity of the Virgin and her Son, but is essentially decorative (Bešlagić, *Leksikon stećaka*, 90). Given this symbol's role in Muslim heritage and its clear esoteric meaning, Bešlagić's claim that this and other symbols are merely decorative and without explicit meaning should be regarded as flawed.

43 See Wenzel, *Ukrasni motivi na stećcima*, 253–54; Bešlagić, *Stećci – kultura i umjetnost*, 272–79; idem, *Leksikon stećaka*, 99.

44 See Bešlagić, *Nišani XV i XVI vijeka u Bosni i Hercegovini*, 24, 36–38; Ćurčić, "Ptice na našim srednjovječnim nadgrobnim spomenicima i starim muslimanskim nišanima," 2.

45 See Mujezinović, *Islamska epigrafika Bosne i Hercegovine*, 3:382.

46 See *Qur'an*, 13:13.

47 *John*, 3:8.

48 See *Qur'an*, 6:38.

49 Ibid., 27:16.

50 Ibid., 21:79; 24:41; 34:10; 38:18–19.

51 Ibid., 36:19.

52 See e.g.: Solovjev, "Engleski izvještaj XVII vijeka o bosanskim poturima," 104–105; see also *John*, 1:32.

any clear prophetic warrant.[53] In very troubled times, the prophet Zachariah was entrusted with the mystery of the Virgin as the centre, doctrine, ritual and virtue in the Temple, and before whose eyes the murders of Zachariah and John and the persecution and passion of her son took place. Zachariah bore witness to her mystery and to the potential that anywhere can be a mihrab of our return to God. Zachariah and the Virgin are present in different ways in churches and mosques. Following the Praised, in peaceable love of God, includes connecting with Zachariah and his son and with the Virgin and hers, as suggested by their presence in mihrabs and ecclesiastical images.

Figure 5.13. Hands and arms are often depicted on *stećci* and *nišani*,[54] either as an open hand or an arm to the elbow or to the shoulder and bent at the elbow. In some cases they form an isolated image and are sometimes depicted close to a crescent moon, rosette or cross, but only on *stećci*. Hands are usually shown with a sword, shield or spear, sometimes a bow or mace. Many guesses have been made as to their meaning. From the esoteric perspective, they are a sign of greeting and of oath-taking. The five fingers indicate our senses in connection with the world axis or upright path, by which means we turn to Unity through the Anointed and the Praised, designated by a crescent moon, rose or cross, in fealty to God. "Those who swear fealty to thee swear fealty in truth to God; God's hand is over their hands. Then whosoever breaks his oath breaks it but to his own hurt; and whoso fulfils his covenant made with God, God will give him a mighty wage."[55] Depictions of weapons beside or in the hand denote the mihrab in the self through which we return from this world's illusion to the self's reality.

Figure 5.14. Ropes are depicted in a variety of ways on *stećci*[56] and are also found on *nišani*.[57] They join and separate, surround and frame. As threads twisted into a single rope, they denote a bond of union; they also symbolize various kinds of oaths, covenants, agreements and alliances. We are split within, and our two sides, higher and lower, are in a constant state of tension. For the higher, illumined side to triumph over the lower, obscured side, we

53 For attitudes to the original and rebuilt temple of Sion, see Barker, *Temple Theology: An Introduction*.

54 See Wenzel, *Ukrasni motivi na stećcima*, 291–303; Bešlagić, *Stećci – kultura i umjetnost*, 290–96; idem, *Leksikon stećaka*, 100; idem, *Nišani XV i XVI vijeka u Bosni i Hercegovini*, 51–56.

55 *Qur'an*, 48:10.

56 See Wenzel, *Ukrasni motivi na stećcima*, 32–51; Bešlagić, *Stećci – kultura i umjetnost*, 140–43; idem, *Leksikon stećaka*, 109–110.

57 See Bešlagić, *Nišani XV i XVI vijeka u Bosni i Hercegovini*, 57–58, 61.

discover, renew and strengthen our original covenant with God Who sends down to us a redemptive rope. God calls to us through the signs in the world and the self and through the Praised and the Book: "And hold you fast to God's bond, together, and do not scatter; remember God's blessing upon you when you were enemies, and He brought your hearts together, so that by His blessing you became brothers."[58]

Figure 5.15. The staff is a symbol of spiritual leadership, of the elders, and denotes the upright path to which the good or perfect bear witness. On *stećci* the staff is usually depicted alone, though some show a hand or a man holding a staff.[59] Staffs are also found on *nišani*.[60] Whoever these staffs may have belonged to – a *did* (elder), *gost* (senior figure) or other dignitary of the Bosnian Church, or a sheikh, *dede* or other dervish – they signify only one thing: a connection with the perfect man or fairest nature by which the traveller ascends the upright path of return to God. Return is through the Anointed and the Praised and the staff is a sign of covenant with God through them as closest to each other in this and the next world. Depictions of it as a weapon or its use in defence may be interpreted symbolically. Receiving the staff in sign of initiation into the spiritual chain of transmission connects the initiate with the Praised, our highest potential. Moses received his staff from the prophet Shuaib as a sign of his connection with Adam, who brought his staff out of Eden.

Figure 5.16. Spears are depicted on *stećci*, with other weapons – bow and arrow, sword or sabre, battle axe and shield.[61] Similar things are found on *nišani*.[62] Constantly focused on the centre, so as to destroy all illusions of independence from God and to find ourselves inwardly and outwardly as received, we are in a constant state of war, on a battlefield. Any weapon can symbolize this struggle. The spear is the most explicit symbol of ascent and descent, height and depth. It was used by the Praised to denote himself in the mihrab of the world. The point of the spear corresponds to witness to God's oneness, our holding it to our connection with the Praised. When the spear is driven point

58 *Qur'an*, 3:103.

59 See Bešlagić, *Stećci – kultura i umjetnost*, 243–49; idem, *Leksikon stećaka*, 103.

60 See Mujezinović, *Islamska epigrafika Bosne i Hercegovine*, 1:11–12. Calling these staffs "bludgeons" or "cudgels" in no way calls into question their symbolic meaning. It is only in crude modern ideological images of the world that traditional signs have lost their symbolic meaning and become mere decorations or seem to depict only the material level. For bludgeons on *nišani* see Bešlagić, *Nišani XV i XVI vijeka u Bosni i Hercegovini*, 57–61.

61 See Ćurčić, "Starinsko oružje u Bosni i Hercegovini," 29–53; Wenzel, *Ukrasni motivi na stećcima*, 223–49; Bešlagić, *Stećci – kultura i umjetnost*, 232–34; idem, *Leksikon stećaka*, 85.

62 See Bešlagić, *Nišani XV i XVI vijeka u Bosni i Hercegovini*, 57–60.

down into the ground, it denotes the relationship of the depths and the height. The Praised is a mercy to the worlds, for God's mercy embraces all things. The spear, point in the ground, towards the grave and the dead, recalls resurrection and ascent and the hand of the Praised who guides us to and pleads with God for us. It symbolizes the peace towards which the people of peace are turned to identify with.

Figure 5.17. Battle axes are found on both *stećci*[63] and *nišani*.[64] In the symbolism of weapons, the battle axe stands for the equilibrium between wood's passive warmth and iron's active coldness. It is used to smash and dismember, the opposite of composition. A double-headed, spiked battle axe is a dervish's staff, denoting spiritual authority or a balance between opposites.

Figure 5.18. Sabres and swords are similar, but not identical. Their symbolic meaning in traditional doctrine is almost identical. They are found on both *stećci*[65] and *nišani*.[66] The sabre is the symbol of righteousness, of acting with knowledge. In human hands, it acts in every direction, but its goal is to be vertical, to come to rest in the position of the upright on the scales of justice, where it stands for rising from the dead to be judged by God for every atom of good and every atom of evil done.

Figure 5.19. The bow and arrow are important for the depiction of weapons on *stećci*[67] and *nišani*.[68] The bow is the clearest possible representation of tension. Initially this tension seems directed towards the outside world: the arrow loosed from the bowstring flies away from the archer, but its destination is the uncreated centre of the self. Every movement of eye and hand, of tongue and foot that we think is ours, begins in that uncreated, uncreatable centre. This is the meaning of God's words sent down to the heart of the Praised: "When thou threwest, it was not thyself that threw, but God threw, and that He might confer on the believers a fair benefit; surely God is All-hearing, All-knowing."[69]

---

63 See Wenzel, *Ukrasni motivi na stećcima*, 223, 246–47; Bešlagić, *Stećci – kultura i umjetnost*, 237–39; idem, *Leksikon stećaka*, 104.

64 See Bešlagić, *Nišani XV i XVI vijeka u Bosni i Hercegovini*, 57–60.

65 See Ćurčić, "Starinsko oružje u Bosni i Hercegovini," 104–121; Wenzel, *Ukrasni motivi na stećcima*, 223–49; Bešlagić, *Stećci – kultura i umjetnost*, 222–25; idem, *Leksikon stećaka*, 90–91.

66 See Bešlagić, *Nišani XV i XVI vijeka u Bosni i Hercegovini*, 57–61.

67 See Ćurčić, "Starinsko oružje u Bosni i Hercegovini," 54–63; Wenzel, *Ukrasni motivi na stećcima*, 224, 248–49; Bešlagić, *Stećci – kultura i umjetnost*, 234–36; idem, *Leksikon stećaka*, 89–90.

68 See Ćurčić, "Starinsko oružje u Bosni i Hercegovini," 59; Bešlagić, *Nišani XV i XVI vijeka u Bosni i Hercegovini*, 57–60.

69 *Qur'an*, 8:17.

The bow is thus the symbol of an arc of the horizon, the cosmos in its perfect order. The archer may think he is at the centre of that order, planning, in the illusion of power, to act on the circumference, as one who hears and knows all things, but it is not so, as God tells him plainly: "But will you shall not, unless God wills, the Lord of all Being."[70] God is the absolute centre and circumference of all things, the inward-most and outward-most of all things. Whenever we do something without testifying to His oneness, the Praised's apostolate and return, it obscures, wounds and ultimately kills our heart.

Figure 5.20. Solomon's seal, also known as the Star of David, is a very widespread symbol among Bosnia's Muslims. It is drawn, carved in wood and stone and wrought in metal in mosques and homes, on *nišani* and public buildings, in books and on amulets. It is also associated with sheikhs' caps,[71] and is to be found in Bosnian churches. It denotes human perfection, union in the equilibrium of giving and receiving, the discovery of the heart in the outside world and of the outside world in the heart. The seal of Solomon is an inscription of the sacred name of the Praised, the sign of prostration: our most sublime position is prostration in humility before the Lord, in which we unite seven: forehead, palms, knees and toes. This denotes the seven heavens and seven earths in clear manifestation of Unity.

Figure 5.21. Bowl-like or shell-like hollows are often carved into *stećci*.[72] Imam ʿAli referred to the human heart as a bowl,[73] into which the Word is sent down as rain falls upon the earth. Purity and soundness of heart are thus a condition of remembrance or of maintaining our covenant with god. The rainwater that gathers in the hollows on *nišani* is believed to have healing powers, in that it connects those who take it with the mercy of God and the sound heart of the good.[74] Such hollows on headstones indicate that they belong to the good.[75]

Figure 5.22. Writing is the most important feature of any tombstone, forming words and epitaphs, announcing our coming from and returning to mystery and silence. Both the grave and tombstones are writing of a type, which keep the living on the border of death. It is on the border that the potential of

70 Ibid., 81:29.

71 See Hadžijahić, "Badžijanije u Sarajevu i Bosni," 131 n 69.

72 See Wenzel, *Ukrasni motivi na stećcima*, 129–39; Bešlagić, *Stećci – kultura i umjetnost*, 382–84.

73 See *Nahj al-Balaghā*, 244.

74 See Ćurčić, "Zanimljivi pabirci iz narodne medicine," 129; idem, "Nadgrobni spomenici u narodnoj medicini u Bosni i Hercegovini," 141–45.

75 Hadžijahić, "Badžijanije u Sarajevu i Bosni," 116.

doctrine, ritual and virtue to convince the living of the resurrection of the dead is measured out. All the Books, all our weapons, all our property and pleasures reveal themselves on the brink as scales directing and measuring our campaigns against imperfection and violence. The Book and doctrine, the mihrab and ritual, humility and generosity, everything that is concentrated in the testimony to God's oneness and the Praised's apostolate is inscribed on the border towards death which has no reality.

Post Scriptum: Witnesses and Witnessing

Bosnian tombstones, whatever their form – *stećci*, crosses or *nišani* – present the same teaching in different languages: God is One, His apostles were sent to us for our self-realization and redemption, and all things return to God that each of us may be rightly judged for our use of the debt incurred by the act of creation. Whatever the differences in form, doctrine or ritual, it is incumbent on those who have inherited and study them to discern the unity they affirm.

As tombstones delineating Bosnia's spiritual space, subject over the centuries to destruction without replenishment, the *stećci* remain a mystery, prompting us to decipherment of the One's eternal language in His different manifestations. Disagreements over their name provide the clearest indication of our limited human ability to see the One behind the many forms that manifest Him.

The noun *stećak* is used for the Bosnian tombstones located in the regions that made up or were influenced by the mediaeval Bosnian state.[1] In western Bosnia they are often called *mašeti* or *mašeta*,[2] while in the east of the country they are also known as Greek gravestones.[3] Their epigraphs refer to them as *bilig* or *kam*. According to Petar Skok, the term *bilig* was adopted in Avar times and comes from the northern Turkic language.[4] The Persian word *nišan*, which

1 Bešlagić, *Leksikon stećaka*, 185–86.

2 Ibid., 180.

3 Ibid. In some cases the terms "Greek graveyard" and *mašeta* are both used for the same burial ground and its *stećci*. See Anđelić, *Historijski spomenici Konjica i okoline*, 216, 218. Petar Skok suggests that the noun *mašet* could derive from the Italian *masseto* (*Etimologijski rječnik hrvatskoga ili srpskoga jezika*, 2:381), a view shared by Šefik Bešlagić (*Leksikon stećaka*, 180). It is a simple matter to demonstrate the untenability of this speculation. There are no traces of this word along the eastern Adriatic coast, from Istria to Albania in the south, but it is commonly used in western Bosnia to denote both *stećci* and where they stand. See, e.g., Bešlagić, *Kupres: srednjovjekovni nadgrobni spomenici*, 11, 35. Ibrahim Pašić has reviewed the appearances of this name and the main hypotheses concerning its origins and concludes that it might be of Gothic origin and perhaps reached Bosnia under Arian influence (see Pašić, *Mile i Moštre*, 500–505). The origins of the name and the ways in which it entered the Bosnian language need further investigation. Simple solutions are both challenging and seductive. Of interest may be the Aramaic noun *maštit*, meaning "basis," "foundation," and "foundation stone."

4 Skok, *Etimologijski rječnik hrvatskoga ili srpskoga jezika*, 1:150.

 | DOI 10.1163/9789004279407_126

means much the same as *bilig*, is used to denote a Muslim gravestone.[5] The Arabic *shāhid* also means gravestone.[6]

These three terms – *mašeta*, Greek gravestone and *bilig* – are of particular importance for understanding their relationship with Muslim witness to God's unity and the Praised's apostolate across the Bosnian religious tradition. This is denied both openly and covertly in the construction of Bosnia's history. The continuity of its Muslim content over time is repudiated, represented as forcibly imposed or alien. This construct of a history of discontinuity considers the Muslim presence to be unconnected with what they define as "pre-Muslim." This is a key factor in every anti-Muslim ideology.

It is a well known fact that old Muslim burial grounds are often found alongside *stećci*, as a sort of temporal annex.[7] The oldest of these burial grounds around Bosnia are usually called *šehit* cemeteries (from *shahīd*) or *šehitluci*, as in, for example, saying that "many shahid graves in the village of Sebin are from the time of the *fatḥ*" [see below].[8] The number of such burial grounds and the fact they are so often located alongside *stećci*, together with the normal interpretation of the term *shahīd*, raises the question what the words *mašeta* and *šehiti* really mean when applied to a Bosnian burial ground in which the dead lie beneath tombstones of various forms.

---

5 Ibid., 2:520.

6 Muftić, *Arapsko-bosanski rječnik*, 764.

7 See, e.g., Ćorović, "Prilog proučavanju načina sahranjivanja i podizanja nadgrobnih spomenika u našim krajevima u Srednjem vijeku," 145. Mak Dizdar writes in his notes to the poem "Pravednik": "Legend has it that *good people*, killed in battle against all the evils of their time, lie buried beneath the old gravestones of mediaeval Bosnian necropolises. Wherever there are *stećci* that are cared for and looked after, the town will not fall. In times of summer drought, the tombstones are visited with prayers for rain. As a child, the author of these lines visited the Nekuk and Radimlja necropolises near Stolac along with a group of people praying for rain. The women scraped at some of the *stećci*, made of soft *miljevina* limestone, believing that the dust they scraped from them could heal various diseases." (Dizdar, *Kameni spavač/Stone Sleeper*, 192). At both these sites where the Muslims of Stolac went to pray for rain, there are old *nišani* alongside the *stećci*. When Dizdar says "Radimlja," the meaning of the name is wider than its present use, which refers only to the necropolis by the River Radimlja; he means the necropolis or harem at Gorica, where the people of Stolac used to come to pray for rain. The necropolises at Nekuk and Gorica are also known to the people of Stolac as *šehiti*.

8 In *Srpski etnografski zbornik*, 43:498, 557; quoted in Musulin, *Rječnik hrvatskog ili srpskog jezika*, 17:526.

The name *mašet* is undoubtedly the most widespread vernacular name for these Bosnian gravestones. It has the same meaning as *stećak* but is also applied to *nišani*.[9] The word *mašet* also features in folk songs:

Do mašeta doru dogonio	He pushed the roan to the tombstone,
Po kamenu čordom udario	And struck the stone with his sword
I duboko biše zafatio.[10]	And clove it deep within.
Po mašetu čordom udario.[11]	He struck the tombstone with his sword.

More than a century ago, in 1891, Ćiro Truhelka suggested that the Bosnian word *mašet* is derived from the Turkish *meşet*, meaning the grave of a hero killed for his faith.[12] He saw nothing in this suggestive fact that might contribute

9 Local people call the famous *nišan* of Omeraga Bašić near Glamoč, which is 4.35m in height, Bašić's *mašet*. (Mujezinović, *Islamska epigrafika Bosne i Hercegovine*, 3:138–39)

10 Jukić, *Narodne piesme bosanske i hercegovačke*, 457.

11 Idem, 458.

12 Truhelka, "Starobosanski mramorovi," 369. Abdulah Škaljić writes that the noun *mašet* derives from the Turkish *meșhed*, or in common speech *meşat*, itself in turn from the Arabic *mäshhäd*. (Škaljić, *Turcizmi u srpskohrvatskom-hrvatskosrpskom jeziku*, 448). The term *mešatluk* is used to mean burial ground three times in Bašeskija's *Ljetopis*: (1) a manuscript of the *Ljetopis* (fol. 31a, line 17) gives an account of gunpowder blown up in a *mešatluk* (Bašeskija, *Ljetopis*, 211), a passage that is missing from Mujezinović's translation; (2) it is related that the bier bearing the body of a particularly great man was carried to the *mešatluk* by six to eight men (idem, 398); and (3) there is a reference to some deceased persons being taken to the *mešatluk* (idem, 400). The manuscript of Bašeskija's *Ljetopis* is in the Gazi Husrev-bey Library in Sarajevo (see Nametak, *Katalog arapskih, turskih, perzijskih i bosanskih rukopisa*, 279–80). It is clear if one simply consults a Turkish dictionary that this Bosnian word and its Turkish forms are of Semitic origin. The following are the forms associated with the word *mašet* and its meanings in Turkish: *meşhed*, pl. *meşâhid*: (1) a place where people assemble, especially for the performance of a special sacred rite; (2) a field of battle, a battle; (3) a place of martyrdom; (4) a funeral assembly; (5) the aspect of a person; *muşhed*, fem. *muşhede*: (1) made or called to be a witness, or to see an act or state; (2) martyred; *muşhid*, fem. *muşhide*: (1) who calls or produces a witness or evidence; (2) who makes another see and become aware of anything; (3) who attains to puberty; *meşhûd*, fem. *meşhûde*, pl. fem. *meşhûdât*: witnessed, seen (Redhouse, *Turkish and English Lexicon Shewing in English the Signification of the Turkish Terms*); *meşhet*: (1) şehit düşülen yer, meaning "a place where a *shahīd* fell;" (2) şehidin gömüldüğü yer, meaning "a place where a *shahīd* is buried" (Akalın, et al., *Türkçe sözlük*); *maşatlık*: müslüman olmayanların, özellikle Yahudilerin mezarlığı, meaning "a burial ground where non-Muslims are buried, especially Jews" (idem). Kerima Filan, who teaches Turkish at the Faculty of the Humanities in Sarajevo, is of the view that the word *mešatluk* can be read as *mašetluk, mašatluk* and *mešetluk*. According to Professor Filan, the etymology of the word

to a deeper understanding of the continuity between the *stećak* and the *nišan*, however, even though it becomes clear as soon as one considers their relationship in the context of the semantic field of the Arabic root *sh-h-d*, a semantic field of such significance that one can hardly discuss Muslim intellectual heritage or of the history of the Bosnian Muslims without giving it the most thorough consideration.

There is a long history of understanding the terms *šehit, mašet* and *fet* in terms of a fairly exclusively anti-Muslim view of history: a *šehit* is a fallen Muslim soldier whose enemies are the Christians and *fet* the conquest or occupation of a Christian country. These are key features of the definition of the Muslim, often equated with the "Turk," as the absolute enemy of the Christian.[13] It follows that all *shahīd* burial grounds in Bosnia are seen as monuments to Muslim violence and Christian suffering, an inverted view central to the construction of a particular historical image of Bosnia and its Muslims. A close study of the relationship and close connection between burial grounds with *stećci* and those with *nišani* and the original meanings of the terms *šehit, mašet* and *fet* makes clear that these interpretations are untenable.

The first condition of being a Muslim is to bear witness to no god but God and the Praised as His apostle. Nothing replaces the primacy of this testimony. Everything else Muslim derives from it as from a living spring. In Arabic, it is expressed in the words *ashhadu an lā ilāha illāllāh wa ashhadu anna muḥammadan rasūlallāh.* One who acknowledges the primacy of this testimony is a *shahīd* or *shāhid*, a witness or martyr in the original meaning of that term. What the *shahīd* utters is *shahāda*, testimony. This is expressed in Arabic, but forms of the same testimony are to be found in every language and at every time and place. The truth of the One and the apostolate of the perfect individual belong to all times, all people, and all languages.

Regarding the apostle, every other prophet and sage has always known whom God announced to Moses in the Torah,[14] of whom Jesus spoke in the Gospel as the Paraclete, the Spirit of Truth and the Holy Spirit,[15] who was

---

is absolutely clear. The shift from the original Arabic *mäshhäd* to the Turkish arises from the customary loss of the consonant "h" in a medial position, since no such consonant exists in Turkish, and the transformation from a voiced to an unvoiced consonant at the end of the word, a feature of the Turkish language.

13 For more on the figure of the Muslim as the enemy of the Christian, see Tolan, *Saracens: Islam in the Medieval European Imagination*; Zirojević, "Turci u našem ogledalu"; and Dukić, *Sultanova djeca*.

14 See *Deuteronomy*, 18:18.

15 John refers to the Paraclete explicitly in three chapters of his Gospel: 14–16. Identifying Jesus' prophecy with the expectation of the coming of the Praised is an inextricable part

awaited in his day but who was not him, the Anointed, the prophet John, nor the prophet Elijah,[16] the witness responds with *shahāda*, witness that this original prophet who is the seal of the prophets was made manifest in the person of the historical Praised, son of ʿAbdullah and Amina, born in Becca in 570 AD. His historical manifestation is but a sign of his metahistorical nature and of the principle of all creation, the primal apostle who, for Muslim witness, is the reason and purpose of all things.

For such witnesses to the Praised, the reasons for their testimony lie in all things, as he is first and last of creation. There is nothing in all our metaphysical, cosmological, anthropological or psychological knowledge that, for Muslims, is not a reason to bear witness to the Praised as perfect and paragon in relation to the All-praised (*al-ḥamid*). This perfect humanity concerns every one of us always and so in all things, for it defines us in our reason and purpose for being in this world.

Nothing we can achieve brings our journey towards the One to an end. Whatever stage we reach, the Praised's perfection represents a higher potential, a reason to follow on in ascent or return to the One. Whatever stage we reach, we never attain our ultimate potential, but it is the only goal that justifies life as a journey towards absolute meaning. The more aware we are of our perfect goal, the greater our reasons for humility and generosity. It is in these virtues that we realize our liberation from seeming in the world and in the self.

Without truth as universal principle, the traditional perspective would be literally impossible. Existence is truth's manifestation and externalization. Both existence and its individual manifestations are created or appear with truth.[17] Everything created with truth gathers in us, as both self and world reveal truth. Wherever we are, this manifestation remains clear. The vault of the heavens and the expanses of the earth and all that lies between bear witness. We can confess it or conceal or associate something other than the truth with it. In each case, witness is of our very core.

To bear witness to the truth entails living, willing, power, knowing, speaking, hearing and seeing. But, however necessary, they are not enough. Witness includes its opposite. Witnesses may suppress, deny or distort the representation of what they know. The perennial human question concerns witness to the truth of our origins and purpose, to what gives meaning to life, will, power,

---

of Muslim witness to God's oneness and the apostolate of the Praised (see Ibn Isḥāq, *Sīrat Rasūl Allāh*, 104; for the meaning of the name *Paraclete* in the Gospel according to John, see also: Knohl, *The Messiah before*, 68–71).

16 See *John*, 1:19–21.

17 See *Qur'an*, 6:73.

knowledge, speech, hearing and seeing at every moment, in the full reality of the "now." We can do either – testify to the truth or conceal it. Bearing witness enables us to find and maintain ourselves in the truth of our creation. Concealing the truth and uttering lies distances us from our own nature. God's discourse to and through the Praised points to this eternal meaning of witness:

> And when thy Lord took from the Children of Adam, from their loins, their seed, and made them testify touching themselves, "Am I not your Lord?" They said, "Yes, we testify" – lest you should say on the Day of Resurrection, "As for us, we were heedless of this," or lest you say, "Our fathers were associators aforetime, and we were seed after them. What, wilt Thou then destroy us for the deeds of the vain-doers?"[18]

This mystical speech concerning our witness to His lordship and our service is at the heart of the cosmic covenant which relates us as faithful to the Faithful through faith, as God says in the Recitation: "We offered confidence [good faith] to the heavens and the earth and the mountains, but they refused to carry it and were afraid of it; and man carried it. Surely he is sinful, very foolish."[19] Faith is knowledge of the beloved and love of the known. With our covenant of confidence, trust or good faith, we stand out from existence; our path remains open either way, towards plenitude or nothing.

Our little knowledge connects us with God as Absolute and does so through our love for That we know little of but have infinite love for. This love unceasingly increases us in knowledge on our journey towards the goal nothing confines or limits. Every bit player in the cosmic covenant joins us on that journey, as God says: "Hast thou not seen how before God prostrate themselves all who are in the heavens and all who are in the earth, the sun and the moon, the stars and the mountains, the trees and the beasts, and many of mankind?"[20] The difference is in the will – everything but us refused to have any will but His, while we agreed that we may take His will as ours.

Presented thus, our self-witness as servants of our Lord marks our relationship as created with our Creator, as debtors and the One we owe our debt to. The Lord Creator to Whom we owe our debt manifests His oneness through His most beautiful names. All of existence, the heavens, the earth and what lies between them gives those names external form, spread far and wide, while we

18 *Qur'an*, 7:172–73.

19 Ibid., 33:72.

20 Ibid., 22:18.

internalize them, concentrating them. Discovering the names in our original nature, we discover ourselves as witnesses of our Lord. We have no knowledge of ourselves without knowing our Lord, no knowledge of Him without knowing ourselves.

Witnesses are Muslims, people of peace, related to God as Peace through being-at-peace. The Bosnian word "mirenje," which may be translated into English as "being at or in peace" and which includes connotations of rest and quiet, corresponds very well to the Arabic verbal noun *islam*. The Praised, as God's servant and apostle, is the perfect example of this mode of being and represents our reason and purpose. The first prerequisite for being-at-peace is witness or *shahāda*. No other requirement is valid without it, for its absence means existence and knowledge of it is unfounded.

Since the Praised is God's first manifestation, he is present in everything and in each of us, directly or indirectly, consciously or unconsciously, as our always higher potential, towards which we are directed by our original nature. His every manifestation is a sign of perfection as the reason and purpose for our creation. We confess him in infinite ways, but they are all versions of God's unique, eternal manifestation: God is first giver, creation the recipient; once His gift has been received, it may be given on. This giving and receiving is the constant, perfect manifestation of God as One.

In the Praised, as universal, firstness of manifestion is achieved in his receptive, maternal and giving, masculine and sealing nature. How we shape our witness is inextricable from our freedom and confidence in God as Faithful (*al-Mu'min*). Seen in terms of historical communities, some of these ways may seem irreconcilable, as a given witness may seem to deny others.

As a community with twenty-six revealed books, the Torah being the first and Malachi the twenty-sixth, and with many others associated with or derived from them in an uninterrupted course of transmission, Jews recognize and bear witness to the apostle whose coming among their brethren God announced through Moses. They also recognize the Anointed, who will be raised from the descendants of David. What they do not admit is that this prophet foretold to them is the Praised Muslims bear witness to as Muhammad born in Becca, nor do they admit that Jesus, Mary's son, to whom Christians and Muslims bear witness, is the Anointed they are waiting for. Muslims do confess that the Anointed Christians recognize was indeed born of the Virgin Mary and later raised up by God that he might come again.

As a people of twenty-seven revealed books, the first being the Gospel according to Matthew and the last Revelation, with which an uninterrupted course of tradition is also associated, Christians recognize and confess God's announcement to Moses of an apostle not John nor Elijah nor the Awaited One of whom the priests and Levites asked John during the time of Jesus.[21] They recognize and confess Jesus' promise of the Paraclete. But for Christians, the historical Praised to whom Muslims bear witness is not the Paraclete they recognize as foretold by Jesus. For Christians, the Praised is neither the prophet foretold to Moses nor the Paraclete.

For Muslims, the Jewish and Christian books, all fifty-three of them, are evidential witness of the Praised as prophet. In principle, they are Muslim books. Over the centuries Muslims have said that the number of the books that precede the Recitation corresponds to the numerical value of the sacred name *Aḥmad* by which Jesus, in the discourse of the Qur'an, foretells and bears witness to the Praised.[22] Given that the revelations are in different languages and the Arabic names *Aḥmad* and *Muḥammad* are both present and can be translated into all languages, Muslims seek and find them in the books of all God's apostles.[23]

In Bosnia, when the *stećci* are referred to as *mašeta* and the *nišani* alongside them as *šehitski*, there is no good reason for not assuming this reflects a fateful duality in witness of the Praised, warrant for whose apostolate, such witnesses believe, lies everywhere, including in the Torah and the Gospel and in the entire sacred heritage associated with them. The Anointed said: "For had ye believed Moses, ye would have believed me: for he wrote of me. But if ye believe not his writings, how shall ye believe my words?"[24]

God said to Moses: "I will raise them up a prophet from among their brethren, like unto thee, and will put my words in his mouth; and he shall speak unto them all that I shall command him."[25] In the same book and with the same significance, we find: "And there arose not a prophet since in Israel like unto Moses, whom the Lord knew face to face."[26] But the Anointed is of the children of Israel – born and raised in Israel of the generation of David.

It cannot be true that Jesus is similar to Moses, for it is said through Moses that there has never been one like him in Israel. Jesus says of the Paraclete,

---

21 See *John*, 1:19–21.

22 See *Qur'an*, 61:6.

23 There is a rich tradition of Muslims seeking and finding prophecies of the Praised in the books of the Bible; for example: Tabari, *The Book of Religion and Empire*. The subtitle of the book is: *A Semi-official Defence and Exposition of Islām Written by Order at the Court and with the Assistance of the Caliph Mutawakkil* (A.D. *847–861*).

24 *John*, 5:46–47.

25 *Deuteronomy*, 18:18.

26 Ibid., 34:10.

whom he foretells as one to come from the Lord after he has gone, "He shall testify of me."[27] In Muslim belief, this prophet like unto Moses and raised up from among the brethren of the Israelites – who are the Ishmaelites – is the Praised, whose name, in the language of the Qur'an, is *Aḥmad*, a prophet who bears firm witness to Jesus as the Anointed and his mother, the Virgin Mary. Thus Moses "writes" of Jesus through the Praised, who says: "I am most close to Jesus, son of Mary, among the whole of mankind in this worldly life and the next life."[28]

No prophet but John bore witness to Jesus knowing him by name and addressing him as such. But John, too, was from Israel. The only prophet who was not an Israelite to bear witness to Jesus, knowing of him and what was revealed to him, was the Praised.[29] Moses "writes" about Jesus, bearing witness to the Praised as one similar to him and as from the brethren of the Israelites. Witnesses to the Praised are thus also witnesses to the Anointed and to Moses.

The commonly accepted prayer that follows *tarāwīḥ* worship[30] – *rabbanā āmannā bimā anzalta wattbaʿnā al-rasūla faktubnā maʿa-shshāhidīn,*[31] which means "Lord, we believe in that Thou hast sent down, and we follow the apostle. Inscribe us therefore with those who bear witness" – also attests to the closeness of the Anointed and the Praised in the witness of Bosnian Muslims. These words are said aloud by the muezzin on completion of worship and as an introduction to congregational prayer. Then, in the mosques of Bosnia, all present – men and women, old and young – raise their arms and said aloud "Amin" after each section of the prayer spoken by the leader.[32]

---

27 *John*, 15:26.

28 Muslim, 4:1260–61.

29 In response to the question of the prophet whom God announces through Moses, like him but not of Israel, rabbis refer to the prophet Balaam (see Finkelstein, *Sifre on Deuteronomy*, 430). There is a clear difference between Moses and Balaam, however – a book was sent down to Moses, but not to Balaam (see Numbers 22 et. seq. on Balaam).

30 *Tarāwīḥ* prayers (Ar. plural of *tarwīḥa*) are the ritual congregation of Muslims during the month of Ramadan following the night prayer. Everyone takes part – men and women, young and old – as they pray twenty *rakaʿāt* (cycles) behind the leader, with a pause between each pair or four cycles. The noun *tarāwīḥ* means "breaks."

31 *Qur'an*, 3:53.

32 This introductory section has for centuries been recited in every Bosnian mosque, but in recent decades it is increasingly being replaced by verse 2:185 of the Qur'an: "The month of Ramadan, wherein the Recitation was sent down to be a guidance to the people, and as a clear signs of the Guidance and the Salvation!" The reasons for this are the same as for the omission or deletion of verse 3:37: "Whenever Zachariah went in to her in the Mihrab." Calligraphic inscriptions of these words from the Qur'an were standard in the mihrabs of

According to the Recitation, Jesus' disciples and apostles conclude their response to him with introductory prayers: "And when Jesus perceived their concealing, he said, 'Who will be my helpers unto God?' The apostles said, 'We will be helpers of God; we believe in God; witness thou that we are people of Peace.' "[33] The connection with the Anointed and his disciples is thus at the heart of the congregation and witness of Bosnian Muslims. In their belief, Muslim witness is inseparable from the witness of Christians as their spiritual and native forebears and as believing brothers at all times.

Being a person of peace (*muslim*) is a necessary but not sufficient condition for being faithful (*mu'min*). The first is a voluntary capacity of the individual, leading to a state of the self in which the will of the Self is revealed, as may be seen from something God says through the Praised:

> The Bedouins say "We believe." Say: "You do not believe; rather say, 'We are at peace;' for faith has not yet entered your hearts. If you obey God and His apostle, He will not diminish you anything of your works."[34]

Like Muslims, both Christians and Jews can be faithful. Simply claiming to be so does not make them so, as the Recitation tells us, when God says through the Praised: "Surely they that believe, and those of Jewry, and the Christians, and those Sabaeans, whoso believes in God and the Last Day and works righteousness – their wage awaits them with their Lord, and no fear shall be on them, neither shall they sorrow."[35]

---

old Bosnian mosques, but in recent decades some have been erased and they are often replaced in the mihrabs of new mosques by part of verse 2:144: "Turn thy face towards the Holy Mosque." One could see in this change ideological influences that attest to the modern loss of awareness of the unbroken course of the Bosnian tradition. The verses that are removed bear ritual and doctrinal witness to the unbroken link between the Muslim heritage and the Christian past, which is incomprehensible to the fundamentalist view of history, in which God is reduced to history and equated with the goal defined and attained by the religious community. The transcendent unity of the different paths to God is thus replaced by the horizontal link between nations and separate teleologies, in which the unity of God is replaced by the unity of the nation.

33 *Qur'an*, 3:52. The phrase "the people of peace" corresponds to the Arabic *muslimūn*. It should not be forgotten that in the Gospel, Jesus son of Mary refers to such people by the Greek noun *eirēnopoioi* (*Matthew*, 5:9).

34 *Qur'an*, 49:14.

35 Ibid., 2:62.

Faith is a condition of the heart. It eludes the will, being absolute certainty, as God says in the Recitation: “God knows what is in your hearts.”[36] The Praised says of human hearts that they are like one of the All-merciful’s two fingers and He turns them where He will.[37] All of us are concentrated in one heart as our supreme, greatest and finest potential. Those who are conscious of that original oneness in will, love, knowledge and beauty[38] are brothers, as God says: “The faithful indeed are brothers; so set things right between your two brothers, and be mindful of God; haply so you will find mercy.”[39]

Witnesses to His unity and the Praised’s apostolate discover in themselves and all things, including their spiritual and native forebears, evidence of the Praised as the prophets’ maternal seal, admonisher and encourager, mercy and light. Muslims bear witness to the Book God revealed to him: “That is the Book, wherein is no doubt, a guidance to the mindful who believe in the Unseen, and perform the prayer, and expend of that We have provided them; who believe in what has been sent down to and what has been sent down before thee, and have faith in the Hereafter.”[40]

In confessing the Book the Praised received and what other apostles have received as books before him, the people of peace are responding to God Who said, speaking in pre-existence to the apostles about the Praised: “Bear witness so, and I shall be with you among the witnesses.”[41] An indivisible element of this witness is willingness to endure, sacrifice and suffer with and for his sake. This willingness is justified by the conviction that following him as our best example redeems us. Witness is the manifestation of His oneness and the Praised’s apostolate.

According to the Revelation God sent down to the Praised, God and the angels, prophets and the faithful are witnesses. In the Recitation, God’s knowledge of our deeds is stressed: “God bears witness to that He has sent down to thee; He has sent it down with His knowledge; and the angels also bear witness; and God suffices for a witness.”[42] And He says of the prophets and faithful as

36 Ibid., 33:51.

37 See Muslim, 4:1397.

38 For the semantic fields of the verbal noun “being-at-peace” or *islām*, faith, to which love and knowledge are concomitant, (*īmān*), doing that which is beautiful (*iḥsān*) and their temporal concentration or dispersal (*sāʿa*) in accordance with God’s discourse in the *Qur’an*, as well as their psychological, anthropological, cosmological and ontological reach, see Murata, *The Vision of Islam*.

39 *Qur’an*, 49:10.

40 Ibid., 2:2–4.

41 Ibid., 3:81.

42 Ibid., 4:166.

witnesses: "We appointed you a midmost nation that you might be witnesses to the people, and that the apostle might be a witness to you."[43]

A.J. Wensinck's studies of the double meaning of the term "witness" in the Jewish, Eastern Christian and Muslim traditions, namely the original meaning of witness and the derived meaning of martyr, lead him to conclude:

> The twofold use of the term shahīd discussed above, proves to be a reflex of the use of the term *mártys* (*mártyr*) in the New Testament on the one hand and in the old Christian literature on the other. The latter uses the word in its technical sense, whereas the former – just as the Kor'ān does – applies it to God as a witness of the deeds of men, to Christ and the apostles as God's witnesses. It is to be observed, that this Christian terminology goes back to the Old Testament, where it is again God who is a witness of the deeds of men, and the pious who are God's witnesses. So the use of the word in the Kor'ān appears to be identical with that in the New Testament; and the latter appears to be dependent upon the Old Testament.[44]

The supreme degree of that testimony is martyrdom for the sake of God and the Praised. All who persist in witness to death – whether they die or are killed – are witnesses. Witness is thus a highly present element of Muslim being as a whole. Every call to prayer includes it. Muslims repeat it countless times throughout their lives, with the desire that they breathe their last breath with the *shahāda*, in witness of no god but God and the Praised as His apostle.

Bearing witness to God's oneness as All-praised is inseparable from bearing witness to His apostle, the Praised, who is human and God's servant. The Praised to whom Muslims bear witness is both the origin and seal of the prophets. They seek and find him in all things within themselves and in the world about them. There is nothing in the seen or unseen world, in the outer horizons or in the self that does not offer signs of the truth of his apostolate and his redemptive warnings to us. He is the witness and seal for all the prophets and good people at all times, and they for him.

The noun *šehit* is the Bosnian version of the Arabic *shahīd*, which features in the Recitation in its primary meaning of "witness" and only later as "martyr." A similar semantic shift from witness to martyr can be found in the Greek *mártys* and the Syriac *sāhdā*.[45] Witness is thus the relationship between the person

---

43 Ibid., 2:143.

44 Wensinck, "The Oriental Doctrine of the Martyrs," 97.

45 See Goldziher, *Muslim Studies*, 2:350–51.

bearing witness and God as Witness. In the case of the peoples or communities of the Book, their individual members are witnesses in relation to the original Revealer of the Book, its carrier and all other people. The entire community of peace is called upon in the name of God to bear witness for the individual, whereas the apostle is a witness in the name of God for all people.[46]

Since every community is bound by its book,[47] which determines its witness, God ordered the Praised to say: "People of the Book, why do you conceal the signs of God? Surely God is witness of the things you do."[48] The books that have been sent down differ, and may be accepted or rejected. For the people of peace (*muslim*) to be faithful (*mu'min*) they must accept the revealed books.

The best known of the books God reveals through His prophets are the Torah, Psalms and Gospel. God's address to the "people of the Book" refers to all of them: Jews as the people of the Torah, Christians as the people of the Gospel, and Muslims as the people of the Recitation. These books set forth the key measures that determine the limits of human responsibility. They are the watershed between our wrongdoings and merits, which meet with punishment or reward.

Being peaceful and faithful means the self is connected with God as Peace and as Faithful through being-at-peace and faith. The self thus discovers itself in its original potential. The opposite of which, of being created on the sublime height, is obscuration, concealment and isolation. None of which is beyond the reach of two wills, the divine and the human. The human will turns either to obscuration, concealment and isolation or to their opposite, illumination, disclosure and openness. When we remove the veils in the self and bear witness to God, the apostle and return, our relationship as witness with God as Witness is open. It encompasses everything in the world and self.

The noun *mašet* may correspond in origin to the Arabic noun of place *mashhad*, derived from the verb *shahida*, "to testify," "to be present in," and hence "to be a *shahīd*," "to be a martyr." Ignaz Goldziher connects and compares these two meanings with features of Eastern Christianity.[49] The noun *mashhad* denotes any sacred place with a defining structure, though the latter is not essential.

A *mashhad* or *mašet* is often the grave of an earlier prophet, righteous person or predecessor of the Praised – of people who knew of him as human perfection and aspired to it after their original nature in conformity with their

46 See *Qur'an*, 22:78.

47 Ibid., 45:28.

48 *Qur'an*, 3:98.

49 See Goldziher, *Muslim Studies*, 2:350–52.

knowledge and circumstances and the times in which they lived. However little their knowledge, they were never without it. Those who came after could see it as clearly foreshadowing their own witness, in which they realized the expectations of their forebears.

Obedience to God and the apostle leads to the assembly in bliss of all prophets, righteous people, witnesses and the sincere.[50] Connection with these people and preservation of their memory is mentioned in the Recitation: "In their stories is surely a lesson to men possessed of minds; it is not a tale forged, but a confirmation of what is before it, and a distinguishing of everything, and a guidance, and a mercy to a people who believe."[51]

The reference to these burial grounds as Greek may be seen as the Bosnian Church demarcating itself in relation to the Serbian version of the Greek or old Eastern rite, as well as from Roman Catholicism.[52] Both the Bosnian *krstjan* and Serbian Christian heritage belong to the eastern Rite; they are Greek, transmitted in the Slavonic translation of Cyril and Methodius.[53] When this translation came to be ritually adapted to the Rascian or Serbian and therefore associated with the ruling Serbian dynasty, the Bosnian version remained, in a sense, more Greek.[54] This may explain the fact that Bosnia's ecclesiastical books are more directly related to earlier versions than to the Rascian, of which they are almost entirely independent.[55]

The noun *fet* is the Bosnian version of the Arabic *fatḥ*, with which the Hebrew *pātah*, the Aramaic and Syriac *petah* and the Ethiopian *fatḥa* are cognate. In each case, the corresponding verb means "to open," "to unfetter," "to release." According to the revelations in the Recitation, this opening relates primarily to the gates of heaven and passage into the garden or into hell, which is the split in the self between its original, redemptive height and the uttermost depths it contains. Our redemption and realization is ascent by the open path to the One.[56]

The notion of "opening" inheres in the semantic fields of the Recitation, all of which are informed by the crucial, central position of the name "God."

---

50 See *Qur'an*, 4:69.

51 *Qur'an*, 12:111.

52 Mavro Orbini wrote of Stjepan II Kotromanić that he was "true to the Greek rite" (Orbini, *Kraljevstvo Slavena*, 414).

53 For the tradition of Cyril and Methodius and its part in Bosnian heritage, see Hadžijahić, *Povijest Bosne u IX i X stoljeću*, 224 et.seq.

54 For the adjective "Greek" to denote the rite and canon that is distinct from the Latin, see the entries in: Budmani, *Rječnik hrvatskog ili srpskog jezika*, 3:397.

55 See Jurić-Kappel, "Bosanske apokalipse u svome (južno)slavenskom kontinuitetu."

56 See *Qur'an*, 7:40; 15:14; 38:50; 39:71, 73; 78:19.

Opening thus denotes our relationship as open with God as Opener (*al-fattāḥ*). This opening means eradicating from the self that which separates it from God, which conceals and isolates it. God orders the Praised to say: "Our Lord will bring us together, then make opening between us by the truth. He is the Opener, All-knowing."[57]

Those who are open or openers (*al-fātiḥ*) are in a relationship with God as Opener (*al-Fattāḥ*). Being an opener attests to what we have received from God as Opener; we are openers, because we have been opened. This is comparable with being people of peace: we are so because we have first received peace from God as Peace.

Opening (*al-fātḥ*) is the relation between the open person and God as Opener. The key sign of that relationship is the holy recitation – the chapter known as the "Opener" (*sūra al-fātiḥa*), the first sura of the Recitation. It is known as the Opening of the Book, the Mother of the Book, the Image of Praise and the Essence of the Recitation.[58] It has seven signs or verses and is also referred to in the Recitation as the Seven oft-repeated Verses.[59] It is second only to the phrase of witness to God's oneness and the Praised's apostolate as most repeated text in the life of the people of peace. They teach it to their children as early as possible and repeat it throughout life, in each cycle of prayer and on many other occasions.

For the people of peace, who relate to God as Peace by finding peace in His will, the Recitation is the key linguistic object of study. Nothing informs the self more than the two words – testimony (*shahāda*) and opening (*al-fātḥ*). The nouns witness (*shahīd*) and opener (*fātiḥ*) are inherent in our relationship with God, whose names, Witness (*al-Shāhid*) and Opener (*al-Fattāḥ*), denote our intellectual adherence to the community of the Praised, every member of which, living or dead, is properly called a witness and opener, a *shahīd* and *fātiḥ*.

Qur'an is a verbal noun denoting "incessant recitation," "teaching," or a text constantly recited and heard, over and over again. The Recitation was spoken by God through the Praised as His apostle and we recite it by listening and repeating, writing and reading, seeing and remembering it. The response of the people of peace to God's teachings through the Praised is: "We hear and are at peace. Our Lord, grant us Thy forgiveness; unto Thee is the homecoming."[60]

57 *Qur'an*, 34:26.

58 The Arabic versions of these are: *Fātihat al-Kitāb, Umm al- Kitāb, Sūrat al-Ḥamd* and *Asās al-Qur'ān*.

59 See *Qur'an*, 15:87.

60 *Qur'an*, 2:285.

It is fair to say that there is no path to God without human perfection or the Praised, and that ignorance of the Recitation is ignorance of him as apostle.

The self is shaped by opening (*al-fāth*) in relation to God as Opener (*al-Fattāḥ*). This is the eternal centre of everything Muslim or related to being-at-peace in and with the will of God. The opening or liberation by which one becomes open or free for our sublime potential concerns us as individuals and therefore all of humankind. No historical, political or ideological construct can deny or substitute for the centrality of the openness of the individual self to God as Opener.

In many anti-Muslim constructs of history, distorted meanings are imposed on these terms and many Muslims, ignorant of the purposes this imposition serves, have adopted and passed on these meanings. In consequence they do not recognize the anti-Muslim ideologies that have deprived them of their foundations. Teleologically speaking, God is the foundation of all things. When His presence is excluded, and ideological teleology is confined to this world, it is possible to deprive people of their historical foundations, as precursor to denying, excluding, persecuting and killing them. Whenever someone deprives others of their foundation, it should be recognized as an incitement to crimes against them.

The village of Babunovići, near Srebrenik, around which are many *šehitluks*, contains the oldest mosque in the region, in a part of the village known as Šehovina. When the imam descends from the mimber on Fridays and the two mandatory cycles of prayer have been completed, all the worshippers stand up and listen to the muezzin saying aloud these words: "Help from God and a nigh victory. Give thou good tidings to the believers!"[61]

61 Ibid., 61:13. On 12 March 2010, the writer was told of this custom in the old mosque in Babunovići, continued in the new one, by Mehmedalija Hadžić, who has himself taken part in it. The residents of the village are aware of the antiquity of this custom. The present imam of the mosque in Babunovići, Ahmed Mujkić, told the author that the villagers say the custom has been transmitted from imam to imam and that he himself received it from his predecessor, Mustafa Sarajlić, who had it from Mustafa Mujkić, who in turn had it from Ibrahim Sarajlić, to whom it was conveyed by mulla Omer Ferizović, who had it from mulla Meho Ferizović. This is as far back as Ahmed Mujkić knows in the chain of transmission.

FIGURE 5.1 *Map of carved stones from the illustrations: in each pair, the first is a mediaeval* stećak, *the second a Muslim* nišan, *both with the same motifs, demonstrating continuity.*

FIGURE 5.3 *Stolac*

FIGURE 5.2 *Krupac*

FIGURE 5.4 *The Sun (upper Opličići, lower Šišići)*

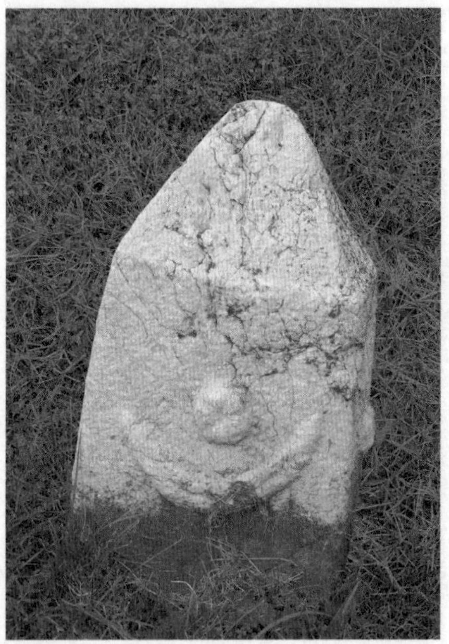

FIGURE 5.5 *The Moon* (*upper Tarevo, lower Sarajevo*)

FIGURE 5.6 *The Cross (upper Grahovčići, lower Ljubina)*

FIGURE 5.7 *Apple (upper Varošište, lower Čevljanovići)*

FIGURE 5.8 *Vine (upper Radimlja, lower Bakići)*

FIGURE 5.9 *Rose (upper Dugo polje, lower Čajniče)*

FIGURE 5.10 *Fleur de lis (upper Opličići, lower Travnik)*

FIGURE 5.11 *Birds (upper Čerin, lower Sarajevo)*

FIGURE 5.12 *Zachariah and Mary (upper Lomnica, lower Sarajevo)*

FIGURE 5.13 *Hand (upper Donji Bratoč, lower Sarajevo)*

FIGURE 5.14 *Rope (upper Sarajevo, lower Bakići)*

FIGURE 5.15 *Staff (upper Gorani, lower Stupari – Vinište)*

FIGURE 5.16 *Spear (upper Podlipnik, lower Brankovići)*

FIGURE 5.17 *Axe (upper Kiseljak, lower Sarajevo)*

FIGURE 5.18 *Sabre (upper Lopoč, lower Foča)*

FIGURE 5.19 *Bow and arrow (upper Delijaš, lower Foča)*

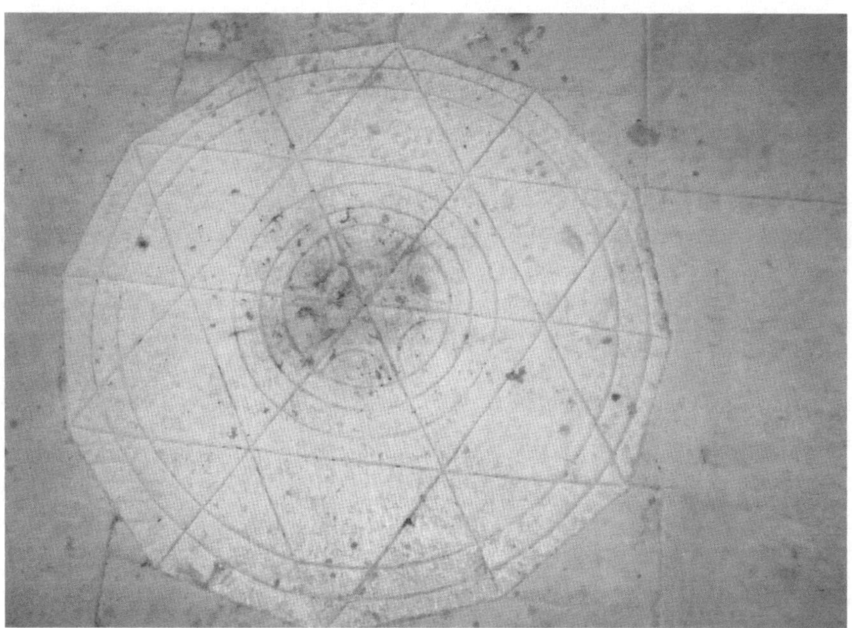

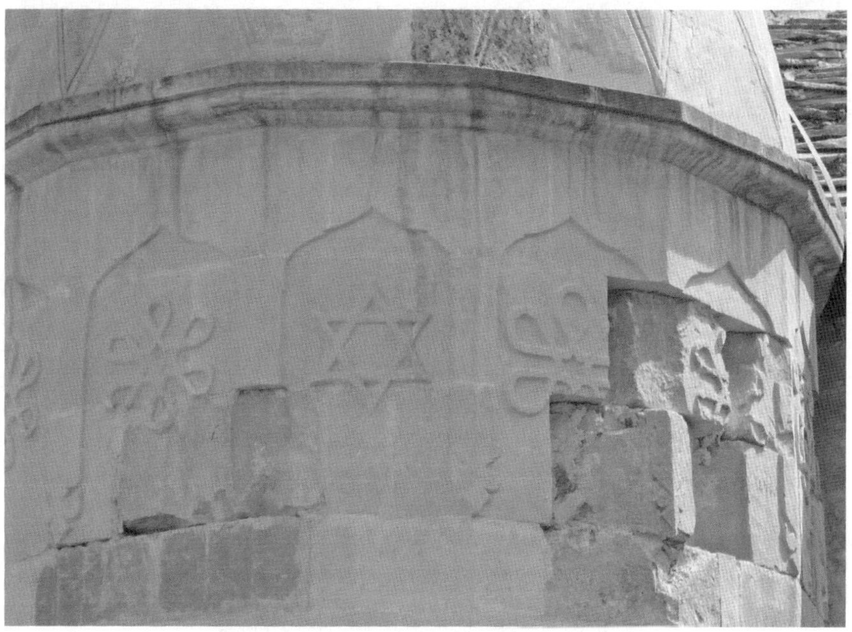

FIGURE 5.20 *The Seal of Solomon (upper Ošanići, lower Stolac)*

FIGURE 5.21 *Bowl (upper Panik, lower Predolje)*

FIGURE 5.22 *Words (upper Veličani, lower Dumanjići)*

Afterword: The Face of the Praised

I have fashioned thee as
a work of art for Myself.
QUR'AN, 20:41

I will raise them up a prophet
from among their brethren,
like unto thee.
DEUTERONOMY, 18:18

Verily of an immense magnitude
is thy nature.
QUR'AN, 68:4

Almost as a rule, one finds the following calligraphic inscription in the mihrabs of Bosnian mosques: "Whenever Zachariah went in to her in the mihrab."[1] One finds similar inscriptions in the mosques of other areas, but little detailed research has been done on them. The Zachariah in the inscription is the prophet of God and priest at the Mosque or Temple in Sion, the father of the prophet John, the Baptist, and the person upon whom he enters is the Virgin Mary, the mother of the Messiah Jesus. The inscription is one part of a Qur'anic verse that refers to Mary in the mihrab of the Mosque.

For Muslim tradition, the mihrab is the symbolic centre or focus of the mosque and so of all human life. What does the inscription mean and why is it found at this central place?

Those who first wrote this unfinished sentence in their mihrabs must have had clear answers to these questions. Their descendants today do not. They have either lost or forgotten them. What has been forgotten can be recalled, however, as there is no true forgetting, at least in the core of the self or for the real. Forgetting is simply a condition of the self where its indomitable core is obscured by false representations and false knowledge.

1 The full verse runs as follows (*Qur'an*, 3:37): "Her Lord received the child with gracious favour, and by His goodness she grew up comely, Zachariah taking charge of her. Whenever Zachariah went in to her in the *miḥrāb*, he found her provisioned. 'Mary,' he said, 'how comes this to thee?' 'From God', she said. Truly God provisions whomsoever He will without reckoning.' "

 | DOI 10.1163/9789004279407_127

The core is cut off from the periphery, which comprises the body, analytic reason, the passions, and so forth. The periphery then appears to be the entire self, but what is lost can be found, so long as it is true. The truth cannot be lost. Only human beings can be lost. When we find ourselves, we also find the truth hidden from us. The inscription at the heart of the mihrab offers us signifiers with ontological, cosmological, anthropological, and psychological references. To understand them, we must have recourse to the framework of traditional intellectuality and perennial wisdom.

The disclosure of these signifiers is of crucial importance for the process of liberation from forgetting or oblivion. Liberating ourselves, we disclose or discover our hearts as treasuries of immediate knowledge – knowledge which does not depend on anything external, but on which human self-realization itself depends.[2] In this way, we may realize ourselves in line with our authentic nature. Memory or recollection is therefore our highest possibility. In it, we find both our beginning and our end.

Finding our beginning and end entails the discovery of both arcs of our existence – the first marking universal descent from the One, the other ascent to the same One. This descent begins in the Light of the Praised, the universal "seed," the maternal prophecy, and the principle of reception in absolute purity, quietude, and service. The end of ascent is the Praised as the universal "fruit."

2 The heart is one of the key concepts for this discourse. The immediate reference is the physical heart, the central organ of the individual through which the blood, as bearer of life, must pass. In the modern period, this meaning has become practically the only one, while for traditional intellectuality it has always been peripheral. In traditional teachings, the heart is considered the core of the self and the principle of the unity of human existence. As such, it is both source and end. All existence comes from it and returns to it, less in a temporal sequence than in absolute unity. The entire self is a manifestation of the heart. The human self entirely depends on the heart, but the reverse is not true. When a condition of the self is taken as independent of the heart and sufficient in itself, it may present an apparent obstacle to the harmony of the One in the many. In such a case, a departure takes place within the self, as it travels down within itself towards its lower and darker parts. Consciousness and power lack guidance and are applied as violence and ignorance: a boundary develops between the heart and the self in the form of hardening, rusting, and corruption. That the heart is the principle of the self does not mean it gives birth to phenomena or they to it. It is in and with all things and beyond them. The Holy Spirit descends upon and in it, so that it reveals the Living, through all His names scattered across the horizons and focused in the self. The heart is thus flow, the coincidence of coming into being and going out of being, of giving and receiving, waning and waxing, of inhalation and exhalation. It is Intellect as the recipient of knowledge and the maximum of closeness to the One.

1

The mihrab inscription in question is from the Recitation, the Word God sent down through the Holy Spirit to the Praised.[3] That Word captures all of existence in verbal form as it relates to God, the only true Being. In this way, existence and its relationship to God are brought together in human language. The focus of the entire discourse is the name of God. Nothing can contradict or equal it. Human being, however, is duality, male and female, as the obverse of the revelation of Unity. This is why we must look for answers in the Recitation as to why Mary was in the mihrab.

God told Moses that He had shaped him as a work [of art] for Himself.[4] He told him that He would raise up a prophet like him,[5] to whom all the prophets had sworn oaths in pre-existence.[6] That prophet's nature is of an immense magnitude[7] and he is our most beautiful example.[8] This is why the Word was revealed to him as the Book from which the text on the Virgin was copied.

Many and complex forms of relationship between God and humankind are described in the Recitation. God is first cause and source of existence. We reflect and focus existence. God owes nothing to anyone. We owe our existence to God. We are related as creature and Creator.

We are always in some form of relation to God, Who is always absolutely near *and* absolutely far, alike *and* incomparable. He has every claim on us, but indulges us and counters our ability to sink to the lowest depth in this, our existential battlefield, through redemption and return to Him. This relation is both in language and non-linguistic and exists in both directions.

The bond in language descends from above, from God to humanity, as the Revelation. Ascending from below, from humanity to God, it assumes various forms of address – witness, praise, prayer, repentance, sacrifice, etc. The non-linguistic bond from above includes signs on the horizons of the world and in history, that from below involves various forms of human duty, ritual, and art.

God is the Lord to Whom the most beautiful names belong. We are His servants, and, as such, our part is to receive and put on that through which our

3 See *Qur'an*, 16:102.

4 Ibid., 20:41. Martin Lings has translated God's words to Moses into English as follows: "I have fashioned thee as a work of art for Myself." Lings, *Splendours of Qur'an Calligraphy and Illumination*, 17.

5 See *Deuteronomy*, 18:18.

6 See *Qur'an*, 7:157.

7 Ibid., 68:4.

8 Ibid., 33:21.

Lord reveals Himself. To be worthy to serve our Lord, we must display absolute humility, quietude, loyalty, and openness to receive and bear what He gives us. In this way, we stand between the annihilation of mere appearance and rising up in the reality received from our Lord as His revelation. Where we stand is determined by our willing agreement to relate to God through confidence and trust. Without this faith in God, our action becomes violent and ignorant, out of arrogance, rebellion, resistance, and closure.

God offers His perfect or rebellious servants two options. Either He is infinitely good and merciful, clement and kind, loving and forgiving of the servant bound to Him in a bond of peace, or wrathful, severe, jealous and chastizing, but always absolutely just. These two possibilities take the forms of being-at-peace, faith, and beauty, or rebellion, concealment, and idolatrous association.

2

Although in constant discovery, our self as a whole remains concealed. Revelation and concealment gather and are reflected in the face. What is revealed speaks of what lies hid, as its higher reality. From moment to moment, we turn our faces to the world and to other people, searching for this higher reality, but they find rest nowhere. We find no quiet repose in which to stand in absolute peace before the Face. No matter where we turn our face or what we encounter in the world, we cannot abide there forever. We are searching for more than is in all the world. It is only through the eternal higher world that our path towards our goal makes any sense at all.

So, we change from moment to moment, as the self alters with each new moment. Our face also changes, as in each new moment it engages with some aspect of the Divine Face Which is both revealed to and hidden from us. And so we may well ask: where does it lead, this change in our face?

The answer remains hidden, so long as we look for it in terms of being-within-change. No final answer is ever possible, though it become the focus of our life, will, knowledge, power, hearing and sight. None of the potential answers can transcend the difference to which our inability to turn our faces to and abide in Peace testifies.

This invincible difference appears in the form of a relationship between seeker and Sought, face and Face. There are always two, but we yearn for One revealed in and affirmed by the pair. We are always in duality, constantly reminded of our higher, more beautiful faculties. However high we rise, this higher, more beautiful state remains out of reach, but we want union with it, nonetheless.

This aspirational wish takes on the form of desire. We want the Face of our Lord, in Which we will find everything our original and final potential promises us. Our life and our death, ritual and sacrifice are the way of virtue on which we are guided by our desire for His face.[9] Our quest becomes witness: "All that dwells upon the earth is perishing, yet still abides the Face of thy Lord, majestic, splendid."[10]

3

As individuals, we experience the duality that runs throughout existence primarily in terms of the opposition between self and world. We are turned towards this world with all our being. This turn would seem to be focused in our face. It is through our face that we address the world, but the world is a mirror of our face, just as our face is of the world.

Everything we learn in our relationship with the world comes about or quickens within us. Our face expresses this interior, as well as the exterior with which it is constantly relating. We and the world are then two aspects of one face, as every pair affirms and reveals one.

The world and the self are differentiated into an infinity of signs in continuous flux. Each sign has two sides and a contrary, as everything in existence is part of a pair.[11] Neither world nor self contains anything that is not part of a pair. The members of a pair can never be reduced to each other nor their differences obliterated. Only absolute unity encompasses them and their differences. It is the same with the face. What it brings together and reflects takes on a different aspect with each new moment, irreducibly different from what is just past or coming. Whatever its condition, the self always partakes of the pair of the face and the Face.

Having turned our faces towards the horizons to gaze at the heavenly expanse, we then retire to the self tired and confused. In the majesty and beauty we have seen, we do not find the Face clearly turned towards us, the Face Which unites everything that spurs us on to ceaseless searching and turning, the Face in Which all duality is resolved. But we desire that turn. Wherever we look, we are looking for ourselves. Returning from the wide horizons, we

---

9 See *Qur'an*, 2:272–73. The prophet David said: "When thou saidst, seek ye my face; my heart said unto thee, Thy face, Lord, will I seek. Hide not thy face far from me; put not thy servant away in anger." (Psalm 27:8–9)

10 *Qur'an*, 55:26–27.

11 See *Qur'an*, 43:12.

are recalled to the inner self as the likely abode of the Face we seek. In this act of recollection, the horizons and the signs they contain cease to be sources of knowledge and become reminders of what is always already within.

4

The beauty revealed to us on the horizons and in others' faces does not last. It calls to us continuously, only to fade. It appears briefly, but the memory of it stimulates us all the more to search for it. Our experience of beauty in the horizons of the world recalls us to the self as beauty's real abode. Nowhere in the world can it take root and become permanently available. It resides in us: we belong to beauty and bear witness of it. But the signs in the world also recall it and the veil of forgetting over it.

What we see as beautiful is in fact how we would like to see ourselves refracted through the vision of the Beautiful. This desire pervades our entire being, inside and out, beginning and end. We are always somewhere between inside and outside, beginning and end. These are pairs in the fullest sense, which is to say they reveal the Unity towards which we aspire.

We and the world form a pair. Nothing in the self or world is so stable or all-embracing as to satisfy our quest: there is no level we can reach that is not a depth in comparison to the One and the Most-High. Our face turns continuously to look for the Face Which will unite and bring fulfilment to all and before Whom we will be alone before the Alone, standing before the Upright, sufficient before the All-sufficient, and praised before the All-praised.

So, we search continuously for our own face, to find and realize all that our highest moment entails and take on the aspect of the Face in undifferentiated fullness, in union with what we know as beauty. This endeavour steers us towards the horizons, which nonetheless remind us of the core or heart of the self. There is nothing in the external world which is not related in some way to our core, as the point of confluence where all distinctions disappear and differences appear as Unity. This possibility is above and beyond all finitude. Only Unity is independent of everything but itself, while what is outside Unity depends on It. To return and ascend to the self means to find one's all in Unity.

5

Experienced by the self as good news welling up from its core, majesty and beauty deserve praise. Whenever we find full confirmation in world or self of identity that transcends duality, we recognise in it that self for which we are looking. When we find it, it appears as a flash of the absolute. As soon as we see it, it disappears. We bear witness, however, as we recall that it came from our own centre. In the indestructible core of our being, we know that what has been shown us in the world and in our own self is the one truth. This is why our consciousness is always discovering and recovering the crucial confession that there is no self but the Self, no face but the Face.

Revealing and remembering beauty speak of the human heart as comprehending beyond time and space, as comprehending all time and all space. Drawing our attention to this possibility, to our return to it, God spoke to us through the Praised, commanding him: "Say: 'Believe in it, or believe not; those who were given the knowledge before it when it is recited to them, fall down upon their faces prostrating,' and say, 'Glory be to our Lord! Our Lord's promise is performed.' And they fall down upon their faces weeping; and it increases them in humility."[12]

We all have knowledge of this, thanks to the act of our creation. We all have one and the same original nature, pure and endowed with everything we need to return to God, as He told us: "So set thy face to the debt of the pure – God's original upon which He originated mankind."[13]

Whenever that which we already know within ourselves is revealed to us in the course of our quest for the self, it becomes all our desire to abnegate this pair, to realize ourselves in Unity as the source and end of all things manifest, and to abnegate our own face before the Face, which is our greatest promise in eternity and infinity. Thus, we bear witness that there is no face but the Face and that we can realize our selves only in the Face.

6

The world reveals us to ourselves. The horizons are in our image writ large, while we are the image of those same horizons writ little. Whatever we comprehend in the external world is comprehended in our heart. The visible world is our face. In this way, we and the world are a pair, each reflecting the other.

We are in the world and whatever confirms our expectations is worthy of praise. But we also bring together within our own selves all that is worthy of praise in ourselves and the world. We bring it together, firstly as recipients

12 *Qur'an*, 17:107–109.

13 Ibid., 30:30.

of the praise by which God self-reveals as the All-praised and then as givers of what we have received through Praise of the Giver.

No matter how high we climb on the heavenly heights or how low descend within ourselves, we remain within limits, which we can never abolish. This is why existence seems, in world and self, dual – as one world accessible to perception and another beyond its reach. We cannot overcome this duality, as it is through duality that Unity is revealed as universal source and end.

While the first world seems closer, it is not. The principle of the second is higher in value: everything visible derives from the invisible. The invisible and the inaudible are the principles of the visible and the audible. We are always hanging between two possibilities: falling into the material depth or rising to the height of the Spirit. Every level we reach displays a visible sign of its essence, a sign whose purpose is to remind us of our essence. The Praised said:

> This house (*Kaʿba*) is one of fifteen, seven in the heavens up to the throne and seven up to the limits of the lowest earth. The highest situated one, which is near the throne, is the "visited house." Every one of these houses has a sacred territory, like that of the Kaʿba. If any one of them fell down, the rest would fall down, one upon the other, to the limits of the lowest earth. And every house has its heavenly or earthly worshippers, like the Kaʿba.[14]

Knowledge relates knower to known. Unity, even if known, is unlimited by anything. No knowledge determines our approach to Unity. No point on the path of approach is final. So long as we are in duality, the upward path to Unity remains open. Our ascent depends on the heart, which contains all the points or degrees, from the lowest to the highest. Once the heart falls, the entire revelation of the One has fallen.

7

We want to be what we know, to know what we are. This is desire for union. As a knowing subject, we need what we know. Nothing can remove this need. This is because the Known is always beyond our knowledge, irresistible, unfailingly attractive. We call this inextinguishable desire of the self love. Unity constantly attracts whatever serves to reveal It in the world of duality. It attracts because

14 Wüstenfeld, *Die Chroniken der Stadt Mekka*, 1:6, 10; cited in: Wensinck, "The Ideas of the Western Semites Concerning the Navel of the Earth," 51–52.

there is nothing real in existence that does not come from and belong to It. In this process, pairs want to appear to and return to the One. Our love for what we know is manifest in confession of no self but the Self.

Through the continuous discovery of beauty and majesty the self that seeks the Self shows its inexhaustible nature, its concealment and its disclosure. The Self cannot be reduced to any appearance, any more than any appearance has reality without It. Every manifestation of the One includes two. The terms of the pair are irreducible to each other, an impossibility that takes on the form of witness of the One in their irresistible attraction for the One. In any such act of witness, both turn to Peace as the Goal in Which all differences will be resolved. Each thing is thus recipient and revelation of Peace, just as being-at-peace is our way of relating to beginning and end.

The Face we seek, in and through Which we want to see ourselves, is irresistibly attractive. We love this perfect Face, but It remains out of our grasp. It reveals and conceals itself before us. To attain It, to be completely at peace before It is not enough, we must set out on the upright road, the road of the blessed, with the Praised as our example and guide. He reveals duality as the in-differentiation of perfect masculinity and perfect femininity in one self.

8

Dis-unity confirms Unity as the ineffable principle of all things. Duality and limitless multiplicity confirm Unity. As multiplicity announces Unity, it also announces the most beautiful name of the One. The most beautiful names are scattered throughout the cosmos, but brought together in us. To accomplish this gathering of the names, their uncreated principle, the Breath of the Creator was inspired into us, that we might gather them and return them to Unity and so to dis-Unity.

We transcend boundaries through thought and it is this which enables us to seek the Named among the names and return to or discover Him in His own Breath at our core. The earth and the heavens extend before us, far exceeding us in magnitude, but we have our place within them and another beyond them, in consciousness and thought, which contain nothing real but the Real. Consciousness of this is our most profound content, as is clear from the words God spoke through the Praised: "My earth and My heaven embrace Me not, but the heart of My believing servant does embrace me."[15] The heart of the faithful

15 Ghazālī, *Iḥyāʾ ʿulūm al-dīn*, 3:12. This sacred tradition is generally accepted among Sufis, but is not to be found in the exoteric collections of the prophet's sayings. See: Hakīm, *al-Muʿjam al-ṣūfī*, 1265–66.

servant mentioned in this holy tradition is that essential place in which all contradictions are reconciled.

Faith is our relationship, as beings of faith, with God the Faithful. This relationship takes place on the basis of what can only be a little knowledge, regardless how great it may appear. Even such knowledge, however, is sufficient for us to recognise the Face which irresistibly attracts our own faces. This force of attraction is love. In faith, knowledge and love are one.

In this mutual attraction of the face and the Face, our external horizons and the self and the world of scattered signs are oriented along an axis that passes through all the worlds towards the throne of the One. Through the Praised, God said of this: "We have seen thee turning thy face about in the heaven; now We will surely turn thee to a direction that shall satisfy thee. Turn thy face towards the Inviolable Mosque; and wherever you are, turn your faces towards it."[16]

9

We are male and female. Our form of being is manifest in or through this division into two that together reveal the One. The full discovery of humanity requires that we transcend this division. To transcend division is to be on the path of return to the One. The full manifestation of the One is the fullness of humanity. For we are fullness; not male or female, but at once male and female. This means that the full human being is the union of all divisions. This is shown at the level of signs in the praise of the One as All-praised.[17] When individual things, their contraries and existence as a whole praise their reason and end, they return the praise with which the One as All-praised revealed Himself. The All-praised is beyond difference, even though He reveals Himself through differences.

When an individual reaches perfection and recognises in him or herself the vicegerent, which is to say a follower of the complete human being, it is in and through the perfect balance of male and female aspects. God is All-praised.

16 *Qur'an*, 2:144.

17 The most important semantic field in the discourse given in this text is formed around the divine name of the All-praised (Ar. *al-Ḥamīd*). This field also contains the human name of the Praised (Ar. *al-Muḥammad*) as the first revelation of God's being praised. The relationship between the All-praised and his revelation through the Praised is the act of praise (Ar. *al-ḥamd*). These forms correspond to the verb "to praise" (Ar. *ḥamida*). In this relationship, God is Creator, human beings created. This relationship does not change. This is why every semantic field in any discourse on this relationship is subordinate and dependent on the field centred around the name of God. See Izutsu, *God and Man in the Koran*, 75–77.

His Self-revelation is like an emanation of His praise. This emanation is creation as the reception of praise and being from the All-praised. Everything through which God reveals Himself as All-praised receives His praise. As this revelation contains nothing that has not been received from the All-praised, praise is the mode of existence for all things. The most sublime sign of this praise is the Praised as maternal prophet who corresponds to the maternal Book, as at once first and last in creation.

God's first manifestation is Praise and the Praised in witness that none are praised but the All-praised. All we find on the lower levels of existence is a series of images of the Praised revealing the All-praised. They are bound by the relation of praise. When praise is focused and flowers in the self, human being is perfected and reaches its fullness. The Praised is thus the perfect example to all others in all their circumstances and conditions.[18] Through him, Light is sent down from on high to the lowest level of existence,[19] a shining lamp to every self on every level of existence.[20] The path back to the All-praised lies through him.

10

The All-praised spoke plainly in the Recitation of this revelation through the Praised of the complete individual and first recipient of praise and fairest example, as well as of the sending down of praise into all the worlds and of how they gather in our essence:

> To God belongs all that is in the heavens and in the earth. We have charged those who were given the Book before you, and you, to remain conscious of God. Conceal not, for, to God belongs all that is in the heavens and in the earth; God is All-sufficient, All-praised.[21]
>
> And it is He who sends down the rain after they have despaired, and He unfolds His mercy.[22]
>
> All that is in the heavens and the earth magnifies God. His is the Kingdom, and His is the praise, and He is powerful over everything.[23]

---

18 See *Qur'an*, 33:21.

19 Ibid., 7:157.

20 Ibid., 33:46

21 *Qur'an*, 4:131.

22 Ibid., 42:28.

23 Ibid., 64:1.

And He is God; there is no god but He. His is the praise in the former as in the latter; His too is the Judgment, and unto Him you shall be returned.[24]

Proclaim thy Lord's praise, and be of those who prostrate themselves, and serve thy Lord, until the Certain comes to thee![25]

Surely thou art before Our eyes. And proclaim the praise of thy Lord when thou arisest, and proclaim the praise of thy Lord in the night, and at the declining of the stars.[26]

But those who believe and do righteous deeds and believe in what is sent down to the Praised – and it is the truth from their Lord – He will acquit them of their evil deeds, and dispose their minds aright.[27]

The Praised is not the father of any one of your men, but the apostle of God, and the seal of the prophets; God has knowledge of everything.[28]

11

When a woman addresses the sought-after Face as perfection of the self, she perceives it as the Praised in male form. When a man is the appellant, he addresses it as the Praised in female form. As the Face brings together and meets all expectations, It is beyond distinction. It is neither the female nor the male Praised, but both. His face resolves all differences: "And call not upon another god with God; there is no god but He. All things perish, except His face."[29] This is the Face Which is before and beyond everything in existence. In and through It we accomplish our ascent and return to our highest moment.

This return includes realization of witness that there is no face but the Face. Conscious of this and mindful of the Unity Which encompasses all things in Its revelation, we abnegate ourselves before the Face that we might be made in Its fullness. God said in the Recitation: "Hast thou not seen how to God prostrate all who are in the heavens and all who are in the earth, the sun and the moon, the stars and the mountains, the trees and the beasts, and many of mankind?"[30]

24 Ibid., 28:70.
25 Ibid., 15:98–99.
26 Ibid., 52:48–49.
27 Ibid., 47:2.
28 Ibid., 33:40.
29 Ibid., 28:88.
30 Ibid., 22:18.

This abnegation is the rejection of mere appearance for the sake of the Real, the annihilation of the face to reveal the Face. In this way the self shows its dissatisfaction with all its conditions except that of being a face before the Face, of looking upon the Beloved and being looked upon by His eyes alone.

In this process of discovery, the world appears as glory thanks to the praise of the Lord. This discovery is expressed perfectly by the ascent through the night to the Light, through the flesh to the Spirit. The path is trod from the lowest depth to the highest height. One who has experience of standing before the Upright and being praised before the All-praised can fall to the lowest depth again and from it call the self to embark upon the upright path towards the realization of our authentic potential.

The One confirms this essential state of affairs, while duality affirms Him, as One. As the first revelation of the Lord as All-praised and as universal humanity, the Praised must be fully dual, for nothing can affirm the One that is not duality. Such a duality is made up of the perfect or first reception and the perfect or first giving, perfect femininity and perfect masculinity. The One sends down and publishes His Word through the Praised. This Word is the Book. Having received it, the Praised is a maternal prophet. The Book he has received is maternal. It contains everything that reveals the One.

This same One sent down and revealed His Word through the Virgin. This perfect Word was the Anointed. It contained nothing not received: like the Praised, the Anointed said nothing on his own account.[31] The nature of the Praised and that of the Virgin are determined by the Book and the Anointed, respectively. The only woman mentioned by name in the Book sent down to the Praised is Mary. She is a sign of the perfect duality that reveals the One. The Praised and the Virgin are one revelation of the One at the beginning of the arc of descent and at the end of the arc of ascent.

12

To glorify and praise the Lord means standing before the Face and the Praised and willing exit from duality: to become That Which one stands in front of and watches and nothing more. This desire is affirmed symbolically by falling in prostration, denying any form of self but the Self, and sacrificing all mortal things for the Living.

---

31 See *John*, 7:18, 14:10 and *Qur'an*, 26:192–95, 16:102.

The world is continuously revealed within us in ever-changing ways, as it itself changes from moment to moment. Duality cannot be mastered, but we do not accept this. For us, the world becomes a battlefield on which to master duality and realize ourselves in the One and the Beautiful. Attaining the goal of our endeavour can seem impossible. But that is precisely what we desire, to launch a war against the impossible, for no incomplete apprehension of existence can satisfy any self open to the Self. In this way, we are always striving against what appears before us, as we crave the Real Which nothing can mimic or transform into seeming.

All our powers are trained on that goal. They are our enemies who obstruct this endeavour. Our greatest enemies are those conditions of the self which imprison us in our sensual nature, the passions which take the form of enjoyment in the beauties of the world, stripped from their authentic Owner, for the sake of Whom they are present and towards Whom they lead.

The battlefield (*miḥrāb*) is therefore a key symbol of our effort to overcome the internal split and to see in the Beloved such a one as the Beloved sees in us as His lover. The attractiveness of the Beloved, whether experienced as male or female, is movement towards Peace and being-at-peace. The further from the apparent and the closer to Him Who is manifest in it, the closer we are to Peace and so to union as our goal. Union means sacrificing duality for realization in the One.

One should stress that the mihrab, in some of its forms in different types of mosque, is also a place of sacrifice. This is because every ritual is at heart a sacrifice. The self is split between two extremes – death and immortality. Presence in the world of disorder and suffering is an aspect of the mortal self. Transcending this via immortality means leaving the world of death and suffering for the triumph of eternity over all forms of appearance. This means suffering the blows and shocks due to the self's attachment to sensation and the things of the world, unmindful of the Beauty they reveal.

What the self of the lower levels experiences as suffering and pain is the passage from closure to individuation and realization in the Self, the move from the signs to the Signified. Bearing witness of no self but the Self and dying in our mortal self, we are born to uprightness in the Self. The battlefield within both self and world involves sacrificing the mortal to attain the Eternal. The Praised, as goal and model, becomes an example of dying for life, giving to receive, leaving to return.

In the mihrab, we are alone. It is a place for the individual to withdraw from his or her own diversity, from being in duality, so as to return to Unity as the Real. We ascend to the mihrab for the sake of the Beloved, to be with Him alone and that He might be with us alone, rapt in mutual regard.

13

That the world glorifies its Lord through praise means it reveals what it has received. The act of praise thus relates the All-praised with the world as praised. God is the Possessor and Giver of praise, while the world is its recipient and promulgator. God alone possess and gives, so that what He is not is nothing, save it be His face. Both the world and man are essentially or ontically poor in comparison to the All-sufficient. The truth of this cannot be altered. It cannot wane, but it may be that forgetting covers it with a veil of ignorance.

There is nothing in the self that has not been received from God. We are fully in debt, and God is our Creditor. We are bound by debt. In this way, God's absolute claim on us is established, so that we have a duty towards God, which means towards all of existence with all its contents. But, we did not arrive in existence of our own will. That was just the will of the Creator.

His will is to lead us to our goal. Everything comes from God and it all returns to Him as the Gatherer-in and the Goal of the journey being taken by all of existence and each thing within it. This all, each and every particle, is under a debt to what is other, in the fullest meaning of that term. There is no atom or butterfly, no animal or constellation, no angel or spirit that does not participate in this com-union whereby everything is at once alone and with all the rest.

Our will is also involved in how we relate to God. We have countless duties towards Him, but also have one claim on Him. This claim is our right to return and self-realization and is both absolute and perfect. Each and every self was made for it in accordance with our original nature. God has opened to us the path to Himself: to see Unity in duality as Its perfect revelation, in that duality that appears as the union of male and female in pure and full self-realization through return to Unity.

We recognise what we have received in the world only by rejecting any illusion of possessing it other than through the Giver. When this relationship to the totality of existence as recipient of praise from God, its Giver, finds expression in us, as existence's focus, then we can speak of human being as praised and praiser of the All-praised. For God and human beings relate through the act of praise.

The perfect reception of praise from God and the restoration of life, will, power, knowledge, speech, hearing, and sight to the Giver is our highest faculty. It affirms the Praised as source and refuge of all existence. All prophecy is discourse on this faculty of humanity. Through such discourse we receive news and are reminded of that part of the self in which God resides. In our constant quest for the One we turn towards the horizons, the ends of the earth, and the heavenly height, but none of this satisfies us. We are just reminded of our highest and most sublime faculty, so that we ask: Where is God? The Praised answers this question: "In the hearts of his faithful servants."[32] He also says: "The hearts of all of Adam's children are as one heart held between the fingers of the All-merciful. He turns it where He will."[33]

14

The Praised is the most beautiful example, a mercy to the worlds, our highest moment. As the most sublime and mightiest pattern, he is important for each of us as we realize our selves after him. To do this we must follow the Praised on the path from periphery to core of our humanity, where all differentiation fades. This is the confession of Unity and return.

Nothing satisfies us but this sublime moment. It may appear to lie outside the self, somewhere in space and time, in culture and history, but if it does, it is only as a sign for the self that it cannot attain realization anywhere but in the self. Realization is only through, above, and beyond sensible things. We are fitted by our authentic nature, the principle given to us at creation, to find and realize ourselves. Each of us is aware of this possibility of self-realization in our original nature as equivalent to the oath sworn to God in pre-existence to bear witness to what we know, our highest faculty, the Praised as the mighty pattern and light sent down.

Prophets are those who swear to God to bear witness amongst their fellows of that which they know in their hearts as God's news. They accept God's choice to remind others of their primordial oath and help free them from oblivion. Through this act of liberation, they are reveal as fully their own, with nothing in their hearts but that fullness for which and with which we are made to travel through the worlds. They are witnesses of the Praised as a mercy to the worlds, the apostle who is always and everywhere the best example borne in the self.

While there have been one hundred and twenty four thousand prophets, none of them is before or after the Praised. He is their seal in pre-existence, when we were all just intentions of the Creator. The Praised remains the seal of the prophets, even now that they have all entered existence and borne witness to what they swore an oath to in pre-existence.

---

32 This tradition may be found in: Ghazālī, *Iḥyā' 'ulūm al-dīn*, 3:1238.

33 Muslim, 4:1397.

15

The Praised is that individual and prophet who testifies from the fullness of human nature that one can pass from the battlefield in this world of duality to the fullness of Peace. And so, he is the champion of the people of peace. This does not mean his condition can be distinguished from his desire, as peaceful and a person of peace, to connect with Peace through being-at-peace.

The Praised is in the world of duality, but as perfect reception of God and the restitution of what has been received in accordance with His will. Receiving, he reveals the Giver; giving, he reveals the God to Whom all returns. Standing in the mihrab, he gazes upon the Virgin Mary as chosen above all women in all the worlds. In her, he regards himself, and through her he sees himself as she sees him out of that perfect duality which is the revelation of the One. The Word was sent down into the world – once as the Anointed, again as the Recitation.

The Word was sent down into the world through Mary and the Praised so that whoever received it might arise through its agency to his or her authentic nature in which everything has been received in all fullness. The Praised and Mary regard each other without cease, as in the eyes of the other they see their own self-realization in Peace and the resolution of duality. In this perfect example, our division into male and female is unriddled as duality that reveals the One. Mary looking at the Praised and he looking back, they share the form of perfect human recollection of God.

The faces of Mary and the Praised, turned to each other, reveal the perfection of the One and the unity of the Perfect. These two know each other by means of their original perfection and the Unity their faces reveal, through the same single heart held in the fingers of the All-merciful. Neither Mary nor the Praised seek in the byways of the world the Face of Him they praise, to Whom they return what they have received. They are before the Face, looking at It and through It alone, bearing witness of It in all they do. God said of this: "To God belong the East and the West; whithersoever you turn, there is the Face of God; God is All-embracing, All-knowing."[34]

As the perfect example of being in the mihrab, the Praised is both alone and together with all of existence. The Holy Spirit came down to him there, on account of his perfect receptivity, which is marked by the face of Mary, just as It did to her, bearing the word of God. Through this Word that descended, the Praised rose up to Peace. For those who desire that path of ascent, God told his apostle: "Say: 'I turn in Peace my face to God, and whosoever follows

34 *Qur'an*, 2:115.

me.' "[35] Turning his face to God, the Praised sees Mary. And Mary, turning her face to God, sees the Praised. This is how the One is revealed in perfect duality through the confession that there is no face but the Face.

God enlightens the face of the Praised with the Light of heaven and earth. This same Light bathes Mary's face. Those who seek the Face yearn for this Light revealed through the face of the Praised, who said of such seekers: "The people most loved by me from my community would be those who would come after me but everyone amongst them would have the keenest desire to catch a glimpse of me even at the cost of his family and wealth."[36]

16

The Praised and Mary, as a pair, are the perfect revelation of the One. The reference to the prophet Zachariah in the inscription in the mihrab relates to the word of God: "So remember Me, and I will remember you."[37] Whenever we are such that we remember God, then God remembers us. When we remember God, we are following the most beautiful example of the Praised as the perfect apostle and the incarnation of the fullness of humanity. This remembrance and this following are our path to self-awareness and flourishing in knowledge.

The Praised is the perfect example for those who have hope in God and the Last Day and who remember. It was to them that God said: "I am with My servant whenever he remembers Me and his lips move."[38] To remember God is to discover the beauty at the core of the self. This discovery draws us irresistibly to union with the beautiful as our means of ascent out of duality. The Praised is perfect in remembrance and so in his love of God. The Virgin Mary is also perfect in remembrance and so in her love of God. Facing each other, the Praised and Mary reveal the Face in contrast to Which everything in existence fades and with Which the many are revealed as union.

God promised us that we will find Him, on condition that we seek Him with all our heart and self.[39] When we attain that level of full seeking, then we are

35 Ibid., 3:20.

36 Muslim, 4:1478.

37 *Qur'an*, 2:152.

38 The sources for these traditions are given in Graham, *Divine Word and Prophetic Word in Early Islam*, 130.

39 See *Deuteronomy*, 11:13. Referring to this command, Mary's son said: "Thou shalt love the Lord thy God with all thy heart, with all thy soul, and with all thy mind, and with all thy strength." (*Mark*, 12:30) The addition "with all thy mind and with all thy strength" reflects

turned towards the Face, enlightened by It, and through It we see ourselves. Then, the Face is all there is for us. This is why the Praised sees himself through Mary's face. He is in the world, but always turned towards God. In this way, he is the example of perfect seeking and of being on the path back to God. Only love, the yearning of the separated to be united, can guarantee that the traveller will find what he or she seeks.[40]

17

God is All-merciful, Ever-merciful. His mercy encompasses all. The Praised, as his first revelation, is the most beautiful example to us all, a mercy to the worlds. This mercy takes the form of the receiving and passing on of Peace. God speaks of this in the Recitation:

> We have not sent thee, save as a mercy unto all Worlds. Say: "It is revealed unto me only that your God is One God; are you then people of Peace?"[41]
>
> Say: "My prayer, my ritual sacrifice, my living, my dying – all belongs to God, the Lord of all Worlds. No associate has He. Even so I have been commanded, and I am the first of those that are in Peace."[42]

---

the condition of humanity in the end times of this period. See Lings, *A Return to the Spirit*, 29–43 and especially the associated footnote on 79.

40 In *Deuteronomy* (6:5): "And thou shalt love the Lord thy God with all thine heart, and with all thy soul, and with all thy might." This sequence of "with all thine heart," "all thy soul," and "all thy might" represents the condition of humanity after the Fall. In the condition of original purity, the heart, as the centre of being, represented the perfect balance of everything peripheral. In similar fashion, Intellect, as the unification of everything in existence, is the link of everything revealed with the Revealer. Once the limits of the world in which we had been placed had been insulted, the periphery, and so the self and power, came to appear separate and independent of the heart, and so there was a process of falling or "development." The heart remains the unquailing core of the self, that lies in a twilight of forgetting and somnolence. For the self to be turned towards the heart as its core, there must come some stimulus from the self, from the will, and from the power still at our disposal. This possibility is from time to time reinforced by the direct sending down of additional aids in this endeavour: through the prophecies by which we are reminded of all the heart comprehends. See Lings, *A Return to the Spirit*, 29–43.

41 *Qur'an*, 21:107–108.

42 Ibid., 6:162–63.

Peace is our highest possibility. God is Peace and Peace comes from Him.[43] All of His creation and everything in it reveal Peace. They are at-peace and relate to God through being-at-peace.[44] This is also the case for us, in our authentic and original condition, and so also as we finally resolve our involvement in their world of duality. In realizing or discovering our original nature-in-peace, we discover the Praised as our highest moment, the moment of the self for which we should be willing to give everything – our family and all our wealth.

Any turn towards God on the upright path leads us to bear witness to the Praised as our champion and our highest possibility. The Praised, as servant to his Lord, says "I." His "I" is dual, as it was created to reveal the uncreated "I" of the One. The dual "I" of the Praised bears within itself the Virgin as perfect and so the feminine aspect of perfect masculinity. This pair is made one in the mighty nature of full humanity.

Being a person-of-peace is a reflection of our will. While always such in our original nature, which is realized through return to God, it is within the bounds of our will to deny this aspect of our being. Once we have brought our will into line with our nature and assumed the mantle of a person of peace, our little knowledge never ceases to grow with regard to the All-knowing, Who encompasses everything with His knowledge. This orientation reflects faith as the mode whereby the faithful relate to the Faithful.

In our little knowledge, we bear witness of the One, turning towards Him. Only in union with Him are we satisfied. This is why we are always striving to be beautiful, in order that the Beloved will look upon us and see that we are so. We are always looking at ourselves through the eyes of the Beloved. We look and we hear. In equating ourselves thus, we do nothing that God does not do.

18

That the Praised was sent as a mercy to the worlds and a witness to the unity of God was revealed through him, as God's servant. It is as such that he is revealed in full perfection through his other aspect, through the perfect pair and the full witness of Peace. Each self is constantly turning. This means that the face is in constant quest for peace or for the condition in which there will be no further turning, nor any face but the Face of the One.

When the face and the Face are related in this way, it is the most beautiful state achievable, the mighty nature of the Praised. God, the angels, and all His

---

43 See *Qur'an*, 59:23. The Praised said: "O God, Thou art Peace, and Peace comes from Thee; Blessed are Thou, O Possessor of Glory and Honour!" (Muslim, 1:292)

44 See *Qur'an*, 3:83.

friends testify to this. Acceding to this witness is the only proof for his followers. When the Praised, as the maternal prophet, is denied and insulted, he cannot be hurt by it. Denial and insult only harm the deniers and insulters, as by it they remove themselves even further from their higher aspects.

No condition of the human self on the path of ascent and return can supplement the model of most beautifully standing before God. This is why the Praised is the seal of the prophets. He is the true self of the faithful which is satisfied only by identification with the Praised, the servant and the apostle of God. The faithful recognise the condition of their selves as insufficient for what is needed to follow the Praised as the closest and dearest of humankind.[45]

Our knowledge is constantly growing. Whatever it may be, it is always enough to point us towards God and the Praised. Ignorance is never an excuse for denying and insulting our higher possibilities. It cannot be, because, independently of everything outside, we bear within ourselves knowledge of our Lord and redeemer. Given that we recognise our higher possibilities in the Praised, our love for him transcends all others.

This is a conscious choice which transforms the meanings of everything within the horizons or in the self. "None of you are faithful," said the Praised, "unless I am dearer to him than his child, his father, and all others."[46] Following the Praised is inseparable from the faithful servant's love for the Faithful Lord. Only in such love and discipleship does the Faithful Lord love His faithful servant.[47]

Zachariah was a man remembered by God and mindful of God. He saw human perfection in the Virgin Mary. What he saw in her was just the image of the Praised as the sublime potential in each of us. Her reception of perfection was revealed in the Recitation: "And when the angels said, 'Mary, God has chosen thee, and purified thee; He has chosen thee above all women. Mary, be obedient to thy Lord, prostrating and bowing before Him.' "[48]

19

The war in the world of the manifold can never be brought to a close on the basis of confidence in our own powers. We realize ourselves in and through Beauty, against Which we cannot war. We can love It, because Beauty attracts

45 Ibid., 33:6.

46 Muslim, 1:31.

47 See *Qur'an*, 3:31.

48 *Qur'an*, 3:42–43.

us irresistibly and increases us in knowledge thereby. The closer we are to It, the better we know It, and the better we know It, the more we love It. This is why the Praised, who wants to see us attain perfection, says it is not war, but beauty. It is in relation to God as Beautiful that we discover the beauty in our own selves and act in all we do out of our connection to Beauty as Owner of all beauty.[49]

However close we come to the boundaries of the world, piercing ever higher, they remain, so that in our feeling of weakness new veils fall upon our face. Unwilling to remove these veils or confess our love has ensured that we can only know a little of the everything that is in us without division and so we become opponents of the Praised and so turn against ourselves. The more resolutely we oppose the Praised, God's servant and apostle, the higher the dark tide rises within the self, urging us on to evil. The Praised, the mercy sent to the worlds, never abandons us, remaining as witness to our discipleship *and* our apostasy.

God has not left any one of us without the possibility of meeting our purpose. His mercy exceeds His wrath.[50] This mercy comprehends everything that is and all things end in it, but with the just distinction of the righteous and the guilty, with just wages for good and evil. As the mercy to the worlds, the Praised will be our advocate, as he himself told us, on that day of resurrection when we shall all be in fear:

> I shall start off and come below the Throne and prostrate myself before my Lord; then God will reveal to me and inspire me with some of His Praises and Glorifications which He will not have revealed to anyone before me. Then it will be said: "O, Praised! Raise your head; ask and it will be granted; intercede and the intercession will be accepted." I will then raise my head and say: "O my Lord, my community, my community." It will be said: "O, Praised! Bring in by the right gate of Paradise those of your community who have no account to render." They will share with the people some other door besides this door.[51]

---

49 Imam ʿAli ibn Abī Ṭālib, said: "When the Beautiful One (*Ḥasan*) was born, I gave him the name of War (*Ḥarb*). God's apostle came – may he always be with the Peace of God! – and said: 'Show me my son! What name have you given him?' I said: 'War.' He said: 'No, for he is the Beautiful One.' " (Ibn Ḥanbal, 2:164, tradition 730)

50 God says: "My mercy exceeds My wrath." (Bukhārī, 9:483)

51 Muslim 1:131–32.

Bibliography

Acta Bosnae: Potissimum Ecclesiastica cum insertis editorum documentorum Regestis ab anno 925. usque ad annum 1752., Zagrabiae: Academia scientiarum et artium Slavorum meridionalium, 1892.

Adorno, Theodor W., "On Tradition", *Telos* 94 (1992–1993): 75–82.

———, *Negative Dialectics*, 1–3, New York: Seabury, 1973.

Afifi, Abul Ela, *The Mystical Philosophy of Muḥyid Din Ibnul 'Arabī*, Cambridge: Cambridge University Press, 1939.

Agović, Bajro, *Džamije u Crnoj Gori*, Podgorica: Almanah, 2001.

'Ajlūnī, Muḥammad b. Ismā'īl, al-, *Kashf al-khafā wa muzīl al-ilbās 'ammā ishtahara min al-aḥādīth 'alā alsīnat al-nās*, Beirut: Mu'assasa al-Risāla, s.a.

Akalın, Şükrü Halûk et al., *Türkçe sözlük*, Ankara: Türk Dil Kurumu, 2005.

Aljović, Vejsil, "Odrazi odanosti islamu vjernika u Umoljanima", *Glasnik Vrhovnog islamskog starješinstva u SFRJ*, 11/12 (1966): 585–586.

Anđelić, Pavao, *Historijski spomenici Konjica i okoline*, Konjic: Skupština opštine Konjic, 1975.

Anon., "Gospina svetišta u našoj domovini", *Dobri pastir*, 1–2 (1951): 49–56.

Arberry, Arthur J., *Discourses of Rūmī*, Richmond: Curzon Press, 1993.

———, *The Koran Interpreted*, London: George Allen & Unwin, 1980.

Arendt, Hannah, "Thinking and Moral Consideration", *Social Research*, 38 (1971): 417–446.

———, *Eichmann in Jerusalem: A report on the Banality of Evil*, New York: Viking, 1963.

Asad, Muhammad, *The Message of the Qur'an*, Gibraltar: Dar al-Andalus, 1980.

Babić, Mirko, "Rezultati arheoloških istraživanja lokaliteta Atik džamije u Bijeljini", *Glasnik Udruženja muzejskih radnika*, 2 (2004): 48–70.

Babylonian Talmud: A Translation and Commentary, trans. Neusner Jacob, Massachusetts: Hendrickson Publishers, 2007.

Bacon, Francis, *Novum Organum*, Oxford: Clarendon Press, 1889.

Badawi, Elsaid M., and Muhammad Abdel Haleem, *Arabic-English Dictionary of Qur'anic Usage*, Leiden/Boston: Brill, 2008.

Ballanfat, Paul, "Mary as a melting of spiritual significations: The case of Rūzbehān Baqlī (d. 1209)", *Forum Bosnae*, 51 (2010): 211–243.

———, *Quatre traités inédifs de Rūzbehān Baqlī Shīrāzī*, Téhéran/Paris; Institut fraçais de recherches en Iran, 1998.

Barker, Margaret, *Temple Theology: An Introduction*, London: Society for Promoting Christian Knowledge, 2004.

Bašeskija, Mula Mustafa Ševki, *Ljetopis (1746–1804)*, trans. Mehmed Mujezinović, Sarajevo: Veselin Masleša, 1968.

Bauman, Zygmunt, *Modernity and Holocaust*, Cambridge, UK: Polity, 1989.

Bayhaqī, Abū Bakr Aḥmad, al-, *Sunan al-Bayhaqī al-kubrā*, 1–10, Makka al-Mukarrama: Maktaba Dār al-Bāz, 1994.

Bećirbegović, Medžida, *Džamije sa drvenom munarom u Bosni i Hercegovini*, Sarajevo: Sarajevo-Publishing, 1999.

———, *Džamije sa drvenom munarom u Bosni i Hercegovini*, Sarajevo: Veselin Masleša, 1990.

Bećirević, Edina, *Genocid on the Drina River*, New Haven: Yale University Press, 2014.

Bejtić, Alija, "Jedno viđenje sarajevskih evlija i njihovih grobova kao kultnih mjesta", *Prilozi za orijentalnu filologiju*, 31 (1981): 111–129.

Benac, Alojz, *Široki brijeg*, Sarajevo: Zemaljski muzej, 1952.

———, *Radimlja*, Sarajevo: Zemaljski muzej, 1950.

Bešlagić, Šefik, *Leksikon stećaka*, Sarajevo: Svjetlost, 2004.

———, *Stećci – kultura i umjetnost*, Sarajevo: Veselin Masleša, 1982.

———, *Nišani XV i XVI vijeka u Bosni i Hercegovini*, Sarajevo: Akademija nauka i umjetnosti Bosne i Hercegovine, 1978.

———, *Kupres: Srednjovjekovni nadgrobni spomenici*, Sarajevo: Zemaljski zavod za zaštitu spomenika kulture i prirodnih rijetkosti Narodne Republike Bosne i Hercegovine, 1954.

Bjelokosić, Luka, "Amajlije i zapisi", *Bosanska vila*, 1 (1912): 11–12.

Bojanić-Lukač, Dušanka, "Un chant a la gloire de Mahomet en Serbe", *Wiener Zeitschrift für die Kunde des Morgenlandes*, 76 (1986): 57–63.

Boss, Sarah Jane, *Empress and Handmaid: On Nature and Gender in the Cult of the Virgin Mary*, London: Cassell, 2000.

Bošnjak, Slavoljub, (fra. Ivan Frano Jukić), *Zemljopis i Poviestnica Bosne*, Zagreb: Narodna tiskarnica dr. Ljudevita Gaja, 1851, in: Jukić, *Sabrana djela*, 171–249.

Böwering, Gerhard, *The Mystical Vision of Existence in Classical Islam*, Berlin: Walter de Gruyter, 1980.

Budmani, Pero, ed., *Rječnik hrvatskog ili srpskog jezika*, 1–3, Zagreb: Jugoslavenska Akademija znanosti i umjetnosti, 1887–1891.

Bukhārī, Imām, al-, *Ṣaḥīh al-Bukhārī*, 1–9, trans. Muhammad Muhsin Khan, Beirut: Dar al-Arabia, 1985.

Bullarium Franciscanum, N.S., 1–2, Firenze: Ad Claras Aquas, 1929–1939.

Burckhardt, Titus, *Art of Islam: Language and Meaning*, London: World of Islam Festival Publishing Company, 1976.

Campbell, Joseph, ed., *Man and Time: Papers from the Eranos Yearbooks*, London: Routledge & Kegan Paul Ltd., 1958.

Cassirer, Ernst, *Substance and Function*, trans. W.C. and M.C. Swabey, Mineola, N.Y.: Dover Publications, 1980.

———, *An Essay on Man: An Introduction to a Philosophy of Human Culture*, New Haven: Yale University Press, 1944.

Charbonneau-Lassay, Louis, *The Bestiary of Christ*, trans. D.M. Dooling, Arkana: A Parabola Book, 1992.

Chenique, François, *Le Buisson ardent, Essai sur la métaphysique de la Vierge*, Paris: La pensée universelle, 1972.

Chittick, C. William, *Science of the Cosmos, Science of the Soul: The Pertinence of Islamic Cosmology in the Modern World*, Oxford: Oneworld, 2007.

———, *Ibn ʿArabī: Heir to the Prophets*, Oxford: One World Publications, 2005.

———, "Weeping in Classical Sufism", in: Patton, *Holy Tears*, 132–134.

———, "Time, Space and the Objectivity of Ethical Norms: The Teaching of Ibn al-ʿArabī", *Islamic Studies* 39/4 (2000): 581–596.

———, *The Self-Disclosure of God: Principles of Ibn al-ʿArabī's Cosmology*, Albany: Suny Press, 1998.

———, *The Sufi Path of Knowledge: Ibn al-ʿArabi's Metaphysics of Imagination*, Albany: State University of New York Press, 1989.

———, "Death and the World of Imagination: Ibn al-ʿArabī's Eschatology", *The Muslim World*, 78 (1988): 51–82.

Cohen, Jeremy, *The Friars and the Jews: The Evolution of Medieval Anti-Judaism*, Ithaca: Cornell University Press, 1982.

Cole, Penny, *The Preaching of the Crusades to the Holy Land, 1095–1270*, Cambridge, Mass.: Medieval Academy, 1991.

Corbin, Henry, *Swedenborg & Esoteric Islam*, trans. Leonard Fox, West Chester, Pennsylvania: Swedenborg Foundation, 1999.

———, *Alone with the Alone: Creative Imagination in the Sufism of Ibn ʿArabi*, trans. Ralph Manheim, Princeton: Princeton University Press, 1998.

———, *The Man of Light in Iranian Sufism*, trans. Nancy Parson, New Lebanon, NY: Omega Publications, 1994.

———, "On the Meaning of Music in Persian Mysticism", *Temenos*, 13 (1992): 49–52.

———, *Temple and Contemplation*, trans. Philip Sherrard, London: Islamic Publications, 1986.

———, *Face de Dieu, face de L'homme: Herméneutique et soufisme*, Paris: Flammarion, 1983.

———, *The Concept of Comparative Philosophy*, trans. Peter Russell, Cambridge: Golgonooza Press, 1981.

———, "The Dramatic Element Common to the Gnostic Cosmogonies of Religions of the Book", *Studies in Comparative Religion*, 14 (1980): 119–221.

———, "For the Concept of Irano-Islamic Philosophy", *The Philosophical Forum* 4/1 (1972): 114–123.

———, *Creative Imagination in the Sūfism of Ibn ʿArabī*, trans. Ralph Manheim, Princeton, N.J.: Princeton University Press, 1969.

———, *Avicenna and the Visionary Recital*, trans. Willard R. Trask, New York: Pantheon Books, 1960.

———, "The Time of Eranos", in: Cambpell, *Man and Time*, xiii–xx.

Cutsinger, James S., ed., *Paths to the Heart: Sufism and the Christian East*, Bloomington: World Wisdom, Inc., 2002.

———, "The Virgin", *Sophia: The Journal of Traditional Studies*, 6/2 (2000): 115–194.

Čelebi, Evlija, *Putopis: Odlomci o jugoslovenskim zemljama*, Sarajevo: Veselin Masleša, 1973.

Čolaković, Zlatan, "Post-traditionality of Homer and Avdo Međedović", *Forum Bosnae: Unity and Plurality in Europe: "The Roma Question"*, 44 (2008): 359–393.

———, "Bosniac Epics – Problems of Collecting and Editing the Main Collections", *Forum Bosnae: Unity and Plurality in Europe*, 39 (2007): 323–361.

Ćatić, Alija, "Božić kod muslimana (Prozor u Bosni)", *Zbornik za narodni život i običaje Južnih Slavena*, 26 (1928): 379–380.

Ćirković, Sima, "Dualistička heterodoksija u ulozi zemaljske crkve: Bosanska crkva", *Srpska akdemija nauka i umetnosti: Glasnik odjeljenja društvenih nauka*, 9 (1995): 7–34.

———, "Glose Srećkovićevog jevanđelja bosanske crkve", in: *Bogomilstvoto na Balkanot vo svetlinata na najnovite istražuvanja*, Skopje: Makedonska akademija na naukite i umetnostite, 1982, 207–222.

———, *Istorija srednjovekovne bosanske države*, Belgrade: Srpska književna zadruga, 1964.

Ćorović, Vladimir, "Prilog proučavanju načina sahranjivanja i podizanja nadgrobnih spomenika u našim krajevima u srednjem vijeku", *Naše starine*, 3 (1956): 127–147.

Ćošković, Pejo, *Crkva bosanska u XV. stoljeću*, Sarajevo: Institut za istoriju, 2005.

———, "Tomašev progon sljedbenika Crkve bosanske 1459.", in: *Zbornik radova naučnog skupa "Migracioni procesi: Bosna i Hercegovina od ranog srednjeg vijeka do najnovijih dana – njihov uticaj i posljedice na demografska kretanja i promjene u našoj zemlji"*, Sarajevo: Institut za istoriju, 1989, 43–48.

———, "Bosanski krstjani u očima svojih kršćanskih suvremenika", *Nastava povijesti*, 3/4 (1988): 183–191.

Ćurčić, Vejsil, "Starinsko oružje u Bosni i Hercegovini", *Glasnik Hrvatskog državnog muzeja u Sarajevu*, 55 (1943): 21–226.

———, "Ptice na našim srednjovječnim nadgrobnim spomenicima i starim muslimanskim nišanima", *Zadružni glasnik*, 3 (1939): 2–3.

———, "Oružje u narodnoj medicini", *Napredak*, 10/5 (1935): 55–56.

———, "Zanimljivi pabirci iz narodne medicine", *Gajret*, 7–8 (1933): 127–129.

———, "Nadgrobni spomenici u narodnoj medicini u Bosni i Hercegovini", *Napredak*, 11–12 (1933): 141–145.

Dārimī, Abū ʿAbd al-Raḥmān al-, *Sunan al-Dārimī*, 2, Beirut: Dār al-Kitāb al-ʿArabī, 1407.

Déclais, Jean-Louis, "Names of the Prophet", in: McAuliffe, *Encyclopaedia of the Qurʾān*, 3:501–505.

Denny, Federick Mathewson, "The meaning of the *ummah* in the Qurʾan", *History of Religions*, 15/1 (1975): 34–70.

Dhahabī, Shams al-Dīn, al-, *Siyar aʿlām al-nubalāʾ*, ed. Bashīr ʿAwwād Maʿrūf, Beirut: Muʾassasa al-Risāla, 1992.

Dialogus inter christianum romanum et patarenum bosnensem, in: Rački, "Prilozi za povijest bosanskih Patarena", 109–110.

Dizdar, Mak, *Stone Sleeper*, trans. Francis R. Jones, London: Anvil Press Poetry, 2009.

———, *Kameni spavač/Stone Sleeper*, trans. Francis R. Jones, Sarajevo: DID, 1999.

Djedović, Rusmir, "Dovište na Ratišu kod Srebrenika", in: Kulenović, ed., *Srebrenik: historijsko-etnografske skice*, 69–76.

Dobrača, Kasim, *Katalog arapskih, turskih, perzijskih i bosanskih rukopisa*, 1, London/Sarajevo: Al-Furqan/Rijaset Islamske zajednice u Bosni i Hercegovini, 2000.

Douglas, Mary, *Jacob's Tears: The Priestly Work of Reconciliation*, New York: Oxford University Press, 2004.

———, *Impurity and Danger*, New York: Praeger, 1966.

Dukić, Davor, *Sultanova djeca: Predodžbe Turaka u hrvatskoj književnosti ranog novovjekovlja*, Zadar: Thema, 2004.

Duvnjak, Stjepan, "Razvoj teologije slike u otačkom razdoblju", *Jukić*, 19–20 (1989/90): 29–62.

Đorđević, Tihomir R., "Preislamski ostaci među jugoslavenskim muslimanima", *Naš narodni život*, Belgrade: Izdavačka knjižarnica Gece Kona, 1932, 1–6.

Džaja, Srećko M., *Konfesionalnost i nacionalnost Bosne i Hercegovine: Predemancipacijsko razdoblje 1463.–1804.*, trans. Ladislav Z. Fišić, Mostar: Ziral, 1999.

———, "Dobri bošnjani" and "Boni Homines", *Dijalog*, 1–2 (2006): 105–130.

Ehlers, Benjamin, *Between Christians and Moriscos*, Baltimore, Maryland: The John Hopkins University Press, 2006.

Eliade, Mircea, "The Sacred in the Secular World", in: Rennie, *Mircea Eliade: A Critical Reader*, 57–67.

———, *Images and Symbols: Studies in Religious Symbolism*, trans. Philip Mairet, Princeton: Princeton University Press, 1991.

———, "The Sacred in the Secular World", *Cultural Hermeneutics*, 1 (1973): 101–113.

———, *Two and the One*, trans. J.M. Cohen, Chicago: The University of Chicago Press, 1965.

Ettinghausen, Richard, ed., *Islamic Art in the Metropolitan Museum of Art*, New York: The Metropolitan Museum of Art, 1972.

Fajić, Zejnil, *Katalog arapskih, turskih, perzijskih i bosanskih rukopisa*, 11, London/ Sarajevo: Al-Furqan/Rijaset Islamske zajednice u Bosni i Hercegovini, 2003.

Farlati, Daniele, *Illiricum sacrum*, 1–9, Venetiis: Apud Sebastianum Coleti, 1751–1819.

Faruque, Muhammad al-, "Emigration", in: McAuliffe, *Encyclopedia of the Qur'ān*, 2:18–23.

Fehérvári, Géza, "Tombstone or Mihrab: A Speculation", in: Ettinghausen, *Islamic Art in the Metropolitan Museum of Art*, 241–254.

Fermendžin, Eusebius, *Acta Bulgariae ecclesiastica ab anno 1565. usque ad annum 1799.*, Zagrabiae: Academia scientiarum et artium Slavorum meridionalium, 1887.

Filipović, Milenko S., "Uskrs kod muslimana", *Hrišćansko delo*, 4/2 (1938): 128–131.

———, *Visočka nahija*, Belgrade: Srpska kraljevska akademija, 1928.

Fine, John, *The Bosnian Church: A New Interpretation*, Boudler: East European Quaterly, 1975.

Finkelstein, Luis, ed., *Sifre on Deuteronomy*, New York: The Jewish Teological Seminary, 2001.

Firestone, Reuven, "Abraham's journey to Mecca in Islamic Exegesis: A form-critical study of a tradition", *Studia islamica*, 76 (1992): 5–24.

Fleischener, Eva, ed., *Auschwitz: Beginning of a new Era?*, New York: KTAV, 1977.

Foley, John Miles, *Traditional Oral Epic: The Odyssey, Beowulf and the Serbo-Croatian Return Song*, Berkley: University of California Press, 1993.

Ford, David, F., "An Interfaith Wisdom: Scriptural Reasoning Between Jews, Christians and Muslims", *Modern Theology*, 22/3 (2006): 345–366.

Fortis, Alberto, *Viaggio in Dalmazia*, 1, Venezia: Presso Alvise Milocco, All' Appoline, 1774.

Freud, Sigmund, "Splitting of the Ego in the Process of Defence", in: Strachey, *The Standard Edition of the Complete Psychological Works of Sigmund Freud*, 23:271–278.

Furūzānfar, Badīʿ al-Zamān, *Ahādīs-i Masnavī*, Tehran: Amīr Kabīr, 1968.

Ghazālī, Abū Ḥāmid, al-, *The Ninety-nine Beautiful Names of God*, trans. David B. Burrell and Nazih Daher, Cambridge: The Islamic Texts Society, 1992.

———, *Iḥyāʾ ʿulūm al-dīn*, 1–4, Cairo: Maṭbaʿa al-ʿĀmira al-Sharafiyya, 1908–1909.

Gimaret, Daniel, *Dieu à l'image de l'homme: les anthropomorphisimes de la sunna et leur interprétation par les théologiens*, Paris: Cerf, 1997.

Goldfeld, Isaiah, "The Illiterate Prophet (*Nabī Ummī*): An inquiry into the development of a dogma in Islamic tradition", *Der Islam*, 57/2 (1980): 58–67.

Goldziher, Ignaz, *Introduction to Islamic Theology and Law*, trans. Andras and Ruth Hamori, Princeton, N.J.: Princeton Univeristy Press, 1981.

———, *Muslim Studies*, 1–2, trans. C.R. Barber and S.M. Stern, London: George Allen & Unwin, 1971.

———, "Veneration of Saints in Islam", in: ibid., *Muslim Studies*, 2:255–341.

Gospel according to Thomas, The, trans. A. Guillamont, H. Ch. Puech, G. Quispel, W. Till and Yassah ʿAbd al Masīḥ, Leiden: E.J. Brill, 1976.

Grabar, Oleg, *The Shape of the Holy: Early Islamic Jerusalem*, Princeton: Princeton University Press, 1996.

Graham, William A., "Scripture and the Qurʾan", in: McAuliffe, *Encyclopaedia of the Qurʾān*, 4:558–569.

———, *Beyond the Written Word: Oral aspects of Scripture in the History of Religion*, Cambridge: Cambridge University Press, 1993.

———, *Divine Word and Prophetic Word in Early Islam: A Reconsideration of the Sources, with Special Reference to the Divine Saying on Hadith Qudsi*, The Hague: Mouton, 1977.

Greenberg, Irving, "Cloud of Smoke, Pillar of Fire: Judaism, Christianity and Modernity after the Holocaust", in: Fleischener, *Auschwitz: Beginning of a new Era?*, 7–57.

Guénon, Réné, *Prespectives on Initiation*, trans. Henry D. Fohr, Ghent, N.Y.: Sophia Perennis, 2001.

———, *Fundamental Symbols: The Universal Language of Sacred Science*, trans. Alvin Moore, Jnr, Cambridge: Quinta Essentia, 1995.

———, *Autorité spirituelle et pouvoir temporel*, Paris: Véga, 1984.

———, "Oriental Metaphysics", in: Needleman, *The Sword of Gnosis, Metaphysics, Cosmology, Tradition, Symbolism*, 40–57.

———, *Symboles de la Science sacrée*, Paris: Gallimard, 1962.

———, *Le Symbolisme de la Croix*, Paris: Véga, 1931.

Hadžijahić, Muhamed, *Povijest Bosne u IX i X stoljeću*, Sarajevo: Preporod, 2004.

———, "Badžijanije u Sarajevu i Bosni: Prilog historiji duhovnosti u nas", *Anali Gazi Husrev-begove biblioteke*, 7–8 (1982): 109–133.

———, "Jedan nepoznati tuzlanski hagiološki katalog", *Članci i građa za kulturnu istoriju istočne Bosne*, 13 (1980): 212–235.

———, "Sinkretistički elementi u islamu u Bosni i Hercegovini", *Prilozi za orijentalnu filologiju*, 28/29 (1978/79): 301–329.

———, "Zemljišni posjedi 'crkve bosanske'", *Historijski zbornik*, 25/26 (1972/73): 461–480.

Hadžimuhamedović, Amra, "Rušenje i građenje mesdžida u Bosni", *Blagaj*, 1/1 (1996): 64–72.

Ḥakīm, Suʿād, al-, *al-Muʿjam al-ṣūfī*, Beirut: Dandara, 1981.

Hamidullah, Muhammad, *Muhammad, A.S.: Život*, trans. Nerkez Smailagić, Sarajevo: Starješinstvo Islamske zajednice u Bosni i Hercegovini, Hrvatskoj i Sloveniji, 1983.

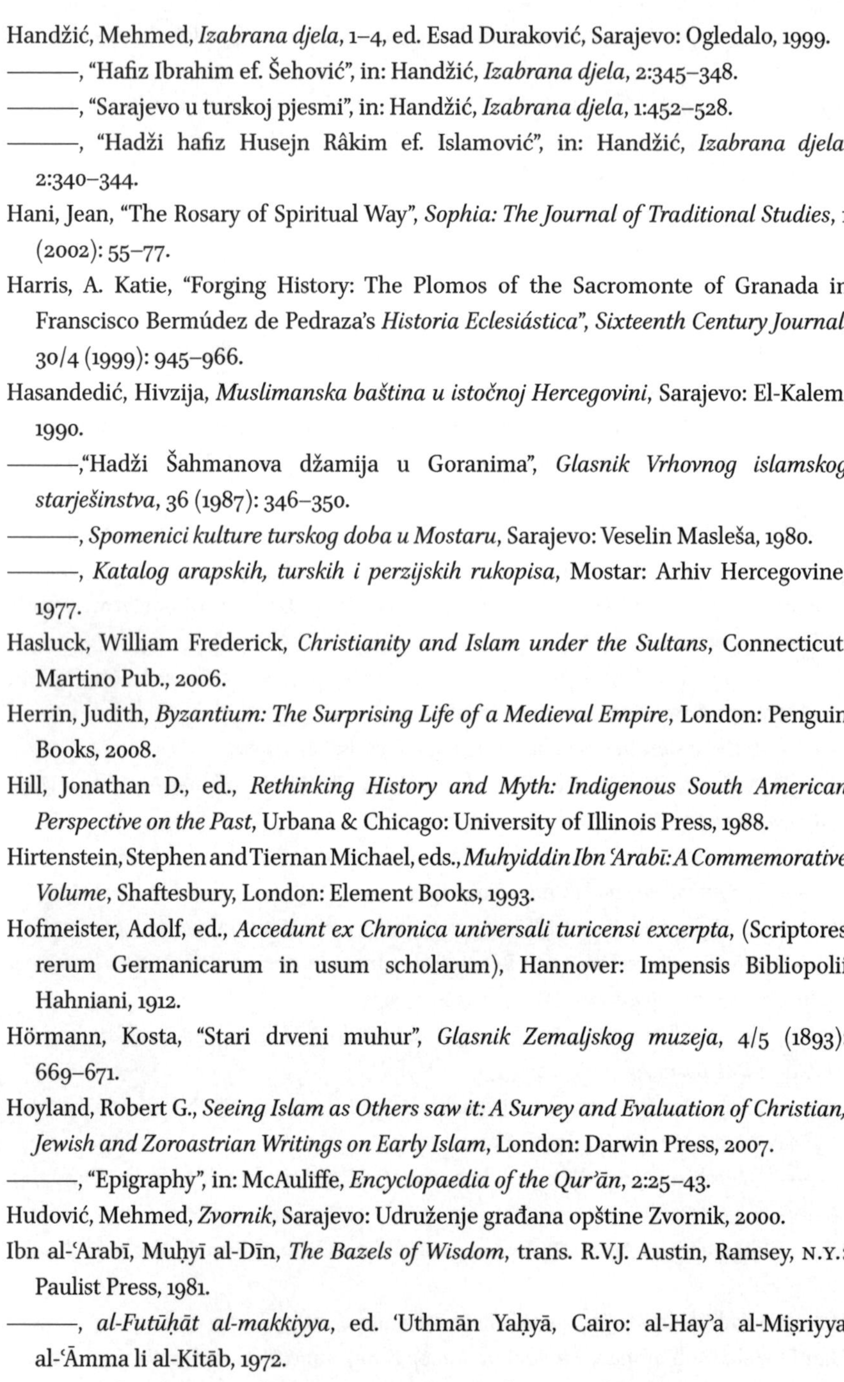

Handžić, Mehmed, *Izabrana djela*, 1–4, ed. Esad Duraković, Sarajevo: Ogledalo, 1999.

———, "Hafiz Ibrahim ef. Šehović", in: Handžić, *Izabrana djela*, 2:345–348.

———, "Sarajevo u turskoj pjesmi", in: Handžić, *Izabrana djela*, 1:452–528.

———, "Hadži hafiz Husejn Râkim ef. Islamović", in: Handžić, *Izabrana djela*, 2:340–344.

Hani, Jean, "The Rosary of Spiritual Way", *Sophia: The Journal of Traditional Studies*, 1 (2002): 55–77.

Harris, A. Katie, "Forging History: The Plomos of the Sacromonte of Granada in Franscisco Bermúdez de Pedraza's *Historia Eclesiástica*", *Sixteenth Century Journal*, 30/4 (1999): 945–966.

Hasandedić, Hivzija, *Muslimanska baština u istočnoj Hercegovini*, Sarajevo: El-Kalem, 1990.

———,"Hadži Šahmanova džamija u Goranima", *Glasnik Vrhovnog islamskog starješinstva*, 36 (1987): 346–350.

———, *Spomenici kulture turskog doba u Mostaru*, Sarajevo: Veselin Masleša, 1980.

———, *Katalog arapskih, turskih i perzijskih rukopisa*, Mostar: Arhiv Hercegovine, 1977.

Hasluck, William Frederick, *Christianity and Islam under the Sultans*, Connecticut: Martino Pub., 2006.

Herrin, Judith, *Byzantium: The Surprising Life of a Medieval Empire*, London: Penguin Books, 2008.

Hill, Jonathan D., ed., *Rethinking History and Myth: Indigenous South American Perspective on the Past*, Urbana & Chicago: University of Illinois Press, 1988.

Hirtenstein, Stephen and Tiernan Michael, eds., *Muhyiddin Ibn 'Arabī: A Commemorative Volume*, Shaftesbury, London: Element Books, 1993.

Hofmeister, Adolf, ed., *Accedunt ex Chronica universali turicensi excerpta*, (Scriptores rerum Germanicarum in usum scholarum), Hannover: Impensis Bibliopolii Hahniani, 1912.

Hörmann, Kosta, "Stari drveni muhur", *Glasnik Zemaljskog muzeja*, 4/5 (1893): 669–671.

Hoyland, Robert G., *Seeing Islam as Others saw it: A Survey and Evaluation of Christian, Jewish and Zoroastrian Writings on Early Islam*, London: Darwin Press, 2007.

———, "Epigraphy", in: McAuliffe, *Encyclopaedia of the Qur'ān*, 2:25–43.

Hudović, Mehmed, *Zvornik*, Sarajevo: Udruženje građana opštine Zvornik, 2000.

Ibn al-ʿArabī, Muḥyī al-Dīn, *The Bazels of Wisdom*, trans. R.V.J. Austin, Ramsey, N.Y.: Paulist Press, 1981.

———, *al-Futūḥāt al-makkiyya*, ed. ʿUthmān Yaḥyā, Cairo: al-Hayʾa al-Miṣriyya al-ʿĀmma li al-Kitāb, 1972.

———, *Tafsīr al-Qurʾān al-Karīm*, 1–2, Beirut: Dār al-Yaqaẓa al-ʿArabiyya, 1968.

———, *Inshāʾ al-dawāʾir*, Leiden: Brill, 1918.

———, "The Book of the Description of the Encompassing Circles" trans. Paul B. Fenton, and Maurice Gloton, in Hirtenstein, *Muhyiddin Ibn 'Arabi: A Commemorative Volume*, 13–43.

Ibn Ḥanbal, Aḥmad, *al-Musnad*, Beirut: Dār al-Ṣādir, s.a.

———, *al-Musnad*, 1–2, Cairo: Mu'assasa Qurṭuba, s.a.

Ibn Ishāq, *The Life of Muhammad (A Translation of Ibn Ishaq's Sirat Rasūl Allāh)*, trans. Alfred Guillaume, Karachi: Oxford University Press, 1980.

Ibn Kathīr, 'Imād al-Dīn Abū al-Fidā' Ismā'īl, *Tafsīr al-Qur'ān al-'Aẓīm*, 1–4, Cairo: Dār Iḥyā' al-Kutub al-'Arabiyya, s.a.

Ibn Māja, al-Ḥāfiẓ Abū 'Abdullāh Muḥammad bin Yazīd al-Qazvīnī, *Sunan Ibn Māja*, 1–2, ed. Muḥammad Fu'ād 'Abd al-Bāqī, Cairo: Dār al-Ḥadīth, 1994.

———, *al-Sunan*, ed. M.F. 'Abd al-Bāqī, Cairo: Dār Iḥyā' al-Kutub al-'Arabiyya, 1952.

Ibn Ṣabbāgh, 'Alī b. Muḥammad b. Aḥmad, *al-Fuṣūl al-muhimma fī ma'rifat al-a'imma*, Qum: Mu'assasa Dār al-Ḥadīth al-Thaqafiyya, 1422.

Ibn Sa'd, Muḥammad, *al-Ṭabaqāt al-kubrā*, 1–9, Beirut: Dār al-Ṣādir, 1985.

Ibn Sīda, 'Alī ibn Ismā'īl, *al-Muḥkam wa al-muḥiṭ al-a'ẓam fī al-lugha*, 1–3, ed. 'Ā'isha 'Abd al-Raḥmān, Cairo: s.n., 1958.

Idel, Moshe, *Ben: Sonship and Jewish Mysticism*, New York: Continuum, 2007.

Iṣfahānī, Rāghib, al-, *al-Mufradāt fī gharīb al-Qur'ān*, ed. Muḥammad Sayyid Kīlānī, Cairo: Sharika Maktaba wa Maṭba'a Muṣṭafā al-Bābī al-Ḥalabī wa awlādih, 1371/1961.

Izutsu, Toshihiko, *Sufism and Taoism: A Comparative Study of Key Philosophical Concepts*, Berkeley: University of California Press, 1984.

———, *God and Man in the Koran: Semantics of the Koranic Weltanschauung*, Tokyo: The Keio Institute of Cultural and Linguistic Studies, 1964.

Jahić, Mustafa, *Katalog arapskih, turskih, perzijskih i bosanskih rukopisa*, 12, London/ Sarajevo: Al-Furqan/Rijaset Islamske zajednice u Bosni i Hercegovini, 2003.

Jazūlī, Muḥammad Sulaymān, al-, *Dalā'il al-khayrāt*, Constantinople: Muḥammad Hāshim al-Kutubī wa shurakā'uh, 1331.

Johnson, Elizabeth A., *Truly Our Sister: A Theology of Mary in the Communion of Saints*, New York: Continuum, 2006.

Jukić, Ivan Frano, *Sabrana djela*, 1, Sarajevo: Svjetlost, 1973.

———, Banjalučanin and Ljubomir Hercegovac, eds., *Narodne piesme bosanske i hercegovačke*, Osiek: Filip Kunić, Kuprješanin, 1858.

Jurić-Kappel, Jagoda, "Bosanske apokalipse u svome (južno)slavenskom kontekstu", *Wiener slavistisches Jahrbuch*, 48 (2002): 75–94.

Kačić Miošić, Andrija, *Razgovor ugodni naroda slovinskoga*, Zagreb: Školska knjiga, 2006.

Kajmaković, Zdravko, *Zidno slikarstvo u Bosni i Hercegovini*, Sarajevo: Veselin Masleša, 1971.

Kamber, Dragutin, "Kardinal Torquemada i tri bosanska bogomila", *Croatia Sacra: arkiv za crkvenu povijest Hrvata*, 3 (1932): 27–93.

Kanic, Feliks, *Srbija, zemlja i stanovništvo*, 1–2, trans. Gligorije Ernjaković, Belgrade: BMG, 1999.

Kepnes, Steven, "Islam as Our Other, Islam as Ourselves", in: Koshul and Kepnes, *Scripture, Reason, and the Contemporary Islam – West Encounter*, (2007): 107–121.

Khoury, Nuha N.N., "The Mihrab: From Text to Form", *International Journal of Middle East Studies*, 30/1 (1998): 1–27.

———, "The Dome of the Rock, the Kaʿba, and Ghumdan: Arab Myths and Umayyad Monuments", *Muqarnas*, 10 (1993): 57–65.

———, "The Mihrab Image: Commemorative Themes in Medieval Islamic Architecture", *Muqarnas*, 9 (1992): 11–28.

———, *The Mihrab Concept*, Ph. D. diss., Harvard: Harvard University, 1992.

Kisāʾī, Muḥammad ibn ʿAbdallāh, al-, *Qiṣaṣ al-anbiyāʾ* (*Tales of the Prophets*), trans. Wheeler M. Thackston Jr., Chicago: Great Books of the Islamic World, 1997.

Kniewald, Dragutin, "Vjerodostojnost latinskih izvora o bosanskim krstjanima", *RAD JAZU*, 1 (1949): 115–276.

Knohl, Israel, *The Messiah before Jesus: The Suffering Servant of the Dead Sea Scrolls*, trans. David Maisel, Berkeley and Los Angeles: University of California Press, 2000.

Kočović, Bogoljub, *Žrtve Drugog svjetskog rata u Jugoslaviji*, Sarajevo: Svjetlost, 1990.

Koshul, Basit B. and Steven Kepnes, ed., *Scripture, Reason, and the Contemporary Islam-West Encounter: Studying the "Other", Understanding the "Self"*, New York: Palgrave Macmillan, 2007.

Krauss, Friedrich S., "Riječ", in: *Smajlagić Meho*, vii–xv.

———, *Smajlagić Meho: Pjesan naših Muhamedovaca*, Dubrovnik: Knjižarnica D. Pretner, 1886.

Kreševljaković, Hamdija, "Stari bosanski gradovi", *Naše starine*, 1 (1953): 7–44.

Kulenović, Salih, Rusmir Djedović and Enes Mutapčić, eds., *Srebrenik: historijsko-etnografske skice*, Srebrenik: Centar za kulturu i informisanje, 2007.

Kuna, Herta, *Srednjovjekovna bosanska književnost*, Sarajevo: Međunarodni forum Bosna, 2008.

Küng, Hans, *The Catholic Church: A Short History*, trans. John Bowden, New York: Modern Library, 2003.

Lavić, Osman, *Katalog arapskih, turskih, perzijskih i bosanskih rukopisa*, 15, London/Sarajevo: Al-Furqān/Rijaset Islamske zajednice u Bosni i Hercegovini, 2006.

Lea, Henry Charles, *A History of the Inquisition of the middle ages*, 1–3, London: Adamant Media Corporation, 2005.

———, *The Moriscos of Spain: Their Conversion and Expulsion*, Philadelphia: Lea Brothers & Co., 1901.

Leach, Edmund, *Culture and Communication: The Logic by which Symbols are Connected*, Cambridge: Cambridge University Press, 1976.

Leibniz, Gottfried W. von, *New Essays on Human Understanding*, eds., Peter Remnant and Jonathan Bennett, Cambridge: Cambridge University Press, 1996.

Lings, Martin and Clinton Minnaar, ed., *The Underlying Religion: An Introduction to the Perennial Philosophy*, Bloomington, Ind.: World Wisdom, 2007.

Lings, Martin, *A Return to the Spirit: Questions and Answers*, Louisville, KY: Fons Vitae, 2005.

———, *Splendours of Qur'an Calligraphy and Ilumination*, Vaduz: Thesaurus Islamicus Foundation, 2005.

———, *Mecca: From before Genesis until now*, Cambridge: Archetype, 2004.

———, *A Sufi Saint of the Twentieth Century: Shaikh Ahmad al-'Alawi: His Spiritual Heritage and Legacy*, Cambridge: The Islamic Texts Society, 1993.

———, *Symbol and Archetype: A Study of the Meaning of Existence*, Cambridge: Quinta Essentia, 1991.

———, *Muhammad: His Life Based On the Earliest Sources*, London: Allen & Unwin, 1988.

López-Baralt, Luce, *Islam in Spanish literature: From the Middle Ages to the Present*, trans. Andrew Hurley, Leiden: E.J. Brill, 1992.

Loos, Milan, *Dualist Heresy in the Middle Ages*, Prague: Academia, 1974.

Lord, Albert B., *The Singer of Tales*, Cambridge, Mass.: Harvard University Press, 2003.

Maglajlić, Munib, "Nikola Tordinac i usmeno pjesništvo", in: ibid., *Usmeno pjesništvo od stvaralaca do sakupljača*, 16–34.

———, *Usmeno pjesništvo od stvaralaca do sakupljača*, Tuzla: Univerzal, 1989.

Mahmutćehajić, Rusmir, *Maintaining the Sacred Center: The Bosnian city of Stolac*, trans. Desmond Maurer, Bloomington, Indiana: World Wisdom Inc., 2011.

———, *Across the River: On the Poetry of Mak Dizdar*, New York: Fordham University Press, 2010.

———, *Tajna Hasanaginice*, Sarajevo: Buybook, 2010.

———, "Good people: A goal reached by many paths", *Forum Bosnae*, 44 (2008): 5–17.

———, *The Mosque: The Heart of Submission*, New York: Fordham University Press, 2006.

———, *Prozori: Riječi i slike*, Sarajevo/Zagreb/Tuzla/Ljubljana: Did/Durieux/Radio Kameleon/Mladinska knjiga, 2000.

———, *The Denial of Bosnia*, Pennsylvania: The Pennsylvania State University Press, 2000.

Majlisī, Muḥammad Bāqir, *Biḥār al-anwār*, Beirut: Mu'assasa al-Wafā', 1983.

Makkī, Abū Ṭālib, al-, *Qūt al-qulūb*, Cairo: Muṣṭafā al-Bābi al-Ḥalabī, 1961.

Makkī, ʿAlī, al-, *Fatḥ al-karīm al-khāliq fī ḥall alfāẓ al-durr al-fāʾiq fī al-ṣalāt ʿalā ashraf al-khalāʾiq (Ṣ) li al-shaykh Muṣṭafā al-Bakrī*, Beirut: Dār al-Kutub al-ʿIlmiyya, 2010.

Mālik b. Anas, Imām, *al-Muwaṭṭaʾ*, trans. ʿAʾisha ʿAbdarahman at-Tarjumana and Yaʿqub Johnson, London: Diwan Press, 1982.

Mandić, Dominik, *Bogomilska crkva bosanskih krstjana*, Chicago: The Croatian Historical Institute, 1962.

Markešić, Luka, *Crkva Božja: Postanak, povijest, poslanje*, Sarajevo: Svjetlo riječi, 2005.

———, "Štovanje Bl. Dj. Marije u bosansko-hercegovačkoj tradiciji", *Nova et vetera*, 36/1–2 (1988): 101–117.

Mastnak, Tomaž, *Crusading Peace: Christendom, the Muslim World, and Western Political Order*, Berkeley: University of California Press, 2002.

Maybūdī, Rashīd al-Dīn, *Kashf al-asrār wa ʿuddat al-abrār*, 1–6, ed. ʿAlī Asghar Ḥikmat, Tehran: Dānishgāh, 1952–1960.

McAuliffe, Jane Dammen, ed., *Encyclopaedia of the Qurʾān*, 1–5, Leiden: Brill, 2001–2006.

McCarthy, Justin, *Death and Exile: The Ethnic Cleansing of Ottoman Muslims, 1821–1922*, Princeton: The Darwin Press, 1995.

Melikian-Chirvani, Assadullah Souren, "The Light of Heaven and Earth: From the *Chahār-tāq* to the *Mihrab*", *Bulletin of the Asia Institute*, 4 (1990): 95–131.

Miles, George C., ed., *Archaeologia Orientalia in Memoriam Ernest Herzfeld*, New York: J.J. Augustin Publisher, 1952.

———, "Mirab and ʿAnaza: A Study in Early Islamic Iconography", in: ibid., ed., *Archaeologia Orientalia in Memoriam Ernest Herzfeld*, 156–171.

Molé, Marijan, *Les mystiques musulmans*, Paris: Presses Universitaires de France, 1965.

Mošin, Vladimir, "Rukopisi bivše Beogradske Narodne biblioteke u Dablinu i u Zagrebu", *Bibliotekar*, 5 (1968): 349–359.

———, "Rukopis Pljevaljskog sinodika pravoslavlja", *Slovo*, 6–8 (1957): 154–176.

Muftić, Teufik, *Arapsko-bosanski rječnik*, Sarajevo: El-Kalem, 2008.

Mujezinović, Mehmed, *Islamska epigrafika Bosne i Hercegovine*, 1–3, Sarajevo: Veselin Masleša, 1974, 1977 and 1982.

———, "Diplome kaligrafa Islamovića u Gazi Husrev-begovoj biblioteci u Sarajevu", *Anali Gazi Husrev-begove biblioteke*, 1 (1972): 91–95.

Mulla Sadra, *The Wisdom of the Throne*, trans. James Winston Morris, Princeton: Princeton University Press, 1981.

Murata, Sachiko, William C. Chittick, and Tu Weiming, *The Sage Learning of Liu Zhi: Islamic Thought in Confucian Terms*, Cambridge: Harvard University Asia Center, 2009.

Murata, Sachiko, and William C. Chittick, *The Vision of Islam: The Foundations of Muslim Faith and Practice*, London: I.B. Tauris Publishers, 1996.

Murata, Sachiko, *The Tao of Islam: A Sourcebook on Gender Relationship in Islamic Thought*, Albany: State University of New York Press, 1992.

Musallam, Basim F., *Sex and Society in Islam*, Cambridge: Cambridge University Press, 1983.

Muslim, Imam, *Ṣaḥīḥ Muslim*, 1–4, trans. 'Abdul Hamid Siddiqi, Riyadh: International Islamic Publishing House, s.a.

Musulin, Stjepan, ed., *Rječnik hrvatskog ili srpskog jezika*, Zagreb: Jugoslavenska Akademija znanosti i umjetnosti, 1959–1962.

Muttaqī al-Hindī, 'Alī b. Ḥusām al-Dīn, al-, *Kanz al-'ummāl fī sunan al-aqwāl wa al-af'āl*, Beirut: Mu'assasa al-Risāla, 1989.

Nahj al-balāgha: Sermons, Letters and Sayings of Imam 'Ali, Qum: Ansaryan Publication, 1989.

Nametak, Fehim, *Katalog arapskih, turskih, perzijskih i bosanskih rukopisa*, 4, London/Sarajevo: Al-Furqān/Rijaset Islamske zajednice u Bosni i Hercegovini, 1998.

Nasafī, 'Azīz, *The Furthest Goal*, in: Ridgeon, *Persian metaphysics and Mysticism*, 41–128.

Nasā'ī, Aḥmad Abū 'Abd al-Raḥmān, al-, *Sunan al-kubrā*, Beirut: Dār al-Kutub al-'Ilmiyya, 1991.

———, *al-Sunan*, 1–8, Cairo: Dār al-Ḥadīth, 1987.

Nasr, Seyyed Hossein, *Islamic Philosophy from its Origin to the Present: Philosophy in the Land of Prophecy*, Albany: State University of New York Press, 2006.

———, "The Heart of the Faithful is the Throne of the All-Merciful", in: Cutsinger, ed., *Paths to the Heart*, 32–45.

Nazor, Anica, *Radosavljeva bosanska knjiga: Zbornik krstjanina Radosava*, Sarajevo: Međunarodni forum Bosna, 2008.

———, "Rukopisi crkve bosanske", in: Šanjek, *Fenomen "krstjani" u srednjovjekovnoj Bosni i Hercegovini: Zbornik radova*, 539–560.

Needleman, Jacob, ed., *The Sword of Gnosis, Metaphysics, Cosmology, Tradition, Symbolism*, Baltimore: Penguin, 1974.

Nikaido, Scott, "Hagar and Ishmael as Literary Figures: An Intertextual study", *Vetus Testamentum*, 51/2 (2001): 219–242.

Njegoš, Petar II Petrović, *Lažni car Šćepan Mali*; in idem, *Djela*, ed. Drago Ćupić, Podgorica: CID, 2001, 149–279.

———, *Ogledalo srbsko*, Belgrade: Knjaž. Srbska knjigopečatnja, 1845.

Nūr al-Ḥaqq, *Sharḥ al-laṭā'if*, Kanpur: Maḥmūd al-Maṭābi', 1343/1924–25.

Okiç, Taib M., "Les Kristians (Bogomiles Parfaits) de Bosnie d'aprés des documents inédits", *Südos-Forschungen*, 19 (1960): 108–133.

Orbini, Mavro, *Kraljevstvo Slavena*, trans. Snježana Husić, Zagreb: Golden Marketing, 1999.

Otašević, Danica, "Nikoljsko jevanđelje: Od originala do digitalne kopije", *Glas biblioteke*, 12 (2005): 33–46.

Padwick, Constance E., *Muslim Devotions: A Study of Prayer-Manuals in Common Use*, Oxford: Oneworld Publications, 1996.

Pantelič, Nikola, ed., *Etnički odnosi Srba sa drugim narodima i etničkim zajednicama*, Belgrade: Etnografski institut Srpske akademije nauka i umjetnosti, 1998.

Papadopoulo, Alexandre, ed., *Le Mihrāb dans l'architecture et la religion musulmanes*, Leiden: E.J. Brill, 1988.

Partner, Peter, *The Knights Templar and Their Myth*, Vermont: Destiny Books, 1990.

———, *The Murdered Magicians: The Templars and Their Myth*, New York: Barnes and Noble, 1987.

Pašić, Ibrahim, *Mile i Moštre: Ilirsko-gotski korijeni bosanske vladarske dinastije, stećaka i Crkve bosanske*, Sarajevo: Ibrahim Pašić, 2009.

Patton, Kimberley C., *Religion of the Gods: Ritual, Paradox, and Reflexivity*, New York: Oxford university Press, 2009.

Patton, Kimberley C., and John S. Hawley, eds., *Holy Tears: Weeping in Religious Imagination*, Princeton: Princeton University Press, 2005.

Pelikan, Jaroslav, *Mary through the Centuries: Her place in the history of culture*, New Haven: Yale University Press, 1996.

Pelusi, Simonetta, *Novum Testamentum Bosniacum Marcianum*, Padova: Studio Editoriale Programma, 1991.

Perry, Mary E., *The Handless Maiden: Moriscos and the Politics of Religion in Early Modern Spain*, Princeton: Princeton University Press, 2005.

Peters, Francis E., *A Reader on Classical Islam*, Princeton: Princeton University Press, 1994.

Piccolomini, Aeneas Sylvius, *Commentarii rerum memorabilium, quae temporibus suis contigerunt*, Romae: ex typographia Dominici Basae, 1584, Frankfurt am Main: Minerva, 1974. The first critcal edition, ed. Adrian van Heck, Città del Vaticano: Biblioteca Apostolica Vaticana, 1984.

Planck, Max, *Die Einheit des physikalischen Weltbildes*, Vortrag, gehalten am 9. Dezember 1908 in der naturwiss, Leiden: Hirzel, 1909.

Popara, Haso, "Idžazetname u rukopisima Gazi Husrev-begove bibioteke: Prilog proučavanju historije obrazovanja u BiH", *Anali Gazi Husrev-begove biblioteke*, 25–26 (2007): 5–41.

Qāḍī ʿIyāḍ ibn Mūsā, *Kitāb al-shifāʾ bi-taʿrīf ḥūquq al-muṣṭafā*, 1–2, Damascus: Dār al-Wafā li al-Ṭibāʿa wa al-Nashr, 1972.

Qārī, ʿAlī ibn Sulṭān Muḥammad, al-, *Mirqāt al-mafātīḥ sharḥ Mishkāt al-maṣābīḥ*, 1–11, Beirut: Dār al-Kutub al-ʿIlmiyya, 2001.

———, *al-Asrār al-marfūʿa fī akhbār al-mavḍūʿa*, 1–30, Beirut: Muʾassasa al-Risāla, 1971.

Rački, Franjo, "Dva nova priloga za povijest bosanskih Patarena", *Starine Jugoslavenske akademije znanosti i umjetnosti*, 14 (1882): 1–29.

———, "Prilozi za povijest bosanskih Patarena", *Starine JAZU*, 1 (1869): 98–140.

Radojičić, Đorđe Sp., ed., *Antologija stare srpske književnosti (XI–XVIII veka)*, Belgrade: Nolit, 1960.

Radojković, Bojana, *Filakteriji, enamluci, pripojasnice*, Belgrade: Muzej primenjene umetnosti, 1974.

Radonić, Jovan, *Dubrovačka akta i povelje*, 1, Belgrade: Srpska kraljevska akademija, 1934.

Rahner, Karl, *Mary, Mother of the Lord: Theological meditations*, New York: Herder and Herder, 1963.

Radtke, Bernd and John O'Kane, *The Concept of Sainthood in Early Islamic Mistycism: Two works of al-Hakīm al-Tirmidhī*, London/ New York: Routledge Curzon, 1996.

Rāzī, Fakhr al-Dīn Muḥammad bin ʿUmar al-Tamīmī, al-, *al-Tafsīr al-kubrā wa mafātīḥ al-ghayb*, 1–32, Beirut: Dār al-Kutub al-ʿIlmiyya, 2000.

Rāzī, Najm al-Dīn, *The Path of God's Bondsmen from Origin to Return*, trans. Hamid Algar, Delmar, N.Y.: Caravan Books, 1982.

Redhouse, James W., *Turkish and English Lexicon Shewing in English the Signification of the Turkish Terms*, Istanbul: Çağrı yayınları, 2006.

Rengeo, Ivan, "Sredovječni nadgrobni spomenici – stećci", in: *Bibliografija i građa za umjetnost i srodne struke, 8*, Zagreb, 1953.

Rennie, Bryan, ed., *Mircea Eliade: A Critical Reader*, London: Equinox, 2006.

Ridgeon, Lioyd, *Persian metaphysics and Mysticism: Selected Treatises of ʿAzīz Nasafī*, Richmond, Surrey: Curzon, 2002.

Riedlmayer, András J., "*Convivencia* under Fire: Genocide and Book-burning in Bosnia", in: Rose, *The Holocaust and the Book*, 266–291.

Roberts, Nancy, "God as Father-Mother, and More", *The Muslim World*, 99 (2009): 102–123.

Robson, James, "Blessings on the Prophet", *Muslim World*, 26 (1936): 365–371.

Rose, Jonathan, ed., *The Holocaust and the Book: Destruction and Preservation*, Amherst: University of Masschusetts, 2001.

Ruderman, David B., *Between Cross and Crescent*, Chantilly, VA.: The Teaching Company, 2005.

Rūmī, Jalāl al-Dīn, *The Mathnawi*, 1–6, trans. Reynold A. Nicholson, London: Luzac, 1997.

———, *Discourses of Rūmī (Fīhi mā fīhi)* trans. Arthur J. Arberry, London & New York: Routledge, 1995.

Rycaut, Paul, *The Present State of the Ottoman Empire, Containing the Maxims of the Turkish Politie, the Most Material Points of the Mahometan Religion, Their Sects and Heresies, Their Convents and Religious Votaries. Their Military Discipline with and*

Exact Computation of Their Forces Both by Land and Sea. Illustrated with Diverse Pieces of Sculpture, Representing the Variety of Habits among the Turks, 1–3, London: John Starkey and Henry Brome, 1670.

Schimmel, Annemarie, *And Muhammad is His Messenger: The Veneration of the Prophet in Islamic Piety*, Chapel Hill: The University of North Carolina Press, 1985.

Schleifer, Aliah, *Mary the Blessed Virgin of Islam*, Louisville: Fons Vitae, 1998.

Schneemelcher, Wilhelm, *New Testament Apocrypha: Gospels and Related Writings*, trans. R. McL. Wilson, Louisville: Westminster John Knox Press, 1991.

Scholem, Gershom, *On the Possibility of Jewish Mysticism in Our Time and Other Essays*, trans. Jonathan Chipman, Philadelphia: Jewish Publication Society, 1997.

———, "The People of the Book"; in ibid., *On the Possibility of Jewish Mysticism in Our Time and Other Essays*, 167–175.

———, *Origins of the Kabbalah*, ed. R.J. Zwi Werblowsky, trans. Allan Arkush, Princeton: Princeton University Press, 1990.

———, "Opening Address", in: Werblowsky, *Types of Redemption*, 5–12.

Schuon, Frithjof, *Spiritual Perspectives and Human Facts*, trans. Peter N. Townsend, Pates Manor: Perennial Books Limited, 1987.

———, *The Transcendent Unity of Religions*, Wheaton: The Theosophical Publishing House, 1984.

———, *From the Divine to the Human: Survey of Metaphysics and Epistemology*, trans. Gustavo Polit and Deborah Lambert, Bloomington: World Wisdom Books, 1982.

———, *Castes and Races*, New York: Sophia Perennis, 1982.

———, *Dimensions of Islam*, London: Allen & Unwin, 1970.

———, *Understanding Islam*, London: Allen & Unwin, 1963.

Seligman, Adam B., Robert P. Weller, Michael J. Puett, and Bennett Simon, *Ritual and Its Consequences: An Essay on the Limits of Sincerity*, New York: Oxford University Press, 2008.

Shah-Kazemi, Reza, *Justice and Remembrance: Introducing the Spirituality of Imam 'Ali*, New York: I.B. Tauris, 2006.

Skok, Petar, *Etimologijski rječnik hrvatskoga ili srpskoga jezika*, 1–4, Zagreb: Jugoslavenska akademija znanosti i umjetnosti, 1971–1974.

Smailbegović, Esma, *Narodna predaja o Sarajevu*, Sarajevo: Institut za jezik i književnost, 1986.

Smith, Jane I. and Yvonne Y. Haddad, "The Virgin Mary in Islamic tradition and commentary", *The Muslim World*, 79/3–4 (1989): 161–187.

Softić, Aiša, *Zbornik bošnjačkih usmenih predaja*, Sarajevo: Sarajevo Publishing, 2005.

Solovjev, Aleksandar, "Simbolika srednjevjekovnih nadgrobnih spomenika u Bosni i Hercegovini", *Godišnjak Istorijskog društva Bosne i Hercegovine*, 8 (1956): 5–67.

———, "Engleski izvještaj XVII vijeka o bosanskim poturima", *Glasnik zemaljskog muzeja u Sarajevu*, 7 (1952): 101–109.

———, "Nestanak bogumilstva i islamizacija Bosne", *Godišnjak Istorijskog društva Bosne i Hercegovine*, 1 (1949): 66–69.

———, "Vjersko učenje bosanske crkve", *Rad JAZU*, 270 (1948): 5–46.

Southern, Richard W., *Western Views of Islam in the Middle Ages*, Harvard University Press, 1978.

———, *The Making of the Middle Age*, Connecticut: Yale University Press, 1961.

Speranskij, Mihail, "Ein Bosnischein Evangelium in der Handschriftensamlung Srećković's", *Archiv für slavische Philologie*, 24 (1902): 172–182.

Strachey, James and Anna Freud, eds., *The Standard Edition of the Complete Psychological Works of Sigmund Freud*, 1–23, London: Hogarth Press, 1938.

Suyūṭī, Jalāl al-Dīn ʿAbd al-Raḥmān, al-, *al-Ḥirz al-manīʿ min al-qawl al-badīʿ fī al-ṣalāt ʿalā al-ḥabīb al-shafīʿ*, al-Khurunfush, Cairo: al-Maṭbaʾa al-ʿĀmira al-Sharqiyya, 1323. a.h.

Šaković, Edin, "Stara džamija u Sokolu", *Gračanički glasnik*, 11 (2001): 75–78.

Šanjek, Franjo, ed., *Fenomen "krstjani" u srednjovjekovnoj Bosni i Hercegovini: Zbornik radova*, Sarajevo/Zagreb: Institut za istoriju/Hrvatski institut za povijest, 2005.

———, *Bosansko-humski krstjani u povijesnim vrelima (13.–15.st.)*, Zagreb: Barbat, 2003.

———, *Bosansko-humski krstjani i katarsko-dualistički pokret u srednjem vijeku*, Zagreb: Kršćanska sadašnjost, 1975.

Šidak, Jaroslav, *Studije o "crkvi bosanskoj" i bogumilstvu*, Zagreb: Liber, 1975.

Šilić, Rufin, "Stoljeće i po bosansko-hercegovačkog vjerovanja u Marijino uznesenje", *Dobri Pastir*, 1–2 (1951): 3–48.

Škaljić, Abdulah, *Turcizmi u srpskohrvatskom-hrvatskosrpskom jeziku*, Sarajevo: Svjetlost, 1973.

Šunjić, Marko, "Jedan novi podatak o gostu Radinu i njegovoj sekti", *Godišnjak Društva istoričara Bosne i Hercegovine*, 11 (1960): 265–268.

Ṭabarānī, Abū al-Qāsim Sulaymān, al-, *al-Muʿjam al-kabīr*, 1–20, Mosul: Maktaba al-ʿUlūm wa al-Ḥikam, 1983.

Ṭabarī, Abū Jaʿfar Muḥammad b. Jarīr, al-, *The History of Prophets and Kings*, 1, trans. Franz Rosenthal, Albany: State University of New York Press, 1989.

———, *Tārīkh al-rusul wa al-mulūk*, (*The History of Prophets and Kings*), 2, trans. William M. Brinner, Albany: State University of New York Press, 1987.

Ṭabarī, ʿAlī, *The Book of Religion and Empire: A Semi-official Defence and Exposition of Islām Written by Order at the Court and with the Assistance of the Caliph Mutawakkil (A.D. 847–861)*, trans. Alphonse Mingana, Manchester: Longmans, Green and Co, 1922.

Ṭabaṭabāʾī, Allama Sayyid Muḥammad Ḥusayn, *Shīʿa*, trans. Sayyid Hossein Nasr, Qum: Ansariyan Publications, 1989.

Tatić-Đurić, Mirjana, *Studije o Bogorodici*, Belgrade: Jasen, 2007.

Thaʿlabī, Ibn Ibrahim, al-, *ʿArāʾis al-majālis fī qiṣaṣ al-anbiyāʾ: Lives of the Prophets*, trans. William M. Brinner, Leiden: E.J. Brill, 2002.

Thallóczy, Ludwig von, *Studien zur Geschichte Bosniens und Serbiens im Mittelalter*, München: Verlag von Duncker, 1914.

Tijānī, Aḥmad, al-ʿAbbās Sayyid Aḥmad ibn Muḥammad, al-, *al-Ṣalāt al-ghaybiyya fī al-ḥaqīqa al-aḥmadiyya*, Marrakesh: al-Zāwiyya al-Kubrā li Sayyidī Muḥammad al-Kabīr al-Tijānī, 2009.

Tirmidhī, Muḥammad b. ʿĪsā Abū ʿIsā, al-, *Sunan*, ed. Aḥmad Muḥammad Shākir et al., 1–5, Cairo: Dār al-Ḥadīth, s.a.

Tirmidhī, al-Ḥakīm, al-, *The Life of the Friends of God*, in: Radtke, *The Concept of Sainthood in Early Islamic Mistycism*, 38–239.

Tolan, John V., *Saracens: Islam in the Medieval European Imagination*, New York: Columbia University Press, 2002.

Trako, Salih, "Ibrahim Zikrija iz Užica, komentator Sulejman Čelebijina djela *Vesilet en-nedžat* ('Sredstvo spasa')", *Anali Gazi Husrev-begove biblioteke*, 11–12 (1985): 165–173.

Trako, Salih and Lejla Gazić, "Rukopisna zbirka Orijentalnog instituta u Sarajevu", *Prilozi za orijentalnu filologiju*, 25 (1975): 15–30.

Traljić, Mahmud, "Hafizi-kutubi Gazi Husrevbegove biblioteke: Prilog historiji Biblioteke", *Anali Gazi Husrev-begove biblioteke*, 5–6 (1978): 54–55.

Truhelka, Ćiro, "Grobnica bosanskog tepčije Batala, obretena kod Gornjeg Turbeta (kotar Travnik)", *Glasnik Zemaljskog muzeja u Bosni i Hercegovini*, 3–4 (1915): 365–374.

———, "Još o testamentu gosta Radina i o patarenima", *Glasnik Zemaljskog muzeja u Bosni i Hercegovini*, 25 (1913): 365–381.

———, "Testament gosta Radina: Prinos patarenskom pitanju", *Glasnik Zemaljskog muzeja u Bosni i Hercegovini*, 23 (1911): 355–375.

———, "Nekoliko hercegovačkih natpisa", *Glasnik Zemaljskog muzeja u Bosni i Hercegovini*, 1 (1892): 24–32.

———, "Starobosanski mramorovi", *Glasnik Zemaljskog muzeja u Bosni i Hercegovini*, 4 (1891): 368–387.

Tustarī, Sahl b. ʿAbdallāh, al-, *Tafsīr al-Qurʾān al-ʿaẓīm*, Cairo: Dār al-Kutub al-ʿArabiyya al-Kubrā, 1911.

Vego, Marko, *Zbornik srednjovjekovnih natpisa Bosne i Hercegovine*, 1–4, Sarajevo: Izdanja Zemaljskog muzeja, 1964.

Vidyarthi, Abdul Haque, *Muhammad in World Scriptures*, Lahore: Dar-Ul-Kutub Islamia, 1940.

Voegelin, Eric, *The New Science of Politics: An Introduction*, Chicago: University of Chicago Press, 1987.

Wadding, Luke, *Annales Minorum seu trium ordinum a.s. Francisco institutorum*, 8–13, ad Florence: Ad Claras Aquas (Quaracchi), 1932.

Wasserstrom, Steven M., *Religion after Religion: Gershom Scholem, Mircea Eliade, and Henry Corbin at Eranos*, Princeton: Princeton University Press, 1999.

Wensinck, Arent J., *Studies of A.J. Wensinck*, New York: Arno Press, 1978.

———, "The Ideas of the Western Semites Concerning the Navel of the Earth", in: idem, *Studies of A.J. Wensinck*, 1–65.

———, *Semietische studiën uit de nalatenschap*, Leiden: A.W. Sijthoff's uitgevers-maatachappij N.V., 1941.

———, "The Oriental Doctrine of the Martyrs", in: idem, *Semietische studiën uit de nalatenschap*, 90–113.

Wensinck, Arent J., J.P. Mensing and J. Brugman, *Concordance et indices de la tradition musulmane*, Leiden: E.J. Brill, 1936–1969.

Wenzel, Marian, *Ukrasni motivi na stećcima/Ornamental Motifs on Tombstones from Medieval Bosnia and Surrounding Regions*, Sarajevo: Veselin Masleša, 1965.

Werblowsky, R.J. Zwi and Bleeker C. Jouco, eds., *Types of Redemption: Contributions to the Theme of the Study-Conference held at Jerusalem 14th to 19th July 1968*, Leiden: E.J. Brill, 1970.

Wheeler, Brannon, *Mecca and Eden: Ritual, Relics, and the Territory in Islam*, Chicago: The University of Chicago Press, 2006.

Winter, Tim, "Jesus and Muhammad: New convergences", *The Muslim World*, 99 (2009): 21–38.

Wüstenfeld, Ferdinand, *Die Chroniken der Stadt Mekka*, Leipzig: Olms Verlag, 1858.

Zirojević, Olga, *Islamizacija na južnoslovenskom prostoru: Dvoverje*, Belgrade: Srpski genealoški centar, 2003.

———, "Turci u našem ogledalu", in: Pantelič, *Etnički odnosi Srba sa drugim narodima i etničkim zajednicama*, 107–113.

Zlatović, Stipan, *Franovci države presvetoga Odkupitelja i hrvatski puk u Dalmaciji*, Zagreb: Knjigotiskara i litografija C. Albrechta, 1888.

Ždralović, Muhamed, *Bosanskohercegovački prepisivači djelā u arabičkim rukopisima*, 1–2, Sarajevo: Svjetlost, 1988.

———, "Bilješke u orijentalnim rukopisima", *Prilozi za orijentalnu filologiju*, 35 (1985): 107–132.

Žerjavić, Vladimir, *Opsesije i megalomanije oko Jasenovca i Bleiburga*, Zagreb: Globus, 1992.

Žitja Konstantina Ćirila i Metodija, trans. Josip Bratulić, Zagreb: Kršćanska sadašnjost, 1998.

Index

This index is of names and places. It does not include the names The Praised, Jesus or The Anointed, or their various synonyms because they appear too frequently. The names Muhammad and Ahmad are included, because in most cases these refer to instances where the Arabic word is being discussed. For reasons of space, it was not considered practical to provide an index of Qur'anic or Biblical passages or of references to the collections of the traditions of the Praised. For similar reasons, concepts and abstract nouns were not included.